Silver Burdett Ginn
Mathematics
VOLUME 1

W9-AVI-327

Program Authors

Francis (Skip) Fennell, Ph.D.
Professor of Education and Chair, Education Department

Western Maryland College
Westminster, Maryland

Joan Ferrini-Mundy, Ph.D.
Professor of Mathematics

University of New Hampshire
Durham, New Hampshire

Herbert P. Ginsburg, Ph.D.
Professor of Psychology and Mathematics Education

Teachers College, Columbia University
New York, New York

Carole Greenes, Ed.D.
Professor of Mathematics Education and Associate Dean,
   School of Education

Boston University
Boston, Massachusetts

Stuart J. Murphy
Visual Learning Specialist

Evanston, Illinois

William Tate, Ph.D.
Associate Professor of Mathematics Education

University of Wisconsin-Madison
Madison, Wisconsin

0-382-34910-5

4 5 6 7 8 9-W 06 05 04 03 02 01

Silver Burdett Ginn
Parsippany, NJ
Atlanta, GA • Deerfield, IL • Irving, TX • Needham, MA • Upland, CA

Grade Level Authors

Jennie Bennett, Ed.D.
Instructional Mathematics Supervisor

Houston Independent School District
Houston, Texas

Charles Calhoun, Ph.D.
Associate Professor of Elementary
  Education Mathematics

University of Alabama at Birmingham
Birmingham, Alabama

Lucille Croom, Ph.D.
Professor of Mathematics

Hunter College of the City University
  of New York
New York, New York

Robert A. Laing, Ph.D.
Professor of Mathematics Education

Western Michigan University
Kalamazoo, Michigan

Kay B. Sammons, M.S.
Supervisor of Elementary Mathematics

Howard County Public Schools
Ellicott City, Maryland

Marian Small, Ed.D.
Professor of Mathematics Education

University of New Brunswick
Fredericton, New Brunswick, Canada

Contributing Authors

Stephen Krulik, Ed.D.
Professor of Mathematics Education

Temple University
Philadelphia, Pennsylvania

Donna J. Long
Mathematics/Title 1 Coordinator

Metropolitan School District of
  Wayne Township
Indianapolis, Indiana

Jesse A. Rudnick, Ed.D.
Professor Emeritus of Mathematics
  Education

Temple University
Philadelphia, Pennsylvania

Clementine Sherman
Director, USI Math and Science

Dade County Public Schools
Miami, Florida

Bruce R. Vogeli, Ph.D.
Clifford Brewster Upton Professor of
  Mathematics

Teachers College, Columbia University
New York, New York

Silver Burdett Ginn
299 Jefferson Road, P.O. Box 480
Parsippany, NJ 07054-0480

Program Reviewers

Sandy Adelstein
First Grade Teacher

Quail Valley Elementary School
Missouri City, Texas

Randa Alford
Sixth Grade Teacher

Lura B. Kean Elementary School
Wooster, Ohio

Mary Almaraz
Elementary Math Technology Teacher

Cypress-Fairbanks Independent School District
Houston, Texas

Betty S. Blake
Fourth Grade Teacher

Nathan Adams Elementary School
Dallas, Texas

Denise Dutcher Bolebruch
Second and Third Grade Teacher

Apex Gifted and Talented Elementary School
Apex, North Carolina

Amanda Borysiewicz
Third Grade Teacher

Metro West Elementary School
Orlando, Florida

David Bush
Fifth Grade Teacher

Ortiz Elementary School
Abilene, Texas

Richard J. Callan
Third Grade Teacher and
   Educational Consultant
1995 Presidential Awardee

Bunker Hill Elementary School
New Whiteland, Indiana

Beverly Carson
Kindergarten Teacher

Sudie L. Williams Elementary School
Dallas, Texas

Anita Carter
Math Coordinator

Northeast IST, Dunbar 6
Fort Worth, Texas

Connie L. Clark
First and Eighth Grade Teacher

Raymore Elementary School
Raymore, Missouri

Joan Conca
Multiage Third and Fourth Grade Teacher

Church Street School
White Plains, New York

Judy Curtis
Gifted and Talented Program Facilitator

Bowie Elementary School
Rosenberg, Texas

Gloria G. Dantzler, Ed.D.
Curriculum Specialist

Cumberland County Schools
Fayetteville, North Carolina

Brenda DeBorde
Director of Mathematics

Grand Prairie ISD
Grand Prairie, Texas

Albertine Douglas
Sixth Grade Teacher

Blackshear Elementary
Houston, Texas

Brenda Durst
Third Grade Teacher

Crown Point Elementary School
Matthews, North Carolina

Audrey Ferguson
Title 1 Math Teacher

Laclede Elementary School
St. Louis Public Schools
St. Louis, Missouri

Andria M. Fields
Fourth Grade/Computer Teacher

Wake County Public Schools
Raleigh, North Carolina

Gail Carter Filson
Elementary Math/Science
   Specialist

Volusia County Schools
Daytona Beach, Florida

Susan Flax
First Grade Teacher

Eagle Point Elementary School
Ft. Lauderdale, Florida

Victoria Fu, Ed.D
Professor of Child Development

Virginia Polytechnic Institute and State
   University
Blacksburg, Virginia

Wayne Gable
First Grade Teacher
1990 Presidential Awardee

Langford Elementary School
Austin, Texas

Marjorie Gross
Fifth/Sixth Grade Mathematics
   Teacher

Actionville
Hommocks School
Mamaroneck Union Free Public School
   District
Mamaroneck, New York

Lisa Gurganus
Kindergarten Teacher

Conway Elementary School
Orlando, Florida

Carole Harper
Fifth Grade Teacher

R.S. Walton School
Philadelphia School District
Philadelphia, Pennsylvania

Marguerite Hart, Ed.D.
Director of Technology, Math, and
   Science

Metropolitan School District of Washington
   Township
Indianapolis, Indiana

Polly Haynes
K–3 Mathematics Teacher
1995 Presidential Awardee

Kyle Elementary School
Hays Consolidated Independent School
   District
Kyle, Texas

Ilene Hoenig
First Grade Teacher

Henry Barnard School
New Rochelle, New York

Suzanne J. James
Third Grade Teacher

Indianapolis Public School #56
Indianapolis, Indiana

Joanne Johnson
Kindergarten Teacher

Woodbine Elementary School
Cicero, Illinois

Liz Jones
Kindergarten Team Leader

English Estates Elementary School
Fern Park, Florida

Mary Kay Karl
Mathematics Teacher

Frost Junior High School
Schaumburg, Illinois

Martha R. Kilgore
First Grade Teacher
1994 Presidential Awardee
E.S. Richardson Elementary School
Minden, Louisiana

Emily Lamont
Kindergarten Teacher
1993 Presidential Awardee
Episcopal School
Baton Rouge, Louisiana

Barbara Leos
Fourth Grade Teacher
Sewell Elementary School
Garland, Texas

Deborah Little
First Grade Teacher
Irving Elementary School
Altoona, Pennsylvania

Sharon Lomas
First Grade Teacher
Hoover Elementary School
Tulsa, Oklahoma

Virginia Madden
Second Grade Teacher
Public School #81
Riverdale, New York

Victoria Magness
Fifth Grade Teacher
Lewis Cassidy Elementary School
Philadelphia, Pennsylvania

Jo Martin
Kindergarten Teacher
Field Slevenson Elementary School
Forest Park, Illinois

Jill McKenzie
Bilingual Second Grade Teacher
Garden Oaks Elementary School
Houston Independent School District
Houston, Texas

Deborah Moilanen
Second Grade Teacher
Miller Elementary
Plano School District
Richardson, Texas

Ingrid Nystrom
Fourth Grade Teacher
Homer Davis Elementary School
Tucson, Arizona

Melinda Ossorio
Elementary Curriculum Specialist
Lauderhill Paul Turner Elementary School
Lauderhill, Florida

Sheridan C. Rayl
First Grade Teacher
Leach Elementary School
Frankton-Lapel Community Schools
Anderson, Indiana

Peggy Roberts
Gifted and Talented Third and Fourth Grade
  Teacher
Pine Tree Intermediate School
Longview, Texas

Jean Rogers
Sixth Grade Teacher
Walter C. Young Middle School
Pembroke Pines, Florida

Janice Russell
Seventh Grade Teacher
1991 Presidential Awardee
Vance Middle School
Bristol Tennessee City School System
Bristol, Tennessee

Flo Sessoms
Sixth Grade Teacher
Charlotte-Mecklenburg School System
Charlotte, North Carolina

Kathleen A. Severns
Fourth Grade Teacher
1995 Presidential Awardee
Dolby Elementary School
Lake Charles, Louisiana

Deborah Shahinian
Fourth Grade Teacher
Casselberry Elementary School
Casselberry, Florida

Lenore Shellman
Kindergarten Teacher
B.H. Macon Elementary School
Dallas, Texas

Debbie Shoulders
Second Grade Teacher
Northeast Elementary School
Clarksville, Tennessee

Wendee Siegel
Sixth Grade Math Coordinator
Orchard Park School District
Williamsville, New York

Susan B. Slesnick
Math Department Chair
Louisville Collegiate School
Louisville, Kentucky

Miguel Soares
Fourth Grade Teacher
Braeburn Elementary School
Houston, Texas

Scott Steinman
Third Grade Teacher
Old Turnpike School
Califon, New Jersey

Annette P. Stigall
First Grade Teacher
Indianapolis Public Schools
Indianapolis, Indiana

Mary D. Thornburg
First Grade Teacher
Carr Elementary School
Dallas, North Carolina

Michael E. Thorson
Ninth and Tenth Grade
  Mathematics Teacher
East Central High School
Tulsa, Oklahoma

Sara Talley Tune
Equity 2000 Coordinator
Metro-Nashville Public Schools
Nashville, Tennessee

Sharon Walker
Educational Coordinator
Kideology
Ontario, New York

Jill P. Weber
Third Grade Teacher
Midland Elementary School
Roy, Utah

Lynn Wolf
Coordinator of Technology Training
Bismarck Public School
Bismarck, North Dakota

Mary Branch Wyatt
Second Grade Teacher
1995 Presidential Awardee
Robert E. Lee Elementary School
Spotsylvania, Virginia

Maria Elena Zavala
ESL Consultant
Corpus Christi ISD
Corpus Christi, Texas

Contents

$5.80

$8.95

Chapter 2 — Addition and Subtraction

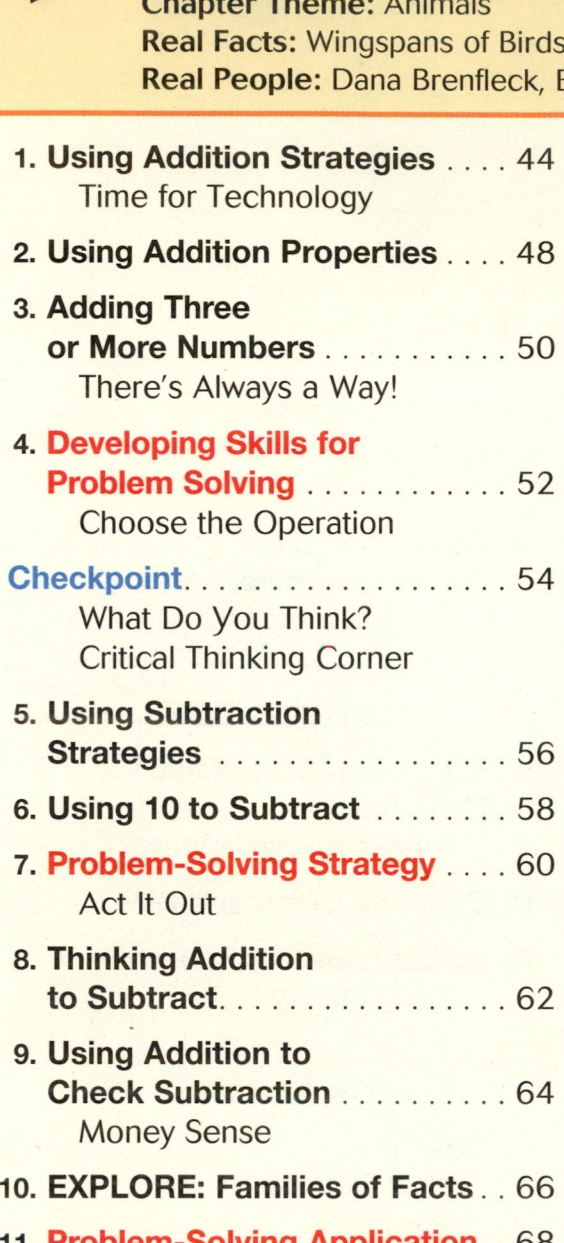

Chapter Theme: Animals

Chapter 3
Addition and Subtraction With Greater Numbers

Chapter Theme: Travel
Real Facts: Number of People on Rafting Trips 78
Real People: Keith Jardine, Rafting Guide 78

4 Time and Measurement

Chapter Theme: Sports and Fitness

Chapter 5 — Multiplication Concepts

Chapter Theme: School Activities

Chapter 6 Multiplication Facts

Chapter Theme: Transportation

Chapter 7 — Using Data and Probability

Chapter Theme: Our Earth

Division Concepts

Chapter Theme: Communities
Real Facts: Balloons Needed for Animal Sculptures. 286
Real People: Lisa Geiger, Juggler 286

Chapter 9 Division Facts

Chapter Theme: Performing Arts

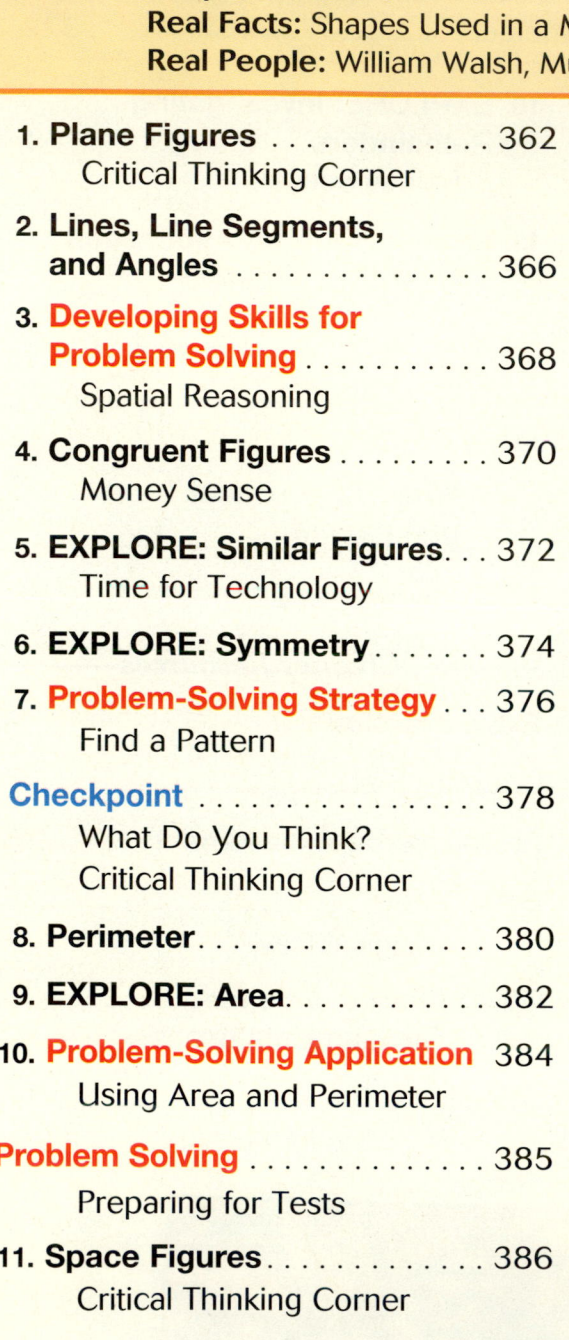

Chapter 10 Geometry

Chapter Theme: Fine Arts

Chapter 11 — Fractions and Decimals

Chapter Theme: Food

Chapter 12 — Multiplying and Dividing Greater Numbers

Chapter Theme: The Future

Starting Off Right!

All aspects of **Silver Burdett Ginn Mathematics** have been carefully developed to help your students travel the path to math success. The program will also help parents understand the math that their children are learning. Let's look at some aspects of the program that will help you make the most of the learning that takes place in the classroom.

There's Always a Way!

There's Always a Way! shows students several strategies to solve a problem. These strategies incorporate different ways of thinking about math ideas and appeal to a variety of learning styles. *There's Always a Way!* often creates a bridge between concrete and abstract solution strategies, allowing your students to build on the math skills and concepts they already possess.

Teaching Tips

- When appropriate, discuss why one solution method might be more practical or efficient than another.
- Foster a classroom environment in which finding many solution methods is encouraged.
- Focus on the process of finding an answer, not the answer itself.

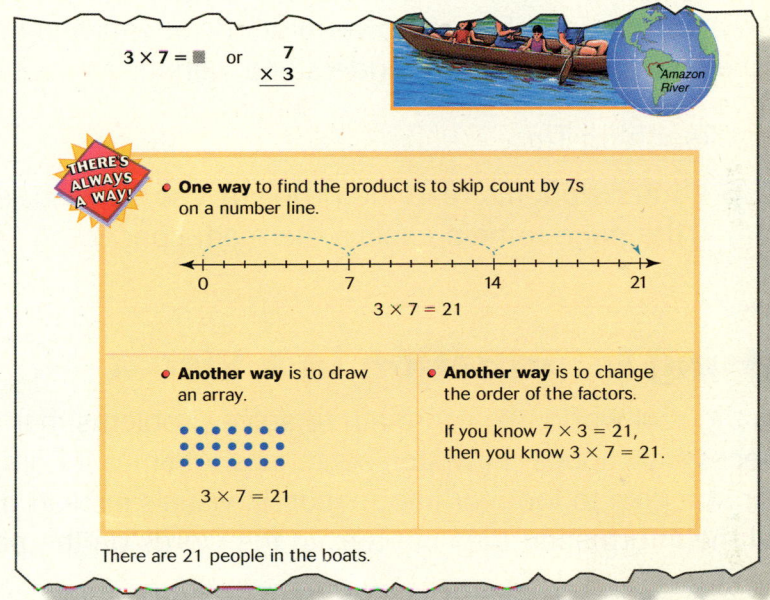

Connecting Ideas

The *Connecting Ideas* section of a lesson extends the skill or concept presented in the lesson. Through *Connecting Ideas,* students are able to see that many math concepts and skills are related to one another and build upon one another.

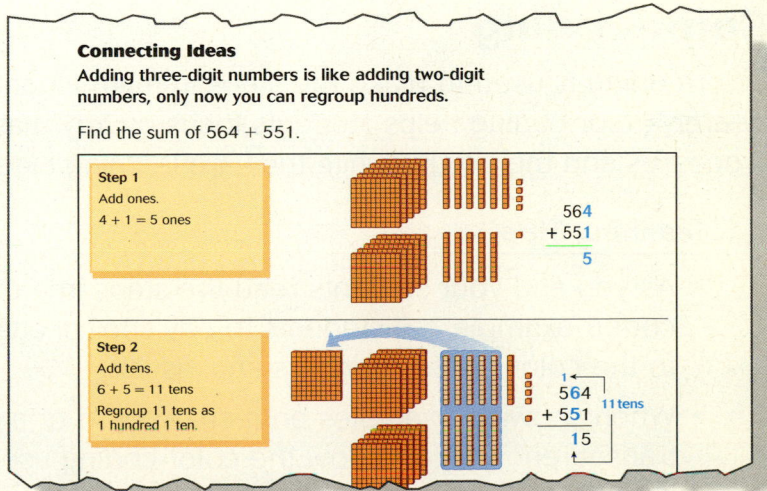

Using the Art and Photographs

The art and photographs in this program have been carefully created to illustrate the math that is being taught. The following are some of the ways that art and photographs will help your students better understand the math skills and concepts they are learning this year.

Visualizing a Math Concept

Art and photographs are powerful tools for showing math concepts that are hard to understand without a visual example.

Teaching Tip

- After students read the problem, use the visuals on the page to help explain the math concept.

Using Information in a Visual

In the real world, we use math to solve problems that do not necessarily appear in written sentences. At times it is important for students to look for information in visuals instead of getting all the information they need from the words on the page.

Teaching Tip

- Have students read the problem first, then look at the visuals on the page to get all the information needed.

Color-coding

Color-coding is used to make the steps in math algorithms clearer. Color-coding helps students focus on key math processes and their order while they are learning algorithms.

Teaching Tips

- As you and your students read the steps in a color-coded example, tell students to pay special attention to the color-coded numbers and visuals.
- When showing examples on a chalkboard or a transparency, try to follow the color-coding used in the textbook.

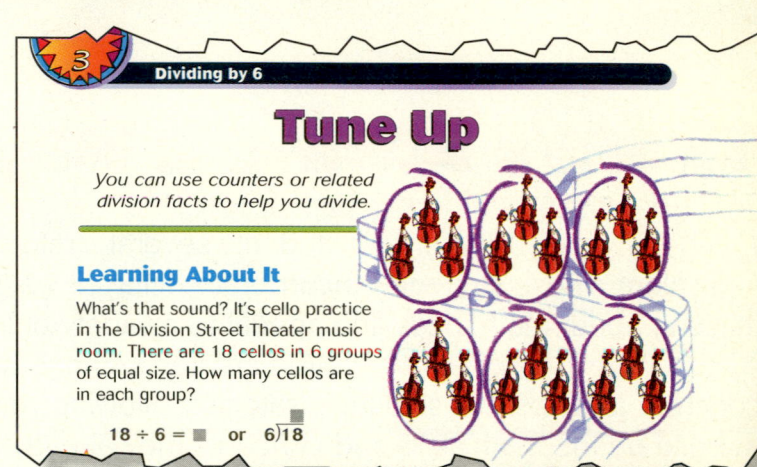

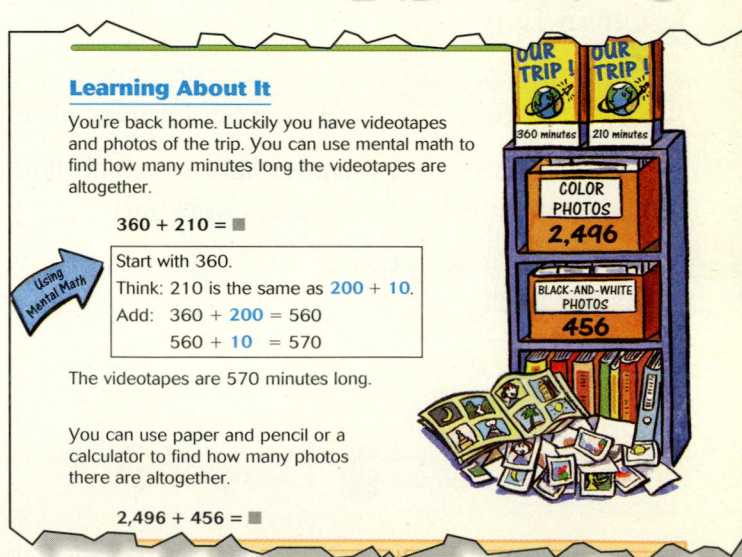

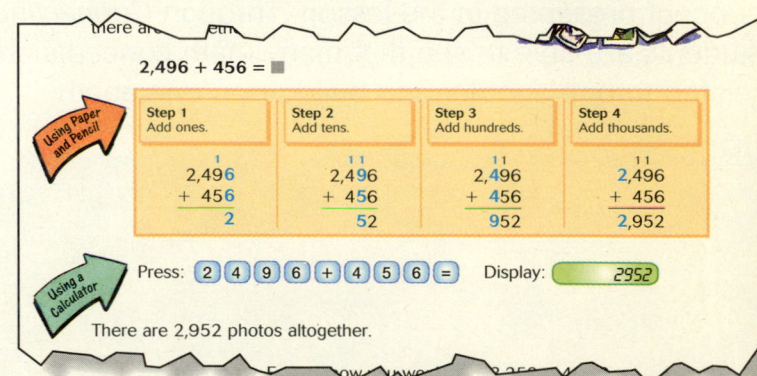

Developing Algebraic Thinking

You will find lessons and exercises throughout **Silver Burdett Ginn Mathematics** that will help students develop a strong foundation in algebraic thinking. Some of the concepts covered in Grade 3 that foster algebraic thinking are described below.

Patterns

Students work with pictorial, numerical, and geometric patterns.

Numerical Relationships

Students investigate properties of numbers as well as numerical relationships such as
- doubles
- odd and even numbers
- square numbers

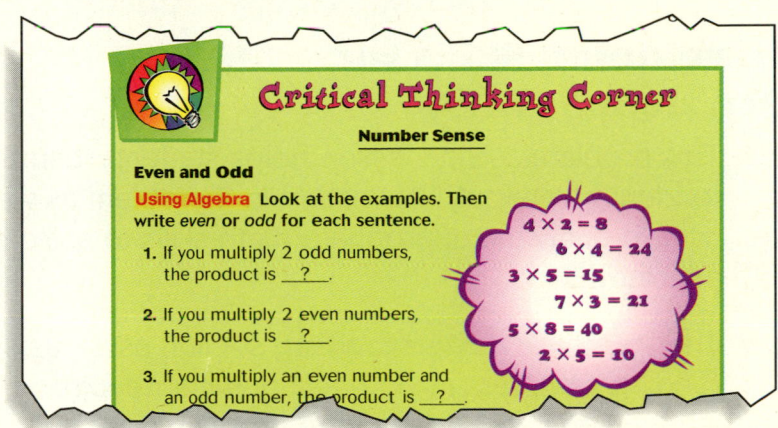

Example of **Numerical Relationships**

Variables, Equations, and Inequalities

Students explore these concepts by
- finding the value of missing numbers
- writing number sentences

Functions and Formulas

Students explore functional relationships by
- following rules to complete tables
- graphing ordered pairs

Example of **Functions**

Proportional Relationships

Students explore proportional relationships such as
- equivalent coin relationships
- equivalent measurements

Representation

Students represent mathematical relationships by using
- counters
- number lines
- tables and graphs

Example of **Representation**

Developing Problem Solving Skills

Each chapter in **Silver Burdett Ginn Mathematics** includes four problem-solving lessons designed to provide students with practice in using a variety of problem-solving skills.

Developing Skills for Problem Solving

▶ This problem-solving lesson helps students learn how to identify relevant information in a problem as well as how to apply the appropriate math skills to solve the problem.

▶ The **Read for Understanding** section asks basic reading-comprehension questions that require students to carefully read the problem.

▶ The **Math Focus** box helps students concentrate on the problem-solving skill that they will need to answer more complex questions.

▶ The **Multiple Choice** questions have been constructed so that students need to think about the process of problem solving as well as the correct answer.

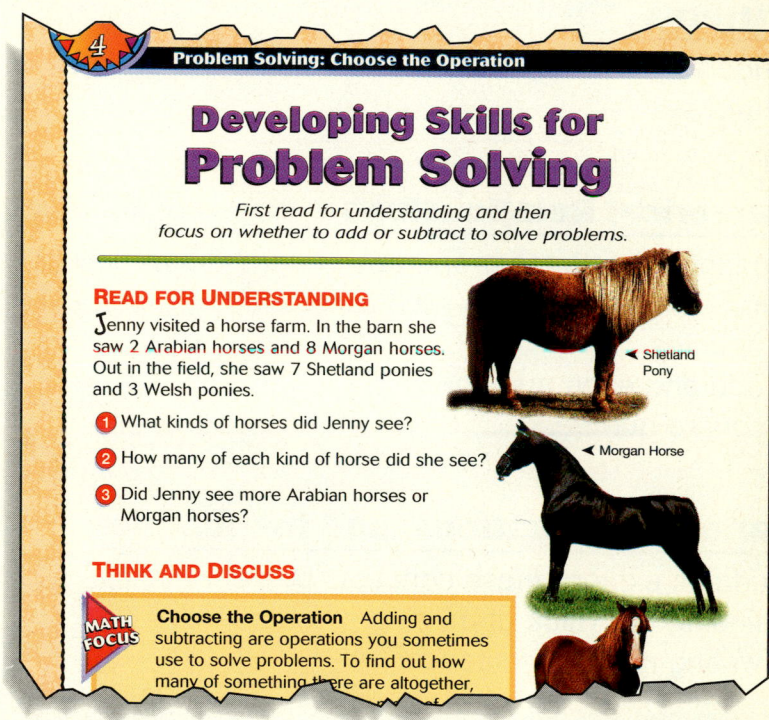

4 Problem Solving: Choose the Operation

Developing Skills for Problem Solving

First read for understanding and then focus on whether to add or subtract to solve problems.

READ FOR UNDERSTANDING

Jenny visited a horse farm. In the barn she saw 2 Arabian horses and 8 Morgan horses. Out in the field, she saw 7 Shetland ponies and 3 Welsh ponies.

1. What kinds of horses did Jenny see?
2. How many of each kind of horse did she see?
3. Did Jenny see more Arabian horses or Morgan horses?

◄ Shetland Pony

◄ Morgan Horse

THINK AND DISCUSS

MATH FOCUS **Choose the Operation** Adding and subtracting are operations you sometimes use to solve problems. To find out how many of something there are altogether,

7 Problem-Solving Strategy

Problem Solving Act It Out

Sometimes acting out a problem will help you solve it.

Billy, Millie, and Tillie are seals. They like to play catch. First their trainer tosses the ball to Billy. Then Billy tosses it to Millie. Millie tosses it to Tillie. Tillie tosses it back to Billy. And around it goes again and again. If Billy catches the ball first, which seal makes the twelfth catch?

⇨ **UNDERSTAND**

What do you need to know?

You need to know that the ball is tossed from Billy to Millie to Tillie and then back to Billy.

⇨ **PLAN**

How can you solve the problem?

One strategy you could use is to **act it out**. Three students can pretend to be

Problem-Solving Strategy

▶ The Problem-Solving Strategy lesson focuses on common strategies used to solve problems. For a complete list of the strategies included, see page T1.

▶ Each lesson guides students through the four-step problem-solving process.
Understand, Plan, Solve, Look Back

▶ Each lesson also has a Mixed Strategy Review, which provides opportunities for students to apply previously learned strategies to solve problems.

Problem-Solving Application

▶ In the Problem-Solving Application lesson, students apply problem-solving skills to a variety of math situations.

▶ Students apply the four-step problem-solving process as they think through and solve a wide variety of problems.

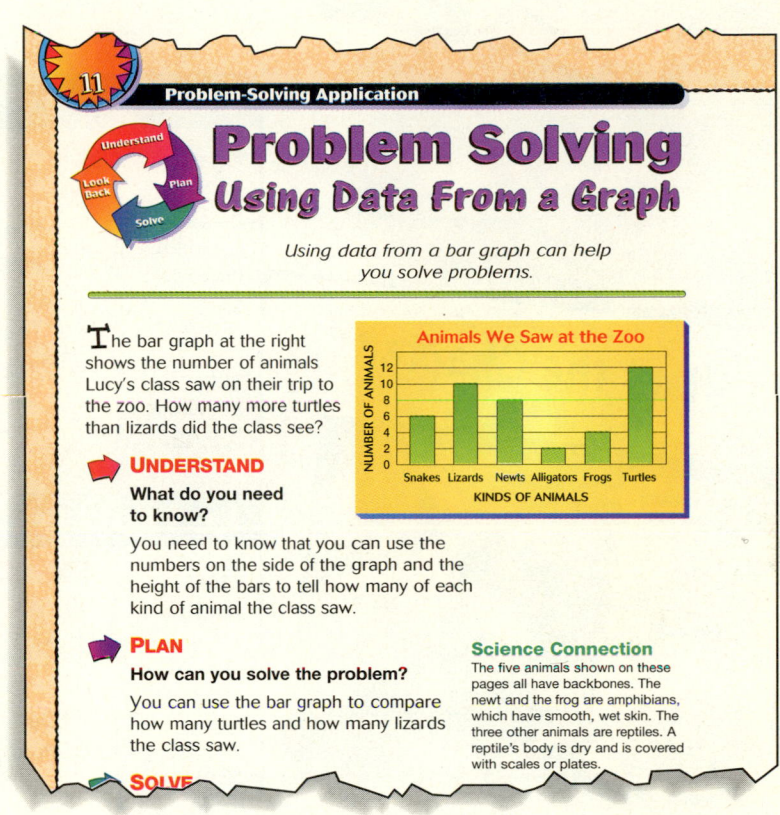

Problem Solving: Preparing for Tests

▶ This problem-solving lesson prepares students for the type of problem-solving questions they are likely to encounter on standardized tests.

▶ **Tips** are provided to help students become successful test takers.

▶ The **Multiple Choice** questions reflect standardized test formats and give students practice in choosing the correct answer.

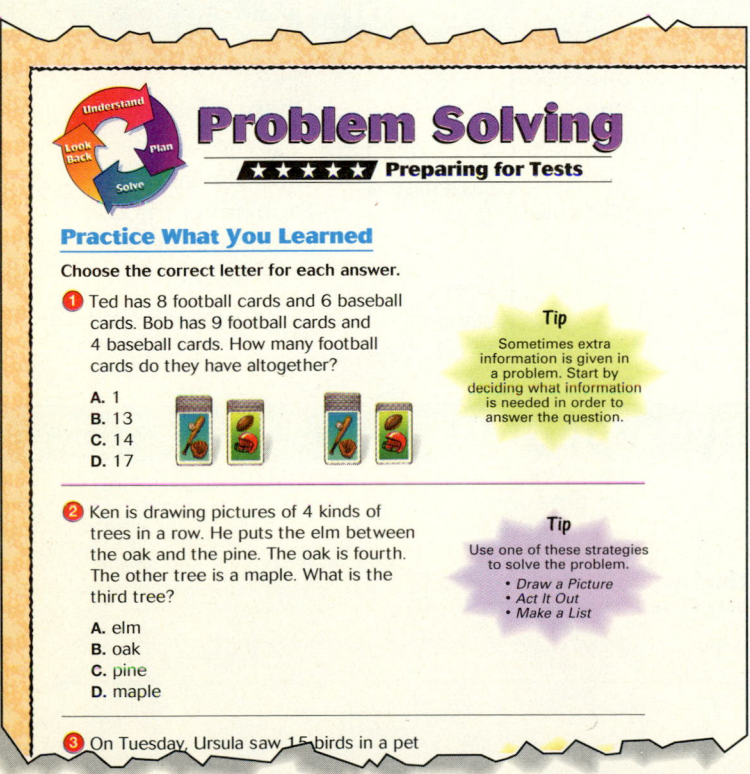

Daily Lesson Planner

Place Value and Money

To Start the Chapter

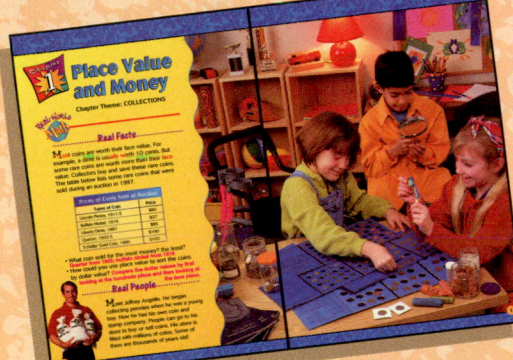

Chapter Opener

Resources

- Chapter Opener
  Career Spotlight
  Chapter Project, *Teacher Guide*,
  pages 1I–1

- Chapter Pretest, *Assessment Guide*,
  pages 63–66

- Family Letter With Activity,
  Home-School Connection,
  pages 1–2

- Internet Activity,
  pages 5, 31

Lesson 1

PAGES 2–3	**EXPLORE: Investigating Number Patterns**

LEARNING OBJECTIVES 1A	**Manipulatives:** counters
	Chapter File Folder
	  Practice, Reteach, Extend 1-1
	  Teaching Tool 10
	Daily Review 1-1
	Practice Workbook, p. 1
	Problem of the Day 1-1

NCTM STANDARDS 3, 6, 13	*p. 2*

Lesson 2

PAGES 4–5	**Ordinal Numbers**
LEARNING OBJECTIVES 1A	**Chapter File Folder** Practice, Reteach, Extend 1-2 Daily Review 1-2 Problem of the Day 1-2
NCTM STANDARDS 1, 3, 6, 8	*p. 5*

Lesson 6

PAGES 18–19B	**EXPLORE: Understanding Thousands**
LEARNING OBJECTIVES 1A	**Chapter File Folder** Practice, Reteach, Extend 1-6 Daily Review 1-6 Problem of the Day 1-6 Teaching With Technology
NCTM STANDARDS 2, 3, 6	

Lesson 7

PAGES 20–21	**Reading and Writing Four-Digit Numbers**

LEARNING OBJECTIVES 1A	**Manipulatives:** base-ten blocks (optional)
	Chapter File Folder
	  Practice, Reteach, Extend 1-7
	  Teaching Tools 12, 22, 23
	Daily Review 1-7
	Practice Workbook, p. 3
	Problem of the Day 1-7

NCTM STANDARDS 1, 3, 6	

Lesson 11

PAGES 30–31	**Counting Coins and Bills**

LEARNING OBJECTIVES 1D	**Manipulatives:** bill and coin set (optional)
	Chapter File Folder
	  Practice, Reteach, Extend 1-11
	  Teaching Tool 21
	Daily Review 1-11
	Practice Workbook, p. 5
	Problem of the Day 1-11

NCTM STANDARDS 1, 2, 3, 6, 8, 12	*p. 31*

Lesson 12

PAGES 32–33A	**Problem-Solving Application**
LEARNING OBJECTIVES 1E	**Chapter File Folder** Practice, Reteach, Extend 1-12 Daily Review 1-12 Problem of the Day 1-12 Problem Solving: Preparing for Tests
NCTM STANDARDS 1, 3, 4, 7	**Checkpoint, pp. 34–35**

Correlation to Investigations

Investigations in Number, Data, and Space
Dale Seymour Publications

Lessons 1-12 **Mathematical Thinking at Grade 3**
Investigations 1, 4; Ten-Minute Math, 87-90

 Algebra   **Time for Technology**   **Time for Technology**   **Critical Thinking**

Lesson 3

PAGES 6–9

Understanding Numbers to 999

Manipulatives: base-ten blocks

Chapter File Folder
Practice, Reteach, Extend 1-3
Teaching Tools 12, 22
Daily Review 1-3
Problem of the Day 1-3

LEARNING OBJECTIVES
1A

NCTM STANDARDS
1, 3, 6, 8

 p. 8   p. 9

Lesson 4

PAGES 10–13

Rounding to the Nearest Ten and Hundred

Chapter File Folder
Practice, Reteach, Extend 1-4
Teaching Tool 19
Daily Review 1-4
Practice Workbook, p. 2
Problem of the Day 1-4

LEARNING OBJECTIVES
1B

NCTM STANDARDS
1, 3, 5, 6

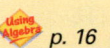 p. 13

Lesson 5

pages 14–15

Developing Skills for Problem Solving

Chapter File Folder
Practice, Reteach, Extend 1-5
Daily Review 1-5
Problem of the Day 1-5

✔ **Checkpoint, pp. 16–17**

LEARNING OBJECTIVES
1E

NCTM STANDARDS
1, 3, 5, 7

 p. 16   p. 17

Lesson 8

PAGES 22–25

Comparing and Ordering Numbers

Chapter File Folder
Practice, Reteach, Extend 1-8
Teaching Tool 12
Daily Review 1-8
Practice Workbook, p. 4
Problem of the Day 1-8

LEARNING OBJECTIVES
1C

NCTM STANDARDS
1, 3, 6, 8

p. 25 p. 25

Lesson 9

PAGES 26–27

Problem-Solving Strategy

Chapter File Folder
Practice, Reteach, Extend 1-9
Daily Review 1-9
Problem of the Day 1-9

LEARNING OBJECTIVES
1E

NCTM STANDARDS
1, 3, 6, 8

Lesson 10

pages 28–29

Extending Place-Value Concepts

Chapter File Folder
Practice, Reteach, Extend 1-10
Teaching Tool 12
Daily Review 1-10
Problem of the Day 1-10

LEARNING OBJECTIVES
1A

NCTM STANDARDS
1, 3, 6, 13

p. 29

Chapter End

PAGES 36–41

Chapter Assessment

Extra Practice, pp. 36–38
Chapter Test, p. 39
Performance Assessment, p. 40
Extension, p. 41
Cumulative Review

In the *Assessment Guide*
Chapter Posttest, pp. 67–70
Interview Activity, p. 35
Long-Answer Question, p. 8

LEARNING OBJECTIVES
**1A 1B 1C
1D 1E**

NCTM STANDARDS
**1, 2, 3, 5, 6,
7, 8, 12, 13**

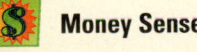 **Money Sense**   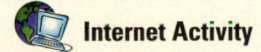 **Internet Activity**

Meeting Individual Needs

Learning Styles vary from student to student. Every Meeting Individual Needs activity focuses on one of the following learning styles. The variety of styles enables students to learn math in ways that are most comfortable to them.

- **AUDITORY**
- **INDIVIDUAL**
- **KINESTHETIC**
- **LINGUISTIC**
- **LOGICAL/MATHEMATICAL**
- **SOCIAL/COOPERATIVE**
- **VISUAL/SPATIAL**

Acquiring English Proficiency

Materials: Teaching Tool 12 (Place-Value Chart)

Have students name items that people collect. List them on the chalkboard. Ask volunteers to make statements about imaginary collections. For example, Sara has 376 stamps. Have other students write that number in a place-value chart. Volunteers then write each number in standard, expanded, and word form on the chalkboard.

For additional activities, see Acquiring English Proficiency, pp. 5, 25.

AUDITORY

For Extra Help

Manipulatives: spinner with numbers 1–9, base-ten blocks*

Have pairs practice modeling, writing, and comparing 3-digit numbers. Each student spins 3 times; then models the number of hundreds, tens, and ones; and writes the number. The student with the greater number earns 1 point. Play continues until one student earns 3 points.

For additional activities, see For Extra Help, pp. 3, 13, 32A.

KINESTHETIC

For Early Finishers

Materials: almanacs

Have students use almanacs to find the 5 tallest buildings in the world. Each student records his or her findings in a table that includes the building's name, location, and height in feet. Students write, exchange, and solve problems, using the information in the table.

For additional activities, see For Early Finishers, pp. 3, 5, 9, 13, 15, 19, 21, 25, 27, 29, 31, 32A.

LOGICAL/MATHEMATICAL

Gifted and Talented

Explain that the ancient Egyptians used hieroglyphs to write numbers. Single strokes represented ones, an arch represented 10, and a coiled rope represented 100. Ask students to research and find pictures of Egyptian hieroglyphs and use them to write a variety of numbers or to make a number chart.

For additional activities, see Gifted and Talented, p. 15.

LOGICAL/MATHEMATICAL

Inclusion

Materials: Teaching Tool 12 (Place-Value Chart)

Have students write pairs of 2-, 3- and 4-digit numbers in place-value charts. Students then cover with sheets of paper all places except those being compared. Students compare the numbers place by place, beginning with the greatest place.

For additional activities, see Inclusion, pp. 27, 31.

VISUAL/SPATIAL

*These Manipulatives are found in the Manipulatives Kit.

MATH CENTER

Cooperative Learning

Present statements containing exact and rounded numbers. For example, "Ed has about 400 coins in his collection. He has coins from 27 different countries." Have students decide which number is exact and which is rounded. Then have them change each statement so that the exact number becomes rounded and the rounded number becomes exact (398 coins from about 30 countries).

For additional activities, see Cooperative Learning, pp. 19, 29.

SOCIAL/COOPERATIVE

Manipulatives

Manipulatives: dollars and coins, spinner labeled 1–9*

Have students work in pairs. One student spins 3 times and uses the numbers to write a money amount. The other student tries to use the least number of bills and coins to show that amount. If the first student can use fewer bills and coins to show the amount, then he or she does so. Students switch roles and repeat the activity.

For additional activities, see Manipulatives, pp. 9, 21.

KINESTHETIC

Using Data

Students round the height of each building to the nearest hundred feet. Then they use their data to complete a pictograph. After students complete their graphs, remind them to count the pictures to make sure all buildings have been included.

For review, see pages 10–15.

Answers: About 600 ft: 3; about 700 ft: 5; about 800 ft: 1; about 900 ft: 1; most of the skyscrapers are about 700 ft.

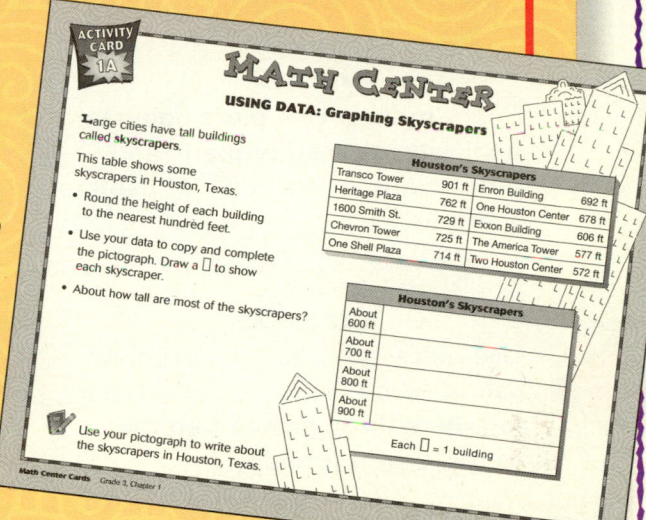

Problem Solving

Materials: base-ten blocks

Students toss 4 clips on the game board, write the scores, and use place-value blocks to show each score. Students combine the place-value blocks and regroup. Then they write the total score. Students play 4 times and order their total scores from least to greatest.

For review, see pages 18–25.

Answers: The lowest possible score is 20; the highest possible score is 2,000.

Assessment

Skills Trace
Skills Assessed at Each Grade

Grade 2
Count money. Use place value to hundreds. Write, compare, and order numbers to 1,000. (Chapters 4 and 9)

Grade 3
Use place value to hundred thousands. Write, compare, and order numbers through hundred thousands. Count money.

Grade 4
Use place value to millions. Write, compare, and order numbers through hundred thousands. (Chapter 1)

Informal Assessment

Informal assessments provide day-to-day feedback. In conjunction with more formal assessments, they give a complete picture of conceptual development.

In the Student Book

What Do You Think?
student pages 17, 35
Students explain what they have learned.

Create Your Own
student pages 25, 32A, 41
Students create their own problems.

Journal Idea
student pages 15, 17, 19, 35
Students communicate mathematically.

Self-Check
student pages 39, 40
Students evaluate their own work.

In the Teacher Guide

Baseline Assessment
teacher page 1I
Helps you assess prior knowledge

Ongoing Assessment

ASSESS UNDERSTANDING
Helps you assess students' understanding

WRAP-UP
Helps you monitor students' progress

JOURNAL IDEA
teacher pages 1, 3, 13, 15, 17, 19, 27, 31, 32A, 35
Helps you assess students' communication of math ideas

Portfolio Ideas

Portfolio opportunities appear on Student Book pages 35 and 40, and Teacher Guide pages 19A–B, 35, and 40.

Other items that you may wish to include in your student portfolios are:

- **Completed Chapter Projects**
- **Journal Entries**
- **CD-ROM and Internet Activities**
- **Informal Observations and Interview Activities**

For further suggestions for organizing and using portfolios, see **Assessment Guide,** pages 50–54.

Formal Assessment

Formal assessment can occur before and after the chapter, as well as at natural breaking points in the chapter.

In the Student Book

Checkpoints
student pages 16–17, 34–35
Use for assessing progress as students work through the chapter.

Chapter Test
student page 39

Performance Assessment
student page 40
The Performance Assessment helps you evaluate the skills and concepts developed in Chapter 1 through hands-on activities.

 CD-ROM Test Generator

This software allows you to customize your own chapter test. Formats include:
- **Multiple Choice**
- **Free Response**
- **Standardized Test**

Assessment Guide

You may choose among the following pages in the *Assessment Guide*.

Pretest Options
- Free Response, pages 63–64
- Multiple Choice, pages 65–66

Posttest Options
- Free Response, pages 67–68
- Multiple Choice, pages 69–70

Interview Activity
page 35

Long-Answer Question
page 8

Correlation to Standardized Tests

Learning Objectives	ITBS K/M	CTBS/5 (Terra Nova)	SAT9	MAT7	CAT5	*Pre/Post-Test Items	Lesson Pages
1A Read and write whole numbers through hundred thousands and ordinal numbers through ninety-ninth	MC: 1	17, 20, 21, 41	PS: 1, 2, 6	CPS: 1–3, 33	MC: 8, 29, 32	1–4	2–9 18–21 28–29
1B Round to the nearest ten or hundred	MC: 11–17	11	PS: 19, 20, 21	CPS: 27, 28 P: 22–24	MC: 2, 6, 20	5–8	10–13
1C Compare and order whole numbers through hundred thousands	MC: 1, 2, 6, 8 ME: 11–17 MDI: 25, 27, 28, 30	14, 33	PS: 3, 4	CPS: 2, 10–12, 29, 30, 33, 35, 37, 39, P: 9	MC: 1, 3, 24	9–12	22–25
1D Determine the value or compare sets of coins and bills; make change up to $10.00			PS: 30, 31, 40 P: 24, 27		MC: 2, 37	13–18	30–31
1E Analyze and solve problems using skills and strategies	PS: 18–24 ME: 11–13, 17	8, 14, 15, 23–25, 29, 47	PS: 4, 5, 44–46	CPS: 33–40 P: 1–12	MC: 8, 17, 19, 39, 40	19–20	14–15 26–27 32–32A 33–33A

MC = Math Concepts, **COM** = Math Computation, **PS** = Problem Solving, **P** = Procedures, **CPS** = Math Concepts & Problem Solving, **ME** = Math Estimation, **MDI** = Math Data Interpretation, **PB** = Math Problems

*Pretests and Posttests are found in the *Assessment Guide*.

Linking Technology

Develop and Reinforce Concepts

MathProcessor™

CD-ROM Activities use MathProcessor™ Tools to help build critical thinking skills and develop problem-solving strategies.

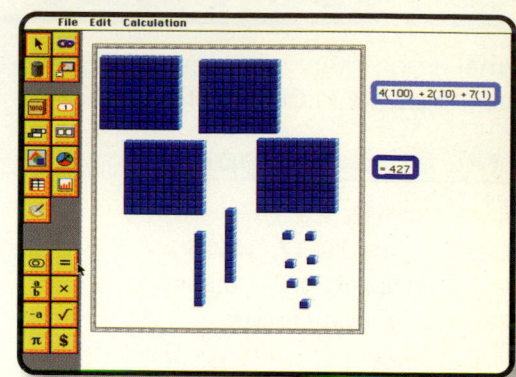

Lesson	Tools	Skill
3	Base-Ten Blocks Number spaces	Students use Manipulatives to model three-digit numbers.
8	Spreadsheet Writing space	Students use a Spreadsheet to compare and order three- and four-digit numbers.
11	Money	Students use Money Manipulatives to show different ways to pay for a purchase.

Review and Practice Skills

Math Blaster® 1

This **CD-ROM** program provides exercises and activities to practice basic math facts and develop mastery of mathematical operations. The chart below lists specific lessons where activities and references can be found.

Lesson	Activity	Subject/Level
1	Trash Zapper	Number Patterns—Level 3: counting by 2s, 3s, 4s from 26 through 60
4	Trash Zapper	Estimation—Levels 1, 2, 3

Extend and Enrich

Internet

Students can use real data in lesson-related math activities.
Teachers can find activities and resources for Lessons 2 and 11.
Parents can find home connections to help reinforce concepts.

Visit our Web site at:

www.sbgmath.com

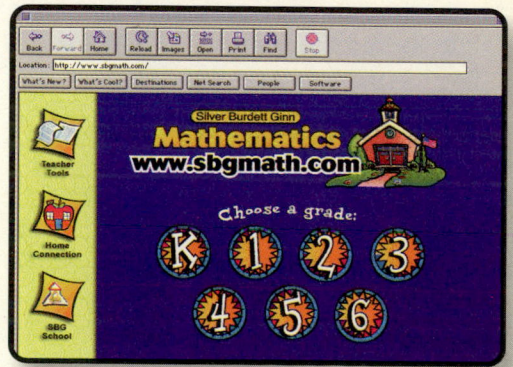

Making Connections

Literature

For the Chapter Activity

Find this book in your local or school library. Use it with the Math & Literature activity on page 11.

- **Marge's Diner**
  by Gail Gibbons
  Thomas Y. Cromwell, 1989

Additional Resources

These books, found in your local or school library, can be used to build math concepts.

- **Big Meeting**
  by Dee Parmer Woodtor
  Atheneum, 1996
- **Numbers**
  by Henry Pluckrose
  Children's Press, 1995

Home-School

Family Letter With Activity
Home-School Connection Booklet

The Family Letter for Chapter 1 practices using place value to read large numbers and comparing them to each other. A family activity suggests using cards numbered 0–9 to build and compare three-, four-, five-, and six-digit numbers.

Study Buddies
Home-School Connection Booklet

Study Buddies pages provide reinforcement activities for students to work on with a partner.

- Study Buddies 1A offers practice rounding to the nearest ten and hundred.
- Study Buddies 1B provides reinforcement for comparing and ordering numbers.

Math Backpack
Take-Home Activities

Math Backpack activities provide a link between the classroom and the home. Activity Cards 1–6 can be used with this chapter. Parents and students alike will enjoy using these laminated cards and accompanying manipulatives.

Cross-Curricular Integration

 Science

- Find out about insects, pp. 6, 8.
- Take a look at rocks and minerals, pp. 22–25.

 Language Arts

- Discover symbols and create your own code, p. 41.
- Interpret ads, p. 15.

 Social Studies

- Explore hobbies, pp. 4, 6, 10, 14, 18, 22.
- Learn about Native American dolls, pp. 10–11, 13.
- Learn about ancient Babylon, p. 41.

 Art

- Design a coin, Teacher Guide pp. 1I–1.
- Learn how jade is used in Chinese carvings, p. 25.

Place Value and Money

Theme: COLLECTIONS

Chapter Overview

In this chapter students will read and write whole numbers through hundred thousands, use ordinal numbers, and count coins and bills.

Activating Prior Knowledge

Discuss with students what they already know about place value and money. Record responses on the chalkboard.

Baseline Assessment

Ask questions such as:

- **How can you tell how many tens and ones are in a number?** *(By looking at the digit in the tens place and the digit in the ones place)*

- **How can you count a group of coins?** *(Possible response: Begin with the coin of greatest value and count on from one coin to the next.)*

Save student responses to use with the **Ongoing Assessment** section in the chapter Checkpoints on pages 17 and 35.

Place Value and Money

Chapter Theme: COLLECTIONS

·······Real Facts·······

Most coins are worth their face value. For example, a dime is usually worth 10 cents. But some rare coins are worth more than their face value. Collectors buy and save these rare coins. The table below lists some rare coins that were appraised in 1999.

Prices of Coins Appraised	
Types of Coin	**Price**
Lincoln Penny, 1911-S	$120
Buffalo Nickel, 1916	$32
Liberty Dime, 1887	$100
Quarter, 1932-S	$240
5-Dollar Gold Coin, 1880	$195

Prices are Brilliant Uncirculated

- What coin sold for the most money? the least? **Quarter from 1932; buffalo nickel from 1916**
- How could you use place value to sort the coins by dollar value? **Compare the dollar values by first looking at the hundreds place and then looking at the tens place.**

·······Real People·······

Meet Jeffrey Angello. He began collecting pennies when he was a young boy. Now he has his own coin and stamp company. People can go to his store to buy or sell coins. His store is filled with millions of coins. Some of them are thousands of years old!

xvi

Design a Coin

INDIVIDUAL
Materials
▶ white paper or construction paper
▶ pencils
▶ markers or crayons (including metallic gold and silver, if possible)

Here is a project that will help your students learn more about the values of coins. Specific lessons are referenced to help you work on the project throughout the chapter.

Getting Started

Distribute a few coins to students. Ask them to name some things that are pictured on the coins, and to suggest reasons why these are pictured. Then have students make drawings of their own coins. Remind them that a coin has two sides, so each coin should have two different pictures.

- The first Greek coins, invented around 650 B.C., were egg-shaped mounds of gold and silver. On one side of the coin were scratched lines indicating its weight and value. On the other side was the seal of the person who had guaranteed the weight of the coin.

Using the Data

As students review the table on page 1-I, make sure they understand that the numbers given after the coins are dates. The letters that follow some of the dates show where the coin was minted. Some additional questions you may wish to ask include:

- Are the oldest coins always the most valuable? Explain. *(No; for example, the 1932 quarter is worth more than the 1887 dime.)*

- What kind of graph might you use to show the data in the table? *(A bar graph)*

.........Real People..........

Jeffrey Angello is the president of American Coin and Stamp Co., Inc., the largest coin, gold, and silver exchange in New Jersey. The value of a coin that collectors like Jeffrey buy and sell is determined foremost by how many like it were made that year. Thus, a coin that is 1,500 years old may be worth only about $2, while a coin that is 40 years old may be worth more than $2,000.

Building Vocabulary

These key words will be found in this chapter.

even	place-value blocks
odd	place-value chart
ordinal numbers	expanded form
rounded	standard form

Journal Idea You may wish to have students write about each vocabulary term in their journals at the beginning and end of the chapter.

Project Links

▶ **Lesson 3** Have students use **geometry** to decide on their coin's size and shape. Point out that the coin could be a circle, square, or other shape.

▶ **Lesson 8** Have students use **place value** to decide how much their coin will be worth in dollars and cents. Then they can make their final drawings.

Project Wrap-up

Have students create a class coin collection. Encourage them to **count** the number of coins in the class collection and to **organize** the coins from those of the least value to those of the greatest value. You might also suggest that they **compare** their different coin designs.

Portfolio Students may wish to include their project work in their portfolios.

Lesson Organizer

Objective: Use patterns to identify odd and even numbers.

- **NCTM Standards:** 3, 6, 13
- **Vocabulary:** even, odd
- **Manipulatives:** counters
- **Materials:** hundreds chart, crayons
- **Lesson Resources:**
  Chapter File Folder
    Practice, Reteach, Extend 1-1
    Teaching Tool 10
  Daily Review 1-1
  Practice Workbook, p. 1
  Transparency 14

Problem of the Day   1-1

Each time Nadia picks 2 handfuls of berries, Emma picks 1. If Nadia picks 6 handfuls, how many handfuls does Emma pick? **3 handfuls**

Math Minute

Complete each pattern.
red, blue, red, blue, red, *(blue)*
red, blue, blue, red, blue, *(blue)*
dash, dot, dash, dot, dash, *(dot)*

Even It Out

Using Algebra

You can use patterns to find out if a number is even or odd!

Learning About It

How do you know if a number is even or odd?

Work with a group.

Step 1 Use a hundreds chart like the one shown.

Step 2 Use counters to show each number from 1 to 10. Put the counters into pairs whenever you can.

Word Bank
even
odd

What You Need

For each group:
  hundreds chart
  counters
  blue crayons
  red crayons

  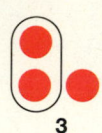
1   2   3

- Which numbers have no counter left over? Circle those numbers on your chart in blue.
  2, 4, 6, 8, 10
- Which numbers have a counter left over? Circle those numbers on your chart in red.
  1, 3, 5, 7, 9

1	2	3	4	5	6	7	8	9	10
11	12	13	14	15	16	17	18	19	20
21	22	23	24	25	26	27	28	29	30
31	32	33	34	35	36	37	38	39	40
41	42	43	44	45	46	47	48	49	50
51	52	53	54	55	56	57	58	59	60
61	62	63	64	65	66	67	68	69	70
71	72	73	74	75	76	77	78	79	80
81	82	83	84	85	86	87	88	89	90
91	92	93	94	95	96	97	98	99	100

All numbers that make pairs and have no counters left over are **even.**

All numbers that make pairs but have 1 counter left over are **odd.**

Step 3 Use counters to show each number from 11 to 20. On your chart, circle even numbers in blue and odd numbers in red. **Blue: 12, 14, 16, 18, 20 Red: 11, 13, 15, 17, 19**

 2

---

1 Introduce

Cooperative Activity

KINESTHETIC

 SMALL GROUPS   10–15 MINUTES

Materials: two-color counters, 6 paper cups

1. Students create patterns by placing different numbers of counters in cups.

2. Students record the pattern they make by writing the number of counters placed in each cup.

3. Students predict the next term of other students' patterns. Then students share their patterns.

2 Teach   Pages 2–3

Discuss how knowing which single-digit numbers are odd and which are even helps you know if two-digit numbers are odd or even.

- Ask: **How does knowing that 9 is odd help you know if 89 is odd or even?** *(Since 9 is odd, 89 is odd.)* **How does knowing that 2 is even help you know if 32 is odd or even?** *(Since 2 is even, 32 is even.)*

Critical Thinking   ANALYSIS

After Think and Discuss, ask: **Why are the odd-even patterns for skip counting by 3 and 7 the same?** *(All odd numbers have the same odd-even pattern.)*

Assess Understanding

After Practice, ask: **Are the number patterns in Exercises 1–4 odd or even?** *(1. odd, 2. even, 3. odd, 4. even)*

 **USING TECHNOLOGY**

Math Blaster® 1, Trash Zapper
Number Patterns: Level 3
Counting by 2s, 3s, 4s
from 26 through 60

Step 4 What pattern do you see on the chart? Use the pattern to complete the chart. Circle even numbers in blue and odd numbers in red.

Some possible answers are: the numbers in the chart alternate odd, even; the columns in the chart also alternate odd, even.

- Look at the even numbers. Which digits are in the ones place? **2, 4, 6, 8, 0**

- Look at the odd numbers. Which digits are in the ones place? **1, 3, 5, 7, 9**

Think and Discuss Use your chart to skip count aloud by 3s. Describe the pattern you see in the even and odd numbers you say. **The pattern is odd, even, odd, even, and so on.**

Practice

Use the hundreds chart. Write the missing numbers in each pattern.

1. 1, 3, 5, ■, ■, 11, ■
   7 9   13

2. 0, 2, ■, 6, ■, ■, 12
   4   8 10

3. 93, ■, 73, 63, ■, ■, 33
   83   53 43

4. ■, 10, ■, 30, 40, ■, 60
   0   20   50

5. 21, 24, 27, ■, ■, ■
   30 33 36

6. 95, 90, 85, ■, ■, ■
   80 75 70

7. Which numbers between 60 and 74 are odd? **61, 63, 65, 67, 69, 71, 73**

 8. Skip count by 10s. Start at 32. Press ③②＋①⓪＝. Continue pressing ＝ five times. Which digit changes each time? Why? **The tens digit; because you are adding 10 each time**

③

Using Algebra

In this lesson, students use **patterns** to identify odd and even numbers.

---

3 Wrap-up

 Journal Idea Your sister wants to split her marble collection with you. How will she know if the collection can be split evenly? *(Sample answer: Group the marbles into pairs. If no marbles are left over, they can be split evenly.)*

Common Error Alert

Watch for students who think numbers ending in zero are neither even nor odd. Have them count by 2s from 2 to 30 and note the numbers that end in zero.

Meeting Individual Needs

For Early Finishers

Students create patterns using odd or even numbers, leaving the last three numbers blank. Students swap patterns with one another and solve.
LOGICAL/MATHEMATICAL

For Extra Help

Play musical chairs. Before each round, ask: **How many children are playing? How many chairs? Are those numbers odd or even?**
VISUAL/SPATIAL

Practice

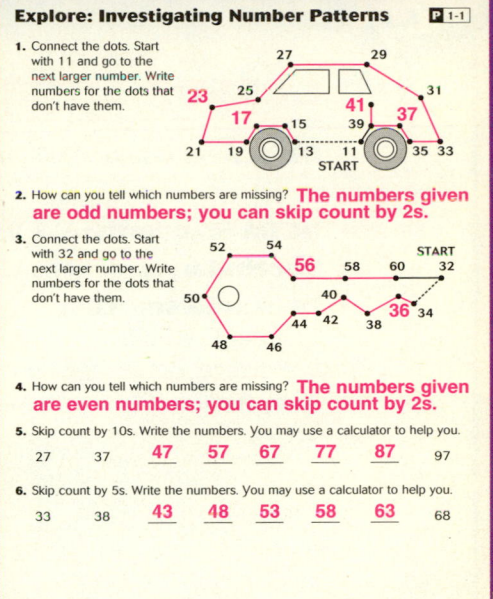

Explore: Investigating Number Patterns P 1-1

1. Connect the dots. Start with 11 and go to the next larger number. Write numbers for the dots that don't have them.

2. How can you tell which numbers are missing? **The numbers given are odd numbers; you can skip count by 2s.**

3. Connect the dots. Start with 32 and go to the next larger number. Write numbers for the dots that don't have them.

4. How can you tell which numbers are missing? **The numbers given are even numbers; you can skip count by 2s.**

5. Skip count by 10s. Write the numbers. You may use a calculator to help you.
27   37   **47   57   67   77   87**   97

6. Skip count by 5s. Write the numbers. You may use a calculator to help you.
33   38   **43   48   53   58   63**   68

© Silver Burdett Ginn Inc. (1)   Use with Grade 3, text pages 2–3.

Reteach

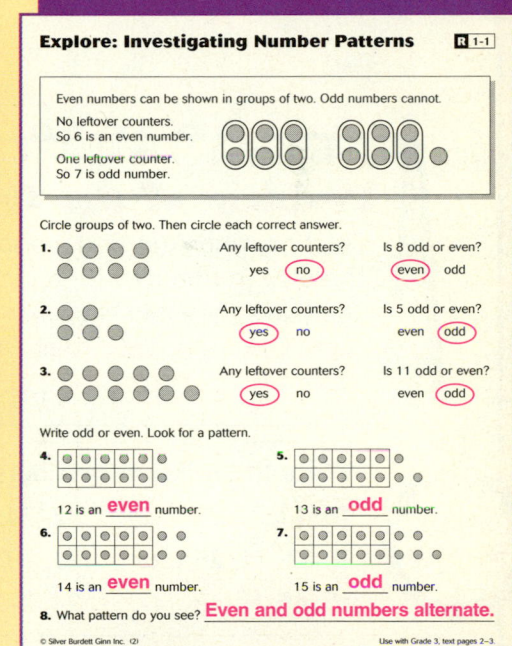

Explore: Investigating Number Patterns R 1-1

8. What pattern do you see? **Even and odd numbers alternate.**

© Silver Burdett Ginn Inc. (2)   Use with Grade 3, text pages 2–3.

Extend

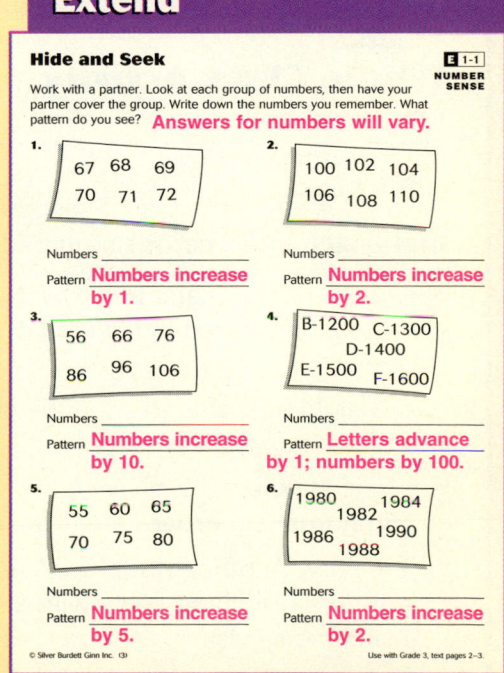

Hide and Seek E 1-1 NUMBER SENSE

Work with a partner. Look at each group of numbers, then have your partner cover the group. Write down the numbers you remember. What pattern do you see? **Answers for numbers will vary.**

1. 67 68 69 70 71 72
   Numbers ___
   Pattern **Numbers increase by 1.**

2. 100 102 104 106 108 110
   Numbers ___
   Pattern **Numbers increase by 2.**

3. 56 66 76 86 96 106
   Numbers ___
   Pattern **Numbers increase by 10.**

4. B-1200 C-1300 D-1400 E-1500 F-1600
   Numbers ___
   Pattern **Letters advance by 1; numbers by 100.**

5. 55 60 65 70 75 80
   Numbers ___
   Pattern **Numbers increase by 5.**

6. 1980 1982 1984 1986 1988 1990
   Numbers ___
   Pattern **Numbers increase by 2.**

© Silver Burdett Ginn Inc. (3)   Use with Grade 3, text pages 2–3.

Lesson Organizer

Objective: Use ordinal numbers 1–100.

- **NCTM Standards:** 1, 3, 6, 8
- **Vocabulary:** ordinal numbers
- **Lesson Resources:**
  Chapter File Folder
    Practice, Reteach, Extend 1-2
  Daily Review 1-2

Problem of the Day   1-2

Chi, Lori, and Ann find a photo booth. All three sit in one row for a picture. Show all the ways they can sit. **6 ways: Chi, Lori, Ann; Chi, Ann, Lori; Ann, Chi, Lori; Ann, Lori, Chi; Lori, Chi, Ann; Lori, Ann, Chi**

Math Minute

Write the missing numbers.

10, 11, ■, 13 *(12)*   72, 74, ■, 78 *(76)*

■, 22, 24, 26 *(20)*   97, 98, ■, 100 *(99)*

45, 46, ■, 48 *(47)*   24, 27, ■, 33 *(30)*

Get in Line

Sometimes numbers are used to show the order of objects or people.

First Mitsu   Second Joe   Third Anna

Learning About It

Many people like to collect things as a hobby. These students are in line to share their collections with the class.

Anna is third in line. Chris is fifth in line. The numbers *third* and *fifth* are ordinal numbers.

▶ **Ordinal numbers** are used to tell the order or position of something.

Word Bank

ordinal numbers

Here are the first twenty-one ordinal numbers.

1st first	2nd second	3rd third	4th fourth	5th fifth	6th sixth	7th seventh
8th eighth	9th ninth	10th tenth	11th eleventh	12th twelfth	13th thirteenth	14th fourteenth
15th fifteenth	16th sixteenth	17th seventeenth	18th eighteenth	19th nineteenth	20th twentieth	21st twenty-first

Think and Discuss Suppose you got in line behind the last student in the picture. What ordinal number would name your position in line? **sixth, 6th**

Try It Out

Write the word name for each ordinal number.

1. 3rd **third**
2. 21st **twenty-first**
3. 9th **ninth**
4. 14th **fourteenth**
5. 11th **eleventh**
6. 1st **first**
7. 18th **eighteenth**
8. 25th **twenty-fifth**
9. 7th **seventh**
10. 68th **sixty-eighth**

4

---

1 Introduce

Whole Class Activity

KINESTHETIC

WHOLE CLASS   10–15 MINUTES

Materials: index cards numbered 25–32

1. Arrange eight chairs in a row. Randomly place a numbered index card on each chair.
2. Ask eight students to sit in the chairs and hold up their cards.
   - Say: **Now switch places until you are in numerical order.**
3. Repeat with other students. Alternate students switching seats with students switching cards.

---

2 Teach   Pages 4–5

Point out that the word *ordinal* comes from the word *order*.

- Ask: **If Anna and Mitsu switched places, who would be first?** *(Anna)*
- Ask: **What place would you be in if the person ahead of you was tenth and the person behind you was twelfth?** *(Eleventh)*

Critical Thinking   SYNTHESIS

After Think and Discuss, ask: **In a line of people, a person is fourth from the front. This person is also second from the back. How many people are in the line?** *(5)*

Assess Understanding

After Try It Out, ask: **What are the word names of the ordinal numbers between 21st and 25th?** *(Twenty-second, twenty-third, twenty-fourth)*

CHALLENGE

How can you be the last person in a line if you are the second person in that line? *(If there are only two people in line)*

Fourth — David

Fifth — Chris

Use the picture of the children in line to answer these questions.

11. What position in line is David? **fourth, 4th**

12. If you are the last person in a line, how many people are behind you? **None**

13. Five people are in line behind Chris. What ordinal number tells the position of the last person? **tenth, 10th**

14. **What If?** Suppose Joe got in line in front of Mitsu. What position would Mitsu be in? **second, 2nd**

Practice

Write the word name for each ordinal number.

INTERNET ACTIVITY
www.sbgmath.com

15. 2nd **second** 16. 12th **twelfth** 17. 16th **sixteenth** 18. 4th **fourth** 19. 20th **twentieth**

20. 8th **eighth** 21. 13th **thirteenth** 22. 5th **fifth** 23. 46th **forty-sixth** 24. 99th **ninety-ninth**

Problem Solving

Use the list at the right for Problems 25–34.

Name the collection in each position.

25. 3rd **dolls** 26. 15th **leaves** 27. 9th **books**

28. 4th **stamps** 29. 6th **coins** 30. 16th **rocks**

In which position is each type of collection?

31. teddy bears **tenth, 10th** 32. stickers **eighth, 8th**

33. sports cards **first, 1st** 34. marbles **seventh, 7th**

Types of Collections
- sports cards
- animal figures
- dolls
- stamps
- action figures
- coins
- marbles
- stickers
- books
- teddy bears
- postcards
- buttons
- video games
- seashells
- leaves
- rocks

Review and Remember

Add or subtract.

35. 1 + 0 **1** 36. 3 + 4 **7** 37. 2 − 2 **0** 38. 1 + 3 **4** 39. 0 + 4 **4**

40. 7 − 2 **5** 41. 9 − 1 **8** 42. 4 + 4 **8** 43. 5 − 3 **2** 44. 6 − 4 **2**

For Extra Practice, see Set A, page 36. **5**

Internet Activity
www.sbgmath.com

Students examine the U.S. Census Bureau rankings of people's first names and write the ordinal number for each ranking.

Practice

Ordinal Numbers
P 1-2

1. Sara has written a list of her favorite animals. In what position is each animal listed? Write the ordinal name.

horses **second**
cats **third**
rabbits **sixth**
monkeys **eighth**
giraffes **ninth**
elephants **tenth**

1. dogs 6. rabbits
2. horses 7. lions
3. cats 8. monkeys
4. hamsters 9. giraffes
5. turtles 10. elephants

Use ordinal numbers to name the position of each shaded triangle. Start from the left.

2. **first, third, sixth, tenth**

3. **second, sixth, tenth, fourteenth**

4. **third, sixth, ninth, twelfth, fifteenth, eighteenth, twenty-first, twenty-fourth**

5. Shade some triangles. Make your own pattern. Name the position of each triangle you shade. Start from the left.
Check that students correctly name the positions of their shaded triangles.

© Silver Burdett Ginn Inc. (4)   Use with Grade 3, text pages 4–5.

Reteach

Ordinal Numbers
R 1-2

Ordinal numbers are used to show the order of people or objects. Here are the first 24 ordinal numbers.

1st first	2nd second	3rd third	4th fourth	5th fifth	6th sixth
7th seventh	8th eighth	9th ninth	10th tenth	11th eleventh	12th twelfth
13th thirteenth	14th fourteenth	15th fifteenth	16th sixteenth	17th seventeenth	18th eighteenth
19th nineteenth	20th twentieth	21st twenty-first	22nd twenty-second	23rd twenty-third	24th twenty-fourth

A	B	C	D	E	F	G	H	I	J	K	L	M
1	**2**	**3**	**4**	**5**	**6**	**7**	**8**	**9**	**10**	**11**	**12**	**13**

N	O	P	Q	R	S	T	U	V	W	X	Y	Z
14	**15**	**16**	**17**	**18**	**19**	**20**	**21**	**22**	**23**	**24**	**25**	**26**

Underneath each letter above, write the number of its order in the alphabet. Now write the ordinal name for each of the following letters in the alphabet.

1. The letter A comes **first** 2. The letter N comes **fourteenth**

3. The letter W comes **twenty-third** 4. The letter J is **tenth**

5. The letter G is **seventh** 6. The letter P is **sixteenth**

7. The letter C is **third** 8. The letter Z is **twenty-sixth**

© Silver Burdett Ginn Inc. (5)   Use with Grade 3, text pages 4–5.

Extend

Racing Results
E 1-2
REASONING

Solve each puzzle.

HINT: Draw a picture to help you solve each problem.

1. Shaun, Angel, and Chris ran in a race. One finished 3rd, one finished 5th, and one finished 8th. If Chris ran faster than Shaun, and Angel ran faster than Chris, who finished 5th? **Chris**

2. The 4 winners of a race posed for a picture. Margaret stood between Pete and Isaac. Isaac stood between Margaret and Isabel. What 2 winners stood at the ends of the line? **Pete and Isabel**

3. Three of the Cougars finished 1st, 4th, and 6th in the 100-meter dash. If Sara ran faster than Carol, and Carol ran faster than Nicole, who finished 4th? **Carol**

4. Tara has not won as many medals as Nadia. Grace has won two more medals than Nadia. Which of the three runners has won the most medals? **Grace**

Try these tough teasers.

5. The Gazelles, the Cheetahs, and the Falcons competed in a track meet. The coaches of these teams are Stan, Pam, and Ted. Stan's team won. Pam's team beat the Gazelles. If Stan coaches the Falcons, what team does Ted coach? **The Gazelles**

6. Three boys watched their sisters run the 50-yard dash. Sue beat Meg. Jim's sister beat Max's sister, and Max's sister beat Josh's sister. If Jill came in 1st, who is Josh's sister? **Meg**

© Silver Burdett Ginn Inc. (6)   Use with Grade 3, text pages 4–5.

---

3 Wrap-up

Julio is first in line. Pati is third. Douglas is between Julio and Pati. In what position is Douglas? *(Second)* Pati lets Monique in front of her. In what position is Monique? *(Third)*

Common Error Alert

Watch for students who confuse cardinal and ordinal numbers. Remind them that ordinal numbers show the order of something, for example first, tenth, twelfth.

Meeting Individual Needs

For Early Finishers

Using ordinal numbers, students list all the steps it takes to tie shoelaces, then follow the steps to see if they included all the steps needed.
KINESTHETIC

Acquiring English Proficiency

Write the names of ordinal numbers to twentieth on index cards. Children take turns putting them in order.

LINGUISTIC

Lesson Organizer

Objective: Read and write numbers to 999.

- **NCTM Standards:** 1, 3, 6, 8
- **Manipulatives:** base-ten blocks (optional)
- **Lesson Resources:**
  Chapter File Folder
     Practice, Reteach, Extend 1-3
     Teaching Tools 12, 22
  Daily Review 1-3
  Transparencies 7, 10, 17

Problem of the Day   1-3

Dolls are arranged in a pattern. The first shelf has 3 dolls. The second has 5 dolls. The third has 7 dolls. The fifth has 11 dolls. How many dolls are on the fourth shelf? **9 dolls**

Math Minute

Write the numeral.

ten *(10)*	eighteen *(18)*
nineteen *(19)*	fourteen *(14)*
twenty *(20)*	forty *(40)*

1 Introduce

Cooperative Activity
KINESTHETIC

🔆 PAIRS   ⏱ 5–10 MINUTES

Materials: spinners (1–9), base-ten blocks

1. One student spins twice to make a two-digit number. The other student models the number, using base-ten blocks.

2. Students switch roles and continue with other two-digit numbers.

3. Partners keep a list of the numbers spun. After students have modeled three or more numbers, say: **Write the numbers in order from least to greatest.**

Name That Number

You can show and describe numbers in many different ways.

Learning About It

James Fujita has an amazing collection—of bugs. He has been collecting them since he was in first grade. Among his many insects, James has 26 butterflies.

You can show the number 26 in different ways.

THERE'S ALWAYS A WAY!

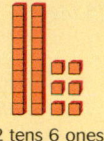 You can use **place-value blocks**.	You can use a **place-value chart**.
2 tens 6 ones	tens | ones 2 | 6

You can use **expanded form**.	You can use **standard form**.	You can use **words**.
20 + 6	26	twenty-six

Kid Connection ➤
James Fujita, of California, has hundreds of bugs. He finds bugs everywhere he goes. He even found a new kind of cricket. James gives some of his bugs to museums and zoos. He brought two of his largest bugs to a TV talk show. They became the stars of the show.

 6

2 Teach   Pages 6–9

Have students study the There's Always A Way! box, which displays different ways of showing 26.

- Ask: **How is the expanded form related to the model with place-value blocks?** *(The 2 tens blocks stand for 20; the 6 ones blocks stand for 6.)*

Connecting Ideas

Once students understand the different ways they can show 2-digit numbers, they are ready to find ways to show 3-digit numbers.

- Have students study the different ways to show 348 in the There's Always A Way! box on page 7.

- Ask: **Suppose there were 6 hundreds in the number instead of 3. What number would that be?** *(648)*

Connecting Ideas

You can also show three-digit numbers in a different way.

Here are some ways to show the number 348.

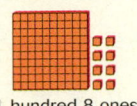

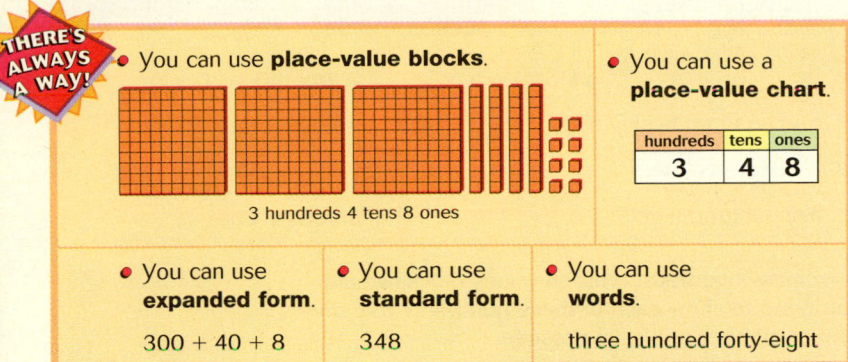

- You can use **place-value blocks**.

3 hundreds 4 tens 8 ones

- You can use a **place-value chart**.

hundreds	tens	ones
3	4	8

- You can use **expanded form**.

300 + 40 + 8

- You can use **standard form**.

348

- You can use **words**.

three hundred forty-eight

Another Example

Here are some ways to show the number 108.

- place-value blocks

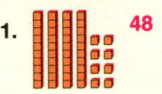

1 hundred 8 ones

- place-value chart

hundreds	tens	ones
1	0	8

- expanded form

100 + 8

- standard form

108

- words

one hundred eight

Think and Discuss Look at the place-value chart for the example above. What does the digit 0 mean? **There are no tens.**

Try It Out

Write each number in standard form.

1. 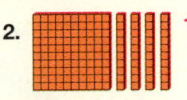 **48**

2. 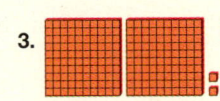 **140**

3. 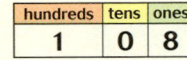 **204**

4. 300 + 60 + 8
368

5. 500 + 30
530

6. 400 + 60 + 5
465

7. 6 hundreds 7 ones
607

8. forty-seven
47

9. six hundred two
602

Using Technology
CD-ROM

MathProcessor™

Tools: Base-Ten Blocks, Number spaces
Objective: Model Three-Digit Numbers

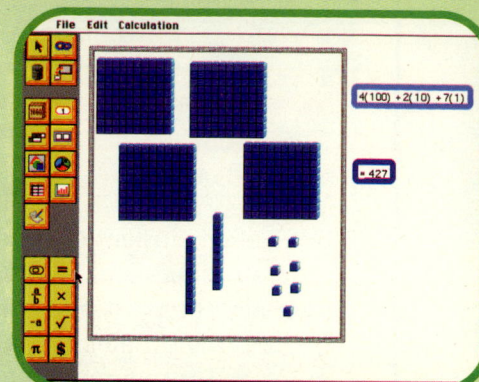

- Link Base-Ten Blocks to two Number spaces.

- Show 427. Click catalog items or use the Stamp tool. Separate items so that the model shows clearly hundreds, tens, and ones.

- Click one Number space.

- Click.

Additional Activities

See also **Activities 1 and 2** in the MathProcessor™ Activity Cards.

Practice

Write each number in standard form.

10.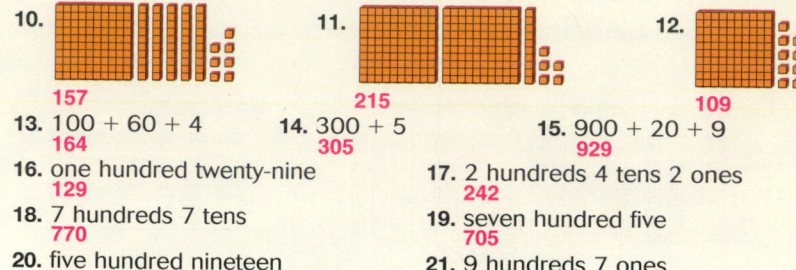
157

11.
215

12.
109

13. $100 + 60 + 4$
164

14. $300 + 5$
305

15. $900 + 20 + 9$
929

16. one hundred twenty-nine
129

17. 2 hundreds 4 tens 2 ones
242

18. 7 hundreds 7 tens
770

19. seven hundred five
705

20. five hundred nineteen
519

21. 9 hundreds 7 ones
907

How many hundreds, tens, and ones blocks would you need to show each of these numbers? Use the fewest number of blocks possible.

22. 341 **3 hundreds 4 tens 1 one**   23. 30 **3 tens**   24. 829 **8 hundreds 2 tens 9 ones**   25. 704 **7 hundreds 4 on**

26. 48 **4 tens 8 ones**   27. 507 **5 hundreds 7 ones**   28. 600 **6 hundreds**   29. 396 **3 hundreds 9 tens 6 one**

Using Algebra Complete each pattern.

30. 486, 586, 686, ■, ■, ■   **786 886 986**

31. 799, 699, 599, ■, ■, ■   **499 399 299**

32. 68, 168, 268, ■, ■, ■   **368 468 568**

33. 574, 474, 374, ■, ■, ■   **274 174 74**

34. 335, 330, 325, ■, ■, ■   **320 315 310**

35. 216, 226, 236, ■, ■, ■   **246 256 266**

Problem Solving

36. James has 100 beetles in one tray and 30 spiders in another tray. He put 1 walking stick next to the 2 trays. How many bugs are there in all? **131 bugs**

37. Suppose you had a collection of two hundred fifty-four bugs. Write the number that shows how many that is. **254**

◄ **Science Connection**
Walking sticks look like real sticks. Their shape and color helps to hide them from enemies when on a branch.

8

---

2 Teach (continued)

★ GIFTED AND TALENTED

Using Ordinal Numbers Have students work in pairs and use ordinal numbers to explain how to get from their classroom to some other familiar place, such as the basketball court in the gym or playground.

38. Using Algebra What missing number would make this sentence true? 800 + ■ + 3 = 863
60

39. Analyze A number has the same number of hundreds, tens, and ones. If the sum of the digits is 6, what is the number? **222**

40. You Decide Suppose you had 50 ones cubes and 3 tens blocks. How could you use them to show the number 48? Explain your reasoning.
Use 3 tens blocks and 18 ones cubes or use 48 ones cubes. Explanations will vary.

41. Explain How do you know that 398 is greater than 389? **There are 9 tens in 398 and only 8 tens in 389.**

Review and Remember
Add or subtract.

42. 7 + 6 **13**	**43.** 15 − 8 **7**	**44.** 13 − 8 **5**	**45.** 6 − 6 **0**
46. 6 − 3 **3**	**47.** 18 − 9 **9**	**48.** 8 + 5 **13**	**49.** 10 + 10 **20**
50. 6 + 3 + 2 **11**	**51.** 5 + 1 + 4 **10**	**52.** 7 + 5 + 2 **14**	**53.** 8 + 1 + 9 **18**

Time for Technology
Using a Calculator

Showing Numbers

To show the number nine hundred three on a calculator, press 9 0 3 .

Show each of the numbers below on a calculator. Write the keys you pushed. Then write the number in standard form.

1. forty-seven
  4 7; 47
2. six hundreds four ones
  6 0 4; 604
3. fifty
  5 0; 50
4. two hundred fifteen
  2 1 5; 215
5. seventy-four
  7 4; 74
6. eight hundreds
  8 0 0; 800

For Extra Practice, see Set B, page 36. **9**

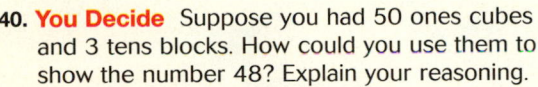
Using Algebra

Students use **patterns** to complete a number sequence. In Exercise 38, students find a value to solve an **equation**.

Time for Technology

Students use a calculator to show numbers written in standard form.

---

3 Wrap-up

How can you show the number 909, using base-ten blocks? *(Nine flats, nine cubes)* using a place-value chart? *(9 hundreds, 0 tens, 9 ones)* in expanded form? *(900 + 9)* in words? *(Nine hundred nine)*

Common Error Alert

Watch for students who forget to use zero in a place to indicate that there are zero ones, tens, hundreds, etc. Have students copy numbers in place-value charts.

Meeting Individual Needs

For Early Finishers

Provide used newspapers and magazines and challenge children to find at least five numbers written in standard form and five numbers written in words.
LINGUISTIC

Manipulatives

One student writes a three-digit number. The partner asks questions to determine the number and uses place-value blocks to show it.
KINESTHETIC

Practice

Understanding Numbers to 999 P 1-3

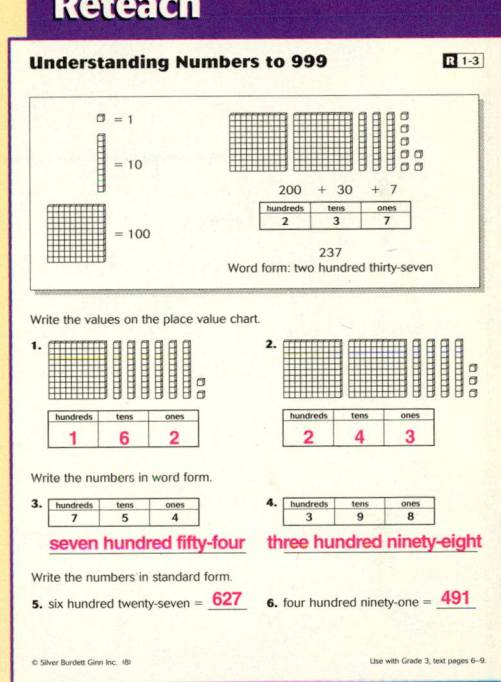

Reteach

Understanding Numbers to 999 R 1-3

Extend

Mystery Numbers E 1-3 NUMBER SENSE

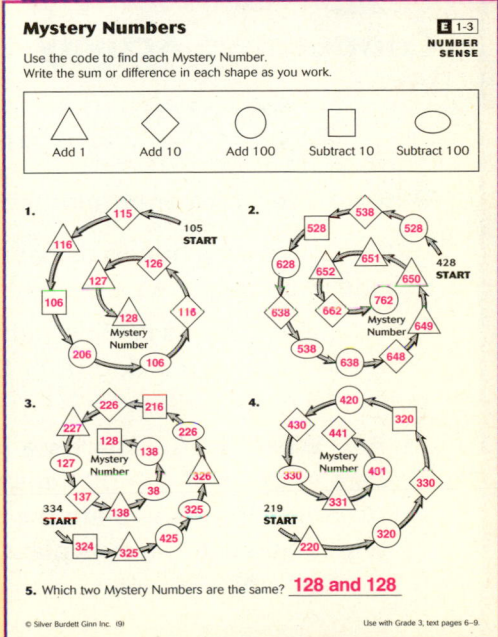

Lesson Organizer

Objective: Round numbers to the nearest ten or hundred.

- **NCTM Standards:** 1, 3, 5, 6
- **Lesson Resources:**
  Chapter File Folder
     Practice, Reteach, Extend 1-4
     Teaching Tool 19
  Daily Review 1-4
  Practice Workbook, p. 2
  Study Buddies 1A
  Transparency 16

Problem of the Day   1-4

Use the digits 2, 3, and 5. What is the greatest 3-digit number you can make? What is the least 3-digit number? **Greatest: 532; least: 235**

Math Minute

How many tens?

55 *(5)*	89 *(8)*
326 *(2)*	490 *(9)*
905 *(0)*	72 *(7)*

Close Enough

You can round numbers when you do not need an exact number.

Learning About It

Many people collect dolls. Three kinds of Native American dolls are shown at the right. Suppose you had 22 patchwork dolls, 25 corn husk dolls, and 28 rag dolls. You could say that you have about 20 patchwork dolls, about 30 corn husk dolls, and about 30 rag dolls.

The word *about* means that the numbers are not exact. The numbers have been **rounded** to the nearest 10.

▲ Iroquois corn husk doll

Seminole palmetto and patchwork dolls ◄

▲ Plains rag doll

25 rounds up to

rounds down to **22**

28 rounds up to

| 20 | 21 | 22 | 23 | 24 | 25 | 26 | 27 | 28 | 29 | 30 |

22 is closer to 20 than to 30.
22 rounds down to 20.

28 is closer to 30 than to 20.
28 rounds up to 30.

25 is halfway between 20 and 30.
If a number is halfway between 2 tens, you round up.
25 rounds up to 30.

More Examples

You can round money to the nearest ten cents.

A. 84¢ rounds down to 80¢.   **B.** 86¢ rounds up to 90¢.

rounds down to **84**   **86** rounds up to

| 80 | 81 | 82 | 83 | 84 | 85 | 86 | 87 | 88 | 89 | 90 |

10

---

1 Introduce

Cooperative Activity
VISUAL/SPATIAL

PAIRS   15–20 MINUTES

Materials: grid paper or hundreds chart

1. Students make a hundreds chart similar to the chart on page 2.

2. Students take turns circling numbers on the chart that have a 1, 3, 7, or 8 in the tens place.

- Ask: **Where on the chart are the numbers with 1 and 3 in the tens place?** *(Near the top)* **Where are the numbers with 7 and 8 in the tens place?** *(Near the bottom)*

---

2 Teach   Pages 10–13

Explain that one instance in which rounding is important is when deciding how much money to give a cashier when buying something.

- Ask: **What two tens does 44 come between?** *(40 and 50)*

- Ask: **What number is halfway between 40 and 50?** *(45)*

- Ask: **Which ten is 44 closer to?** *(40)*

Connecting Ideas

Once students know how to round 2-digit numbers, they can make the connection to rounding 3-digit numbers.

- Be sure students realize that they will now be thinking about the two hundreds a number comes between.

- Ask: **What is a 3-digit number that would round to 500? to 800? to 1,000?** *(Sample answers: 500: 462 or 501; 800: 778 or 842; 1,000: 975 or 987)*

Connecting Ideas

You can use what you learned about rounding two-digit numbers to round three-digit numbers.

This is how you would round 215, 250, and 275 to the nearest hundred.

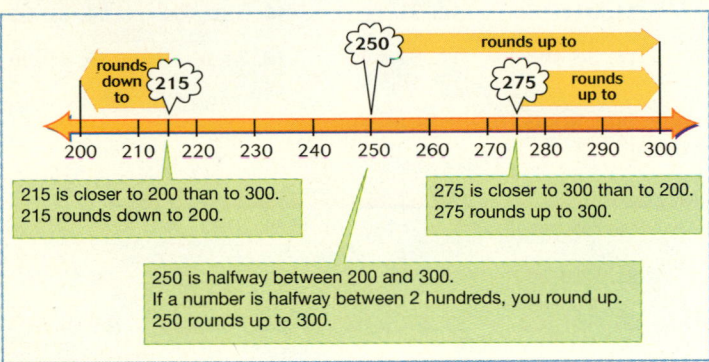

215 is closer to 200 than to 300.
215 rounds down to 200.

275 is closer to 300 than to 200.
275 rounds up to 300.

250 is halfway between 200 and 300.
If a number is halfway between 2 hundreds, you round up.
250 rounds up to 300.

More Examples

You can round money to the nearest dollar.

A. $5.49 rounds down to $5.00.   **B.** $5.74 rounds up to $6.00.

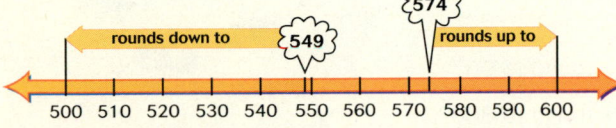

Think and Discuss Explain how you would round the number 958 to the nearest hundred.

Explanations will vary. One possible answer is that 958 is closer to 1,000 than to 900, so 958 rounds up to 1,000. Another answer is to look at the tens digit. It is 5, so you round the number up to the next hundred. So 958 rounds up to 1,000.

Try It Out

What number is halfway between these numbers?

1. 20 and 30
25

2. 60 and 70
65

3. 10 and 20
15

4. 80 and 90
85

5. 200 and 300
250

6. 400 and 500
450

7. 600 and 700
650

8. 800 and 900
850

9. 100 and 200
150

▲ Hopi kachina doll

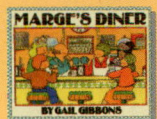

Using Technology
CD-ROM

Math Blaster® 1, Trash Zapper

Estimation: Levels 1, 2, 3

- In Levels 1 and 2, students estimate numbers 0–60, rounding to the nearest 10.
- In Level 3, students estimate numbers 50–499, rounding to the nearest 100.

Sample Problems:

Level 1: 12 rounds to 10

Level 2: 57 rounds to 60

Level 3: 235 rounds to 200

Use the number line. Round to the nearest ten or ten cents.

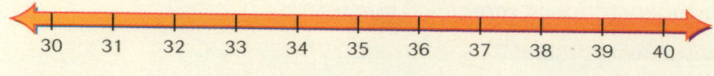

| | | | | | | | | | | |
|30|31|32|33|34|35|36|37|38|39|40|

10. 36 **40**   **11.** 31¢ **30¢**   **12.** 35 **40**   **13.** 39¢ **40¢**   **14.** 32 **30**

15. 33¢ **30¢**   **16.** 38 **40**   **17.** 37¢ **40¢**   **18.** 31 **30**   **19.** 40 **40**

Use the number line. Round to the nearest hundred or dollar.

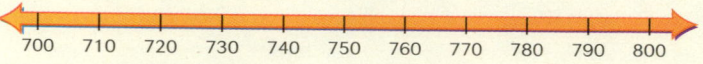

| | | | | | | | | | | |
|700|710|720|730|740|750|760|770|780|790|800|

20. 719 **700**   **21.** 754 **800**   **22.** 748 **700**   **23.** 726 **700**   **24.** $7.76 **$8.00**

25. $7.03 **$7.00**   **26.** 781 **800**   **27.** $7.99 **$8.00**   **28.** 760 **800**   **29.** $7.30 **$7.00**

Practice

Use the numbers at the right to answer Exercises 30–33.

30. Which numbers round to 80?
81, 84

31. Which numbers round to 90?
85, 93

32. Which numbers round to 800?
795, 843

33. Which numbers round to 700?
730, 749

85 84 93 795 81 843 730 749

Round to the nearest ten or ten cents.

34. 55 **60**   **35.** 87 **90**   **36.** 34 **30**   **37.** 49¢ **50¢**   **38.** 22 **20**

39. 56¢ **60¢**   **40.** 16 **20**   **41.** 93¢ **90¢**   **42.** 45¢ **50¢**   **43.** 76¢ **80¢**

Round to the nearest hundred or dollar.

44. $7.49 **$7.00**   **45.** 571 **600**   **46.** 360 **400**   **47.** 852 **900**   **48.** 442 **400**

49. $1.30 **$1.00**   **50.** $4.18 **$4.00**   **51.** $9.78 **$10.00**   **52.** 323 **300**   **53.** $2.60 **$3.00**

 12

---

2 Teach (continued)

Assess Understanding

After Try It Out, ask: **How do you know that 35 is halfway between 30 and 40?** *(It is 5 more than 30 and 5 less than 40.)*

★ GIFTED AND TALENTED

Go Shopping Provide students with a newspaper advertisement or a list of school supplies and prices. Ask: **How many items cost about a dollar? What are they? Which items cost about two dollars? What could you buy if you had five one-dollar bills?**

Problem Solving

54. A museum has 32 storytelling dolls in a special display case. About how many dolls are in the case? **About 30 dolls**

55. What If? Suppose the museum had 38 storytelling dolls in the display case. About how many dolls would there be in the case? **About 40**

56. Analyze A number has the digits 3, 4, and 6. When you round the number to the nearest hundred, you get 500. What is the number? **463**

▲ Cochiti Pueblo storytelling doll

Review and Remember

Add or subtract.

57. 4 + 7 **11** **58.** 15 − 6 **9** **59.** 6 + 9 **15** **60.** 3 + 8 **11** **61.** 12 − 7 **5**

62. 18 − 9 **9** **63.** 5 + 7 **12** **64.** 8 + 6 **14** **65.** 16 − 8 **8** **66.** 14 − 7 **7**

Critical Thinking Corner

Number Sense

Rounding Up and Rounding Down

This number line shows the numbers that round to 600.

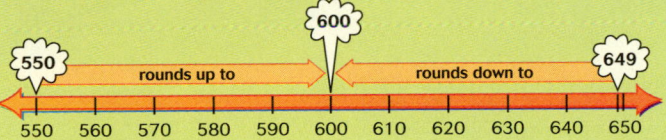

- 550 is the least whole number that rounds up to 600.
- 649 is the greatest whole number that rounds down to 600.

What are the least and the greatest whole numbers that round to each number?

1. 700 **650, 749**   **2.** 500 **450, 549**   **3.** 900 **850, 949**   **4.** 400 **350, 449**

For Extra Practice, see Set C, page 36. **13**

Critical Thinking

Discuss the greatest and least two-digit number that will round to 100. *(99 and 50)*

---

3 Wrap-up

Tell how to round 310 to the nearest hundred. *(Since the 1 in the tens place is less than 5, round down to 300.)*

Journal Idea List grocery store items. Assign each a price. Add the cost and round to the nearest dollar.

Common Error Alert

Watch for students who make the decision to round up or down without using the digit immediately to the right of the rounding place.

Meeting Individual Needs

For Early Finishers

A student uses the spinner to form a three-digit number, then rounds it to the nearest 10 or 100. A partner tells how the number was rounded.
KINESTHETIC

For Extra Help

Students round 33, 38, 110, and 198. Then they use number lines to explain their answers. *(30, 40, 100, 200)*

KINESTHETIC

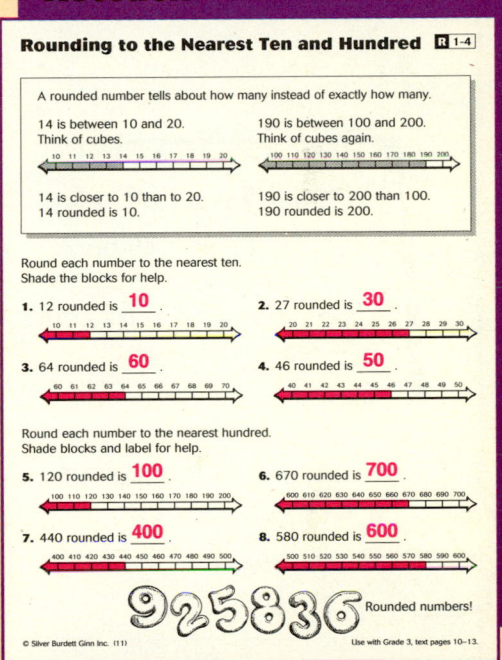
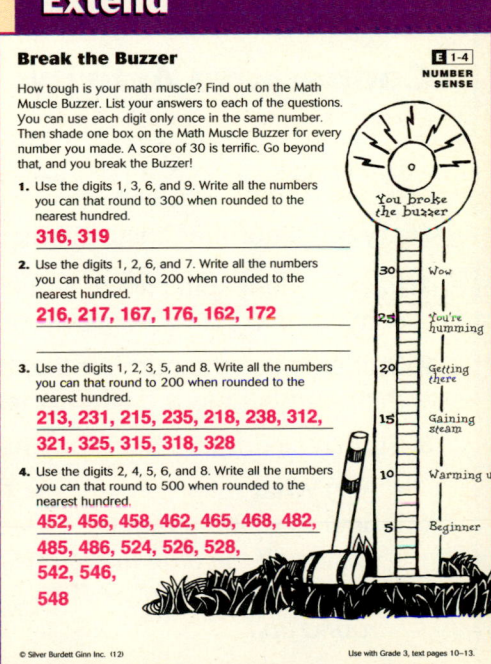

Lesson Organizer

Objective: Use estimates or exact numbers to solve problems.

- **NCTM Standards:** 1, 3, 5, 7
- **Lesson Resources:**
  Chapter File Folder
    Practice, Reteach, Extend 1-5
  Daily Review 1-5

Problem of the Day   1-5

"I read about 40 books," Al said. The number 40 is rounded to the nearest 10. How many books could Al actually have read? **Between 35 and 44**

Math Minute

Round to the nearest ten.

18 *(20)*	42 *(40)*
56 *(60)*	68 *(70)*
77 *(80)*	23 *(20)*

Developing Skills for Problem Solving

First read for understanding and then focus on whether the numbers are exact numbers or estimates.

READ FOR UNDERSTANDING

*E*mma has more than 500 stamps in her stamp collection. She has almost 40 flower stamps. She also has 22 bird stamps and 12 stamps from foreign countries. Her bird stamps cost $0.32 each.

1. How many stamps does Emma have? **More than 500 stamps**
2. How many flower stamps does she have? **Almost 40 stamps**
3. How many stamps from foreign countries does she have? **12 stamps**

THINK AND DISCUSS

MATH FOCUS

Exact Numbers or Estimates
Estimates are not exact numbers. Words like *more than*, *almost*, and *about* can tell you that numbers are estimated, not exact.

Reread the paragraph at the top of the page.

4. Does Emma have exactly 40 flower stamps? If not, does she have more or fewer? How can you tell? **No; she has fewer. The problem states that she has "almost 40."**
5. Does Emma have exactly 12 stamps from foreign countries? If not, does she have more or fewer? How can you tell?
   See Additional Answers, pages 36–37.
6. When might the number 30 stand for an exact amount? When might it be an estimate?
   See Additional Answers, pages 36–37.

14

1 Introduce

Cooperative Activity
LOGICAL/MATHEMATICAL

PAIRS   **10–15 MINUTES**

Materials: number lines, spinners (0–9)

1. Each student spins twice and uses the spins to make a two-digit number.
2. Students use the number line to round their numbers to the nearest ten.
3. Students compare how they rounded.

- Ask: **What rules can you use to decide how to round a number?** *(Sample answer: If the digit in the ones place is 4 or less, round down; if it's 5 or more, round up.)*

2 Teach   Pages 14–15

Read for Understanding Have students read the paragraph. The questions below it are reading comprehension questions based on information that can be found in the paragraph.

Think and Discuss As you discuss the math focus, have students use the words *more than, almost,* and *about* to describe the number of items in the classroom.

After discussing the questions, ask: **Is $0.32 an exact or estimated number?** *(Exact)* **Is 22 bird stamps an exact or estimated number?** *(Exact)*

Critical Thinking ANALYSIS
After Think and Discuss, ask: **How many students are in your school? Give an example of a situation where you would use an estimated number for the student population.**

Assess Understanding
Before Show What You Learned, ask: **What words tell you that a number is an estimate?** *(Sample answer:* nearly, more than, about*)*

Show What You Learned

Answer each question. Give a reason for your choice.

*E*d's aunt gave him almost 300 stamps. His grandfather gave him 50 airplane stamps and 30 dog stamps. His uncle gave him about 100 stamps of famous people.

1 Which word helps you know that 300 stamps is an estimate?

a. gave

b. stamps

c. almost

2 Which word helps you know that 100 stamps is an estimate?

a. gave

b. about

c. stamps

3 Which sentence tells how many airplane stamps Ed received from his grandfather?

a. Ed received exactly 50 airplane stamps.

b. Ed received almost 50 airplane stamps.

c. Ed received less than 50 airplane stamps.

Use the ad at the right to answer Problems 4–7.

4 There are 4 numbers in the ad. How many of the numbers are estimates?

a. two of the numbers

b. three of the numbers

c. all of the numbers

> **STAMP IT!**
>
> Open 6 Days a Week
>
> More than 700 stamps available!
> Over 30 kinds to choose from!
>
> **Only 10¢ each!**

5 How much would 4 stamps cost altogether?

a. less than 40¢

b. more than 40¢

c. exactly 40¢

6 Which of the following could be the number of stamps available?

a. 700 stamps

b. 697 stamps

c. 720 stamps

7 **Journal Idea** Explain how you can tell which numbers in the ad are estimates and which numbers are exact. **When words like *more than* and *over* are used to describe a number, the number is an estimate. Otherwise, the number is usually exact.**

15

---

3 Wrap-up

Mae received $5.00 as change from a purchase. Is this an exact or estimated number? *(Exact)*

Journal Idea Have students list additional examples of when estimated numbers might be used.

Common Error Alert

Watch for students who think that using the word *about* is the only way you can tell if a number is estimated. Have them list other words that might be used.

Meeting Individual Needs

For Early Finishers

Have students create a two-column chart with the headings *Exact Numbers* and *Estimated Numbers*. Students list examples under each heading.

LOGICAL/MATHEMATICAL

Gifted and Talented

Using the phrases listed in the Math Focus on p. 14, challenge students to list estimated numbers they use during a typical school day.

SOCIAL/COOPERATIVE

Problem-Solving Strategy: Use Logical Reasoning

Lesson Organizer

Objective: Use logical reasoning to solve problems.

- **NCTM Standards:** 1, 3, 6, 8
- **Lesson Resources:**
  Chapter File Folder
     Practice, Reteach, Extend 1-9
  Daily Review 1-9
  Transparency 8

Problem of the Day   1-9

Use only the digits 9, 8, and 7. Make five number sentences that compare 2-digit numbers. Use the < sign. You can repeat digits. **Sample answers: 77 < 78, 79 < 87, 77 < 99**

Math Minute

Fill in the blank.

68, 78, __, 98, 108 *(88)*

__, 310, 410, 510 *(210)*

999, 888, 777, 666, __ *(555)*

1,020, 1,030, 1,040, __, 1,060 *(1,050)*

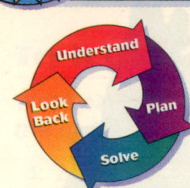

Problem Solving
Use Logical Reasoning

Sometimes you can use logical reasoning to solve problems.

Sam and Leah are arranging four model cars. Leah puts the red car in front of the blue car. Sam puts the yellow car between the blue car and the red car. Leah puts the purple car next to the red car but not next to the yellow car. What is the order of the cars?

 UNDERSTAND

What do you need to find?

You need to find how Sam and Leah are arranging the four model cars.

 PLAN

How can you solve the problem?

You can use **logical reasoning** to help you organize the facts. As you read each sentence of the problem, start listing the order of the cars. Adjust your list each time you find new information.

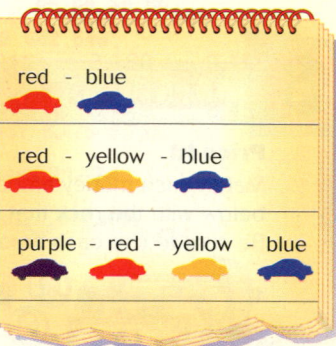

red - blue

red - yellow - blue

purple - red - yellow - blue

 SOLVE

The order of the cars is purple, red, yellow, and blue.

 LOOK BACK

Compare your answer with the facts in the problem. Does your answer match the facts? **The answer should match each fact in the problem.**

26

---

1 Introduce

Whole Class Activity
KINESTHETIC

 WHOLE CLASS   5–10 MINUTES

Materials: taped music

1. Students place their chairs in a row in the middle of the room.

2. When the music plays, students walk around the chairs in a circle. When the music stops, they sit in any chair.

3. Students identify which classmates are in the following positions: *first, last, before the 6th place, after the 8th place.*

---

2 Teach   Pages 26–27

Have students read the introduction.

Understand Ask: **Could a yellow car be between a blue and a green car and not next to either of them? Explain.** *(Yes; a car can be between two cars and not immediately next to either of them.)*

Plan Make sure students read the clues in the problem in the order in which they appear.

Solve Remind students that there is more than one way to solve a problem. For example, they can make drawings or use manipulatives to help visualize the problem.

Look Back Students can point to the cars in their answer as they read the clues in the problem.

Critical Thinking   ANALYSIS

After Look Back, ask: **What if Leah put the red car after the blue car? What would have been the order of the cars?** Have the students redo the problem. *(Blue, red, yellow, purple)*

Assess Understanding

Before Using the Strategy, ask: **How can drawing a picture help you solve a problem?** *(Sample answer: It helps you visualize clearly the problem and see its parts.)*

Using the Strategy

Use logical reasoning to solve each problem.

1 Julie has 4 glass horses on a shelf. The black horse is between the brown horse and the silver horse. The brown horse is fourth. The other horse is red. What is the color of the third horse? **Black**

2 Mary is thinking of an even number that uses the digits 0, 1, 2, and 3. The number is greater than 2,000 but less than 3,000. There is a 3 in the tens place. What is the number? **2,130**

3 Aaron gave Melinda a hint about the number of trucks in his collection. He said, "It is an odd number less than 20 and greater than 10. The sum of the digits is 6." How many trucks are in Aaron's collection? **15 trucks**

4 Kent is looking at a picture of himself and his family. His mom and dad are on each end. Kent's brother is next to Kent and to the left of his dad. Kent's sister is to the right of his mom. Who is in the middle of the picture? **Possible answers: Kent or his brother**

Mixed Strategy Review

Try these or other strategies to solve each problem.
Tell which strategy you used. **Strategies may vary. Possible strategies are given.**

Problem Solving Strategies
- *Write a Number Sentence*
- *Use Logical Reasoning*
- *Find a Pattern*
- *Draw a Picture*

5 Jeff arranges fall leaves around the bulletin board in this order: brown, green, red, yellow. If he continues the pattern, what color will the 16th leaf be? *Draw a Picture;* **yellow**

6 Josh is thinking of a number between 25 and 60. There is a 4 in the ones place. The sum of the digits is 9. What is the number? *Use Logical Reasoning;* **54**

7 You have 11 toy boats. Eight of them are red. If you want 15 red boats, how many more red boats do you need? *Write a Number Sentence;* **7 red boats**

27

3 Wrap-up

Journal Idea Write a problem that requires finding a number based on at least three clues. Solve it, then challenge a classmate to solve it.

Common Error Alert

Watch for students who do not use all of the facts in a logic problem. Ask them to compare their answers against each fact to see if their answers are correct.

Meeting Individual Needs

For Early Finishers

Challenge students to write a word problem that is solved by using logical reasoning. They can model it after one of the problems in the lesson.

LOGICAL/MATHEMATICAL

Inclusion

Using colored counters, have students take turns creating sequences and then writing problems for the sequences.

VISUAL

Lesson Organizer

Objective: Write five- and six-digit numbers.

- **NCTM Standards:** 1, 3, 6, 13
- **Lesson Resources:**
  Chapter File Folder
    Practice, Reteach, Extend 1-10
    Teaching Tool 12
  Daily Review 1-10
  Transparencies 7, 10, 17

Problem of the Day   1-10

Pictures of oak, elm, fir, and pine trees must be placed on a page. There are four pictures of each kind of tree. How can you arrange the pictures so that each row and column has one of each kind of tree?

Math Minute

Write the number.

three thousand, eighty-five *(3,085)*

two hundred ninety-eight *(298)*

one thousand, nineteen *(1,019)*

seven hundred sixty-seven *(767)*

Mounds of Marbles

You can use what you know about place value to write five-digit and six-digit numbers.

 13,783

Learning About It

How many marbles do you think fit into a backpack? This backpack holds 13,783 marbles. Here are some ways to show this number.

THERE'S ALWAYS A WAY!

- Use a **place-value chart**.

ten thousands	thousands	hundreds	tens	ones
1	3,	7	8	3

- Use **expanded form**. 10,000 + 3,000 + 700 + 80 + 3
- Use **standard form**. 13,783
- Use **words**. thirteen thousand, seven hundred eighty-three

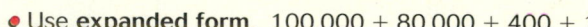

Another Example

Here are some ways to show the number 180,401.

- Use a **place-value chart**.

hundred thousands	ten thousands	thousands	hundreds	tens	ones
1	8	0,	4	0	1

- Use **expanded form**. 100,000 + 80,000 + 400 + 1
- Use **standard form**. 180,401
- Use **words**. one hundred eighty thousand, four hundred one

Think and Discuss Suppose you could put 100 more marbles in the backpack. How many marbles would be in the backpack then? **13,883 marbles**

 28

---

1 Introduce

Cooperative Activity

VISUAL/SPATIAL

 **PAIRS**    **10–15 MINUTES**

Materials: spinners (0–9), four-digit place-value charts

1. Each student spins three numbers to write the greatest possible three-digit number on the chart. Students compare numbers.

   - Ask: **Which number is greatest? Which is least?**

2. Repeat the activity with students spinning to write four-digit numbers.

Problem of the Day: See p. 37.

2 Teach   Pages 28–29

Guide students to understand that the pattern of having a ones, tens, and hundreds column continues with numbers in the thousands.

Critical Thinking   ANALYSIS

After Think and Discuss, ask: **How would you change the place-value chart if you put 4,000 more marbles in the backpack?** *(The chart would have a 7 instead of a 3 in the thousands place.)*

Assess Understanding

After Try It Out, ask: **How do you know where to place commas and zeros in Exercise 2?** *(A comma goes between the thousands and hundreds; the zeros are in the thousands and tens places.)*

CHALLENGE

Look at the place-value chart under Another Example on page 28. Suppose you wanted to write a seven-digit number on the chart. Predict the name of the seventh place. *(Millions)*

Try It Out

Write each number in standard form.

1. 200,000 + 30,000 + 6,000 + 400 + 50 + 9 **236,459**

2. four hundred thirty thousand, two hundred six **430,206**

3. 9 hundred thousands 2 ten thousands 4 hundreds 3 ones **920,403**

Practice

Write the value of the underlined digit.

4. 866,<u>5</u>04 **500**
5. 11,06<u>5</u> **5**
6. <u>5</u>92,124 **500,000**
7. 7<u>5</u>7,492 **50,000**
8. 34,6<u>5</u>2 **50**
9. <u>6</u>32,191 **600,000**
10. 124,8<u>3</u>0 **800**
11. 42<u>7</u>,931 **7,000**
12. <u>2</u>3,507 **20,000**
13. 889,41<u>6</u> **6**
14. <u>2</u>5,422 **20,000**
15. 19,0<u>9</u>7 **90**
16. 651,4<u>6</u>4 **400**
17. <u>3</u>48,770 **300,000**
18. 21,0<u>8</u>0 **80**

Write each number in expanded form.
See Additional Answers, pages 36–37.

19. 824,034
20. 55,312
21. 890,760
22. 1,003
23. 888,888
24. 9,640

Problem Solving

25. A store has 100,000 blue marbles, 30,000 red marbles, and 800 green marbles. How many marbles does the store have? How do you know your answer is reasonable? **130,800 marbles; Explanations will vary.**

26. Suppose a museum has a collection of 354,000 clay marbles. If another 10,000 marbles are brought to the museum, how many marbles will be in the collection? **364,000 marbles**

▲ Kid Connection
A secret spin on her shooter marble helped Amanda Burn, from Tennessee, win the national marbles championship.

Review and Remember

Using Algebra Complete each pattern.

27. 997, 998, 999, ▆, ▆ **1,000 1,001**
28. 176, 175, 174, ▆, ▆ **173 172**
29. 322, 321, 320, ▆, ▆ **319 318**
30. 470, 480, 490, ▆, ▆ **500 510**

For Extra Practice, see Set F, page 38. **29**

Using Algebra

In Exercises 27–30, students use **patterns** to complete number sequences.

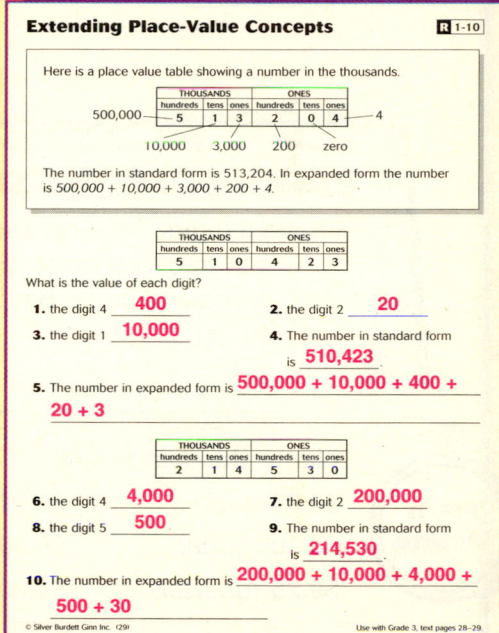
---

3 Wrap-up

Show three ways to write two hundred thousand, nine hundred forty-two. *(200 thousands, 9 hundreds, 4 tens, 2 ones; 200,000 + 900 + 40 + 2; 200,942)*

Common Error Alert

Watch for students who don't use zeros as placeholders when rewriting numbers from word names to standard form. Have students use place-value charts.

Meeting Individual Needs

For Early Finishers

Students use place-value charts to model 109,823. Then students show the number in as many ways as they can.

LOGICAL/MATHEMATICAL

Cooperative Learning

One student writes a five-digit number and reads it to a partner, who writes the number down. They check numbers and switch roles.

AUDITORY

Checkpoint

Vocabulary Review

You may wish to review these terms before students begin the Checkpoint.

expanded form   A number written as the sum of the value of its digits.

standard form   A number written with commas separating groups of three digits.

word form   A number written in words.

Using the Page

Purpose To review concepts and skills presented since the last Checkpoint.

- If necessary, discuss the directions and content of each section of the Checkpoint with the class.

- Page numbers associated with each group of items refer to the pages on which the skill or concept was presented. Those students needing review should turn to the appropriate lessons.

Using Algebra

In Exercise 35, students use what they know about **numerical relationships** to solve a math riddle.

Understanding Numbers to 999,999

Vocabulary

Match each number with its name.

1. 400,000 + 20,000 + 300 + 5
   expanded form

2. seven thousand, nine hundred eighty-five
   word form

3. 519,082
   standard form

Word Bank

expanded form
standard form
word form

Concepts and Skills

Write the value of the digit 7 in each number. (pages 20–21, 28–29)

4. 2,307   **7**
5. 5,790   **700**
6. 8,378   **70**
7. 7,023   **7,000**
8. 83,709   **700**
9. 30,007   **7**
10. 570,020   **70,000**
11. 987,002   **7,000**

Compare. Write >, <, or = for each ●. (pages 22–25)

12. 34 **<** 43
13. 57 **<** 60
14. 235 **<** 237
15. 7,503 **<** 7,511
16. 3,823 **>** 3,799
17. 2,802 **>** 2,799
18. 605 **>** 506
19. 1,244 **<** 1,422
20. 3,589 **<** 3,627

Write the numbers in order from least to greatest. (pages 22–25)

21. 26 14 28   **14 26 28**
22. 19 37 2   **2 19 37**
23. 4,223 4,232 4,242   **4,223 4,232 4,242**
24. 305 289 351   **289 305 351**
25. 703 699 694   **694 699 703**
26. 3,580 3,780 3,680   **3,580 3,680 3,780**
27. 479 362 299   **299 362 479**
28. 1,752 899 1,538   **899 1,538 1,752**
29. 921 1,011 899   **899 921 1,011**

Write each amount. (pages 30–31)

30. **$6.45**

31. **$5.18**

34

Reinforcement and Remediation

 PAIRS

- Provide each pair with index cards numbered 0–9, place-value chart, paper, and base-ten blocks. Have students shuffle the index cards and place them face down.

- Students draw three cards and use the numbers to write the greatest possible number on the place-value chart. Students compare digits and use base-ten blocks to decide which number is greatest.

- Students repeat the activity using 4–6 cards. A variation is to use decimal points and dollar signs to write and compare monetary amounts.

Problem Solving

32. Risa has 1,249 stamps in her stamp collection. Miguel has 1,439 stamps in his collection. Who has more stamps? **Miguel**

33. Wayne has 2 quarters, 3 dimes, 3 nickels, and 3 pennies. A super pack of baseball cards costs $1.00. Does he have enough money to buy the cards? **No, he has only $0.98.**

34. Rodney has a ten-dollar bill, 2 five-dollar bills, and 8 one-dollar bills. He wants to use as few bills as he can to pay for a sticker album that costs $17.98. How should he pay? **With the ten-dollar bill and the 2 five-dollar bills**

35. **Using Algebra** I am a number less than 800 and greater than 500. I have a 4 in the tens place. My ones digit is less than 3 but greater than 0. All of my digits are even numbers. What number am I? **642**

What do you think?
When you count coins, why is it usually better to start with the coin that has the greatest value?

If you start with the coin of the greatest value, you can often skip count to add the remaining coins.

 Journal Idea

How does knowing place value help you understand the difference between 20 and 200? **Students should demonstrate understanding that adding a zero to a number changes its place value.**

You Decide

Activity

Money Matters

You have 2 one-dollar bills, 5 quarters, 7 dimes, and 5 nickels. You want to save as much money as you spend.

Make a list of 5 or more different ways you can save and spend the money. Use play money to help you.

 You might wish to include this work in your portfolio.

Answers will vary. Sample answer: save 1 one-dollar bill, 4 quarters, 1 dime and spend 1 one-dollar bill, 1 quarter, 6 dimes, 5 nickels.

35

Scoring Rubric

3 EXCELLENT Students find the total amount of money they are given. Students then realize that they need to try different combinations of coins and bills to form half of that amount, which is $2.10. Students then use a chart to organize their work and list five or more different ways to save and spend the money equally.

2 SATISFACTORY Students may first try to come up with combinations of bills and coins that are equal in value, but whose combined value is not the entire amount. At some point, students realize that they need to try different combinations of coins and bills to form half of the total amount of money they have. Students may use a chart to organize their work and list several different ways to save and spend the money equally.

1 NEEDS IMPROVEMENT Students have little or no understanding of how to make combinations with the given denominations of money to obtain a certain value. Students cannot make a list of different ways to spend and save money.

Ongoing Assessment

You may want to have students review their responses to the Baseline Assessment questions presented at the beginning of the chapter. Have students discuss what they have learned in this chapter to help them answer the "What do you think?" question.

What do you think?

Accept reasonable responses. Students may say that it's more difficult to count money if you start with the coin that has the least value.

Journal Idea

Suggest that students describe how place value helps them understand how to write greater numbers.

You Decide

This activity allows you to evaluate students' understanding of money. As students do the activity, encourage them to make a chart to keep track of the amounts they try. Be sure students understand that the amounts of money spent and saved are to be the same and the sum of the two amounts is to be the entire amount of money.

Portfolio Activity

You may wish to have students include their work from the You Decide activity in their portfolios.

The scoring rubric on the left may be used to help you assess students' work.

Chapter 2

Linking Technology

Develop and Reinforce Concepts

MathProcessor™

CD-ROM Activities use MathProcessor™ Tools to help build critical thinking skills and develop problem-solving strategies.

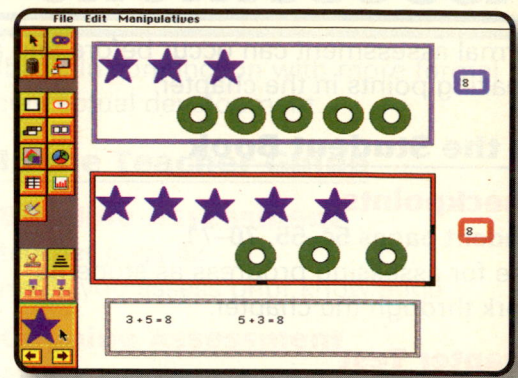

Lesson	Tools	Skill
2	Manipulatives	Students use Manipulatives to explore addition strategies.
3	Manipulatives	Students use Manipulatives to find the sum of 4 one-digit numbers.
9	Large Frames	Students use addition to check subtraction.

Review and Practice Skills

Math Blaster® 1

This **CD-ROM** program provides exercises and activities to practice basic math facts and develop mastery of mathematical operations. The chart below lists specific lessons where activities and references can be found.

Lesson	Activity	Subject/Level
1	Trash Zapper	Addition—Levels 1, 2, 3
6	Number Recycler	Subtraction—Levels 1, 2, 3

Extend and Enrich

Internet

Students can use real data in lesson-related math activities.
Teachers can find activities and resources for Lessons 3 and 8.
Parents can find home connections to help reinforce concepts.

Visit our Web site at:

www.sbgmath.com

Making Connections

Literature

Chapter Resources

These books, found in your local or school library, can be used to help build math concepts.

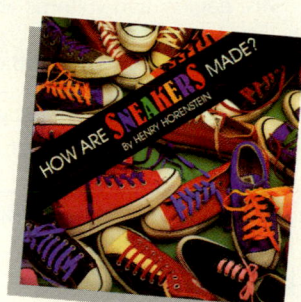

- **How Are Sneakers Made?**
  by Henry Horenstein
  Simon & Schuster Books for Young Readers, 1993
- **Let's Investigate Estimating**
  by Marion Smoothey
  Marshall Cavendish Corporation, 1995

Home-School

Family Letter With Activity
Home-School Connection Booklet

The Family Letter for Chapter 2 introduces the idea of using fact families as a strategy to add and subtract. The activities included in the letter offer practice recognizing and completing fact families.

Study Buddies
Home-School Connection Booklet

Study Buddies pages provide reinforcement activities for students to work on with a partner.

- Study Buddies 2A provides practice using the ten frame to subtract.
- Study Buddies 2B guides students in writing addition sentences to check subtraction.

Math Backpack
Take-Home Activities

Math Backpack activities provide a link between the classroom and the home. Activity Cards 1–6 can be used with this chapter. Parents and students alike will enjoy using these laminated cards and accompanying manipulatives.

Cross-Curricular Integration

 Science

- Read these interesting animal facts, pp. 42–43, 46, 47, 56, 59, 63, 64, 68, 73.
- Explore animal habitats, pp. 42–43, 57, 58, 62, 63, 64, 71.

 Art

- Create an animal poster, Teacher Guide pp. 42–43.

 Social Studies

- Read about Chinese goldfish ponds, p. 49.
- Learn about birds that live in Florida, p. 51.
- Find out how alpaca wool is used in South America, pp. 64–65.

 Language Arts

- Learn the terminology for measuring the height of horses, p. 53.

Addition and Subtraction

Theme: ANIMALS

Chapter Overview

In this chapter students will learn different strategies to add and subtract.

Activating Prior Knowledge

Discuss with students what they already know about addition and subtraction facts. Record responses on the chalkboard.

Baseline Assessment

Ask questions such as:

- **What are some activities you do where you need to add?** *(Possible responses: Keeping score in a game; Counting baseball cards)*

- **What are some activities you do where you need to subtract?** *(Possible response: Figuring out how much money I have left after buying my sister a birthday present)*

Save student responses for use with the **Ongoing Assessment** section in the chapter Checkpoints on pages 55 and 71.

Addition and Subtraction

Chapter Theme: ANIMALS

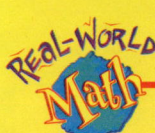

·········· Real Facts ··········

Hawks, eagles, and vultures are known as birds of prey. They catch animals, fish, and other birds for food. Birds are measured by their wingspans. The wingspan is the distance between the wing tips. The wings have to be spread wide to be measured. Below is a list of wingspans for a few birds of prey.

Type of Bird	Wingspan in Feet
African Little Sparrow Hawk	1
Golden Eagle	7
Rough-legged Hawk	5
Vulture	10
Martial Eagle	8

- What is the difference in size of wingspan between the largest and smallest birds listed? **9 feet**

- Two of which kind of bird have the same total wingspan as a vulture? **Rough-legged Hawk; 5 + 5 = 10**

········· Real People ·········

Meet Dana Brenfleck. She trains birds of prey. She began working with birds more than 10 years ago. Today she works for the Arizona-Sonora Desert Museum. She teaches people about desert birds. The birds with her in the photograph are called Harris Hawks.

42

Create an Animal Poster

 INDIVIDUAL

Materials
- ▶ posterboard or other heavy paper
- ▶ glue
- ▶ crayons and markers
- ▶ optional: magazines and books about animals and their habitats

Here is a project that will help your students practice addition and subtraction. Specific lessons are referenced to help you work on the project throughout the chapter.

Getting Started

Start the project by explaining that a desert is one kind of *habitat*, a place where a certain kind of animal or plant is normally found. Other habitats include a rain forest, the Arctic, or an ocean. Tell students that they will make a poster showing a habitat and some of the animals and plants that live there.

..........Real Facts..........

- Golden Eagles swoop down on their prey at speeds of up to 95 miles an hour.
- The Martial Eagle can spot prey more than a mile away.

Using the Data

When students review the table on page 42, make sure they understand that wingspans are given in feet. Some additional questions you may wish to ask include:

- Which two birds' wingspans together add up to the wingspan of one Martial Eagle? *(The African Little Sparrow Hawk and Golden Eagle)*
- List the birds in order from greatest to least wingspan. *(Vulture, Martial Eagle, Golden Eagle, Rough-legged Hawk, African Little Sparrow Hawk)*

..........Real People..........

Dana Brenfleck is a *falconer,* a person who trains birds of prey. Some of the birds she has worked with include peregrine falcons, kestrels, and Cooper's hawks. At the Arizona-Sonora Desert Museum, she trains Harris hawks and demonstrates their capabilities to visitors. You might ask students to discuss how animal trainers could use math in their work.

Project Links

▶ **Lesson 5** Students should select two animals for their posters. Have them draw or find magazine pictures of each. Then ask them to **count** the number of pictures they have of each animal.

▶ **Lesson 9** Now students can make their posters. Ask them **addition** and **subtraction questions** such as: How many of each animal are on your poster? What kind of animal do you have the most pictures of?

Project Wrap-up

Have students display their posters. Then they can meet with other students who chose the same habitat. Each group should **add** to find the total number of animals on their posters and **subtract** to compare the number of animals on their posters with that of another group.

Portfolio Students may wish to include their project work in their portfolios.

Building Vocabulary

These key words will be found in this chapter.

count on	count up
addends	missing addend
sum	difference
count back	fact family

Journal Idea You may wish to have students write about each vocabulary term in their journals at the beginning and end of the chapter.

Using Addition Strategies

Lesson Organizer

Objective: Use addition strategies.

- **NCTM Standards:** 1, 6, 8, 13
- **Manipulatives:** counters (optional)
- **Lesson Resources:**

  Chapter File Folder
  Practice, Reteach, Extend 2-1
  Teaching Tool 8

  Daily Review 2-1
  Practice Workbook, p. 6
  Transparencies 23, 23A

Problem of the Day 2-1

I used 1 quarter and 3 dimes to buy something. I got 1 nickel back. How much money did I spend? **$0.50**

Math Minute

Add.

6 + 3 = *(9)*	3 + 4 = *(7)*
6 + 2 = *(8)*	6 + 1 = *(7)*
7 + 1 = *(8)*	3 + 2 = *(5)*

Using Addition Strategies

A Real Plus

There are different strategies you can use to add.

Learning About It

There are 7 skunks hunting for insects. Then 2 more skunks join them. To find how many skunks there are in all, you can add.

To add 1, 2, or 3, you can **count on**.

7 + 2 = ■

Start with 7.
Count 2 more.

You end at 9.   So 7 + 2 = 9.
There are 9 skunks in all.

Suppose 5 skunks joined the 7 skunks. How many skunks would there be?

To add numbers greater than 3, sometimes you can **make a ten**.

7 + 5 = ■

Make a ten. Then add the rest.

7   +   5   =   ■

10   +   2   =   12   So 7 + 5 = 12.

There would be 12 skunks.

44

---

1 Introduce

Whole Class Activity

VISUAL

WHOLE CLASS   5–10 MINUTES

1. Draw six circles on the board.

2. Draw two more circles on the board in a separate group.

   - Ask: **How many circles do you count in the first group?** *(6)* **How many in the second group?** *(2)* **How many circles are on the board?** *(8)*

   - Discuss: **How did you count the total number of circles?** *(Sample answer: Start with 6 and then count two more to get 8.)*

2 Teach Pages 44–47

Explain to students that strategies such as counting on and making a ten can help them find sums more easily.

Have a volunteer explain how each strategy works. Then ask:

- **What strategy would you use to add 6 + 3?** *(Counting on)*

- **What strategy would you use to add 8 + 5?** *(Making a ten)*

Then have students create a fact that could be solved using each of the strategies.

Connecting Ideas

After students have worked with counting on and making a ten, they can find the sums for new double facts.

Discuss why two different doubles could be used to find 7 + 8.

- Ask: **What do you have to do when you use 7 + 7?** *(Add one to the sum)* **What do you have to do when you use 8 + 8?** *(Take one away from the sum)*

Then have students name another fact in which they could use 7 + 7 to help find the sum. *(Sample answer: 7 + 6)*

- Ask: **What other fact could you use to find the answer to 7 + 6?** *(6 + 6)*

More Examples

Count on to find these sums.

A. $6 + 3 = 9$

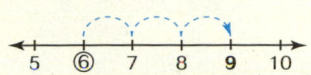

B. $9 + 2 = 11$

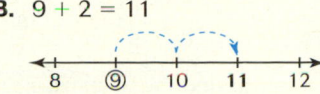

Make a ten to find these sums.

C. $9 + 5 = 14$

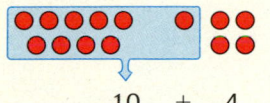

$$10 \quad + \quad 4 \quad = \quad 14$$

D. $8 + 3 = 11$

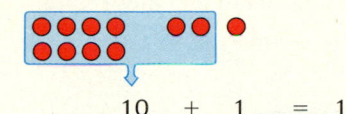

$$10 \quad + \quad 1 \quad = \quad 11$$

Connecting Ideas

So far you have learned strategies for counting on and for making a ten. When numbers are close to each other, you can use doubles to add them.

Suppose 8 skunks joined 7 skunks. How many skunks would there be?

$$7 + 8 = \blacksquare$$

You can use the **doubles** $7 + 7$.

$7 + 7 = 14$
$7 + 8$ is one more.
So $7 + 8 = 15$.

Or you can use the doubles $8 + 8$.

$8 + 8 = 16$
$7 + 8$ is one less.
So $7 + 8 = 15$.

There would be 15 skunks.

Think and Discuss Explain how you could use doubles to find the sum of $4 + 5$.
Use $4 + 4 = 8$ and add 1 $(8 + 1 = 9)$ or use $5 + 5 = 10$ and subtract 1 $(10 - 1 = 9)$.

45

Number Concepts and Quantitative Reasoning

Math Connections

 PAIRS

Have each pair of students choose a two-digit number whose digits are different and each digit is 5 or less. Then have them reverse the digits and add the two numbers. Ask students to describe the sum and write an explanation telling why the sum is always a number that has the same two digits. Then have them explore what happens if the digits of each number are greater than 5.

▲ This activity can be used at any time to reinforce or extend math connections.

Critical Thinking   ANALYSIS

After Think and Discuss, ask: **Would you use the strategy counting on for adding 4 + 5? Why or why not?** *(Answer could be* yes *or* no *depending upon each student's ability to remember the number of times he or she counted on.)*

Using Technology
CD-ROM

**Math Blaster® 1,
Trash Zapper**

Addition: Levels 1, 2, 3

- In Level 1, students solve addition problems with sums 0–9.
- In Level 2, students solve addition problems with sums 10–14.
- In Level 3, students solve addition problems with sums 15–18.

Sample Problems:

Level 1: 6 + 3 = 9

Level 2: 10 + 4 = 14

Level 3: 8 + 7 = 15

Try It Out

Count on to find these sums.

1. 9 + 1 **10**	2. 9 + 3 **12**	3. 5 + 2 **7**	4. 8 + 2 **10**	5. 7 + 3 **10**

Make a ten to find these sums.

6. 5 + 8 **13**	7. 4 + 7 **11**	8. 9 + 6 **15**	9. 9 + 7 **16**	10. 4 + 8 **12**

Use doubles to find these sums.

11. 6 + 7 **13**	12. 9 + 8 **17**	13. 3 + 4 **7**	14. 5 + 6 **11**	15. 8 + 7 **15**

Practice

Add.

16. 2 + 2 = **4**	17. 4 + 2 = **6**	18. 5 + 1 = **6**	19. 3 + 1 = **4**	20. 3 + 3 = **6**	21. 3 + 7 = **10**
22. 4 + 1 = **5**	23. 6 + 4 = **10**	24. 8 + 6 = **14**	25. 8 + 0 = **8**	26. 1 + 9 = **10**	27. 5 + 9 = **14**
28. 5 + 3 = **8**	29. 2 + 4 = **6**	30. 8 + 9 = **17**	31. 6 + 5 = **11**	32. 8 + 8 = **16**	33. 3 + 8 = **11**
34. 1 + 6 = **7**	35. 5 + 5 = **10**	36. 2 + 7 = **9**	37. 5 + 0 = **5**	38. 8 + 5 = **13**	39. 7 + 9 = **16**

Using Algebra Compare. Write >, <, or = for each .

40. 2 + 6 **<** 6 + 3   41. 8 + 0 **<** 9 + 0

42. 8 + 5 **>** 0 + 5   43. 7 + 4 **=** 9 + 2

44. 6 + 1 **>** 1 + 2   45. 3 + 0 **<** 7 + 0

◄**Science Connection** Animals have ways to protect themselves from other animals. A skunk protects itself with a spray. The spray has a very unpleasant smell.

46

---

2 Teach (continued)

Assess Understanding

After Try It Out, ask: **Which strategy would you use to find 6 + 9?** *(Sample answer: Make a ten)*

GIFTED AND TALENTED

Use Addition Strategies Have students make conjectures about how they would find the sum of three numbers, each less than 10.

Problem Solving

46. Jasmin saw 5 chipmunks by a tree and 2 more on a log. How many did she see in all? **7 chipmunks**

47. Fred counted 4 squirrels and 9 rabbits. How many animals did Fred count? **13 animals**

48. Science Connection Some skunks can spray as far as 15 feet. Suppose a skunk is 9 feet from a rabbit. The rabbit moves back 7 more feet. Could the spray reach the rabbit? Explain your answer. **No; 9 + 7 = 16 feet.**

— 9 feet —

Review and Remember

Compare. Write >, <, or = for each.

49. 12 **>** 8 **50.** 25 **<** 41 **51.** 126 **>** 83

52. 345 **=** 345 **53.** 1,746 **<** 1,764 **54.** 4,965 **>** 3,285

Time for Technology
Using the MathProcessor™ CD-ROM

Names for Ten

Use manipulatives to show different names for 10.

- Link a connecting cubes space 🟩 to a number space 🔲.
- Click 1 blue cube and 9 red cubes. Click in the number space, then 🟰.
- Show different names for 10. Use other colors.

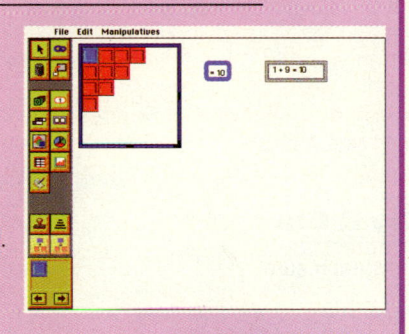

For Extra Practice, see Set A, page 72. **47**

Using Algebra

In Exercises 40–45, students use symbols to create **inequalities** that are true.

Time for Technology

Click = to change from expanded notation to the standard form of a number and vice versa.

---

3 Wrap-up

How could you add 9 + 2? *(Make a ten or count on)* **What is the sum of 9 + 2?** *(11)*

Journal Idea Write 3 addition sentences whose answers can be found using one of the strategies—counting on, making a ten, or using doubles.

Common Error Alert

Watch for students who make ten but then incorrectly subtract from the other addend before finding the sum. For example, 9 + 5 = 10 + 3 rather than 10 + 4.

Meeting Individual Needs

For Early Finishers

Pairs of students name a double, then name the addition facts for which they could find the sum using the double.

AUDITORY

For Extra Help

Have students use pennies to act out the make-a-ten strategy for adding 8 and 9 to any number.

KINESTHETIC

Practice

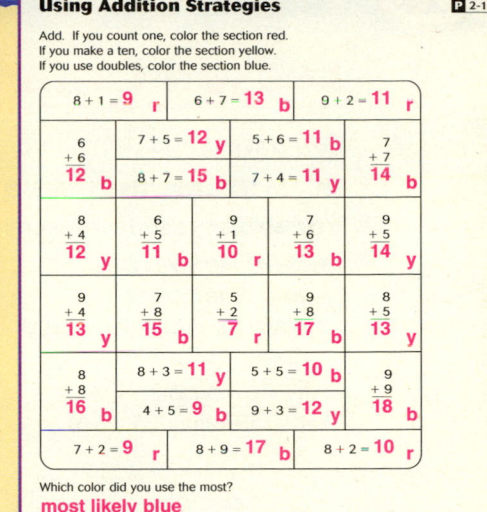

Using Addition Strategies P 2-1

Add. If you count one, color the section red. If you make a ten, color the section yellow. If you use doubles, color the section blue.

8 + 1 = **9** r	6 + 7 = **13** b	9 + 2 = **11** r
6 + 6 = **12** b	7 + 5 = **12** y	5 + 6 = **11** b	7 + 7 = **14** b
8 + 7 = **15** b	7 + 4 = **11** y
8 + 4 = **12** y	6 + 1 = **7**	9 + 1 = **10** r	7 + 6 = **13** b	9 + 5 = **14** y
9 + 4 = **13** y	7 + 8 = **15** b	5 + 2 = **7** r	9 + 8 = **17** b	8 + 5 = **13** b
8 + 8 = **16** b	8 + 3 = **11** y	5 + 5 = **10** b	9 + 9 = **18** b
7 + 2 = **9** r	4 + 5 = **9** b	9 + 3 = **12** y
	8 + 9 = **17** b	8 + 2 = **10** r

Which color did you use the most?
most likely blue

Why do you think that is?
Most of the numbers were close to each other.

© Silver Burdett Ginn Inc. (41) Use with Grade 3, text pages 44–47.

Reteach

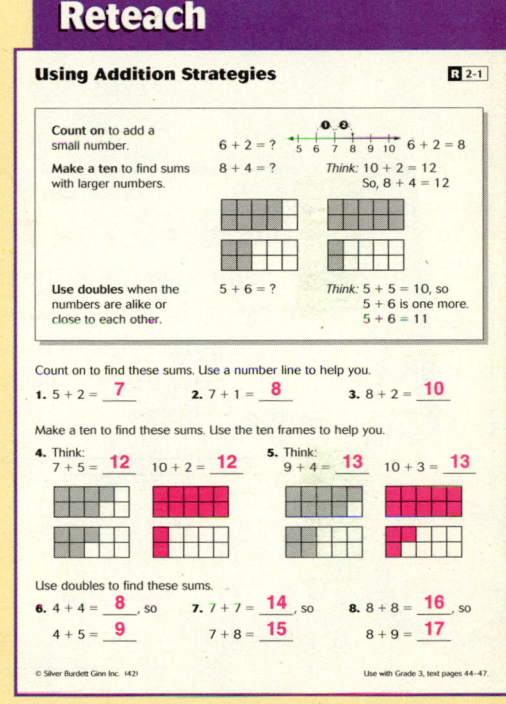

Using Addition Strategies R 2-1

Count on to add a small number. 6 + 2 = ? 6 + 2 = 8

Make a ten to find sums with larger numbers. 8 + 4 = ? *Think:* 10 + 2 = 12 So, 8 + 4 = 12

Use doubles when the numbers are alike or close to each other. 5 + 6 = ? *Think:* 5 + 5 = 10, so 5 + 6 is one more. 5 + 6 = 11

Count on to find these sums. Use a number line to help you.

1. 5 + 2 = **7** **2.** 7 + 1 = **8** **3.** 8 + 2 = **10**

Make a ten to find these sums. Use the ten frames to help you.

4. *Think:* 7 + 5 = **12** 10 + 2 = **12** **5.** *Think:* 9 + 4 = **13** 10 + 3 = **13**

Use doubles to find these sums.

6. 4 + 4 = **8**, so 4 + 5 = **9** **7.** 7 + 7 = **14**, so 7 + 8 = **15** **8.** 8 + 8 = **16**, so 8 + 9 = **17**

© Silver Burdett Ginn Inc. (42) Use with Grade 3, text pages 44–47.

Extend

Double Puzzle E 2-1 VISUAL THINKING

Work with a partner. Cut your puzzles into pieces. Mix the two sets together. Then work together to make two completed puzzles that are the same.

© Silver Burdett Ginn Inc. (43) Use with Grade 3, text pages 44–47.

Lesson Organizer

Objective: Add using properties.

- **NCTM Standards:** 1, 3, 6, 8
- **Vocabulary:** addends, sum
- **Lesson Resources:**
  Chapter File Folder
    Practice, Reteach, Extend 2-2
    Teaching Tool 8
  Daily Review 2-2
  Transparencies 23, 23A

Problem of the Day   2-2

Nine children went to the park. There were twice as many children climbing the rope ladders as there were on the swings. How many children were on the swings? **See answer, page 73.**

Math Minute

Add.

$6 + 3 = $ *(9)* $7 + 8 = $ *(15)*

$2 + 9 = $ *(11)* $4 + 8 = $ *(12)*

$6 + 5 = $ *(11)*

Using Algebra

Facts About Facts

There are special rules that can help you remember your addition facts.

Learning About It

Amanda is buying goldfish. She buys 3 lionhead goldfish and 4 fantail goldfish. How many goldfish does she buy in all?

Word Bank
addends
sum

$$3 + 4 = 7$$
↑ addend ↑ addend ↑ sum

$$4 + 3 = 7$$
↑ addend ↑ addend ↑ sum

She buys 7 goldfish.

▶ Changing the order of the **addends** does not change the **sum**.

Kyle buys 5 fantail goldfish and 0 lionhead goldfish. How many goldfish does he buy?

He buys 5 goldfish.

$$5 + 0 = 5$$

▶ When you add 0 to a number, the sum is that number.

Think and Discuss How does knowing $5 + 2 = 7$ help you find $2 + 5$? **The order of the numbers does not change the sum. Since $5 + 2 = 7$, $2 + 5 = 7$.**

Try It Out

Find each sum.

1. $2 + 3$ **5**   **2.** $8 + 1$ **9**   **3.** $0 + 7$ **7**   **4.** $6 + 2$ **8**
    $3 + 2$ **5** $1 + 8$ **9** $7 + 0$ **7** $2 + 6$ **8**

48

---

1 Introduce

Whole Class Activity
KINESTHETIC

WHOLE CLASS   **5–10 MINUTES**

1. Three students stand in a group in front of the class.

2. Then two more students stand in front of the class, but apart from the others.
   - Ask: **How many students are at the front of the class?** *(5)*

3. The two groups switch places.
   - Ask: **How many students are in front of the class?** *(5)* **When the groups switch places, does the number of students change?** *(No)*

2 Teach   Pages 48–49

Have students verify that both $4 + 3$ and $3 + 4$ equal 7. Then have students discuss that $5 + 0 = 5$.

- Ask: **Why doesn't $5 + 0 = 0$?** *(Sample answer: If you add nothing to 5 you still have 5.)*

Finally, have students give you another pair of facts to show the Order Property.

Critical Thinking   SYNTHESIS

After Think and Discuss, say: **Draw pictures to show that $2 + 1 = 1 + 2$.**

Assess Understanding

After Try It Out, ask: **Is it easier to add $6 + 3$ or $3 + 6$? Explain.** *(Sample answer: $6 + 3$; it is easier to count on 3 than to count on 6.)*

USING TECHNOLOGY

MathProcessor™ Activities
See **Activities 7 and 8** in the MathProcessor™ Activity Cards.

Practice

Find each sum.

5. $7 + 1 = 8$	6. $1 + 7 = 8$	7. $9 + 4 = 13$	8. $4 + 9 = 13$	9. $7 + 5 = 12$	10. $5 + 7 = 12$
11. $0 + 6 = 6$	12. $4 + 3 = 7$	13. $9 + 0 = 9$	14. $3 + 5 = 8$	15. $6 + 1 = 7$	16. $6 + 6 = 12$
17. $5 + 8 = 13$	18. $9 + 9 = 18$	19. $5 + 4 = 9$	20. $7 + 6 = 13$	21. $6 + 9 = 15$	22. $8 + 4 = 12$

Follow each rule to complete each table.

Rule: Add 2

Input	Output
5	7
7	9
23. 0	2
24. 9	11

Rule: Add 8

Input	Output
2	10
8	16
25. 1	9
26.	
27. 5	13

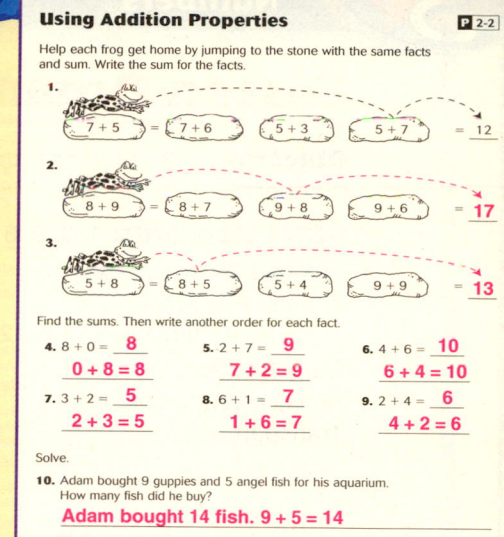

▲**Social Studies Connection**
For years Chinese people have used goldfish ponds to make their gardens more beautiful.

Problem Solving

28. Amanda visited a goldfish pond. She saw 8 tiger head goldfish, 4 bubble eye goldfish, and 3 frogs. How many goldfish did she see?
12 goldfish

29. **You Decide** A pet shop has 10 red, 9 black, and 8 white goldfish. You want to buy 15 goldfish for your tank. Which fish will you choose? **A possible answer is 7 red, 6 black, and 2 white goldfish.**

30. **Analyze** The sum of two numbers is 13. One number is 1 more than 5. What are the numbers?
6, 7

Review and Remember

Write the next four numbers in each pattern.

31. 100, 90, 80, ■, ■, ■, ■
70 60 50 40

32. 48, 46, 44, ■, ■, ■, ■
42 40 38 36

33. 150, 250, 350, ■, ■, ■, ■
450 550 650 750

34. 125, 130, 135, ■, ■, ■, ■
140 145 150 155

For Extra Practice, see Set B, page 72. **49**

Using Algebra

Using Algebra

In this lesson, students use the order property to investigate **numerical relationships.**

---

3 Wrap-up

How can you find the sum of 8 + 0? *(The sum of any number plus 0 is that number.)*
How can you find 5 + 7 if you know 7 + 5? *(5 + 7 equals 7 + 5.)*

Common Error Alert

Watch for students who think zero plus any number equals zero. Have them use counters to model a few exercises.

Meeting Individual Needs

For Early Finishers

One student creates an input/output table, filling in both columns and not including the rule. The partner tells the rule. Students switch roles.
LOGICAL/MATHEMATICAL

Acquiring English Proficiency

Students can create a poster showing the names of different properties and several examples to illustrate each property.
LOGICAL/MATHEMATICAL

Practice

Using Addition Properties P 2-2

Help each frog get home by jumping to the stone with the same facts and sum. Write the sum for the facts.

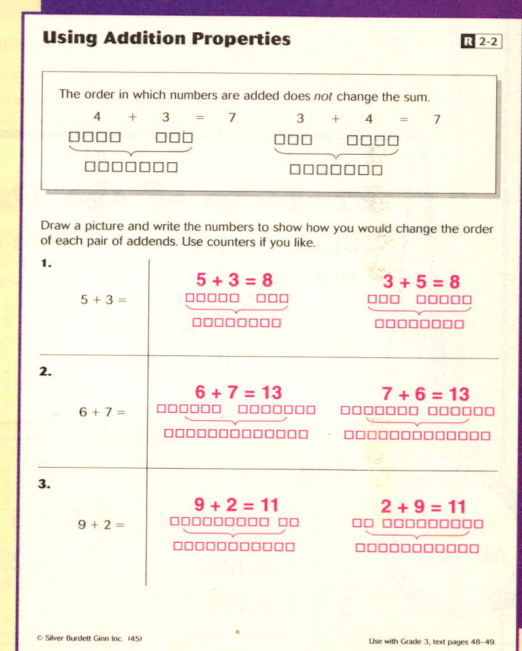

1. $7 + 5 = 7 + 6$ $5 + 3$ $5 + 7$ $= 12$
2. $8 + 9 = 8 + 7$ $9 + 8$ $9 + 6$ $= 17$
3. $5 + 8 = 8 + 5$ $5 + 4$ $9 + 9$ $= 13$

Find the sums. Then write another order for each fact.

4. $8 + 0 = 8$	5. $2 + 7 = 9$	6. $4 + 6 = 10$
$0 + 8 = 8$	$7 + 2 = 9$	$6 + 4 = 10$
7. $3 + 2 = 5$	8. $6 + 1 = 7$	9. $2 + 4 = 6$
$2 + 3 = 5$	$1 + 6 = 7$	$4 + 2 = 6$

Solve.

10. Adam bought 9 guppies and 5 angel fish for his aquarium. How many fish did he buy?
Adam bought 14 fish. 9 + 5 = 14

11. Heather saw 8 cardinals on one nature walk and 7 cardinals on another nature walk. How many cardinals did she see in all?
Heather saw 15 cardinals. 8 + 7 = 15

© Silver Burdett Ginn Inc. (44) Use with Grade 3, text pages 48–49.

Reteach

Using Addition Properties R 2-2

The order in which numbers are added does *not* change the sum.

$4 + 3 = 7$ $3 + 4 = 7$

□□□□ □□□   □□□ □□□□
□□□□□□□   □□□□□□□

Draw a picture and write the numbers to show how you would change the order of each pair of addends. Use counters if you like.

1. $5 + 3 =$ **5 + 3 = 8**   **3 + 5 = 8**

2. $6 + 7 =$ **6 + 7 = 13**   **7 + 6 = 13**

3. $9 + 2 =$ **9 + 2 = 11**   **2 + 9 = 11**

© Silver Burdett Ginn Inc. (45) Use with Grade 3, text pages 48–49.

Extend

Around Town E 2-2 VISUAL THINKING

Look at the map. Then answer each question.

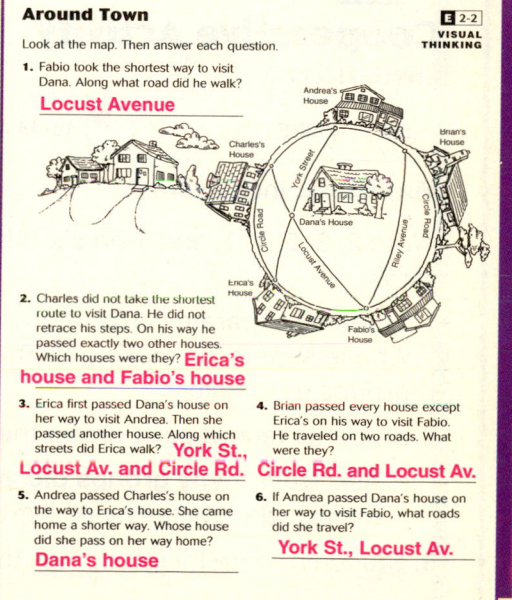

1. Fabio took the shortest way to visit Dana. Along what road did he walk?
Locust Avenue

2. Charles did not take the shortest route to visit Dana. He did not retrace his steps. On his way he passed exactly two other houses. Which houses were they? **Erica's house and Fabio's house**

3. Erica first passed Dana's house on her way to visit Andrea. Then she passed another house. Along which streets did Erica walk?
York St., Locust Av. and Circle Rd.

4. Brian passed every house except Erica's on his way to visit Fabio. He traveled on two roads. What were they? **Circle Rd. and Locust Av.**

5. Andrea passed Charles's house on the way to Erica's house. She came home a shorter way. Whose house did she pass on her way home?
Dana's house

6. If Andrea passed Dana's house on her way to visit Fabio, what roads did she travel?
York St., Locust Av.

© Silver Burdett Ginn Inc. (46) Use with Grade 3, text pages 48–49.

Lesson Organizer

Objective: Use addition to check subtraction.

- **NCTM Standards:** 1, 4, 6, 8
- **Lesson Resources:**
  Chapter File Folder
    Practice, Reteach, Extend 2-9
  Daily Review 2-9
  Study Buddies 2B

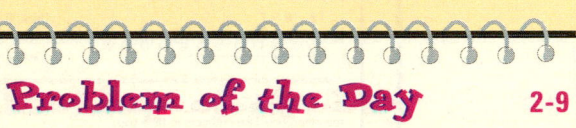

Problem of the Day 2-9

I had 5 stickers. Molly gave me 4 more stickers. Then my brother gave me some. Now I have 20 stickers. How many stickers did my brother give me? **11 stickers**

Math Minute

Add.

3 + 2 = (5)   2 + 7 = (9)

4 + 3 = (7)   6 + 2 = (8)

8 + 1 = (9)

Time for a Checkup

You can use addition to check subtraction.

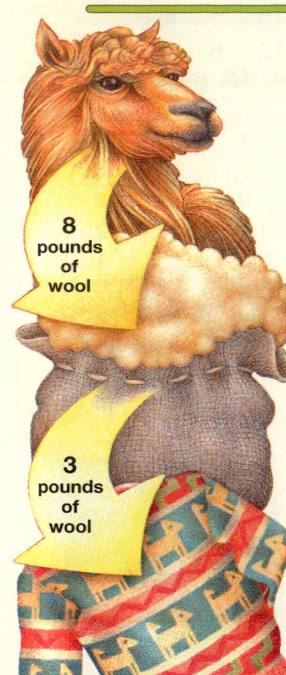

8 pounds of wool

3 pounds of wool

Learning About It

Pedro and his father have sheared 8 pounds of wool from an alpaca. So far 3 pounds of wool have been used to make a sweater. How many pounds of wool are left?

8 − 3 = ■
8 − 3 = 5

Five pounds of wool are left.

Addition and subtraction are opposite operations, so you can use addition to check subtraction.

$$\begin{array}{r} 8 \\ -3 \\ \hline 5 \end{array} \quad same \quad \begin{array}{r} 5 \\ +3 \\ \hline 8 \end{array}$$

Since 5 + 3 = 8, you know that 8 − 3 = 5.

More Examples

A. $\begin{array}{r} 6 \\ -2 \\ \hline 4 \end{array}$ same $\begin{array}{r} 4 \\ +2 \\ \hline 6 \end{array}$ B. $\begin{array}{r} 15 \\ -9 \\ \hline 6 \end{array}$ same $\begin{array}{r} 6 \\ +9 \\ \hline 15 \end{array}$

Think and Discuss What addition sentence could you use to check that 13 − 6 = 7?
7 + 6 = 13 or 6 + 7 = 13

Try It Out *Order of addends shown below may vary.*
Write an addition sentence to check each subtraction sentence.

1. 12 − 8 = 4   **2.** 14 − 9 = 5   **3.** 10 − 3 = 7
■ + ■ = 12   ■ + ■ = 14   ■ + ■ = 10
4 8   **5 9**   **7 3**

▲ The alpaca is related to the camel. It lives in the Andes Mountains in South America. Alpacas are very good at climbing steep hills and mountains.

64

1 Introduce

Cooperative Activity

KINESTHETIC

SMALL GROUPS   5–10 MINUTES

Manipulatives: counters

1. Students arrange nine counters in a group, then move four counters aside.
   - Ask: **What subtraction problem did you model?** *(9 − 4 = 5)*

2. Students add the four counters back to the other five.
   - Ask: **What addition problem did you model?** *(5 + 4 = 9 or 4 + 5 = 9)*

3. Groups model 7 − 3 = 4 and 4 + 3 = 7.

2 Teach   Pages 64–65

Read the problem with students. Discuss each step of the solution, giving students an opportunity to use their own words to explain how addition and subtraction are related.

- Ask: **Can you use addition to check subtraction?** *(Yes)* **How? Give an example.** *(Sample answer: 7 − 4 = 3 can be checked using 3 + 4 = 7.)*

Critical Thinking   ANALYSIS

After Think and Discuss, say: **If you subtract 3 and then add 3 to a number, you end up where you started. What happens if you add 3 and then subtract 3?** *(You still end up with the original number.)*

Assess Understanding

After Try It Out, ask: **What addition sentence could you use to check 8 − 4 = 4?** *(4 + 4 = 8)*

USING TECHNOLOGY

MathProcessor™ Activities
See **Activities 11 and 12** in the MathProcessor™ Activity Cards.

Practice

Subtract. Use addition to check your answer.

4. 9 − 2 **7**	5. 6 − 5 **1**	6. 6 − 3 **3**	7. 8 − 0 **8**	8. 10 − 6 **4**	9. 11 − 7 **4**
10. 15 − 6 **9**	11. 17 − 9 **8**	12. 12 − 3 **9**	13. 8 − 6 **2**	14. 4 − 2 **2**	15. 7 − 3 **4**

Problem Solving

16. Luisa sheared 9 pounds of wool from one alpaca and 8 pounds of wool from another. How many pounds did she shear in all? **17 pounds**

17. **Social Studies Connection** Many Latin American clothes and blankets are made from alpaca wool. Often the wool is dyed different colors. Suppose a weaver makes 9 blankets to sell at the market. If 5 are sold, how many are left? **4 blankets**

Review and Remember

Write the value of the underlined digit.

18. 6<u>4</u>2 **40** 19. 35<u>9</u> **9** 20. <u>2</u>,410 **400** 21. <u>9</u>,005 **9,000** 22. <u>1</u>4,028 **10,000**

Money $ense

A Fair Share
Look at the money below. How can you divide it equally among 4 people? How much money would each person have? Draw a picture or make a list to show your work.

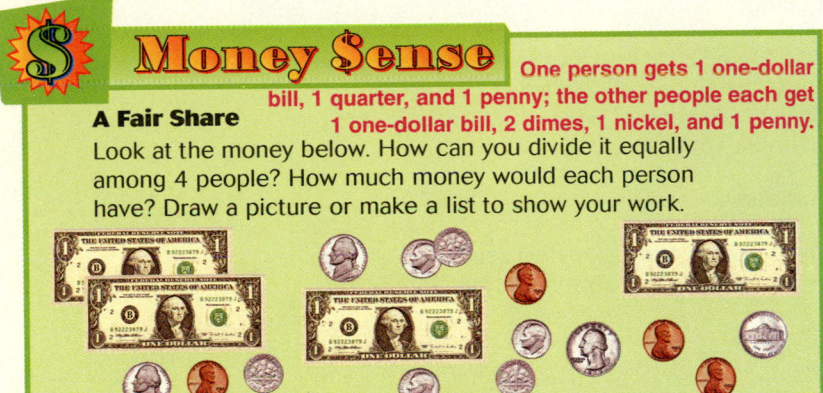

One person gets 1 one-dollar bill, 1 quarter, and 1 penny; the other people each get 1 one-dollar bill, 2 dimes, 1 nickel, and 1 penny.

For Extra Practice, see Set G, page 74. 65

Money Sense

Suggest that students find coins equivalent to those pictured to help them divide the money equally.

---

3 Wrap-up

How can you use addition to check **15 − 6 = 9?** *(Add 9 + 6 or 6 + 9.)*

📔 **Journal Idea** You had $5.00 and gave $2.00 to a friend. Now how much do you have? How can addition help you check your answer?

Common Error Alert

Watch for students who add the wrong numbers when using addition to check subtraction. Have students add the numbers from the bottom up.

Meeting Individual Needs

For Early Finishers

Each student writes 5 incorrect subtraction problems, then switches papers with another student and uses addition to correct each one.
LOGICAL/MATHEMATICAL

Inclusion

A student models 14 − 6 = 8 by moving 6 counters away from a group of 14. The partner adds 6 counters to the group of 8 counters to model 8 + 6 = 14.
VISUAL/SPATIAL

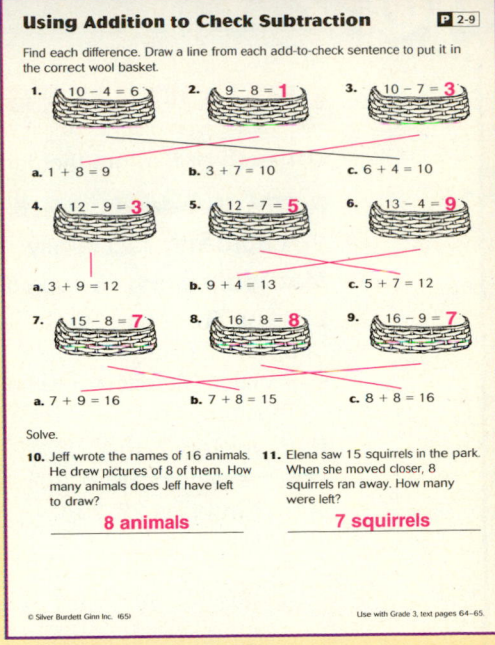
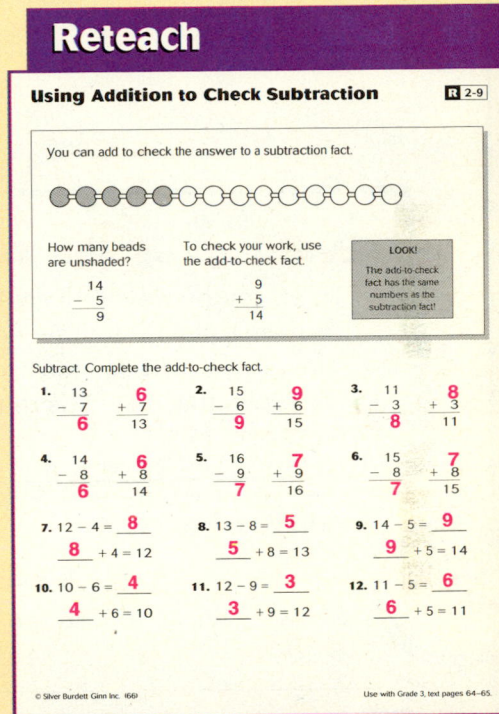
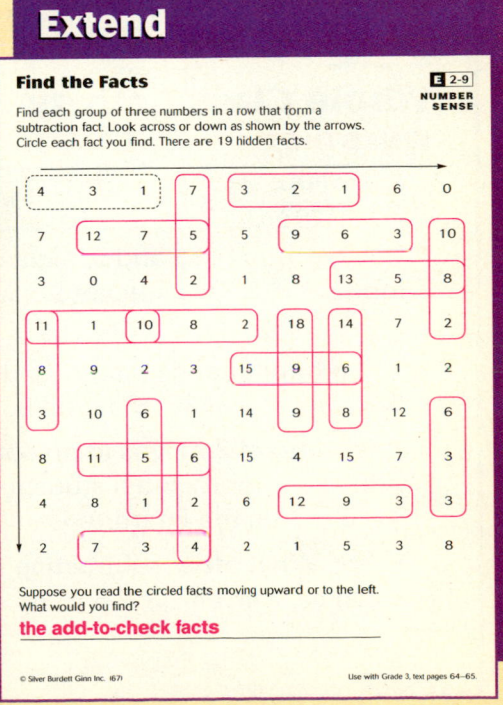
LESSON 9 65

Lesson Organizer

Objective: Explore fact families.

- **NCTM Standards:** 1, 4, 6, 8
- **Vocabulary:** fact family
- **Manipulatives:** 18 two-color counters
- **Lesson Resources:**
  Chapter File Folder
     Practice, Reteach, Extend 2-10
     Teaching Tool 8
  Daily Review 2-10
  Practice Workbook, p. 10
  Transparencies 23, 23A

Problem of the Day 2-10

The 6 key on Kevin's calculator is broken, but all the other keys work fine. How can Kevin use his broken calculator to prove that $14 - 6$ is really 8? **Sample answer: $14 - 1 - 1 - 1 - 1 - 1 - 1 = 8$**

Math Minute

Add or subtract.

$4 + 2 = (6)$	$6 - 2 = (4)$
$2 + 4 = (6)$	$6 - 4 = (2)$

A Family of Facts

You can use counters to discover addition and subtraction facts that are related.

Word Bank
fact family

Learning About It

Work with a partner.

Step 1 Use counters to show how the rabbits are grouped.

Write two addition sentences to show how many rabbits there are in all. Write two subtraction sentences to show how you could separate the rabbits into the two groups.

What number sentences did you write? **$5 + 3 = 8$; $3 + 5 = 8$; $8 - 5 = 3$; $8 - 3 = 5$**

▶ When addition and subtraction sentences all use the same numbers, they make a **fact family**.

5, 3, and 8 make a fact family.

$5 + 3 = 8$	$8 - 5 = 3$
$3 + 5 = 8$	$8 - 3 = 5$

What You Need

For each pair:
18 two-color counters

66

---

1 Introduce

Whole Class Activity

KINESTHETIC

 WHOLE CLASS   5–10 MINUTES

1. Using groups of 3 and 5, eight students model $3 + 5$. One student writes $3 + 5 = 8$ on the board.

2. The groups change places, and a student writes $5 + 3 = 8$ on the board.

3. The group of 3 moves to an opposite side of the room and a student writes $8 - 3 = 5$ on the board.

- Ask: **What other subtraction sentence can be written?** $(8 - 5 = 3)$

2 Teach   Pages 66–67

As students work through each step, they should discover that fact families use the same numbers and include related addition and subtraction sentences.

Critical Thinking   ANALYSIS

After Think and Discuss, ask: **Can any three numbers form a fact family? Explain.** *(Sample answer: No; two of the numbers must equal the third number for them to make a fact family.)* **Give an example of three numbers that do not form a fact family.** *(Sample answer: 2, 5, and 9)*

Assess Understanding

Before Practice, discuss: **One fact family is 3, 6, 9. Does the sentence $6 + 9 = 15$ belong in the family? Explain.** *(No; 15 is not one of the family members.)*

CHALLENGE

Write the fact family for 8, 8, and 16. $(8 + 8 = 16; 16 - 8 = 8)$

Step 2 Use 8 counters. Show the fact family that uses the numbers 6, 2, and 8. Then write the addition and subtraction sentences for the fact family.

$2 + 6 = 8$
$6 + 2 = 8$
$8 - 2 = 6$
$8 - 6 = 2$

Step 3 Now make other fact families, using only 8 counters. Write the addition and subtraction sentences for each fact family. **Answers may vary.**

Think and Discuss Look at all the fact families you wrote. Do they all have 2 addition and 2 subtraction sentences? Why or why not? **No, the fact family 4, 4, 8 only has one addition and one subtraction sentence because both addends are the same number.**

Practice

1. Can 5, 8, and 12 make a fact family? Explain why or why not. **No; $5 + 8 = 13$, not 12**

2. How does knowing the addition facts in a fact family help you find the subtraction facts? **The addition facts and the subtraction facts use the same numbers.**

3. Ricky used 9, 9, and 18 to make a fact family. How many addition and subtraction sentences can he make? **1 addition and 1 subtraction sentence**

4. Which of the pictures below could be used to show the fact family for 2, 3, and 5? **a, c**

a.    b.    c.

67

---

3 **Wrap-up**

What is the fact family for 5, 6, and 11?
(5 + 6 = 11; 6 + 5 = 11; 11 − 5 = 6; 11 − 6 = 5)

 Journal Idea Write one addition and one subtraction word problem for the fact family 3, 4, and 7.

Common Error Alert

Watch for students who repeat an addition or subtraction sentence in their fact family. Have students check that they have four different facts.

Meeting Individual Needs

For Early Finishers

Challenge students to list as many facts as they can think of where the sum is 9.
(0 + 9, 1 + 8, 2 + 7, 3 + 6, 4 + 5, 9 + 0, 8 + 1, 7 + 2, 6 + 3, 5 + 4)
LOGICAL/MATHEMATICAL

Cooperative Learning

Assign each group a different fact family. Groups determine how they will represent the fact family, such as with flowers on a poster. Display posters.
VISUAL/SPATIAL

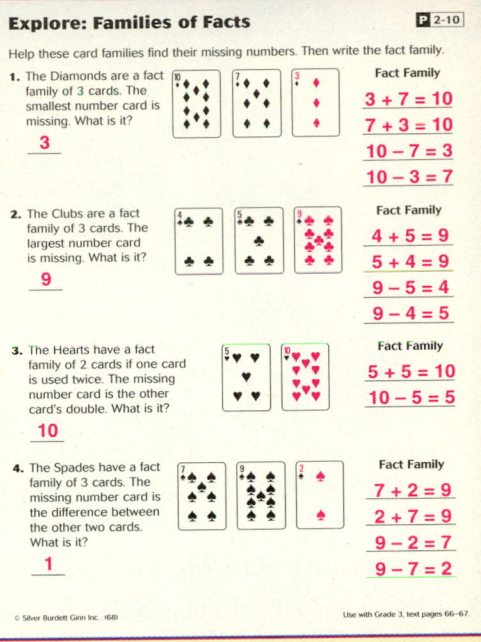

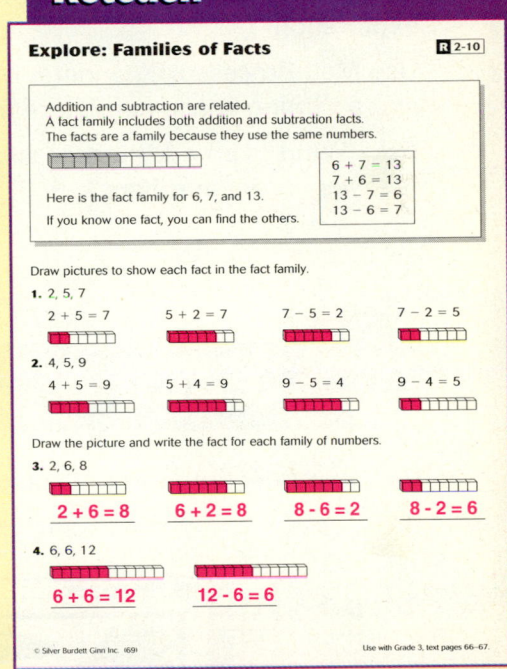

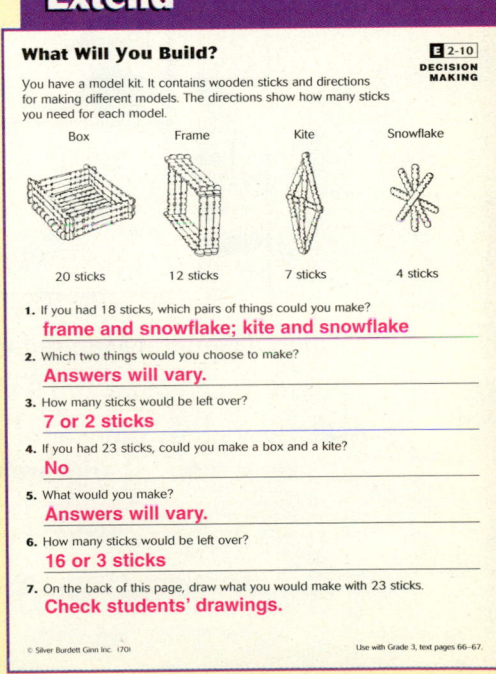

Teaching With Technology

Explore: Families of Facts

1 Introduce

Objective: Students will explore fact families using General Manipulatives on the computer.

Resources: MathProcessor™ Version 1.1

MathProcessor™ User Guide: Sections C, D, E, L

In Lesson 10, students use concrete materials to explore fact families. The MathProcessor™ Tools can also be used for this exploration.

Use MathProcessor™ General Manipulatives, a Number space, and a Writing space to explore the fact family 4, 5, 9.

Ask: What is an addition or subtraction sentence we can write using the numbers 2, 3, 5? (Sample answers: 2 + 3 = 5; 5 − 3 = 2)

2 Teach

As you model the examples below for the fact family 4, 5, 9, discuss the steps.

Step 1

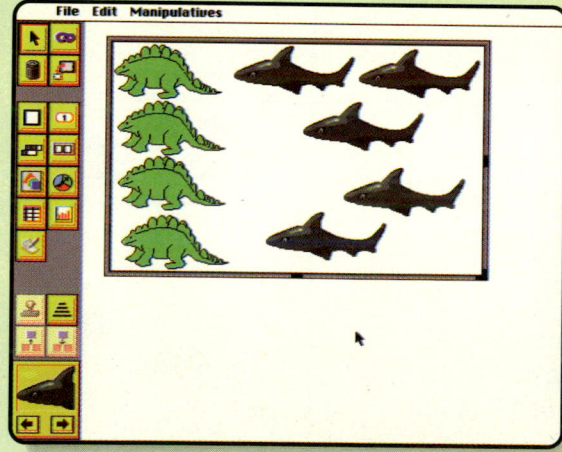

- Open a General Manipulatives workspace ▢.
- Show 4 dinosaurs and 5 sharks.

Ask: How many dinosaurs are there? (4 dinosaurs)
How many sharks are there? (5 sharks)

Step 2

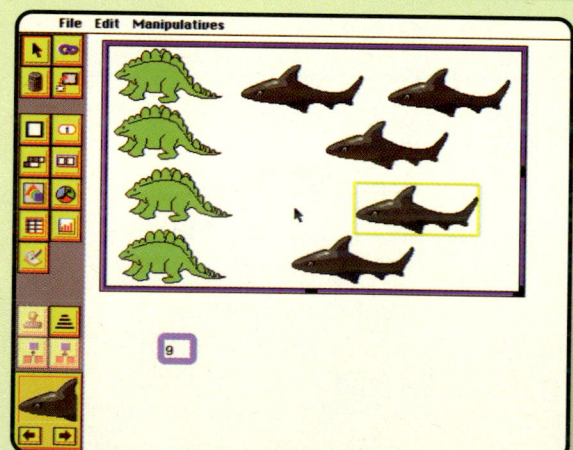

- Open a Number space 🔢.
- Link 🔗 the workspace to the Number space.

Ask: How many animals are there in all? (9 animals)
Write two addition sentences to show how many animals there are in all. (4 + 5 = 9; 5 + 4 = 9)

Step 3

- Drag 4 dinosaurs out of the workspace.

Ask: How many animals are left in the workspace? *(5 animals)* **What subtraction sentence can we write to describe the number of animals that remain in the workspace?** *(9 − 4 = 5)*

Step 4

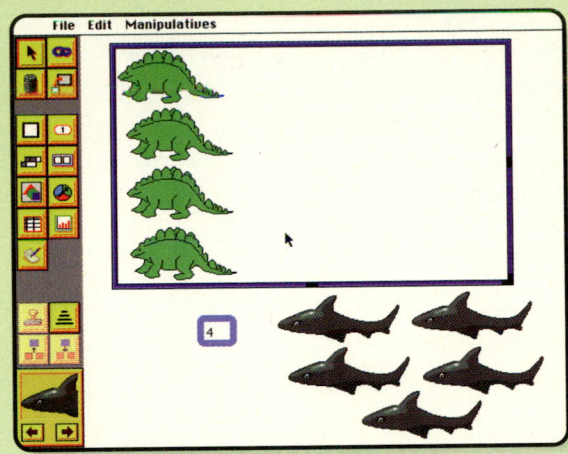

- Drag the 4 dinosaurs back into the workspace.
- Drag the 5 sharks out of the workspace.

Ask: What subtraction sentence can we write to describe this picture? *(9 − 5 = 4)* **What does each number stand for?** *(9, total number; 5, number taken out; 4, number remaining)*

Step 5

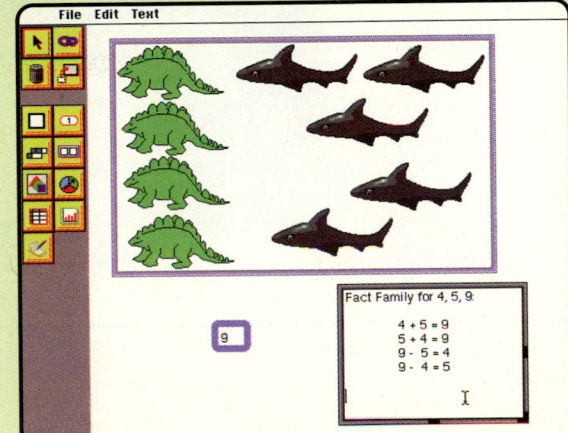

Fact Family for 4, 5, 9:
$4 + 5 = 9$
$5 + 4 = 9$
$9 - 5 = 4$
$9 - 4 = 5$

- Open a Writing space .

Ask: What addition and subtraction sentences can we write for the fact family 4, 5, 9? *(4 + 5 = 9; 5 + 4 = 9; 9 − 4 = 5; 9 − 5 = 4)*

3 Wrap-up

Allow students to use MathProcessor™ to explore fact families.

Write the fact families.

1. 6, 3, 9   **2.** 2, 4, 6   **3.** 8, 2, 10

 **Portfolio Opportunity** You may wish to have students open a Writing space and explain their responses for the exercises above and below. You may also wish to have students make printouts of their responses and add them to their portfolios.

Can 6, 9, and 17 make a fact family? Explain why or why not. *(No; 6 + 9 = 15, not 17)*

Write one addition word problem and one subtraction word problem for the fact family 6, 3, 9. *(Check students' responses.)*

Meeting Individual Needs

Cooperative Learning

Students work in pairs and take turns. One student uses **MathProcessor**™ General Manipulatives to model a fact family. The partner writes the addition and subtraction sentences in a Writing space.

For Early Finishers

Math Blaster® software and **MathProcessor**™ **Activity Cards 7–12** provide opportunities for students to practice skills learned in this chapter.

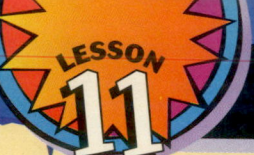

Lesson Organizer

Objective: Use data from graphs to solve problems.

- **NCTM Standards:** 1, 2, 3, 4, 7
- **Lesson Resources:**
  Chapter File Folder
    Practice, Reteach, Extend 2-11
  Daily Review 2-11

Problem of the Day   2-11

$A + B = C \qquad B - A = A$

Each letter stands for a different number. A letter has the same value each time it appears. Find a value for each letter.
Sample answer: A = 2, B = 4, and C = 6

Math Minute

Add.

7 + 3 *(10)*	9 + 7 *(16)*
4 + 8 *(12)*	2 + 5 + 8 *(15)*
2 + 4 + 9 *(15)*	1 + 6 + 6 *(13)*

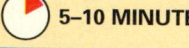

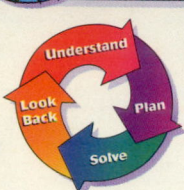

Problem Solving
Using Data From a Graph

Using data from a bar graph can help you solve problems.

The bar graph at the right shows the number of animals Lucy's class saw on their trip to the zoo. How many more turtles than lizards did the class see?

Animals We Saw at the Zoo

NUMBER OF ANIMALS — 12, 10, 8, 6, 4, 2, 0

Snakes Lizards Newts Alligators Frogs Turtles

KINDS OF ANIMALS

UNDERSTAND

What do you need to know?

You need to know that you can use the numbers on the side of the graph and the height of the bars to tell how many of each kind of animal the class saw.

PLAN

How can you solve the problem?

You can use the bar graph to compare how many turtles and how many lizards the class saw.

Science Connection
The five animals shown on these pages all have backbones. The newt and the frog are amphibians, which have smooth, wet skin. The three other animals are reptiles. A reptile's body is dry and is covered with scales or plates.

SOLVE

The class saw 12 turtles and 10 lizards.

12 − 10 = 2 turtles

The class saw 2 more turtles than lizards.

LOOK BACK

How many turtles and lizards did the class see altogether?
22 turtles and lizards

▲ Red-bellied turtle

68

---

1 Introduce

Cooperative Activity
KINESTHETIC

👥 PAIRS   🕐 5–10 MINUTES

Manipulatives: counters (10 red and 10 blue), spinner (0–9)

1. One student spins and arranges that number of red counters in a column.

2. The partner repeats Step 1, using a different color.

   - Ask: **How can you tell which color you have more of?** *(Compare the column heights and count.)* **How can you find the total number of counters?** *(Add the number of red and blue counters.)*

2 Teach   Pages 68–68A

Understand Emphasize that students need to only look at the bars for turtles and lizards.

Plan Ask: **How do you know the number of lizards and turtles they saw?** *(Sample answer: You look at the bars for turtle and lizard, then read the numbers to the left of the bars.)*

Solve Ask: **Why do you subtract to find the answer?** *(Sample answer: Because you want to find how many more)*

Look Back Students can check their answer by looking at the difference in the heights of the bars and using the scale on the graph.

Critical Thinking APPLICATION
After Look Back, ask: **What is the difference between the greatest and the least number of animals seen?** *(10)*

Assess Understanding
Before Show What You Learned, ask: **How does looking at a bar graph help you solve problems?** *(Sample answer: The different heights of the bars make it easy to compare data.)*

Show What You Learned

Use the graph on page 68 to help you solve these problems.

◀ Alpine newt ▶

1 Which kind of animal did the class see the least on their trip to the zoo?
Alligators

2 Which kind of animal did the class see the most?
Turtles

3 How many lizards and snakes did the class see altogether?
16 lizards and snakes

4 How many more lizards than snakes did the class see?
4 lizards

5 How many turtles and frogs did the class see altogether?
16 turtles and frogs

6 How many more turtles than frogs did the class see?
8 turtles

7 List the animals the class saw in order from the least animals seen to the most animals seen.
Alligators, frogs, snakes, newts, lizards, and turtles

8 What is the total number of animals the class saw on their trip to the zoo? **42 animals**

9 Analyze Sarah said she saw two large snakes, a green sea turtle and a painted turtle. Can you tell for certain if this is true by looking at the graph? Tell why or why not. **See Additional Answers, pages 72–73.**

10 Analyze Henry said he saw a bullfrog, a grass frog, a toad frog, and a red-eyed tree frog. Look at the graph. Could this be true? Tell why or why not.
See Additional Answers, pages 72–73.

11 Explain Which animals did the class see more of: frogs and newts or turtles and snakes? Explain how you know. **See Additional Answers, pages 72–73.**

12 Create Your Own Write a problem using the information in the bar graph. Then give your problem to a classmate to solve.
Check students' problems.

▼ Harlequin flying tree frog

▼ Boa constrictor

American alligator ▶

68A

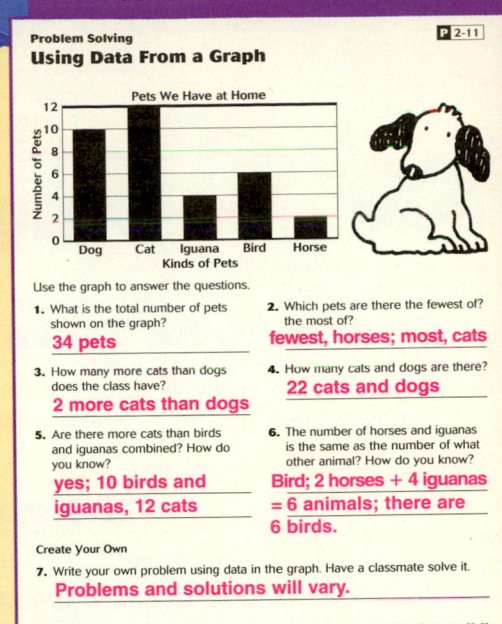
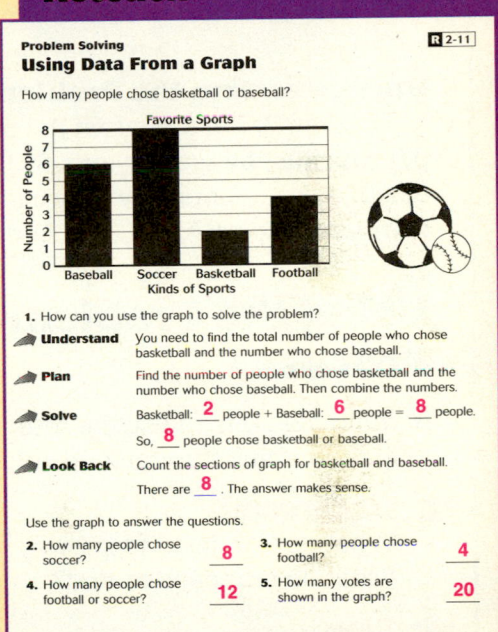
---

3 Wrap-up

How can you find the total number of animals seen on the trip? *(Sample answer: Add the number of each kind of animal.)*

Journal Idea Students choose a bar graph from a magazine or newspaper and write a sentence about it.

Common Error Alert

Watch for students who do not match graph bars with correct numbers. Suggest that they use a ruler or other straightedge to line up numbers with tops of bars.

Meeting Individual Needs

For Early Finishers

Students use the symbols < and > to compare the different animals Lucy's class saw. For example, 6 snakes < 10 lizards.
KINESTHETIC

Gifted and Talented

Have students take a survey of their classmates' favorite type of books, such as mystery or humor. Students compile the data and create a bar graph.
KINESTHETIC

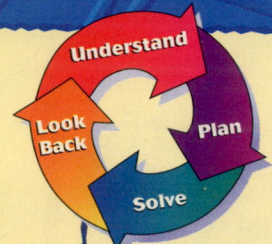

Problem Solving

Preparing for Tests

Purpose To apply problem-solving strategies and skills in a multiple-choice testing format

Reading for Problem Solving

Building Vocabulary

Students will need to understand the phrase *2 fewer birds* to solve Problem 3. Point out that each day after the first day, the number of birds decreases by 2. Students can thus eliminate Choice D, since it is greater than 15.

Understanding the Problem

In Problem 7, point out that the amount spent on pencils must be greater than $1.50 and less than $2.00. Ask students why they can therefore eliminate Choice A. *($1.25 is less than $1.50.)*

Using the Problem-Solving Process

Remind students to use the four steps below to help them think through and solve problems.

Understand
What do you need to know?
What do you need to find?

Plan
How can you solve the problem?

Solve
How can you use your plan?

Look Back
Have you solved the problem?
How can you check your answer?

Common Error Alert

For Problem 9 Students may choose the wrong number from the graph. Have them place their finger on the label for fish, then move their finger to the top of the bar and across to see what number the bar stops at.

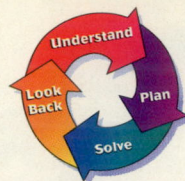

Problem Solving
★★★★★ **Preparing for Tests**

Practice What You Learned

Choose the correct letter for each answer.

1 Ted has 8 football cards and 6 baseball cards. Bob has 9 football cards and 4 baseball cards. How many football cards do they have altogether?

A. 1
B. 13
C. 14
D. 17

Tip
Sometimes extra information is given in a problem. Start by deciding what information is needed in order to answer the question.

2 Ken is drawing pictures of 4 kinds of trees in a row. He puts the elm between the oak and the pine. The oak is fourth. The other tree is a maple. What is the third tree?

A. elm
B. oak
C. pine
D. maple

Tip
Use one of these strategies to solve the problem.
• *Draw a Picture*
• *Act It Out*
• *Make a List*

3 On Tuesday, Ursula saw 15 birds in a pet store window. Each day after that, there were 2 fewer birds. How many birds were there on Friday?

A. 9
B. 11
C. 13
D. 17

Tip
Try making a table to show how many birds there are on Wednesday, Thursday, and Friday.

4 There were 3 squirrels and 8 birds in the backyard. Then 2 more squirrels joined the others. Which number sentence shows the number of squirrels in the backyard now?

A. $8 + 2 = \blacksquare$
B. $3 + 2 = \blacksquare$
C. $3 - 2 = \blacksquare$
D. $3 + 8 + 2 = \blacksquare$

5 Lynn is 3 years older than Tim. Angie is 3 years younger than Tim. Which of the following is true?

A. Tim is older than Lynn.
B. Angie is older than Lynn.
C. Lynn is older than Angie.
D. Angie is older than Tim.

6 There are 15 books on sale at a yard sale. More than 10 of the books are sold. What is reasonable for the number of books that are left?

A. Less than 5
B. Between 5 and 10
C. Between 10 and 15
D. More than 15

7 Nan spent $1.50 on pens and $2.00 on markers. She bought pencils which cost more than the pens but less than the markers. Which is a reasonable amount Nan might have spent on the pencils?

A. $1.25   C. $1.75
B. $1.50   D. $2.00

8 Patricia has 29 red hearts and 42 blue hearts in her sticker collection. **About** how many red and blue hearts does Patricia have?

A. 10
B. 20
C. 40
D. 70

Use the graph for Problems 9–10.

This graph shows the number of pets that the students in Karen's class have.

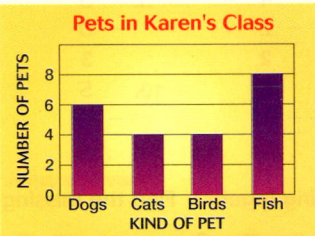

Pets in Karen's Class

9 How many fish do the students in Karen's class have?

A. 4
B. 6
C. 8
D. 9

10 How many more dogs than cats do the students in Karen's class have?

A. 2
B. 3
C. 6
D. 10

69A

Tips for Test-Taking

Is there extra information?
In Problem 4, ask students if any information is extra and have them explain their responses. *(The number of birds is extra; the question asks only about the number of squirrels.)*

Is an estimate or an exact answer needed?
In Problem 8, ask students whether they need to find an exact number or an estimate. *(An estimate; the question asks about how many.)*

What strategy can be used? In Problem 5, suggest that students use the *Make A List* strategy. They can make a list of the three friends in order of their ages. Then they can compare their list with the answer choices to find the correct answer.

Is the answer reasonable? In Problem 6, have students read the problem. Then ask them why Choice D is not reasonable. *(There were 15 books and some were sold, so there cannot be more than 15 books left.)*

Chapter 3

Daily Lesson Planner

Addition and Subtraction With Greater Numbers

To Start the Chapter

Chapter Opener

Resources

- Chapter Opener
  Career Spotlight
  Chapter Project, *Teacher Guide*,
  pages 78–79

- Chapter Pretest, *Assessment Guide*,
  pages 79–82

- Family Letter With Activity,
  Home-School Connection,
  pages 13–14

- Internet Activity,
  pages 93, 95, 105

Lesson 1

PAGES 80–81	**Using Mental Math**
	Chapter File Folder
LEARNING OBJECTIVES 3B, 3D	Practice, Reteach, Extend 3-1
	Daily Review 3-1
	Problem of the Day 3-1
NCTM STANDARDS 1, 6, 8	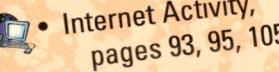 p. 81

Lesson 2

PAGES 82–83	**Estimating Sums**
	Chapter File Folder
LEARNING OBJECTIVES 3A	Practice, Reteach, Extend 3-2
	Teaching Tools 19, 20
	Daily Review 3-2
	Problem of the Day 3-2
NCTM STANDARDS 1, 3, 5, 7	p. 83

Lesson 6

PAGES 92–93	**Adding Greater Numbers**
	Chapter File Folder
LEARNING OBJECTIVES 3B	Practice, Reteach, Extend 3-6
	Teaching Tool 13
	Daily Review 3-6
	Practice Workbook, p. 11
	Problem of the Day 3-6
NCTM STANDARDS 1, 6, 8	p. 93

Lesson 7

PAGES 94–95	**Adding More Than Two Numbers**
	Chapter File Folder
LEARNING OBJECTIVES 3C	Practice, Reteach, Extend 3-7
	Daily Review 3-7
	Problem of the Day 3-7
	✓ Checkpoint, pp. 96–97
NCTM STANDARDS 1, 4, 8	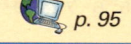 p. 95 p. 96 p. 97

Lesson 11

PAGES 104–107	**Subtracting Two- and Three-Digit Numbers**
	Manipulatives: base-ten blocks
	Chapter File Folder
LEARNING OBJECTIVES 3D	Practice, Reteach, Extend 3-11
	Teaching Tools 14, 22, 23
	Daily Review 3-11
	Practice Workbook, p. 13
	Problem of the Day 3-11
NCTM STANDARDS 1, 6, 8	p. 104 p. 106 p. 107

Lesson 12

PAGES 108–109	**Subtracting Greater Numbers**
	Chapter File Folder
LEARNING OBJECTIVES 3D	Practice, Reteach, Extend 3-12
	Teaching Tool 14
	Daily Review 3-12
	Practice Workbook, p. 14
	Problem of the Day 3-12
NCTM STANDARDS 1, 6, 7, 8	p. 109

Chapter End

PAGES 118–125	**Chapter Assessment**
	Extra Practice, pp. 118–120
LEARNING OBJECTIVES 3A 3B 3C 3D 3E	Chapter Test, p. 121
	Performance Assessment, p. 122
	Extension, p. 123
	Using Math in Science, p. 124
	Cumulative Review
NCTM STANDARDS 1, 2, 3, 4, 5, 6, 7, 8, 12, 13	**In the *Assessment Guide***
	Chapter Posttest, pp. 83–86
	Interview Activity, p. 37

 Algebra   **Time for Technology**    **Time for Technology**   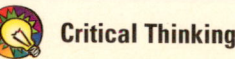 **Critical Thinking**

LEARNING OBJECTIVES

3A Estimate sums and differences

3B Add two-, three-, and four-digit numbers, including money

3C Add more than two numbers

3D Subtract two-, three-, and four-digit numbers, including money

3E Analyze and solve problems using skills and strategies

NCTM STANDARDS

1 Problem Solving
2 Communication
3 Reasoning
4 Mathematical Connections
5 Estimation
6 Number Sense and Numeration
7 Whole Number Operations
8 Whole Number Computation
9 Geometry and Spatial Sense
10 Measurement
11 Statistics and Probability
12 Fractions and Decimals
13 Patterns and Relationships

Lesson 3

PAGES 84–85

LEARNING OBJECTIVES 3E

NCTM STANDARDS 1, 3, 7

Developing Skills for Problem Solving

Chapter File Folder
Practice, Reteach, Extend 3-3
Daily Review 3-3
Problem of the Day 3-3

Lesson 4

PAGES 86–87B

LEARNING OBJECTIVES 3B

NCTM STANDARDS 3, 6, 8, 13

EXPLORE: Regrouping in Addition

Manipulatives: base-ten blocks
Chapter File Folder
Practice, Reteach, Extend 3-4
Teaching Tools 22, 44
Daily Review 3-4
Problem of the Day 3-4
Teaching With Technology

Lesson 5

PAGES 88–91

LEARNING OBJECTIVES 3B

NCTM STANDARDS 1, 3, 8

Adding Two- and Three-Digit Numbers

Manipulatives: base-ten blocks (optional)
Chapter File Folder
Practice, Reteach, Extend 3-5
Teaching Tools 13, 22, 23
Daily Review 3-5
Problem of the Day 3-5

💲 p. 90   🖥 p. 91

Lesson 8

PAGES 98–99

LEARNING OBJECTIVES 3E

NCTM STANDARDS 1, 2, 3, 7

Problem-Solving Strategy

Chapter File Folder
Practice, Reteach, Extend 3-8
Daily Review 3-8
Problem of the Day 3-8

Lesson 9

PAGES 100–101

LEARNING OBJECTIVES 3A

NCTM STANDARDS 1, 3, 4, 5

Estimating Differences

Chapter File Folder
Practice, Reteach, Extend 3-9
Teaching Tools 19, 20
Daily Review 3-9
Practice Workbook, p. 12
Problem of the Day 3-9

Using Algebra p. 101

Lesson 10

PAGES 102–103

LEARNING OBJECTIVES 3D

NCTM STANDARDS 3, 6, 8

EXPLORE: Regrouping in Subtraction

Manipulatives: base-ten blocks
Chapter File Folder
Practice, Reteach, Extend 3-10
Teaching Tools 22, 43
Daily Review 3-10
Problem of the Day 3-10

Using Algebra p. 103

Lesson 13

PAGES 110–111

LEARNING OBJECTIVES 3D

NCTM STANDARDS 1, 3, 8

Subtracting Across Zeros

Chapter File Folder
Practice, Reteach, Extend 3-13
Teaching Tool 14
Daily Review 3-13
Practice Workbook, p. 15
Problem of the Day 3-13

Lesson 14

PAGES 112–113

LEARNING OBJECTIVES 3B 3D

NCTM STANDARDS 1, 3, 8

Choosing a Computation Method

Chapter File Folder
Practice, Reteach, Extend 3-14
Daily Review 3-14
Problem of the Day 3-14

Lesson 15

PAGES 114–115A

LEARNING OBJECTIVES 3E

NCTM STANDARDS 1, 3, 4, 7

Problem-Solving Application

Chapter File Folder
Practice, Reteach, Extend 3-15
Daily Review 3-15
Problem of the Day 3-15
Problem Solving: Preparing for Tests

✓ Checkpoint, pp. 116–117

Using Algebra p. 116

Correlation to Investigations

Investigations in Number, Data, and Space
Dale Seymour Publications

Lessons 1-15   **Combining and Comparing**
Investigations 1, 3, 4

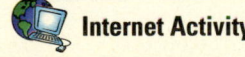

Meeting Individual Needs

Learning Styles vary from student to student. Every Meeting Individual Needs activity focuses on one of the following learning styles. The variety of styles enables students to learn math in ways that are most comfortable to them.

- AUDITORY
- INDIVIDUAL
- KINESTHETIC
- LINGUISTIC
- LOGICAL/MATHEMATICAL
- SOCIAL/COOPERATIVE
- VISUAL/SPATIAL

Acquiring English Proficiency

Materials: magazines and newspapers

Ask students to look through magazines and newspapers to find 2-, 3-, and 4-digit numbers that provide data related to travel, such as airfare or hotel room rates. Have students create and solve their own addition and subtraction story problems about travel.

For additional activities, see Acquiring English Proficiency, pp. 85, 91, 107, 113.

LINGUISTIC

For Extra Help

Manipulatives: base-ten blocks (hundreds, tens, and ones) in separate bags*

Have students work in pairs to practice modeling addition. One student takes a handful of models from each bag and writes the 3-digit number. The other student does the same. Students then add the numbers by combining the 2 sets of models, regrouping when necessary.

For additional activities, see For Extra Help, pp. 81, 83, 93, 109.

KINESTHETIC

For Early Finishers

Have students draw simple maps that show road distances between imaginary cities. The maps can also show other data, such as heights of mountains or lengths of rivers. Students write addition and subtraction problems about their maps, then solve one another's problems.

For additional activities, see For Early Finishers, pp. 81, 83, 85, 87, 91, 93, 95, 99, 101, 103, 107, 109, 111, 113, 114A.

VISUAL/SPATIAL

Gifted and Talented

Present addition and subtraction problems with missing digits, such as these.

$$\begin{array}{r} \square\,6\,8 \\ +\;5\,3\,\square \\ \hline 9\,0\,2 \end{array} \qquad \begin{array}{r} 7\,\square\,5 \\ +\;2\,\square\,5 \\ \hline 1{,}0\,0\,0 \end{array} \qquad \begin{array}{r} 4\,8\,\square \\ +\;\square\,7\,5 \\ \hline 8\,\square\,2 \end{array}$$

After students have solved each problem, they can create, exchange, and solve each other's problems.

For additional activities see Gifted and Talented, p. 101.

LOGICAL/MATHEMATICAL

Inclusion

Materials: base-ten blocks, Teaching Tool 14 (Subtraction Place-Value Work Form)

Have students write problems, such as 800 − 254, in a place-value form, then model the regrouping. Ask guiding questions such as: "Are there enough ones to subtract? Can I regroup a ten to make ones? How can I regroup a hundred to make tens and ones?"

For additional activities, see Inclusion, p. 99.

KINESTHETIC

*These Manipulatives are found in the Manipulatives Kit.

MATH CENTER

Cooperative Learning

Manipulatives: base-ten blocks*

Students work in small groups. One student creates a story problem that requires adding or subtracting 3- or 4-digit numbers. The second student explains whether to add or subtract. The third student finds the answer. The fourth student uses base-ten blocks to check the answer. Students continue until all have participated in each role.

For additional activities, see Cooperative Learning, pp. 95, 114A.

SOCIAL/COOPERATIVE

Manipulatives

Manipulatives: base-ten blocks, spinner labeled 1–9*

Have pairs play "Try for 1,000." One student spins twice and shows those numbers of tens and ones. Another student does the same. In the next round, students spin and add tens and ones to those they have, regroup if necessary, and write the addition problem. Play continues until someone reaches 1,000.

For additional activities, see Manipulatives, pp. 87, 103, 111.

KINESTHETIC

Using Data

Materials: base-ten blocks

Students gather base-ten blocks—hundreds, tens, and ones—that add up to 500. They put the blocks in 2 groups. Then they make a table and write the 2 addends. They move blocks from one group to another and write the new addends. Students repeat until they have found 10 ways to make 500.

For review, see pages 26–27, 88–91, and 98–99.

Answers: Answers will vary.

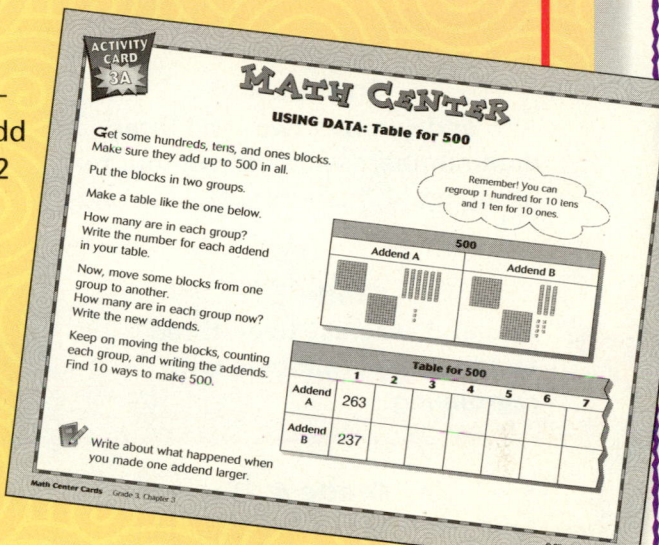

Problem Solving

Students round prices to the nearest dollar to find the total rounded cost. They add the actual prices to find the difference. Students subtract 20¢ from each actual price, round the new prices to the nearest dollar, and identify which prices have changed.

For review, see pages 80–85 and 114–114A.

Answers: Rounded prices: eggs = $1.00; orange juice = $2.00; milk = $2.00; cereal = $2.00; soup = $2.00; total rounded cost = $9.00; $0.95; eggs; rounded prices of orange juice and soup change to $1.00.

Assessment

Skills Trace
Skills Assessed at Each Grade

Grade 2
Add and subtract two- and three-digit numbers with and without regrouping. (Chapters 5, 6, and 11)

Grade 3
Add and subtract two-, three-, and four-digit numbers with regrouping.

Grade 4
Add and subtract five-digit numbers with regrouping. (Chapter 2)

Informal Assessment

Informal assessments provide day-to-day feedback. In conjunction with more formal assessments, they give a complete picture of conceptual development.

In the Student Book

What Do You Think?
student pages 97, 117
Students explain what they have learned.

Create Your Own
student pages 95, 114A
Students create their own problems.

Journal Idea
student pages 87, 97, 117
Students communicate mathematically.

Self-Check
student pages 121, 122
Students evaluate their own work.

In the Teacher Guide

Baseline Assessment
teacher page 78
Helps you assess prior knowledge

Ongoing Assessment

ASSESS UNDERSTANDING

Helps you assess students' understanding

WRAP-UP

Helps you monitor students' progress

JOURNAL IDEA
teacher pages 79, 81, 87, 97, 101, 103, 111, 117
Helps you assess students' communication of math ideas

Portfolio Ideas

Portfolio opportunities appear on Student Book pages 117 and 122, and Teacher Guide pages 87A–B, 117, and 122.

Other items that you may wish to include in your student portfolios are:

- **Completed Chapter Projects**
- **Journal Entries**
- **CD-ROM and Internet Activities**
- **Informal Observations and Interview Activities**

For further suggestions for organizing and using portfolios, see **Assessment Guide,** pages 50–54.

Formal Assessment

Formal assessment can occur before and after the chapter, as well as at natural breaking points in the chapter.

In the Student Book

Checkpoints
student pages 96–97, 116–117
Use for assessing progress as students work through the chapter.

Chapter Test
student page 121

Performance Assessment
student page 122
The Performance Assessment helps you evaluate the skills and concepts developed in Chapter 3 through hands-on activities.

 CD-ROM Test Generator

This software allows you to customize your own chapter test. Formats include:

- **Multiple Choice**
- **Free Response**
- **Standardized Test**

Assessment Guide

You may choose among the following pages in the *Assessment Guide.*

Pretest Options
- Free Response, pages 79–80
- Multiple Choice, pages 81–82

Posttest Options
- Free Response, pages 83–84
- Multiple Choice, pages 85–86

Interview Activity
page 37

Long-Answer Question
page 9

Performance Assessment 1
pages 15–17

Cumulative Test 1
pages 87–90

Correlation to Standardized Tests

Learning Objectives	ITBS K/M	CTBS/5 (Terra Nova)	SAT9	MAT7	CAT5	*Pre/Post- Test Items	Lesson Pages
Standardized Test Items							
3A Estimate sums and differences	MC: 11–17	11, 12	PS: 41	CPS: 27 P: 22, 23	MC: 6	1–3	82–83 100–101
3B Add two-, three-, and four-digit numbers, including money	PS: 19, 22, 23, COM: 2, 7, 9, 13, 15 MC: 2, 10 ME: 11, 15–17	1, 3	P: 11, 2, 22, 24	P: 1, 2, 6, 13, 14, 22 CPS: 35	COM: 2–6, 9, 10	4–8	80–81 86–93 112–113
3C Add more than two numbers	COM: 7 PS: 22		PS: 3, 23	P: 6	COM: 1, 7	9–11	94–95
3D Subtract two-, three-, and four-digit numbers, including money	PS: 18, COM: 3, 5, 6, 8, 12, 16 ME: 12–14	2, 4	P: 3, 23	P: 3–5, 7–9, 15, 23	COM: 12–24	12–17	80–81 102–113
3E Analyze and solve problems using skills and strategies	PS: 18–24 ME: 11–13, 17	12, 48–50, 50	PS: 4, 43–46	CPS: 33–40 P: 1–12	MC: 20, 25–27, 38	18–20	84–85 98–99 114–114A 115–115A

MC = Math Concepts, **COM** = Math Computation, **PS** = Problem Solving, **P** = Procedures, **CPS** = Math Concepts & Problem Solving, **ME** = Math Estimation, **MDI** = Math Data Interpretation, **PB** = Math Problems

*Pretests and Posttests are found in the *Assessment Guide.*

Chapter 3

Linking Technology

MathProcessor™

CD-ROM Activities use MathProcessor™ Tools to help build critical thinking skills and develop problem-solving strategies.

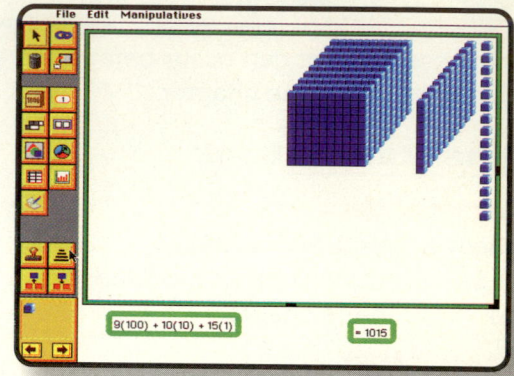

Lesson	Tools	Skill
5	Base-Ten Blocks Number space	Students explore regrouping ones and tens in addition.
10	Base-Ten Blocks Number space	Students use manipulatives to regroup hundreds, tens, and ones in subtraction.
13	Base-Ten Blocks Number space	Students use manipulatives to subtract across zeros.

Review and Practice Skills

Math Blaster® 1

This **CD-ROM** program provides exercises and activities to practice basic math facts and develop mastery of mathematical operations. The chart below lists specific lessons where activities and references can be found.

Lesson	Activity	Subject/Level
1	Cave Runner	Addition—Level 6: sums 22–25
11	Math Blaster	Subtraction—Levels: 1–5
12	Math Blaster	Subtraction—Level 6: Differences 10–18

Extend and Enrich

Internet

Students can use real data in lesson-related math activities.
Teachers can find activities and resources for Lessons 6, 7, and 11.
Parents can find home connections to help reinforce concepts.

Visit our Web site at:

www.sbgmath.com

Making Connections

Literature

For the Chapter Activity

Find this book in your local or school library. Use it with the Math & Literature activity on page 105.

- **Night of the Moonjellies**
  by Mark Shasha
  Simon & Schuster Books for
  Young Readers, 1992

Additional Resources

These books, found in your local or school library, can be used to help build math concepts.

- **Alexander, Who Used to Be Rich Last Sunday**
  by Judith Viorst
  Atheneum, 1985
- **Let's Investigate Estimating**
  by Marion Smoothey
  Marshall Cavendish Corporation, 1995

Home-School

Family Letter With Activity
Home-School Connection Booklet

The Family Letter for Chapter 3 introduces the idea of using mental math to find sums and differences and to estimate sums and differences. Family activities suggest ways to reinforce mental math skills by playing games while carrying out daily activities.

Study Buddies
Home-School Connection Booklet

Study Buddies pages provide reinforcement activities for students to work on with a partner.

- Study Buddies 3A provides help with rounding to the nearest ten and using tens to estimate sums.
- Study Buddies 3B offers practice adding more than two numbers.
- Study Buddies 3C provides practice subtracting greater numbers.

Math Backpack
Take-Home Activities

Math Backpack activities provide a link between the classroom and the home. Activity Cards 1–6 can be used with this chapter. Parents and students alike will enjoy using these laminated cards and accompanying manipulatives.

Cross-Curricular Integration

Language Arts

- Keep a travel log, Teacher Guide pp. 78–79.
- Write your own palindromes, p. 123.

Social Studies

- Learn about different careers, pp. 78, 101.
- Visit people and places around the world, pp. 83, 84, 88, 91, 95, 109, 111.
- Travel in time to the California Gold Rush, pp. 98, 99.

Science

- Read about a Hawaiian volcano, p. 83.
- Read about digging for dinosaur bones, p. 101.

Art

- Take a look at traditional Mayan pottery, p. 91.

Chapter 3

Addition and Subtraction With Greater Numbers

Theme: TRAVEL

Chapter Overview

In this chapter students will learn strategies for addition and subtraction and will add and subtract two-, three-, and four-digit numbers.

Activating Prior Knowledge

Discuss with students what they already know about addition and subtraction of greater numbers. Record responses on the chalkboard.

Baseline Assessment

Ask questions such as:

- **What are some strategies that can help you add?** *(Drawing a picture, using counters, using paper and pencil, using mental math)*

- **How are addition and subtraction different?** *(In addition, you join groups to find how many in all; in subtraction, you take away from a group to find a difference.)*

Save student responses to use with the **Ongoing Assessment** section in the chapter Checkpoints on pages 97 and 117.

Addition and Subtraction With Greater Numbers

Chapter Theme: TRAVEL

Real-WORLD Math

·············Real Facts·············

White water rafting is a fun way to see a river! The Arkansas River Tours of Colorado plans rafting trips. The chart below shows how many people went on trips during five months in 1997 and 1998.

Arkansas River Tours Rafting Trips

Month	Number of People (1998)	Number of People (1997)
May	970	665
June	3,242	3,133
July	5,358	4,542
August	2,623	2,763
September	176	104

- In 1997, about how many more people went rafting in July than in June?

- Which month do you think would be the busiest in 1999? Use the data to decide.

·········Real People·········

Meet Keith Jardine. He guides rafting trips on America's rivers. He makes sure people know how to safely paddle rafts. River guides use mathematics to find out how fast the river flows. If the water is too fast, the river is not safe for rafting.

78

Chapter Project

Keep a Travel Log

 PAIRS

Materials
- ▶ construction paper or posterboard
- ▶ markers and crayons
- ▶ scissors
- ▶ glue or tape

Here is a project that will help your students practice addition and subtraction with greater numbers. Specific lessons are referenced to help you work on the project throughout the chapter.

Getting Started

Explain that students will work with a partner to take a "trip" in a Math Mobile. Each pair will choose a real or make-believe place to visit. They will use a Travel Log to keep track of the places they go, the number of miles they travel, and other "facts" about their trip.

..........Real Facts..........

- The longest time anyone has survived alone on a raft is 133 days. Poon Lim of Great Britain's Merchant Navy did so after his ship was torpedoed in the Atlantic Ocean on November 23, 1942.

- At 1,460 miles, the Arkansas is the fifth longest river in the United States. The longest river is the Mississippi-Missouri-Red Rock at 3,710 miles.

Using the Data

When students review the table on page 78, make sure they read *across* to compare the numbers of people for 1996 and for 1997. Explain that the numbers for May and September are low because the trips begin in mid-May and end on Labor Day. Some questions you may wish to ask include:

- About how many more people went rafting in May 1997 than in May 1996? *(Estimates will vary. Possible estimate: 300 people)*

- Which month had about 50 more people in 1997 than in 1996? *(September)*

..........Real People..........

Keith Jardine raced with a ski team in California when he was a teenager. Later, he worked as a ski instructor and coach. He began working as a river guide in 1985, and now teaches people to paddle safely as he guides trips along rivers in California, Oregon, and the Grand Canyon.

Building Vocabulary

These key words will be found in this chapter.

estimate   palindromes

front-end estimation

Journal Idea You may wish to have students write about each vocabulary term in their journals at the beginning and end of chapter.

Project Links

▶ **Lesson 5** Partners should decide where the Math Mobile will go, then write **math "facts"** about their trip in a Travel Log. For example: "Our Math Mobile will go to 34 different places. It will travel 32,640 miles and carry 1,722 people."

▶ **Lesson 9** Partners should discuss the numbers they came up with in the previous link. They can then use the numbers to write **addition and subtraction problems** in their Travel Log.

Project Wrap-up

Have each pair finish its Travel Log and show it to the class. Encourage pairs to share their math problems with their classmates. Challenge the class to solve each problem by **adding** or **subtracting**.

Portfolio Students may wish to include their project work in their portfolios.

Lesson Organizer

Objective: Add and subtract mentally.

- **NCTM Standards:** 1, 6, 8
- **Lesson Resources:**
  Chapter File Folder
  Practice, Reteach, Extend 3-1
  Daily Review 3-1

Problem of the Day 3-1

Jenny is making a calendar for the month of May. She wrote one 1 for May 1. She wrote one 1 and one 0 for May 10. She wrote in all of the dates on her calendar. How many 1s did she write? **14 ones**

Math Minute

Add.

4 + 3 *(7)*	8 + 2 *(10)*
2 + 5 *(7)*	9 + 1 *(10)*
6 + 2 *(8)*	7 + 3 *(10)*

 1

Using Mental Math

Get a Head Start

Sometimes you can solve problems in your head.

Learning About It

Your class is going on a trip in the Math Mobile! There are 20 seats upstairs and 30 seats downstairs. How many seats are on the Math Mobile?

20 + 30 = ■

You can use mental math to find the sum. Use addition facts you know.

Think:
$$\begin{array}{r} 2 \\ + 3 \\ \hline 5 \end{array}$$
So
$$\begin{array}{r} 2 \text{ tens} \\ + 3 \text{ tens} \\ \hline 5 \text{ tens} \end{array}$$
So
$$\begin{array}{r} 20 \\ + 30 \\ \hline 50 \end{array}$$

There are 50 seats on the Math Mobile.

If 40 seats on the Math Mobile are blue and the rest are green, how many seats are green?

50 − 40 = ■

You can use mental math to find the difference. Use subtraction facts you know.

Think:
$$\begin{array}{r} 5 \\ - 4 \\ \hline 1 \end{array}$$
So
$$\begin{array}{r} 5 \text{ tens} \\ - 4 \text{ tens} \\ \hline 1 \text{ ten} \end{array}$$
So
$$\begin{array}{r} 50 \\ - 40 \\ \hline 10 \end{array}$$

There are 10 green seats.

More Examples

A.
$$\begin{array}{r} 500 \\ + 300 \\ \hline 800 \end{array}$$
B.
$$\begin{array}{r} 900 \\ - 200 \\ \hline 700 \end{array}$$
C.
$$\begin{array}{r} 3{,}000 \\ + 4{,}000 \\ \hline 7{,}000 \end{array}$$
D.
$$\begin{array}{r} 8{,}000 \\ - 7{,}000 \\ \hline 1{,}000 \end{array}$$

Think and Discuss Use 7 + 3 = 10 and mental math to find 70 + 30. Explain your thinking.
7 + 3 = 10, 7 tens + 3 tens = 10 tens, 70 + 30 = 100

80

---

1 Introduce

Cooperative Activity
KINESTHETIC

PAIRS   ⏱ 5–10 MINUTES

Manipulatives: base-ten rods

1. Each student takes a handful of rods from a pile.
2. Each student records the number of rods that were taken.
3. Both students add the total number of rods.

- Ask: **How many rods do you have together? What whole number does the total number of rods represent?**

2 Teach   Pages 80–81

Allow students to use base-ten rods to check answers after using mental math.

- Ask: **What operation would you use to find how many seats there are altogether?** *(Addition)*
- Ask: **What operation would you use to find how many seats are green?** *(Subtraction)*

Critical Thinking   APPLICATION

After Think and Discuss, ask: **How can you use mental math to find 100 − 80?** *(Sample answer: 10 − 8 = 2, and 10 tens − 8 tens = 2 tens, so 100 − 80 = 20)*

Assess Understanding

After Try It Out, say: **Explain how to find the sum for 500 + 300.** *(5 + 3 = 8, and 5 hundreds + 3 hundreds = 8 hundreds, so 500 + 300 = 800)*

 USING TECHNOLOGY

Math Blaster® 1, Cave Runner
Addition: Level 6
Sums 22–25

Try It Out

Use mental math to find each sum.

1. $\begin{array}{r} 4 \\ + 2 \\ \hline 6 \end{array}$	**2.** $\begin{array}{r} 40 \\ + 20 \\ \hline 60 \end{array}$	**3.** $\begin{array}{r} 400 \\ + 200 \\ \hline 600 \end{array}$	**4.** $\begin{array}{r} 4{,}000 \\ + 2{,}000 \\ \hline 6{,}000 \end{array}$

Practice

Find each sum or difference.

5. $\begin{array}{r} 60 \\ + 50 \\ \hline 110 \end{array}$	**6.** $\begin{array}{r} 80 \\ - 20 \\ \hline 60 \end{array}$	**7.** $\begin{array}{r} 100 \\ + 700 \\ \hline 800 \end{array}$	**8.** $\begin{array}{r} 700 \\ - 500 \\ \hline 200 \end{array}$	**9.** $\begin{array}{r} 6{,}000 \\ - 2{,}000 \\ \hline 4{,}000 \end{array}$
10. $\begin{array}{r} 500 \\ + 0 \\ \hline 500 \end{array}$	**11.** $\begin{array}{r} 700 \\ + 600 \\ \hline 1{,}300 \end{array}$	**12.** $\begin{array}{r} 120 \\ - 80 \\ \hline 40 \end{array}$	**13.** $\begin{array}{r} 900 \\ - 600 \\ \hline 300 \end{array}$	**14.** $\begin{array}{r} 9{,}000 \\ + 8{,}000 \\ \hline 17{,}000 \end{array}$
15. $\begin{array}{r} 600 \\ + 400 \\ \hline 1{,}000 \end{array}$	**16.** $\begin{array}{r} 700 \\ - 200 \\ \hline 500 \end{array}$	**17.** $\begin{array}{r} 900 \\ + 400 \\ \hline 1{,}300 \end{array}$	**18.** $\begin{array}{r} 8{,}000 \\ + 1{,}000 \\ \hline 9{,}000 \end{array}$	**19.** $\begin{array}{r} 5{,}000 \\ - 3{,}000 \\ \hline 2{,}000 \end{array}$

Using Algebra Complete each pattern.

20. 20, 30, 40, ■, ■, ■
               50 60 70

21. 2, 12, 22, ■, ■, ■
             32 42 52

22. 103, 203, 303, ■, ■, ■
            403 503 603

23. 80, 70, ■, ■, 40, ■
           60 50   30

24. 540, ■, ■, 240, ■, 40
        440 340   140

25. 215, ■, ■, ■, 615, 715
         315 415 515

Problem Solving

26. Each television on the Math Mobile has 200 regular channels and 400 cable channels. How many channels are there in all? **600 channels**

27. Mega computers on the Math Mobile have 900 games. Mini computers only have 700 games. How many more games are there on the Mega computer? **200 games**

Review and Remember

Round each number to the nearest ten.

28. 59   **29.** 31   **30.** 65   **31.** 87
   60   30   70   90

For Extra Practice, see Set A, page 118. **81**

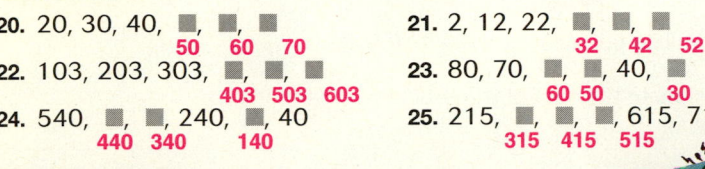

Using Algebra

In Exercises 20–25, students use **patterns** to make complete number sequences.

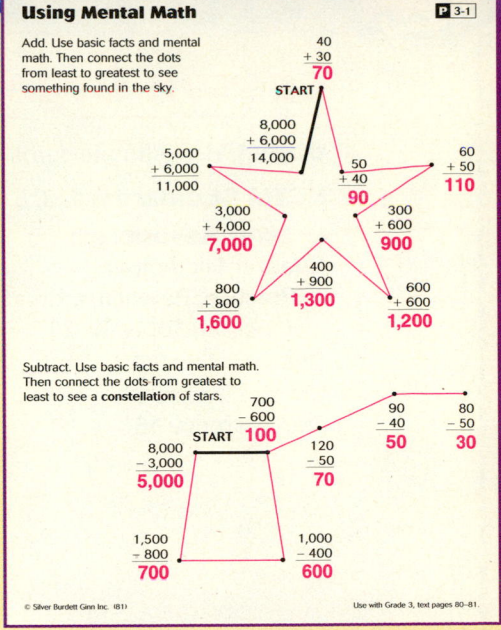

3 Wrap-up

Journal Idea Write sentences to describe the steps for using mental math to add and subtract. *(Sample answer: Think of the numbers as groups of tens; use addition or subtraction facts to find the answer.)*

Common Error Alert

Watch for students who may only add the number of tens, hundreds, or thousands and forget to put the 0s where needed as placeholders. Place-value charts may help.

Meeting Individual Needs

For Early Finishers

Have students write problems in which they add three multiples of 10, 100, and 1,000. Students exchange problems and solve.
LOGICAL/MATHEMATICAL

For Extra Help

Write 3 + 6, 30 + 60, 300 + 600, 3,000 + 6,000 on the board. Students solve. Ask students to write similar problems and have classmates solve them.
LOGICAL/MATHEMATICAL

Lesson Organizer

Objective: Estimate sums.

- **NCTM Standards:** 1, 3, 5, 7
- **Lesson Resources:**
  Chapter File Folder
     Practice, Reteach, Extend 3-2
     Teaching Tools 19, 20
  Daily Review 3-2
  Study Buddies 3A
  Transparency 16

Problem of the Day   3-2

There are twelve 50-cent postcards in a dozen. How much would 2 dozen of these postcards cost? **$12**

Math Minute

Add.

$1 + \blacksquare = 10$ *(9)* $4 + \blacksquare = 10$ *(6)*

$2 + \blacksquare = 10$ *(8)* $5 + \blacksquare = 10$ *(5)*

$3 + \blacksquare = 10$ *(7)*

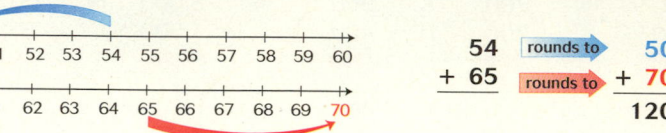

Estimating Sums

That's About It

Rounding can help you estimate greater sums.

Learning About It

The Math Mobile's first stop is inside a volcano! The Math Mobile goes down 54 feet. Then it goes down 65 feet more. About how many feet does it go down in all?

Since you want to know *about* how many feet, you do not need an exact answer. You can round to **estimate** the sum.

54 feet

65 feet

Round to the nearest ten.

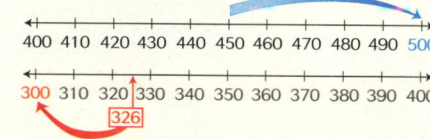

Add the rounded numbers.

$$\begin{array}{r} 54 \\ + \ 65 \end{array} \quad \begin{array}{l} \text{rounds to} \\ \text{rounds to} \end{array} \quad \begin{array}{r} 50 \\ + \ 70 \\ \hline 120 \end{array}$$

The Math Mobile goes down *about* 120 feet.

You can estimate the sum of three-digit numbers the same way.

Estimate 450 + 326.

Round to the nearest hundred.

Add the rounded numbers.

$$\begin{array}{r} 450 \\ + \ 326 \end{array} \quad \begin{array}{l} \text{rounds to} \\ \text{rounds to} \end{array} \quad \begin{array}{r} 500 \\ + \ 300 \\ \hline 800 \end{array}$$

450 + 326 is *about* 800.

Think and Discuss Would you round $3.54 up to $4.00 or down to $3.00? Explain how you know.
Round up to $4.00, since $3.54 is closer to $4.00 than to $3.00.

82

---

1 Introduce

Whole Class Activity

VISUAL

 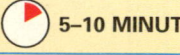 WHOLE CLASS   ⏱ 5–10 MINUTES

Materials: number line transparency

Write *Round 27* on the transparency.

1. One student draws a red line on the number line from 27 to 20. Another student draws a blue line from 27 to 30.

- Ask: **Is 27 closer to 20 or to 30? Explain.** *(Sample answer: 30; the line from 27 to 30 is shorter than the line from 27 to 20.)*

2. Students repeat the activity by rounding 34.

2 Teach   Pages 82–83

Discuss how rounding can result in a sum that is greater than or less than the actual sum.

- Ask: **How can you tell if the estimated sum is going to be greater than or less than the exact answer?** *(If you round all the numbers down, the estimated sum will be less; the estimated sum will be greater if you round all the numbers up.)*

Critical Thinking   ANALYSIS

After Think and Discuss, say: **Find the missing digit in the addition sentence $230.39 + $1■4.00 if the estimated sum is $400.00.** *(Sample answers: 5, 6, 7, 8, or 9)*

Assess Understanding

After Try It Out, ask: **What is the rule for rounding to the nearest ten?** *(Digits in the ones place ending in 5 or more cause the tens place to round up, and those ending in 4 or less cause the tens place to remain the same.)*

CHALLENGE

Write a story problem that involves addition of numbers that are to be rounded. Share your work with a classmate.

Try It Out

Estimate by rounding to the nearest ten.

1. 62 + 38 **100** 2. 45 + 72 **120** 3. 96 + 28 **130** 4. 74 + 76 **150**

5. 29 + 53 **80** 6. 58 + 17 **80** 7. 40 + 68 **110** 8. 21 + 93 **110**

Estimate by rounding to the nearest hundred or dollar.

9. 421 + 683 **1,100** 10. $9.85 + $3.12 **$13.00** 11. 513 + 891 **1,400** 12. $4.95 + $7.86 **$13.00**

Practice

Estimate by rounding to the nearest ten.

13. 57 + 36 **100**	14. 24 + 37 **60**	15. 51 + 65 **120**	16. 98 + 21 **120**	17. 33 + 22 **50**

Estimate by rounding to the nearest hundred or dollar.

18. 186 + 321 **500**	19. 495 + 384 **900**	20. $ 2.06 + 9.18 **$11.00**	21. 715 + 850 **1,600**	22. 521 + 649 **1,100**
23. $ 4.81 + 2.53 **$8.00**	24. 690 + 280 **1,000**	25. 718 + 531 **1,200**	26. $ 9.27 + 4.63 **$14.00**	27. 361 + 417 **800**

Problem Solving

28. The volcano was hot! The Math Mobile made 425 ice cubes. Then it made 861 ice cubes. About how many ice cubes did it make?
Estimates will vary. A possible answer is 1,300 ice cubes.

29. Andy found 2 lava rocks near the volcano. Together they weighed 100 pounds. One rock weighed 40 pounds. How much did the other rock weigh? **60 pounds**

▲ **Social Studies Connection**
Kilauea is a volcano in Hawaii. Visitors can see lava flow from it!

Review and Remember

Using Algebra Complete each pattern.

30. 4, 5, 6, ▨, ▨, ▨
7 8 9

31. 6, 8, ▨, ▨, ▨,16
10 12 14

32. 420 ▨, ▨, 720, ▨ , 920
520 620 820

33. 135, 140, ▨, ▨,155, ▨
145 150 160

For Extra Practice, see Set B, page 118. **83**

Using Algebra

In Exercises 30–33, students use **patterns** to complete number sequences.

---

3 Wrap-up

Maya bought two paperback books for $5.63 each. How can you estimate how much she spent? *(Round each cost to the nearest dollar. Then add the amounts: $6.00 + $6.00 = $12.00.)*

Common Error Alert

Watch for students who look in the ones place instead of the tens place before rounding three-digit numbers to the nearest hundred. Point to the tens place.

Meeting Individual Needs

For Early Finishers

Each student writes down four different dollar amounts, such as $23.39. Students switch papers and estimate each sum.

LOGICAL/MATHEMATICAL

For Extra Help

Write *22 + 28* on the board. Students can use number lines to round each number and then estimate the sum.

KINESTHETIC

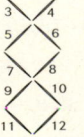
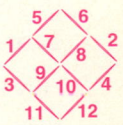
LESSON 2 83

Lesson Organizer

Objective: Decide when an estimate is enough to solve a problem.

- **NCTM Standards:** 1, 3, 7
- **Lesson Resources:**
  Chapter File Folder
      Practice, Reteach, Extend 3-3
  Daily Review 3-3

Problem of the Day   3-3

A book is open on the table. The page numbers that are showing have a sum of 85 and a difference of 1. What are the page numbers? **Page 42 and page 43**

Math Minute

Estimate.

25 + 33 *(60)*	45 + 53 *(100)*
18 + 27 *(50)*	64 + 83 *(140)*
33 + 28 *(60)*	62 + 23 *(80)*

---

1 Introduce

Cooperative Activity
LOGICAL/MATHEMATICAL

 PAIRS   **5–10 MINUTES**

Manipulatives: spinner (0–9)

1. Each student spins two numbers to create a 2-digit number. Have students round each number.

2. The first student estimates the sum of the numbers. The partner finds the exact sum.

3. Have students compare answers to see how close their estimates were to the actual sum.

Developing Skills for Problem Solving

First read for understanding and then focus on whether you need an exact answer or an estimate.

Hawaii

READD FOR UNDERSTANDING

The Math Mobile has landed in Hawaii, a state known for its friendly people and tasty pineapples. Suppose a restaurant there needs 100 pineapples for a party. The restaurant only has the 2 crates of pineapples shown.

1 How many pineapples does the restaurant need? **100 pineapples**

2 How many pineapples are in each crate? **39 pineapples and 42 pineapples**

THINK AND DISCUSS

MATH FOCUS

Deciding When to Estimate
Sometimes all you need to solve a problem is an estimate. If the question asks "about how many" or "are there enough", often you just need to find an estimate.

Reread the paragraph at the top of the page.

3 Would you estimate or find an exact answer to find *about* how many pineapples the restaurant has? **Estimate**

4 Does the restaurant have enough pineapples for the party? Can you estimate to solve the problem? Why or why not? **See Additional Answers, pages 118–119.**

5 Why is it sometimes helpful to be able to estimate instead of finding an exact answer?
A possible answer is that it often takes less time to estimate large sums or differences than to add or subtract to find an exact number.

▲ Social Studies Connection
Hawaii is a group of islands. It became the fiftieth state in 1959. Almost all the pineapples grown in the United States come from Hawaii.

84

---

2 Teach   Pages 84–85

Read for Understanding Have students read the paragraph. The questions below it are reading comprehension questions based on information that can be found in the paragraph and in the pictures.

Think and Discuss Discuss the math focus. Ask students to give you examples of situations when they would estimate.

After Question 4, ask: **If the restaurant needs a pineapple for every guest at a party, would they estimate or get an exact number?** (Sample answer: Exact or estimate is acceptable as long as students can support their choice.)

Critical Thinking APPLICATION

After Think and Discuss, ask: **What if the pineapple crates on page 84 have 48 and 47 pineapples? Why is it better to find the exact sum to decide if the restaurant will have enough pineapples?** (Sample answer: When you round both numbers up, you need to be sure that you have not overestimated.)

Assess Understanding

Before Show What You Learned, say: **You have $5 and want to buy a hat for $1.90. Would you estimate to decide if you have enough money?** (No; you would compare the numbers.)

Show What You Learned

Answer each question. Give a reason for your choice.

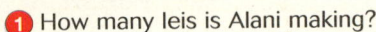

Alani wants to make 4 flower necklaces, called leis. She uses 48 flowers for each lei.

1 How many leis is Alani making?
   a. 48
   (b.) 4
   c. 220

2 Which of the following is true?
   (a.) 100 flowers is enough for 2 leis.
   b. 100 flowers is enough for 3 leis.
   c. 100 flowers is enough for 4 leis.

3 Which number sentence should you use to estimate how many flowers Alani needs for 4 leis?
   a. 48 + 48 + 48 + 48 = ■
   (b.) 50 + 50 + 50 + 50 = ■
   c. 48 + 4 = ■

4 Which number sentence should you use to find *exactly* how many flowers Alani needs for 4 leis?
   (a.) 48 + 48 + 48 + 48 = ■
   b. 50 + 50 + 50 + 50 = ■
   c. 48 + 4 = ■

Nick hiked 2 miles alongside a waterfall. It took him 124 minutes to hike up and 105 minutes to hike down. About how long did Nick hike?

5 What are you asked to find?
   a. the exact time it took to hike up and down
   (b.) about how long it took to hike up and down
   c. how much longer it took to hike up than to hike down

6 Which do you need to know?
   a. the distance of the hike
   b. the name of the waterfall
   (c.) the number of minutes it took Nick to hike up and down the waterfall

7 **Explain** Do you need to find an exact answer or an estimate to solve the problem? **The problem asks *about* how long, so an estimate is enough.**

85

 **Wrap-up**

Explain why you can use an estimate to find about how many pineapples a restaurant needs for 2 weeks if it uses 78 pineapples a week. *(Sample answer: You just need to find about how many pineapples the restaurant needs.)*

Common Error Alert

Watch for students who write exact sums when they should be estimating. Have them reread the problem and discuss why it is appropriate to estimate.

Meeting Individual Needs

For Early Finishers

Students solve this problem: Kim's van makes 5 trips from the airport to a hotel. 17 people fit in the van at once. How many people get a ride? *(85)*
LOGICAL/MATHEMATICAL

Acquiring English Proficiency

Ask students to write definitions for the words *estimate* and *exact*. Help students create word webs with examples of related words and phrases.
LINGUISTIC

Practice

Reteach

Extend

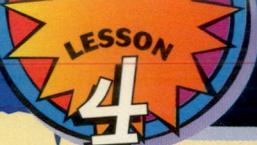

Lesson Organizer

Objective: Use base-ten blocks to add.

- **NCTM Standards:** 3, 6, 8, 13
- **Manipulatives:** base-ten blocks
- **Lesson Resources:**
  Chapter File Folder
     Practice, Reteach, Extend 3-4
     Teaching Tools 22, 44
  Daily Review 3-4

Problem of the Day   3-4

Sela has a dollar. Item A costs $0.32, item B costs $0.49, and item C costs $0.31. About how much more does she need to buy all 3 items?

About $0.10 more

Math Minute

Add.

10 + 8 *(18)*	40 + 50 *(90)*
20 + 8 *(28)*	70 + 30 *(100)*
30 + 20 *(50)*	

Lots of Blocks

You can use base-ten blocks to add numbers.

Learning About It

Work with a group.

Use base-ten blocks to add 356 + 67.

What You Need

For each group: base-ten blocks

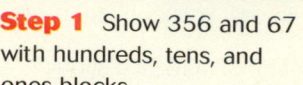

Step 1 Show 356 and 67 with hundreds, tens, and ones blocks.

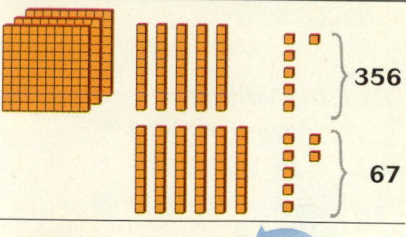
} 356
} 67

Step 2 Look at the ones. Regroup 10 ones as 1 ten.

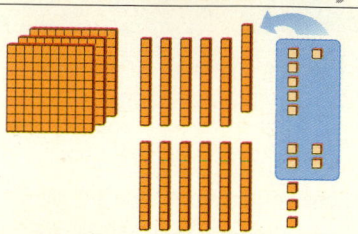

Step 3 Look at the tens. Regroup 10 tens as 1 hundred.

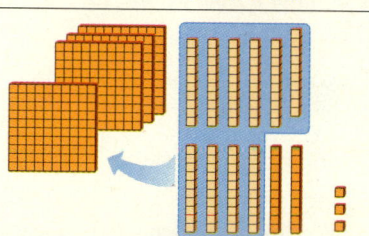

Step 4 Look at the hundreds. There are not enough hundreds to regroup.

Count the blocks you have. What is the sum of 356 + 67? **423**

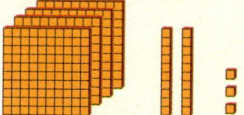

---

1 Introduce

Whole Class Activity

VISUAL

 WHOLE CLASS   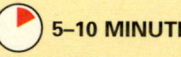 **5–10 MINUTES**

Materials: overhead base-ten blocks

1. A volunteer shows 1 hundred, 9 tens, and 10 ones using the overhead blocks.
   - Ask: **How many tens can you regroup the ones for?** *(1)*

2. A volunteer regroups 10 ones for 1 ten.
   - Ask: **How many hundreds can you regroup the tens for?** *(1)*

3. Then 10 tens are regrouped for 1 hundred.
   - Ask: **How many hundreds in all?** *(2)*

---

2 Teach   Pages 86–87

Discuss regrouping using base-ten blocks.

When regrouping 356 + 67, ask: **Will the sum have at least 1 thousand? Explain your answer.** *(No; there are not enough hundreds to regroup as 1 thousand.)*

Critical Thinking   ANALYSIS

After Think and Discuss, ask: **Can you have an addition problem in which you have to regroup more than ten ones?** *(No, if you add only two addends; yes, if you add more than two addends.)*

Assess Understanding

Before Practice, ask: **To find 29 + 57, do you need to regroup? Explain.** *(Yes; you need to regroup 10 ones as 1 ten.)*

CHALLENGE

Model 48 + 127 + 283 using base-ten blocks and find the sum. *(458)*

1. They can regroup 10 ones for 1 ten and 10 tens for 1 hundred.

Step 5 Record your work in a chart like this.

Addition Sentence	Did I regroup 10 ones for 1 ten?	Did I regroup 10 tens for 1 hundred?	Did I regroup 10 hundreds for 1 thousand?
356 + 67 = 423	yes	yes	no

Step 6 Repeat Steps 1 to 5 four or more times. Take turns picking different numbers each time. Regroup when you can.

Think and Discuss How can you know just by looking at an exercise whether or not you need to regroup? **If you have more than 9 ones, 9 tens, or 9 hundreds, you need to regroup.**

Practice

1. **What If?** Suppose Ann and Sal's blocks looked like this after they put them together. What regrouping can they do? **See above.**

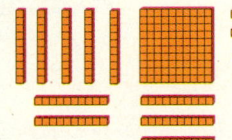

2. Manolo looked at the problem 347 + 158. He said he needs to regroup 10 tens for 1 hundred. Is he right? Explain your answer. **Yes; 7 ones + 8 ones = 15 ones, which are regrouped for 1 ten 5 ones. Then there will be 10 tens, since 4 tens + 5 tens + 1 ten = 10 tens.**

3. **Journal Idea** Karen and Teri showed the numbers 621 and 238 with blocks. Will they need to regroup when they add their numbers together? Explain your answer. **Students should realize that the answer is no, since the ones, tens, and hundreds all add to 9 or less.**

87

---

3 Wrap-up

Describe the regrouping for 462 + 539. *(Regroup 10 ones as 1 ten; 10 tens for 1 hundred; 10 hundreds as 1 thousand.)*

Journal Idea For Exercise 3, suggest that students draw a picture to help them explain the regrouping.

Common Error Alert

Watch for students who miscount and regroup 9 or 11 ones as 1 ten. Tell students to count carefully.

Meeting Individual Needs

For Early Finishers

Two students write addition problems that include a two-digit and a three-digit number, then sort problems into those that do and do not need regrouping.
LOGICAL/MATHEMATICAL

Manipulatives

Using a coin set, a student models 16 cents using pennies. Ask the student to exchange pennies for dimes. Repeat, using 27 pennies and then 32 pennies.
KINESTHETIC

Explore: Regrouping in Addition P 3-4

Combine base-ten blocks.

Exchange to show the sum using the fewest blocks possible. The first one is done for you.

				tens	ones
1.	3 tens	6 ones	Regroup	8	1
	+ 4 tens	5 ones			
	7 tens	11 ones			

				tens	ones
2.	5 tens	3 ones	Regroup	8	0
	+ 2 tens	7 ones			
	7 tens	**10 ones**			

				tens	ones
3.	4 tens	7 ones	Regroup	7	8
	+ 2 tens	11 ones			
	6 tens	**18 ones**			

				hundreds	tens	ones
4.	5 tens	6 ones	Regroup	1	3	1
	+ 7 tens	5 ones				
	12 tens	**11 ones**				

					hundreds	tens	ones
5.	3 hundreds	5 tens	6 ones	Regroup	6	0	6
	+ 2 hundreds	4 tens	10 ones				
	5 hundreds	**9 tens**	**16 ones**				

Solve.

6. Neil and Judith walked on the moon's surface. Neil walked 118 paces in one direction. Judith walked 225 paces in the opposite direction. How many paces apart are Neil and Judith? **343 paces apart**

7. Neil finds 187 moon rocks to bring back to Earth. Judith finds 243 moon rocks. How many moon rocks did Neil and Judith find?
430 moon rocks

Reteach

Explore: Regrouping in Addition R 3-4

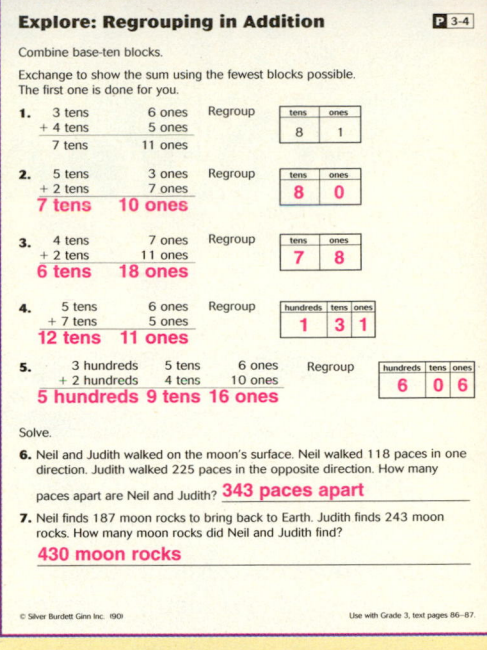

Add. Use base ten blocks to help you. Regroup ones into tens and tens into hundreds where possible. The first problem is done for you.

Regroup

1.	5 tens	7 ones		57
	+ 2 tens	6 ones		+ 26
	7 tens	13 ones	**8** tens **3** ones	83

2.	4 tens	2 ones		42
	+ 4 tens	9 ones		+ 49
	8 tens	**11** ones	**9** tens **1** ones	**91**

3.	6 tens	4 ones		64
	+ 1 tens	8 ones		+ 18
	7 tens	**12** ones	**8** tens **2** ones	**82**

4.	2 tens	7 ones		27
	+ 3 tens	6 ones		+ 36
	5 tens	**13** ones	**6** tens **3** ones	**63**

5.	9 tens	1 ones		91
	+ 1 tens	9 ones		+ 19
	10 tens	**10** ones	**1** hundreds **1** tens **0** ones	**110**

Extend

What Could It Be? E 3-4 **NUMBER SENSE**

Use numbers from the box to answer each problem. You may use a number more than once.

1. Which numbers could be a phone number?
7371092, 2803613, 6161385

2. Which numbers could be the year someone in your family was born?
1962, 1956, 1987

3. Which numbers could be a street address number?
4, 18, 1962, 25, 62, 1956, 19, 1,000 726, 9, 1987, 1999, 3,334

4. Which numbers could be a zip code?
23065, 70607

5. Which numbers could be the sum of two one-digit numbers?
4, 18, 9, 3

6. Which numbers could be the sum of a three-digit number and a two-digit number? **1000, 726**

7. Which numbers have a 3 in the thousands place?
23065, 2803613, 3334

8. Which numbers could be the difference between two two-digit numbers?
4, 18, 25, 0, 62, 19, 9, 3

9. Which number has the same digit in the ones place as it has in the ten thousands place? **70607**

4	18	1962
23065	25	
0	7371092	
62	1956	
2803613	19	
70607	1000	
726	6161385	
9	3334	
1987	1999	3

Teaching With Technology
Explore: Regrouping in Addition

1 Introduce

Objective: Students will use Base-Ten Blocks to add on the computer.

Resources: MathProcessor™ Version 1.1
MathProcessor™ User Guide: Sections C, D, E, L

In Lesson 4, students use Base-Ten Blocks to explore regrouping in addition. The MathProcessor™ Tools can also be used for this exploration.

Use MathProcessor™ Base-Ten Blocks and a Number space to explore regrouping 346 + 78.

Say: Using the least number of Base-Ten Blocks, show the number 346. *(3 hundreds flats, 4 tens rods, 6 ones cubes)*

2 Teach

As you model 346 + 78 below, discuss the steps.

Step 1

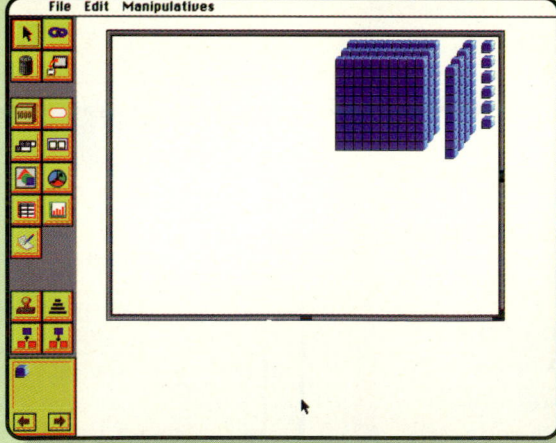

- Open a Base-Ten Blocks workspace .
- Show 346. Click to arrange the workspace.

Ask: How many hundreds flats are there? *(3 hundreds flats)* **tens rods?** *(4 tens rods)* **ones cubes?** *(6 ones cubes)* **How can we show 78?** *(7 tens rods, 8 ones cubes)*

Step 2

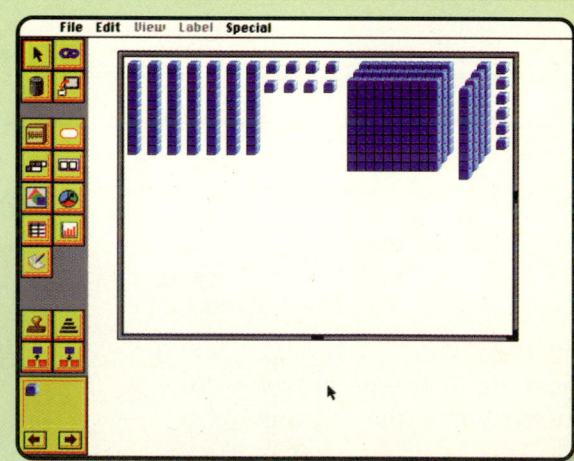

- Add 78 blocks to the workspace.

Ask: What operation can be used to describe putting 78 more blocks into the workspace? *(Addition)*

Step 3

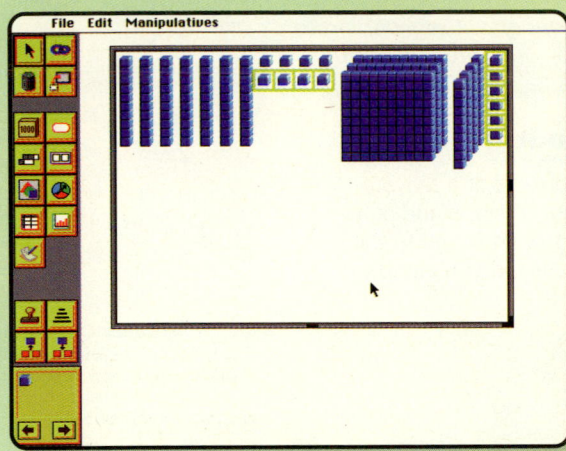

Ask: **How many ones cubes are there in all?** *(14 ones cubes)*

How can the ones cubes be regrouped? *(Sample answer: Regroup 10 ones cubes into 1 tens rod.)*

• Select 10 ones cubes.

Step 4

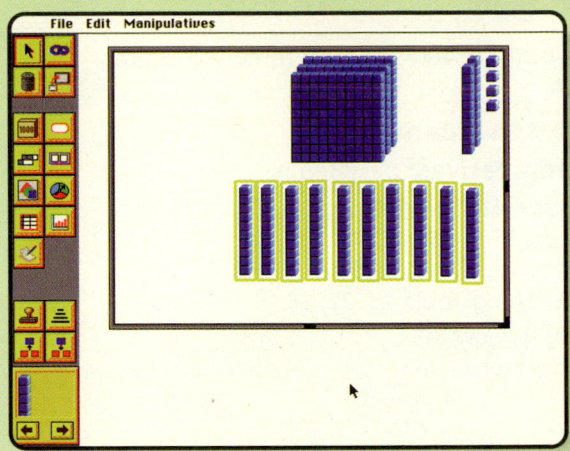

• Click to regroup 10 ones cubes to 1 tens rod.

Ask: **How many tens rods are there in all ?** *(12 tens rods)*

How can the tens rods be regrouped? *(Regroup 10 tens rods into 1 hundreds flat.)*

• Select 10 tens rods.

Step 5

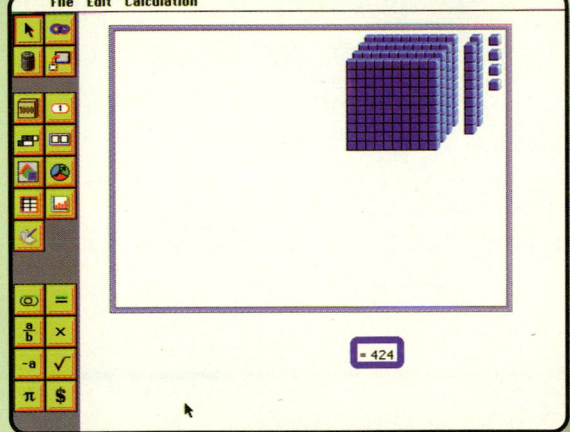

• Regroup 10 tens rods into 1 hundreds flat.

Ask: **Do we need to regroup the hundreds flats? Explain.** *(No; there are not enough flats to regroup.)* **What is the sum of 346 + 78?** *(424)*

• Link the workspace to a Number space 🔲. Click = in the Number space to reveal the answer.

3 Wrap-up

Allow students to use MathProcessor™ to explore regrouping in addition.

Add. Regroup when you can.

1. 259 + 87 *(346)*   **2.** 396 + 48 *(444)*   **3.** 599 + 99 *(698)*

Portfolio Opportunity You may wish to have students open a Writing space and explain their responses for the exercises above and for the question below. You may also wish to have students make printouts of their responses and add them to their portfolios.

How can you know just by looking at an exercise whether or not you need to regroup? *(Sample answer: If you have more than 9 ones or 9 tens or 9 hundreds, you need to regroup.)*

 ## Meeting Individual Needs

For Extra Help

Students take turns choosing a three-digit number and a two-digit number to add. One student models the addition with **MathProcessor**™ Base-Ten Blocks. The other student uses paper and pencil to add. Students compare answers.

For Early Finishers

Math Blaster® software and **MathProcessor**™ **Activity Cards 13–18** provide opportunities for students to practice skills learned in this chapter.

Adding Two- and Three-Digit Numbers

Lesson Organizer

Objective: Add two- and three-digit numbers.

- **NCTM Standards:** 1, 3, 8
- **Manipulatives:** base-ten blocks (optional)
- **Lesson Resources:**
  Chapter File Folder
    Practice, Reteach, Extend 3-5
    Teaching Tools 13, 22, 23
  Daily Review 3-5
  Transparency 18

Problem of the Day   3-5

Each letter of the alphabet has a value. A = 1, B = 2, C = 3, D = 4 and so on up to Z = 26. So, the word CAB has a value of 6. Find the value of your first name.
Check students' answers.

Math Minute

Estimate.

19 + 8 *(30)*	20 + 11 *(30)*
24 + 9 *(30)*	9 + 17 *(30)*
16 + 14 *(30)*	12 + 18 *(30)*

Step by Step

Use what you know about regrouping to help you add two- and three-digit numbers.

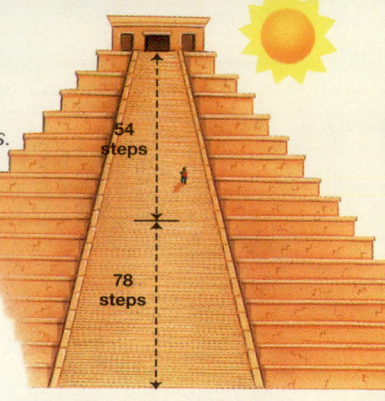
54 steps
78 steps

Learning About It

OLÉ! The Math Mobile is at a Maya pyramid. You climb 78 steps and stop. Then you climb 54 steps to get to the top. How many steps did you climb?

$$78 + 54 = \blacksquare$$

▲ **Social Studies Connection**
The Maya people lived hundreds of years ago in Mexico, Guatemala, and Honduras. They built stone pyramids that are still standing today.

Estimate first.

78	rounds to		80
+ 54	rounds to		+ 50
			130

Then add to find the exact answer.

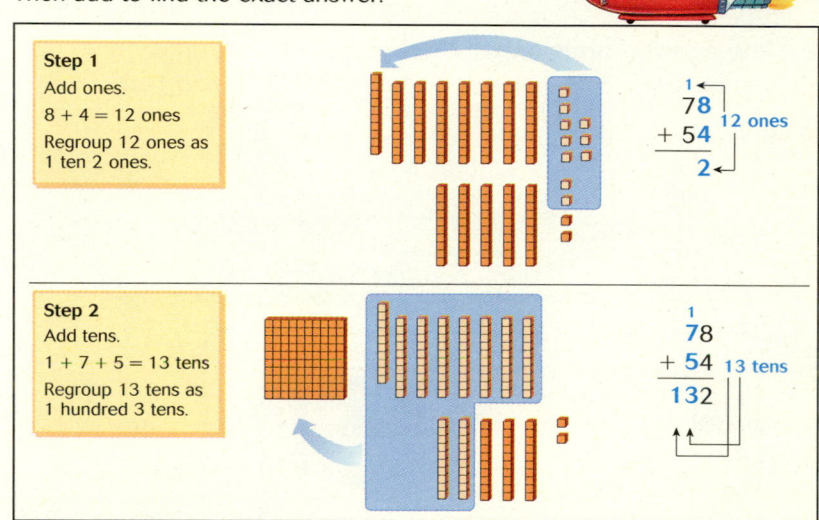

Step 1
Add ones.
8 + 4 = 12 ones
Regroup 12 ones as 1 ten 2 ones.

$$\begin{array}{r} 1 \\ 78 \\ + 54 \\ \hline 2 \end{array}$$ 12 ones

Step 2
Add tens.
1 + 7 + 5 = 13 tens
Regroup 13 tens as 1 hundred 3 tens.

$$\begin{array}{r} 1 \\ 78 \\ + 54 \\ \hline 132 \end{array}$$ 13 tens

You climbed 132 steps in all.
Look at the estimate of 130. Is 132 a reasonable answer? **Yes**

 88

---

1 Introduce

Cooperative Activity

KINESTHETIC

 PAIRS   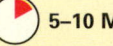 **5–10 MINUTES**

Manipulatives: coin set, bill set, spinner (1–6)

1. Each student spins twice to make a two-digit number representing cents.

2. Each student models his or her number using dimes and pennies.

3. Pairs work together to add their two-digit numbers and model the sum using the fewest possible number of coins and bills.

- Ask: **If you only spin digits less than 5, do you need to regroup?** *(No)*

2 Teach   Pages 88–91

Discuss how estimating before adding can be helpful. Ask: **Why should you estimate first?** *(Estimating helps determine if your answer is reasonable.)*

- Say: **Explain how you know when to regroup ones.** *(When there are 10 or more ones)*

- Ask: **Why is there a one in the hundreds place in the sum?** *(Because there are more than 10 tens in the tens place)*

Connecting Ideas

After learning to add two-digit numbers, students are ready to add three-digit numbers.

- Ask: **What do you think will be the same as adding 2-digit numbers?** *(Sample answer: Start on the right and work left; regroup when there are 10 or more in any place in the answer.)*

- Ask: **What do you do when you have 10 or more tens in the tens place?** *(Regroup 10 tens as 1 hundred)*

- Ask: **Why is there a one in the thousands place of the sum?** *(Because there were more than 10 hundreds.)*

Connecting Ideas

Adding three-digit numbers is like adding two-digit numbers, only now you can regroup hundreds.

Find the sum of 564 + 551.

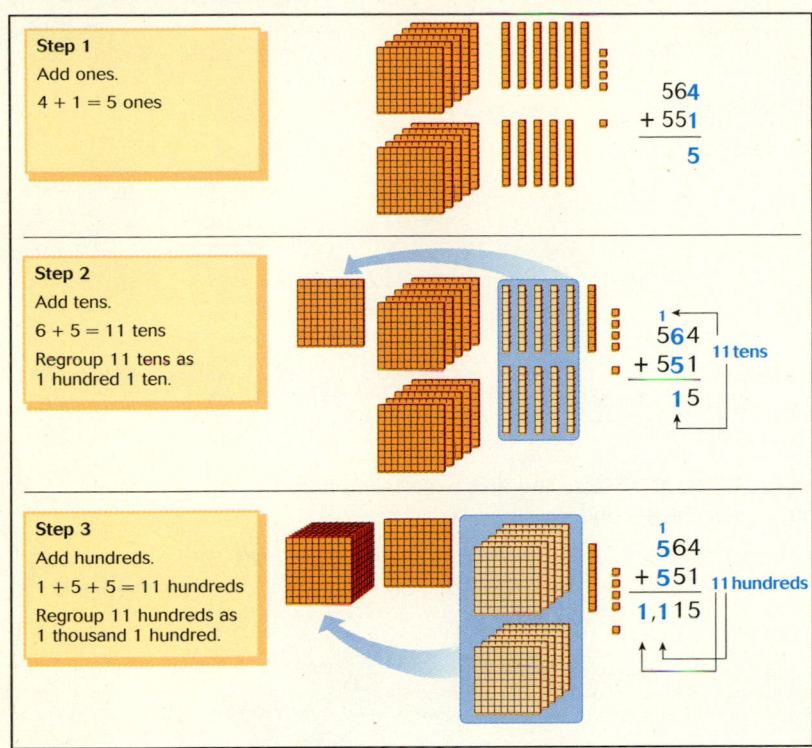

Step 1
Add ones.
4 + 1 = 5 ones

564
+ 551
  5

Step 2
Add tens.
6 + 5 = 11 tens
Regroup 11 tens as
1 hundred 1 ten.

564
+ 551   11 tens
 15

Step 3
Add hundreds.
1 + 5 + 5 = 11 hundreds
Regroup 11 hundreds as
1 thousand 1 hundred.

564
+ 551   11 hundreds
1,115

The sum of 564 + 551 is 1,115.

More Examples

A.
$5.49
+ 2.13
$ 7.62   12 pennies = 1 dime 2 pennies

B.
$ 5.92
+ 3.47
$ 9.39   13 dimes = 1 dollar 3 dimes

Think and Discuss How can the sum of 2 three-digit numbers be a four-digit number?
The sum can be a four-digit number if there are more than 9 hundreds.

 89

Critical Thinking   ANALYSIS

After Think and Discuss, say: **Create a problem adding two-digit numbers that makes the greatest sum possible using each of the following digits once: 7, 3, 4, and 8.** *(Sample answers: 83 + 74, 84 + 73, 73 + 84, 74 + 83)*

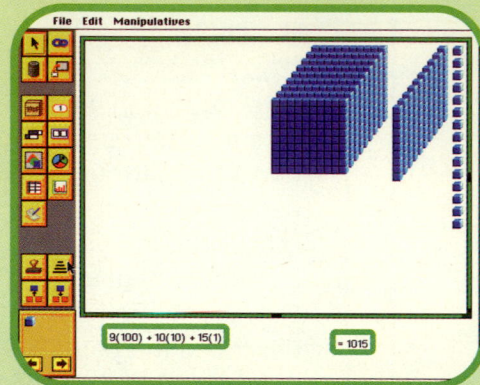

Using Technology
CD-ROM

MathProcessor™

Tools: Base-Ten Blocks; Number spaces
Objective: Adding Three-Digit Numbers

```
File  Edit  Manipulatives
```

9(100) + 10(10) + 15(1)   = 1015

- To model 586 + 429 = 1,015, link
  Base-Ten Blocks and two Number
  spaces. Click catalog items to model
  586. Separate the blocks so the model
  shows clearly the hundreds, tens, and
  ones.

- Add 429 blocks to the workspace.

- Click to sort blocks. Blocks may
  overlap.

- Click one Number space. Click.

- Click to regroup.

Additional Activities

See also **Activities 13 and
14** in the MathProcessor™
Activity Cards.

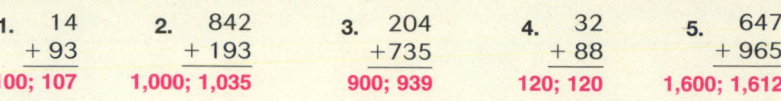

Try It Out

Estimate first. Then add.
Use base-ten blocks if you wish.

1. 14	2. 842	3. 204	4. 32	5. 647
+ 93	+ 193	+735	+ 88	+ 965
100; 107	**1,000; 1,035**	**900; 939**	**120; 120**	**1,600; 1,612**

Practice

Find each sum.

6. 29	7. 403	8. 64	9. 312	10. 486
+ 32	+ 256	+ 87	+ 98	+ 975
61	**659**	**151**	**410**	**1,461**
11. 52	12. 563	13. 212	14. 47	15. $ 7.18
+ 98	+ 139	+ 500	+ 6	+ 3.90
150	**702**	**712**	**53**	**$11.08**
16. $ 6.84	17. 70	18. $ 4.08	19. 95	20. 374
+ 2.71	+ 46	+ 7.65	+ 87	+ 992
$9.55	**116**	**$11.73**	**182**	**1,366**

Using Mental Math Use the first exercise to help
you answer the second.

21. 462 + 375 = 837
462 + 475 = ■ **937**

22. 289 + 706 = 995
286 + 706 = ■ **992**

23. 537 + 246 = 783
537 + 146 = ■ **683**

  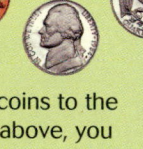

Money Sense

Money Riddles

Solve each money riddle below.

1. Ricky replaced one of the
coins shown above with a
different coin. The value of
the coins changed to 46¢.
Which coin did Ricky replace?
What did he replace it with?
Nickel; dime

2. If you add 2 coins to the
coins shown above, you
can divide all the coins into
two equal amounts. Which
coins should you add? How
much money will be in each
equal group?
Penny and dime; 26¢

90

2 Teach (continued)

Assess Understanding

After Try It Out, say: **Estimate, then add,
128 + 394.** *(500, 522)*

 ### GIFTED AND TALENTED

Compare Prices Give students a list of
five items that can commonly be bought
at a grocery store. Have students record
the prices for these items at different grocery stores by visiting the stores or by
finding the prices in newspaper advertise-
ments.

Have students bring their findings to class,
compare prices, and subtract to find the
differences from store to store.

Problem Solving

24. Explain Lina helps her mother make pottery. One week, Lina makes 12 bowls and her mother makes 17 bowls. They sell 27 of them. How many bowls are left? Explain your answer. **2 bowls; 12 + 17 = 29 and 29 − 27 = 2**

25. A large bowl costs $63 and a small bowl costs $49. How much would 2 small bowls cost? **$98**

26. Handmade necklaces cost $16. Is $30 enough money to buy 2 necklaces? Explain. **No; $16 + $16 = $32 so $30 is not enough.**

27. Toni, Meg, and Jim are waiting in the line to buy souvenirs. Toni is behind Meg and Jim. Jim is in front of Meg. Who is first in line? **Jim**

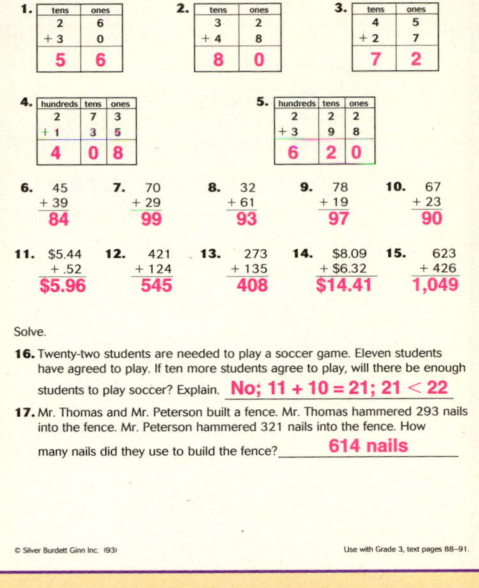

▲ **Social Studies Connection** Traditional Maya pottery is still made today in Chiapas and other Mexican states.

Review and Remember

What time does each clock show?

28.  **2:30**

29.  **4:00**

30.  **10:30**

31.  **7:00**

Time for Technology
Using the MathProcessor™ CD-ROM

Use base-ten blocks to show
234 + 678 = ▇.

- Click ▇. Link it to two number spaces ▇.
- Show 234 with base-ten blocks. Click a number space, then ▇. Add 678 more blocks.
- Click trade up ▇ until regrouping is no longer possible.

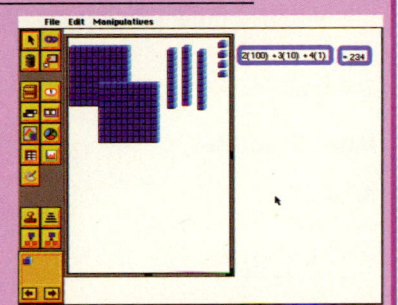

For Extra Practice, see Set C, page 118. **91**

---

3 Wrap-up

Find the sum for 958 + 654. Then describe the sum for each place value. *(1,612; ones: 1 ten + 2 ones, tens: 1 hundred + 1 ten, hundreds: 1 thousand + 6 hundreds)*

Common Error Alert

Watch for students who write the regrouped ones above the wrong place. Place-value charts may help students line up numbers correctly.

Meeting Individual Needs

For Early Finishers

Using base-ten blocks, a student shows 2 three-digit numbers, knowing that a partner will regroup when adding the numbers. The partner adds the blocks.
VISUAL/SPATIAL

Acquiring English Proficiency

Have students sort addition examples, explaining what *regrouping* means and how it does or does not happen in each example.
VISUAL/SPATIAL

Money Sense

Provide students with coin sets if help is needed.

Time for Technology

Students use the computer to add with base-ten blocks.

Practice

Adding Two- and Three-Digit Numbers P 3-5

Add.

1.	tens	ones
	2	6
+3		0
	5	**6**

2.	tens	ones
	3	2
+4		8
	8	**0**

3.	tens	ones
	4	5
+2		7
	7	**2**

4.	hundreds	tens	ones
	2	7	3
+1		3	5
	4	**0**	**8**

5.	hundreds	tens	ones
	2	2	2
+3		9	8
	6	**2**	**0**

6.	45	7.	70	8.	32	9.	78	10.	67
+39		+29		+61		+19		+23	
84		**99**		**93**		**97**		**90**	

11.	$5.44	12.	421	13.	273	14.	$8.09	15.	623
+.52		+124		+135		+$6.32		+426	
$5.96		**545**		**408**		**$14.41**		**1,049**	

Solve.

16. Twenty-two students are needed to play a soccer game. Eleven students have agreed to play. If ten more students agree to play, will there be enough students to play soccer? Explain. **No; 11 + 10 = 21; 21 < 22**

17. Mr. Thomas and Mr. Peterson built a fence. Mr. Thomas hammered 293 nails into the fence. Mr. Peterson hammered 321 nails into the fence. How many nails did they use to build the fence? **614 nails**

© Silver Burdett Ginn Inc. (93)   Use with Grade 3, text pages 88–91.

Reteach

Adding Two- and Three-Digit Numbers R 3-5

To add two three-digit numbers:

Step 1 Add the ones. Regroup if you need to.
Step 2 Add the tens. Regroup if you need to.
Step 3 Add the hundreds.

hundreds	tens	ones
2	2	3
+1	2	8
3	5	1

3 + 8 = 11. Add a regrouped ten to the tens place.

1. 367 + 128 = **495**

2. 552 + 319 = **871**

3. 271 + 443 = **714**

© Silver Burdett Ginn Inc. (94)   Use with Grade 3, text pages 88–91.

Extend

Mathlandia E 3-5 NUMBER SENSE

Each island in Mathlandia is divided into two secret regions. You can show the regions by drawing boundary lines. Just remember that the sum of the numbers in one region must equal the sum of the numbers in the other region.

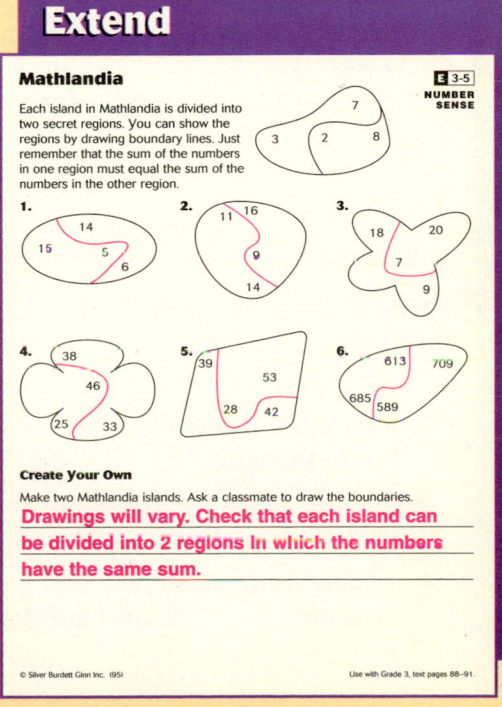

Create Your Own

Make two Mathlandia islands. Ask a classmate to draw the boundaries. **Drawings will vary. Check that each island can be divided into 2 regions in which the numbers have the same sum.**

© Silver Burdett Ginn Inc. (95)   Use with Grade 3, text pages 88–91.

Lesson Organizer

Objective: Add four-digit numbers.

- **NCTM Standards:** 1, 6, 8
- **Lesson Resources:**
  Chapter File Folder
     Practice, Reteach, Extend 3-6
     Teaching Tool 13
  Daily Review 3-6
  Practice Workbook, p. 11
  Transparencies 7, 18

Problem of the Day   3-6

Use the digits 2, 3, 4, 5, 6, and 7. Make two sets of 3-digit numbers that add to 999. **Sample answer:**
235 + 764 = 999 and 325 + 674 = 999

Math Minute

Add.

195 + 350 *(545)*   432 + 542 *(974)*

250 + 178 *(428)*   645 + 754 *(1,399)*

301 + 521 *(822)*   528 + 302 *(830)*

6

Adding Greater Numbers

Floating Along

You can regroup ones, tens, hundreds, and thousands to add four-digit numbers.

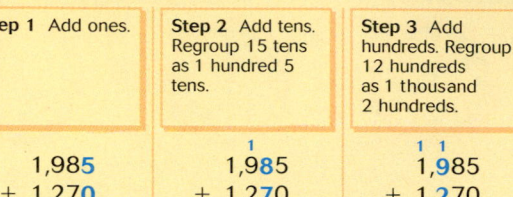

First Rapids 1,985 feet

Second Rapids 1,270 feet

Learning About It

Splash! The Math Mobile lands in some river rapids. The first rapids are 1,985 feet long. The second rapids are 1,270 feet long. How long are the rapids altogether?

1,985 + 1,270 = ■

THERE'S ALWAYS A WAY!

- **One way** to find the sum is to use paper and pencil.

Step 1 Add ones.	Step 2 Add tens. Regroup 15 tens as 1 hundred 5 tens.	Step 3 Add hundreds. Regroup 12 hundreds as 1 thousand 2 hundreds.	Step 4 Add thousands.
1,98**5** + 1,27**0** **5**	¹ 1,9**8**5 + 1,2**7**0 **55**	¹ ¹ 1,**9**85 + 1,**2**70 **255**	¹ ¹ **1**,985 + **1**,270 **3,255**

- **Another way** is to use a calculator.

Press: ① ⑨ ⑧ ⑤ ⊕ ① ② ⑦ ⓪ ⊜   Display: ⟨ *3255* ⟩

The rapids are 3,255 feet long altogether.

More Examples

A.	¹ $ 23.96 + 45.62 $ 69.58	B.	¹ ¹ $ 39.64 + 28.71 $ 68.35

Think and Discuss Why should you always estimate before using a calculator to solve a problem? **To make sure the calculator answer is reasonable**

92

---

1 Introduce

Cooperative Activity
KINESTHETIC

PAIRS   ⏱ 10–15 MINUTES

Materials: base-ten blocks, spinner (1–6)

1. One student spins to make 2 three-digit numbers and represents the numbers using base-ten blocks.

2. The partner mentally adds the ones and shares the sum.

3. The first student models how to regroup if necessary to match the sum.

4. Students repeat Steps 2 and 3 to find the sum of the tens and hundreds.

2 Teach   Pages 92–93

Discuss regrouping and when it is needed. Have students find the sums of 2,345 + 5,432 and 1,492 + 1,638. *(7,777; 3,130)*

- Say: **Explain why regrouping was needed only some of the time.** *(Regrouping can only be done when a place value is 10 or more.)*

Critical Thinking   ANALYSIS

After Think and Discuss, ask: **How do you know that the sum of 8,978 + 7,816 will be a five-digit number?** *(Because the thousands place needs to be regrouped.)*

Assess Understanding

After Try It Out, say: **Describe the regroupings for 1,956 + 1,344 and find the sum.** *(Ones: 1 ten and 0 ones; tens: 1 hundred and 0 tens; hundreds: 1 thousand and 3 hundreds; 3,300)*

CHALLENGE

Write a story problem that involves adding five-digit numbers that require regrouping in four place values.

Try It Out

INTERNET ACTIVITY
www.sbgmath.com

Find each sum.

1. 4,836
    + 3,053
    7,889

2. 6,394
    + 5,735
    12,129

3. $ 4.08
    + 2.96
    $7.04

4. 5,241
    + 6,593
    11,834

5. 6,498
    + 3,795
    10,293

Practice

Choose a Method Use paper and pencil or a calculator to find each sum. Tell which method you used. **Methods will vary.**

6. 1,316
    + 4,802
    6,118

7. 2,614
    + 7,210
    9,824

8. 5,469
    + 3,275
    8,744

9. 6,378
    + 7,225
    13,603

10. 5,062
    + 8,761
    13,823

11. 3,025
    + 4,365
    7,390

12. $62.24
    + 16.40
    $78.64

13. 6,387
    + 5,984
    12,371

14. 8,627
    + 499
    9,126

15. $86.20
    + 3.49
    $89.69

16. 4,329
    + 8,990
    13,319

17. 2,536
    + 4,718
    7,254

18. $68.21
    + 47.14
    $115.35

19. 1,473
    + 914
    2,387

20. $23.65
    + 58.77
    $82.42

Problem Solving

21. One month, 3,642 people went rafting. The next month 4,396 people went rafting. How many people went rafting in the two months? **8,038 people**

22. A small life vest costs $34.99, a medium life vest costs $50.99, and a large life vest costs $63.95. How much would it cost to buy both a medium and a large life vest? **$114.94**

23. **Analyze** A number is less than 3,425 + 8,630 and greater than 7,614 + 4,429. What could the number be? **Any number from 12,044 to 12,054**

Review and Remember

Add or subtract.

24. 7 + 6 **13**

25. 12 − 8 **4**

26. 15 − 6 **9**

27. 9 + 8 **17**

For Extra Practice, see Set D, page 119. **93**

Internet Activity

www.sbgmath.com

Students use information found on river rafting Web sites to practice math skills.

Practice

Adding Greater Numbers P 3-6

1. 473
    + 6,138
    6,611

2. 5,752
    + 3,523
    9,275

3. 8,648
    + 6,372
    15,020

4. 1,374
    + 6,211
    7,585

5. $49.50
    + 28.90
    $78.40

6. $39.28
    + 50.63
    $89.91

7. $38.76
    + 25.40
    $64.16

8. $22.48
    + 98.75
    $121.23

9. 5,720 + 3,376 = **9,096**

10. 7,483 + 4,631 = **12,114**

11. 3,287 + 4,165 = **7,452**

12. 2,760 + 1,404 = **4,164**

Use the numbers on the number cards. Find the sum of every possible number pair. Then use your answers to complete the sentences below.

| 7,475 | 7,924 | 7,478 | 7,923 |

13. Write the pair of numbers with the greatest sum:
    7,924 + 7,923 = 15,847

14. The number pair with smallest sum is: **7,475 + 7,478 = 14,953**

15. The number pair with a sum that has all odd number digits is:
    7,475 + 7,924 = 15,399

Solve.

16. Shelly has $14.50 in her bank. She adds $5.50 baby-sitting money to her bank account. How much does Shelly have now? **$20.00**

17. A trip down the Moon Rapids costs $12.95. You also want to rent an underwater camera for $2.79. What will the rapids trip cost? **$15.74**

© Silver Burdett Ginn Inc. (96)   Use with Grade 3, text pages 92–93.

Reteach

Adding Greater Numbers R 3-6

Adding four-digit numbers is like adding two-digit and three-digit numbers: sometimes you have to regroup.

	thousands	hundreds	tens	ones	
	4	0	9	8	
+1		6	3	5	
Step 1 Add ones.			1	3	13 ones
Step 2 Add tens.		1	2		12 tens
Step 3 Add hundreds.		6			6 hundreds
Step 4 Add thousands.	5				5 thousands
Step 5 Find the sum.	5	7	3	3	sum

Use the place value charts to find the sums.

thousands	hundreds	tens	ones
5	3	6	4
2	4	2	6
		1	0
		8	
7			
7	7	9	0

5,364
+ 2,426
7,790

thousands	hundreds	tens	ones
1	7	3	5
7	1	9	6
		1	1
	1	2	
8			
8	9	3	1

1,735
+ 7,196
8,931

© Silver Burdett Ginn Inc. (97)   Use with Grade 3, text pages 92–93.

Extend

Pinball Wizard E 3-6 REASONING

Your scores for each round of pinball are shown below. Which two targets did you hit? Write the numbers.

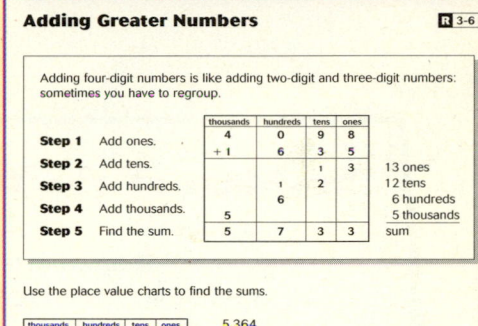

1. 3,928
    + 6,211
    10,139

2. 4,929
    + 9,999
    14,928

3. 2,387
    + 6,784
    9,171

4. 2,998
    + 9,999
    12,997

5. 6,784
    + 6,211
    12,995

6. 4,929
    + 6,784
    11,713

7. 2,998
    + 3,928
    6,926

8. 3,829
    + 4,929
    8,758

9. 3,829
    + 2,998
    6,827

10. 2,387
    + 6,211
    8,598

11. 4,929
    + 3,928
    8,857

12. 9,999
    + 2,387
    12,386

Suppose you hit two targets and each target is different.

13. What is the highest possible score you could get? **16,783**

14. What is the lowest possible score you could get? **5,385**

© Silver Burdett Ginn Inc. (98)   Use with Grade 3, text pages 92–93.

---

3 Wrap-up

Explain how to add 9,999 and 9,999.
(Sample answer: Add the 9s in the ones place. Regroup 10 ones as 1 ten. Add the 9s in the tens place and the regrouped ten. Regroup 10 tens as 1 hundred. Repeat for each place value.)

Common Error Alert

Watch for students who forget to write a ten thousands digit in the sum when 10 thousands are regrouped as 1 ten thousand. Remind them to add carefully.

Meeting Individual Needs

For Early Finishers

One student adds 1,111 + 1,111 *(2,222)*. Another adds 2,222 to the answer. They add until the answer is 17,776. Why did the pattern change? *(Regrouping)*

LOGICAL/MATHEMATICAL

For Extra Help

Write an addition problem on the board using 2 four-digit numbers involving regrouping. Ask students to tell you, step by step, how to solve the problem.

LOGICAL/MATHEMATICAL

Adding More Than Two Numbers

Lesson Organizer

Objective: Add three and four numbers.

- **NCTM Standards:** 1, 4, 8
- **Lesson Resources:**
  Chapter File Folder
  Practice, Reteach, Extend 3-7
  Daily Review 3-7
  Study Buddies 3B
  Transparency 7

Problem of the Day   3-7

There are two digits: ▲ and ■. All ▲ are the same. All ■ are the same. ▲ is not the same as ■. What are the digits if ▲▲▲ + ■■ = 288?

▲ = 2 and ■ = 6

Add.

$2 + 2 + 2$ *(6)* $2 + 4 + 2$ *(8)*

$1 + 5 + 3$ *(9)* $6 + 2 + 4$ *(12)*

$4 + 3 + 2$ *(9)*

 **Math Minute**

Line Up!

Use what you know about adding two numbers to add three or four numbers.

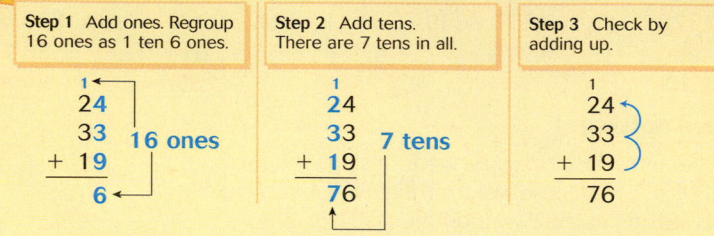

Learning About It

Brrr! The Math Mobile has landed at a sled-dog race. Kipanik and his dog team are in the race. How far is it from Start to Checkpoint 3?

$$24 + 33 + 19 = ■$$

 THERE'S ALWAYS A WAY!

- **One way** to find the sum is to use paper and pencil.

Step 1 Add ones. Regroup 16 ones as 1 ten 6 ones.	**Step 2** Add tens. There are 7 tens in all.	**Step 3** Check by adding up.
$\begin{array}{r} 1 \\ 24 \\ 33 \\ + 19 \\ \hline 6 \end{array}$ **16 ones**	$\begin{array}{r} 1 \\ 24 \\ 33 \\ + 19 \\ \hline 76 \end{array}$ **7 tens**	$\begin{array}{r} 24 \\ 33 \\ + 19 \\ \hline 76 \end{array}$

- **Another way** to find the sum is to use a calculator.

Press: ② ④ + ③ ③ + ① ⑨ =   Display: 76

It is 76 miles from Start to Checkpoint 3.

More Examples

A.
$$\begin{array}{r} 1 \\ 524 \\ 203 \\ + 691 \\ \hline 1{,}418 \end{array}$$

B.
$$\begin{array}{r} 1 \\ 2{,}431 \\ 6{,}350 \\ + 4{,}912 \\ \hline 13{,}693 \end{array}$$

Think and Discuss What are the most ones you could regroup as tens when you add three numbers? Explain how you know.
20 ones; the most ones you could have is 9 + 9 + 9 or 27.

---

1 Introduce

Cooperative Activity

VISUAL

PAIRS   **5–10 MINUTES**

Manipulatives: spinners (1–6)

1. Each student spins the spinner three times and adds the numbers.
2. Students exchange numbers and add them in a different order.
3. Students compare answers.

- Ask: **If you change the order of the numbers, do you still get the same sum?** *(Yes.)*

2 Teach   Pages 94–95

Remind students that they can add the digits in the same place value in any order. Tell them to look for doubles and numbers that add to 10.

- Ask: **Why do you add ones before you add tens?** *(Because you might need to regroup, so you must start on the right and work to the left)*

Critical Thinking   ANALYSIS

After Think and Discuss, ask: **What digits are missing in the problem $15 + ■8 + 3■ = 120$?** *(6; 7)*

Assess Understanding

After Try It Out, say: **Add 58 + 34 + 21 and explain the steps.** *(113; Add ones: 1 ten 3 ones; add tens: 1 hundred 1 ten.)*

 CHALLENGE

Using only mental math, will the sum of 15 + 32 + 26 be the same as the sum of 47 + 26? Explain. *(Yes; 15 + 32 = 47)*

Try It Out

Add. Check each answer by adding up.

1.	2.	3.	4.	5.
64	311	712	6,012	8,341
21	926	260	294	2,965
+ 38	+ 475	+ 49	+ 658	+ 3,477
123	**1,712**	**1,021**	**6,964**	**14,783**

Practice

Choose a Method Use paper and pencil or a calculator to find each sum. Tell which method you used.

6.	7.	8.	9.	10.
58	35	627	437	2,600
62	46	480	652	354
+ 19	+ 99	+ 71	+ 801	+ 896
139	**180**	**1,178**	**1,890**	**3,850**

11.	12.	13.	14.	15.
427	$7.34	$18.51	9,462	42
614	2.50	22.45	5,021	36
+ 182	+ 3.69	+ 96.83	+ 4,934	15
1,223	**$13.53**	**$137.79**	**19,417**	+ 98
				191

16. 51 + 84 + 23 **158**

17. 60 + 71 + 84 **215**

18. 200 + 400 + 850 **1,450**

Problem Solving

19. Suppose a sled-dog team travels 13 miles in one hour, 11 miles the next hour, and 12 miles the hour after that. How many miles does the sled-dog team travel? **36 miles**

20. Create Your Own Write a problem about a sled-dog race. Use the numbers from the map on page 94. Have a friend solve your problem. **Problems will vary.**

Review and Remember

Add.

21.	22.	23.	24.
2	3	9	7
6	2	2	4
+ 1	+ 4	+ 4	+ 3
9	**9**	**15**	**14**

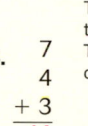

INTERNET ACTIVITY
www.sbgmath.com

Social Studies Connection
The Iditarod is a sled-dog race that is held every year in Alaska. The race is over 1,000 miles and can last more than 20 days. ▼

For Extra Practice, see Set E, page 119. **95**

Internet Activity

www.sbgmath.com

Students use information from the Internet to calculate the distance of a race.

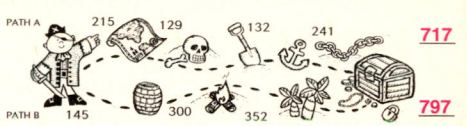
---

3 Wrap-up

Explain the steps you use to find the sum of 125 + 189 + 166. (Add the ones: regroup 20 ones as 2 tens; add the tens: regroup 18 tens as 1 hundred and 8 tens; add the hundreds.)

Common Error Alert

Watch for students adding wrong digits together in horizontal addition sentences. Suggest students rewrite them vertically and line up the places.

Meeting Individual Needs

For Early Finishers

Students use a spinner to create 3 four-digit numbers and write them down to create an addition problem. Students solve and check using a calculator.
LOGICAL/MATHEMATICAL

Cooperative Learning

Each group creates a story problem with a picture that involves adding four or more numbers. Groups exchange problems and find sums.
VISUAL/SPATIAL

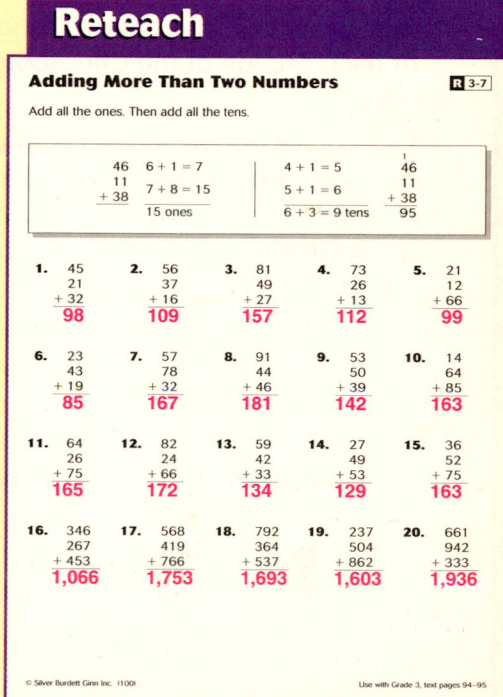

Lesson Organizer

Objective: Subtract across zeros with three- and four-digit numbers.

- **NCTM Standards:** 1, 3, 8
- **Lesson Resources:**
  Chapter File Folder
    Practice, Reteach, Extend 3-13
    Teaching Tool 14
  Daily Review 3-13
  Practice Workbook, p. 15
  Transparency 19

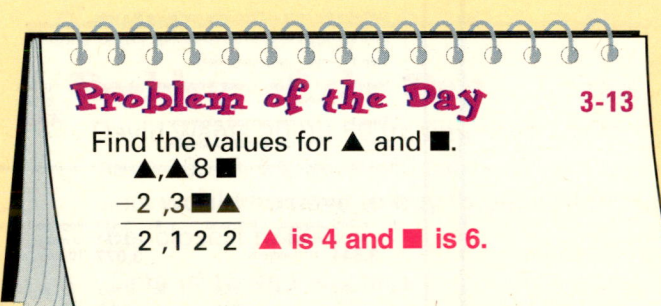

Problem of the Day 3-13

Find the values for ▲ and ■.

▲,▲ 8 ■
− 2 ,3 ■ ▲
_____
2 ,1 2 2   **▲ is 4 and ■ is 6.**

Math Minute

Subtract.

107 − 68 *(39)*	620 − 580 *(40)*
431 − 282 *(149)*	6,273 − 5,737 *(536)*
263 − 81 *(182)*	7,342 − 2,658 *(4,684)*

Zeroing In

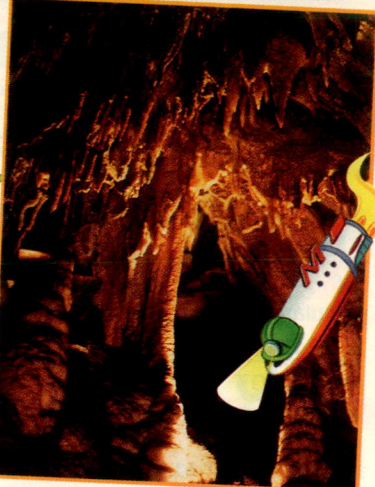

Sometimes when you subtract, you need to subtract across zeros.

Learning About It

Who turned out the lights? The Math Mobile is underground. You are in Mammoth Cave! Suppose there are 300 passages you can explore. If your class explores 124 passages, how many passages are left to explore?

$$300 − 124 = \blacksquare$$

▲ **Social Studies Connection**
Mammoth Cave National Park in Kentucky is the largest cave system in the world.

Step 1	**Step 2**	**Step 3**	**Step 4**
0 ones < 4 ones, so you need more ones to subtract. There are no tens, so regroup 1 hundred as 10 tens. Then regroup 1 ten as 10 ones.	Subtract ones.	Subtract tens.	Subtract hundreds.
9 2 10 10 3̸0̸0̸ − 124	9 2 10 10 3̸0̸0̸ − 124 ___ 6	9 2 10 10 3̸0̸0̸ − 124 ___ 76	9 2 10 10 3̸0̸0̸ − 124 ___ 176

There are 176 passages left to explore.

More Examples

A.
9
5 10 13
1,603
− 275
_____
1,328

3 ones < 5 ones
There are no tens, so regroup 1 hundred as 10 tens. Then regroup 1 ten as 10 ones.

B.
9
1 10 10
$2,004
− 1,521
_____
$483

0 tens < 2 tens
There are no hundreds, so regroup 1 thousand as 10 hundreds. Then regroup 1 hundred as 10 tens.

Think and Discuss To find 6,000 − 8, would you use paper and pencil or mental math? Explain why. **Choices and explanations will vary.**

110

1 Introduce

Whole Class Activity

VISUAL

 WHOLE CLASS   5–10 MINUTES

Materials: overhead base-ten blocks

1. A volunteer writes *508 − 137* on the overhead.
   - Ask: **Is regrouping needed?** *(Yes.)*
2. Using the overhead blocks, another student shows how to regroup to get tens.
   - Ask: **How can you use numbers to show the regrouping?** *(Cross out the 5 and write 4 above it; cross out the 0 in the tens place and write 10 above it.)*

2 Teach   Pages 110–111

Discuss each of the steps for subtracting across zeros.

- Ask: **If the class had already visited 234 of the 300 passages, how many would be left to explore?** *(66)* **Explain how you used regrouping to get the answer.**
  (1 hundred was regrouped as 10 tens, 1 ten was regrouped as 10 ones.)

Critical Thinking   ANALYSIS

After Think and Discuss, say: **Find the difference for 300 − 150** *(150)* **and 30 − 15** *(15).* **How did knowing the answer to one help you to solve the other using mental math?** *(Sample answer: The only difference is a zero in the ones place.)*

Assess Understanding

After Try It Out, ask: **Where is regrouping across zeros needed in the example 3,804 − 2,630?** *(Regroup 1 hundred as 10 tens.)*

 **USING TECHNOLOGY**

MathProcessor™ Activities
See **Activities 17 and 18** in the MathProcessor™ Activity Cards.

Try It Out

Find each difference.

1.	2.	3.	4.	5.
600 − 348 **252**	8,000 − 4,291 **3,709**	5,000 − 241 **4,759**	703 − 659 **44**	$4,000 − 2,360 **$1,640**

Practice

Subtract.

6.	7.	8.	9.	10.
900 − 349 **551**	4,000 − 2,056 **1,944**	200 − 58 **142**	307 − 158 **149**	600 − 419 **181**

11.	12.	13.	14.	15.
6,020 − 4,340 **1,680**	$25.00 − 12.65 **$12.35**	502 − 279 **223**	$7.00 − 2.94 **$4.06**	100 − 37 **63**

Using Mental Math Use mental math to find each difference.

16. 500 − 80 **420**   **17.** 7,000 − 160 **6,840**   **18.** $4.00 − $1.36 **$2.64**

19. $9.00 − $1.50 **$7.50**   **20.** $40.00 − $4.99 **$35.01**   **21.** 8,000 − 2,459 **5,541**

Problem Solving

22. The Math Mobile has 200 kneepads to help you crawl through passages. The 28 children in your class each used 2 kneepads. How many are left? Explain how you solved the problem.
144 kneepads; accept all reasonable explanations.

23. Suppose you bring 105 meals to eat as you explore the cave. If 27 meals are left at the end of the trip, how many meals were eaten? How do you know your answer is reasonable?
78 meals; accept all reasonable explanations.

▲
Social Studies Connection
Stephen Bishop was the first modern-day explorer of Mammoth Cave. He began exploring the cave in 1838.

Review and Remember

Find each answer.

24.	25.	26.	27.	28.	29.
7 + 6 **13**	9 − 9 **0**	14 − 8 **6**	6 + 9 **15**	12 − 7 **5**	7 + 8 **15**

For Extra Practice, see Set I, page 120. **111**

---

3 Wrap-up

How can you subtract from a number that has zeros? *(Regroup across the zeros.)*

✏️ **Journal Idea** Write a word problem in which the solver must subtract across zeros.

Common Error Alert

Watch for students who may get confused and lose track of zeros and nines as they regroup. Remind them to cross out each zero and write the regrouped number.

Meeting Individual Needs

For Early Finishers

Two students write out 3 subtraction problems involving subtracting across zeros. They trade problems, solve, then use addition to check answers.
LOGICAL/MATHEMATICAL

Manipulatives

Write *$300 − $147* on the board. Students use a bill set to show each amount in the problem. Students trade in bills to find the difference. *($153)*
VISUAL/SPATIAL

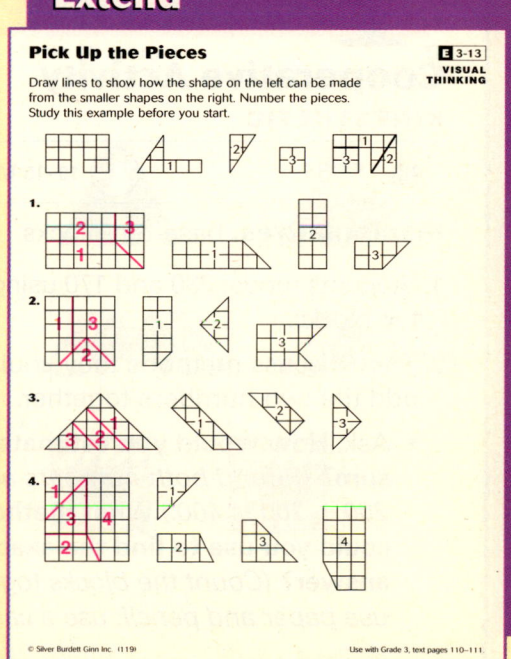
LESSON 13   111

Checkpoint

Vocabulary Review

You may wish to review these terms before students begin the Checkpoint.

addend   A number that is added to another number.

estimate   To give an approximate rather than an exact answer.

sum   The answer in addition.
        Example: 8 + 7 = 15
        The sum is 15.

Using the Page

Purpose To review concepts and skills presented since the last Checkpoint

- If necessary, discuss the directions and content of each section of the Checkpoint with the class.

- Page numbers associated with each group of items refer to the pages on which the skill or concept was presented. Those students needing review should turn to the appropriate lessons.

 Using Algebra

In Exercises 29–32, students solve **equations** and compare sums.

Subtracting Numbers

Vocabulary

Use the words from the Word Bank to fill in the blanks.

1. When you round a number you get an <u>estimate</u> ?.

2. Each number that is added is called an <u>addend</u> ?.

3. The answer in addition is called the <u>sum</u> ?.

Word Bank
addend
estimate
sum

Concepts and Skills

Estimate each difference by rounding to the nearest ten. (pages 100–101)

4.	5.	6.	7.	8.
92 − 74 **20**	56 − 48 **10**	78 − 22 **60**	61 − 28 **30**	93 − 49 **40**

Estimate each difference by rounding to the nearest hundred or dollar. (pages 100–101)

9.	10.	11.	12.	13.
807 − 296 **500**	434 − 177 **200**	$7.98 − 2.79 **$5.00**	750 − 610 **200**	$9.72 − 1.15 **$9.00**
14.	15.	16.	17.	18.
579 − 365 **200**	$4.68 − 1.51 **$3.00**	812 − 327 **500**	$9.04 − 2.91 **$6.00**	618 − 194 **400**

Subtract. (pages 104–113)

19.	20.	21.	22.	23.
46 − 35 **11**	64 − 31 **33**	74 − 69 **5**	58 − 29 **29**	$6.08 − 4.59 **$1.49**
24.	25.	26.	27.	28.
317 − 108 **209**	$6.15 − 4.28 **$1.87**	817 − 645 **172**	2,211 − 1,788 **423**	$25.01 − 10.75 **$14.26**

Using Algebra Compare. Use >, <, or = for each ●. (pages 100–113)

29. 912 − 412 ● 850 − 350   **=**

30. 810 − 212 ● 810 − 210   **<**

31. 4,936 − 2,102 ● 2,834   **=**

32. 6,008 − 2,216 ● 5,432 − 1,234   **<**

Reinforcement and Remediation

 **PAIRS**

- Provide pairs of students with base-ten blocks, spinner (0–9), and paper.

- Each student spins to create a 2-digit number. Pairs compare numbers and decide which is greater. One student rounds to the nearest ten and estimates the difference. The partner uses base-ten blocks to find the exact difference.

- Students repeat the activity, spinning 3 and 4 numbers to subtract and add 3- and 4-digit numbers. Encourage students to use decimal points and dollar signs to add and subtract monetary values.

Problem Solving

33. The Math Mobile visited a city for two days. On Monday, 2,324 people toured the ship. On Tuesday, 2,499 people toured it. How many people toured the ship in all?
4,823 people

34. Everyone who toured the Math Mobile was given a free lunch. How many more lunches were given on Tuesday than Monday?
175 lunches

35. On Tuesday morning, the Math Mobile's radar showed that a storm was 107 miles from the city. That afternoon the storm was 79 miles away. How many miles had the storm moved? **28 miles**

Journal Idea
Write a word problem about the Math Mobile that can be solved by using addition or subtraction. Then see if a classmate can solve it. **Word problems will vary.**

What do you think?
Would you use mental math or paper and pencil to find 487 − 407? Explain your choice.

A possible answer is mental math; you can use basic subtraction facts to subtract the 7 ones and the 4 hundreds.

You Decide

Activity

Plan a Dinner Menu

Plan a dinner to eat on the Math Mobile. Be sure that the dinner has 800 calories or less.

- Which foods will you choose?
- How many calories will your dinner have? If you want to eat about 2,000 calories a day, about how many calories should you eat the rest of the day?

 You might wish to include this work in your portfolio.

Food	Amount	Calories
Hamburger	3 oz	385
Pizza	1 slice	345
Fruit Salad	1 cup	85
Roll	1 roll	120
Orange Juice	1 cup	120
Whole Milk	1 cup	150

Students' menus will vary. Check to see that the total number of calories for the dinner does not exceed 800.

Ongoing Assessment

You may want to have students review their responses to the Baseline Assessment questions presented at the beginning of the chapter. Have students discuss what they have learned in this chapter to help them answer the "What do you think?" question.

What do you think?

Accept reasonable responses. Some students may choose mental math, and some may choose pencil and paper to determine that 487 − 407 = 80.

Journal Idea
Encourage students to write problems that require regrouping.

You Decide

This activity allows you to evaluate students' understanding of addition, subtraction, and estimation. As students do the activity, encourage them to revise their work as needed. Be sure students' choices total 800 calories or less.

Portfolio Activity
You may wish to have students include their work from the You Decide activity in their portfolios.

The scoring rubric on the left may be used to help you assess students' work.

Scoring Rubric

3 EXCELLENT Using estimation, students create a dinner menu with items whose calories total 800 or less. Students then estimate the amount of calories they should eat for the rest of the day that would combine with the dinner calories to total about 2,000 calories.

2 SATISFACTORY Students create a dinner menu with items whose calories total 800 or less. They may add numbers of calories instead of estimating to decide what combination will give 800 calories or less. Students then estimate the amount of calories they should eat for the rest of the day that would combine with the dinner calories to total about 2,000 calories.

1 NEEDS IMPROVEMENT Students have little or no understanding of how to choose items whose calories total 800 or less. Students cannot make a decision about calories that they should eat for the rest of the day.

Extra Practice

Using the Pages

Purpose To maintain and review skills developed in this chapter

Page numbers associated with each group of items refer to the pages on which the skill or concept was presented. Those students needing review should turn to the appropriate lessons.

Using Technology
For Additional Practice

You may wish to use the following technology resources.

Math Blaster® 1
For Set A: Cave Runner, addition: Level 6; sums 22–25
For Set G: Math Blaster, subtraction: Levels 1–5
For Set H: Math Blaster, subtraction: Level 6

Internet www.sbgmath.com
For Set D: Chapter 3, Whitewater Rafting Activity
For Set E: Chapter 3, Iditarod Activity
For Set G: Chapter 3, Moon Walk Activity

MathProcessor™ CD-ROM Activities
For Set C: Activities 13 and 14
For Set I: Activities 17 and 18

Extra Practice

Set A (pages 80–81)

Find each sum or difference.

1. 50 + 70 = **120**
2. 90 − 30 = **60**
3. 300 + 800 = **1,100**
4. 8,000 − 4,000 = **4,000**
5. 6,000 + 9,000 = **15,000**

6. The first 100 children to sign up for soccer were given a $3 coupon for sports equipment. The next 200 children were given a $1 coupon. How many coupons were given out? **300 coupons**

7. Last week, 580 children signed up for softball. Two hundred of the children have received their team shirts. How many children still need to receive their shirts? **380 children**

Set B (pages 82–83)

Estimate by rounding to the nearest ten.

1. 37 + 54 = **90**
2. 83 + 29 = **110**
3. 45 + 34 = **80**
4. 44 + 34 = **70**
5. 16 + 28 = **50**

Estimate by rounding to the nearest hundred or dollar.

6. 263 + 358 = **700**
7. $9.73 + 2.53 = **$13.00**
8. $8.03 + 4.48 = **$12.00**
9. 595 + 405 = **1,000**
10. 812 + 279 = **1,100**

Set C (pages 88–91)

Estimate first. Then add. **Estimates may vary. Possible estimates are shown.**

1. 57 + 63 = **120; 120**
2. 49 + 58 = **110; 107**
3. $4.35 + 7.80 = **$12; $12.15**
4. 478 + 807 = **1,300; 1,285**
5. $3.13 + 7.29 = **$10; $10.42**

6. Lauren has 119 U.S. stamps and 187 Canadian stamps in her collection. How many stamps does she have? **306 stamps**

7. Lee collects posters. He bought a large poster for $6.95 and a small poster for $3.29. How much money did he spend? **$10.24**

118

Additional Answers

Chapter 3

Lesson 3
Page 84

4. **No; yes; if you estimate the number of pineapples the restaurant has by rounding each crate to the nearest ten and adding the rounded numbers together, you see that there are only about 80 pineapples.**

Lesson 8
Page 99

Table for Problems 1–3

Number of Wagons	Number of Oxen
1	4
2	8
3	12
4	16
5	20
6	24
7	28
8	32
9	36
10	40

Extra Practice

Set D (pages 92–93)

Find each sum.

1. $\begin{array}{r} 1{,}790 \\ + 2{,}304 \\ \hline \mathbf{4{,}094} \end{array}$
2. $\begin{array}{r} 3{,}448 \\ + 7{,}348 \\ \hline \mathbf{10{,}796} \end{array}$
3. $\begin{array}{r} \$35.98 \\ + 14.29 \\ \hline \mathbf{\$50.27} \end{array}$
4. $\begin{array}{r} 6{,}393 \\ + 3{,}744 \\ \hline \mathbf{10{,}137} \end{array}$
5. $\begin{array}{r} \$38.25 \\ + 11.75 \\ \hline \mathbf{\$50.00} \end{array}$

6. Rebecca spent $29.50 for tickets to a game and $10.50 for food. Janet spent $24.00 for tickets and $12.65 for food. Who spent more? **Rebecca**

7. There are 2,350 seats in the lower part of a stadium. There are 1,890 seats in the upper part of the stadium. How many seats are there in the stadium? **4,240 seats**

Set E (pages 94–95)

Find each sum.

1. $\begin{array}{r} 23 \\ 27 \\ + 94 \\ \hline \mathbf{144} \end{array}$
2. $\begin{array}{r} 305 \\ 479 \\ + 813 \\ \hline \mathbf{1{,}597} \end{array}$
3. $\begin{array}{r} 3{,}045 \\ 1{,}989 \\ + 7{,}053 \\ \hline \mathbf{12{,}087} \end{array}$
4. $\begin{array}{r} 6{,}234 \\ 8{,}975 \\ + 3{,}437 \\ \hline \mathbf{18{,}646} \end{array}$
5. $\begin{array}{r} \$82.13 \\ 15.89 \\ + 19.08 \\ \hline \mathbf{\$117.10} \end{array}$

6. Students at Smith School want to collect 1,000 soup labels. The first grade saved 246 labels. The second grade saved 338 labels. The third grade saved 340 labels. Did the students reach their goal? **No**

7. Ray, Bob, and Phil sold plants to raise money for their school band. Ray sold 27 plants. Bob sold 38 plants, and Phil sold 63 plants. How many plants did the three boys sell? **128 plants**

Set F (pages 100–101)

Estimate by rounding to the greatest place value.

1. $\begin{array}{r} 58 \\ - 29 \\ \hline \mathbf{30} \end{array}$
2. $\begin{array}{r} 74 \\ - 53 \\ \hline \mathbf{20} \end{array}$
3. $\begin{array}{r} 36 \\ - 25 \\ \hline \mathbf{10} \end{array}$
4. $\begin{array}{r} 48 \\ - 29 \\ \hline \mathbf{20} \end{array}$
5. $\begin{array}{r} 62 \\ - 45 \\ \hline \mathbf{10} \end{array}$

6. $\begin{array}{r} 536 \\ - 215 \\ \hline \mathbf{300} \end{array}$
7. $\begin{array}{r} 812 \\ - 388 \\ \hline \mathbf{400} \end{array}$
8. $\begin{array}{r} 627 \\ - 289 \\ \hline \mathbf{300} \end{array}$
9. $\begin{array}{r} 587 \\ - 293 \\ \hline \mathbf{300} \end{array}$
10. $\begin{array}{r} 882 \\ - 617 \\ \hline \mathbf{300} \end{array}$

119

Performance Assessment
Page 122

1a. **Possible answers:**
   1 quarter, 1 nickel
   1 quarter, 5 pennies
   3 dimes
   2 dimes, 2 nickels
   2 dimes, 1 nickel, 5 pennies
   2 dimes, 10 pennies
   1 dime, 4 nickels
   1 dime, 3 nickels, 5 pennies
   1 dime, 2 nickels, 10 pennies
   1 dime, 1 nickel, 15 pennies
   1 dime, 20 pennies
   6 nickels
   5 nickels, 5 pennies
   4 nickels, 10 pennies
   3 nickels, 15 pennies
   2 nickels, 20 pennies
   1 nickel, 25 pennies
   30 pennies

Problem of the Day Answers

Lesson 8
Teacher Guide page 98

Sample answer:

4	9	2
3	5	7
8	1	6

Lesson 15
Teacher Guide page 114

Nate could begin at 478 and add on to 591, keeping track of the numbers he uses to reach that goal.

		4. 8,827	**5.** $17.84
/		− 6,987	− 12.19
.6.58		1,840	$5.65

	3. $60.00	**4.** 7,000	**5.** 5,000
.00	− 8.59	− 1,327	− 1,450
9.25			
$16.75	$51.41	5,673	3,550

...ught party decorations
..89. He gave the cashier
..00. How much change did
ne get? **$2.11**

7. Bev has 300 balloons for a party. Sixty-five of them are red. How many balloons are not red?
235 balloons

Set J (pages 112–113)

Choose a Method Use mental math, paper and pencil, or a calculator to add or subtract. Tell which method you chose. **Methods may vary.**

1. 800	**2.** 956	**3.** 7,000	**4.** 9,035	**5.** 7,350
+ 600	− 253	+ 6,000	− 5,035	− 1,728
1,400	703	13,000	4,000	5,622

120

Chapter Test

Estimate by rounding to the greatest place value.

1.	45 + 39 **90**	2.	74 − 62 **10**	3.	282 + 724 **1,000**	4.	782 − 275 **500**	5.	$8.50 + 7.49 **$16.00**

Find each sum.

6.	541 + 306 **847**	7.	26 + 78 **104**	8.	$3.05 + 6.48 **$9.53**	9.	7,356 + 4,732 **12,088**	10.	$81.33 + 15.69 **$97.02**

11. 24 + 36 + 98 **158**   12. 300 + 200 + 720 **1,220**

13. 14 + 22 + 63 **99**   14. $5.15 + $2.08 + $1.35 **$8.58**

Find each difference.

15.	48 − 29 **19**	16.	80 − 44 **36**	17.	$4.39 − 2.47 **$1.92**	18.	6,202 − 5,347 **855**	19.	$30.00 − 25.98 **$4.02**

20. 563 − 473 **90**   21. 5,682 − 4,391 **1,291**

22. 89 − 17 **72**   23. $38.06 − $13.47 **$24.59**

Solve.

24. One week the Math Mobile made a tour of some special places. It visited 624 places in New York, 470 places in Illinois, and 336 places in Nevada. How many places did it visit in all three states? **1,430 places**

25. Students traveled to Paris, France, in the Math Mobile. They found that the Eiffel Tower is 984 feet tall. The Washington Monument in Washington, D.C., is 555 feet tall. How much taller is the Eiffel Tower? **429 feet taller**

 Self-Check
Look back at Exercises 15 to 23. Use addition to check that your answers are correct.

121

Reteaching Chart

Learning Objectives	Test Items	Text Pages	Resources
3A	1–5	82–83, 100–101	P/R3-2, P/R3-9
3B	6–10	80–81, 86–93, 112–113	P/R3-1, P/R3-4, P/R3-5, P/R3-6, P/R3-14
3C	11–14, 24	94–95	P3-7, R3-7
3D	15–23, 25	80–81, 102–113	P/R3-1, P/R3-10, P/R3-11, P/R3-12, P/R3-13, P/R3-14,
3E	24–25	84–85, 98–99 114–114A	P3-3, R3-3, P3-8, R3-8, P3-15, R3-15

The item analysis in the chart may be used to diagnose students' errors and to correlate the lessons and resources appropriate for reinforcement and remediation.

Chapter Test

Assessment Options

This Chapter Test can be used as a review, practice test, or chapter test. The Performance Assessment on page 122 may be used instead of or with this Chapter Test.

Other options are provided in the *Assessment Guide*.

- **Pretest**—multiple-choice or free-response form, pp. 79–82
- **Posttest**—multiple-choice or free-response form, pp. 83–86
- **Interview Activity,** p. 37
- **Long-Answer Question,** p. 9

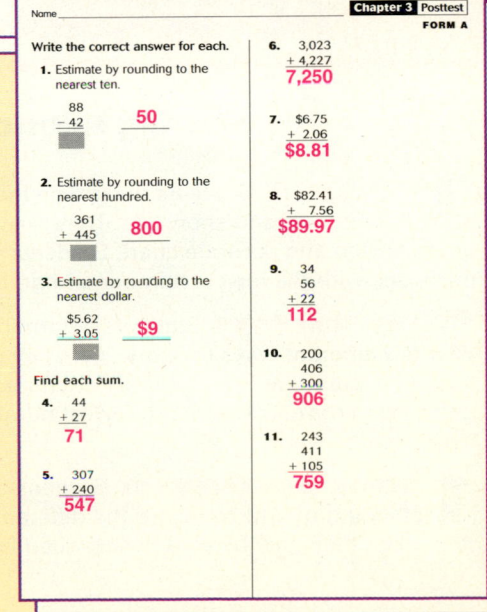

Multiple Choice and Free Response tests assess the same objectives and contain the same number of test items.

Performance Assessment

Using the Page

 PAIRS

Materials: play money: 2 quarters, 5 dimes, 8 nickels, 35 pennies

Purpose Performance Assessment may be used instead of, or in conjunction with, more formal assessments to show what students know about addition and subtraction.

- Problem 1 will help you assess if students have an understanding of the basic concepts and processes of addition and subtraction. Problem 2 will help you assess if students are able to apply their understanding. The Scoring Rubrics below provide specific behaviors and results to look for in Problems 1 and 2.

- Students can evaluate their own work by responding to the Self-Check questions. To further assess their understanding, ask students the following questions: **What part of addition and subtraction do you find the easiest? the most difficult?**

 For Your Portfolio

You may wish to have students include the work from the Performance Assessment in their portfolios.

For an additional Performance Assessment activity, see **Assessment Guide,** pp. 15–17.

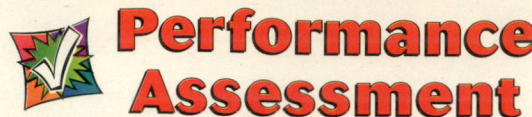

Performance Assessment

Show What You Know About Addition and Subtraction

1 Use play money to answer Questions 1a and 1b.

a. Show 30¢ in as many ways as you can. Make a chart like the one below to show your work. **See Additional Answers, pages 118–119.**

What You Need

play money:
  2 quarters
  5 dimes
  8 nickels
  35 pennies

Quarters	Dimes	Nickels	Pennies	Total

b. How can you make 30¢ with the fewest number of coins? with the greatest number of coins? **1 quarter, 1 nickel; 30 pennies**

Self-Check Did you check that each combination of coins has a sum of 30¢?

Country	Travel Time
France	67 minutes
Colombia	80 minutes
Kenya	156 minutes
Australia	208 minutes

2 This chart shows the time it takes the Math Mobile to travel from the United States to different countries.

a. Pick a country to visit. How many minutes would it take the Math Mobile to travel there and back? **Answer should be double the travel time shown for the country chosen.**

b. Tonya wants to visit each country. If she returns to the United States after each visit, how much time will she spend traveling? **1,022 minutes**

c. Suppose the Math Mobile was scheduled for a flight every 3 hours. Which countries could the Math Mobile visit? **France or Colombia**

Self-Check Did you make sure you included minutes both *to* and *from* each country?

France
Colombia
Kenya
Australia

 For Your Portfolio
You might wish to include this work in your portfolio.

122

Performance Assessment Scoring Rubrics

Scoring Rubric 1

3 EXCELLENT Students determine that there are more than ten different ways to show 30¢. They display the combinations in an organized and accurate chart. Students correctly find how to make 30¢ with the fewest number and greatest number of coins.

2 SATISFACTORY Students determine that there are five to ten different ways to show 30¢. They may display the combinations in a chart that is not entirely organized. Students may correctly find how to make 30¢ with the fewest number or the greatest number of coins.

1 NEEDS IMPROVEMENT Students have little or no understanding of how to record the different combinations of coins. With help, they may be able to show combinations and record them.

Scoring Rubric 2

3 EXCELLENT Students correctly calculate the travel time to and from the country they picked. They correctly calculate the travel time for Tonya's trip. They identify the countries for which a round trip is less than 3 hours.

2 SATISFACTORY Students understand how to calculate the travel times. Some students may forget to include the travel time back from a country.

1 NEEDS IMPROVEMENT Students have little or no understanding of how to calculate the travel times. With help, they can understand how to calculate but make mistakes while calculating.

Extension

Palindromes!

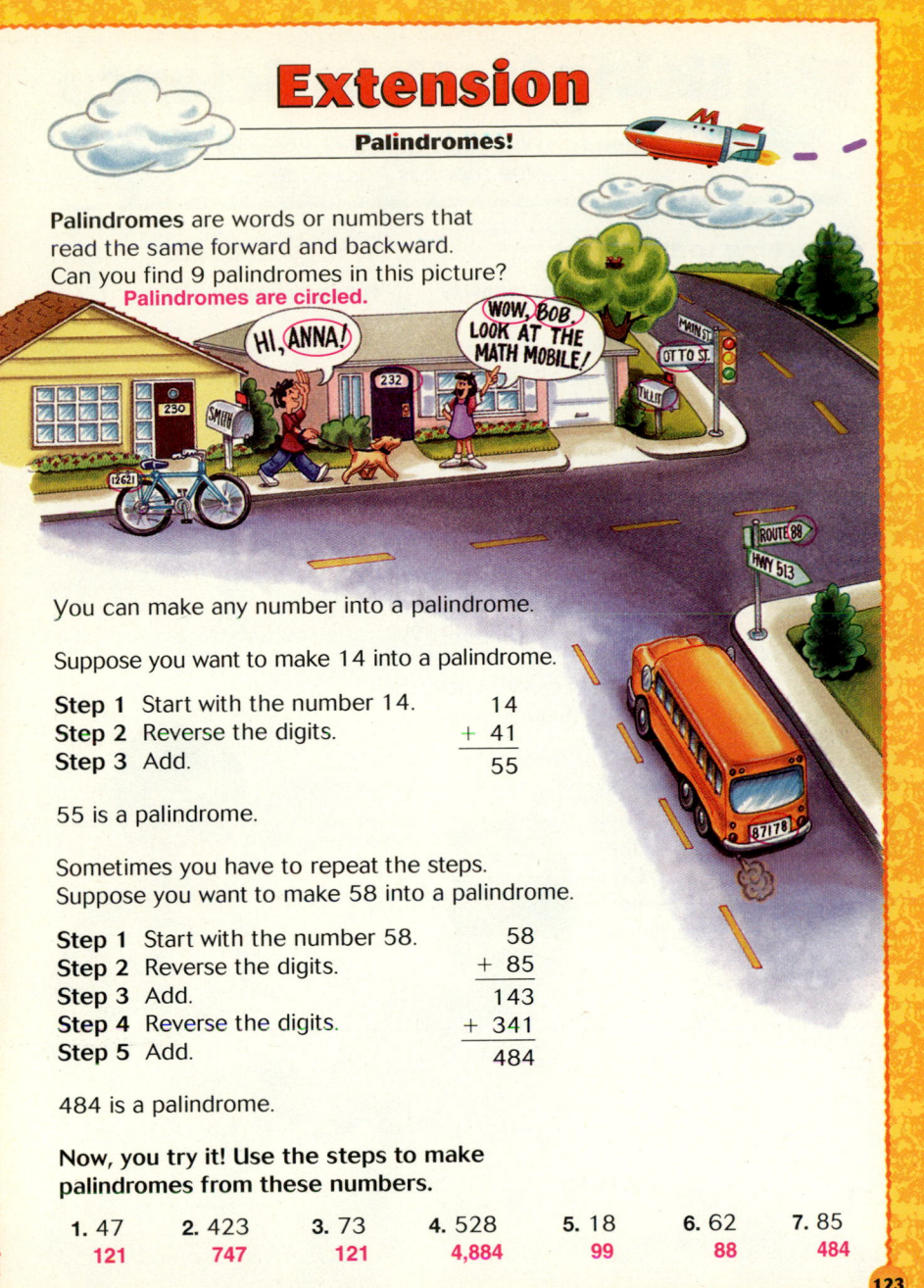

Palindromes are words or numbers that read the same forward and backward. Can you find 9 palindromes in this picture?

Palindromes are circled.

You can make any number into a palindrome.

Suppose you want to make 14 into a palindrome.

Step 1 Start with the number 14.   14
Step 2 Reverse the digits.   + 41
Step 3 Add.   55

55 is a palindrome.

Sometimes you have to repeat the steps.
Suppose you want to make 58 into a palindrome.

Step 1 Start with the number 58.   58
Step 2 Reverse the digits.   + 85
Step 3 Add.   143
Step 4 Reverse the digits.   + 341
Step 5 Add.   484

484 is a palindrome.

Now, you try it! Use the steps to make palindromes from these numbers.

1. 47	**2.** 423	**3.** 73	**4.** 528	**5.** 18	**6.** 62	**7.** 85
121	747	121	4,884	99	88	484

123

Using the Page

🌟 **SMALL GROUPS**

Purpose To identify palindromes

- For each number in the picture, suggest that students reverse the digits to see if the number is the same as in the picture.

- Ask: **How many steps does it take to make 12 a palindrome? 68 a palindrome?** *(3; 7)*

Additional Questions

If you know that you can make the palindrome 88 from 62, what other number can make the palindrome 88? *(26)*

What palindrome can you make from 1,234? *(5,555)*

Using Math in Science

Using the Pages

 **SMALL GROUPS**

Materials: basketball, tennis ball, metric tape measure (or centimeter ruler), string, scissors, calculator

Purpose Use the mathematics skills of measuring and adding to build a model that shows the relative distance between Earth and the moon.

Explore Science

- In this activity, students use a basketball and tennis ball to build a model to demonstrate the relative distance between Earth and the moon. The model is based on the fact that the distance around Earth is roughly $9\frac{1}{2}$ times the distance from Earth to the moon.

- For Step 1, make sure students make their measurements around the middle of the basketball. They should wrap the string as if they are measuring the equator on a globe.

- For Step 2, remind students to record their measurements to the nearest centimeter.

- Inform students that the distance around the middle of Earth is about four times greater than the distance around the middle of the moon. Ask students to determine if that same relationship exists between the basketball and the tennis ball.

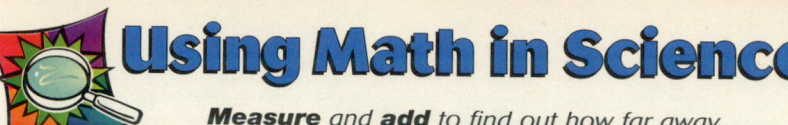

Measure and add to find out how far away the moon is from Earth.

Reaching to the Moon

Have you ever wondered how far away the moon is? It's about the same distance as going around the middle of Earth nine and a half times. Using a basketball as a model for Earth and a tennis ball as a model for the moon, you can make a model to show how far away the moon is.

What You Need

For each group:
  basketball
  tennis ball
  metric tape measure
   (or centimeter ruler)
  string
  scissors
  calculator

Explore

Step 1 To find out the distance around your model of Earth, wrap a piece of string around the middle of the basketball exactly once. Then hold the string there while another group member cuts it.

Step 2 Measure the length of the string. Then round that length to the nearest centimeter. On a piece of paper, write down this measurement nine times.

Assess Performance

✓ **Science Skills Checklist**
- Did students accurately measure the distance around the middle of the model Earth?
- Did students measure in centimeters?
- Did students correctly complete the models of the moon and Earth?

Step 3 Now cut the piece of string in half. Measure the length again to the nearest centimeter. Add this measurement to your list of nine numbers.

Step 4 Using a calculator, add all ten numbers together. Now, measure and cut another piece of string that is equal in length to that total length.

Step 5 Tape one end of the string to the floor, and place your basketball on top of it. Gently stretch the string out in a straight line and tape the other end to the floor. Then place the tennis ball on that end of the string. You have now completed your model!

▲ The photos above show the relationship of the size of the moon to the size of Earth.

Analyze

1. Does it matter in which order you added the numbers in Step 4? Try adding the numbers down and then add the numbers up. Do you get the same answer? **The order does not matter. Students should get the same sum either way.**

2. Did your model of the distance between Earth and the moon match exactly the models of other groups? What are some reasons that the models may be slightly different? **See right.**

Some basketballs might be less inflated than others; one group may have rounded up their measurement to the nearest centimeter while another group rounded down; one group might have measured the string more exactly than another group.

For Your Portfolio

Draw a picture of the model you made. Label the basketball and the tennis ball. Write what each ball stands for. Explain how addition helped you make your model.

Explore Further!

The distance around Earth at the equator is about 24,900 miles. Can you think of a way to use a calculator to figure out the distance in miles from Earth to the moon? **See side column for detailed explanation.**

125

Apply Math

- Students use a centimeter ruler to measure the length of the string that shows the distance around the basketball. If necessary, remind students to measure to the nearest centimeter.

- For Step 3, show the students how to fold the string in half to find where it should be cut. Then if necessary, remind them to measure the length of this piece of string to the nearest centimeter.

- Students then use a calculator to add their measurements. If students are getting different answers for Step 4, remind them that they should be adding a total of 10 numbers. Have them check to be sure that they listed the first measurement 9 times and that they also included the second measurement in their list.

For Your Portfolio

As students draw a picture of their model to record their work, suggest that they label the measurement showing the distance between the basketball and the tennis ball. Have students write a sentence or two explaining what their model shows.

Explore Further!

If students have trouble getting started, explain that 24,900 miles represents the same measurement as the distance around the middle of the basketball. Have students round 24,900 to the nearest thousand. Then help students use division on the calculator to find that half of 25,000 miles is 12,500 miles. Students should then be able to use these numbers to find the approximate distance from Earth to the moon. That distance is approximately 237,000 miles.

Math Skills Checklist

- Did students correctly measure to the nearest centimeter?
- Using a calculator, did students correctly add the 10 numbers together?
- Did students correctly measure the string used in their completed model?

Cumulative Review

Preparing for Tests

Purpose To review and maintain skills and concepts learned in this and previous chapters.

Preparation for Standardized Tests

Exercises in the review are presented in a multiple-choice format similar to that used for most standardized tests. This provides an opportunity for students to practice their test-taking skills. You may wish to have students use Teaching Tool 1, which simulates the format of the answer sheets commonly used with standardized tests.

Continuous Skills Review

The six mathematics strands below are continuously reviewed to help students maintain skills. Each Cumulative Review covers four of the six strands. All six strands are reviewed every 3 chapters. Continuous review will help students retain skills and concepts learned in previous chapters and in the previous grade.

★ Number Concepts
★ Patterns, Relationships, and Algebraic Thinking
★ Geometry and Spatial Reasoning
★ Measurement
★ Probability and Statistics
★ Operations

Cumulative Review

★★★★★ **Preparing for Tests**

Choose the correct letter for each answer.

Operations	Patterns, Relationships, and Algebraic Thinking

1. What is the sum of 679 and 345?

A. 334   **C.** 1,024
B. 914   D. 10,024

2. Tina spent $2.88 on a calculator and $3.99 on a notebook. **About** how much money did she spend?

A. $3.00   **C.** $7.00
B. $5.00   D. $17.00

3. 486
   − 97

A. 389   C. 399
B. 411   D. 583

4. Will has 41¢ in his pocket. His Aunt gave him 55¢. How much money does he have now?

A. 14¢   C. 86¢
B. 92¢   **D.** 96¢

5. Which number makes this sentence true?

$241 + \blacksquare = 245$

A. 3   C. 5
B. 4   D. 6

6. What is the missing number in the number pattern?

48, 44, 40, $\blacksquare$, 32, 28

A. 36   C. 38
B. 37   D. 42

7. Which names the same number as $12 + 14 + 16$?

$$12 + 14 + 16$$

A. $12 + 14 - 16$
B. $12 + 16 + 14$
C. $12 + 14 + 1 + 6$
D. $12 + 1 + 4 + +6$

8. One sticker costs 6¢. Two stickers cost 12¢. Three stickers cost 18¢. How much would 4 stickers cost?

A. 20¢
B. 24¢
C. 30¢
D. 36¢

Chapter 3 Cumulative Review

Reteaching Chart

Strand	Items	Text Pages	Resources
Number Concepts	*	*	*
Patterns, Relationships, & Algebraic Thinking	5–8	2–3, 50–51, 104–107	P/R1–1, P/R2–3 P/R3–11
Geometry	9–12	See Grade 2.	
Measurement	*	*	*
Probability & Statistics	13–16	See Grade 2.	See Activity, next page.
Operations	1–4	82–83, 88–91, 104–107	P/R3–2, P/R3–5, P/R3–11

* Covered in Chapter 1 or 2 Cumulative Reviews.

Geometry and Spatial Reasoning	Probability and Statistics

Geometry and Spatial Reasoning

9. How many sides does this shape have?

A. 3
B. 4
C. 5
D. 6

10. Which numeral has a line of symmetry?

A.   C.

B.   D.

11. Which object is shaped like a cone?

A.

B.

C. SOUP

D.

12. Which space shape could you use to draw a circle?

A. C.

B. D.

Probability and Statistics

13. Look at the bag. If you pick one tile, what color will you most likely pick?

A. green
B. red
C. blue
D. yellow

Use the graph for Questions 14–16.

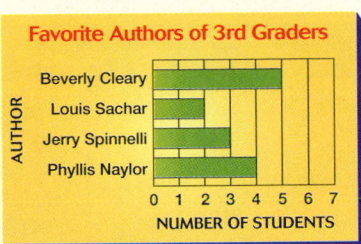

Favorite Authors of 3rd Graders

14. Which author was chosen most often?

A. Beverly Cleary
B. Jerry Spinnelli
C. Louis Sachar
D. Phyllis Naylor

15. How many students chose Phyllis Naylor?

A. 5   C. 3
B. 4   D. 2

16. How many more students chose Beverly Cleary than chose Jerry Spinnelli?

A. 2   C. 4
B. 3   D. 5

Chapter 3 Cumulative Review

Reteaching Activity

Graphing Birthdays

 WHOLE CLASS   **15–20 MINUTES**

This activity is based on content taught in Grade 2. Graphing is covered in Chapter 7 at Grade 3.

Materials: For the whole class — colored chalk and chalkboard or markers and grid paper

On the chalkboard or on grid paper, draw a grid with 4 columns and 8 rows. (Add more rows as needed depending upon the number of students in your class). Write the following labels at the bottom of each of the columns: *Spring, Summer, Fall, Winter.*

Tell students the beginning and ending dates for each season. Then ask each of them to color in one box over the season in which his or her birthday falls.

Remind students that they are making a bar graph. After the graph is completed, ask questions that the students can answer by looking at the graph. Then challenge students to make up their own questions.

Chapter 4

Daily Lesson Planner

Time and Measurement

To Start the Chapter

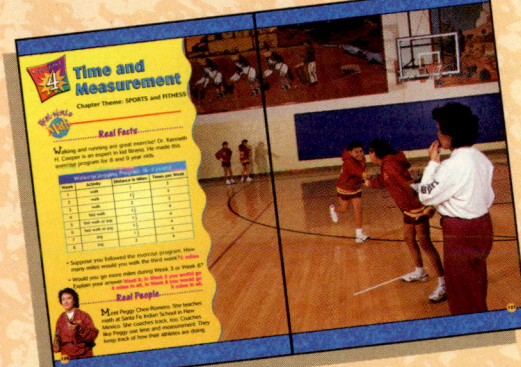

Chapter Opener

Resources

- Chapter Opener
  Career Spotlight
  Chapter Project, *Teacher Guide*,
  pages 126–127

- Chapter Pretest, *Assessment Guide*,
  pages 91–94

- Family Letter With Activity,
  Home-School Connection,
  pages 21–22

-  Internet Activity,
  pages 137, 161

Lesson 1

PAGES 128–129	**Telling Time to the Quarter Hour**
LEARNING OBJECTIVES **4A**	**Chapter File Folder** Practice, Reteach, Extend 4-1 Teaching Tools 24, 25, 26 Daily Review 4-1 Problem of the Day 4-1
NCTM STANDARDS **1, 3, 4, 8, 10, 12**	

Lesson 2

PAGES 130–131	**Telling Time to the Minute**
LEARNING OBJECTIVES **4A**	**Chapter File Folder** Practice, Reteach, Extend 4-2 Teaching Tools 24, 25 Daily Review 4-2 Problem of the Day 4-2
NCTM STANDARDS **1, 2, 3, 4, 8, 10**	

Lesson 6

PAGES 140–143	**Using Customary Units of Length**
LEARNING OBJECTIVES **4C**	**Chapter File Folder** Practice, Reteach, Extend 4-6 Teaching Tool 32 Daily Review 4-6 Problem of the Day 4-6
NCTM STANDARDS **1, 2, 3, 4, 8, 10**	$ p. 143

Lesson 7

PAGES 144–145	**EXPLORE: Using Customary Capacity**
LEARNING OBJECTIVES **4C**	**Chapter File Folder** Practice, Reteach, Extend 4-7 Teaching Tool 45 Daily Review 4-7 Practice Workbook, p. 17 Problem of the Day 4-7
NCTM STANDARDS **1, 2, 3, 5, 10, 13**	

Lesson 11

PAGES 152–155	**Using Metric Units of Length**
LEARNING OBJECTIVES **4D**	**Chapter File Folder** Practice, Reteach, Extend 4-11 Teaching Tool 31 Daily Review 4-11 Problem of the Day 4-11
NCTM STANDARDS **1, 2, 3, 5, 6, 10**	p. 155

Lesson 12

PAGES 156–157	**Using Milliliters and Liters**
LEARNING OBJECTIVES **4D**	**Chapter File Folder** Practice, Reteach, Extend 4-12 Daily Review 4-12 Practice Workbook, p. 18 Problem of the Day 4-12
NCTM STANDARDS **1, 2, 3, 5, 6, 10**	

Chapter End

PAGES 166–171	**Chapter Assessment**
LEARNING OBJECTIVES **4A 4B 4C** **4D 4E**	Extra Practice, pp. 166–168 Chapter Test, p. 169 Performance Assessment, p. 170 Extension, p. 171 Cumulative Review **In the *Assessment Guide*** Chapter Posttest, pp. 95–98 Interview Activity, p. 8 Long-Answer Question, p. 9
NCTM STANDARDS **1, 2, 3, 4, 5, 8, 10, 12, 13**	

Algebra   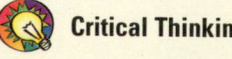 **Time for Technology**   **Time for Technology**   **Critical Thinking**

Lesson 3

PAGES 132–133

LEARNING OBJECTIVES 4B

NCTM STANDARDS 1, 2, 3, 5, 8, 10, 13

Elapsed Time

Chapter File Folder
Practice, Reteach, Extend 4-3
Teaching Tools 24, 25
Daily Review 4-3
Practice Workbook, p. 16
Problem of the Day 4-3

Lesson 4

PAGES 134–135

LEARNING OBJECTIVES 4E

NCTM STANDARDS 1, 3, 4, 7

Developing Skills for Problem-Solving

Chapter File Folder
Practice, Reteach, Extend 4-4
Daily Review 4-4
Problem of the Day 4-4

Lesson 5

PAGES 136–137

LEARNING OBJECTIVES 4A

NCTM STANDARDS 1, 3, 4, 13

Using a Calendar

Chapter File Folder
Practice, Reteach, Extend 4-5
Teaching Tool 32
Daily Review 4-5
Problem of the Day 4-5

✔ **Checkpoint, pp. 138–139**

Using Algebra p. 137   💻 p. 137   ⏰ p. 139

Lesson 8

PAGES 146–147

LEARNING OBJECTIVES 4C

NCTM STANDARDS 1, 2, 3, 5, 10

Using Ounces and Pounds

Chapter File Folder
Practice, Reteach, Extend 4-8
Daily Review 4-8
Problem of the Day 4-8

Lesson 9

PAGES 148–149

LEARNING OBJECTIVES 4C

NCTM STANDARDS 1, 2, 3, 5, 10

Temperature in Degrees Fahrenheit

Chapter File Folder
Practice, Reteach, Extend 4-9
Daily Review 4-9
Problem of the Day 4-9

💻 p. 149

Lesson 10

PAGES 150–151B

LEARNING OBJECTIVES 4E

NCTM STANDARDS 1, 3, 4, 7, 10

Problem-Solving Strategy

Chapter File Folder
Practice, Reteach, Extend 4-10
Teaching Tool 24
Daily Review 4-10
Problem of the Day 4-10
Teaching With Technology

Lesson 13

PAGES 158–159

LEARNING OBJECTIVES 4D

NCTM STANDARDS 1, 2, 3, 5, 6, 10

Using Grams and Kilograms

Chapter File Folder
Practice, Reteach, Extend 4-13
Daily Review 4-13
Practice Workbook, p. 19
Problem of the Day 4-13

Lesson 14

PAGES 160–161

LEARNING OBJECTIVES 4D

NCTM STANDARDS 1, 2, 3, 5, 6, 8, 10

Temperature in Degrees Celsius

Chapter File Folder
Practice, Reteach, Extend 4-14
Daily Review 4-14
Practice Workbook, p. 20
Problem of the Day 4-14

💻 p. 161

Lesson 15

PAGES 162–163A

LEARNING OBJECTIVES 4E

NCTM STANDARDS 1, 3, 4, 7, 9, 10

Problem-Solving Application

Chapter File Folder
Practice, Reteach, Extend 4-15
Daily Review 4-15
Problem of the Day 4-15
Problem Solving: Preparing for Tests

✔ **Checkpoint, pp. 164–165**

Using Algebra p. 162A

Correlation to Investigations

Investigations in Number, Data, and Space
Dale Seymour Publications

Lessons 1-5   **Combining and Comparing**
Investigations 3, 5

Lessons 6-15   **From Paces to Feet**
Investigations 1-4

Combining and Comparing
Investigations 2-3

Exploring Solids and Boxes
Investigation 5

Meeting Individual Needs

Learning Styles vary from student to student. Every Meeting Individual Needs activity focuses on one of the following learning styles. The variety of styles enables students to learn math in ways that are most comfortable to them.

- **AUDITORY**
- **INDIVIDUAL**
- **KINESTHETIC**
- **LINGUISTIC**
- **LOGICAL/MATHEMATICAL**
- **SOCIAL/COOPERATIVE**
- **VISUAL/SPATIAL**

Acquiring English Proficiency

Have students make a measurement bulletin board. Post index cards with units, such as *Cups, Pints, Quarts,* and *Gallons,* on the bulletin board. Each day, challenge students to describe situations in which they have seen or heard these units used. Students create pictures about the situations and add them to a corresponding section of the bulletin board.

For additional activities, see Acquiring English Proficiency, pp. 133, 143, 149.

LINGUISTIC

For Extra Help

Materials: ruler; 1 lb weight

Have students practice comparing objects to benchmark units, such as 1 foot or 1 pound. Students work in pairs. One student chooses an object, such as a pencil. The second student says whether the length is more or less than 1 foot. Students switch roles and repeat. Students check their estimates by measuring.

For additional activities, see For Extra Help, pp. 129, 137, 145, 151, 155, 161.

LOGICAL/MATHEMATICAL

For Early Finishers

Materials: almanacs, sports reference books, newspapers

Have students research Olympic track and field events, such as the high jump or the discus throw. Each student finds at least three events of this type, and lists the Olympic record for each event.

For additional activities, see For Early Finishers, pp. 129, 131, 133, 135, 137, 143, 145, 147, 149, 151, 155, 157, 159, 161, 162A.

LINGUISTIC

Gifted and Talented

Materials: calculators

Have students use calculators and these rules to estimate their weights on different planets.

- Mercury or Mars: Divide Earth weight by 5, then multiply by 2.
- Venus: Divide Earth weight by 8, then multiply by 7.
- Jupiter: Divide Earth weight by 2, then multiply by 5.

For additional activities, see Gifted and Talented, pp. 131, 157.

LOGICAL/MATHEMATICAL

Inclusion

Students who are distractible may benefit from activities in which the procedural steps of measurement are outlined. For example, create a poster that lists and illustrates steps for measuring length.

1. Line up the left end of the ruler with the object you are measuring.

2. Find the ruler mark that is closest to where the object ends.

3. Write the measurement.

For additional activities, see Inclusion, p. 147.

VISUAL/SPATIAL

MATH CENTER

Cooperative Learning

Materials: books about animals, set of encyclopedias

Students work in small groups. One student writes the name of an animal or draws its picture. Each student writes an estimate about a different measurement of the animal, such as its height, length, or weight. The activity continues until each student has had a chance to choose an animal.

For additional activities, see Cooperative Learning, pp. 159, 162A.

SOCIAL/COOPERATIVE

Manipulatives

Materials: Teaching Tool 24 (Clock Face), index cards with numbers 5, 11, 17, 33, 40, 57

One student uses a clock face to show a time, and says and writes that time. The second student picks a card from the pile, then shows, says, and writes the time that is that many minutes *later*. Students switch roles and repeat the activity.

For additional activities, see Manipulatives, p. 135.

VISUAL

Using Data

Materials: Teaching Tool 24

Students copy and complete a bus schedule. Remind students to work backward to find a departure time when the arrival and elapsed times are given.

For review, see pages 132–133 and 150–151.

Answers: Departure Times: Manassas—9:55, Philadelphia—11:00, Wilmington—11:55; Elapsed Times: Annapolis—55 min, Richmond—1 hr, 45 min; Arrival Times: Baltimore–10:25, NYC—3:00; Manassas, Annapolis, and Baltimore are less than 50 mi from Wash., D.C.

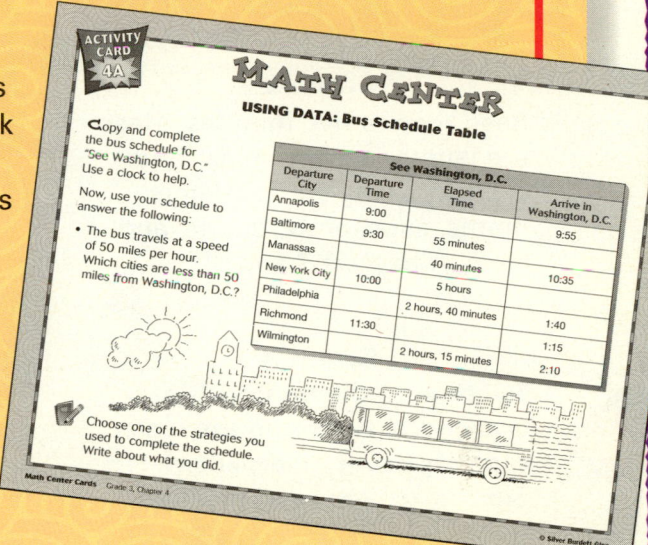

Problem Solving

Materials: centimeter ruler, meterstick, 1 kilogram weight, balance scale

Students will find classroom items whose measurements they think will match the estimates given in the table. Then they will use tools to measure the items and record the actual measurements. Students compare the estimates with the actual measurements.

For review, see pages 26–27, 60–61, 152–155, and 158–159.

Answers: Answers will vary.

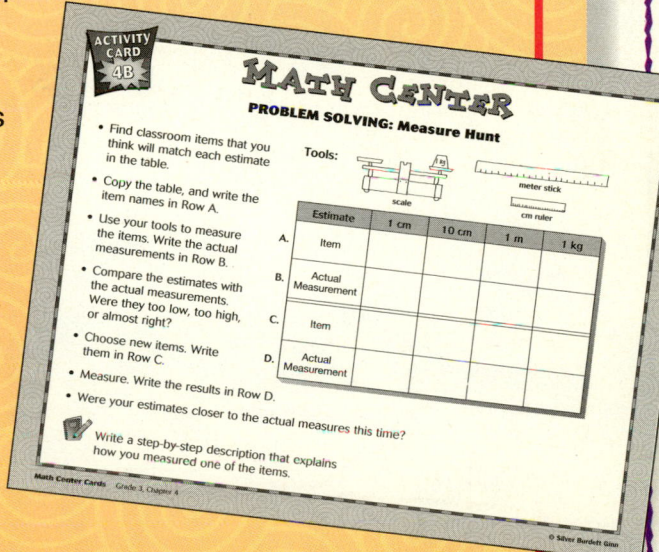

Assessment

Skills Trace
Skills Assessed at Each Grade

Grade 2
Read time to five minutes. Measure length, weight, mass, and capacity using yards, meters, grams, cups, pints, quarts, and liters. (Chapters 7 and 8)

Grade 3
Tell time to the minute. Measure length, weight, mass, and capacity using miles, kilometers, ounces, gallons, and milliliters.

Grade 4
Tell time to the second. Measure length, weight, mass, and capacity using millimeter, ton, and fluid ounce. (Chapter 7)

Informal Assessment

Informal assessments provide day-to-day feedback. In conjunction with more formal assessments, they give a complete picture of conceptual development.

In the Student Book

What Do You Think?
student pages 139, 165
Students explain what they have learned.

Create Your Own
student pages 137, 149, 162A
Students create their own problems.

Journal Idea
student pages 129, 139, 143, 165
Students communicate mathematically.

Self-Check
student pages 169, 170
Students evaluate their own work.

In the Teacher Guide

Baseline Assessment
teacher page 126
Helps you assess prior knowledge

Ongoing Assessment

ASSESS UNDERSTANDING
Helps you assess students' understanding

WRAP-UP
Helps you monitor students' progress

JOURNAL IDEA
teacher pages 127, 129, 131, 135, 137, 139, 143, 165
Helps you assess students' communication of math ideas

Portfolio Ideas

Portfolio opportunities appear on Student Book pages 165 and 170, and Teacher Guide pages 151A–B, 165, and 170.

Other items that you may wish to include in your student portfolios are:

- **Completed Chapter Projects**
- **Journal Entries**
- **CD-ROM and Internet Activities**
- **Informal Observations and Interview Activities**

For further suggestions for organizing and using portfolios, see *Assessment Guide,* pages 50–54.

Formal Assessment

Formal assessment can occur before and after the chapter, as well as at natural breaking points in the chapter.

In the Student Book

Checkpoints
student pages 138–139, 164–165
Use for assessing progress as students work through the chapter.

Chapter Test
student page 169

Performance Assessment
student page 170
The Performance Assessment helps you evaluate the skills and concepts developed in Chapter 4 through hands-on activities.

 CD-ROM Test Generator

This software allows you to customize your own chapter test. Formats include:

- **Multiple Choice**
- **Free Response**
- **Standardized Test**

Assessment Guide

You may choose among the following pages in the *Assessment Guide*.

Pretest Options
- **Free Response,** pages 91–92
- **Multiple Choice,** pages 93–94

Posttest Options
- **Free Response,** pages 95–96
- **Multiple Choice,** pages 97–98

Interview Activity
page 38

Long-Answer Question
page 9

Correlation to Standardized Tests

Learning Objectives	ITBS K/M	CTBS/5 (Terra Nova)	SAT9	MAT7	CAT5	*Pre/Post-Test Items	Lesson Pages
4A Tell and use time, including the calendar	**MC:** 9	46	**PS:** 36	**CPS:** 14, 15	**MC:** 16	1–3, 7–8	128–131 136–137
4B Estimate time; determine elapsed time		13, 49	**PS:** 36			4–6	132–133
4C Estimate, measure, and convert U.S. customary units of length, capacity, weight, and temperature	**MC:** 5 **ME:** 12, 13, 17	30, 34, 39, 44	**PS:** 32–34, 37–39	**CPS:** 13, 16, 17, 26	**MC:** 4, 22, 31, 43	9–13	140–149
4D Estimate, measure, and convert metric units of length, capacity, mass, and temperature						14–17	152–161
4E Analyze and solve problems using skills and strategies	**PS:** 18–24 **ME:** 11–13, 17	34, 46	**PS:** 44–46	**CPS:** 33–40 **P:** 1–12	**CPS:** 16–19, 40	18–20	134–135 150–151 162–162A 163–163A

MC = Math Concepts, **COM** = Math Computation, **PS** = Problem Solving, **P** = Procedures, **CPS** = Math Concepts & Problem Solving, **ME** = Math Estimation, **MDI** = Math Data Interpretation, **PB** = Math Problems

*Pretests and Posttests are found in the *Assessment Guide*.

Chapter 4

Linking Technology

Develop and Reinforce Concepts

MathProcessor™

CD-ROM Activities use MathProcessor™ Tools to help build critical thinking skills and develop problem-solving strategies.

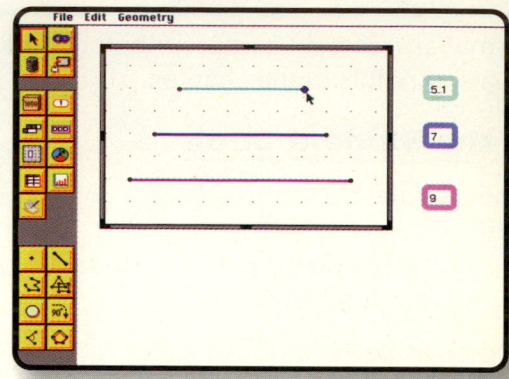

Lesson	Tools	Skill
5	Spreadsheet	Students use a Spreadsheet to organize data.
6	Frames Number spaces	Students convert linear measures.
11	Geometry Number spaces	Students use Geometry Tools to draw and measure various line segments.

Review and Practice Skills

Math Blaster® 1

This **CD-ROM** program provides exercises and activities to practice basic math facts and develop mastery of mathematical operations. The chart below lists specific lessons where activities and references can be found.

Lesson	Activity	Subject/Level
1	Begin Short Mission	Subtraction—Level 3: differences 8–14. Save Mission before exiting.
9	Continue Short Mission	Subtraction—Level 3: Restore Mission. Differences 8–14. Save Mission before exiting.
14	Complete Short Mission	Subtraction—Level 3: Restore Mission. Differences 8–14. Save results.

Extend and Enrich

Internet

Students can use real data in lesson-related math activities.
Teachers can find activities and resources for Lessons 5, 9, and 14.
Parents can find home connections to help reinforce concepts.

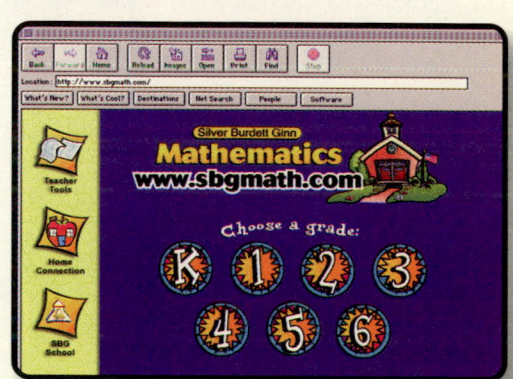

Visit our Web site at:

www.sbgmath.com

Making Connections

Literature

For the Chapter Activity

Find this book in your local or school library. Use it with the Math & Literature activity on page 153.

- **Inch by Inch**
  by Leo Lionni
  Astor-Honor, 1960

Additional Resource

This book, found in your local or school library, can be used to build math concepts.

- **The Young Gymnast**
  by Joan Jackman
  Dorling Kindersley, 1995

Home-School

Family Letter With Activity
Home-School Connection Booklet

The Family Letter for Chapter 4 introduces the skills of telling time and reading a calendar. Family activities suggest looking for opportunities for children to tell time using both digital and analog clocks, writing an evening schedule, and making a calendar to display at home.

Study Buddies
Home-School Connection Booklet

Study Buddies pages provide reinforcement activities for students to work on with a partner.

- Study Buddies 4A provides practice counting ahead to find elapsed time.
- Study Buddies 4B helps students understand and estimate capacity using milliliters and liters.

Math Backpack
Take-Home Activities

Math Backpack activities provide a link between the classroom and the home. Activity Cards 1–6 can be used with this chapter. Parents and students alike will enjoy using these laminated cards and accompanying manipulatives.

Cross-Curricular Integration

Technology

- Use the Internet to explore calendars, p. 137.
- Use the Internet to find out about weather around the world, p. 149.
- Use the Internet to compare temperatures of different cities, p. 161.

Health & Fitness

- Read about a track-and-field coach, p. 126.
- Find out how much water you should drink each day, p. 145.
- Compare the weights of different sports equipment, p. 147.

Social Studies

- Read about an 18th-century clockmaker, p. 129.
- Find out how ancient Egyptians kept track of time, p. 131.

Science

- Find out at what temperatures water boils and freezes, p. 148.

Chapter 4 Time and Measurement

Theme: SPORTS AND FITNESS

Chapter Overview

In this chapter students will tell, use, and estimate time and use standard and metric units to measure distance, weight, capacity, and temperature.

Activating Prior Knowledge

Discuss with students what they already know about time and measurement. Record responses on the chalkboard.

Baseline Assessment

Ask questions such as:

- **Why is it important to be able to tell time?** *(Possible response: So you won't be late for school.)*

- **What are some things that are important to measure?** *(Possible responses: Medicine; the distance in a race; fruit sold by weight at the market)*

Save student responses for use with the **Ongoing Assessment** section in the chapter Checkpoints on pages 139 and 165.

Chapter 4 Time and Measurement

Chapter Theme: SPORTS and FITNESS

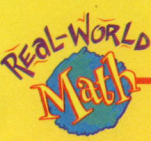
Real-World Math

·················Real Facts·················

Walking and running are great exercise! Dr. Kenneth H. Cooper is an expert in kid fitness. He made this exercise program for 8 and 9 year olds.

Walking/Jogging Program (8–9 years)			
Week	Activity	Distance in Miles	Times per Week
1	walk	1	3
2	walk	$1\frac{1}{2}$	3
3	walk	2	3
4	fast walk	$1\frac{1}{2}$	4
5	fast walk or jog	$1\frac{1}{2}$	4
6	fast walk or jog	$1\frac{1}{2}$	4
7	jog	$1\frac{1}{2}$	4
8	jog	2	4

- Suppose you followed the exercise program. How many miles would you walk the third week? **6 miles**

- Would you go more miles during Week 3 or Week 8? Explain your answer. **Week 8; in Week 3 you would go 6 miles in all, in Week 8 you would go 8 miles in all.**

················Real People·················

Meet Peggy Chee-Romero. She teaches math at Santa Fe Indian School in New Mexico. She coaches track, too. Coaches like Peggy use time and measurement. They keep track of how their athletes are doing.

126

Chapter Project

Here is a project that will help your students learn more about measurement and graphing. Specific lessons are referenced to help you work on the project throughout the chapter.

Run a Relay Race

 SMALL GROUPS

Materials
► slips of paper
► paper bag
► old newspapers
► masking tape
► measuring tape
► construction paper or tagboard

Getting Started

Tell students that they are going to plan and hold a relay race. Remind them that in a relay race, each team member runs only a part of the whole distance. Use a random method to make teams of four students. Have each team meet to choose a team name.

...........Real Facts...........

- The Cooper Institute for Aerobics Research in Dallas, Texas, estimates that about 1 out of 3 school-age children do not engage in enough physical activity.

- An exercise program should begin with a warm-up (2 to 5 minutes of light activity such as stretching) and end with a cool-down (a slow 5-minute walk, followed by gentle stretches).

Using the Data

As students review the table on page 126, make sure they understand how to read *across* the columns. Some questions you may wish to ask include:

- How does the distance in miles change between Week 1 and Week 8? *(Week 1: 1 mile per day, 3 miles per week. Week 8: 2 miles per day, 8 miles per week.)*

- During which week do you walk or jog a total of $4\frac{1}{2}$ miles? *(Week 2)*

..........Real People..........

Peggy Chee-Romero has many responsibilities as a coach. She encourages athletes, shows them techniques, and makes suggestions for improvement. Ask students to discuss how a coach might use math in his or her work.

Project Links

▶ **Lesson 3** Have teams practice for the relay race, using a stopwatch or a watch with a second hand to **time** their runners.

▶ **Lesson 6** Choose a place for the race. Students should decide how far each runner will run, then **measure** and mark the course.

▶ **Lesson 11** Explain how the baton is passed. Then have teams use items such as rolled newspapers to make batons.

Project Wrap-up

Have the teams race, one team at a time. Invite four students to work as timers, and assign one runner to each timer. Have the team **record** its times. Then help students **calculate** the team time by adding the individual times of the four runners. Conclude by having the class make a **bar graph** to record and compare the race times of each team.

Portfolio Students may wish to include their project work in their portfolios.

Building Vocabulary

These key words will be found in this chapter.

calendar	minutes	hours
inch (in.)	foot (ft)	yard (yd)
mile (mi)	capacity	cup (c)
pint (pt)	quart (qt)	gallon (gal)
ounce (oz)	pound (lb)	centimeter
decimeter	meter	kilometer
liter	milliliter	
kilogram	degrees Celsius (°C)	
gram	degrees Fahrenheit (°F)	

Journal Idea You may wish to have students use each vocabulary term in their journals at the beginning and end of the chapter.

Lesson Organizer

Objective: Tell time to the hour, quarter hour, and half hour.

- **NCTM Standards:** 1, 3, 4, 8, 10, 12
- **Lesson Resources:**
  Chapter File Folder
    Practice, Reteach, Extend 4-1
    Teaching Tools 24, 25, 26
  Daily Review 4-1
  Transparency 37

Problem of the Day   4-1

A nickel wrapper holds 40 nickels. A dime wrapper holds 50 dimes. What's the total if you have one full wrapper of each?
$7.00

Math Minute

Add.

5 + 5 *(10)*	30 + 15 *(45)*
5 + 5 + 5 *(15)*	45 + 15 *(60)*
15 + 15 *(30)*	30 + 30 *(60)*

1
Telling Time to the Quarter Hour

Right on Time!

You can tell time to the hour, quarter hour, and half hour.

Learning About It

The community center has sports activities after school. Look at the schedule. Here's how the times look on a clock.

Schedule

Lesson	Time
Soccer	4:00
Tennis	4:15
Karate	4:30
Volleyball	4:45

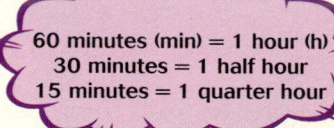

Soccer	Tennis	Karate	Volleyball
4:00	**4:15**	**4:30**	**4:45**
• 4:00	• 4:15	• 4:30	• 4:45
• four o'clock	• four-fifteen	• four-thirty	• four forty-five
	• quarter past four	• half past four	• quarter to five
	• fifteen minutes after four	• thirty minutes after four	• forty-five minutes after four

The short hand, or hour hand, on a clock shows hours. It takes 60 minutes, or 1 hour, for the hour hand to move from one number to the next number.

The long hand, or minute hand, shows minutes. It takes 5 minutes for the minute hand to move from one number to the next number.

A day has 24 hours. The hours from 12 midnight to 12 noon are A.M. The hours from 12 noon until 12 midnight are P.M.

> 60 minutes (min) = 1 hour (h)
> 30 minutes = 1 half hour
> 15 minutes = 1 quarter hour

Think and Discuss Where is the hour hand when the clock shows half past five?
Halfway between the 5 and the 6

128

---

1 Introduce

Cooperative Activity
KINESTHETIC

SMALL GROUPS   10–15 MINUTES

Materials: paper plates, metal brads, poster-board clock hands, crayons

1. Students fold paper plates into four equal sections, then unfold the plates.
2. Students use the creases as guides to label the plate with 12, 3, 6, and 9.
3. Students write the missing clock numbers. After attaching hands to the clock, students show and discuss times.

2 Teach   Pages 128–129

On the board, draw two clocks. Divide one clock into two equal sections. Divide the other into four equal sections. Guide students to understand that each of the two sections is one-half of an hour, and each of the four sections is one-quarter of an hour.

Critical Thinking   ANALYSIS

After Think and Discuss, ask: **How does the position of the minute hand differ at quarter to the hour from quarter past the hour?** *(If the minute hand is on the 9, it is quarter to the hour and if it is on the 3, it is quarter past the hour.)*

Assess Understanding

After Try It Out, ask: **In Exercises 5–7, how do you know which time is morning and which is night?** *(A.M. stands for morning hours; P.M. stands for night hours.)*

USING TECHNOLOGY

Math Blaster® 1, Short Mission
Subtraction: Level 3
Differences 8–14
Save Mission before exiting.

Try It Out

Write the correct time.

1.
10:00

2.
12:30

3.
8:45

4.
3:15

Choose the time when each activity is more likely to happen.

5. going to school
  a. 8 A.M. **b.** 8 P.M. **a**

6. going to sleep
  a. 9 A.M. **b.** 9 P.M. **b**

7. eating dinner
  a. 6 A.M. **b.** 6 P.M. **b**

Practice

Write each time in two ways using words. **See Additional Answers, pages 166–167.**

8.

9.

10.
6:45

11.
8:30

Write each time using numbers.

12. quarter to ten **9:45**
13. thirty minutes after two **2:30**
14. seven-fifteen **7:15**
15. eight-forty **8:40**
16. three forty-five **3:45**
17. twelve-fifty **12:50**

Problem Solving

18. Suppose you arrive at soccer practice at 4:15. Practice starts at 4:00. Are you early or late? **Late**

19. The soccer game begins at 11:45. Is this time closer to 11:00 or 12:00? **12:00**

20. **Journal Idea** Write the time quarter to six in three other ways.
5:45; five forty-five; forty-five minutes after five

▲ **Social Studies Connection**
In 1753, an African American named Benjamin Banneker built a clock entirely of wood. The clock kept perfect time for over 50 years.

Review and Remember

Add or subtract.

21. 14 + 32
46
22. 243 − 115
128
23. 64 − 47
17
24. 437 + 287
724

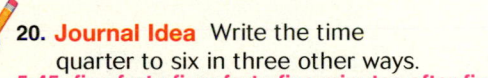
For Extra Practice, see Set A, page 166. **129**

---

3 Wrap-up

List two ways to describe the time when the hour hand is on 7 and the minute hand is on 3. *(7:15, or quarter past seven)*

Journal Idea Suggest that students write an additional time, such as quarter to ten in three other ways.

Common Error Alert

Watch for students who confuse quarter to the hour with quarter past the hour. Review the meaning of *to* and *past*.

Meeting Individual Needs

For Early Finishers

Students use paper-plate models to make clocks that show the times of daily school events. Students write how digital clocks would display each time.
KINESTHETIC

For Extra Help

Using model clocks, show a time such as 4:00. Ask students to tell you the time shown. Then have students show 4:15, 4:30, 4:45, and 5:00.
VISUAL/SPATIAL

Practice

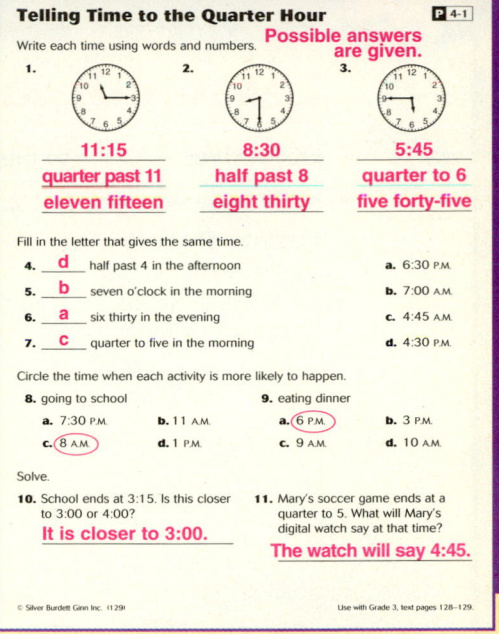

Reteach

Extend

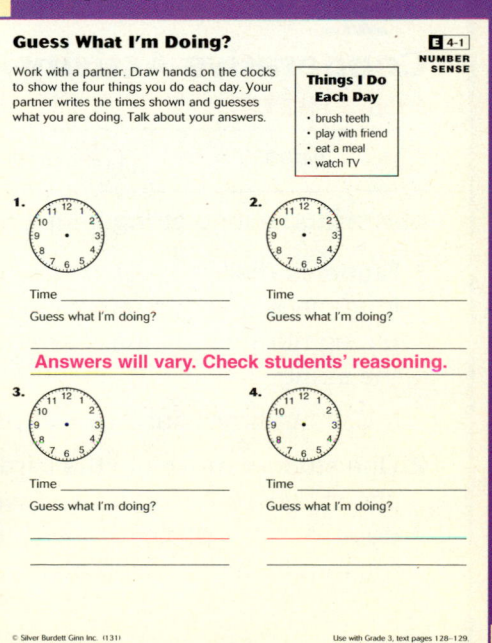

Lesson Organizer

Objective: Tell time to the minute.

- **NCTM Standards:** 1, 2, 3, 4, 8, 10
- **Lesson Resources:**
  Chapter File Folder
  Practice, Reteach, Extend 4-2
  Teaching Tools 24, 25
  Daily Review 4-2
  Transparency 37

Problem of the Day   4-2

You read for 2 hours. Then you stopped 45 minutes before dinner. You ate dinner at 6:30 P.M. What time did you start reading? **3:45 P.M.**

Math Minute

Add.

5 + 5 + 5 + 5 *(20)*	25 + 15 *(40)*
30 + 20 *(50)*	45 + 15 *(60)*
15 + 10 *(25)*	45 + 10 *(55)*

Every Minute Counts

You can use a clock to tell time to the minute.

Learning About It

The swim team started warm-up laps at 3 o'clock. They finished at five minutes after three. How does this look on a clock?

Start at 12. Count 5 minutes. Read this time as 3:05.

Kickboard practice started at 4 o'clock. It ended at seventeen minutes after four. How does this look on a clock?

Start at 12. Count 15 minutes by 5s. Then count 2 minutes more. Read this time as 4:17.

Think and Discuss How long does it take the minute hand to move once around the clock? How long does it take the hour hand to move once around the clock? **60 minutes; 12 hours**

Try It Out

Write each time using numbers.

1.	2.	3.	4.

5:50	**3:10**	**11:31**	**5:34**

130

---

1 Introduce

Cooperative Activity

KINESTHETIC

 PAIRS   10–15 MINUTES

Materials: a long string, index cards

1. Students make a clock by forming a long piece of string into a circle and taping numbered index cards onto the string.
   - Call out times such as half past ten.
2. One student moves to the card that shows where the hour hand would point, and the partner moves to where the minute hand would point.

2 Teach   Pages 130–131

Guide students to understand that each mark on the clock represents one minute.

- Ask: **Kickboard practice ended at 4:17. If practice had lasted four more minutes, what time would the clock show?** *(4:21)*

Critical Thinking   SYNTHESIS

After Think and Discuss, ask: **How many times does the hour hand move around the clock in one day?** *(Two)*

Assess Understanding

After Try It Out, ask: **How can you write the time four minutes past ten, using numbers?** *(10:04)*

CHALLENGE

Jean began swimming at 3:02. She swam until 3:15. She rested 15 minutes, then swam 15 more minutes before going home. What time did the clock show when she finished swimming? *(3:45)*

Practice

Write each time in two ways. See Additional Answers, pages 166–167.

5.  6.   7.  8.

9.  10.  11.  12.

13. one forty-three   14. three forty-six   15. five minutes to six

16. eleven-fourteen   17. nine-eleven   18. seven twenty-one

Problem Solving

19. It is 6 minutes after 10 in the morning. Write the time in numbers. Use P.M. or A.M. to show the time of day. **10:06 A.M.**

20. A sundial tells time by using a shadow made by sunlight shining on a stick. Why couldn't you use a sundial all the time? **Because the sun doesn't shine at night or when it is cloudy**

▲ **Social Studies Connection**
The ancient Egyptians used sundials to keep track of time.

21. Find the number of minutes in 1 day. First press ⑥ ⓪ for the number of minutes in 1 hour. Then press ✕ ② ④ to multiply the minutes by 24 hours. What does the display show? How could you find the number of minutes in 2 days? **1,440; multiply 1,440 minutes by 2 days or multiply 60 minutes by 48 hours = 2,880.**

Review and Remember

Round to the greatest place value.

22. 33 **30**	23. 48 **50**	24. $1.49 **$1.00**	25. 53 **50**	26. $6.89 **$7.00**
27. 861 **900**	28. 28 **30**	29. $9.12 **$9.00**	30. 656 **700**	31. $3.59 **$4.00**

For Extra Practice, see Set B, page 166. **131**

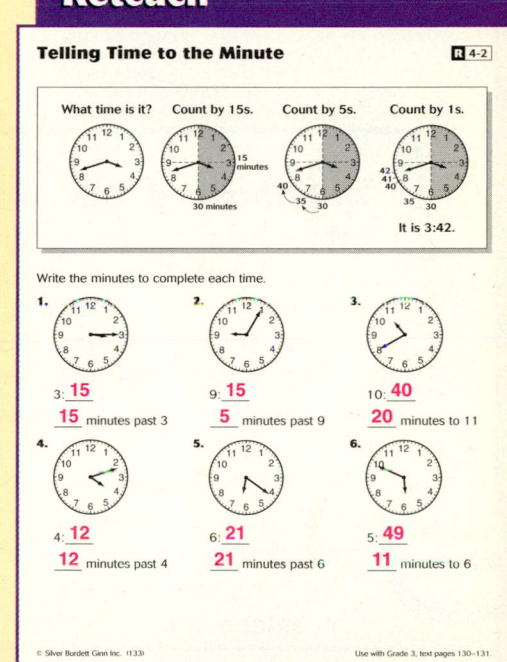
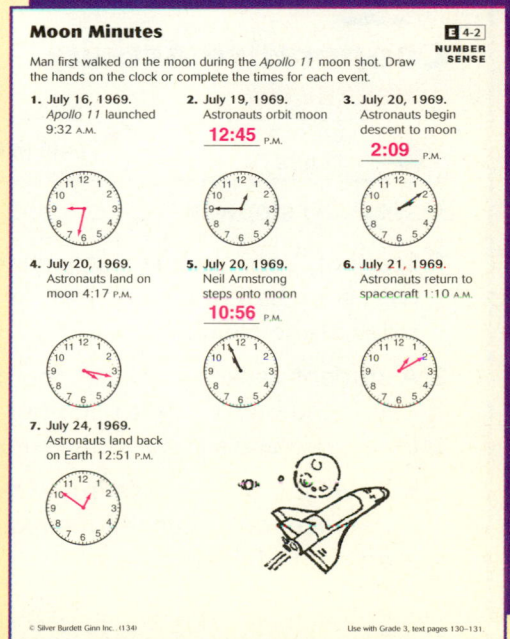
---

3 Wrap-up

📓 **Journal Idea** Keep track of your before- and after-school schedule. Record the times you wake up, leave for school, arrive home, do your homework, eat dinner, and go to sleep. Write the times, using words or numbers.

Common Error Alert

Watch for students who have difficulty counting the minute tick marks on a clock face. Have them use a piece of paper to cover each mark as they count it.

Meeting Individual Needs

For Early Finishers

Two students work together to create a class schedule of their school day. Have pairs compare the schedules with other students.
KINESTHETIC

Gifted and Talented

Say: **The big hand is on the 2 and the little hand is on the 7.** What time is it? *(10 minutes after 7)* Challenge students with other examples.
AUDITORY

Lesson Organizer

Objective: Find elapsed time.

- **NCTM Standards:** 1, 2, 3, 5, 8, 10, 13
- **Lesson Resources:**
  Chapter File Folder
    Practice, Reteach, Extend 4-3
    Teaching Tools 24, 25
  Daily Review 4-3
  Practice Workbook, p. 16
  Study Buddies 4A
  Transparency 37

Problem of the Day 4-3

Think about reading the time on a digital clock. Which 3-digit times show the digits in counting order (forward or backward)? Could you find at least four?
Sample answers: 2:34, 3:45, 6:54, 5:43

 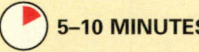

Math Minute

Write each time, using numbers.
quarter past eleven *(11:15)*
half past four *(4:30)*
five minutes to five *(4:55)*
seventeen after nine *(9:17)*

As Time Goes By

A clock can help you find out how much time has passed.

Learning About It

Little League baseball is popular all over the world. Suppose a game in Chinese Taipei starts at 2:00. It lasts two hours and forty-five minutes. When does it end?

 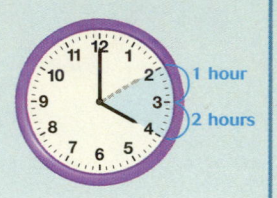 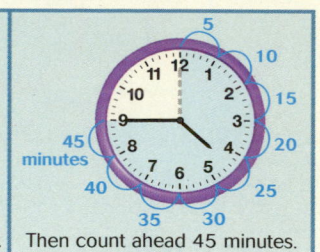

Start at 2:00.

Count ahead 2 hours to 4:00.

Then count ahead 45 minutes. The time is 4:45.

The game ends at 4:45.

The first inning of a game started at 11:05. If it ended at 11:27, how long did the inning last?

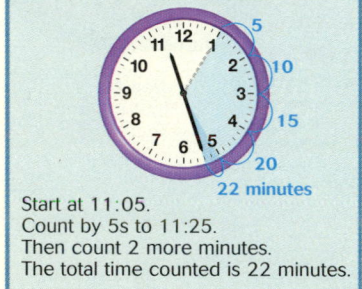 

Start at 11:05.
Count by 5s to 11:25.
Then count 2 more minutes.
The total time counted is 22 minutes.

▲ **Kid Connection** This Little League team from Chinese Taipei won the 1996 World Series Championship.

The inning lasted 22 minutes.

Think and Discuss You want to be at a game at 3:30. It takes 20 minutes to get there. When should you leave? **3:10**

 132

---

1 Introduce

Cooperative Activity
KINESTHETIC

WHOLE CLASS   **5–10 MINUTES**

Materials: stopwatch, index card

1. Students race against a stopwatch. Start with each half of the class on opposite sides of the room.
2. A student walks across the room and hands the index card to another student until everyone's crossed the room.
   - Have students first estimate how long the race took, then tell the exact amount of time it took.

2 Teach   Pages 132–133

You might wish to use a demonstration clock to act out the elapsed time. Have students discuss what is going on in each section of the example for the Little League game.

- Ask: **If the game in Taipei had lasted another fifteen minutes, at what time would it have ended?** *(5:00)*

Critical Thinking   APPLICATION

After Think and Discuss, ask: **When should you arrive for a thirty-minute practice that ends at 12:15?** *(11:45)*

Assess Understanding

After Try It Out, ask: **How many minutes pass from 7:55 to 8:27?** *(32 minutes)*

CHALLENGE

Juan wakes up at 6:15 in the morning. His bus arrives at 7:00. If he takes 45 minutes to get dressed and 20 minutes to do morning chores, will he catch his bus on time? How many minutes late will he be? *(No; 20 minutes late)*

Try It Out

Write the time each clock will show in 5 minutes.

1.  **10:05**
2.  **10:40**
3.  **8:00**
4. **8:32**

5. Look at Exercises 1 and 2. How much time has passed from the first clock to the second clock?
35 minutes

Practice

Write the time each clock will show in 20 minutes.

6.  **1:20**
7. 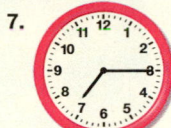 **7:35**
8.  **3:50**
9.  **7:27**

Look at each pair of times. Write how much time has passed.

10. Start 10:50 P.M.
    End 11:50 P.M.
    1 hour
11. Start 6:17 A.M.
    End 6:20 A.M.
    3 minutes
12. Start 7:35 A.M.
    End 8:00 A.M.
    25 minutes

Problem Solving

13. A ball game begins at 10:00 A.M. It lasts 2 hours and 30 minutes. When does it end?
    12:30 P.M.

14. **Analyze** The swimming pool is open from 9:00 A.M. to 11:30 A.M and from 1:00 P.M. to 5:00 P.M. each day. How long is the pool open each day?
    6 hours and 30 minutes

Review and Remember

Choose a Method Use paper and pencil or mental math to solve. Name your method.
Methods will vary.

15. 7 + 4 + 8 + 2 **21**
16. 246 + 110 **356**
17. 49 − 38 **11**
18. 77 − 22 **55**
19. 18 + 9 + 3 **30**
20. 66 − 4 **62**
21. 50 − 26 **24**
22. 164 − 27 **137**
23. 119 + 83 **202**

For Extra Practice, see Set C, page 166. **133**

---

3 Wrap-up

How can you tell how much time passed between 6:15 and 6:37? *(Start at 6:15; count by 5s to 6:35; count 2 more minutes; 22 minutes.)*

Common Error Alert

Watch for students who miscount when calculating elapsed time because they begin counting from 12 rather than from the starting time.

Meeting Individual Needs

For Early Finishers

Ask: **How would you find the amount of time that passes between 2:15 and 2:43?** *(Count by 5s to 2:40; then count 3 more minutes.)*
LINGUISTIC

Acquiring English Proficiency

Write the words *before, to, after,* and *past* on index cards. One student chooses a card and states a time, using the word.
AUDITORY

 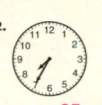 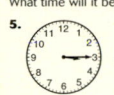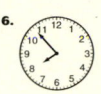
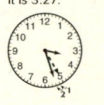

Lesson Organizer

Objective: Understand the meaning of exact and estimated numbers in problems.

- **NCTM Standards:** 1, 3, 4, 7
- **Lesson Resources:**
  Chapter File Folder
      Practice, Reteach, Extend 4-4
  Daily Review 4-4

Problem of the Day 4-4

Al phoned home at 4:30 P.M. "I'll be home in an hour and a half," he said. If Al arrived home 10 minutes later than he planned, what time was it? **6:10 P.M.**

Math Minute

Estimate the minutes.

22 minutes + 12 minutes *(30)*
18 minutes + 56 minutes *(80)*
14 minutes + 35 minutes *(50)*
55 minutes + 14 minutes *(70)*

Developing Skills for Problem Solving

In this lesson you'll first read for understanding and then focus on whether numbers are exact numbers or estimates.

READ FOR UNDERSTANDING

In an exciting soccer game yesterday the Eagles beat the Hornets 8 goals to 5. Over 120 fans watched the game, which lasted about 90 minutes. After the game, Coach Ramos and 4 parents treated the winning team to ice cream.

1. How many goals did the Eagles score? **8 goals**
2. How long did the game last? **About 90 minutes**
3. Who treated the players to ice cream? **Coach Ramos and 4 parents**

THINK AND DISCUSS

MATH FOCUS

Exact Numbers or Estimates Estimates are not exact numbers. Words like *about*, *over*, *less than*, and *almost* can tell you that numbers are estimated, not exact.

Reread the paragraph at the top of the page.

4. Can you tell exactly how many fans there were? Why or why not? **No; the article says there were over 120 fans, so all you know is that the number of fans was more than 120.**
5. How many people treated the winning team to ice cream? Is your answer an exact number or an estimate? Explain how you know. **5 people; Exact number; The article states a specific amount, not about 5 people.**
6. When could a number like 30 be used to show an exact amount? When could it be used to show an estimated amount? **Answers will vary. A possible answer is that 30 could be the exact number of students in a class; 30 could be about how many minutes are spent playing a kickball game.**

134

---

1 Introduce

Whole Class Activity

VISUAL

WHOLE CLASS   5–10 MINUTES

Materials: clock face with hands

1. On the overhead, show students 2:15.
2. Have students write an estimate of what the time will be in 26 minutes. *(2:45)*
3. Have students use model clocks to show the exact time. *(2:41)*

   - Discuss: **When might you estimate time?** *(Sample answer: When you want to know about how much time you have before the bus arrives)*

2 Teach   Pages 134–135

Read for Understanding If students have difficulty with the reading comprehension questions (Questions 1–3), have them find the sentence in the paragraph that relates to each question. Then pair the information in the sentence with the question.

Think and Discuss As you discuss the Math Focus, have students use words such as *over, less than*, and *almost* to describe estimates of the number of books in their classroom.

After Question 5, ask: **If the article stated that more than 4 people treated the winning team to ice cream, would that be an exact or estimated number? Explain.** *(Estimated number; more than indicates there are not exactly 4 people.)*

Critical Thinking ANALYSIS

After Think and Discuss, ask: **Do you think you use more estimated or exact numbers in your everyday activities? Give examples.** *(Estimated; I wake up at about 6:00 every day, but not exactly at 6:00; I drink about 3 glasses of milk a day.)*

Assess Understanding

Before Show What You Learned, ask: **How many students are in our class? Is your number exact or estimated?** *(Sample answer: There are exactly 25 students in the class; exact.)*

Show What You Learned

Answer each question. Give a reason for your choice.

Cara played in a soccer game for almost 15 minutes. Her team scored 2 goals in that time. Then a rainstorm stopped the game for over 30 minutes. About 25 fans left the game during the storm. Two of them returned when the rain stopped.

1 How long was the game stopped by rain?

a. Exactly 30 minutes

b. Less than 30 minutes

c. More than 30 minutes

2 Which of these numbers is *not* an estimate?

a. 15 minutes

b. 2 goals

c. 30 minutes

3 Which of these words tells you that 25 fans is an estimate?

a. game

b. about

c. left

One Eagles game that was played during a light rain, lasted for over 50 minutes. About 40 people watched the game. Only 8 people had umbrellas. The Eagles won 2 to 1.

4 How many people might have watched the game?

a. 42 people

b. 20 people

c. 73 people

5 How many people at the game had umbrellas?

a. 8 people

b. More than 8 people

c. Fewer than 8 people

6 **Explain** Is it correct to say that the Eagles played for almost 50 minutes? Why or why not? **No, they played for *over* 50 minutes, not *almost* 50 minutes.**

135

3 Wrap-up

Explain how you can tell if a number is estimated. *(Sample answer: Words like about, over, less than, and almost are hints that numbers are estimates.)*

 Journal Idea Write a sentence using an estimated number.

Common Error Alert

Watch for students who use a word and a phrase to give an estimate of a number. Example: "There are about hundreds of books in this classroom."

Meeting Individual Needs

For Early Finishers

Have students estimate the number of students in your school, assuming 25 in each class. Provide the exact numbers and check the estimates for accuracy.
LOGICAL/MATHEMATICAL

Manipulatives

Students use counters to show *about 8*, *less than 8*, *greater than 8*, and *exactly 8*. A partner checks for accuracy. Students switch roles, using 5.
VISUAL/SPATIAL

Lesson Organizer

Objective: Use a calendar to identify specific dates.

- **NCTM Standards:** 1, 3, 4, 13
- **Lesson Resources:**
  Chapter File Folder
    Practice, Reteach, Extend 4-5
    Teaching Tool 32
  Daily Review 4-5
  Transparency 20

Problem of the Day   4-5

How many times does the minute hand pass the 8 in 24 hours: 2 times, 4 times, or 24 times? **24 times**

 Math Minute

Add.

4 + 3 *(7)*	4 + 4 + 4 *(12)*
5 + 2 *(7)*	3 + 3 + 3 + 3 *(12)*
7 + 7 + 7 + 7 *(28)*	28 + 1 *(29)*

It's a Date

A calendar helps you know the date.

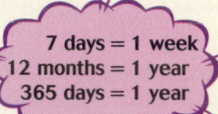

7 days = 1 week
12 months = 1 year
365 days = 1 year

Learning About It

A **calendar** shows the days, weeks, and months of the year in order. Look at the calendar below. A karate class starts on Saturday, June 12.

You can write that date in two ways.

June 12, 1999   6/12/99
↑   ↑   ↑   ↑   ↑   ↑
month day year   month day year

SUNDAY	MONDAY	TUESDAY	WEDNESDAY	THURSDAY	FRIDAY	SATURDAY
		1	2	3	4	5
6	7	8	9	10	11	12 Karate Class
13	14 Flag Day	15	16	17	18	19
20 Father's Day	21	22	23	24	25	26
27	28	29	30			

June

Now look at the months of the year at the left. June is the 6th month of the year. What is the 10th month? **October**

Think and Discuss What is today's date? What day of the week is it?
Answer will depend on date book used.

Try It Out

Use the calendar pages for Exercises 1–6. Write the name of the month.

1. 9th month **September**
2. 1st month **January**
3. 12th month **December**

Write the day of the week.

4. June 22 **Tuesday**
5. June 16 **Wednesday**
6. June 25 **Friday**

136

---

1 Introduce

Cooperative Activity

VISUAL

 PAIRS   ● **5–10 MINUTES**

Materials: 12 index cards, each labeled with a month and its number of days

1. Place the cards face down on a desk.
2. Students play a memory game by turning over two cards. If the cards have the same number of days, the cards are kept. If not, they are returned.

- Discuss: **Which months have the most days? Which one has the fewest?**
  (January, March, May, July, August, October, December; February)

2 Teach   Pages 136–137

Review ordinal numbers. Ask students to identify the 1st, 6th, and 12th months. *(January, June, December)*

- Ask: **What date is 2 weeks after June 12?** *(June 26)* **Explain how you know.** *(1 week = 7 days; 14 + 12 = 26)*
- Ask: **What date is 2 weeks after June 26?** *(July 10)*

Critical Thinking   APPLICATION

After Think and Discuss, ask: **What will the date be on Saturday of this week?** *(Sample answer: December 4, 1999)*

Assess Understanding

After Try It Out, ask: **What day is the first day of the third month of this year?** *(Sample answer: Monday)*

 **USING TECHNOLOGY**

MathProcessor™ Activities
See **Activities 19 and 20** in the MathProcessor™ Activity Cards.

Practice

Use the calendar below for Exercises 7–11.

7. What is honored throughout the month of February? **Black History**

8. What holiday do we celebrate on February 21? What day of the week is that? **Presidents' Day; Monday**

9. What is the date of the fourth Monday? **February 28**

10. What is the date of the bowling party? **February 26**

11. On what day is the basketball game? **Friday**

BLACK HISTORY MONTH!
February

SUNDAY	MONDAY	TUESDAY	WEDNESDAY	THURSDAY	FRIDAY	SATURDAY
		1	2	3	4	5
6	7	8	9	10	11 Basketball Game	12
13	14 Valentine's Day	15	16	17	18	19
20	21 Presidents' Day	22	23	24	25	26 Bowling Party
27	28	29				

▲ Every fourth year is called a **leap year**. A leap year has 366 days. The extra day in a leap year is February 29.

Name the month that is 4 months before each month.

12. May **January**
13. December **August**
14. July **March**
15. February **October**

16. April **December**
17. September **May**
18. October **June**
19. March **November**

Problem Solving

20. If today is Saturday, August 3, what will be the date in two weeks? **August 17**

21. **Analyze** What will the date be exactly 1 year after January 1, 1999? **January 1, 2000**

22. A basketball game will be held on October 12. Today is October 2. In how many days will the game be played? **10 days**

23. **Create Your Own** Make up two questions about the calendar above. Ask a classmate to answer your questions. **Check students' questions.**

INTERNET ACTIVITY
www.sbgmath.com

Review and Remember

Using Algebra Complete each pattern.

24. 383, 483, 583, ■, 783, ■
683 883

25. 625, 525, 425, ■, 225, ■
325 125

26. 49, 149, 249, ■, ■, ■
349 449 549

27. 382, 482, ■, ■, 782, ■
582 682 882

28. 921, 821, 721, ■, ■, 421
621 521

29. 704, 604, ■, ■, ■, 204
504 404 304

For Extra Practice, see Set D, page 166. **137**

Internet Activity

www.sbgmath.com

Students perform an on-line calendar activity.

Using Algebra

In Exercises 24–29, students use **patterns** to complete number sentences.

Practice

Using a Calendar   P 4-5

Use the calendar to answer the questions.

1998	MAY				1998	
SUN	MON	TUE	WED	THU	FRI	SAT
					1	2
3	4	5 Cinco de Mayo	6	7	8	9
10 Mother's Day	11	12	13	14	15	16
17	18	19	20	21	22	23
24	25 Memorial Day	26	27	28	29	30
31						

1. What holiday is on May 5? What day of the week is that?
Cinco de Mayo; Tuesday

2. What is the date of the second Tuesday?
May 12th

3. On what day and date is Memorial Day?
Monday, May 25th

4. How many Fridays are in May this year?
5

Solve.

5. Ms. Russell's class is in a play on March 22. Today is March 13. In how many days is the play?
9 days

6. If today is Tuesday, October 23, what was the date two weeks ago?
Tuesday, October 9

7. What is the date after Sunday, May 31, 1998?
Monday, June 1, 1998

8. **Make Your Own** question for the answer: Wednesday, May 27, 1998.
Questions will vary.

© Silver Burdett Ginn Inc. (141)   Use with Grade 3, text pages 136–137.

Reteach

Using a Calendar   R 4-5

A calendar shows the days and dates for a year. A year has 12 months. A month is made up of days and weeks.

1998	NOVEMBER				1998	
SUN	MON	TUE	WED	THU	FRI	SAT
1	2	3	4	5	6	7
8	9	10	11	12	13	14
15	16	17	18	19	20	21
22	23	24	25	26 Thanksgiving Day	27	28
29	30					

one day →   7 days = 1 week →

The first day of November in 1998 falls on a Sunday. The date is November 1, 1998.

Use the November 1998 calendar. Write your answer.

1. What day is November 11?
Wednesday

2. What is the date of the first Saturday?
November 7

3. What is the date of the third Monday?
November 16

4. What day is the second day in November?
Monday

5. Thanksgiving falls on what date?
November 26

6. What is the 19th of November?
Thursday

© Silver Burdett Ginn Inc. (142)   Use with Grade 3, text pages 136–137.

Extend

Date Book Mix-up   E 4-5   REASONING

The pages of Wesley's date book have gotten mixed up. Help him arrange them correctly. He has figured out the first page. Give the remaining pages a number from 2 to 6 to tell the proper order. If you have trouble remembering the order, cut out the pages and then arrange them in order on a piece of paper. Paste them down.

dentist–3:30	• library books due tomorrow • movies with Mark–3:00	spelling test TODAY!
⑥	②	④
ask Mark to go with me to tomorrow's movie	• library books due today • buy baseball mitt • study for tomorrow's spelling test	• baseball tryouts–4:00 • dentist tomorrow
①	③	⑤

© Silver Burdett Ginn Inc. (143)   Use with Grade 3, text pages 136–137.

---

3 Wrap-up

Write the 26th day of the 1st month of the year 1999 in two ways. (Sample answer: January 26, 1999; 1/26/99)

Journal Idea Make a calendar of your favorite month. Write a few sentences telling why you chose it.

Common Error Alert

Watch for students who do not realize that calendars change from year to year. Remind them to use the calendar for the correct year.

Meeting Individual Needs

For Early Finishers

Students create a calendar for the current month. Have them list all important events, such as national holidays and school events.
KINESTHETIC

For Extra Help

Students create a calendar page for the month of their birthday and circle the day in red crayon. Students write their birth date in two different ways.
KINESTHETIC

 # Checkpoint

Vocabulary Review

You may wish to review these terms before students begin the Checkpoint.

calendar A device that arranges time in days, weeks, months, and years.

minutes Units of time equal to 60 seconds.

hours Units of time equal to 60 minutes.

Using the Page

Purpose To review concepts and skills presented up to this point in Chapter 4.

- If necessary, discuss the directions and content of each section of the Checkpoint with the class.

- Page numbers associated with each group of items refer to the pages on which the skill or concept was presented. Those students needing review should turn to the appropriate lessons.

 # Checkpoint
Time

Complete. Use words from the Word Bank.

Word Bank
calendar
minutes
hours

1. There are 60 __?__ in 1 hour. **minutes**
2. A __?__ shows the months of a year. **calendar**
3. There are 24 __?__ in a day. **hours**

Write each time using numbers. (pages 128–131)

4. **11:15** 5. **5:51** 6. **4:46** 7. **8:10**

8. three twenty-four **3:24** 9. twelve-thirty **12:30** 10. six minutes to two **1:54**

Write the time each clock will show in 5 minutes. (pages 132–133)

11. **2:25** 12. 4:55 **5:00** 13. **3:20** 14. 11:32 **11:37**

Write how much time has passed. (pages 132–133)

15. 5:30 P.M. to 7:00 P.M. **1 hour and 30 minutes**
16. 10:25 A.M. to 11:15 A.M. **50 minutes**

Use the calendar at the right. (pages 136–137)

17. What date is the karate class? **November 27**
18. What is the date of the third Friday? **November 19**
19. What holiday is on November 25? **Thanksgiving**
20. What is the date 2 weeks from November 8? **November 22**
21. On what day of the week is November 1? **Monday**

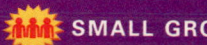

138

Reinforcement and Remediation   SMALL GROUPS

- Provide a model clock and index cards with the following times: 1:45, 2:15, 3:20, and 4:00. Have students place cards face down.

- Ask students to pick a card and arrange themselves in clockwise order according to the times on their cards.

- Have the first student use the clock to show the time on the card and the next student pre-

dict the elapsed minutes or hours between the time on the first card and the time on the second card. Ask students to move the clock hands to check the prediction and record the actual elapsed time.

- Have the next two students in the group repeat the activity.

Problem Solving

22. Suppose you get to a roller skating rink at 4:30 P.M. You leave at 6:00 P.M. How long were you at the rink? **1 hour and 30 minutes**

23. **What If?** Suppose you got to the roller rink at 4:45 P.M. How long would you have been at the rink? **1 hour and 15 minutes**

24. Suppose you go to the playground at 15 minutes after 2 in the afternoon. Write the time in numbers. **2:15 P.M.**

25. The school field day is May 18. Today is May 5. How many days are there until the field day? **13 days**

What do you think?

How much time do you spend in school each day?

How much time do you spend in school each week?

Answers will vary.

 Journal Idea
Write about what you usually do in school at these times: 9:30 A.M., 11:30 A.M., 2 P.M. **Check students' sentences.**

 *Critical Thinking Corner*

Number Sense

Estimating Time

Seconds are a very short period of time. There are 60 seconds in a minute. Estimate whether it will take *seconds, minutes,* or *hours* to complete each of these activities. Explain your answer. **Possible answers are given. Accept all reasonable answers and explanations.**

1.
Minutes

2.
Hours

3.
Seconds

4.
Hours

5.
Seconds

6.
Minutes

139

Ongoing Assessment

You may want to have students review their responses to the questions presented at the beginning of the chapter. Have students discuss what they have learned so far in this chapter that helps them answer the "What do you think?" question.

What do you think?

Accept reasonable responses. Answers will vary according to different school hours.

Journal Idea
Encourage students to describe how the activities during school vary from activities they do at 3:30 P.M., 5:30 P.M., and 8:00 P.M.

Critical Thinking Corner

Number Sense

- For each picture, encourage students to recall how long it takes them to complete the activity.

- Say: **Estimate whether it will take seconds, minutes, or hours for the following activities: reading a title of a book, going through the lunch line, attending three classes.** *(Seconds, minutes, hours)*

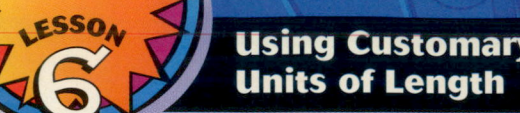
Lesson Organizer

Objective: Use customary units to measure length.

- **NCTM Standards:** 1, 2, 3, 5, 8, 10
- **Vocabulary:** inch, foot, yard, mile
- **Materials:** paper clips, ruler, yardstick or string
- **Lesson Resources:**
  Chapter File Folder
     Practice, Reteach, Extend 4-6
     Teaching Tool 32
  Daily Review 4-6
  Transparency 21

Problem of the Day   4-6

The day before yesterday, Marcia said, "It's five more days until my birthday!" The day after tomorrow is Sunday. On what day is Marcia's birthday? **Monday**

Math Minute

Add.

2 + 4 + 6 *(12)*	36 + 36 + 36 *(108)*
12 + 12 + 12 *(36)*	36 + 12 *(48)*
36 + 36 *(72)*	36 + 12 + 12 *(60)*

Inch by Inch

You can measure length and distance using different units of measurement.

Learning About It

Olympic gymnasts tumble and jump on a bar called a balance beam. How can you find the width of the beam?

You can use paper clips to measure the width of the beam below. Estimate how many clips you can put end to end on the line. Then check. **About 3 paper clips**

You can also use a ruler to measure the width of the beam in inches. An **inch** is a unit used to measure length or distance.

about 1 yard

about 1 foot

◄ In ancient times people used their arms and hands to measure some lengths. What problems might that cause?
The lengths of body parts vary from person to person, so measurements would vary.

Word Bank

inch (in.)
foot (ft)
yard (yd)
mile (mi)

What You Need

For each student:
paper clips
ruler
yardstick or string

◄— 4 inches —►

inches   1   2   3   4

Hint Line up the first mark on the ruler with the left end of the line.

The balance beam is 4 inches wide.

140

---

1 Introduce

Cooperative Activity

LOGICAL/MATHEMATICAL

PAIRS   10–15 MINUTES

Materials: ruler

1. One student stands against the board. The partner uses the ruler to mark the student's height.
2. Students switch roles.
3. The class compares the heights marked on the board.

- Ask: **How can you find out how tall other students are?** *(Sample answer: Use a yardstick to measure from the floor to the mark on the board.)*

2 Teach   Pages 140–143

Discuss units of length and distance. Have students provide examples of lengths measured in inches, feet, yards, and miles.

- Say: **Explain how to line up the ruler to measure.** *(Always line up the left end of the ruler with the left end of the object you are measuring.)*
- Ask: **Why can't you line up the right end of the ruler with the right end of the object?** *(Because you will read the wrong number at the opposite end of the ruler)*

Connecting Ideas

After students have discussed inches, they can make the connection to longer units of length like feet, yards, and miles. Have students discuss the equivalent measures. Then ask the following questions:

- **About how many feet long is your classroom?** *(Sample answer: 20 feet)*
- **About how many classrooms laid end to end would equal 1 mile? Use a calculator to find out.** *(Sample answer: 264)*

More Examples

Some things are not an exact number of inches long. You can measure them using the $\frac{1}{2}$-inch mark and the $\frac{1}{4}$-inch mark on the ruler.

A.

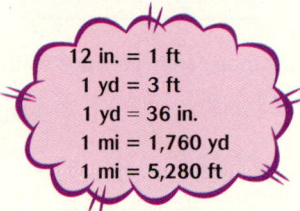

$2\frac{1}{2}$ in.

B.

$1\frac{1}{4}$ in.

Connecting Ideas

Inches are used to measure short lengths. Feet, yards, and miles are units used to measure longer lengths.

Look at the picture of the girl on the balance beam on page 140. On many people, the distance from the elbow to the end of the fingers is about 1 **foot**. The distance from the nose to the end of the fingers is about 1 **yard**. The distance a person can walk in 20 minutes is about 1 **mile**.

12 in. = 1 ft
1 yd = 3 ft
1 yd = 36 in.
1 mi = 1,760 yd
1 mi = 5,280 ft

- Find 3 objects that you think are each about 1 foot long.

- Find 3 objects that you think are each about 1 yard long.

- Check your estimates by measuring each object with a ruler or yardstick.
Check students' measurements.

Think and Discuss How do you decide whether it's best to measure an object using inches, feet, yards, or miles? **Small objects can best be measured by using small units, such as inches; larger objects by using larger units, such as miles; objects of medium size by using feet and yards.**

141

Critical Thinking   ANALYSIS

After Think and Discuss, ask: **What could you use to measure each of the following units: inch, foot, yard, mile?** *(Inches and feet, ruler; yards, yardstick; miles, car odometer)*

Using Technology
CD-ROM

MathProcessor™

Tools: Small Frames; Number spaces
Objective: Converting Linear Measures

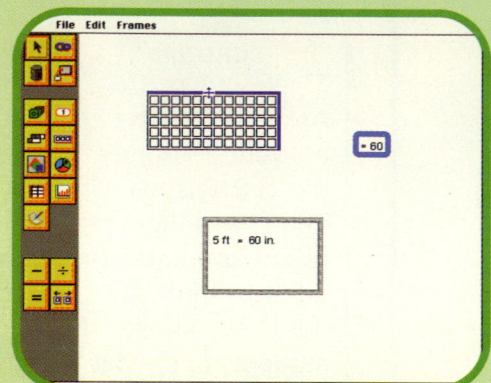

5 ft = ___?___ in.

- Link Small Frames to a Number space. Drag right to show 12 frames.
- Click the Number space. Click =.
- Click-drag the top border up with the cross-hatch cursor to show 5 rows.
- In a Writing space, show the number sentence: 5 ft = 60 in.

Additional Activities

See also **Activities 21 and 22** in the MathProcessor™ Activity Cards.

Try It Out

Using Estimation Estimate the length of each object to the nearest inch. Check your estimate with a ruler.

1.  **2 inches**

2.  **1 inch**

What unit would you use to measure each item?
Write *inch, foot, yard,* or *mile.*

3. length of a finger **Inch**

4. width of your classroom **Yard or foot**

5. height of a door **Foot**

6. length of the Mississippi River **Mile**

Practice

Estimate and measure to the nearest $\frac{1}{2}$ inch.

7.  **3 $\frac{1}{2}$ inches**

8. 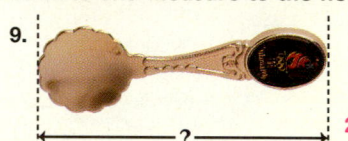 **1 $\frac{1}{2}$ inches**

Estimate and measure to the nearest $\frac{1}{4}$ inch.

9.  **2 $\frac{1}{4}$ inches**

10. **$\frac{3}{4}$ inch**

Use an inch ruler. Draw each length. **Check students' drawings for accuracy.**

11. 4 in.　　12. 6 in.　　13. $3\frac{1}{2}$ in.　　14. $4\frac{1}{4}$ in.　　15. $2\frac{3}{4}$ in.

Choose the best unit.

16. The length of a shoe:
　　10 inches or 10 feet
　　10 inches

17. The distance between two towns:
　　6 inches or 6 miles
　　6 miles

18. The height of a balance beam:
　　4 feet or 4 miles
　　4 feet

19. The length of a room:
　　14 inches or 14 feet
　　14 feet

142

2 Teach (continued)

Assess Understanding

After Try It Out, say: **Tell why it is best to use miles instead of inches to measure the distance from home to school.**
(Sample answer: Inches are used to measure short lengths; the number of inches would be too great.)

⭐ **GIFTED AND TALENTED**

Measuring Systems Have students design their own systems of measurement and use them to measure the tops of their desks. Ask if their systems would be helpful in measuring the height of the school, the distance from school to home, and the width of a hair.

Students may wish to use common items, such as paper clips, as a standard of measure for small objects.

31. Students' answers should demonstrate an understanding that inches are used to measure shorter distances and feet and yards are used to measure longer distances.

Complete.

20. 12 in. = ___ ft
1

21. 3 ft = ___ yd
1

22. 36 in. = ___ ft
3

23. 5,280 ft = ___ mi
1

24. 36 in. = ___ yd
1

25. 2 yd = ___ ft
6

26. 1 yd = ___ in.
36

27. 1,760 yd = ___ mi
1

28. 2 ft = ___ in.
24

Problem Solving

29. The Tumblers Club made a banner that measures 10 feet long. About how many yards long is the banner? **About 3 yards**

30. You Decide If you wanted to measure your bedroom, which units of measurement would you use? Explain your choice. **Answers and explanations will vary.**

31. Journal Idea Name two items that are measured in inches, two items that are measured in feet, and two items that are measured in yards. **See above.**

32. Zoë estimates a balance beam is about 17 feet long. Hy estimates it's about 6 yards long. The balance beam measures 16 feet. Whose estimate is closer? **Zoë's**

Review and Remember

Using Mental Math Find each sum or difference.

33. 60 + 30 **90**   **34.** 70 − 40 **30**   **35.** 90 − 10 **80**   **36.** 20 + 70 **90**

37. 35 + 20 **55**   **38.** 100 + 25 **125**   **39.** 42 − 20 **22**   **40.** 200 − 50 **150**

41. 45 − 30 **15**   **42.** 350 − 75 **275**   **43.** 30 + 25 **55**   **44.** 100 − 95 **5**

Money $ense

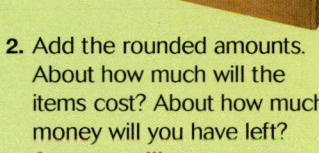

$4.11 $8.17 $9.99 $3.85

Get Ready To Play!
You have $25 to spend on 3 items shown at the right. Follow the steps below to estimate the total cost.

1. Choose the 3 items you want to buy and round each item's price to the nearest dollar. **See below.**

2. Add the rounded amounts. About how much will the items cost? About how much money will you have left? **Answers will vary.**

1. Answers will vary. The rounded prices are: football—$10; frisbee—$4; soccer ball—$8; kickball—$4.

For Extra Practice, see Set E, page 167. **143**

Money Sense

To extend the activity, ask students to find the exact total and change.

3 Wrap-up

Journal Idea Ask students to write an explanation of why some objects are usually measured in inches, others in feet, and others in miles.

Common Error Alert

Watch for students who think that a yard is intermediate in length between a foot and a mile. Point out that yards are much closer in length to feet than to miles.

Meeting Individual Needs

For Early Finishers

Students measure one hand and one foot in inches. They compare with two other students. Then they list measurements from least to greatest.
KINESTHETIC

Acquiring English Proficiency

Create index cards with the words *inch*, *foot*, *yard*, and *mile*. One student chooses a card and names an object that is best measured with that unit.
LINGUISTIC

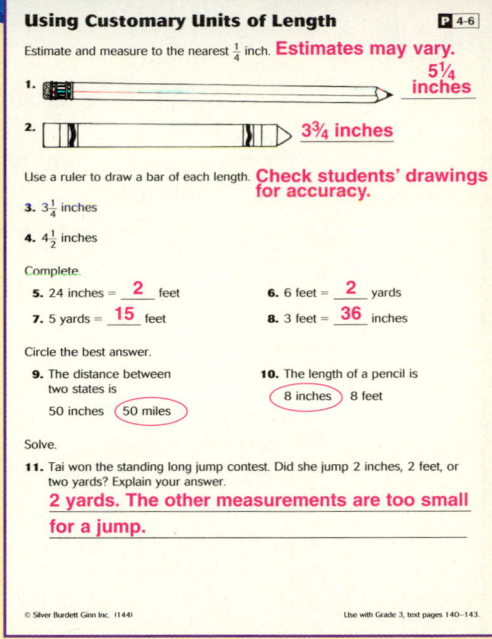

Practice

Using Customary Units of Length   P 4-6

Estimate and measure to the nearest $\frac{1}{4}$ inch. **Estimates may vary.**

1. **5¼ inches**

2. **3¾ inches**

Use a ruler to draw a bar of each length. **Check students' drawings for accuracy.**

3. $3\frac{1}{4}$ inches

4. $4\frac{1}{2}$ inches

Complete.

5. 24 inches = **2** feet   **6.** 6 feet = **2** yards

7. 5 yards = **15** feet   **8.** 3 feet = **36** inches

Circle the best answer.

9. The distance between two states is 50 inches **50 miles**

10. The length of a pencil is **8 inches** 8 feet

Solve.

11. Tai won the standing long jump contest. Did she jump 2 inches, 2 feet, or two yards? Explain your answer.
2 yards. The other measurements are too small for a jump.

© Silver Burdett Ginn Inc. (144)   Use with Grade 3, text pages 140–143.

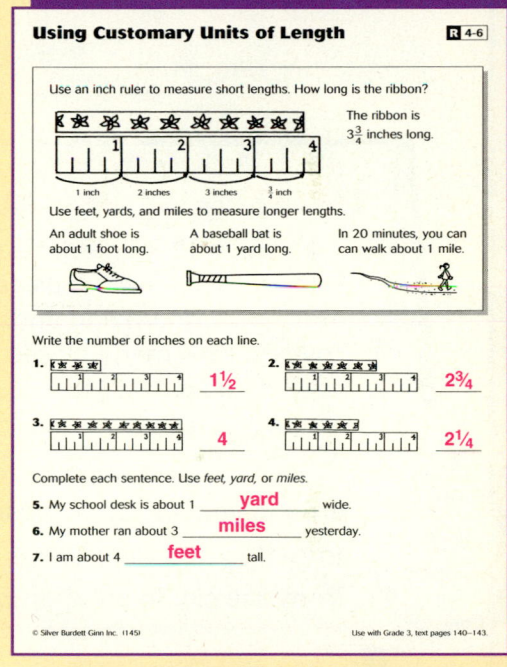

Reteach

Using Customary Units of Length   R 4-6

Use an inch ruler to measure short lengths. How long is the ribbon?

The ribbon is $3\frac{3}{4}$ inches long.

1 inch   2 inches   3 inches $\frac{3}{4}$ inch

Use feet, yards, and miles to measure longer lengths.

An adult shoe is about 1 foot long.
A baseball bat is about 1 yard long.
In 20 minutes, you can can walk about 1 mile.

Write the number of inches on each line.

1. **1½**   **2.** **2¾**

3. **4**   **4.** **2¼**

Complete each sentence. Use *feet*, *yard*, or *miles*.

5. My school desk is about 1 **yard** wide.

6. My mother ran about 3 **miles** yesterday.

7. I am about 4 **feet** tall.

© Silver Burdett Ginn Inc. (145)   Use with Grade 3, text pages 140–143.

Extend

Measure Mania   E 4-6
ESTIMATION

Work with a partner. Choose two different units below to measure the length of your classroom. Estimate first. Then measure.

Unit	Estimate	Actual Measure
inches		
your foot	**Estimates and measurements will vary.**	
feet		
your pace		
yards		

Use the information in your table to answer the questions.

1. What was the least reasonable unit of measure to use? Why?
Possible answer: Inches. The room was too large to measure using such a small unit.

2. Compare your actual measures with classmates. For which units do you have the same measurements? Why?
Feet or yards might be the same; they are large standard units of measure.

© Silver Burdett Ginn Inc. (146)   Use with Grade 3, text pages 140–143.

Lesson Organizer

Objective: Use customary units to measure capacity.

- **NCTM Standards:** 1, 2, 3, 5, 10, 13
- **Vocabulary:** capacity, cup, pint, quart, gallon
- **Materials:** measuring cup; pint, quart, and gallon containers; water; marker; tape
- **Lesson Resources:**
  Chapter File Folder
      Practice, Reteach, Extend 4-7
      Teaching Tool 45
  Daily Review 4-7
  Practice Workbook, p. 17

Problem of the Day   4-7

Jake has a 12-ft board. He wants to cut it into 3-ft, 2-ft, and 1-ft pieces. If he uses the whole board and ends up with six pieces, how many pieces of each length will he have? **2 pieces of each length**

Math Minute

What's the best unit of measure?

around your waist *(inches)*

from floor to ceiling *(feet)*

from one city to another *(miles)*

EXPLORE: Using Customary Capacity

Pour Some More

You can use different units to measure how much a container holds.

Learning About It

The amount of liquid a container holds is called its **capacity**.

Units used to measure capacity include **cups**, **pints**, **quarts**, and **gallons**.

Suppose you want to take 4 cups of water to a track meet. What size container will you take?

Work with a group.

Step 1 Collect empty pint, quart, and gallon containers. Label each container.

> **Word Bank**
> capacity
> cup (c)
> pint (pt)
> quart (qt)
> gallon (gal)

What You Need

For each group:
measuring cup
pint, quart, and
* gallon containers*
water
marker
tape

Step 2 Estimate how many cups of water you think each container will hold. Record your estimates on a chart like the one shown. **Estimates will vary.**

Size of container	Estimate of cups it holds	Actual cups it holds	Actual pints it holds	Actual quarts it holds	Actual gallons it holds
Cup	1	1	0	0	0
Pint	**Estimates**	**2**	**1**	**0**	**0**
Quart	**will**	**4**	**2**	**1**	**0**
Gallon	**vary.**	**16**	**8**	**4**	**1**

144

 **Introduce**

Cooperative Activity

KINESTHETIC

 SMALL GROUPS   ⏱ 5–10 MINUTES

Materials: water, 8-oz cups, quart containers

- Discuss: **Predict the number of cups needed to fill the container.** (Sample answer: four)

  One student fills the cup with water and pours it into the container until it is full.

- Ask: **How many cups did it take to fill the container?** *(four)*

Teach   Pages 144–145

Display an 8-oz juice box and pint, quart, half-gallon, and gallon milk cartons. Discuss the relative sizes of the containers.

After students have completed Step 5, ask:

- **How many cups equal 1 quart?** *(4)*
- **How many cups equal 1 pint?** *(2)*
- **How many pints equal 1 quart?** *(2)*
- **How many quarts equal 1 gallon?** *(4)*

Critical Thinking   SYNTHESIS

After Think and Discuss, ask: **If you have 2 jars with different shapes, how can you tell which has a greater capacity?** (Sample answer: Fill both with water and measure.)

Assess Understanding

Before Practice, say: **Order a quart, pint, gallon, and cup from greatest to least and from least to greatest.** (Gallon, quart, pint, cup; cup, pint, quart, gallon)

CHALLENGE

Sandra made two quarts of orange juice. Her friends drank one pint. How many pints are left? *(Three)*

Step 3 Use a measuring cup to fill a pint container. How many cups of water are needed to fill a pint? Record your results in your chart. **2 cups**

Step 4 Now find out how many cups are needed to fill a quart container. Then do the same for a gallon container. Record your results in your chart.
4 cups in a quart; 16 cups in a gallon

Step 5 Repeat the activity. This time find out how many pints, quarts, or gallons each container can hold. Record what you find. **Check students' charts.**

Think and Discuss Do containers need to have the same shape to hold the same amount? Explain why or why not. **No, a short, wide container could hold the same amount as a taller, narrower one.**

Practice

Choose the best estimate for each container.

1.
1 c or 1 gal **1 c**

2.
1 c or 1 qt **1 c**

3.
50 c or 50 gal **50 gal**

4.
2 pt or 2 gal **2 pt**

5.
1 c or 1 gal **1 gal**

6.
35 qt or 35 gal **35 gal**

7. How many cups are there in 1 quart? in 1 gallon? **4 cups in a quart; 16 cups in a gallon**

8. How many pints are there in 1 gallon? **8 pints**

9. **Health and Fitness Connection** You need to drink about 8 cups of water a day to help you stay healthy. How many quarts is that? **2 quarts**

10. **Analyze** Suppose you want to take 10 cups of water to a track meet. What is the least number of quart containers you should take? **3 quart containers**

145

---

3 Wrap-up

Explain which unit of capacity is best used to determine the amount of water held by an Olympic-sized swimming pool. *(Sample answer: Gallons are best because cups, pints, and quarts are too small and would be too numerous.)*

Common Error Alert

Watch for students who confuse quarts and gallons. Display quart- and gallon-sized containers to help them understand the difference.

Meeting Individual Needs

For Early Finishers

Ask: **If each student in our class drinks 1 cup of milk, how much milk is needed?** The answer is to be stated in the largest containers possible.
LOGICAL/MATHEMATICAL

For Extra Help

Students write words and draw pictures to make charts showing how many cups, pints, and quarts are in 1, 2, and 3 gallons.
LOGICAL/MATHEMATICAL

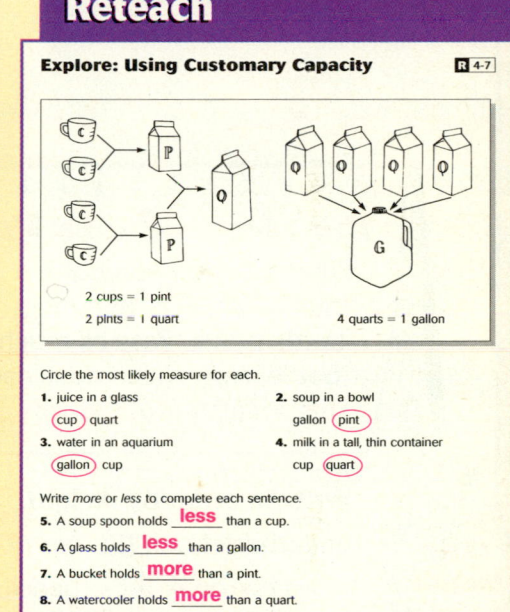
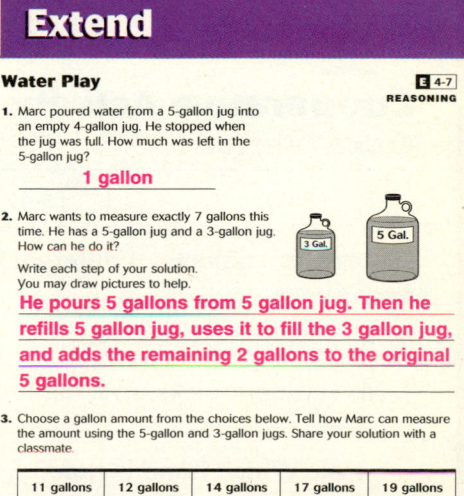

Lesson Organizer

Objective: Use customary units to measure weight.

- **NCTM Standards:** 1, 2, 3, 5, 10
- **Vocabulary:** ounce (oz), pound (lb)
- **Materials:** balance scale, 1-ounce weight (or 10 pennies), 1-pound weight (or 160 pennies)
- **Lesson Resources:**
  Chapter File Folder
    Practice, Reteach, Extend 4-8
  Daily Review 4-8

Problem of the Day   4-8

Ed has 2 shampoo bottles. Their total capacity is 18 ounces. One bottle holds twice as much as the other bottle. How much does each hold?
6 ounces and 12 ounces

 Math Minute

Write in order by weight.

paperback book *(3)*   car *(6)*

math textbook *(4)*   pencil *(2)*

feather *(1)*   refrigerator *(5)*

Bouncing Ounces

You can use customary units to estimate and measure weight.

Learning About It

Ounces and **pounds** are units used to measure weight.

Word Bank
ounce (oz)
pound (lb)

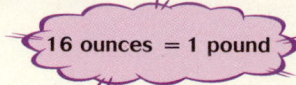 16 ounces = 1 pound

A football weighs about 1 pound.

A tennis ball weighs about 2 ounces.

- Find 3 objects that you think weigh about 1 pound each.
- Find 3 objects that you think weigh about 1 ounce each.
- Check your estimates by weighing each object.
  Check students' measurements.

What You Need

For each class:
  a balance scale
  1-ounce weight
    (or 10 pennies)
  1-pound weight
    (or 160 pennies)

Think and Discuss Which unit would you use to weigh small objects? large objects? Explain why.
Students should realize that small objects are often measured in ounces and large objects are often measured in pounds. However, this is not always the case since small objects can be heavy and large objects can be light.

Try It Out

Choose a unit to measure each item. Write *ounces* or *pounds*.

1. swimsuit
   Ounces
2. jump rope
   Ounces
3. bicycle
   Pounds
4. baseball cap
   Ounces
5. golf ball
   Ounces
6. bowling ball
   Pounds
7. rowboat
   Pounds
8. swimming goggles
   Ounces

Choose the best estimate.

9.
2 lb or 2 oz
2 lb

10.
1 lb or 1 oz
1 lb

11.
8 lb or 8 oz
8 oz

12.
3 oz or 3 lb
3 oz

---

1 Introduce

Cooperative Activity
KINESTHETIC

PAIRS   5–10 MINUTES

Materials: objects of different weights, paper bags

Place each object in a separate paper bag.

1. One student picks up a bag in each hand.
   - Ask: **Which hand is holding the heavier object?**
2. Repeat for each student, using different objects.

2 Teach   Pages 146–147

Make sure students understand how to use the balance scale and weights.

- Ask: **How could you check whether an object weighs more than 2 pounds?** *(Find something that weighs 1 pound and use it with the 1-pound weight.)*

Critical Thinking   ANALYSIS

After Think and Discuss, ask: **Do all objects that weigh 1 pound share the same size or shape? Give an example.** *(Sample answer: No; a pound of margarine and a pound of grapes weigh the same but have different shapes.)*

Assess Understanding

After Try It Out, ask: **What unit would you use to measure the weight of an apple? a watermelon?** *(Ounces; pounds)*

 CHALLENGE

If 160 pennies weigh one pound, how many pennies weigh 3 pounds? *(480)*

Practice

Use the chart for Exercises 13–16.

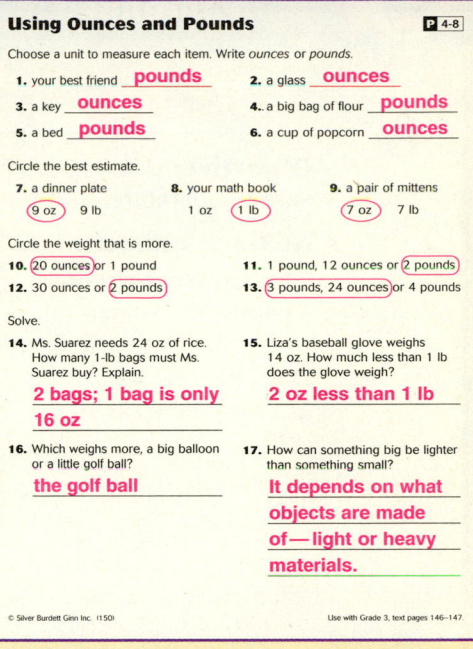

13. Which ball is the lightest? the heaviest?
Tennis ball; child's bowling ball

14. Which ball weighs about 1 pound?
Soccer ball

15. About how heavy is a basketball in pounds and ounces?
About 1 pound, 5 ounces

16. About how heavy is a soccer ball in pounds and ounces?
About 1 pound, 1 ounce

Ball	Weight
basketball	about 21 oz
soccer ball	about 17 oz
tennis ball	about 2 oz
child's bowling ball	about 6 lb

Write the weight that is more.

17. 13 oz or 1 lb
1 lb

18. 2 lb or 35 oz
35 oz

19. 2 lb or 18 oz
2 lb

20. 3 lb or 50 oz
50 oz

Problem Solving

Use the chart above for Problems 21 and 22.

21. Explain Suppose you put five basketballs in a bag. Would the bag weigh more than 5 pounds? How do you know? **See below.**

22. What If? Suppose you put three tennis balls and a soccer ball in the bag with the basketballs. Now how much would the bag weigh?
128 ounces or 8 pounds

23. A badminton racket weighs about 4 ounces. A tennis racket weighs about 12 ounces. How much heavier is the tennis racket?
About 8 ounces

24. Analyze Suppose you have a plastic bag of tennis balls that weighs 1 pound. About how many tennis balls are in the bag?
About 8 tennis balls

Review and Remember

Write the amount.

25.
$2.53

26.
$5.39

27.
$1.85

28.
$6.75

21. Yes; 1 basketball weighs more than 1 pound so 5 basketballs would weigh more than 5 pounds.

For Extra Practice, see Set F, page 167. **147**

---

3 Wrap-up

How many ounces are in a pound? *(16)*
Which balls listed at the top of page 147 weigh more than a pound? *(Basketball, soccer ball, child's bowling ball)*

Common Error Alert

Watch for students who make poor estimates of an object's weight because they are not familiar with the actual weight of an ounce and a pound.

Meeting Individual Needs

For Early Finishers

Write on the board *10 pennies = 1 oz.* Students use a balance scale to weigh objects found in the classroom that are less than, more than, or equal to 1 oz.
KINESTHETIC

Inclusion

Have a student put a different object in each hand. Ask the student to compare and estimate the weights of the objects.

KINESTHETIC

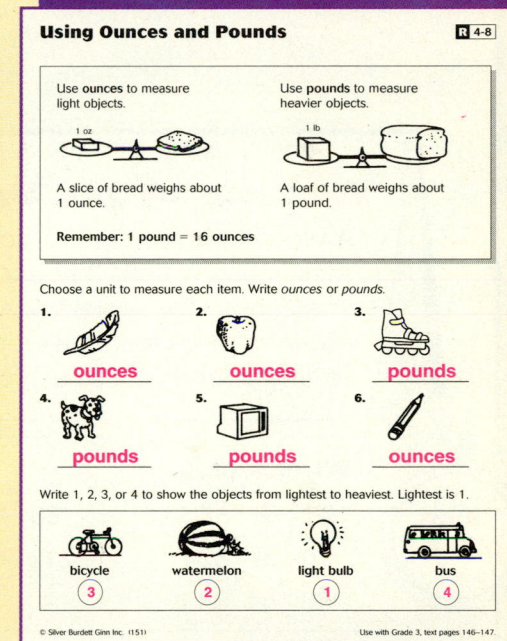
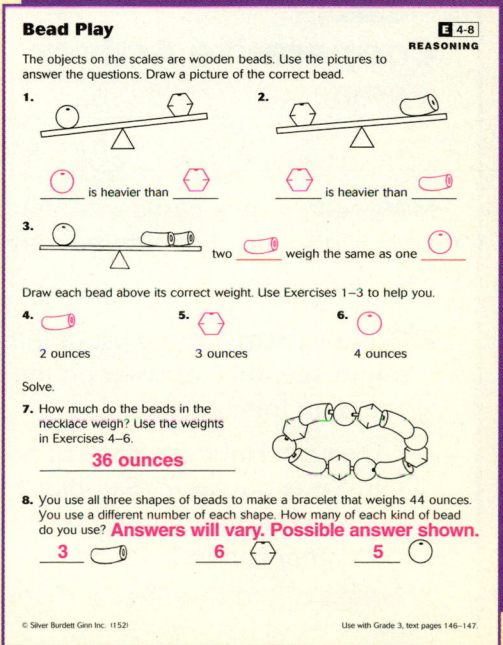
LESSON 8   147

Temperature in Degrees Fahrenheit

Lesson Organizer

Objective: Use degrees Fahrenheit to measure temperature.

- **NCTM Standards:** 1, 2, 3, 5, 10
- **Lesson Resources:**
  Chapter File Folder
  Practice, Reteach, Extend 4-9
  Daily Review 4-9
  Transparency 22

Problem of the Day   4-9

A wooden box weighs 7 pounds. A plastic box weighs 2 pounds less than a metal box. The metal box weighs 6 pounds more than the wooden box. How many pounds does each of them weigh?

 Math Minute

Write > or <.

105 ● 98 *(>)*		68 ● 80 *(<)*
0 ● 32 *(<)*		212 ● 100 *(>)*
80 ● 68 *(>)*		

Fun in the Sun

You can use a thermometer to estimate and measure temperature.

°F

- 130°
- 120° Very hot day 105°F
- 110°
- 100° Normal body temperature 98.6°F
- 90°   Warm day 80°F
- 80°
- 70°   Room temperature 68°F
- 60°
- 50°
- 40°
- 30°   Water freezes 32°F
- 20°
- 10°
- 0°   Very cold day 0°F
- -10°
- -20°

Read: seventy-five degrees Fahrenheit
Write: 75°F

148

Learning About It

To measure temperature, you can use **degrees Fahrenheit** (°F).

- The thermometer shows 75°F.
- Water boils at 212°F.
- Water freezes at 32°F.

Estimate the temperature for each of the activities shown. Use the thermometer to help you. **Accept reasonable estimates. Possible estimates are given below.**

75°F or higher   **30°F or lower**

Think and Discuss What kind of clothing would you wear if the temperature was 10°F? What if it was 89°F?

10°F: heavy coat, gloves, and hat; 89°F: shorts, T-shirts, and swimsuits

Try It Out

Write each temperature. Describe the temperature as *hot, cold, warm,* or *cool*.

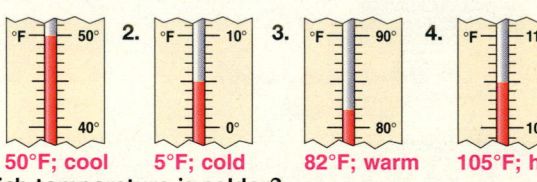

1. **50°F; cool**   2. **5°F; cold**   3. **82°F; warm**   4. **105°F; hot**

Which temperature is colder?

5. 20°F or 30°F **20°F**
6. 60°F or 56°F **56°F**
7. 15°F or 5°F **5°F**

---

1 Introduce

Cooperative Activity

LINGUISTIC

 SMALL GROUPS   5–10 MINUTES

Materials: index cards with the phrases *cold winter day, hot summer day*

1. Students choose an index card.
2. Groups brainstorm a list of things they might see, feel, or wear on the day indicated on their cards.

- Discuss: **How can you tell how cold or hot it is outside?** *(Sample answers: Use a thermometer; listen to a weather report.)*

Problem of the Day: See answer, page 167.

2 Teach   Pages 148–149

Discuss how to read the degree marks on the thermometer.

- Ask: **Which temperature is colder: 10°F or 10°F below zero?** *(10°F below zero is colder.)*

Critical Thinking   ANALYSIS

After Think and Discuss, say: **Suppose the weather forecast says today's high temperature will be 100°F. Is it more likely to be summer or winter?** *(Summer)*

Assess Understanding

After Try It Out, ask: **What is the warmest temperature shown in Exercises 1–4? the coldest?** *(105°F; 5°F)*

 **USING TECHNOLOGY**

Math Blaster® 1, Continue Short Mission
Restore Mission.
Subtraction: Level 3
Differences 8–14
Save Mission.

Practice

Write each temperature. Describe the temperature as *hot, cold, warm,* or *cool.*

8.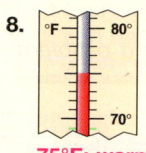
75°F; warm

9.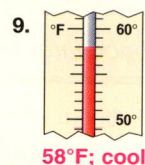
58°F; cool

10.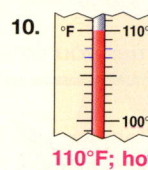
110°F; hot

11.
15°F; cold

Problem Solving

12. The temperature is 92°F in Miami and 41°F in Seattle. In which city would you rather swim outdoors? **Miami**

13. Suppose the temperature in your home freezer is 30°F. Can you make ice? Explain why or why not. **Yes, because water freezes at 32°F.**

14. **Analyze** The temperature in the morning is 72°F. By noon it has risen 6°. Then it drops 10°. What temperature is it then? **68°F**

15. **Create Your Own** Write a problem about a day with three temperature changes. Give your problem to a classmate to solve. **Check students' problems.**

Review and Remember

Add or subtract.

16. 39 + 52
91

17. 190 − 76
114

18. 1,284 + 4,315
5,599

19. 127 + 465
592

20. 31 − 12
19

21. 36 + 93
129

22. 1,740 − 246
1,494

23. 654 − 439
215

Time for Technology

Surf the Net

Check Out the Weather

You can use the internet to find information about weather in other parts of the world.

Explore one of these sites.

www.weather.com   www.usatoday.com   www.intellicast.com

Share your findings with the class.

For Extra Practice, see Set G, page 167.   **149**

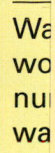

3 Wrap-up

How can a thermometer help you describe a warm day? *(Sample answer: A thermometer measures exactly how warm the day is.)*

Common Error Alert

Watch for students who think that the Fahrenheit scale ends at 0°F. Remind them that there can be temperatures less than, or below, zero.

Meeting Individual Needs

For Early Finishers

Students use today's newspaper to locate your town's temperature in degrees Fahrenheit. Have them find and list 5 major cities and their temperatures.
LINGUISTIC

Acquiring English Proficiency

Make a spinner with sections labeled 15°F, 28°F, 52°F, 75°F, and 98°F. A student spins, then describes something he or she could do at that temperature.
AUDITORY

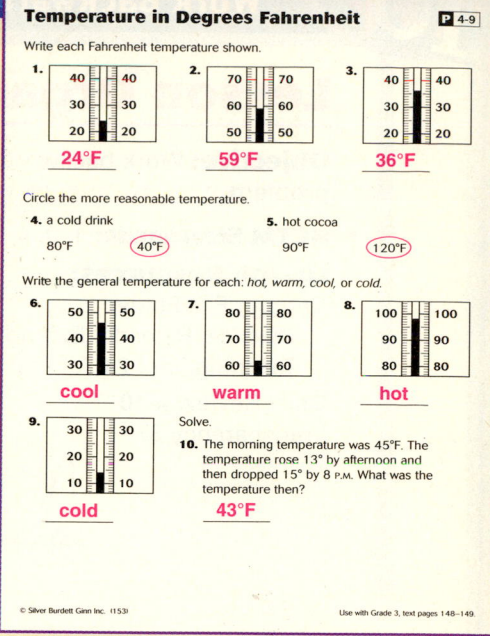
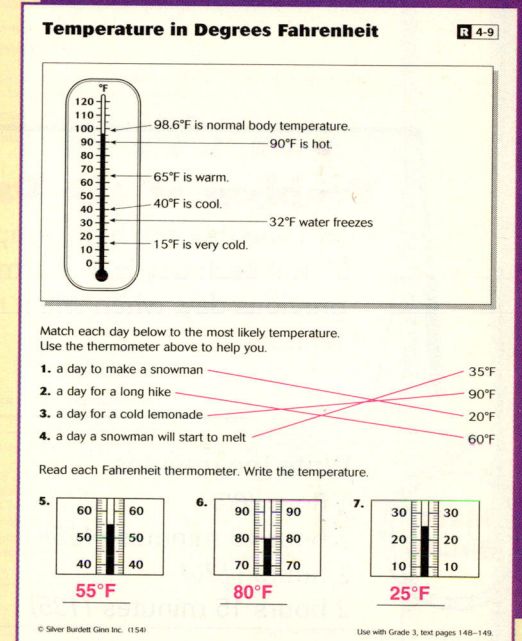
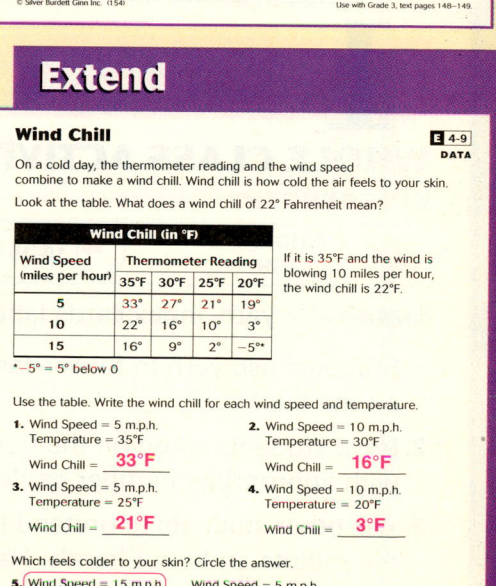

 # Teaching With Technology

Problem Solving: Work Backwards

1 Introduce

Objective: Students will work backwards to solve a problem on the computer.

Resources: MathProcessor™ Version 1.1

MathProcessor™ User Guide: Sections C, D, E, L

In Lesson 10, students are encouraged to solve problems by using the work backwards strategy. The MathProcessor™ Tools can help them use this strategy to solve problems.

Use MathProcessor™ Money manipulatives and Number spaces to work backwards to find the total cost of a purchase.

Ask: Jerome received $5.00 in change when he bought a magazine for $3.50 and bottled water for $1.50. How much money did he give to the salesperson?

2 Teach

As you model the strategy of work backwards to solve the problem above, discuss the steps.

Step 1

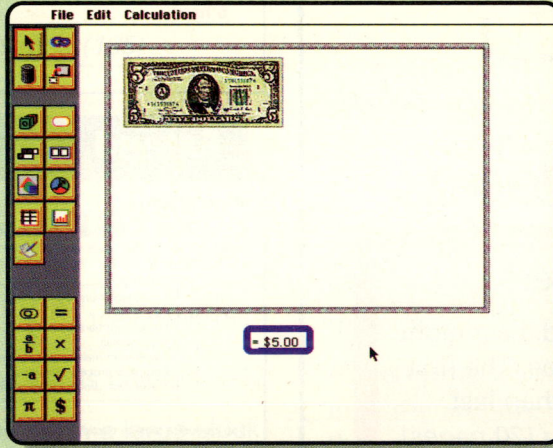

- Open a Money manipulatives workspace  and link it to a Number space.
- **Ask: How much change did Jerome receive?** *($5.00)*
- Show $5.00 in the workspace.
- Click the Number space. Then click $.

Step 2

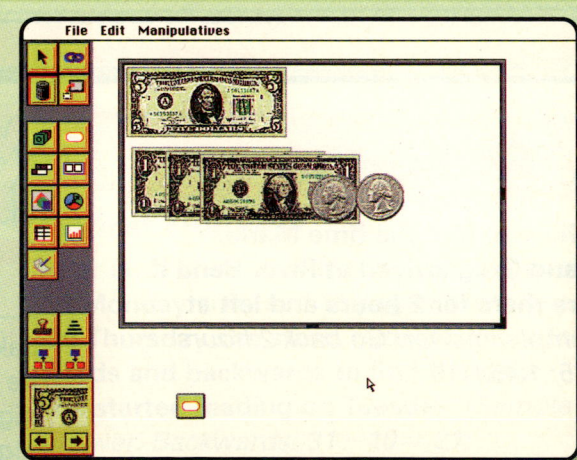

- Click . Then click the Number space.
- **Ask: How can we work backwards to find how much money Jerome gave the salesperson?** *(Sample answer: Add to the $5.00 the cost of the magazine and the cost of the bottled water.)*
- Show $3.50 more in the workspace.

Step 3

Ask: What does the $3.50 represent? *(The cost of the magazine)*

• Show $1.50 more in the workspace.

Ask: What does the $1.50 represent? *(The cost of the bottled water)*

Step 4

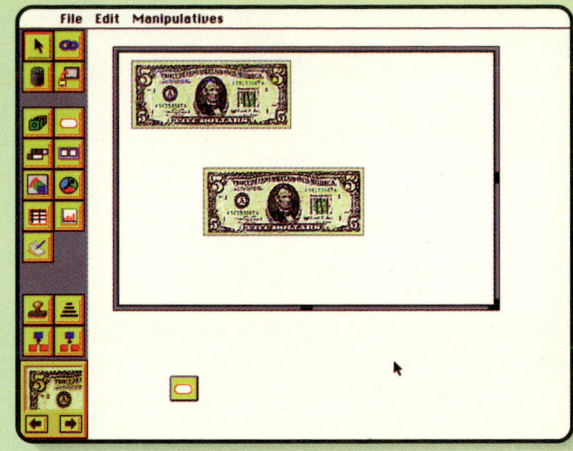

Ask: How much money is in the workspace? *($10.00)*
Can we regroup? *(Yes, $3.50 and $1.50 can be regrouped to $5.00.)*

• Regroup ▓ $3.50 and $1.50 to a $5.00 bill.

Ask: How much money did Jerome give the salesperson? *($10.00)*

Step 5

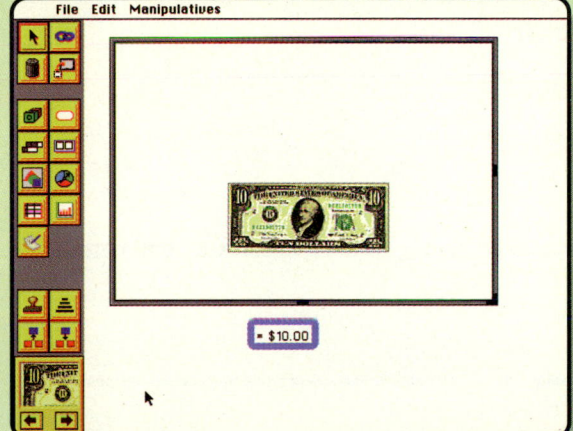

• Select two $5.00 bills. Click ▓ to regroup to a $10.00 bill.

• Double-click Number space to reveal the answer.

Ask: How did we work backwards to solve the problem? *(Started with amount of change received, then added cost of each purchase)*

3 Wrap-up

Allow students to use MathProcessor™ to solve these problems.

Solve each problem. Describe the strategy you used. *(Strategies may vary. Possible strategies shown.)*

1. Students visiting a museum arrived at 1:15 P.M. and left at 2:30 P.M. They spent 15 minutes watching a video and the remainder of the time using computers. How long did they spend working on computers? *(Work Backwards; 1 hour)*

2. Write a word problem and solve it. Describe the strategy you used. Is there another strategy you could have used? If so, describe it. *(Check students' responses.)*

 **Portfolio Opportunity** You may wish to have students open a Writing space and explain their responses for the exercises above.

Meeting Individual Needs

Gifted and Talented

Each student writes a math problem. Partners exchange problems. Each student solves the partner's problem using **MathProcessor™** and describes the strategy used. Partners discuss the problems, the solutions, and the strategies they used.

For Early Finishers

Math Blaster® software and **MathProcessor™ Activity Cards 19–24** provide opportunities for students to practice skills learned in this chapter.

Lesson Organizer

Objective: Use metric units to measure length.

- **NCTM Standards:** 1, 2, 3, 5, 6, 10
- **Vocabulary:** centimeter (cm), decimeter (dm), meter (m), kilometer (km)
- **Materials:** centimeter ruler, meterstick
- **Lesson Resources:**
  Chapter File Folder
  　Practice, Reteach, Extend 4-11
  　Teaching Tool 31
  Daily Review 4-11
  Transparency 21

Problem of the Day   4-11

Ten days from yesterday the date will be May 19. What is today's date? You may use a calendar to help you.
May 10

Math Minute

Round to the nearest ten.

58 *(60)*	79 *(80)*
32 *(30)*	84 *(80)*
95 *(100)*	7 *(10)*

Off by a Centimeter!

You can use metric units to estimate and measure length.

Learning About It

At the Family Fun Park, goofy golf is one of many games people can play.

Tom hit the golf ball. It stopped 1 centimeter from the hole.

A **centimeter** is a metric unit used to measure length.

When Chris hit the golf ball, it stopped 10 centimeters, or 1 **decimeter**, from the hole. That distance would look like this.

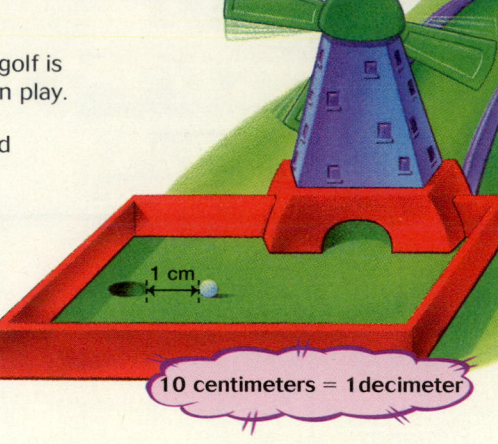

1 cm

10 centimeters = 1 decimeter

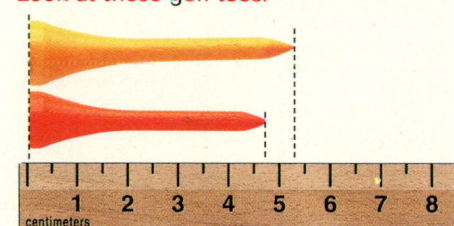

10 centimeters

More Examples

Some objects may not be an exact number of centimeters in length. You can measure them to the nearest centimeter.

Look at these golf tees.

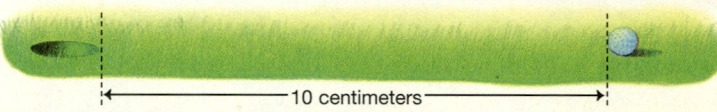

Word Bank

centimeter (cm)
decimeter (dm)
meter (m)
kilometer (km)

What You Need

For each student:
centimeter ruler
meterstick

To the nearest centimeter, each golf tee measures 5 centimeters.

152

---

1 Introduce

Cooperative Activity

KINESTHETIC

PAIRS　　　5–10 MINUTES

Materials: centimeter ruler, spinner (1–9)

1. One student spins a number. The other student uses the ruler to find an object that is about that length in centimeters.
2. Students switch roles.

2 Teach　　Pages 152–155

Have students find a crayon that has a width close to 1 centimeter. They can use the crayon to verify the 10 centimeter (1 dm) length.

- Ask: **How can you decide the length of the yellow golf tee?** *(Sample answer: The end of the tee is closer to 5 than to 6, so it is about 5 centimeters long.)*

- Ask: **About how long is the orange golf tee?** *(About 5 cm)* **How can both golf tees be about 5 cm long when they are different lengths?** *(Sample answer: Both are close to 5 cm long, but one is shorter than 5 cm, and one is longer than 5 cm.)*

Connecting Ideas

After students have discussed centimeters and decimeters, they can make the connection to longer units of measure, such as meters and kilometers.

For students who are not familiar with a baseball bat, they can look at the width of a doorway, which is generally close to 1 meter.

- Ask: **How many meters long do you think our classroom is?** *(Sample answer: about 6 meters)*

- Ask: **How many classrooms laid end to end would equal about 1 kilometer?** *(Sample answer: about 166 classrooms)*

1 m = 100 cm
1 m = 10 dm
1 km = 1,000 m

Connecting Ideas

Centimeters and decimeters are used to measure short lengths. Meters and kilometers are used to measure longer lengths.

At the Fun Park you can hit baseballs in batting cages. The length of each baseball bat is about 1 **meter**.

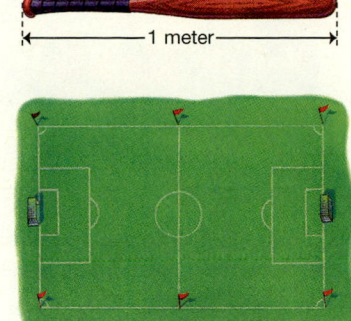
1 meter

There is a soccer field at the Fun Park. The length of 11 soccer fields is about 1 **kilometer**.

- Find three things that you think are each about 1 meter long.

- Use a meterstick or a centimeter ruler to check your estimates.

- Name three things you think you could measure in kilometers.
  Objects will vary.

▲ The length of 11 soccer fields end to end is about 1 kilometer.

Think and Discuss Would you use a strip of paper 1 cm, 1 m, or 1 km long to measure your height? Explain your choice. **1 m; a centimeter would be much too short and a kilometer would be much too long.**

Try It Out

Write the best estimate.

1.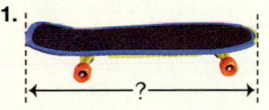
   70 cm or 7 cm
   70 cm

2.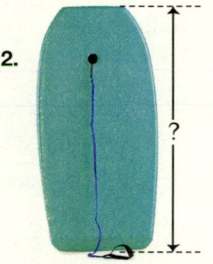
   1 dm or 1 m
   1m

3.
   30 cm or 30 km
   30 cm

153

Critical Thinking   GENERALIZATION

After Think and Discuss, ask: **Why do you think some foot races are measured in kilometers while others are measured in meters?** *(Sample answer: Some races are very short while other races are very long.)*

Assess Understanding

After Try It Out, ask: **Which unit of length would you use to measure the distance between first and second base on a baseball field?** *(Meters)*

Using Technology
CD-ROM

MathProcessor™

Tools: Geometry; Number spaces
Objective: Drawing and Measuring Line Segments

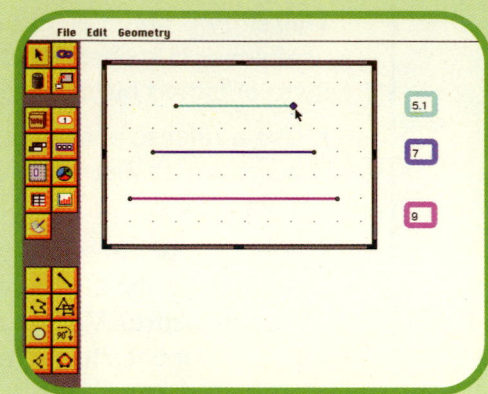

* Open a Square Grid Geometry workspace 🔲.

* Click ◥. Click-drag to draw a line segment. Double-click to end.

* Link 📷 the line segment to a Number space 🔢 to show the length of the segment in units.

* Draw other line segments. Link each to its own Number space.

* If a Number space shows a decimal, click an endpoint and slowly drag the point to increase or decrease the measurement.

Additional Activities

See also **Activities 23 and 24** in the MathProcessor™ Activity Cards.

Practice

Estimate and measure to the nearest centimeter.

4.
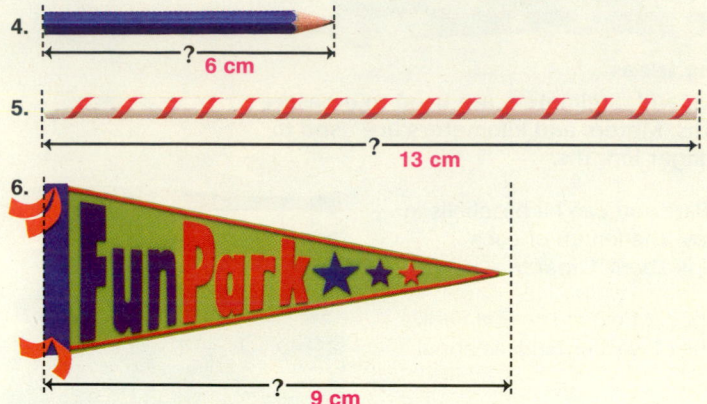
? **6 cm**

5. ? **13 cm**

6. ? **9 cm**

What unit would you use to measure each item?
Write *centimeter, decimeter, meter,* or *kilometer.*

7. length of your foot
Decimeter or centimeter
8. length of a fingernail
Centimeter
9. distance between cities
Kilometer
10. length of your classroom
Meter

Complete. Use the information on pages 152–153 to help you.

11. 100 cm = __?__ m   **1**
12. 1 km = __?__ m   **1,000**
13. 10 cm = __?__ dm   **1**
14. 2,000 m = __?__ km   **2**
15. 3 m = __?__ cm   **300**
16. 400 cm = __?__ m   **4**

The map shows the route of a park path. Use the map for Exercises 17–19.

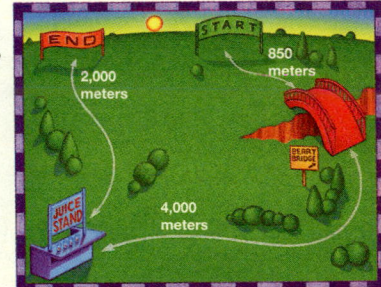

17. Is the distance from Start to Berry Bridge more or less than 1 kilometer?
Less than 1 kilometer

18. How many kilometers is the distance from Berry Bridge to the juice stand?
4 kilometers

19. Is the distance from the juice stand to the end of the path less than, more than, or the same as the distance from Start to Berry Bridge?
More than the distance

 154

2 Teach (continued)

⭐ GIFTED AND TALENTED

Estimate and Measure Have students estimate the lengths, in meters, of objects such as a door, a table, or a wall. Then have students measure these objects with a meterstick or a 1-m long piece of yarn to find the actual lengths. Students can make and display posters of common classroom objects and their measurements. This information can be used for comparison when students encounter measurements of other objects in meters.

Problem Solving

20. Members of a bicycle club rode 5 kilometers around a path before stopping to rest. Did they ride more or less than 1,000 meters?
More

21. A runner ran in an 800-meter race. Did she run more or less than a kilometer? **Less**

22. A shoelace measures 3 decimeters. How many centimeters long is it? **30 centimeters**

23. Jocelyn wants to put posters across a wall that is 3 m wide. Each poster is 65 cm wide. How many posters can she fit on the wall? What strategy did you use to solve the problem?
4 posters; Possible strategies: *Draw a Picture* or *Guess and Check*

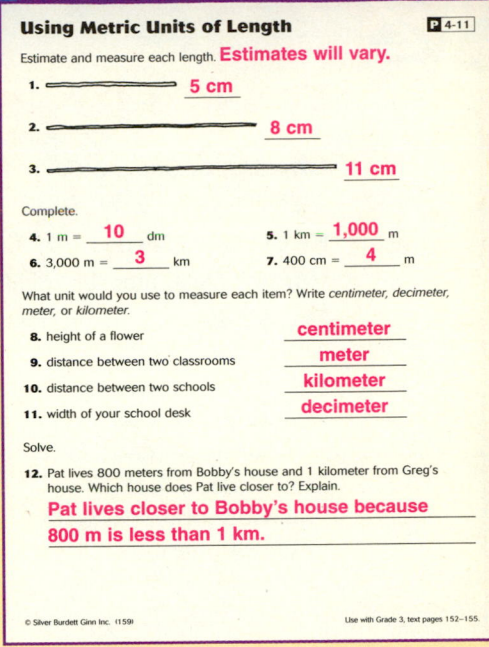

Review and Remember

Add or subtract.

24. $52.79 − $38.08
$14.71

25. 70 − 53
17

26. 4,599 + 1,236
5,835

27. 6,046 + 7,814
13,860

28. 92 − 33
59

29. $46.25 + $19.98
$66.23

Critical Thinking Corner

Visual Thinking

What's Wrong?

Ricki, Joe, and Becky each measured the length of a piece of wood by using a centimeter ruler. The pictures show how they made their measurements. What are they each doing wrong?

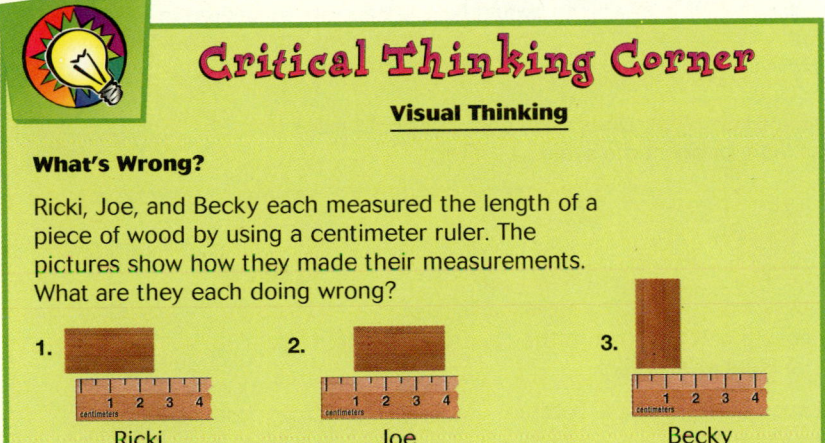

1. Ricki **2.** Joe **3.** Becky

Ricki and Joe lined up the ruler incorrectly. The ruler should be lined up exactly at the first tic mark. Becky measured the width of the wood instead of the length.

For Extra Practice, see Set H, page 168. **155**

Critical Thinking

Ask how the length of the wood could be found using the pictures given. *(In Exercise 2, the wood measures from the 1 cm mark to the 4 cm mark, so it is 3 cm long.)*

---

3 Wrap-up

Describe several things you might measure using the following units: centimeters, decimeters, meters, kilometers.
(Sample answers: cm: paper clips; dm: dictionary; m: student height; km: distance from school to home)

Common Error Alert

Watch for students who measure incorrectly because they do not line up their rulers exactly at one end of the object being measured.

Meeting Individual Needs

For Early Finishers

Students measure one hand and one foot in centimeters. They compare data with two other students, then list measurements from least to greatest.
KINESTHETIC

For Extra Help

Write on the board: *centimeter, decimeter,* and *meter.* Have students find objects in the room to be measured in each unit, then have them measure.
VISUAL/SPATIAL

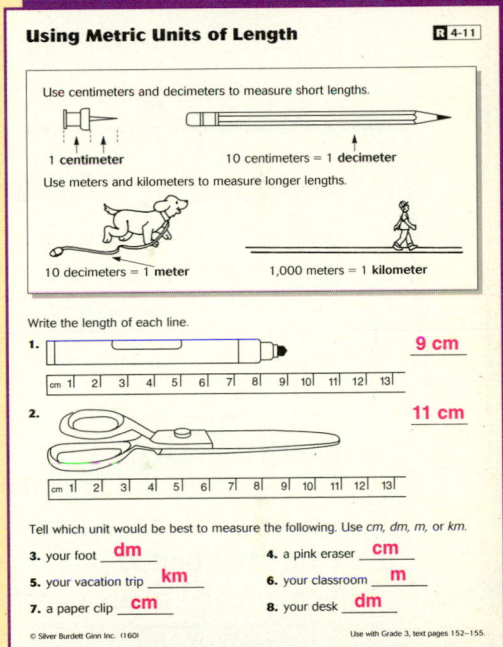
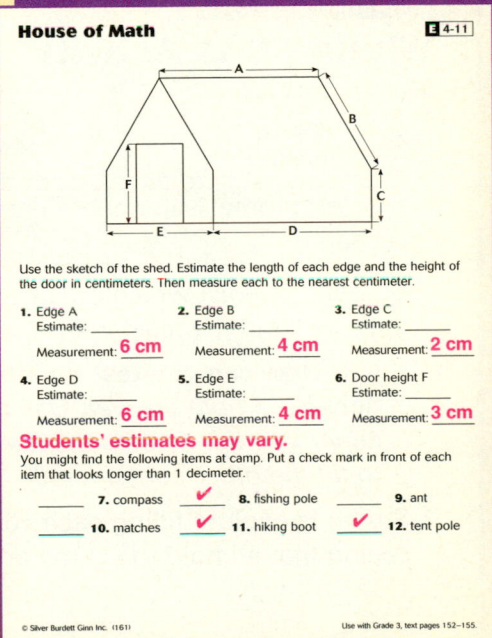

Lesson Organizer

Objective: Use metric units to measure capacity.

- **NCTM Standards:** 1, 2, 3, 5, 6, 10
- **Vocabulary:** liter (L), milliliter (mL)
- **Materials:** 1-liter container, assorted size containers
- **Lesson Resources:**
  Chapter File Folder
    Practice, Reteach, Extend 4-12
  Daily Review 4-12
  Practice Workbook, p. 18
  Study Buddies 4B

Problem of the Day 4-12

A fence is 10 meters long. The fence posts are 2 meters apart. How many posts are in the fence? **6**

Math Minute

Which is greater?
1 pint or 1 gallon *(1 gallon)*
1 quart or 1 cup *(1 quart)*
1 cup or 1 pint *(1 pint)*
1 gallon or 1 quart *(1 gallon)*

12
Using Milliliters and Liters

On the Road

You can use metric units to measure capacity.

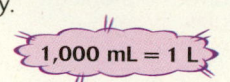

Learning About It

After riding for an hour, the Bicycle Club stops for a drink. Each rider carries 1 liter of water like the one shown.

A **liter** and a **milliliter** are metric units used to measure capacity.

Word Bank
liter (L)
milliliter (mL)

$$1,000 \text{ mL} = 1 \text{ L}$$

This medicine dropper holds about 1 mL.

This water bottle holds about 1 L.

What You Need

For each student:
1-liter container
assorted size containers

- Find three containers that you think will each hold about 1 liter.
- Use water and a 1-liter container to check your estimate. **Check students' measurements.**

Think and Discuss Name two items that would have a capacity measured in milliliters. **Answers will vary. Possible answers include a thimble and a teacup.**

Try It Out

Using Estimation Does each container hold *more than*, *less than*, or *about the same as* 1 liter?

1.  **Less than**
2.  **More than**
3. **More than**
4. 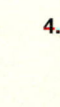 **About the same as**

Choose a unit to measure the capacity of each item. Write *liters* or *milliliters*.

5. spoon **Milliliters**
6. bathtub **Liters**
7. car gasoline tank **Liters**
8. drinking glass **Milliliters**
9. swimming pool **Liters**
10. soup bowl **Milliliters**

156

---

1 Introduce

Whole Class Activity

VISUAL/SPATIAL

WHOLE CLASS — 10–15 MINUTES

Materials: three 1-liter containers of various shapes

1. Students predict which containers hold the most and the least water.
   - Ask: **How can you test your predictions?** *(Sample answer: Use the container you think holds the least water to fill the other containers.)*
2. Students explore filling each container, seeing that all hold the same amount.

2 Teach Pages 156–157

Explain how scientists often use milliliters to measure small amounts of fluid. Ask: **What other groups of people might measure using milliliters?** *(Sample answer: pharmacists)*

- Say: **Name some items you could find in a grocery store that are measured in milliliters.** *(Sample answers: soda, water, juice)*

Critical Thinking APPLICATION

After Think and Discuss, say: **Name two items that would be measured in liters.** *(Sample answer: soft drinks, mouthwashes)*

Assess Understanding

After Try It Out, ask: **Which unit is used when measuring small amounts of a fluid? large amounts?** *(Milliliter; liter)*

CHALLENGE

The bicycle club has five riders, and each is carrying 1 liter of water. How many milliliters of water are the riders carrying? *(5,000)*

Practice

Choose the best estimate.

11.
1 L or 150 mL
150 mL

12.
5 mL or 5 L
5 mL

13.
250 mL or 25 L
250 mL

14.
40 mL or 40 L
40 L

15.
1 mL or 1 L
1 L

16.
115 mL or 115 L
115 L

Choose a unit to measure the capacity of each item.
Write *liters* or *milliliters*.

17. soup ladle
Milliliters
18. paint bucket
Liters
19. soup can
Milliliters
20. pond
Liters
21. perfume bottle
Milliliters
22. pitcher
Liters
23. washing machine
Liters
24. bottle cap
Milliliters
25. cooler
Liters

Problem Solving

26. How many milliliters are in a 5 L container? **5,000 milliliters**

27. Suppose you drank 650 mL of water after riding
your bicycle. How many more mL would you
need to drink to equal 1 liter? **350 mL**

28. **Explain** If you do not know the capacity of a
container, how would you find out how many
liters it holds? **You could fill the container with water and then pour that water
into liter containers to see how many liters it fills. Or you could
use a liter container to fill the container in question.**

Review and Remember

Add or subtract.

29. 7,118 − 6,255
863
30. 65 + 76
141
31. 6,794 + 2,363
9,157
32. 42 − 21
21
33. 826 + 108
934
34. 349 − 149
200

For Extra Practice, see Set I, page 168. **157**

Practice

Using Milliliters and Liters   P 4-12

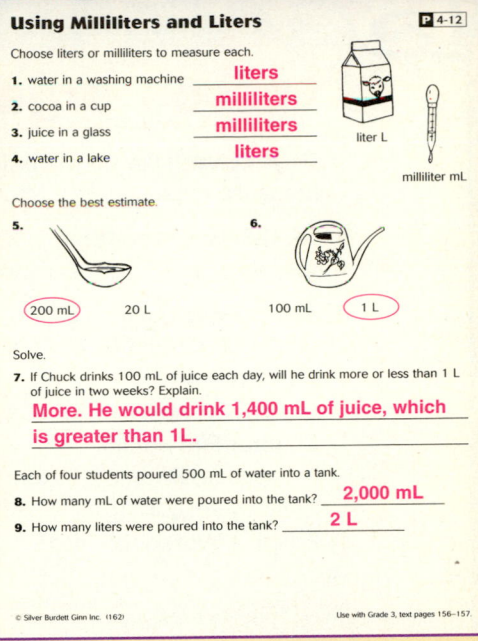

Choose liters or milliliters to measure each.

1. water in a washing machine **liters**
2. cocoa in a cup **milliliters**
3. juice in a glass **milliliters**
4. water in a lake **liters**

liter L
milliliter mL

Choose the best estimate.

5. (200 mL) 20 L
6. 100 mL (1 L)

Solve.

7. If Chuck drinks 100 mL of juice each day, will he drink more or less than 1 L
of juice in two weeks? Explain.
**More. He would drink 1,400 mL of juice, which
is greater than 1L.**

Each of four students poured 500 mL of water into a tank.

8. How many mL of water were poured into the tank? **2,000 mL**
9. How many liters were poured into the tank? **2 L**

© Silver Burdett Ginn Inc. (162)   Use with Grade 3, text pages 156–157.

Reteach

Using Milliliters and Liters   R 4-12

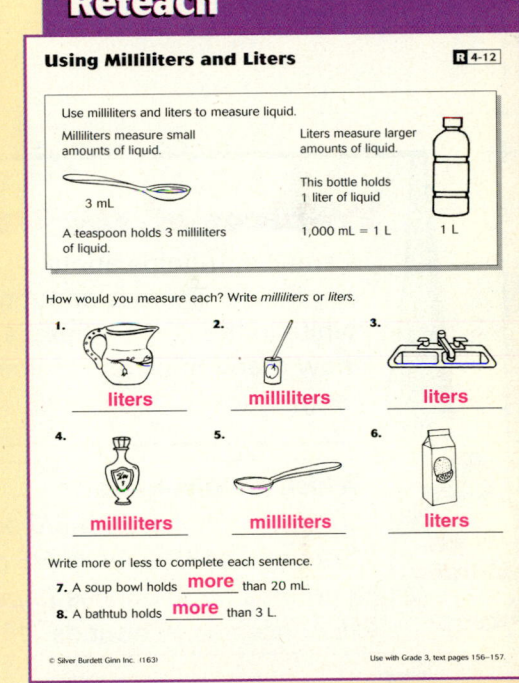

Use milliliters and liters to measure liquid.

Milliliters measure small
amounts of liquid.

3 mL

A teaspoon holds 3 milliliters
of liquid.

Liters measure larger
amounts of liquid.

This bottle holds
1 liter of liquid.

1,000 mL = 1 L   1 L

How would you measure each? Write *milliliters* or *liters*.

1. **liters**
2. **milliliters**
3. **liters**
4. **milliliters**
5. **milliliters**
6. **liters**

Write more or less to complete each sentence.

7. A soup bowl holds **more** than 20 mL.
8. A bathtub holds **more** than 3 L.

© Silver Burdett Ginn Inc. (163)   Use with Grade 3, text pages 156–157.

Extend

All or None?   E 4-12
REASONING

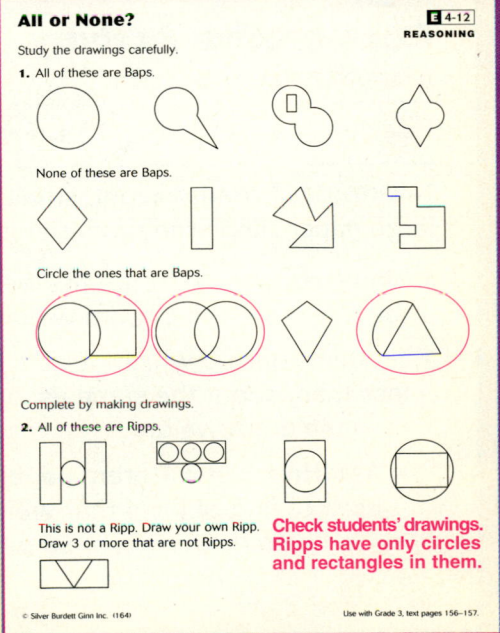

Study the drawings carefully.

1. All of these are Baps.

None of these are Baps.

Circle the ones that are Baps.

Complete by making drawings.

2. All of these are Ripps.

This is not a Ripp. Draw your own Ripp.
Draw 3 or more that are not Ripps.
**Check students' drawings.
Ripps have only circles
and rectangles in them.**

© Silver Burdett Ginn Inc. (164)   Use with Grade 3, text pages 156–157.

---

3 Wrap-up

Explain how you know when to use milliliters and liters to measure fluid amounts.
*(Use milliliters to measure small amounts,
liters to measure large amounts.)*

Common Error Alert

Watch for students who have trouble picturing the actual size of
items shown in the exercises.
Have students describe the sizes
of these items in real life.

Meeting Individual Needs

For Early Finishers

Give students different-shaped bottles
that hold the same amount of liquid. Ask:
**Which container will hold the most
water?** Let students investigate.
VISUAL/SPATIAL

Gifted and Talented

Have students find 2 containers where 1
container holds about 10 times more
than the other container. Students use
beans to check their estimates.
VISUAL/SPATIAL

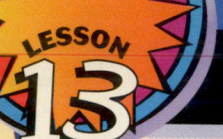

Lesson Organizer

Objective: Use metric units to measure mass.

- **NCTM Standards:** 1, 2, 3, 5, 6, 10
- **Vocabulary:** gram (g), kilogram (kg)
- **Materials:** balance scale, 1-kilogram weight or 400 pennies, 1-gram weight or 1 large paper clip
- **Lesson Resources:**
  Chapter File Folder
    Practice, Reteach, Extend 4-13
  Daily Review 4-13
  Practice Workbook, p. 19

Problem of the Day   4-13

A small egg holds about 30 milliliters of egg inside. There is about twice as much white in the egg as there is yolk. About how many milliliters of yolk are in a small egg? **About 10 milliliters.**

Math Minute

Which weighs more?

20 ounces or 1 pound *(20 ounces)*
2 pounds or 48 ounces *(48 ounces)*
3 pounds or 30 ounces *(3 pounds)*
16 ounces or 16 pounds *(16 pounds)*

Grand Grams

Grams and kilograms help you tell how heavy or light objects are.

Learning About It

Some sports equipment is heavy. Some is light. You can use the metric units **grams** and **kilograms** to measure how heavy objects are.

Word Bank
gram (g)
kilogram (kg)

One large paper clip is about 1 gram.

A baseball bat is about 1 kilogram.

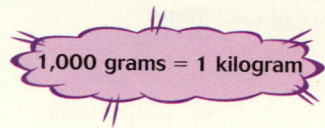

1,000 grams = 1 kilogram

- Find three objects that you think would each measure about 1 kilogram.

- Find three objects that you think would each measure about 1 gram.

- Check your estimates by weighing each object. **Check students' measurements.**

What You Need

*For each class:
  balance scale
  1-kilogram weight
    or 400 pennies
  1-gram weight or
    1 large paper clip*

Think and Discuss Which unit would you use to measure how heavy a single golf ball is? a carton of 1,000 golf balls? Give reasons for your choices.
A single golf ball is light and would best be measured in grams. One thousand golf balls would be heavier and would best be measured in kilograms.

Try It Out

Choose a unit to measure each item. Write *grams* or *kilograms*.

1. baseball cap **Grams**	**2.** dollar bill **Grams**	**3.** bowling ball **Kilograms**	**4.** canoe **Kilograms**
5. penny **Grams**	**6.** bicycle **Kilograms**	**7.** piano **Kilograms**	**8.** golf tee **Grams**

158

---

1 Introduce

Cooperative Activity
KINESTHETIC

 PAIRS   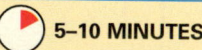 5–10 MINUTES

Materials: 1-gram weight, small and large paper clip, large rubber eraser

1. Have students compare the weight of the objects to the 1-gram weight.

2. Students decide which objects weigh less than, about the same as, or more than the gram weight.

- Ask: **How can a 1-gram paper clip be used to find objects that weigh 50g?** *(Compare the weight to 50 paper clips.)*

2 Teach   Pages 158–159

Discuss how grams are used to measure objects that aren't very heavy and kilograms are used to measure heavier objects.

- Say: **Name some items in a grocery store that are weighed in kilograms.** *(Sample answers: fruit, vegetables, meat)*

Critical Thinking   ANALYSIS

After Think and Discuss, ask: **Why do you think both grams and kilograms are used instead of just kilograms?** *(If just grams were used, the number of grams that heavy objects weigh would be very high.)*

Assess Understanding

After Try It Out, ask: **Which object in Exercises 1–8 weighs the most? the least?** *(Most: piano; least: dollar bill)*

CHALLENGE

List the following objects from least heavy to most heavy: 2-kilogram box, 3,000-gram brick, 100-gram book. *(100-gram book, 2-kilogram box, 3,000-gram brick)*

Practice

Choose the best estimate.

9.

8 g or 800 g
8 g

10.

1 kg or 1 g
1 kg

11.

1 g or 1 kg
1 g

12.

200 kg or 13 kg
13 kg

13.

900 kg or 30 g
900 kg

14.

5 kg or 550 kg
550 kg

Using Estimation Is each item *more than, less than,* or *about the same as* 1 kilogram?

15.

About the same as

16.

Less than

17.

More than

Write which measurement is more.

18. 4 kg or 3,500 kg
3,500 kg
19. 2,500 g or 2 kg
2,500 g
20. 4,000 g or 4,000 kg
4,000 kg
21. 25 g or 1 kg
1 kg
22. 250 g or 25 kg
25 kg
23. 3,000 g or 30 kg
30 kg

Problem Solving

24. One roller skate is about 2 kilograms. How heavy would 2 pairs of skates be? **About 8 kilograms**

25. A soccer ball is about 450 grams. How many more grams would it have to be to be 1 kilogram? **About 550 g**

Review and Remember

Find each sum.

26. 342 + 904 + 65
1,311
27. 2,409 + 371 + 184
2,964
28. $18.37 + $52.44 + $85.99
$156.80
29. 6,435 + 2,114 + 8,790
17,339
30. 51 + 49 + 78 + 19
197
31. 1,234 + 400 + 38
1,672

For Extra Practice, see Set J, page 168. **159**

---

3 Wrap-up

Which unit would you use to weigh your desk? *(Kilograms)*

Common Error Alert

Watch for students who have difficulty keeping track of zeros when converting kilograms to grams. Remind them to add 3 zeros.

Meeting Individual Needs

For Early Finishers

Students use a balance scale to investigate objects found in the classroom that are less than, more than, or equal to one gram.
KINESTHETIC

Cooperative Learning

Have groups create charts with the headings *Gram* and *Kilogram*. Challenge groups to list at least ten items in each column.
LINGUISTIC

 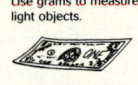
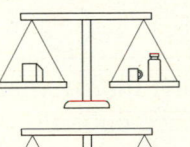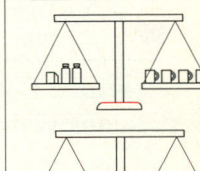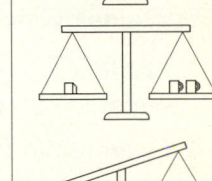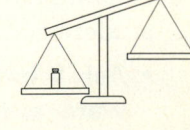
LESSON 13 159

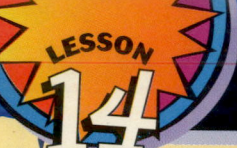

Lesson Organizer

Objective: Measure temperature in degrees Celsius.

- **NCTM Standards:** 1, 2, 3, 5, 6, 8, 10
- **Lesson Resources:**
  Chapter File Folder
    Practice, Reteach, Extend 4-14
  Daily Review 4-14
  Practice Workbook, p. 20
  Transparency 22

Problem of the Day   4-14

Suppose a paper clip weighs 1 gram, a craft stick weighs 3 grams, a penny weighs 5 grams, and a checker weighs 8 grams. How can you balance an eraser that weighs 21 grams? Find at least 3 ways.

 Math Minute

Subtract.

32° − 10° *(22°)*	98° − 65° *(33°)*
48° − 11° *(37°)*	10° − 0° *(10°)*
76° − 25° *(51°)*	85° − 3° *(82°)*

Goose Bumps

You can use a Celsius thermometer (°C) to measure temperature.

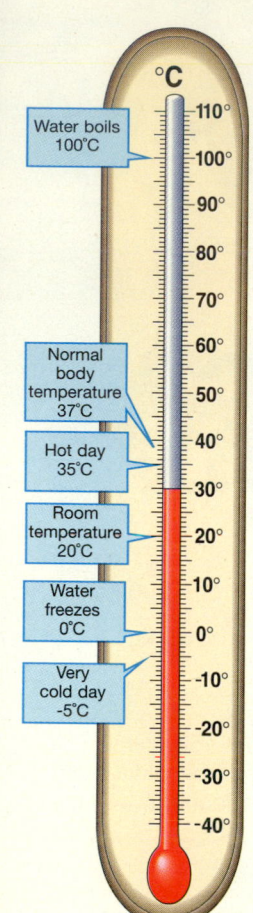

Water boils 100°C — 110°
— 100°
— 90°
— 80°
— 70°
Normal body temperature 37°C — 60°
— 50°
Hot day 35°C — 40°
Room temperature 20°C — 30°
— 20°
Water freezes 0°C — 10°
— 0°
Very cold day -5°C — -10°
— -20°
— -30°
— -40°

Read: thirty degrees Celsius
Write: 30°C

Learning About It

To measure temperature, you can use **degrees Celsius** (°C).

- The thermometer shows 30°C.
- Water boils at 100°C.
- Water freezes at 0°C.

Estimate the temperature for each of the activities shown. Use the thermometer to help you. **Accept reasonable estimates. Possible estimates are given.**

35°C or higher

0°C or lower

Think and Discuss What would you wear outside if the thermometer measured 10°C? What if it was 35°C? **10°C: winter jackets, gloves, hats; 35°C: shorts, T-shirts, swimsuits**

Try It Out

Write each temperature. Describe the temperature as *hot, cold, warm,* or *cool.*

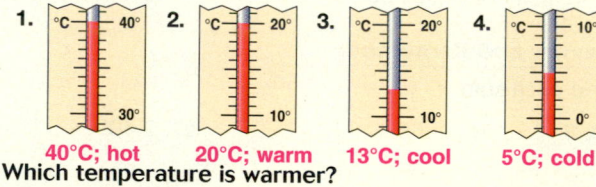

1. °C — 40° / — 30° **40°C; hot**
2. °C — 20° / — 10° **20°C; warm**
3. °C — 20° / — 10° **13°C; cool**
4. °C — 10° / — 0° **5°C; cold**

Which temperature is warmer?

5. 18°C or 28°C   **28°C**
6. 50°C or 60°C   **60°C**
7. 70°C or 65°C   **70°C**

160

---

 1 Introduce

Whole Class Activity

KINESTHETIC

WHOLE CLASS   10–15 MINUTES

Materials: Celsius thermometer, plastic container, water, ice cubes

1. Students measure the temperature of water at room temperature.

2. Leaving the thermometer in the water, students add ice cubes.

- Ask: **What was the temperature of the water at room temperature? after ice was added?** *(Sample answer: about 20°C; about 0°C)*

Problem of the Day: See p. 167.

---

2 Teach   **Pages 160–161**

Have students read the temperatures on the thermometer. Then discuss the benchmarks provided. Ask: **Could you swim in a pool that was heated to 90°C? Why or why not?** *(No; you would get burned.)* **Could you swim in a lake that has a temperature of 5°C? Why or why not?** *(No; you would freeze.)*

Critical Thinking   APPLICATION

After Think and Discuss, ask: **Suppose the temperature outside is 12°C. Should you grab your ice skates and head for the pond? Explain.** *(No; the temperature is above freezing.)*

Assess Understanding

After Try It Out, ask: **In Exercises 1–4, which temperature is hottest? coldest?** *(40°C; 5°C)*

 ### USING TECHNOLOGY

Math Blaster® 1, Complete Short Mission
Restore Mission.
Subtraction: Level 3
Differences 8–14
Complete Mission. Save results.

Practice

Show What ...

Solve.

1. The 3-kilome...
   1:55 P.M. Jed...
   2:10 P.M. How...
   Jed run? **15 m...**

3. When the fiel...
   temperature w...
   At noon it wa...
   2:00 P.M. the...
   2° hotter than...
   was the temp...
   83° Fahrenhe...

5. In one game...
   fill a gallon ju...
   measuring c...
   jug was 3 qu...
   cups did Na...
   4 cups

Use the chart b...

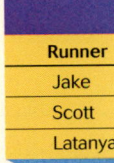

Runner	
Jake	
Scott	
Latanya	

7. Write the o...
   finished the...

8. Write the o...
   finished the...

9. Rachel also...
   4 seconds...
   16 seconds

10. **Analyze** W...
    she was 2...
    came in th...

Practice

Choose the best estimate.

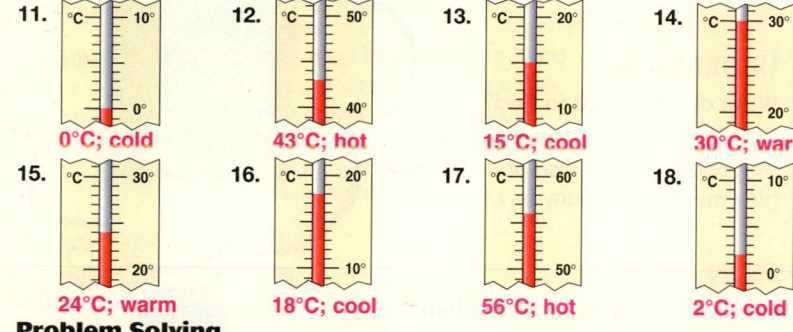

8. 0°C or 20°C — **20°C**
9. 8°C or 100°C — **8°C**
10. 90°C or 32°C — **32°C**

Write each temperature. Describe the temperature as *hot, cold, warm,* or *cool*.

11. **0°C; cold**
12. **43°C; hot**
13. **15°C; cool**
14. **30°C; warm**
15. **24°C; warm**
16. **18°C; cool**
17. **56°C; hot**
18. **2°C; cold**

Problem Solving

19. Water is boiling on the stove. Would the water temperature be 80°C or 100°C? **100°C**

20. A thermometer measures 39°C. Is this warmer or cooler than normal body temperature? **Warmer**

21. **Explain** In Dallas, Texas, the temperature is 34°C. In Chicago, Illinois, the temperature is 15°C. In which city would you be more likely to wear a jacket outside? **Chicago, Illinois; 34°C is hot; 15°C is cool.**

22. When Susan woke up yesterday, the temperature outside was 24°C. By noon, the temperature was 7 degrees warmer. What was the temperature at noon? **31°C**

Review and Remember

Add or subtract.

23. 39 + 23 — **62**
24. 53 − 11 — **42**
25. 767 − 593 — **174**
26. 384 + 295 — **679**
27. 88 + 47 — **135**
28. 98 − 59 — **39**
29. 491 + 456 — **947**
30. 685 − 487 — **198**

For Extra Practice, see Set K, page 168. **161**

Internet Activity

www.sbgmath.com

Students use information from the Internet to compare temperatures from different cities.

Temperature in Degrees Celsius P 4-14

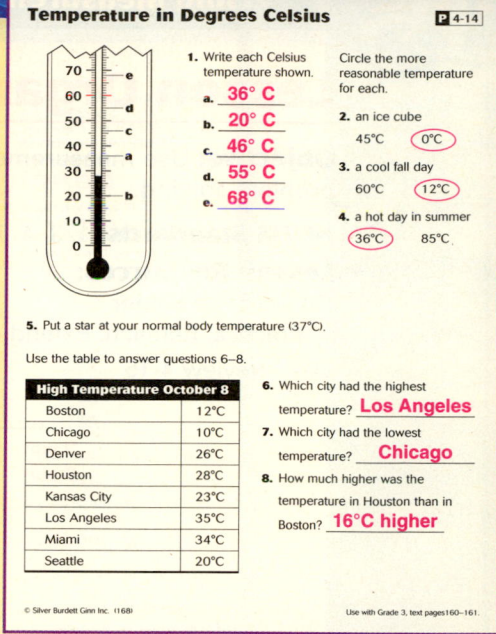

1. Write each Celsius temperature shown.
   a. **36° C**
   b. **20° C**
   c. **46° C**
   d. **55° C**
   e. **68° C**

Circle the more reasonable temperature for each.

2. an ice cube — 45°C ⟨**0°C**⟩
3. a cool fall day — 60°C ⟨**12°C**⟩
4. a hot day in summer — ⟨**36°C**⟩ 85°C.

5. Put a star at your normal body temperature (37°C).

Use the table to answer questions 6–8.

High Temperature October 8	
Boston	12°C
Chicago	10°C
Denver	26°C
Houston	28°C
Kansas City	23°C
Los Angeles	35°C
Miami	34°C
Seattle	20°C

6. Which city had the highest temperature? **Los Angeles**
7. Which city had the lowest temperature? **Chicago**
8. How much higher was the temperature in Houston than in Boston? **16°C higher**

© Silver Burdett Ginn Inc. (168) — Use with Grade 3, text pages 160–161.

Reteach

Temperature in Degrees Celsius R 4-14

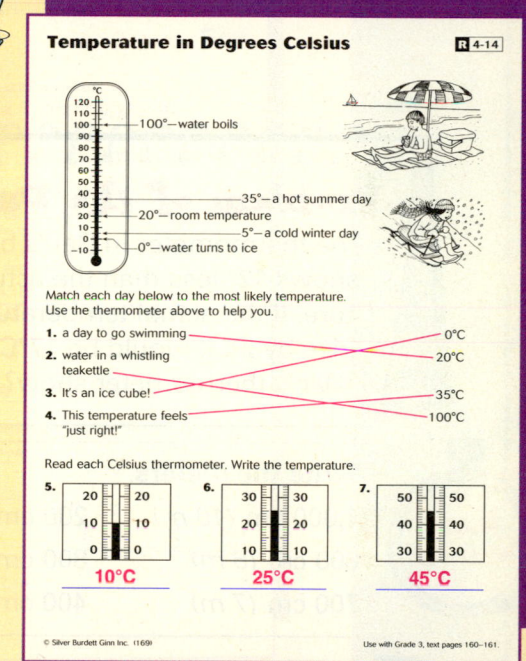

- 100°—water boils
- 35°—a hot summer day
- 20°—room temperature
- 5°—a cold winter day
- 0°—water turns to ice

Match each day below to the most likely temperature. Use the thermometer above to help you.

1. a day to go swimming — 0°C
2. water in a whistling teakettle — 20°C
3. It's an ice cube! — 35°C
4. This temperature feels "just right!" — 100°C

Read each Celsius thermometer. Write the temperature.

5. **10°C**
6. **25°C**
7. **45°C**

© Silver Burdett Ginn Inc. (169) — Use with Grade 3, text pages 160–161.

Extend

Line-Up E 4-14 — VISUAL THINKING

Each row is missing a picture that fits the sequence. Choose the missing picture and draw it in the box.

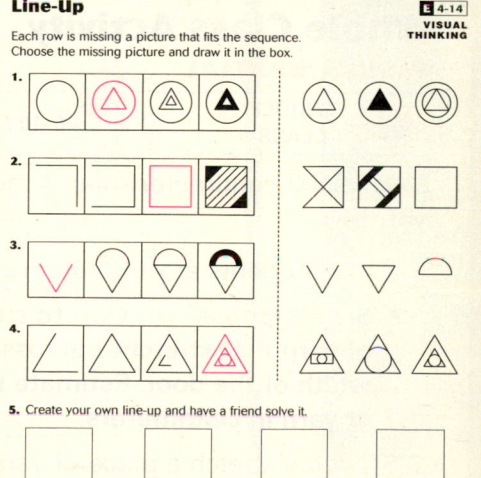

5. Create your own line-up and have a friend solve it.

Answers will vary. Check students' patterns.

© Silver Burdett Ginn Inc. (170) — Use with Grade 3, text pages 160–161.

---

3 W...

Discuss and reco...
meters of fence...
square garden v...
meters long. (Sa...
times (328); 350...

Comm...

Watch for st...
label their a...
that answer...
correct unit...
labeled.

---

3 Wrap-up

The temperature of bath water is greater than the temperature of the human body. Predict the temperature of bath water. Explain your answer. *(Sample answer: Body temperature is 37°C, so bath water might be 40°C.)*

Common Error Alert

Watch for students who use the Fahrenheit temperatures of boiling and freezing points when using the Celsius scale. Review Celsius boiling and freezing points.

Meeting Individual Needs

For Early Finishers

Students use newspapers to locate your town's temperature in degrees Celsius. Then have them find and list 5 major cities and their temperatures.

LINGUISTIC

For Extra Help

Draw several Celsius thermometers. Show pictures of the 4 seasons. Students estimate the temperature of each season and draw in red to show the estimate.

VISUAL/SPATIAL

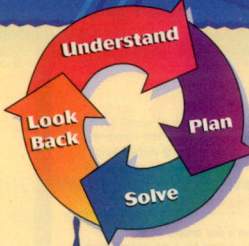

Problem Solving

Preparing for Tests

Purpose To apply problem-solving strategies and skills in a multiple-choice testing format

Reading for Problem Solving

Building Vocabulary
In Problem 1, students need to know that *A.M.* is used for times before noon and *P.M.* is used for times after noon. Ask students which answer choices this eliminates. *(Choices A and C)*

Understanding the Problem
In Problem 8, be sure students know that there are seven days in a week. Ask students how knowing this will help them solve the problem. *(They should add 7 three times to 3 to find the date in three weeks.)*

Using the Problem-Solving Process

Remind students to use the four steps below to help them think through and solve problems.

 Understand
What do you need to know?
What do you need to find?

 Plan
How can you solve the problem?

 Solve
How can you use your plan?

 Look Back
Have you solved the problem?
How can you check your answer?

Common Error Alert

For Problem 6 Students may correctly find how many cars each boy has, but mix the boys up and choose Choice C. Ask students how many cars each boy has, and which boy has fewer cars. Then have students reread the question to see which boy the question asks about.

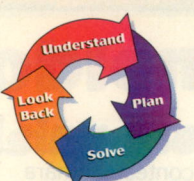

Problem Solving
★★★★★★ **Preparing for Tests**

Practice What You Learned

Choose the correct letter for each answer.

1 Phil left home at 10:50 A.M. He got back three and one-half hours later. What time did Phil get home?

A. 1:50 A.M.
B. 1:50 P.M.
C. 2:20 A.M.
(D.) 2:20 P.M.

Tip
Sometimes you can eliminate some answer choices. Why can you eliminate Choices A and C?

---

2 Over the weekend, 239 people went to the school play on Saturday and 178 people went on Sunday. What is the best way to estimate the total number of people who went to the play in all?

A. 200 + 100
(B.) 200 + 200
C. 300 + 100
D. 300 + 200

Tip
Start by rounding each number to the nearest hundred.

---

3 Jim is fencing in a play area for his dog. He has 75 feet of wire fencing. If he only needs 56 feet of fencing for the play area, how much fencing will Jim have left?

(A.) 19 feet
B. 21 feet
C. 29 feet
D. 131 feet

Tip
You can use the *Draw a Picture* strategy to help you solve this problem.

163

---

4 Mary Beth played soccer for 38 minutes in one game and 42 minutes in another game. **About** how many minutes did she play in the two games?

A. 50 minutes
B. 60 minutes
C. 80 minutes
D. 90 minutes

5 Mark's dog weighs 57 pounds. Jane's dog weighs 42 pounds. Which number sentence would be best to use to estimate the difference in the weights?

A. $60 - 50 = \blacksquare$
B. $60 - 40 = \blacksquare$
C. $60 - 30 = \blacksquare$
D. $50 - 30 = \blacksquare$

6 Gil and Ben collect toy cars. If they combined their collections they would have 14 cars. Ben has 4 more cars than Gil. How many cars does Gil have?

A. 4   C. 9
B. 5   D. 10

7 Will bought a calculator that cost $8 and a battery to go with it. The total cost of his purchase was less than $10. Which is reasonable for the cost of the battery?

A. Less than $1
B. Between $2 and $3
C. Between $3 and $4
D. More than $4

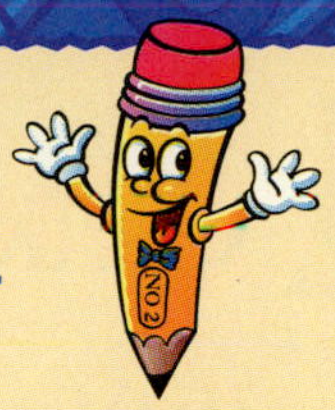

8 If today is July 3, what will the date be in 3 weeks?

A. July 19
B. July 20
C. July 21
D. July 24

Use the graph for Problems 9–10.

This graph shows the number of ice cream cones sold at a school fair in one hour.

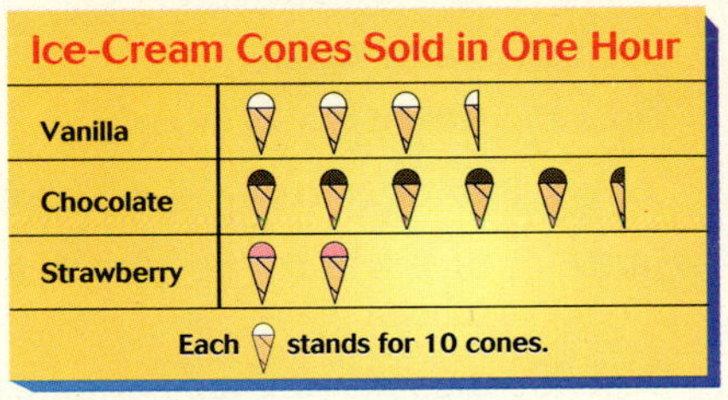

Ice-Cream Cones Sold in One Hour

Vanilla	🍦 🍦 🍦 🍦
Chocolate	🍦 🍦 🍦 🍦 🍦 🍦
Strawberry	🍦 🍦

Each 🍦 stands for 10 cones.

---

9 How many chocolate cones were sold?

A. 6
B. 50
C. 55
D. 60

10 How many more chocolate cones were sold than vanilla cones?

A. 2
B. 6
C. 10
D. 20

163A

# Checkpoint

Vocabulary Review

You may wish to review these terms before students begin the Checkpoint.

inch (in.)	12 inches equal 1 foot.
foot (ft)	1 foot equals 12 inches.
yard (yd)	1 yard equals 3 feet.
mile (mi)	1 mile equals 5,280 feet.
cup (c)	1 cup equals 8 ounces.
pint (pt)	1 pint equals 2 cups.
quart (qt)	1 quart equals 4 cups.
gallon (gal)	1 gallon equals 4 quarts.
ounce (oz)	16 ounces equal 1 pound.
pound (lb)	1 pound equals 16 ounces.
centimeter (cm)	100 centimeters equal 1 meter.
decimeter (dm)	1 decimeter equals 10 centimeters.
meter (m)	1 meter equals 100 centimeters.
kilometer (km)	1 kilometer equals 1,000 meters.
liter (L)	1 liter equals 1,000 milliliters.
milliliter (mL)	1,000 milliliters equal 1 liter.
gram (g)	1,000 grams equal 1 kilogram.
kilogram (kg)	1 kilogram equals 1,000 grams.
Fahrenheit (F)	A unit for measuring temperature.
Celsius (C)	A unit for measuring temperature.

Using the Page

Purpose To review concepts and skills presented since the last Checkpoint

- If necessary, discuss the directions and content of each section of the Checkpoint with the class.

- Page numbers associated with each group of items refer to the pages on which the skill or concept was presented. Those students needing review should turn to the appropriate lessons.

# Checkpoint
Measurement

Vocabulary

Use the words from the Word Bank to fill in the blanks.

1. A ___?___ **foot** is equal to 12 inches.
2. A meter is equal to 100 ___?___. **centimeters**
3. We can use ___?___ **Fahrenheit** to measure temperature.
4. We can use ___?___ **grams** to measure how heavy things are.

Word Bank
centimeters
Fahrenheit
foot
grams

Concepts and Skills

Write the weight that is more. (pages 146–147, 158–159)

5. 1 lb 8 oz or 26 oz **26 oz**
6. 1 kg or 900 g **1 kg**
7. 3 kg or 3,100 g **3,1000 g**
8. 16 oz or 1 lb 2 oz **1 lb 2 oz**
9. 1 lb 15 oz or 32 oz **32 oz**
10. 2 kg or 2,500 g **2,500 g**

Describe the following temperatures as *hot, cold, warm,* **or** *cool.* (pages 148–149, 160–161)

11. 5° F. **cold**
12. 70° F. **warm**
13. 47° F. **cool**
14. 91° F. **hot**
15. 32° F. **cold**
16. 19° F. **cold**
17. 68° F. **warm**
18. 102° F. **hot**

Write the best unit of measure for the following. Write *centimeter, decimeter, meter,* **or** *kilometer.* (pages 152–155)

19. length of a baseball bat **Decimeter or meter**
20. distance you could walk in 2 hours **Kilometer**
21. length of a swimming pool **Meter**
22. distance you could throw a ball **Meter**

Write the best unit of measure for the following. Write *liters* **or** *milliliters.* (pages 156–157)

23. pitcher **Liters**
24. small juice can **Milliliters**
25. bath tub **Liters**
26. lake **Liters**
27. drinking glass **Milliliters**
28. spoon **Milliliters**
29. juice box **Milliliters**
30. fish tank **Liters**
31. swimming pool **Liters**

164

Reinforcement and Remediation 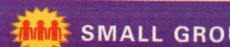 SMALL GROUPS

- Provide each group with standard and metric rulers, Celsius and Fahrenheit thermometers, balance scale with grams and ounces, paper.

- Students estimate and measure the following in standard and metric units: room temperature, length of a dictionary, weight of 4 coins.

- Students record their estimates and measurements on a chart, and compare their findings with other groups.

Problem Solving

32. Which is a better outdoor temperature for a picnic, 20°C or 45°C? **20°C**

33. Suppose it takes 30 minutes to drive in a car from your house to the park. Would the distance be measured in feet, yards, or miles? **Miles**

34. Carrie walks 2 kilometers every day. How many kilometers does she walk in a week? in 2 weeks? **14 kilometers; 28 kilometers**

35. The temperature at noon was 74°F. At night, the temperature was 58°F. How much colder was the temperature at night? **16 degrees colder**

What do you think?

What unit of measure would you use to measure short lengths? Explain your choice.

Centimeters or inches; Explanations may vary but should indicate that these units are shorter lengths than other units.

Journal Idea

Write a short, funny story about what happens when someone uses a ruler incorrectly. Tell what is measured incorrectly and why the result is funny. **Check students' stories.**

You Decide
Activity

Plan a Perfect Day

Work with your group to plan a perfect school day.

- What activities will you do? How long will each activity last?

Make a schedule for your day. List each activity, the time it begins and ends, and how long it will last.

You might wish to include this work in your portfolio.

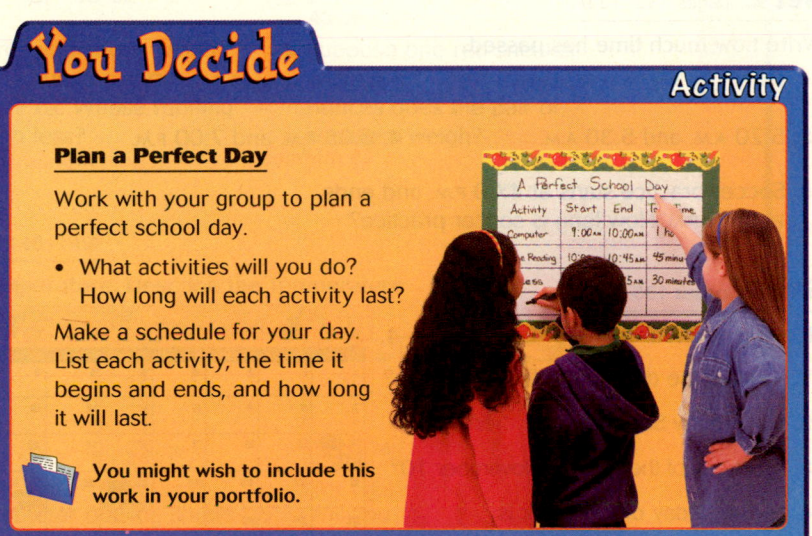

Check students' schedules. Check that times do not overlap and that elapsed time is calculated correctly for each activity.

165

Set E

Use an

1. 3 in

5. 1 $\frac{3}{4}$

9. Fra clo
2 y

Set F

Write t

1. 8 o
8 o

3. 1 p
18

5. 2 lb
2 lb

7. Col 20 wei sho
Col

Set G

Write e as *hot*,

1. °F—

25°

5. The put

10. 9:12; n after ni

11. 4:46; f utes af five

12. 8:54; e utes af

13. 1:43; f sevent

14. 3:46; f fourtee

15. 5:55; fi five fift

16. 11:14;

17. 9:11; e

Scoring Rubric

3 EXCELLENT Students create a schedule for a perfect school day with a number of fun activities and their beginning and ending times. Students then compute the elapsed time for each activity. Students check that the total amount of time for all activities does not exceed the amount of time spent in school.

2 SATISFACTORY Students create a schedule for a perfect school day with a few activities and their beginning and ending times. Students then compute the elapsed time for each activity. Students may not check that the total amount of time for all activities does not exceed the amount of time spent in school.

1 NEEDS IMPROVEMENT Students have little or no understanding of how to make a schedule to cover the amount of time spent in school.

Ongoing Assessment

You may want to have students review their responses to the Baseline Assessment questions presented at the beginning of the chapter. Have students discuss what they have learned in this chapter to help them answer the "What do you think?" question.

What do you think?

Accept reasonable responses. Some students may say centimeters because there are one hundred centimeters in a meter, or inches because they are shorter than feet or yards.

Journal Idea

Encourage students to share and compare journal entries.

You Decide

This activity allows you to evaluate students' understanding of time. As students do the activity, remind them that they need to schedule only the amount of time they spend in school. Be sure students include the beginning and ending time and the total amount of time spent in each activity in their schedule.

Portfolio Activity

You may wish to have students include their work from the You Decide activity in their portfolios.

The scoring rubric on the left may be used to help you assess students' work.

Extra Practice

Set H (pages 152–155)

Estimate and measure to the nearest centimeter.

1.  **2 cm**
←—?—→

2.  **4 cm**
←———?———→

3.  **3 cm**
←——?——→

What unit would you use to measure each?
Write *centimeter, decimeter, meter,* or *kilometer.*

4. length of a toothpick
Centimeter

5. height of a mountain
Kilometer

6. height of a flagpole
Meter

Set I (pages 156–157)

Choose a unit to measure each item.
Write *liters* or *milliliters.*

1. jug
Liters

2. bathtub
Liters

3. medicine dropper
Milliliters

4. teacup
Milliliters

5. perfume bottle
Milliliters

6. truck's gasoline tank
Liters

Set J (pages 158–159)

Choose the best estimate.

1.
50 g or 1 kg
50 g

2.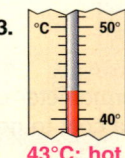
10 kg or 100 kg
10 kg

3.
150 kg or 1 kg
1 kg

Set K (pages 160–161)

Write each temperature. Describe the temperature
as *hot, cold, warm,* or *cool.*

1. °C 20°
10°
19°C; warm

2. °C 10°
0°
3°C; cold

3. °C 50°
40°
43°C; hot

Chapter Test

Write how much time has passed.

1.
21 minutes

2.
18 minutes

Draw each length. **Check students' drawings for accuracy.**

3. $2\frac{1}{2}$ in.
4. $3\frac{3}{4}$ in.
5. $\frac{1}{4}$ in.
6. 4 cm
7. 10 cm
8. 6 cm

Choose cup, pint, or gallon to measure each item.

9. kitchen sink
Gallon
10. mug
Cup
11. bathtub
Gallon
12. shampoo bottle
Pint

Choose liter or milliliter to measure each item.

13. swimming pool
Liter
14. soup spoon
Milliliter
15. medicine dropper
Milliliter

Write each temperature.

16.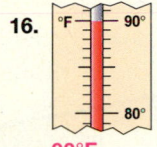
90°F
17.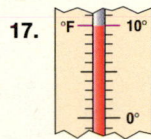
10°F
18.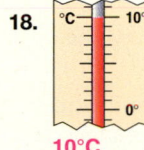
10°C
19.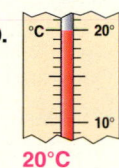
20°C

Write the weight that is more.

20. 1 lb or 14 oz **1 lb**
21. 2 lb 3 oz or 40 oz **40 oz**
22. 700 g or 1 kg **1 kg**
23. 5 kg or 4,500 g **5 kg**

24. Bob lost some money. He has $3.50 now. Yesterday he spent $2.50. He started with $10. How much money did Bob lose? **$4.00**

25. It takes Lily 35 minutes to get home. If she leaves at 4:35 P.M., can she be home by 5:00 P.M.? Explain why or why not.
No; she'll arrive home at 5:10 P.M.

 Self-Check
Did you position your ruler correctly for Exercises 3–8?

169

Reteaching Chart

Learning Objectives	Test Items	Text Pages	Resources
4A	1–2	128–131, 136–137	P4-1, R4-1, P4-2, R4-2, P4-5, R4-5
4B	1, 2, 25	132–133	P4-3, R4-3
4C	3–12, 16–17, 20–21	140–149	P/R4-6, P/R4-7, P/R4-8, P/R4-9
4D	13–15, 18–19, 22–23	152–161	P/R4-11, P/R4-12, P/R4-13, P/R4-14
4E	24–25	134–135, 150–151, 162–162A, 163–163A	P4-4, R4-4, P4-10, R4-10, P4-15, R4-15

The item analysis in the chart may be used to diagnose students' errors and to correlate the lessons and resources appropriate for reinforcement and remediation.

Chapter Test

Assessment Options

This Chapter Test can be used as a review, practice test, or chapter test. The Performance Assessment on page 170 may be used instead of or with this Chapter Test.

Other options are provided in the *Assessment Guide*.

- **Pretest—multiple-choice or free-response form,** pp. 91–94
- **Posttest—multiple-choice or free-response form,** pp. 95–98
- **Interview Activity,** p. 38
- **Long-Answer Question,** p. 9

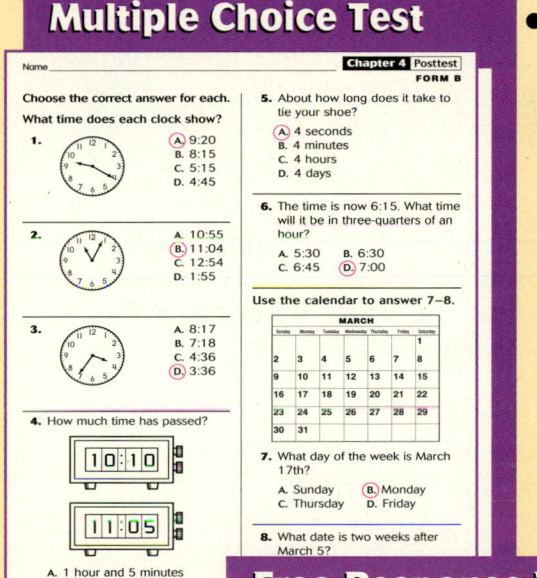

Multiple Choice and Free Response tests assess the same objectives and contain the same number of test items.

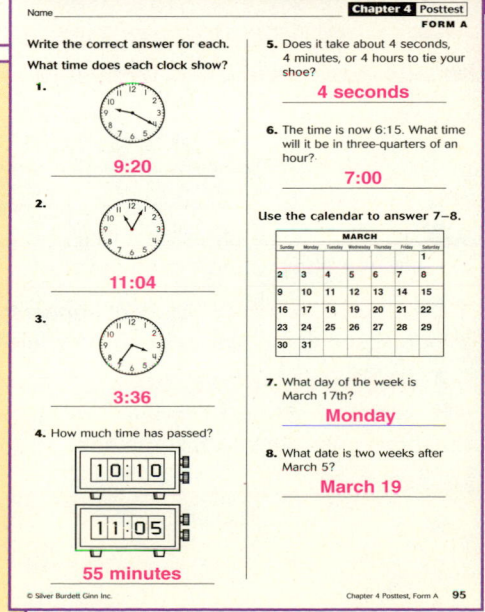

Performance Assessment

Using the Page

 **PAIRS**

Materials: rulers, paper clips, string, tiles, clock

Purpose Performance Assessment may be used instead of, or in conjunction with, more formal assessments to show what students know about time and measurement.

- Problem 1 will help you assess if students have an understanding of the basic concepts and processes of measuring elapsed time. Problem 2 will help you assess if students have an understanding of the basic concepts and processes of measuring length. The Scoring Rubrics below provide specific behaviors and results to look for in Problems 1 and 2.

- Students can evaluate their own work by responding to the Self-Check questions. To further assess their understanding, ask students the following questions: **What part of measuring time and length do you find the easiest? the most difficult?**

For Your Portfolio

You may wish to have students include the work from the Performance Assessment in their portfolios.

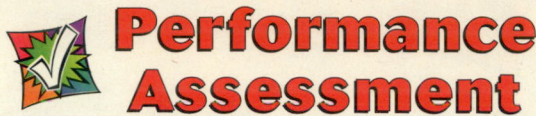

Performance Assessment

Show What You Know About Time and Measurement

1 Use the chart to answer Questions 1a–1c. Show your answers on a clock you have made or drawn.

What You Need
- rulers
- paper clips
- string
- color tiles
- clock

a. You start skating at 3:30 P.M. Show the time that you will be finished. **4:00 P.M.**

b. Some students play 3 games of kickball in a row, without stopping. They start at 10:00 A.M. Show the time that they will be finished. **11:00 A.M.**

c. Basketball starts at 2:25 P.M. The bus will pick up the basketball team 20 minutes after basketball ends. Show the time that the bus will pick up the team. **3:40 P.M.**

Playing Time	
Activity	**Minutes**
Basketball	55
Kickball	20
Skating	30

Self-Check Did you remember to add the time spent playing basketball to the starting time for Question 1c?

2 Use the materials shown below for Questions 2a–2b.

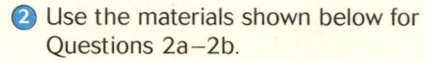

a. Measure the cover of your math book in as many ways as you can. Record your results. Which material is best for measuring your book? Explain why. **The rulers; The other materials do not give exact measurements.**

b. Repeat the activity, measuring two other items in the classroom. **Check students' measurements; Explanations may vary.**

Self-Check Did you find more than one way to measure your book?

For Your Portfolio

You might wish to include this work in your portfolio.

170

Performance Assessment Scoring Rubrics

Scoring Rubric 1

3 EXCELLENT Students correctly calculate the elapsed times. They show the times on a real or drawn clock. Students can explain how they found their answers.

2 SATISFACTORY Students understand how to calculate the elapsed times but make errors while calculating.

1 NEEDS IMPROVEMENT Students have little or no understanding of how to calculate the elapsed times. They can show the times on a clock with some help.

Scoring Rubric 2

3 EXCELLENT Students use customary and noncustomary units to measure the book. They use pictures or words to describe the size of the book in a variety of ways.

2 SATISFACTORY Students have an understanding of how to measure the book using customary and noncustomary units but may not measure correctly. They may need help thinking of different ways to measure the size of the book.

1 NEEDS IMPROVEMENT Students have little or no understanding of how to measure or describe the book. With help, they can measure and describe the size of the book. They need help thinking of different ways to measure the size of the book.

Extension

Making a Schedule

A schedule shows when events or activities will happen. Here's a schedule showing the times for team tryouts.

Use the schedule to answer these questions.

1. What time do swim tryouts start? **4:00**

2. Could you attend both the soccer and the volleyball tryouts? Why or why not? **See above right.**

   2. Yes. Soccer tryouts end before volleyball tryouts begin.

3. How much time is there for baseball tryouts? **Two hours**

Team Tryouts

Time	Activity
10:30 – 12:30	baseball team
1:00 – 3:00	soccer team
3:30 – 4:30	volleyball team
4:00 – 5:30	swim team

4. **Create Your Own** Write a schedule for a class picnic. Include time to eat lunch, play games, and clean up. **Check students' schedules.**

   5. They would want to know, before the picnic began, what time the activities would begin and end so they could plan which ones they would go to.

   - Make two columns. Write *Time* at the top of one column and *Activity* at the top of the other.

   - Under *Activity,* list each of the activities in the order in which they will happen.

   - Under *Time,* write the time each activity will begin and end.

5. Why would students at the picnic want to see the schedule at the start of the picnic? **See above right.**

171

Extension

Using the Page

 SMALL GROUPS

Purpose To read and create schedules

- Discuss: **How can you tell which teams had the longest tryouts?** (*Compare the time for each tryout.*)

- Ask: **How long will the tryouts for the soccer and volleyball teams take?** (*3 hours*)

Additional Questions

Ask: **Why is it a good idea to know how much time you want to schedule for the entire picnic before scheduling time for each activity?** (*It helps you know how much time is available for each activity.*)

Discuss: **How would you decide how much time to schedule for each activity?** (*Sample answer: Estimate the time you want to spend for each activity to decide if there is enough time.*)

Cumulative Review

Preparing for Tests

Purpose To review and maintain skills and concepts learned in this and previous chapters.

Preparation for Standardized Tests

Exercises in the review are presented in a multiple-choice format similar to that used for most standardized tests. This provides an opportunity for students to practice their test-taking skills. You may wish to have students use Teaching Tool 1, which simulates the format of the answer sheets commonly used with standardized tests.

Continuous Skills Review

The six mathematics strands below are continuously reviewed to help students maintain skills. Each Cumulative Review covers four of the six strands. All six strands are reviewed every 3 chapters. Continuous review will help students retain skills and concepts learned in previous chapters and in the previous grade.

★ Number Concepts
★ Patterns, Relationships, and Algebraic Thinking
★ Geometry and Spatial Reasoning
★ Measurement
★ Probability and Statistics
★ Operations

Cumulative Review
★★★★★ **Preparing for Tests**

Choose the correct letter for each answer.

Number Concepts	Measurement

1. What is the value of the digit 1 in the number 981,256?

 A. 1 hundred
 B. 1 thousand
 C. 10 thousand
 D. 100 thousand

2. Which number is the same as fifty thousand, one hundred three?

 A. 501,003
 B. 50,130
 C. 50,103
 D. 5,103

3. Which group of numbers is in order from *greatest* to *least*?

 A. 4,832 3,930 2,749 2,184
 B. 4,832 2,749 3,930 2,184
 C. 2,284 2,749 3,930 4,832
 D. 2,749 2,184 4,832 3,930

4. Which shaded region does **NOT** represent $\frac{3}{4}$ of the figure?

 A.   C.
 B.   D.

5. What is the *perimeter* of this figure?

 A. 10 cm
 B. 15 cm
 C. 24 cm
 D. 25 cm

(2 cm, 3 cm, 4 cm, 1 cm)

6. Tonya's soccer game starts at 4:00 P.M. and ends at 5:15 P.M. How long does it last?

 A. 45 minutes
 B. 1 hour 5 minutes
 C. 1 hour 15 minutes
 D. 1 hour 45 minutes

7. Look at the thermometer. If the temperature goes down by 4°, how warm will it be?

 A. 72°F
 B. 78°F
 C. 80°F
 D. 82°F

8. A party began at 2:30 P.M. It lasted 2 hours 20 minutes. Which clock shows what time the party ended?

 A. 2:50   C. 4:10
 B. 3:20   **D.** 4:50

Chapter 4 Cumulative Review

Reteaching Chart

Strand	Items	Text Pages	Resources
Number Concepts	1–4	22–25, 28–29	P/R1–8, P/R1–10
Patterns, Relationships, & Algebraic Thinking	*	*	*
Geometry	9–12	See Grade 2.	
Measurement	5–8	132–133, 148–149	P/R4–3, P/R4–9 See Activity, next page.
Probability & Statistics	13-16	See Grade 2.	
Operations	*	*	*

* Covered in Chapter 5 or 6 Cumulative Reviews.

Geometry and Spatial Reasoning	Probability and Statistics

Geometry and Spatial Reasoning

9. How many sides does this shape have?

A. 4
B. 6
C. 7
D. 8

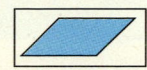

10. Which figure is congruent to (has the same size and shape as) the figure in the box?

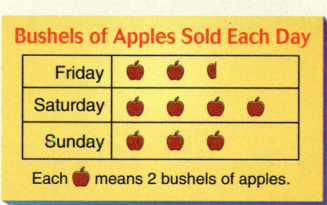

A.
C.
B.
D.

11. How many corners does an octagon have?

A. 10
B. 9
C. 8
D. 7

12. Which letter is inside the circle and outside the triangle?

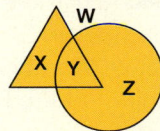

A. W   C. y
B. X   D. Z

Probability and Statistics

13. Which spinner gives you the best chance of landing on red?

A.   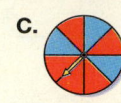   C.

B.   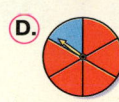   D.

Use the graph for Questions 14–16.

Bushels of Apples Sold Each Day

Friday	🍎 🍎 🍎
Saturday	🍎 🍎 🍎 🍎
Sunday	🍎 🍎 🍎

Each 🍎 means 2 bushels of apples.

14. On which day were the most apples sold?

A. Friday
B. Saturday
C. Sunday
D. Monday

15. How many more bushels were sold on Saturday than on Sunday?

A. 1   C. 4
B. 2   D. 5

16. How many bushels of apples were sold on Friday?

A. 6   C. 3
B. 5   D. $2\frac{1}{2}$

Chapter 4 Cumulative Review

Reteaching Activity

Measuring Perimeters

SMALL GROUPS   10–15 MINUTES

This activity is based on content taught in Grade 2. Perimeter is covered in Chapter 10 at Grade 3.

Materials: For each group — inch ruler

Draw a 4-in. by 7-in. rectangle on the chalkboard. Ask a volunteer to measure the sides with a ruler and then add the lengths of the sides together. Remind students that the distance around the figure is called the perimeter. Ask: **What is the perimeter of the rectangle?** *(22 inches)*

Then have children work in groups to measure the perimeter of the following items in the classroom: their desk, their math book, and their notebook. Have groups compare their findings.

Chapter 5

Daily Lesson Planner
Multiplication Concepts

To Start the Chapter

Chapter Opener

Resources

- Chapter Opener
  Career Spotlight
  Chapter Project, *Teacher Guide*,
  pages 172–173

- Chapter Pretest, *Assessment Guide*,
  pages 99–102

- Family Letter With Activity,
  Home-School Connection,
  pages 27–28

- 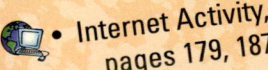 Internet Activity,
  pages 179, 187

Lesson 1

PAGES 174–175B	**EXPLORE: Understanding Multiplication**

LEARNING OBJECTIVES 5A	**Manipulatives:** 36 counters
	Chapter File Folder
	  Practice, Reteach, Extend 5-1
	  Teaching Tool 43
	Daily Review 5-1
	Problem of the Day 5-1

NCTM STANDARDS 1, 3, 7	Teaching With Technology

Lesson 2

PAGES 176–177	**Relating Multiplication and Addition**
LEARNING OBJECTIVES 5A	**Chapter File Folder** Practice, Reteach, Extend 5-2 Daily Review 5-2 Practice Workbook, p. 21 Problem of the Day 5-2
NCTM STANDARDS 1, 3, 6, 7, 8, 13	p. 176

Lesson 6

PAGES 186–187	**Multiplying by 5**
LEARNING OBJECTIVES 5B	**Chapter File Folder** Practice, Reteach, Extend 5-6 Daily Review 5-6 Problem of the Day 5-6 ✓ **Checkpoint, pp. 188–189**
NCTM STANDARDS 1, 3, 6, 7, 8, 13	p. 187 p. 187 p. 189

Lesson 7

PAGES 190–191	**Multiplying by 3**

LEARNING OBJECTIVES 5B	**Chapter File Folder**
	  Practice, Reteach, Extend 5-7
	  Teaching Tools 7, 18
	Daily Review 5-7
	Practice Workbook, p. 22
	Problem of the Day 5-7

NCTM STANDARDS 1, 3, 6, 7, 8, 13	p. 191

Lesson 11

PAGES 198–199	**EXPLORE: Patterns in Multiplication**

LEARNING OBJECTIVES 5B	**Chapter File Folder**
	  Practice, Reteach, Extend 5-11
	  Teaching Tools 4, 8, 9, 43
	Daily Review 5-11
	Practice Workbook, p. 25
	Problem of the Day 5-11

NCTM STANDARDS 3, 6, 7, 8, 13	p. 198

Lesson 12

PAGES 200–201A	**Problem-Solving Application**

LEARNING OBJECTIVES 5C	**Chapter File Folder**
	  Practice, Reteach, Extend 5-12
	  Teaching Tool 21
	Daily Review 5-12
	Problem of the Day 5-12
	Problem Solving: Preparing
	  for Tests

NCTM STANDARDS 1, 2, 3, 7	✓ **Checkpoint, pp. 202–203**

Correlation to Investigations

Investigations in Number, Data, and Space
Dale Seymour Publications

Lessons 1-11	**Things That Come in Groups** Investigations 1-4; Ten-Minute Math, 91-94
	Landmarks in the Hundreds Investigations 1, 3
Lesson 12	**Mathematical Thinking at Grade 3** Investigation 3

 Algebra   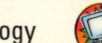 Time for Technology   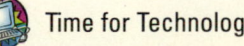 Time for Technology   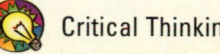 Critical Thinking

LEARNING OBJECTIVES

5A Relate arrays and repeated addition to multiplication

5B Use 0, 1, 2, 3, 4, and 5 as factors

5C Analyze and solve problems using skills and strategies

NCTM STANDARDS

1 Problem Solving
2 Communication
3 Reasoning
4 Mathematical Connections
5 Estimation
6 Number Sense and Numeration
7 Whole Number Operations
8 Whole Number Computation
9 Geometry and Spatial Sense
10 Measurement
11 Statistics and Probability
12 Fractions and Decimals
13 Patterns and Relationships

Lesson 3

PAGES 178–181

LEARNING OBJECTIVES 5A

NCTM STANDARDS 1, 3, 7, 13

Using Arrays
Chapter File Folder
Practice, Reteach, Extend 5-3
Daily Review 5-3
Problem of the Day 5-3

 p. 178   p. 179   p. 181

Lesson 4

PAGES 182–183

LEARNING OBJECTIVES 5C

NCTM STANDARDS 1, 3, 7

Developing Skills for Problem-Solving
Chapter File Folder
Practice, Reteach, Extend 5-4
Daily Review 5-4
Problem of the Day 5-4

Lesson 5

PAGES 184–185

LEARNING OBJECTIVES 5B

NCTM STANDARDS 1, 3, 6, 7, 8, 13

Multiplying by 2
Chapter File Folder
Practice, Reteach, Extend 5-5
Teaching Tool 18
Daily Review 5-5
Problem of the Day 5-5

Lesson 8

PAGES 192–193

LEARNING OBJECTIVES 5B

NCTM STANDARDS 1, 3, 6, 7, 8, 13

Multiplying by 4
Chapter File Folder
Practice, Reteach, Extend 5-8
Daily Review 5-8
Practice Workbook, p. 23
Problem of the Day 5-8

 p. 193

Lesson 9

PAGES 194–195

LEARNING OBJECTIVES 5C

NCTM STANDARDS 1, 3, 7

Problem-Solving Strategy
Chapter File Folder
Practice, Reteach, Extend 5-9
Daily Review 5-9
Problem of the Day 5-9

Lesson 10

PAGES 196–197

LEARNING OBJECTIVES 5B

NCTM STANDARDS 1, 3, 6, 7, 8, 13

Multiplying by 1 or 0
Chapter File Folder
Practice, Reteach, Extend 5-10
Daily Review 5-10
Practice Workbook, p. 24
Problem of the Day 5-10

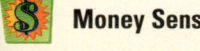 p. 197  p. 197

Chapter End

PAGES 204–209

LEARNING OBJECTIVES 5A 5B 5C

NCTM STANDARDS 1, 3, 6, 7, 8, 13

Chapter Assessment
Extra Practice, pp. 204–206
Chapter Test, p. 207
Performance Assessment, p. 208
Extension, p. 209
Cumulative Review

In the *Assessment Guide*
Chapter Posttest, pp. 103–106
Interview Activity, p. 39
Long-Answer Question, p. 10

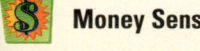 **Money Sense**  **Internet Activity**

Meeting Individual Needs

Learning Styles vary from student to student. Every Meeting Individual Needs activity focuses on one of the following learning styles. The variety of styles enables students to learn math in ways that are most comfortable to them.

- AUDITORY
- INDIVIDUAL
- KINESTHETIC
- LINGUISTIC
- LOGICAL/MATHEMATICAL
- SOCIAL/COOPERATIVE
- VISUAL/SPATIAL

Acquiring English Proficiency

Students work in pairs and clap to model multiplication. Write a multiplication fact, such as 3×2, on the chalkboard. Explain that one student will clap 3 groups of 2 claps each. As one student claps, the partner counts the total number of claps, and then says the multiplication sentence, $3 \times 2 = 6$. Partners repeat, switching roles and using other multiplication facts.

For additional activities, see Acquiring English Proficiency, pp. 175, 185, 197, 200A.

AUDITORY

For Extra Help

Materials: color tiles, index cards with numbers 1–5

Students will use color tiles to make rectangles. Students take two cards from the pile. The first card tells the number of rows in the rectangle; the second card tells the number of tiles in each row. Students write a fact for the rectangle. They turn the rectangle on its side and write the related fact.

For additional activities, see For Extra Help, pp. 177, 183, 199.

VISUAL

For Early Finishers

Materials: construction paper, crayons or markers

Have students draw pictures of situations that show multiplication facts. For example, for 3×4, a student might draw 3 cars with 4 people in each car. Underneath the picture, students write a multiplication sentence and an addition sentence that correspond to the picture.

For additional activities, see For Early Finishers, pp. 175, 177, 181, 183, 185, 191, 193, 195, 197, 199, 200A.

VISUAL/SPATIAL

Gifted and Talented

Materials: 2 sets of index cards with numbers 1–9

One partner takes 2 cards from the pile, uses them to create a 2-digit number, and writes a multiplication fact that has that number as its product. If the student succeeds, he or she earns 1 point. The student returns the cards to the pile. The second student does the same. Play continues until one student earns 5 points.

For additional activities, see Gifted and Talented, pp. 187, 193.

LOGICAL/MATHEMATICAL

Inclusion

Materials: egg carton, 2-color counters

Students may benefit from activities in which they model and link repeated addition and multiplication. Write related addition and multiplication facts, such as 4×2 and $2 + 2 + 2 + 2$. Explain that both sentences show 4 groups of 2. Have students model the sentences by putting 2 counters in each of 4 sections of an egg carton.

For additional activities, see Inclusion, p. 191.

VISUAL/SPATIAL

*These Manipulatives are found in the Manipulatives Kit.

MATH CENTER

Using Data

Materials: coins (pennies)

Students choose an item to buy. Then they make a table to show how much 1, 2, 3, 4, and 5 of that item would cost. Students do the same thing for 2 other items. Encourage them to use pennies to model their purchases.

For review, see pages 68–68A, 184–193, 196–197, and 200–201.

Answers: Ring: 3¢, 6¢, 9¢, 12¢, 15¢; top: 2¢, 4¢, 6¢, 8¢, 10¢; sticker: 1¢, 2¢, 3¢, 4¢, 5¢; pin: 4¢, 8¢, 12¢, 16¢, 20¢; puzzle: 5¢, 10¢, 15¢, 20¢, 25¢.

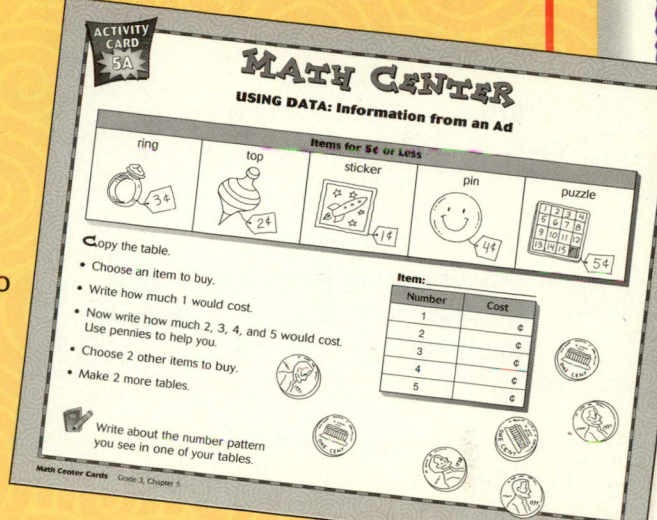

Problem Solving

Materials: Teaching Tool 3 (10 x 10 Grid Paper), crayons

Students may use the guess and check strategy to find rectangles containing 12 squares on the grid paper. Then they outline and color each rectangle they find. Students repeat the activity, this time finding rectangles containing 16 squares.

For review, see pages 178–181.

Answers: Answers will vary; all arrays have 12 squares.

Cooperative Learning

Materials: spinner labeled 2, 2, 3, 4, 5; Teaching Tool 19 (Number Line 0–100)

Have students work in small groups. One student spins the spinner twice and writes a multiplication sentence with those two factors. The second student uses a number line to show the fact. The third student uses repeated addition to show the fact. Students repeat and switch roles.

For additional activities, see Cooperative Learning, pp. 181, 195.

LOGICAL/MATHEMATICAL

Manipulatives

Manipulatives: color tiles*

Have students make a train of 2 tiles. Students then write a multiplication sentence for the train: $1 \times 2 = 2$. Students make another train of 2 tiles and write the multiplication sentence for the total: $2 \times 2 = 4$. They continue until they have 9 trains of 2 tiles. Have students repeat the activity with trains of 3 tiles, 4 tiles, and 5 tiles.

For additional activities, see Manipulatives, p. 187.

VISUAL/SPATIAL

Chapter 5 Assessment

Skills Trace
Skills Assessed at Each Grade

Grade 2
Introduce skip counting by 2s, 3s, 4s, and 5s. (Chapter 3)

Grade 3
Introduce using the multiplication algorithm. Introduce multiplication facts 0–5.

Grade 4
Use basic multiplication facts. (Chapter 3)

Informal Assessment

Informal assessments provide day-to-day feedback. In conjunction with more formal assessments, they give a complete picture of conceptual development.

In the Student Book

What Do You Think?
student pages 189, 203
Students explain what they have learned.

Create Your Own
student pages 197, 200A, 209
Students create their own problems.

Journal Idea
student pages 187, 189, 199, 203
Students communicate mathematically.

Self-Check
student pages 207, 208
Students evaluate their own work.

In the Teacher Guide

Baseline Assessment
teacher page 172
Helps you assess prior knowledge

Ongoing Assessment
ASSESS UNDERSTANDING
Helps you assess students' understanding

WRAP-UP
Helps you monitor students' progress

JOURNAL IDEA
teacher pages 173, 181, 185, 189, 197, 199, 200A, 203
Helps you assess students' communication of math ideas

Portfolio Ideas

Portfolio opportunities appear on Student Book pages 203 and 208, and Teacher Guide pages 175A–B, 203, and 208.

Other items that you may wish to include in your student portfolios are:

- **Completed Chapter Projects**
- **Journal Entries**
- **CD-ROM and Internet Activities**
- **Informal Observations and Interview Activities**

For further suggestions for organizing and using portfolios, see *Assessment Guide,* pages 50–54.

Formal Assessment

Formal assessment can occur before and after the chapter, as well as at natural breaking points in the chapter.

In the Student Book

Checkpoints
student pages 188–189, 202–203
Use for assessing progress as students work through the chapter.

Chapter Test
student page 207

Performance Assessment
student page 208
The Performance Assessment helps you evalutuate the skills and concepts developed in Chapter 5 through hands-on activities.

 CD-ROM Test Generator

This software allows you to customize your own chapter test. Formats include:

- **Multiple Choice**
- **Free Response**
- **Standardized Test**

Assessment Guide

You may choose among the following pages in the *Assessment Guide.*

Pretest Options
- **Free Response, pages 99–100**
- **Multiple Choice, pages 101–102**

Posttest Options
- **Free Response, pages 103–104**
- **Multiple Choice, pages 105–106**

Interview Activity
page 39

Long-Answer Question
page 10

Correlation to Standardized Tests

Learning Objectives	ITBS K/M	CTBS/5 (Terra Nova)	SAT9	MAT7	CAT5	*Pre/Post-Test Items	Lesson Pages
5A Relate arrays and repeated addition to multiplication	MDI: 30	17	PS: 7	CPS: 36	COM: 21	1–4	174–181
5B Use 0, 1, 2, 3, 4, and 5 as factors	COM: 11, 17, MC: 8 MDI: 27, 30		P: 8, PS: 9, 10	P: 10, 11, 16, 17, 24	COM: 25, 27	5–16	184–193 196–199
5C Analyze and solve problems using skills and strategies	PS: 18–24 ME: 11–13, 17	16	PS: 42, 44–46	CPS: 33, 40 P: 1, 12	MC: 19, 21, 40	17–20	182–183 194–195 200–200A 201–201A

MC = Math Concepts, **COM** = Math Computation, **PS** = Problem Solving, **P** = Procedures, **CPS** = Math Concepts & Problem Solving, **ME** = Math Estimation, **MDI** = Math Data Interpretation, **PB** = Math Problems

*Pretests and Posttests are found in the *Assessment Guide.*

Linking Technology

Develop and Reinforce Concepts

MathProcessor™

CD-ROM Activities use MathProcessor™ Tools to help build critical thinking skills and develop problem-solving strategies.

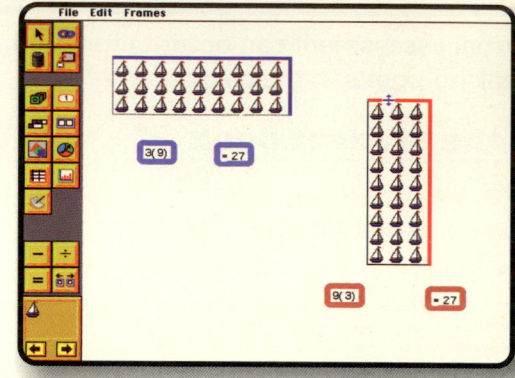

Lesson	Tools	Skill
1	Large Frames Number spaces	Students explore the relationship between addition and multiplication.
3	Large Frames Number spaces	Students use arrays to model multiplication.
11	Spreadsheet	Students enter formulas in a Spreadsheet to make a price list.

Review and Practice Skills

Math Blaster® 1

This **CD-ROM** program provides exercises and activities to practice basic math facts and develop mastery of mathematical operations. The chart below lists specific lessons where activities and references can be found.

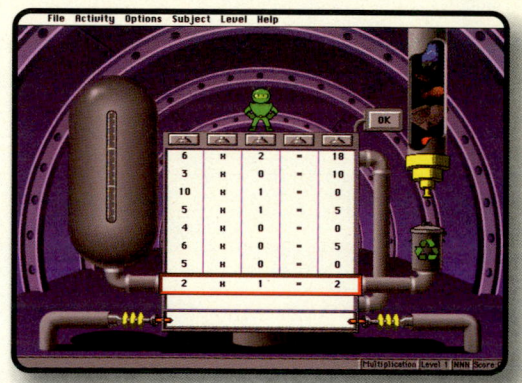

Lesson	Activity	Subject/Level
5	Number Recycler	Multiplication—Level 1: multiply by 0, 1, 2 with products 0–20
10	Trash Zapper	Multiplication—Level 1: multiply by 0, 1, 2 with products 0–20

Extend and Enrich

Internet

Students can use real data in lesson-related math activities.
Teachers can find activities and resources for Lessons 3 and 6.
Parents can find home connections to help reinforce concepts.

Visit our Web site at:

www.sbgmath.com

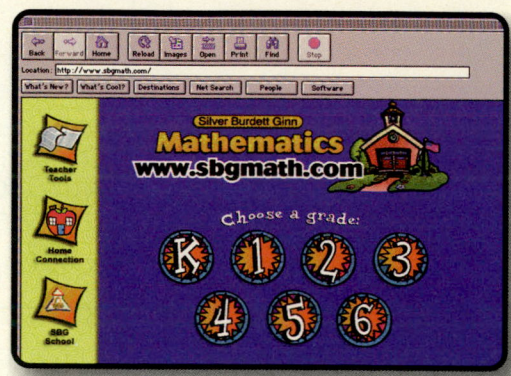

Making Connections

Literature

Chapter Resources

These books, found in your local or school library, can be used to help build math concepts.

- **How Did Numbers Begin?**
  by Mindel and Harry Sitomer
  Thomas Y. Cromwell, 1976
- **Anno's Magic Seeds**
  by Mitsumasa Anno
  Philomel Books, 1982

Home-School

Family Letter With Activity
Home-School Connection Booklet

The Family Letter for Chapter 5 introduces the concept of multiplying by using repeated addition. A family activity suggests reviewing multiplication facts by buying or making a set of flashcards. A riddle game is also provided to practice multiplication skills.

Study Buddies
Home-School Connection Booklet

Study Buddies pages provide reinforcement activities for students to work on with a partner.

- Study Buddies 5A provides practice using repeated addition to multiply.
- Study Buddies 5B reinforces multiplication by the numbers 0 and 1.

Math Backpack
Take-Home Activities

Math Backpack activities provide a link between the classroom and the home. Activity Cards 1–6 can be used with this chapter. Parents and students alike will enjoy using these laminated cards and accompanying manipulatives.

Cross-Curricular Integration

 Technology

- Use computer frames to make an array, p. 181.
- Use on-line data to practice math skills, pp. 178, 186.

 Language Arts

- Keep a reading log, Teacher Guide pp. 172–173.

 Social Studies

- Meet a teacher, p. 172.
- Learn about nations and flags, pp. 178–181.
- Learn about the United Nations, p. 181.

 Music

- Find out what a maraca is, p. 184.
- Read about tabla drums, p. 185.

Multiplication Concepts

Theme: SCHOOL ACTIVITIES

Chapter Overview

In this chapter students will develop the multiplication algorithm and apply it to multiply by the numbers 0 through 5.

Activating Prior Knowledge

Discuss with students what they already know about multiplication. Record responses on the chalkboard.

Baseline Assessment

Ask questions such as:

- **How can you combine equal groups to find how many in all?** *(Add each group one at a time to find how many in all.)*

- **Can you think of another way to find how many in all?** *(Possible responses: Count; multiply)*

Save student responses for use with the **Ongoing Assessment** section in the chapter Checkpoints on pages 189 and 203.

Multiplication Concepts

Chapter Theme: SCHOOL ACTIVITIES

....................**Real Facts**..................

Teachers at The Tome School in Maryland wanted more books for their library. Many families gave teachers thank-you gifts. So, the teachers asked families to buy books instead for $7, $10, $15, or $20. The graph shows books bought in 1997.

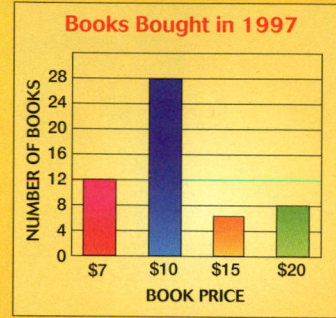

Books Bought in 1997

- How many more $10 books were sold than $20 books? **20 books**

- How could you find out how much money was spent buying books for the library? **Multiply to find the amount of money spent for each price category. Then add all the products together.**

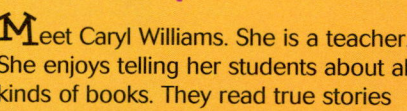

........................**Real People**........................

Meet Caryl Williams. She is a teacher. She enjoys telling her students about all kinds of books. They read true stories about desert animals. They also read tales about mice who ride motorcycles.

172

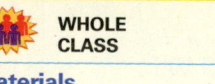

Create a Bookworm

WHOLE CLASS
Materials
▶ construction paper
▶ squares of paper (7" x 7")
▶ crayons or markers

Here is a project that will help your students learn more about multiplication. Specific lessons are referenced to help you work on the project throughout the chapter.

Getting Started

Start by telling students that they are going to make a bookworm like the one shown on pages 172–173. They will make a head for the bookworm, then add a segment for each book that has been read. Each segment should include the book's title, author, and a drawing of an event in the book.

Kids are special people

..........Real Facts..........

- The first library in America was established at Harvard University in 1638.

- The smallest bound printed book ever sold measures $\frac{1}{25}$ by $\frac{1}{25}$ inches. It contains the children's story *Old King Cole!* The pages can be turned only by using a needle.

Using the Data

As students review the bar graph on page 172, make sure they understand that the bars show the number of books bought for each of the given prices. Some additional questions you may wish to ask include:

- How many $15 books were bought? How do you know? *(6 books; the bar is halfway between 4 and 8.)*

- How many books were bought in all? *(12 + 28 + 6 + 8 = 54 books)*

..........Real People..........

Caryl Williams, a teacher, uses math every day, even when she's teaching reading or social studies. She uses numbers to keep track of students and their test grades. She uses multiplication to find supplies needed for various tasks. For example, if she has 20 students who each need 3 sheets of paper, she multiplies 20 x 3 to get the total sheets of paper needed. You might ask students to discuss other ways that teachers use math in their work.

Building Vocabulary

These key words will be found in this chapter.

multiply	**product**
factors	**array**

Journal Idea You may wish to have students write about each vocabulary term in their journals at the beginning of the chapter. At the end of the chapter, suggest that they use the vocabulary to make an acrostic or crossword puzzle.

Project Links

▶ **Lesson 6** Ask students **multiplication** questions about bookworm segments they make. For example: If a reading group of four students each read 2 books, how many segments will they add to the bookworm?

▶ **Lesson 10** Give students a 7-inch square for each book they read. Then ask students to **multiply** 7 times the number of squares they fill in to find how many inches their segments will add to the worm.

Project Wrap-up

Finish by having students attach their segments to the bookworm. Then encourage them to find how long the entire bookworm is. You may wish to continue the project throughout the year. As students read more books, they can attach additional segments to the worm and find the worm's new length.

Portfolio Students may wish to include their project work in their portfolios.

Lesson Organizer

Objective: Identify multiplication as adding equal groups.

- **NCTM Standards:** 1, 3, 7
- **Vocabulary:** multiply
- **Manipulatives:** 36 counters per pair
- **Materials:** 12 index cards, 6 paper plates per pair
- **Lesson Resources:**
  Chapter File Folder
    Practice, Reteach, Extend 5-1
    Teaching Tool 43
  Daily Review 5-1

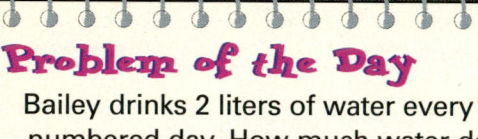

Problem of the Day 5-1

Bailey drinks 2 liters of water every even-numbered day. How much water does she drink in July? **30 liters**

Math Minute

Add.

3 + 3 *(6)*	8 + 8 *(16)*
3 + 3 + 3 *(9)*	8 + 8 + 8 *(24)*
3 + 3 + 3 + 3 *(12)*	8 + 8 + 8 + 8 *(32)*

Counting Counters

Multiplying is like adding equal groups.

Learning About It

Work with your partner. Find out how many counters you need to make 4 groups of 6 counters.

Word Bank
multiply

Step 1 Use 4 paper plates. Put 6 counters on each plate. How many counters are there altogether?

When you have equal groups of objects, you can add or you can **multiply** to find the total number of objects.

$6 + 6 + 6 + 6 = 24$ counters

4 groups of $6 = 24$ counters

$4 \times 6 = 24$ counters

What You Need

For each pair:
  12 index cards
  6 paper plates
  36 counters

Step 2 Use the counters and paper plates to make other equal groups. First write the numbers from 1 to 6 on two sets of index cards.

Step 3 Pick a card from one set to find how many plates you need. Pick a card from the other set to find how many counters to put on each plate.

- What could you do to find out how many counters you need for all the plates?
  You could add or you could multiply.

 174

---

1 Introduce

Whole Class Activity

LOGICAL/MATHEMATICAL

WHOLE CLASS   🕐 **10–15 MINUTES**

1. Twelve students stand to form three equal-sized lines.

2. Students find the total number of people in all three lines.

   - Ask: **How can you find the number of people in the lines?** *(Sample answers: Add the number of students in each line; count off.)* **How many lines of 4 students do you have?** *(3)* **Can you say 3 groups of 4 is 12?** *(Yes)*

3. Repeat using 3 students in each row.

2 Teach   Pages 174–175

Discuss how students found the total number of counters on the plates.

Ask: **Do 6 groups of 4 and 4 groups of 6 represent the same number? Explain your answer.** *(Yes, because changing the way you group the counters does not change how many counters there are)*

Critical Thinking   ANALYSIS

After Think and Discuss, say: **Explain why each of the 8 boxes of crayons needs to have the same number of crayons before you can multiply.** *(Multiplying is the same as adding equal groups.)*

Assess Understanding

Before Practice, show 3 counters on each of 6 plates. Ask: **What multiplication sentence can you write to show the number of counters on the plates?** *(6 × 3 = 18)*

USING TECHNOLOGY

MathProcessor™ Activities
See **Activities 25 and 26** in the MathProcessor™ Activity Cards.

Step 4 Repeat Step 3 five or more times. Record your work in a chart like the one below.

Draw	Think	Write
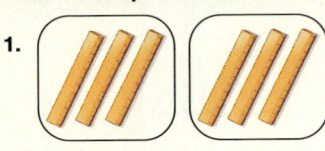	4 groups of 6 = 24	4 × 6 = 24

Think and Discuss Suppose you have 8 boxes of crayons. What must you know before you can multiply to find how many crayons you have in all?
How many crayons are in each box

Practice

Write a multiplication sentence for each picture.

1.

   2 × 3 = 6

2.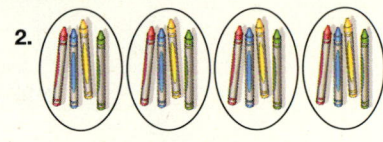

   4 × 4 = 16

3.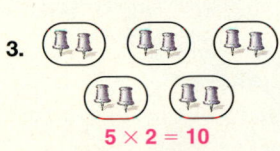

   5 × 2 = 10

4.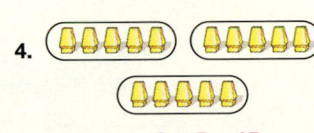

   3 × 5 = 15

For each picture tell whether or not you can write a multiplication sentence. Explain why or why not.

5.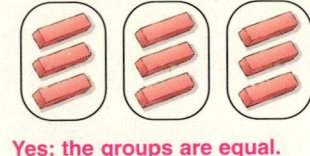

   Yes; the groups are equal.

6.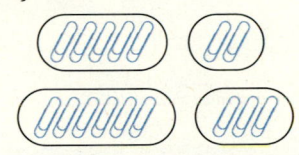

   No; the groups are not equal.

7.

   No; the groups are not equal.

8.

   Yes; the groups are equal.

 175

---

3 Wrap-up

Dorene has 3 bags with 7 oranges in each bag. How can you find how many oranges she has in all? *(Add 7 three times; multiply 3 times 7.)*

Common Error Alert

Watch for students who have difficulty writing multiplication sentences from pictures. Count the number of groups and the number in each group to find the factors.

Meeting Individual Needs

For Early Finishers

Using a spinner labeled 1–5, students spin to find how many in each group, then spin to find how many groups, then write a multiplication fact.
LOGICAL/MATHEMATICAL

Acquiring English Proficiency

Students use counters to create multiplication sentences, stating them in this form: I multiply ❏ times ❏ to get the answer. ❏ times ❏ equals ❏.
AUDITORY

Practice

Explore: Understanding Multiplication P 5-1

 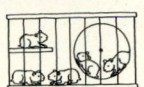

Fill in the table.
1. Write the different kinds of class pets.
2. Write the number of groups.
3. Write the number in each group.

Class Pet	Number of Groups	Number in Each Group
Turtle	2	3
Bird	3	1
Gerbil	2	5

Look at the numbers in your table. Think of different ways to find the total number of each kind of animal. Write a multiplication sentence to answer each question.
3. How many turtles are there in all? 2 × 3 = 6
4. How many birds are there in all? 3 × 1 = 3
5. How many gerbils are there in all? 2 × 5 = 10

© Silver Burdett Ginn Inc. (177)   Use with Grade 3, text pages 174–175.

Reteach

Explore: Understanding Multiplication R 5-1

How many groups of pennants?
How many pennants in each group?
How many pennants in all?
You can use a multiplication table to show the information.

Item	Number of Groups	Number in Each Group	Number in All
pennants	2	6	12

Multiplication sentence: 2 × 6 = 12

Find the total number for each group. Make a table if you need help.

1.  How many groups? 1
   How many in each group? 2
   Multiplication sentence: 1 × 2 = 2

2. 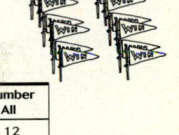 How many groups? 3
   How many in each group? 3
   Multiplication sentence: 3 × 3 = 9

3. How many groups? 4
   How many in each group? 4
   Multiplication sentence: 4 × 4 = 16

© Silver Burdett Ginn Inc. (178)   Use with Grade 3, text pages 174–175.

Extend

Playing Ball E 5-1 NUMBER SENSE

Help the sports director count the sports equipment. Circle like groups of equipment. Draw a line to connect them, then write the missing numbers. One has been started for you.

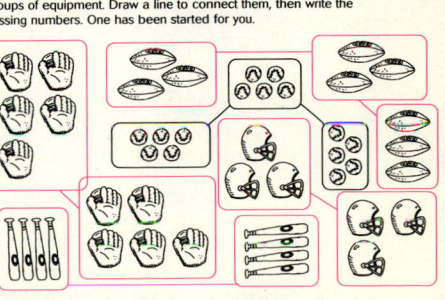

1. baseballs
   3 groups of 5 = 15 in all
2. bats
   2 groups of 4 = 8 in all
3. gloves
   2 groups of 5 = 10 in all
4. helmets
   2 groups of 3 = 6 in all
5. footballs
   3 groups of 3 = 9 in all
6. The equipment list shows that there should be 16 baseballs, 8 bats, 10 gloves, 6 helmets, and 12 footballs. Compare the list with your totals. What has been lost?
   1 baseball and 3 footballs

© Silver Burdett Ginn Inc. (179)   Use with Grade 3, text pages 174–175.

Teaching With Technology
Explore: Understanding Multiplication

1 Introduce

Objective: Students will explore multiplication as adding equal groups on the computer.

Resources: MathProcessor™ Version 1.1

MathProcessor™ User Guide: Sections C, D, I, J, L

In Lesson 1 students use counters to identify multiplication as adding equal groups. The MathProcessor™ Tools can also be used for this exploration.

Use MathProcessor™ Base-Ten Blocks, Spreadsheet, and Number Cubes to explore multiplication.

Ask: How can you show 4 + 4 with Base-Ten Blocks?
(Show 4 ones; add 4 more ones.) **4 + 4 + 4?** *(Show 4 ones; add 4 ones; add 4 ones.)*

2 Teach

As you model the addition and multiplication examples below, discuss the steps.

Step 1

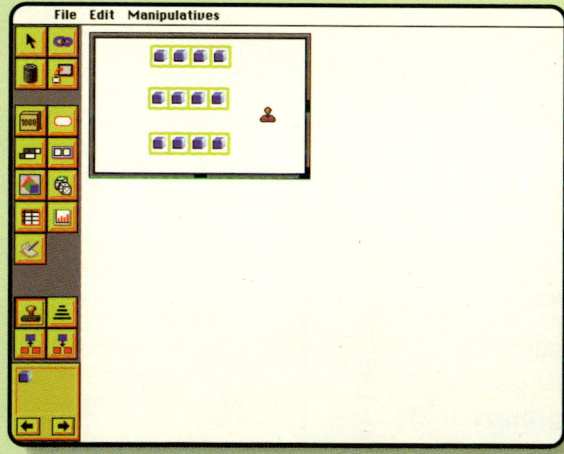

- Open a Base-Ten Blocks workspace ▣ .
- Show 4 ones cubes. Select the cubes and Stamp 🔖 2 more groups.
- **Ask: How many groups of 4 are there?** *(3 groups)* **How many ones cubes are there in all?** *(12)* **What multiplication sentence can we write?** *(3 × 4 = 12)*

Step 2

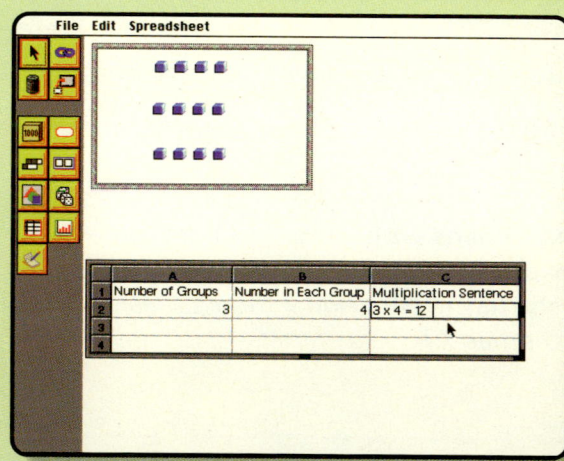

- Open a Spreadsheet ▦ . Label as shown.
- **Ask: How are addition and multiplication related?** *(Sample answer: Multiplication is a quick way of adding equal groups.)*
- Delete the Base-Ten Blocks workspace, and open a new one.

Step 3

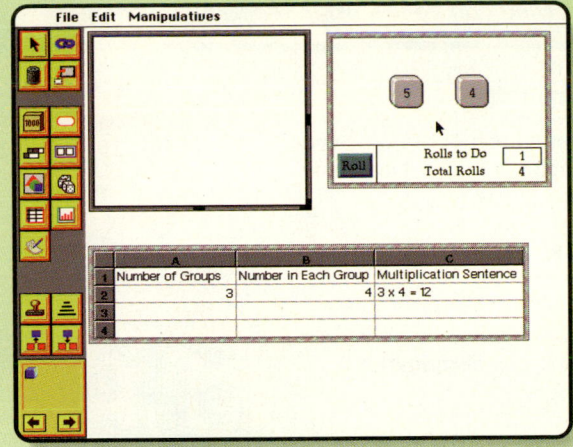

- Click Number Cubes 🎲 . Select and roll 2 cubes.

Ask: The number on the first cube tells how many equal groups. Let the number on the second cube tell how many in each group. How many groups will we make? How many will be in each group? *(Sample shown: 5 equal groups, 4 in each group)*

Step 4

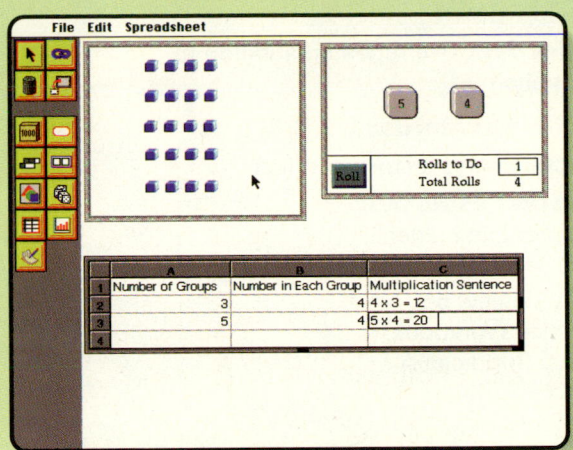

- In the Spreadsheet, enter the number of ones in each group and the number of groups. Show the groups.

Ask: How many cubes in all? What multiplication sentence can we write in the Spreadsheet ? *(Answers will vary. Sample shown)*

- Record the results in the Spreadsheet.

Step 5

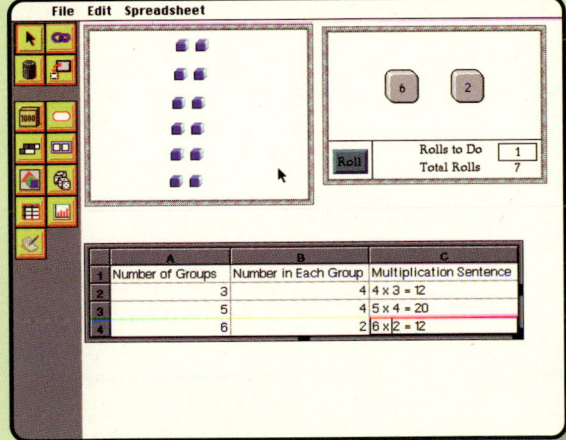

- In a new Base-Ten Blocks workspace, repeat the procedure used in Steps 3 and 4.

Ask: How can we find the total number? *(Multiply number of groups by number in each group.)* **What multiplication sentence can we write?** *(Answers will vary.)*

3 Wrap-up

Allow students to use MathProcessor™ to show the number of groups and number in each group.

Write a multiplication sentence for each exercise.

1. 2 groups of 4 *(2 × 4 = 8)* **2.** 4 groups of 2 *(4 × 2 = 8)*

3. 3 groups of 7 *(3 × 7 = 21)* **4.** 7 groups of 3 *(7 × 3 = 21)*

5. 5 groups of 5 *(5 × 5 = 25)* **6.** 1 group of 8 *(1 × 8 = 8)*

 Portfolio Opportunity You may wish to have students open a Writing space and explain their steps for the exercises above and for the question below. You may also wish to have students make printouts of their responses and add them to their portfolios.

Which addition sentence, 3 + 3 + 3 or 3 + 4 + 5 can you write as a multiplication sentence? Explain. *(3 + 3 + 3 ; to multiply, the groups have to be equal.)*

 ## Meeting Individual Needs

Manipulatives

Students work in pairs and take turns. One student models equal groups of cubes using the **MathProcessor**™ Base-Ten Blocks. The partner writes the multiplication sentence.

For Early Finishers

Math Blaster® software and **MathProcessor**™ **Activity Cards 25–30** provide opportunities for students to practice skills learned in this chapter.

Relating Multiplication and Addition

Lesson Organizer

Objective: Use repeated addition to multiply.

- **NCTM Standards:** 1, 3, 6, 7, 8, 13
- **Vocabulary:** factors, product
- **Lesson Resources:**
  Chapter File Folder
    Practice, Reteach, Extend 5-2
  Daily Review 5-2
  Practice Workbook, p. 21
  Study Buddies 5A

Problem of the Day   5-2

How many ways can you use dimes and nickels to make 25¢? Make a list to show the ways. **2 dimes and 1 nickel; 1 dime and 3 nickels; 5 nickels**

Math Minute

Write as addition sentences.

2 groups of 3 *(3 + 3 = 6)*

3 groups of 2 *(2 + 2 + 2 = 6)*

4 groups of 4 *(4 + 4 + 4 + 4 = 16)*

---

1 Introduce

Cooperative Activity
KINESTHETIC

 SMALL GROUPS   ⏵ 5–10 MINUTES

Materials: coin sets, cups, spinners (1–9)

1. Students spin a number and place that many cups on their desk.

2. Students spin another number and place that many dimes in each cup.

3. Students write an addition sentence and a multiplication sentence for their cups and dimes and find the total number of dimes.

Using Algebra

Book Fair

Multiplying can be like using repeated addition.

Learning About It

The book fair is here! Each of the 4 shelves in this bookcase holds 8 books. How many books are in the bookcase?

You can add to find out.

$8 + 8 + 8 + 8 = 32$

Whenever you add the same number again and again, you can also multiply.

$8 + 8 + 8 + 8 = 32$

4 groups of 8 = 32

So $4 \times 8 = 32$

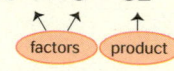
factors   product

There are 32 books in the bookcase.

> The numbers you multiply are called **factors**.
>
> The answer you get when you multiply is called the **product**.

Word Bank

factors
product

More Examples

A.

$3 + 3 = 6$
2 groups of 3 = 6
$2 \times 3 = 6$

B.

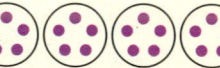

$5 + 5 + 5 + 5 = 20$
4 groups of 5 = 20
$4 \times 5 = 20$

Think and Discuss What multiplication sentence could you use to show $7 + 7 + 7 + 7 + 7 + 7$? **$6 \times 7 = 42$**

176

---

2 Teach   Pages 176–177

Ask: What do factors tell you about the groups? *(Factors tell how many groups there are and how many are in each group.)*

Critical Thinking   SYNTHESIS
After Think and Discuss, say: **Create a picture and an addition sentence that show 6 × 3.** *(Sample answers: picture showing 6 groups of 3; 3 + 3 + 3 + 3 + 3 + 3 = 18)*

Assess Understanding
After Try It Out, ask: **How many factors are in each multiplication sentence?** *(2)*

CHALLENGE

Each compact disc costs $9 and each tape costs $7. How much do three compact discs and four tapes cost? *($55)*

Try It Out

Write a multiplication sentence for each addition sentence.

1. $3 + 3 + 3 + 3 + 3 + 3 = 18$
   $6 \times 3 = 18$
2. $5 + 5 = 10$
   $2 \times 5 = 10$
3. $7 + 7 + 7 = 21$
   $3 \times 7 = 21$
4. $4 + 4 + 4 + 4 = 16$
   $4 \times 4 = 16$
5. $1 + 1 + 1 = 3$
   $3 \times 1 = 3$
6. $0 + 0 = 0$
   $2 \times 0 = 0$

Practice

Write an addition sentence and a multiplication sentence for each set of pictures.

7.
   $3 + 3 + 3 + 3 = 12$
   $4 \times 3 = 12$
8.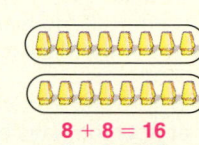
   $2 + 2 + 2 + 2 + 2 + 2 = 12$
   $6 \times 2 = 12$
9. (pencils)
   $8 + 8 = 16$
   $2 \times 8 = 16$

Write a multiplication sentence for each addition sentence.

10. $2 + 2 + 2 + 2 = 8$
    $4 \times 2 = 8$
11. $8 + 8 = 16$
    $2 \times 8 = 16$
12. $9 + 9 + 9 = 27$
    $3 \times 9 = 27$
13. $7 + 7 + 7 + 7 + 7 = 35$
    $5 \times 7 = 35$
14. $5 + 5 + 5 = 15$
    $3 \times 5 = 15$
15. $1 + 1 + 1 + 1 = 4$
    $4 \times 1 = 4$

Problem Solving

Use the chart for Problems 16–18.

16. Which costs less, 9 comic books or 9 picture books?
    9 comic books cost less.
17. Suppose you had $27. Would it be reasonable to say you can buy 6 storybooks? Explain your reasoning.
    No; 6 x $5 = $30 so they cost more than $27.
18. On the last day of the book fair, storybooks go on sale for $4 each. How much money can you save if you buy 6 storybooks on the last day?
    $6

Carver School Book Fair

Picture Books $7

Storybooks $5

Comic Books $2

Review and Remember

Add or subtract.

19. $\begin{array}{r} 34 \\ + 28 \\ \hline 62 \end{array}$
20. $\begin{array}{r} 181 \\ + 125 \\ \hline 306 \end{array}$
21. $\begin{array}{r} 9,004 \\ - 2,506 \\ \hline 6,498 \end{array}$
22. $\begin{array}{r} 372 \\ - 164 \\ \hline 208 \end{array}$
23. $\begin{array}{r} 1,287 \\ - 489 \\ \hline 798 \end{array}$

For Extra Practice, see Set A, page 204. **177**

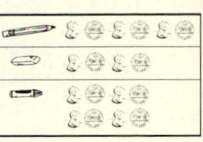

Using Algebra

In this lesson, students investigate the **numerical relationship** between addition and multiplication.

---

3 Wrap-up

How can you use addition to find the total number of oranges if there are four bags of six oranges? *(Add 6 four times.)*

Common Error Alert

Watch for students who confuse *factor* and *product*. Guide them to think of a product as something that is made. In math, the product is made by multiplying the factors.

Meeting Individual Needs

For Early Finishers

Students take a handful of counters and arrange them into equal groups. Then they write addition and multiplication sentences to record the groups.
LOGICAL/MATHEMATICAL

For Extra Help

Using index cards with predrawn groups on them, students can write *add □ + □ + □ = □* or they can say "There are □ groups of □."
LOGICAL/MATHEMATICAL

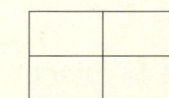
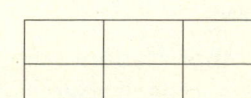

LESSON 2 177

Lesson Organizer

Objective: Use arrays to multiply.

- **NCTM Standards:** 1, 3, 7, 8, 13
- **Vocabulary:** array
- **Lesson Resources:**
  Chapter File Folder
  Practice, Reteach, Extend 5-3
  Daily Review 5-3

Problem of the Day 5-3

Rudy has a secret number. He says it when he counts by twos and by fives. He does *not* say the number when he counts by threes. What could the number be?
Sample answers: 10, 20, 40

Math Minute

Write each using multiplication.

2 + 2 *(2 × 2)*	5 + 5 + 5 *(3 × 5)*
3 + 3 *(2 × 3)*	2 + 2 + 2 *(3 × 2)*
3 + 3 + 3 *(3 × 3)*	3 + 3 + 3 + 3 *(4 × 3)*

Hurray for Arrays!

Using Algebra

Drawing arrays can help you think about multiplication.

Learning About It

It's United Nations Day! You are putting up a display of flags from around the world on your classroom wall. How many flags are in the display?

Wait! Before you start counting, look at how the flags are placed.

> The flags form an **array**. An array shows objects in rows and columns.

Word Bank
array

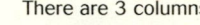
There are 3 columns.

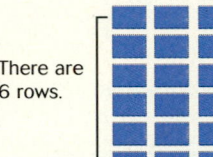
There are 6 rows.

Since an array is made of equal groups, you can multiply to find how many objects are in it.

INTERNET ACTIVITY
www.sbgmath.com

There are 6 rows.
There are 3 flags in each row.
6 × 3 = 18

There are 18 flags in the display.

178

---

1 Introduce

Cooperative Activity

KINESTHETIC

PAIRS   5–10 MINUTES

Materials: 16 color tiles, spinner (1–4)

1. One student spins for the number of rows.

2. The other student spins for the number of tiles in each row.

3. Students arrange the tiles to form a shape that shows the number of rows and the number of tiles in each row.

- Ask: **What shape is your arrangement?** *(Sample answer: Rectangle)*

---

2 Teach   Pages 178–181

Tell students that rows go across like rows in a theater, while columns go up and down like columns that are used to support the roof of a porch.

- Ask: **Is there another array you could make with 18 flags? What happens if you turn the array sideways?** *(Sample answer: Yes, 2 rows with 9 in each row; You have 9 rows with 2 in each row.)*

- Ask: **What arrays can you make with 12 flags?** *(4 rows with 3 in each row; 3 rows with 4 in each row; 2 rows with 6 in each row; 6 rows with 2 in each row; 1 row with 12 in the row; 12 rows with one in each row)*

Have students look at the More Examples section on page 179. Ask them to check that there are the same number of stars in each array in Example A and the same number of rectangles in each array in Example B.

- Ask: **What does turning an array sideways show?** *(Sample answer: The order in which you multiply the number of rows and the number in each row does not change the product.)*

- Ask: **What multiplication sentence can you write for an array with 4 rows with 4 stars in each row?** *(4 × 4 = 16)*

Oh no! The display was put up sideways! Are there still 18 flags?

Compare the two arrays.

How many rows? **6 rows**
How many flags in each row? **3 flags**
How many in all? **18 flags**
$6 \times 3 = 18$ **18 flags**

How many rows? **3 rows**
How many flags in each row? **6 flags**
How many in all? **18 flags**
$3 \times 6 = 18$

Yes, both arrays have 18 flags.

> The order in which you multiply factors does not change the product.

More Examples

A.

$4 \times 2 = 8$ $2 \times 4 = 8$

B.

$5 \times 3 = 15$ $3 \times 5 = 15$

Think and Discuss If you know that $4 \times 8 = 32$, how can that help you find the product of 8×4?
The order in which you multiply factors does not change the product, so 8 x 4 = 32.

179

Using Algebra

In this lesson, students use representations of **numerical relationships** to multiply.

Internet Activity

www.sbgmath.com

Students use on-line data to practice math skills.

Geometry and Spatial Reasoning

Math Connections

WHOLE CLASS

- Have students observe the classroom.

- Say: **Write the name of an object you see. Next to it, write the name of a geometric figure this object reminds you of.**

- Encourage volunteers to share what they wrote with the class. As each figure is named, have students identify as many properties of the figure as they can.

- Invite students to suggest how these figures can be combined, subdivided, or changed to form other figures. You might also ask students to write the names of other objects that have a similar shape and suggest places where these objects might be found.

▲ This activity can be used at any time to reinforce or extend math connections.

Critical Thinking SYNTHESIS

After Think and Discuss, ask: **What happens to a sum if you change the order of the addends?** *(The sum stays the same.)*

Using Technology
CD-ROM

MathProcessor™

Tools: Large Frames; Number spaces
Objective: To use arrays to model multiplication

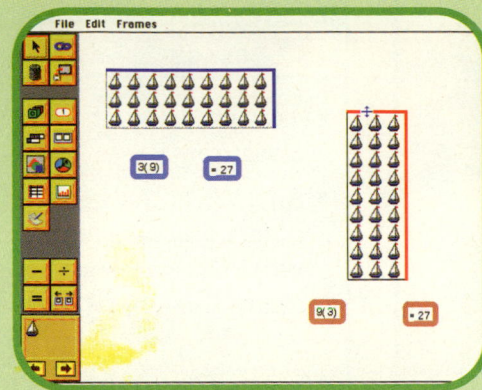

- Link 🔲 a Large Frame 🔲 to two Number spaces 🔲. Drag right to show 9 frames. Drag the top border up to show 3 rows. The array shows 3 × 9.

- Click one Number space. Click 🟨=. Click a catalog item to fill the array.

- Open another Large Frame and link it to two Number spaces. Model 9 × 3. Click-drag right to show 3 frames. Drag up to show 9 rows. Fill the array.

- Click one Number space. Click 🟨=.

Additional Activities

See also **Activities 27 and 28** in the MathProcessor™ Activity Cards.

Try It Out

Complete the multiplication sentence for each array.

1. $2 \times 3 = \blacksquare$ **6**

2. $3 \times 6 = \blacksquare$ **18**

3. $4 \times 5 = \blacksquare$ **20**

Practice

Write a multiplication sentence for each array.

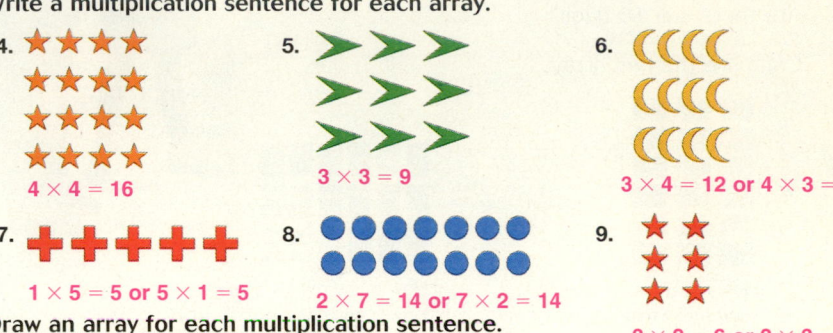

4. $4 \times 4 = 16$

5. $3 \times 3 = 9$

6. $3 \times 4 = 12$ or $4 \times 3 = 12$

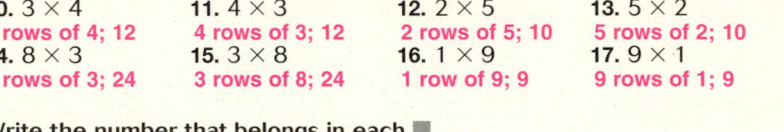

7. $1 \times 5 = 5$ or $5 \times 1 = 5$

8. $2 \times 7 = 14$ or $7 \times 2 = 14$

9. $3 \times 2 = 6$ or $2 \times 3 = 6$

Draw an array for each multiplication sentence. Then find the product. **Check students' drawings.**

10. 3×4
3 rows of 4; 12

11. 4×3
4 rows of 3; 12

12. 2×5
2 rows of 5; 10

13. 5×2
5 rows of 2; 10

14. 8×3
8 rows of 3; 24

15. 3×8
3 rows of 8; 24

16. 1×9
1 row of 9; 9

17. 9×1
9 rows of 1; 9

Write the number that belongs in each ■.

18. $4 \times 6 = 24$, so $6 \times 4 = \blacksquare$ **24**

19. $9 \times 7 = 63$, so $7 \times 9 = \blacksquare$ **63**

20. $5 \times 6 = 30$, so $\blacksquare \times 5 = 30$ **6**

21. $7 \times 4 = 28$, so $\blacksquare \times 7 = 28$ **4**

22. $\blacktriangledown \times \bullet = 35$, so $\bullet \times \blacktriangledown = \blacksquare$ **35**

23. $\blacktriangle \times \bullet = 12$, so $\bullet \times \blacktriangle = \blacksquare$ **12**

Problem Solving

24. Mr. Swinton's class made classroom mailboxes. There are 7 rows. There are 4 mailboxes in each row. How many mailboxes did the class make? **28 mailboxes**

180

2 Teach (continued)

Assess Understanding

After Try It Out, ask: **If you add another row of 5 circles to the array in Exercise 3, how many circles will you have in all? Write the new multiplication sentence.** *(25; 5 × 5 = 25)*

 ## GIFTED AND TALENTED

Making Arrays Give students a cardboard or paper square-foot tile. Have them estimate how many tiles they will need to arrange in each row and column in order to cover the surface of their classroom floor, and use the number of rows and columns to determine the total number of tiles they will need. Students can check their estimates by using a tile to measure the length and width of the room.

25. A flag store has many flags displayed in an array. There are 3 rows of state flags and 3 rows of flags from other countries. If there are 8 flags in each row, how many flags are on display?
48 flags

26. Social Studies Connection In 1945, there were 51 countries that belonged to the United Nations. By 1996 there were 185 countries. How many more countries belonged in 1996 than in 1945?
134 more countries

▲ The United Nations headquarters is in New York City. Its goals include peace, health, and education for all people. Flags of the member countries fly in front of its buildings.

Review and Remember

Give the place value of the underlined digit.

27. 1<u>8</u>
tens

28. 3<u>4</u>
ones

29. <u>1</u>23
hundreds

30. 80<u>6</u>
tens

31. <u>2</u>,970
thousands

32. <u>4</u>5,310
ten thousands

Time for Technology

Using the MathProcessor™ CD-ROM

Making Arrays

Use frames to make an array that shows 8 × 9.

- Open a frames space 🔲. Link it to two number spaces 🔲.

- Click-drag the right bar until 9 frames show. Then click-drag the top bar until 8 frames show.

- Click a catalog item to fill the array. Click one number space. Then, click =.

- Follow the steps to make another array to show 9 × 8.

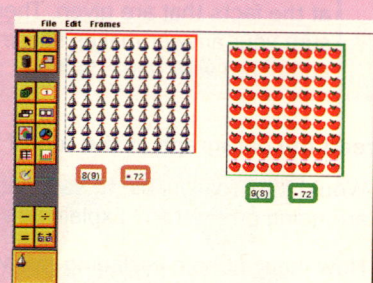

For Extra Practice, see Set B, page 204. **181**

For Extra Practice, see Set B, page 204.

Time For Technology

Students must wait until the arrow turns to a cross-hatch before dragging the right bar and top border.

3 Wrap-up

Describe two arrays that can help you find 4 × 6. *(4 rows of 6; 6 rows of 4)*

📓 **Journal Idea** Write two multiplication sentences. Then make an array to represent each sentence.

Common Error Alert

Watch for students who don't realize that an array can represent 2 multiplication sentences such as 4 × 5 = 20 and 5 × 4 = 20.

Meeting Individual Needs

For Early Finishers

Write the numbers 1–9 on slips of paper. Students pick two numbers, then use cubes to model a multiplication problem and solve.
KINESTHETIC

Cooperative Learning

Student 1 creates an array with cubes. Student 2 writes the multiplication sentence, and then Student 3 tells the factors and product for the array.
LINGUISTIC

Practice

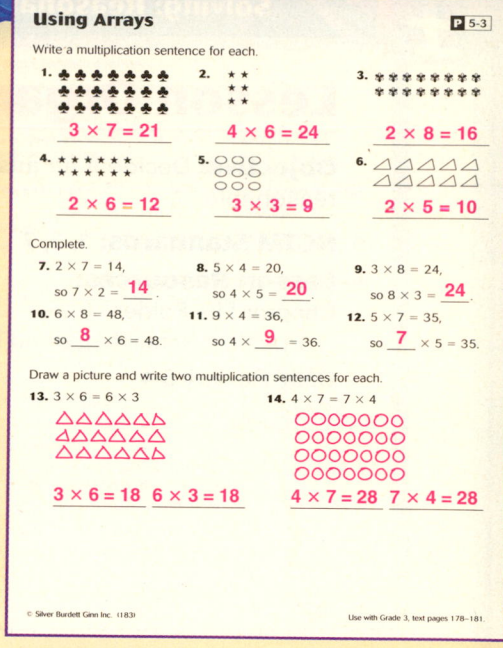

Using Arrays P 5-3

Write a multiplication sentence for each.

1. $3 \times 7 = 21$ **2.** $4 \times 6 = 24$ **3.** $2 \times 8 = 16$

4. $2 \times 6 = 12$ **5.** $3 \times 3 = 9$ **6.** $2 \times 5 = 10$

Complete.

7. $2 \times 7 = 14$, so $7 \times 2 = $ **14**

8. $5 \times 4 = 20$, so $4 \times 5 = $ **20**

9. $3 \times 8 = 24$, so $8 \times 3 = $ **24**

10. $6 \times 8 = 48$, so **8** $\times 6 = 48$.

11. $9 \times 4 = 36$, so $4 \times $ **9** $= 36$.

12. $5 \times 7 = 35$, so **7** $\times 5 = 35$.

Draw a picture and write two multiplication sentences for each.

13. $3 \times 6 = 6 \times 3$
$3 \times 6 = 18 \quad 6 \times 3 = 18$

14. $4 \times 7 = 7 \times 4$
$4 \times 7 = 28 \quad 7 \times 4 = 28$

© Silver Burdett Ginn Inc. (183) Use with Grade 3, text pages 178–181.

Reteach

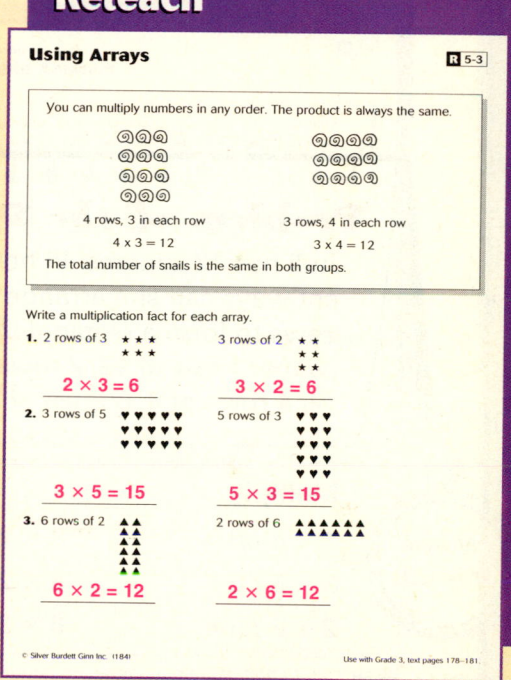

Using Arrays R 5-3

You can multiply numbers in any order. The product is always the same.

4 rows, 3 in each row
$4 \times 3 = 12$

3 rows, 4 in each row
$3 \times 4 = 12$

The total number of snails is the same in both groups.

Write a multiplication fact for each array.

1. 2 rows of 3
$2 \times 3 = 6$

3 rows of 2
$3 \times 2 = 6$

2. 3 rows of 5
$3 \times 5 = 15$

5 rows of 3
$5 \times 3 = 15$

3. 6 rows of 2
$6 \times 2 = 12$

2 rows of 6
$2 \times 6 = 12$

© Silver Burdett Ginn Inc. (184) Use with Grade 3, text pages 178–181.

Extend

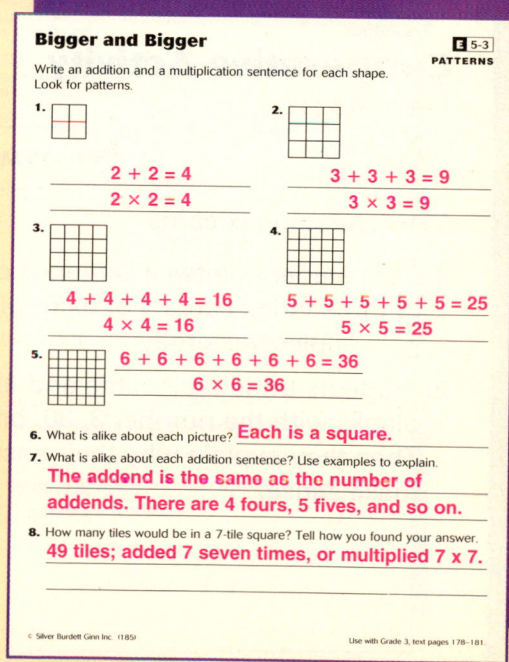

Bigger and Bigger E 5-3
PATTERNS

Write an addition and a multiplication sentence for each shape. Look for patterns.

1. $2 + 2 = 4$
$2 \times 2 = 4$

2. $3 + 3 + 3 = 9$
$3 \times 3 = 9$

3. $4 + 4 + 4 + 4 = 16$
$4 \times 4 = 16$

4. $5 + 5 + 5 + 5 + 5 = 25$
$5 \times 5 = 25$

5. $6 + 6 + 6 + 6 + 6 + 6 = 36$
$6 \times 6 = 36$

6. What is alike about each picture? **Each is a square.**

7. What is alike about each addition sentence? Use examples to explain.
The addend is the same as the number of addends. There are 4 fours, 5 fives, and so on.

8. How many tiles would be in a 7-tile square? Tell how you found your answer.
49 tiles; added 7 seven times, or multiplied 7 x 7.

© Silver Burdett Ginn Inc. (185) Use with Grade 3, text pages 178–181.

Checkpoint

Vocabulary Review

You may wish to review these terms before students begin the Checkpoint. Vocabulary words in Lessons 1–6:

multiply   To find the total number of items in groups of equal size.

factors   The numbers that are multiplied to give a product. *Example:* $3 \times 8 = 24$. The factors are 3 and 8.

product   The answer in multiplication. *Example:* $4 \times 8 = 32$. The product is 32.

array   An arrangement of objects or numbers in rows and columns.

Using the Page

Purpose To review concepts and skills presented up to this point in Chapter 5.

- If necessary, discuss the directions and content of each section of the Checkpoint with the class.

- Page numbers associated with each group of items refer to the pages on which the skill or concept was presented. Those students needing review should turn to the appropriate lessons.

 **Using Algebra**

In Exercises 13–15, students use representations of **numerical relationships** to multiply.

In Exercises 16–21, students draw arrays to represent a multiplication sentence.

Checkpoint
Understanding Multiplication

Write a multiplication sentence for each picture. (pages 174–175)

1. $3 \times 2 = 6$ 2. $6 \times 4 = 24$ 3. $7 \times 5 = 35$

Write a multiplication sentence for each addition sentence. (pages 176–177)

4. $2 + 2 + 2 + 2 + 2$ $5 \times 2 = 10$
5. $7 + 7 + 7$ $3 \times 7 = 21$
6. $5 + 5 + 5 + 5$ $4 \times 5 = 20$
7. $9 + 9 + 9 + 9$ $4 \times 9 = 36$
8. $6 + 6$ $2 \times 6 = 12$
9. $4 + 4 + 4 + 4 + 4 + 4$ $6 \times 4 = 24$
10. $4 + 4$ $2 \times 4 = 8$
11. $8 + 8 + 8$ $3 \times 8 = 24$
12. $3 + 3 + 3 + 3 + 3 + 3 + 3$ $7 \times 3 = 21$

Using Algebra Write a multiplication sentence for each array. (pages 178–181)

13. $4 \times 3 = 12$ or $3 \times 4 = 12$
14. $3 \times 7 = 21$ or $7 \times 3 = 21$
15. $5 \times 6 = 30$ or $6 \times 5 = 30$

Using Algebra Draw an array for each multiplication sentence. (pages 178–181)

16. 2×5 2 rows of 5
17. 4×3 4 rows of 3
18. 2×2 2 rows of 2
19. 6×6 6 rows of 6
20. 8×2 8 rows of 2
21. 3×4 3 rows of 4

Find each product. (pages 184–187)

22. $\begin{array}{r} 2 \\ \times 7 \\ \hline 14 \end{array}$
23. $\begin{array}{r} 4 \\ \times 2 \\ \hline 8 \end{array}$
24. $\begin{array}{r} 6 \\ \times 5 \\ \hline 30 \end{array}$
25. $\begin{array}{r} 9 \\ \times 5 \\ \hline 45 \end{array}$
26. $\begin{array}{r} 5 \\ \times 3 \\ \hline 15 \end{array}$
27. $\begin{array}{r} 4 \\ \times 5 \\ \hline 20 \end{array}$
28. $\begin{array}{r} 2 \\ \times 6 \\ \hline 12 \end{array}$
29. $\begin{array}{r} 7 \\ \times 2 \\ \hline 14 \end{array}$
30. $\begin{array}{r} 9 \\ \times 2 \\ \hline 18 \end{array}$
31. $\begin{array}{r} 6 \\ \times 2 \\ \hline 12 \end{array}$

Reinforcement and Remediation
PAIRS

- Provide pairs with index cards numbered 1–9. Have students place cards face down, pick a card, and draw a picture that shows the number on the card multiplied by 2.

- Have the partner write a multiplication sentence for the picture. Ask the partner to count by 2s to check the product.

- Encourage students to repeat the activity by multiplying the number on the card by 5. Have them compare patterns of products with 2 or 5 as factors.

Problem Solving

32. The Bay School computer lab has 9 tables. There are 5 computers on each of 6 tables. How many computers are in the lab?
30 computers

33. Mrs. Goodman gave 2 pencils to each of 4 students. Mr. Witt gave 3 pencils to each of 5 students. Who gave out more pencils?
Mr. Witt

34. Jack has 3 boxes of markers. Each box has 8 markers in it. If Jack takes 2 out of each box, how many markers are still in the boxes?
18 markers

35. **Analyze** Mr. Ring put his students into groups of 5. He made 4 groups. Three students were left. How many students are in Mr. Ring's class?
23 students

 Journal Idea
Write two addition sentences—one that can be solved by multiplying and one that cannot.

Check students' addition sentences.

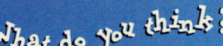 **What do you think?**

Does the order in which you multiply factors change the product?

No; the product will be the same.

 ## Critical Thinking Corner

Visual Thinking

An Array Puzzle

Using Algebra You can use arrays to make a puzzle!

- Use grid paper. Make arrays to show these multiplication examples.

2 × 7	3 × 2	8 × 5
4 × 5	4 × 2	3 × 4

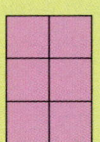

2 × 7

- Cut out each of your arrays. Put them together to make an array that shows the multiplication example 10 × 10.

3 × 2

How many squares are in a 10 × 10 array? **100 squares**

189

Ongoing Assessment

You may want to have students review their responses to the questions presented at the beginning of the chapter. Have students discuss what they have learned so far in this chapter that helps them answer the "What do you think?" question.

What do you think?

Accept reasonable responses. Students should recognize that the order in which you multiply factors does not change the product.

 ## Journal Idea
Encourage students to describe why one sentence can and the other cannot be solved by multiplication.

Critical Thinking Corner

Visual Thinking

A sample answer is shown.
Some arrays have been turned.

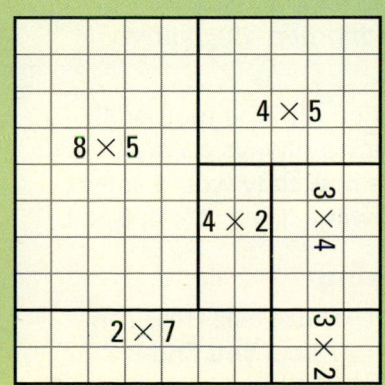

Lesson Organizer

Objective: Multiply by 3.

- **NCTM Standards:** 1, 3, 6, 7, 8, 13
- **Lesson Resources:**
  Chapter File Folder
      Practice, Reteach, Extend 5-7
      Teaching Tools 7, 18
  Daily Review 5-7
  Practice Workbook, p. 22
  Transparency 7

Problem of the Day   5-7

At the music store, you get 1 free CD for every 5 you buy. If you buy 10 CDs, how many CDs will you have in all? **12 CDs**

Math Minute

Add.

3 + 3 *(6)*   3 + 3 + 3 + 3 + 3 *(15)*

3 + 3 + 3 *(9)*

3 + 3 + 3 + 3 *(12)*

---

7 — Multiplying by 3

Jump for Recess

Repeated addition and skip counting can help you multiply by 3.

Learning About It

It's time for recess! There are only 4 jump ropes. If 3 students share each jump rope, how many students can jump rope at one time?

$4 \times 3 = \blacksquare$ or $\begin{array}{r} 3 \\ \times 4 \\ \hline \end{array}$

THERE'S ALWAYS A WAY!

- **One way** to find the product is to draw a picture. Show 4 groups of 3.

12 students in all

- **Another way** is to use repeated addition.

  $3 + 3 + 3 + 3 = 12$

- **Another way** is to skip count.

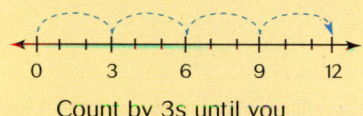

Count by 3s until you have said 4 numbers.

3, 6, 9, 12

- **Another way** is to use a multiplication fact.

  $4 \times 3 = 12$

12 students share the jump ropes.

Think and Discuss How can knowing $4 \times 3 = 12$ help you find 5×3? **5×3 is one more group of 3 than 4×3. $4 \times 3 = 12$ so $5 \times 3 = 12 + 3$, or 15.**

190

---

1 Introduce

Cooperative Activity

KINESTHETIC

SMALL GROUPS   **10–15 MINUTES**

Materials: For each group: 18 counters, 3 plates

1. Students choose a number from 1 to 6 and place this number of counters on each plate.

   - Ask: **How many counters do you have in all? How did you find the total number of counters on all 3 plates?** *(Sample answer: 15; repeated addition)*

2. Students repeat the activity using different numbers from 1 to 6.

2 Teach   Pages 190–191

Discuss the relationship between skip counting and repeated addition.

- **How is counting by 3s different from counting by 5s?** *(Since there's a different number in each group, the pattern is different.)*

For further practice with the methods discussed in There's Always a Way!, have students discuss how they would solve each of the following: 3×3, 7×3, 6×3.

Critical Thinking   ANALYSIS

After Think and Discuss, ask: **How can knowing $9 \times 3 = 27$ help you find 8×3?** *(Sample answer: Subtract one group of 3.)*

Assess Understanding

After Try It Out, say: **Find 3×7. What method did you use?** *(21; Sample answer: multiplication fact)*

CHALLENGE

How many toothpicks do you need to make 8 triangles if each toothpick can only be used for one triangle? *(24)*

Try It Out

Multiply.

1. $\begin{array}{r} 3 \\ \times\, 5 \\ \hline 15 \end{array}$	**2.** $\begin{array}{r} 3 \\ \times\, 1 \\ \hline 3 \end{array}$	**3.** $\begin{array}{r} 4 \\ \times\, 3 \\ \hline 12 \end{array}$	**4.** $\begin{array}{r} 3 \\ \times\, 6 \\ \hline 18 \end{array}$	**5.** $\begin{array}{r} 3 \\ \times\, 9 \\ \hline 27 \end{array}$	**6.** $\begin{array}{r} 8 \\ \times\, 3 \\ \hline 24 \end{array}$

Practice

Multiply.

7. $\begin{array}{r} 2 \\ \times\, 3 \\ \hline 6 \end{array}$	**8.** $\begin{array}{r} 3 \\ \times\, 0 \\ \hline 0 \end{array}$	**9.** $\begin{array}{r} 6 \\ \times\, 3 \\ \hline 18 \end{array}$	**10.** $\begin{array}{r} 3 \\ \times\, 7 \\ \hline 21 \end{array}$	**11.** $\begin{array}{r} 3 \\ \times\, 3 \\ \hline 9 \end{array}$	**12.** $\begin{array}{r} 9 \\ \times\, 3 \\ \hline 27 \end{array}$

13. 3×1 **3** **14.** 3×3 **9** **15.** 9×3 **27** **16.** 0×3 **0** **17.** 3×9 **27**

18. 7×3 **21** **19.** 5×3 **15** **20.** 3×8 **24** **21.** 3×4 **12** **22.** 3×6 **18**

Using Algebra Follow each rule to complete each table.

Rule: Multiply by 3

	Input	Output
	7	21
23.	6	18
24.	4	12
25.	9	27

Rule: Multiply by 5

	Input	Output
	3	15
26.	6	30
27.	2	10
28.	8	40

Problem Solving

29. Each year there is a Double Dutch World Tournament. Each singles team has 3 people. How many people are needed to make 5 singles teams for the tournament? **15 people**

30. What If? Suppose there are 7 singles teams in the tournament. How many people in the tournament are on singles teams? **21 people**

▲ **Kid Connection** Jasmine Manns, Latasha Burnett, and Shaquannah Floyd practice for the Double Dutch World Tournament. Their team, coached by Geraldine Code, is from New Jersey.

Review and Remember

Find each sum or difference.

31. $\begin{array}{r} 56 \\ +\, 43 \\ \hline 99 \end{array}$	**32.** $\begin{array}{r} 693 \\ -\, 212 \\ \hline 481 \end{array}$	**33.** $\begin{array}{r} 682 \\ +\, 320 \\ \hline 1{,}002 \end{array}$	**34.** $\begin{array}{r} 7{,}043 \\ -\, 2{,}578 \\ \hline 4{,}465 \end{array}$	**35.** $\begin{array}{r} 8{,}234 \\ +\, 6{,}918 \\ \hline 15{,}152 \end{array}$

For Extra Practice, see Set E, page 206. **191**

---

3 Wrap-up

What is 10×3? How did you find the product? (30; Sample answer: Add 10 three times.)

Common Error Alert

Watch for students who skip count by 3 incorrectly. Suggest that they use a number line to help them.

Meeting Individual Needs

For Early Finishers

Students spin a spinner, then draw a triangle and write the number in each of its corners. They use the numbers to write a multiplication sentence and solve.
VISUAL

Inclusion

Have students use a floor number line to 30 to solve 3×3, 3×4, 3×7, and 3×9. They should always start at 3, and hop to find the product.
KINESTHETIC

Practice

Multiplying by 3 P 5-7

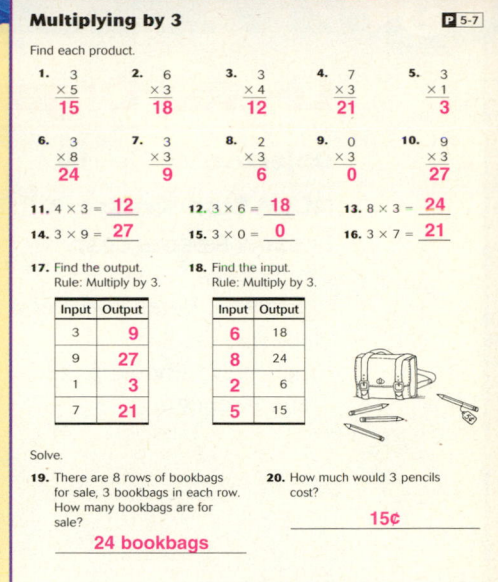

Reteach

Multiplying by 3 R 5-7

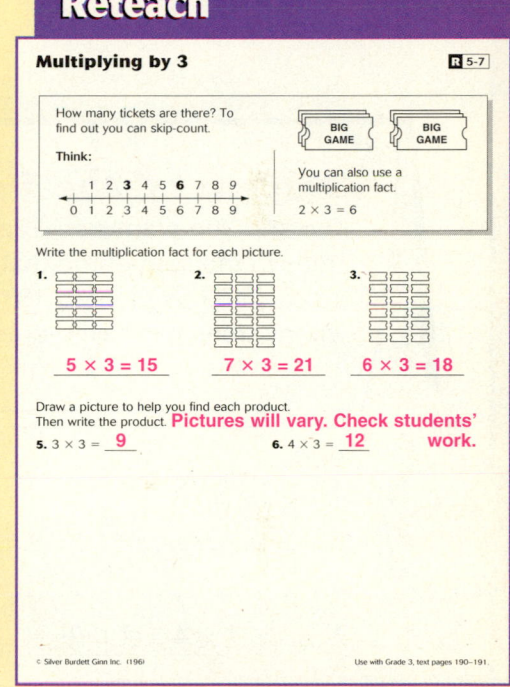

Extend

Triangle Land E 5-7

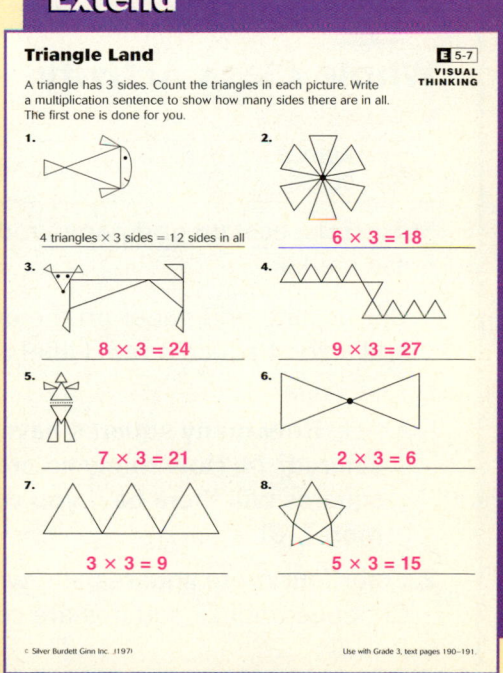

Lesson Organizer

Objective: Multiply by 4.

- **NCTM Standards:** 1, 3, 6, 7, 8, 13
- **Lesson Resources:**
  Chapter File Folder
  Practice, Reteach, Extend 5-8
  Daily Review 5-8
  Practice Workbook, p. 23
  Transparency 7

Problem of the Day 5-8

Ken and Jen plant trees. Jen plants 3 trees in the same time that Ken plants 2 trees. Jen has planted 15 trees. How many trees has Ken planted? **10 trees**

Math Minute

Add.

4 + 4 *(8)*

4 + 4 + 4 *(12)*

4 + 4 + 4 + 4 *(16)*

4 + 4 + 4 + 4 + 4 *(20)*

---

1 Introduce

Whole Class Activity

VISUAL

WHOLE CLASS · 5–10 MINUTES

Materials: acetate grid paper, red dry-erase marker

1. Use acetate grid paper on the overhead and color 4 squares red. Label the grid "4."

   - Ask: **How many squares have been colored?** *(4)* **How many colored squares will there be if you color 4 more?** *(8)*

2. Color four more squares and write "8." Continue until 28 squares are colored.

Computer Lab

There are many ways to multiply by 4.

Learning About It

Your school has a new computer lab. There are 5 rows of computers. There are 4 computers in each row. How many computers are there in the computer lab?

$5 \times 4 = \blacksquare$ or $\begin{array}{r} 4 \\ \times 5 \\ \hline \end{array}$

THERE'S ALWAYS A WAY!

- **One way** to find the product is to draw a picture. Show 5 groups of 4.

20 computers in all

- **Another way** is to skip count.	- **Another way** is to change the order of the factors.
0 4 8 12 16 20 4, 8, 12, 16, 20	If you know $4 \times 5 = 20$, then you know $5 \times 4 = 20$.
- **Another way** is to use repeated addition. $4 + 4 + 4 + 4 + 4 = 20$	- **Another way** is to use a multiplication fact. $5 \times 4 = 20$

There are 20 computers in the lab.

Think and Discuss Which way of finding a product do you like best? **Answers will vary.**

192

---

2 Teach Pages 192–193

Ask: **How would you skip count by 4s to find the product of 4 × 5?** *(4, 8, 12, 16, 20)* **by 5s?** *(5, 10, 15, 20)*

Critical Thinking SYNTHESIS

After Think and Discuss, ask: **Which method helps you find 10 × 4 fastest?** *(Sample answer: skip counting)*

Assess Understanding

After Try It Out, ask: **How does knowing 6 × 4 = 24 help you find 7 × 4?** *(You can add 4 to the product of 6 × 4.)*

CHALLENGE

How would you answer Problem 19 if instead the teacher bought 4 boxes of CDs with 5 CDs in a box and 2 boxes with 4 CDs in a box? *(49 + (4 × 5) + (2 × 4) = 77)*

Try It Out

Multiply. Tell how you found the product. **Methods will vary.**

1. 4×3 **12**   2. 6×4 **24**   3. 1×4 **4**   4. 7×4 **28**   5. 9×4 **36**

Practice

Find each product.

6. $\begin{array}{r} 4 \\ \times 8 \\ \hline \textbf{32} \end{array}$ 7. $\begin{array}{r} 4 \\ \times 1 \\ \hline \textbf{4} \end{array}$ 8. $\begin{array}{r} 9 \\ \times 4 \\ \hline \textbf{36} \end{array}$ 9. $\begin{array}{r} 4 \\ \times 7 \\ \hline \textbf{28} \end{array}$ 10. $\begin{array}{r} 8 \\ \times 4 \\ \hline \textbf{32} \end{array}$ 11. $\begin{array}{r} 1 \\ \times 4 \\ \hline \textbf{4} \end{array}$

12. $\begin{array}{r} 4 \\ \times 4 \\ \hline \textbf{16} \end{array}$ 13. $\begin{array}{r} 3 \\ \times 4 \\ \hline \textbf{12} \end{array}$ 14. $\begin{array}{r} 4 \\ \times 5 \\ \hline \textbf{20} \end{array}$ 15. $\begin{array}{r} 4 \\ \times 6 \\ \hline \textbf{24} \end{array}$ 16. $\begin{array}{r} 2 \\ \times 4 \\ \hline \textbf{8} \end{array}$ 17. $\begin{array}{r} 7 \\ \times 4 \\ \hline \textbf{28} \end{array}$

Problem Solving

18. Four groups of students use the class computer each day. Two students work on the computer at a time. How many students use the computer each day? **8 students**

19. The computer teacher had 49 CDs. She bought 3 boxes of new CDs. Each box has 4 CDs in it. How many CDs does she have now? **61 CDs**

Review and Remember

20. $346 + 694$ **1,040**   21. $74 - 18$ **56**   22. $415 + 987$ **1,402**   23. $561 - 284$ **277**

Critical Thinking Corner
Visual Thinking

Match It!

Match each set of pictures with its number sentence.

1.   b   a. 3×3
2.   c   b. 2×3
3.   a   c. $3 + 2 + 3$

For Extra Practice, see Set F, page 206. **193**

Critical Thinking

After students make matches, ask them to write **a** and **b** as addition sentences. (*a.* 3 + 3 + 3; *b.* 2 + 2 + 2, or 3 + 3)

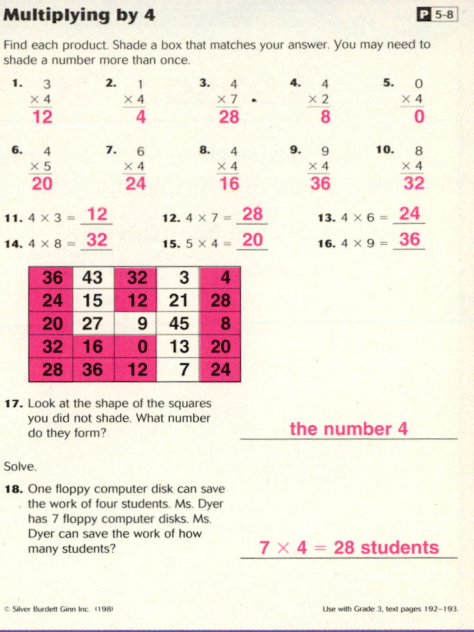
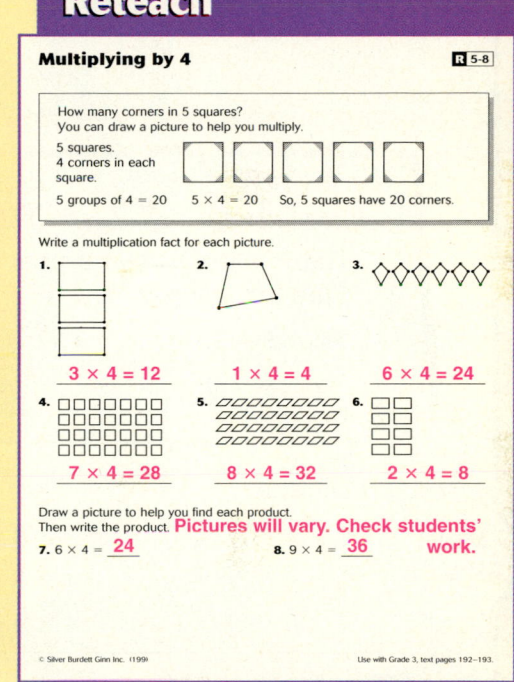

---

3 Wrap-up

You know that $4 \times 3 = 12$. Explain how this fact can help you find the products of 4×4 and 4×5. (*Add 4 to the products; 12 + 4 = 16; 16 + 4 = 20*)

Common Error Alert

Watch for students who group their counters incorrectly. Remind them to think of the number of groups first, and then the number in each group.

Meeting Individual Needs

For Early Finishers

Ask: **How many quarters are in a dollar?** (4) Have students multiply to find the number of quarters in each dollar amount from $1 to $9.

LOGICAL/MATHEMATICAL

Gifted and Talented

Students use a spinner to find how many cars were sold in one day, writing the multiplication sentence that shows how many tires left the car lot that day.

LOGICAL/MATHEMATICAL

Lesson Organizer

Objective: Make an organized list to help solve a problem.

- **NCTM Standards:** 1, 3, 7
- **Lesson Resources:**
  Chapter File Folder
  Practice, Reteach, Extend 5-9
  Daily Review 5-9

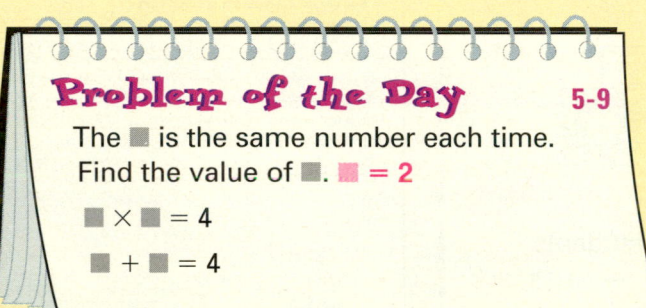

Problem of the Day   5-9

The ■ is the same number each time.
Find the value of ■. ■ = 2

$$■ \times ■ = 4$$
$$■ + ■ = 4$$

Math Minute

Multiply.

3 × 4 *(12)*	2 × 8 *(16)*
3 × 9 *(27)*	4 × 5 *(20)*
4 × 8 *(32)*	4 × 9 *(36)*

Problem Solving
Make a List

Making a list can sometimes help you solve a problem.

Mr. Weaver is taking a picture of Jenny, Liza, and Ryan for the class scrapbook. He asks them, "How many different ways could you three students stand in a line?"

UNDERSTAND

What do you need to know?

You need to know that any of the students can be first, second, or third.

PLAN

How can you solve the problem?

You can **make a list** to help you find all the different ways. Choose one student to be first and another to be second. The last one will be third.

SOLVE

When you make your list, you will notice that there are 2 ways for Jenny to be first, 2 ways for Liza to be first, and 2 ways for Ryan to be first.

So, there are 6 ways that the students could stand in line.

First	Second	Third
Jenny	Liza	Ryan
Jenny	Ryan	Liza
Liza	Ryan	Jenny
Liza	Jenny	Ryan
Ryan	Jenny	Liza
Ryan	Liza	Jenny

LOOK BACK

How is making a list helpful when you want to know if you covered all the ways?
Students should realize that a list helps them organize their work so that they don't miss any of the ways and so that they don't count any of the ways more than once.

194

---

1 Introduce

Whole Class Activity
VISUAL/SPATIAL

WHOLE CLASS	10–15 MINUTES

1. Explain that you want to collect information about favorite TV shows.
2. Ask students to name favorite shows.
3. Ask one student to recall the names of three shows. Then ask another to remember three more shows, etc.
4. Discuss how it would have been helpful if you had made a list.

- Say: **Sometimes making a list can help us organize information.**

---

2 Teach   Pages 194–195

Understand Ask: **Who are the children who will stand in line?** *(Jenny, Liza, and Ryan)*

Plan Ask three students to volunteer to act out the problem. Use name tags to help students remember the names in the problem.

Solve Ask: **Why can't Jenny be first more than two times?** *(Sample answer: You cannot arrange the other two students more than two ways.)*

Look Back Ask: **What other way could you check your answer?** *(Sample answer: Draw a diagram and compare it to the list.)*

Critical Thinking ANALYSIS
After Look Back, ask: **Four students are going to be in a picture. How many different pictures could Mr. Weaver take if the same student is first in line in every picture? Explain.** *(Six; the students can only be arranged six different ways.)*

Assess Understanding
Before Using the Strategy, ask students if making an unorganized list is helpful. Discuss how organizing information could keep you from repeating the same information on the list.

Using the Strategy

Make a list to help you solve Problems 1–4.

1 Rudy must decide what to wear for his school picture. He likes his blue shirt and his yellow shirt. He likes his black pants and his brown pants. What are the ways Rudy could choose a shirt and pair of pants to wear? *See Additional Answers, pages 204–205.*

2 Students get to pick the background for their school pictures. They can choose blue, green, or tan. The color can be solid or striped. List all the different background choices that the students have. *See above.*

2. 2 choices: blue solid; blue striped; green solid; green striped; tan solid; tan striped

3 Jan, Carl, and Peter are standing in line to get their picture taken. What are all the different ways they can stand in line? *6 ways: Jan, Carl, Peter; Jan, Peter, Carl; Carl, Jan, Peter; Carl, Peter, Jan; Peter, Jan, Carl; Peter, Carl, Jan*

4 Tim can sit or stand for his photo. He also has a choice of a blue or black background. What ways can he have his picture taken? *sit/blue; sit/black; stand/blue; stand/black*

Mixed Strategy Review

Try these or other strategies to solve each problem. Tell which strategy you used. *Strategies may vary. Possible strategies are listed.*

Problem Solving Strategies

- Make a List
- Use Logical Reasoning
- Work Backwards
- Guess and Check

5 Jeff is taller than Alan. Sue is shorter than Alan. Gayle is taller than Jeff. The school photographer wants the 4 students to stand in line from tallest to shortest. In what order should they stand? *Use Logical Reasoning; Gayle, Jeff, Alan, Sue*

6 Jon sold 10 picture frames. He sold 4 more wooden frames than plastic frames. How many of each kind of frame did he sell? *See below.*

7 Joan had $2.05 when she got home from school. She had paid $14.95 for her school pictures. She also bought a new pen at the school store for $3.00. How much money did Joan have to start with? *Work Backwards; $20*

6. *Guess and Check;* 3 plastic frames, 7 wooden frames

195

---

3 Wrap-up

Mr. Weaver wants a picture of Sally and Alice standing next to each other for the scrapbook. How many different pictures can he take? *(Two)*

Common Error Alert

Watch for students who have a duplicate arrangement in their list. Have them check that each arrangement has a different order.

Meeting Individual Needs

For Early Finishers

Write: 2, 4, 5, 10, and 17. Ask: **How many sums can you find by adding two numbers and using all of the numbers shown? You can't add a number to itself.** *(10)*
LOGICAL/MATHEMATICAL

Cooperative Learning

Act this out: Lynn is older than David. Dawn is younger than David. Gene is older than Lynn. Order from oldest to youngest. *(Gene, Lynn, David, Dawn)*
KINESTHETIC

Practice

Problem Solving
Make a List

P 5-9

Make a list to solve.

1. Troy has white bread, rye bread, and a roll. He has roast beef and ham. How many different ways can Troy make a sandwich?

roast beef, white
roast beef, rye
roast beef, roll
ham, white
ham, rye
ham, roll
____6____ different sandwiches

2. Gil orders a sandwich. How many different ways can the sandwich-maker arrange turkey, bacon, and cheese on the roll?

turkey, bacon, cheese
turkey, cheese, bacon
bacon, cheese, turkey
bacon, turkey, cheese
cheese, turkey, bacon
cheese, bacon, turkey
____6____ different ways

3. Wanda can buy chips, pretzels, or nuts. She can buy juice or milk. How many different ways can Wanda buy a snack and a drink?

chips, juice
chips, milk
pretzels, juice
pretzels, milk
nuts, juice
nuts, milk
____6____ different ways

4. Jared plays the piano and the organ. Kacey plays the trombone and the trumpet. In how many different ways can they play their instruments?

piano, trombone
piano, trumpet
organ, trombone
organ, trumpet
____4____ different ways

© Silver Burdett Ginn Inc. (2011)   Use with Grade 3, text pages 194–195.

Reteach

Problem Solving
Make a List

R 5-9

A class banner has wide stripes in red, green, and blue. In how many ways can the stripes be ordered on the banner?

Red	Blue	Green

1. How can you find all the ways the stripes can be ordered?

Understand You need to make a list to show the ways.

Plan There are 3 different color stripes. Each color can be the first stripe.

Solve List all the ways you can make the banner.

• red, blue, green	• green, red, blue	• blue, green, red
• red, green, blue	• green, blue, red	• blue, red, green

____3____ groups of ____2____ ways each = ____6____ ways.

Look Back The list includes all the possible ways, so the answer makes sense.

Make a list to solve.

2. Ricky has a sweatshirt and a T-shirt. He has a pair of black jeans and a pair of blue jeans. How many different outfits can he wear?

sweatshirt, black jeans
sweatshirt, blue jeans
T-shirt, black jeans
T-shirt, blue jeans
____4____ different outfits

3. Martha can see a play on Friday, Saturday, or Sunday. She can go at 5:00 or 8:00. How many choices does she have?

Friday, 5:00
Friday, 8:00
Saturday, 5:00
Saturday, 8:00
Sunday, 5:00
Sunday, 8:00
____6____ choices

© Silver Burdett Ginn Inc. (2021)   Use with Grade 3, text pages 194–195.

Extend

Costume Choices

E 5-9
PROBABILITY

Del, Mel, Belle, Nell, and Stella are wearing costumes for the big party. Their choices are shown below.

neckwear	headwear	footwear	outerwear
red bow tie	cowboy hat	shoes	cape
polka dot scarf	wig	boots	jacket
	baseball cap	slippers	

1. Del wants to wear something on his head and something around his neck. How many combinations can he make? ____6____ combinations

2. Mel wants to wear a cape and special shoes. How many combinations can he make? ____3____ combinations

3. Belle wants to wear something special on her head and something special on her feet. How many combinations can she make? ____9____ combinations

4. Stella thinks that she should wear the red bow tie, a wig, and some special footwear. How many different ways can she do this? ____3____ different ways

5. Nell wants to wear something on her head, her feet, and her neck. How many different combinations can Nell wear? You can make a table like this one on another piece of paper. ____18____ combinations

Headwear	Footwear	Neckwear
cowboy hat	boots	bow tie
cowboy hat	boots	scarf

6. Suppose you want to wear a cape, slippers, something around your neck, and something on your head. How many different ways could you do this? ____6____ different ways

© Silver Burdett Ginn Inc. (203)   Use with Grade 3, text pages 194–195.

Lesson Organizer

Objective: Multiply by 1 or 0.

- **NCTM Standards:** 1, 3, 6, 7, 8, 13
- **Lesson Resources:**
  Chapter File Folder
     Practice, Reteach, Extend 5-10
  Daily Review 5-10
  Practice Workbook, p. 24
  Study Buddies 5B

Problem of the Day   5-10

Al has 98¢. He has 10 coins. What coins does Al have? Make a list.

2 quarters, 4 dimes, 1 nickel, 3 pennies

Math Minute

Add.

$1 + 1 + 1 =$ *(3)*

$1 + 1 + 1 + 1 + 1 =$ *(5)*

$0 + 0 + 0 + 0 =$ *(0)*

---

1 Introduce

Cooperative Activity

KINESTHETIC

 PAIRS    5–10 MINUTES

Materials: counters, cups, spinner 0–9

1. A student spins the spinner to know how many cups to place on the desk.

2. The partner places one counter in each cup. Ask: **How many counters do you have in all? What math sentence describes the amount you have?** *(Repeated addition or multiplication)*

3. Students spin three more times and write multiplication sentences.

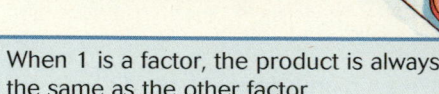

10   **Multiplying by 1 or 0**

Lunch Line

Follow the rules to multiply by 1 or 0.

Learning About It

It's lunchtime! There are 4 plates on the counter. Each plate has 1 cheeseburger on it. How many cheeseburgers are there?

$4 \times 1 = \blacksquare$

$4 \times 1 = 4$

There are 4 cheeseburgers.

> When 1 is a factor, the product is always the same as the other factor.

There are 3 plates on another counter. There are no hot dogs on any of the plates. How many hot dogs are there?

$3 \times 0 = \blacksquare$

$3 \times 0 = 0$

There are 0 hot dogs.

> When 0 is a factor, the product is always 0.

Think and Discuss Is it easier to multiply 3×1 than it is to multiply 345×1? Explain your thinking. **Answers will vary. Students should realize that when one of the factors is 1, the product is the same as the other factor.**

Try It Out

Multiply.

1. 8×1 **8**
2. 0×9 **0**
3. 1×1 **1**
4. 6×0 **0**
5. 2×1 **2**
6. 4×0 **0**
7. 8×0 **0**
8. 1×9 **9**
9. 5×1 **5**
10. 7×1 **7**

---

2 Teach   Pages 196–197

Draw a large zero on the board. Give the zero a big mouth with sharp teeth. Say: **This is the zero monster. It eats other factors.** Write: $\blacksquare \times 0 = 0$ next to the zero monster. Explain: **When you multiply any factor by 0, the zero monster eats the other factor. The product of any number and 0 is always 0.**

Critical Thinking   **APPLICATION**

After Think and Discuss, say: **Find the missing number: $300 \times \blacksquare = 300$.** *(1)*

Assess Understanding

After Try It Out, write the following on the board. Ask students to complete each problem with <, >, or =.

$0 \times 9 \; \bullet \; 1 \times 9 \; (<)$

$1 \times 3 \; \bullet \; 352 \times 0 \; (>)$

$1 \times 0 \; \bullet \; 0 \times 14 \; (=)$

 USING TECHNOLOGY

Math Blaster® 1, Trash Zapper
Multiplication; Level 1
Multiply by 0, 1, 2
With products 0–20

Practice

Find each product.

11.	12.	13.	14.	15.	16.
1 × 6 = 6	9 × 0 = 0	1 × 7 = 7	2 × 0 = 0	1 × 0 = 0	5 × 0 = 0

17.	18.	19.	20.	21.	22.
0 × 3 = 0	1 × 2 = 2	7 × 0 = 0	9 × 1 = 9	1 × 5 = 5	4 × 1 = 4

23. 1 × 8 **8**   24. 0 × 8 **0**   25. 0 × 9 **0**   26. 1 × 6 **6**   27. 3 × 1 **3**

Problem Solving

Use the menu to solve Problems 28–30.

28. How much do 7 tacos cost? **$7**

29. **What If?** You don't buy any tacos. How much money do you spend on tacos? **$0**

30. **Create Your Own** Use the menu to write a multiplication problem of your own. **Problems will vary.**

Menu
Taco $1
Super Salad $2
Giant Sandwich $4

Review and Remember

Using Algebra Compare. Use >, <, or = for each ●.

31. 6 + 6 ● 9 + 3   **=**
32. 11 − 8 ● 13 − 9   **<**
33. 12 − 5 ● 8 + 6   **<**

Money $ense

Think and Drink

Drink Menu
Milk 35¢
Water 65¢
Juice 75¢

1. You have a one-dollar bill, 4 quarters, and a dime. What money would you use to pay for 2 cartons of milk? What would your change be?
Possible answer: 3 quarters; 5¢

2. You give the cashier a one-dollar bill and a quarter to buy two drinks. She gives you back a dime and a nickel as change. What did you buy?
1 milk and 1 juice

For Extra Practice, see Set G, page 206.   **197**

3 Wrap-up

Journal Idea How can you tell when a product will be one of the two factors? *(If one of the two factors is 1 or 0)* How do you know when a product will be zero? *(If one of the factors is 0)*

Common Error Alert

Watch for students who do not differentiate adding with zero from multiplying by zero. Have them draw pictures to show how they are different.

Meeting Individual Needs

For Early Finishers

Write the following: 1, 10, 100, 1,000, 2, 20, 200, 2,000. Have students multiply all numbers by 1 and 0. Discuss the pattern.

LOGICAL/MATHEMATICAL

Acquiring English Proficiency

Write: 2 × 1 = 2 and 15 × 1 = 15. Review the meaning of *product* and *factor*. Students model each using counters, noting which factor is the same. *(1)*

VISUAL

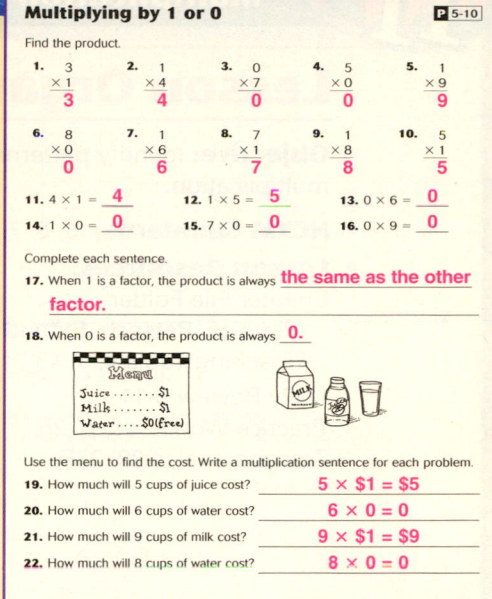
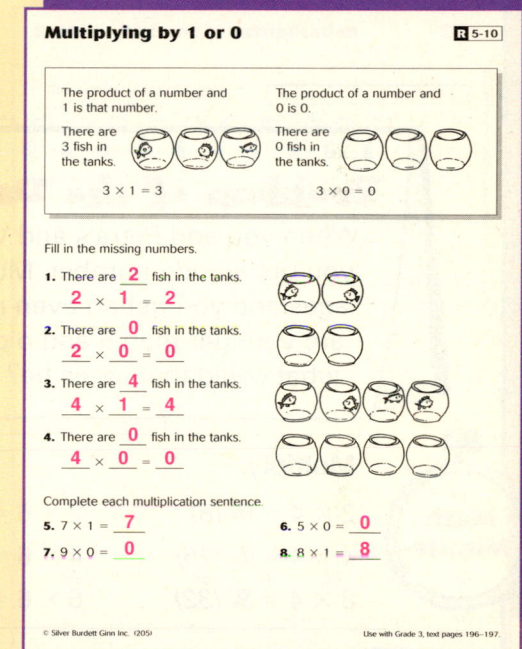
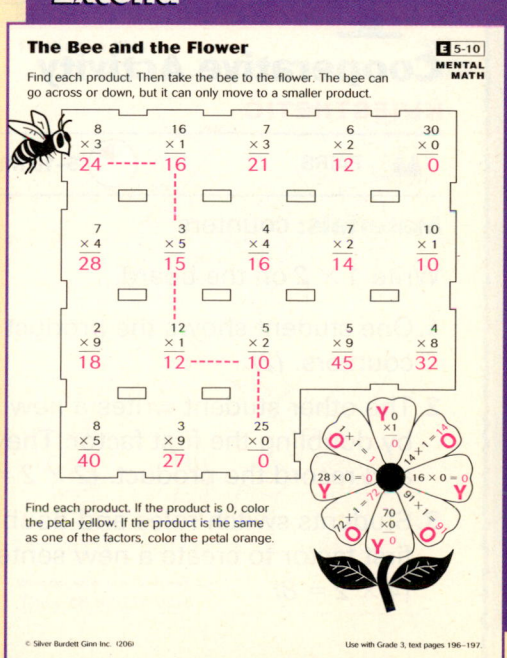

Lesson Organizer

Objective: Use multiplication to solve problems.

- **NCTM Standards:** 1, 2, 3, 7
- **Lesson Resources:**
  Chapter File Folder
    Practice, Reteach, Extend 5-12
    Teaching Tool 21
  Daily Review 5-12

Problem of the Day   5-12

Tia is twice as old as her brother Axel. Tia's brother Chris is twice as old as she is. If Tia is 12, how old are Chris and Axel? **Chris is 24; Axel is 6**

 Math Minute

Multiply.

2 × 4 *(8)*	0 × 7 *(0)*
5 × 9 *(45)*	3 × 9 *(27)*
4 × 6 *(24)*	5 × 1 *(5)*

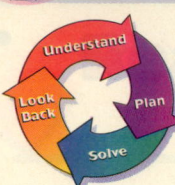
Problem Solving
Using Data From Pictures

Use what you know about problem solving to solve problems involving money.

Lisa is going to the school store to buy some pencils. If she buys 4 or more pencils, she will save 6¢ a pencil. Lisa decides to buy 5 pencils. How much money does she save?

> **School Store Sale**
>
> Regular price: 24¢ each
> Sale price: Buy 4 or more pencils and save 6¢ each!

 UNDERSTAND

What do you need to know?

First you need to know whether or not Lisa is buying 4 or more pencils. If she is buying 4 or more pencils, you need to know that she saves 6¢ on each pencil she buys.

 PLAN

How can you solve the problem?

You can **write a number sentence**. Since Lisa is buying more than 4 pencils, you can multiply 6¢ by 5 to find how much money she saves.

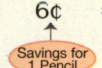 **SOLVE**

$$5 \times 6¢ = 30¢$$

Number of Pencils | Savings for 1 Pencil | Total Savings

Lisa saves 30¢.

 LOOK BACK

How could you use addition to check your answer? **6¢ + 6¢ + 6¢ + 6¢ + 6¢ = 30¢**

200

---

1 Introduce

Whole Class Activity

KINESTHETIC

WHOLE CLASS	5–10 MINUTES

Materials: play coins

1. Show a nickel and three pennies on the overhead.
   - Ask: **If an item costs three times the amount shown, how much would it cost?** *($0.24)*

2. Students use coins at their desks to find the answer.
   - Discuss: **Use the coins in different ways to show $0.24.** *(Sample answer: Two dimes and four pennies)*

2 Teach   Pages 200–200A

Understand   Ask: **Why is it not important to know that the regular price of each pencil is 24¢?** *(Sample answer: You are being asked to find savings, not cost.)*

Plan   Ask: **Why can you multiply to solve this problem?** *(Sample answer: Because you want to find the total, and each group has the same amount, 6 cents)*

Solve   Ask: **Does Lisa save 30 cents on each pencil or 30 cents on all 6 pencils? Explain.** *(She saves 30 cents altogether because she saves 6 cents on each pencil.)*

Look Back   Ask: **Why can you check the problem by adding 6 cents five times?** *(Sample answer: Because you can use both multiplication and addition to find how many in all)*

Critical Thinking   ANALYSIS

After Look Back, ask: **Hassan spent $1.78. He gave the clerk $2.03. What was his change? Why did he give the clerk three extra pennies?** *(25 cents; He wanted the fewest number of coins in change.)*

Assess Understanding

Before Show What You Learned, ask students to describe a situation in which they would need to multiply.

④ In a conte...
were 493...
guess was...
Which is t...
the numb...

A. 400
B. 500
C. 600 (circled)
D. 700

⑤ Small bask...
large bask...
much wou...
bought 5...

A. $2.00
B. $14.00
C. $30.00 (circled)
D. $40.00

⑥ Jill and Is...
4 birds or...
they mak...
8 cards a...
5 cards. ...
has Jill st...

A. 3
B. 12 (circled)
C. 20
D. 32

⑦ Jerry and...
2 dogs. ...
number ...

A. 3 × 2
B. 4 × 2 (circled)
C. 3 + 2
D. 2 + 2

Show What You Learned

Use the information below to answer each question.

ERASER SALE Buy 3 or more and save 5¢ each.

NOTE PADS ON SALE Buy 3 or more and save 9¢ each.

Pens $1.00 · Erasers 50¢ · Calculators $6.00 · Note Pads 79¢ · Stickers 8¢

① How much do 2 pens and 3 stickers cost?
$2.24

② How much money will Tamara pay for a calculator and 2 pens?
$8.00

③ Maya buys 4 note pads on sale. How much money does she save?
36¢

④ Paul and Karen each need 2 erasers. They decide to buy the erasers together. How much money will each of them save?
They each will save 10¢.

⑤ Which costs more, 10 pens or 2 calculators?
2 calculators

⑥ **You Decide** Mrs. Smith wants to buy 4 calculators for her classroom. She has $25. What other items could she buy with the money she has left?
Answers will vary. Cost of additional items should not exceed $1.00.

⑦ **Analyze** You have $1 to spend at the school store. You buy a note pad. Do you have enough money left to buy 4 stickers? How do you know?
No; $1.00 − 79¢ = 21¢ and 4 stickers would cost 4 × 8¢, or 32¢.

⑧ **Create Your Own** Use the information in the picture above to write a problem. Give it to a classmate to solve. **Check students' problems.**

200A

③ Wrap-up

✏️ **Journal Idea** Have students write three problems: One where they need to add money; one where they need to subtract money; and one where they need to multiply money.

Common Error Alert

Watch for students who use the price for one item instead of the price for multiple items. Have them check the number of each item that is purchased.

Meeting Individual Needs

For Early Finishers

Have groups of students use the pictures on page 200A to create problems for others to solve. Exchange papers and check each other's work.
LOGICAL/MATHEMATICAL

Acquiring English Proficiency

Discuss the meaning of *save*: **A pen that costs 50¢ is on sale for 25¢. How much do you save?** *(25¢)* Have students share money-saving problems.
LINGUISTIC

Practice

Problem Solving
Using Data From Pictures
P 5-12

Regular Prices		CLEARANCE SALE!
white T-shirt	$ 6	Buy 5 or more white T-shirts, save $2 on each
color T-shirt	$ 7	Buy 3 or more sweatshirts, save $3 on each
long-sleeve T-shirt	$ 9	Buy 4 or more color T-shirts, save $1 on each
sweatshirt	$10	
hooded sweatshirt	$15	

Use the information above to solve the problems.

1. Valeria buys 3 white T-shirts. How much does she spend?
$18

2. Chuck buys 2 long-sleeve T-shirts. How much does he spend?
$18

3. Hua buys 3 sweatshirts. How much does she save? How much does she spend?
saves $9, spends $21

4. Ron buys 5 white T-shirts. How much does he save? How much does he spend?
saves $10, spends $20

5. What will it cost Ed for a hooded sweatshirt and 2 color T-shirts?
$29

6. What will it cost Jo for a sweatshirt and 3 white T-shirts?
$28

7. Explain Mrs. Yoon has $50 to spend. She buys 5 color T-shirts. What other items can Mrs. Yoon buy with the money she has left?
Possible answer: 5 × $6, or $30 for 5 color T-shirts and 2 × $10, or $20 for 2 sweatshirts

8. Explain Hessa says that if she buys a fourth color T-shirt, it will only cost her $3. What does Hessa mean?
Three color T's cost $21. Four on sale cost $24. $24 − $21 = $3, so the fourth T costs only $3.

© Silver Burdett Ginn Inc. (210) · Use with Grade 3, text pages 200–201.

Reteach

Problem Solving
Using Data From Pictures
R 5-12

You can solve problems by "reading" a picture.

Amusement Park Rides	
Tilt-a-Whirl	3 tickets
Roller Coaster	5 tickets
Fun House	2 tickets
Ferris Wheel	4 tickets
C-Force	6 tickets

1. How many tickets are needed for 2 people to ride the Tilt-a-Whirl?

🔺 **Understand** You need to find the number of tickets needed for 1 person to ride the Tilt-a-Whirl. Then you can use it to find the amount needed for 2 people.

🔺 **Plan** You can multiply the number of tickets needed for 1 person by 2, the total number of people riding.

🔺 **Solve** 2 × 3 tickets = **6** tickets

🔺 **Look Back** The total amount of tickets needed is **6**. What addition sentence can you use to check?
3 + 3 = 6

Use the chart to answer the questions.

2. Jeff and Annie want to ride the C-Force. How many tickets will they need?
12 tickets

3. Five children want to ride the roller coaster. How many tickets will they need?
25 tickets

4. Three people want to ride the Ferris Wheel. They have 10 tickets. Do they have enough? Explain.
No, they would need 12 tickets.

© Silver Burdett Ginn Inc. (211) · Use with Grade 3, text pages 200–201.

Extend

Shopping Detective
E 5-12 DATA

You are the shopping detective. You know how much money each shopper had and how much each shopper has left. Decide what was on their shopping list.

SPECIAL PURCHASES
$4.00 · $2.00 · $3.00 · $5.00

1. Mrs. Stanley had $25, got $4 change, and bought 7 of the same thing. What did she buy?
7 loaves of bread

2. Mr. Black had $10, got $2 change, and bought 4 of the same thing. What did he buy?
4 cartons of milk

3. Ms. Winters had $20, got no change, and bought 5 of the same thing. What did she buy?
5 pieces of watermelon

4. Mr. Sampson had $30, got $5 change and bought 5 of the same thing. What did he buy?
5 bags of apples

5. Mr. Waverly had $10 and got $1 change. He bought 2 of one thing and 1 of another. What did he buy?
2 cartons of milk
1 bag of apples

6. Ms. Calloway had $20 and got $2 change. She bought 3 of one thing and 2 of another. What did she buy?
3 pieces of watermelon
2 loaves of bread

7. Suppose you have $30 to spend. Decide what you would like to buy. Buy at least two of each item you choose. Find out how much you spent.
Answers will vary. Check that 2 items of each are purchased. Check totals.

© Silver Burdett Ginn Inc. (212) · Use with Grade 3, text pages 200–201.

LESSON 12   200A

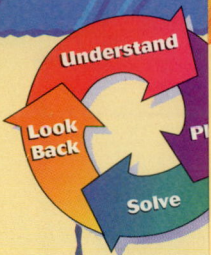

Extra Practice

Extra Practice

Using the Pages

Purpose To maintain and review skills developed in this chapter

Page numbers associated with each group of items refer to the pages on which the skill or concept was presented. Those students needing review should turn to the appropriate lessons.

 **Using Algebra**

In Set B, Exercises 1–9, students use **numerical relationships** to multiply.

In Set C, Exercises 12–19, students use a **function** rule to complete a table.

Using Technology
For Additional Practice

You may wish to use the following technology resources.

Math Blaster® 1
For Set C: Number Recycler, multiplication: Level 1, multiply by 0, 1, 2 with products 0–20
For Set G: Trash Zapper, multiplication: Level 2, multiply by 3, 4 with products 0–48

Internet www.sbgmath.com
For Set B: Chapter 5, Hurray for Arrays! Activity
For Set D: Chapter 5, Crayons Activity

MathProcessor™ CD-ROM Activities
For Set B: Activities 27 and 28

Set A (pages 176–177)

Write an addition sentence and a multiplication sentence for each set of pictures.

$1 + 1 + 1 + 1 + 1 = 5$
$5 \times 1 = 5$

1.
$2 + 2 + 2 = 6$
$3 \times 2 = 6$

2.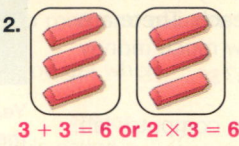

3.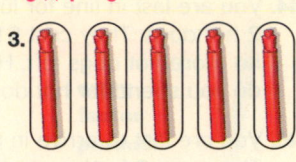

$3 + 3 = 6$ or $2 \times 3 = 6$

Write a multiplication sentence for each addition sentence.

4. $8 + 8 + 8 = 24$
$3 \times 8 = 24$
5. $6 + 6 + 6 + 6 = 24$
$4 \times 6 = 24$
6. $1 + 1 + 1 = 3$
$3 \times 1 = 3$
7. $4 + 4 + 4 + 4 + 4 = 20$
$5 \times 4 = 20$
8. $5 + 5 + 5 + 5 + 5 + 5 = 30$
$6 \times 5 = 30$
9. $2 + 2 + 2 + 2 + 2 + 2 = 12$
$6 \times 2 = 12$

10. One book costs $4. How much money do 5 books cost? **$20**
11. One shelf holds 9 books. How many books can 3 shelves hold? **27 books**

Set B (pages 178–181)

Using Algebra Write a multiplication sentence for each array.

1. $3 \times 5 = 15$ or $5 \times 3 = 15$
2. $4 \times 4 = 16$
3. $3 \times 7 = 21$ or $7 \times 3 = 21$

Draw an array to show each multiplication problem. Then find the product. **Drawings will vary.**

4. 1×6 **1 row of 6; 6**
5. 7×4 **7 rows of 4; 28**
6. 2×3 **2 rows of 3; 6**
7. 6×2 **6 rows of 2; 12**
8. 4×2 **4 rows of 2; 8**
9. 3×5 **3 rows of 5; 15**

10. The music classroom has 5 rows of bells. Each row has 6 bells. How many bells are there in the music classroom? **30 bells**
11. In the gym there are 4 rows of mats. There are 8 mats in each row. How many mats are there? **32 mats**

204

Additional Answers
Chapter 5

Lesson 9
Page 195

1. 4 ways:
   blue shirt, black pants;
   blue shirt, brown pants;
   yellow shirt, black pants;
   yellow shirt, brown pants

Extra Practice

Set C (pages 184–185)

Multiply.

1. $\begin{array}{r} 2 \\ \times 4 \\ \hline 8 \end{array}$	2. $\begin{array}{r} 2 \\ \times 3 \\ \hline 6 \end{array}$	3. $\begin{array}{r} 2 \\ \times 9 \\ \hline 18 \end{array}$	4. $\begin{array}{r} 2 \\ \times 8 \\ \hline 16 \end{array}$	5. $\begin{array}{r} 2 \\ \times 6 \\ \hline 12 \end{array}$	6. $\begin{array}{r} 9 \\ \times 2 \\ \hline 18 \end{array}$

7. 1×2 **2** 8. 2×0 **0** 9. 7×2 **14** 10. 2×8 **16** 11. 5×2 **10**

Using Algebra Complete each table.

Rule: Multiply by 2

	Input	Output
12.	5	10
13.	8	16
14.	2	4
15.	4	8

Rule: Multiply by 2

	Input	Output
16.	1	2
17.	3	6
18.	8	16
19.	6	12

20. The computer lab received 7 new computer games. Two people are needed to play each game. How many people can play in all? **14 people**

Set D (pages 186–187)

Multiply.

1. $\begin{array}{r} 5 \\ \times 3 \\ \hline 15 \end{array}$	2. $\begin{array}{r} 5 \\ \times 2 \\ \hline 10 \end{array}$	3. $\begin{array}{r} 4 \\ \times 5 \\ \hline 20 \end{array}$	4. $\begin{array}{r} 6 \\ \times 5 \\ \hline 30 \end{array}$	5. $\begin{array}{r} 5 \\ \times 5 \\ \hline 25 \end{array}$	6. $\begin{array}{r} 8 \\ \times 5 \\ \hline 40 \end{array}$
7. $\begin{array}{r} 5 \\ \times 6 \\ \hline 30 \end{array}$	8. $\begin{array}{r} 2 \\ \times 5 \\ \hline 10 \end{array}$	9. $\begin{array}{r} 5 \\ \times 4 \\ \hline 20 \end{array}$	10. $\begin{array}{r} 5 \\ \times 1 \\ \hline 5 \end{array}$	11. $\begin{array}{r} 3 \\ \times 5 \\ \hline 15 \end{array}$	12. $\begin{array}{r} 7 \\ \times 5 \\ \hline 35 \end{array}$

13. 5×9 **45** 14. 8×5 **40** 15. 9×5 **45** 16. 5×1 **5** 17. 5×0 **0**

18. A teacher is putting 5 paintings on each bulletin board. After finishing 4 bulletin boards, he has only 2 paintings left. How many paintings did the teacher start with? **22 paintings**

19. The art teacher needs 35 paintbrushes. They come in packages of 8. Will 5 packages be enough? Explain.
Yes; 5 × 8 = 40 paintbrushes and only 35 are needed.

205

Extra Practice

Set E (pages 190–191)

Multiply.

1. 3
   × 2
   6

2. 5
   × 3
   15

3. 3
   × 5
   15

4. 3
   × 8
   24

5. 4
   × 3
   12

6. 8
   × 3
   24

7. 3 × 3 **9**   8. 9 × 3 **27**   9. 6 × 3 **18**   10. 7 × 3 **21**   11. 3 × 6 **18**

12. There are 3 buckets of balls on the playground. Each bucket has 7 balls. Kari takes 4 balls out of one bucket. How many balls are left in the buckets? **17 balls**

13. There are 3 relay teams. There are 7 students and 2 teachers on each team. How many students are there in all? **21 students**

Set F (pages 192–193)

Find each product.

1. 8
   × 4
   32

2. 6
   × 4
   24

3. 2
   × 4
   8

4. 4
   × 4
   16

5. 5
   × 4
   20

6. 4
   × 6
   24

7. 4 × 1 **4**   8. 4 × 3 **12**   9. 3 × 4 **12**   10. 9 × 4 **36**   11. 7 × 4 **28**

Set G (pages 196–197)

Find each product.

1. 3
   × 0
   0

2. 7
   × 1
   7

3. 1
   × 2
   2

4. 0
   × 6
   0

5. 7
   × 0
   0

6. 5
   × 1
   5

7. 9 × 0 **0**   8. 1 × 6 **6**   9. 9 × 1 **9**   10. 1 × 3 **3**   11. 3 × 8 **24**

12. The school store sells colored-pencil sets. How much money would 9 colored-pencil sets cost? **$9**

13. How much money would 3 highlighters cost at the school store? **$6**

School-Store Sale

Colored-Pencil Sets	$1 each
Highlighters	$2 each
Marker Sets	$3 each
Binders	$5 each

Chapter Test

Write a multiplication sentence. Then find the product.

1. 4 + 4 + 4
   3 × 4 = 12
2. 6 + 6 + 6 + 6 + 6 + 6
   6 × 6 = 36
3. 5 + 5 + 5 + 5
   4 × 5 = 20
4. 7 + 7 + 7 + 7 + 7
   5 × 7 = 35

Draw an array for each multiplication exercise. **Check students' drawings.**

5. 9 × 3 **9 rows of 3**
6. 7 × 5 **7 rows of 5**

Find each product.

7. 3
   × 4
   12
8. 5
   × 6
   30
9. 5
   × 9
   45
10. 2
   × 6
   12
11. 2
   × 9
   18

12. 5
   × 5
   25
13. 4
   × 9
   36
14. 3
   × 8
   24
15. 3
   × 6
   18
16. 7
   × 3
   21

17. 0 × 9 **0**
18. 1 × 5 **5**
19. 9 × 1 **9**

Continue each pattern.

20. 2, 4, 6, 8, ▪, ▪, ▪
    10 12 14
21. 5, 10, 15, 20, ▪, ▪, ▪
    25 30 35
22. 4, 8, 12, 16, ▪, ▪, ▪
    20 24 28
23. 3, 6, 9, 12, ▪, ▪, ▪
    15 18 21

Solve.

24. There are 7 groups of students. Each group has 4 students. Suppose you collect 2 papers from each student. How many papers will you collect? **56 papers**

25. In the cafeteria you can buy a vanilla, chocolate, or strawberry frozen yogurt with sprinkles or nuts. What are the different ways you can buy a frozen yogurt with a topping? **Vanilla with nuts, vanilla with sprinkles, chocolate with nuts, chocolate with sprinkles, strawberry with nuts, strawberry with sprinkles**

Self-Check

Look back at Exercise 1. Is the number of addends one of the factors in the multiplication sentence that you wrote?

207

Reteaching Chart

Learning Objectives	Test Items	Text Pages	Resources
5A	1–6, 20–23	174–181, 198–199	P5-1, R5-1, P5-2, R5-2, P5-3, R5-3, P5-11, R5-11
5B	7–23	184–187, 190–193, 196–199	P5-5, R5-5, P5-6, R5-6, P5-7, R5-7, P5-8, R5-8, P5-10, R5-10
5C	24–25	182–183, 194–195, 200–200A, 201–201A	P5-4, R5-4, P5-9, R5-9, P5-12, R5-12

The item analysis in the chart may be used to diagnose students' errors and to correlate the lessons and resources appropriate for reinforcement and remediation.

Chapter Test

Assessment Options

This Chapter Test can be used as a review, practice test, or chapter test. The Performance Assessment on page 208 may be used instead of or with this Chapter Test.

Other options are provided in the *Assessment Guide*.

- **Pretest—multiple-choice or free-response form,** pp. 99–102
- **Posttest—multiple-choice or free-response form,** pp. 103–106
- **Interview Activity,** p. 39
- **Long-Answer Question,** p. 10

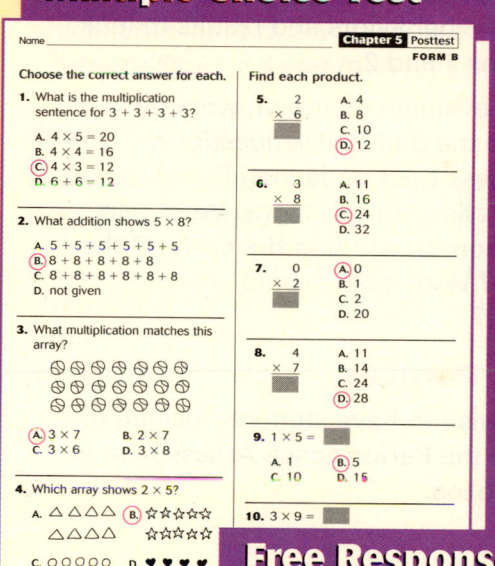

Multiple Choice and Free Response tests assess the same objectives and contain the same number of test items.

Meeting Individual Needs

Learning Styles vary from student to student. Every Meeting Individual Needs activity focuses on one of the following learning styles. The variety of styles enables students to learn math in ways that are most comfortable to them.

- **AUDITORY**
- **INDIVIDUAL**
- **KINESTHETIC**
- **LINGUISTIC**
- **LOGICAL/MATHEMATICAL**
- **SOCIAL/COOPERATIVE**
- **VISUAL/SPATIAL**

Acquiring English Proficiency

Manipulatives: color tiles*

Ask students to think of things that come in groups of 2, 3, 4, 5 or 6. Then have students act out buying these items. The buyer chooses an item, such as 3 sets of markers, with 5 in each set. The seller uses tiles to model the item. Partners work together to write and say a multiplication sentence that describes the total number of items.

For additional activities, see Acquiring English Proficiency, pp. 215, 217, 221, 233.

LINGUISTIC

For Extra Help

Manipulatives: spinner labeled 1–9, 2-color counters*

Have students work in pairs. Each student spins twice, writes a multiplication fact with those two factors, and then uses counters to check the product. The student with the greater product earns 1 point. Play continues until one student earns 5 points.

For additional activities, see For Extra Help, pp. 219, 221, 229, 231, 238A.

LOGICAL/MATHEMATICAL

For Early Finishers

Materials: 4 by 4 grid, spinner labeled 4–9, 2-color counters

Students use these numbers on a 4 × 4 grid to make a Bingo card: 24, 30, 32, 35, 36, 40, 42, 45, 48, 49, 54, 56, 63, 64, 72, 81. Students spin the spinner twice and place a counter on the product of the numbers. The first one to make a line wins.

For additional activities, see For Early Finishers, pp. 215, 217, 219, 223, 227, 233, 235, 237, 238A.

LOGICAL/MATHEMATICAL

Gifted and Talented

Present this problem:

Mark is 2 times as old as Lisa. Jake is 3 times as old as Lisa. The sum of Jake's age and Lisa's age is 16. How old is each person? *(Lisa is 4, Mark is 8, Jake is 12.)*

Have students create, exchange, and solve similar logical reasoning problems.

For additional activities, see Gifted and Talented, pp. 227, 237.

LOGICAL/MATHEMATICAL

Inclusion

Materials: Teaching Tool 4 (Centimeter Grid), spinner labeled 1–9

Have students work with partners to complete multiplication facts to 9 × 9. One student reads a multiplication fact such as 4 × 5, and says what it means: 4 groups of 5. The partner shades 4 rows of 5 squares on a grid, counting each row as he or she shades it. Partners then complete the fact.

For additional activities, see Inclusion, p. 223.

VISUAL/SPATIAL

*These Manipulatives are found in the Manipulatives Kit.

Cooperative Learning

Materials: index cards with these numbers: 16, 18, 20, 24, 25, 27, 30, 32, 35, 36, 40, 42, 45, 48, 49, 54, 56, 63, 64, 72, 81

Have students work in pairs. One student selects a card. Students take turns writing different multiplication facts that have that number for a product. When students have written all the possible multiplication facts for that number, they pick another card and repeat.

For additional activities, see Cooperative Learning, pp. 229, 235.

LOGICAL/MATHEMATICAL

Manipulatives

Materials: Teaching Tool 10 (One-Hundred Chart), 2-color counter, spinner labeled 1–9

Students use a hundred chart to show multiplication facts. One student spins twice, writes a multiplication fact with those 2 factors, such as 6 × 7, then reads it as "six times seven." The second student moves a counter along the hundred chart to show 6 sevens.

For additional activities, see Manipulatives, p. 231.

LOGICAL/MATHEMATICAL

MATH CENTER

Using Data

Materials: 2-color counters

Students make a pictograph using 2-color counters. They will need to discover that one symbol represents 5 chorus members. Then students will figure out the total number of students in the chorus.

For review, see pages 230–231 and 238–238A.

Answers: Each symbol stands for 5 students; 50 students.

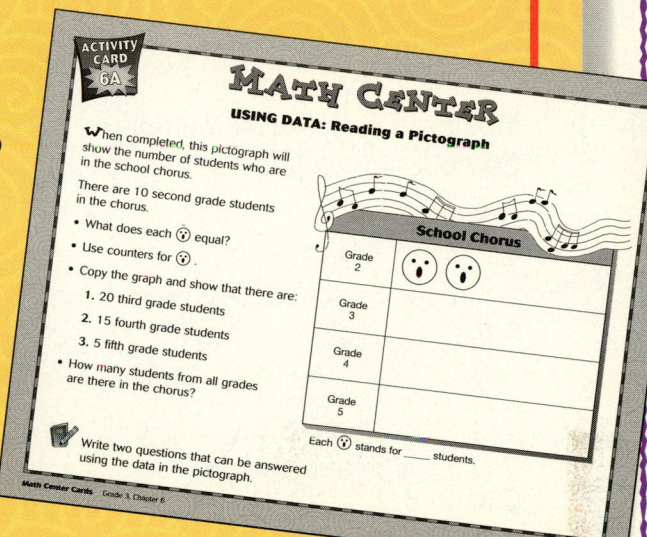

Problem Solving

Materials: spinner, index cards

Students spin the spinner twice and use the 2 numbers to make up a multiplication riddle. They do this 5 times, and then play a game with the riddles they have made up.

For review, see pages 218–221, 226–229, and 232–233.

Answers: The products are greater.

Chapter 6 Assessment

Informal Assessment

Informal assessments provide day-to-day feedback. In conjnction with more formal assessments, they give a complete picture of conceptual development.

In the Student Book

What Do You Think?
student pages 225, 241
Students explain what they have learned.

Create Your Own
student pages 238A, 247
Students create their own problems.

Journal Idea
student pages 221, 225, 234, 241
Students communicate mathematically.

Self-Check
student pages 245, 246
Students evaluate their own work.

In the Teacher Guide

Baseline Assessment
teacher page 210
Helps you assess prior knowledge

Ongoing Assessment
ASSESS UNDERSTANDING
Helps you assess students' understanding

WRAP-UP
Helps you monitor students' progress

JOURNAL IDEA
teacher pages 211, 217, 221, 225, 229, 233, 235, 241
Helps you assess students' communication of math ideas

Portfolio Ideas

Portfolio opportunities appear on Student Book pages 241 and 246, and Teacher Guide pages 217A–B, 241, and 246.

Other items that you may wish to include in your student portfolios are:

- **Completed Chapter Projects**
- **Journal Entries**
- **CD-ROM and Internet Activities**
- **Informal Observations and Interview Activities**

For further suggestions for organizing and using portfolios, see *Assessment Guide,* pages 50–54.

Formal Assessment

Formal assessment can occur before and after the chapter, as well as at natural breaking points in the chapter.

In the Student Book

Checkpoints
student pages 224–225, 240–241
Use for assessing progress as students work through the chapter.

Chapter Test
student page 245

Performance Assessment
student page 246
The Performance Assessment helps you evaluate the skills and concepts developed in Chapter 6 through hands-on activities.

 CD-ROM Test Generator

This software allows you to customize your own chapter test. Formats include:

- **Multiple Choice**
- **Free Response**
- **Standardized Test**

Assessment Guide

You may choose among the following pages in the *Assessment Guide.*

Pretest Options
- **Free Response, pages 107–108**
- **Multiple Choice, pages 109–110**

Posttest Options
- **Free Response, pages 111–112**
- **Multiple Choice, pages 113–114**

Interview Activity
page 40

Long-Answer Question
page 10

Performance Assessment 2
pages 19–21

Cumulative Test 2
pages 115–118

Correlation to Standardized Tests

	Standardized Test Items						
Learning Objectives	**ITBS K/M**	**CTBS/5 (Terra Nova)**	**SAT9**	**MAT7**	**CAT5**	***Pre/Post-Test Items**	**Lesson Pages**
6A Use arrays to show multiplication			P: 28, 29			1–3	212–217
6B Use 3, 6, 4, 8, 7, and 9 as factors	COM: 4, 11, 17 MC: 8	6	P: 7, 9	P: 10, 11, 17, 18	COM: 28	4–13	218–221 226–231
6C Find missing factors; multiply three numbers				P: 16		14–17	234–237
6D Analyze and solve problems using skills and strategies	PS: 18–24 ME: 11–13, 15, 17 MC: 6	29, 47	PS: 44–46	CPS: 33–40 P: 1–12	MC:19–40	18–20	222–223 232–233 238–238A 239–239A

MC = Math Concepts, **COM** = Math Computation, **PS** = Problem Solving, **P** = Procedures, **CPS** = Math Concepts & Problem Solving, **ME** = Math Estimation, **MDI** = Math Data Interpretation, **PB** = Math Problems

*Pretests and Posttests are found in the *Assessment Guide.*

Chapter 6 Linking Technology

Develop and Reinforce Concepts

MathProcessor™

CD-ROM Activities use MathProcessor™ Tools to help build critical thinking skills and develop problem-solving strategies.

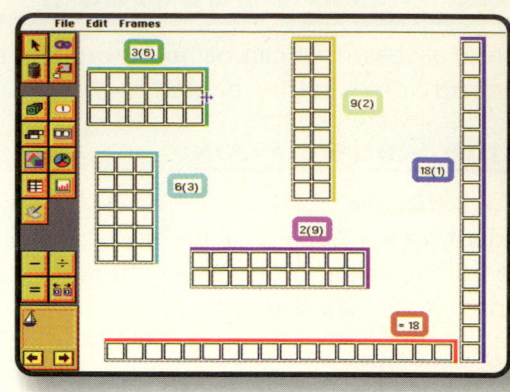

Lesson	Tools	Skill
1	Large Frames Number spaces	Students use arrays to model factors of 18.
8	Large Frames	Students use Large Frames to multiply one-digit by one-digit factors.
10	Large Frames	Students use Large Frames to multiply three factors.

Review and Practice Skills

Math Blaster® 1

This **CD-ROM** program provides exercises and activities to practice basic math facts and develop mastery of mathematical operations. The chart below lists specific lessons where activities and references can be found.

Lesson	Activity	Subject/Level
3	Cave Runner	Multiplication—Level 3: multiply by 5, 6 with products 0–72
7	Math Blaster	Multiplication—Level 5: multiply by 7, 8, 9 with products 1–108

Extend and Enrich

Internet

Students can use real data in lesson-related math activities.
Teachers can find activities and resources for Lessons 6 and 8.
Parents can find home connections to help reinforce concepts.

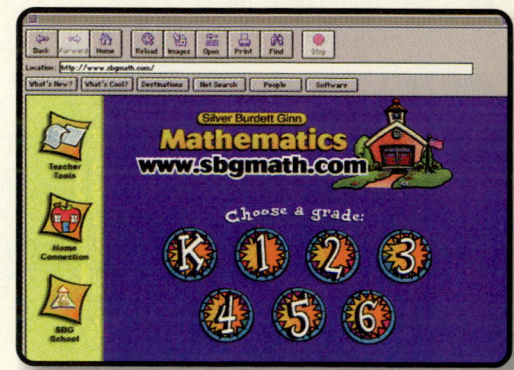

Visit our Web site at:

www.sbgmath.com

Making Connections

Literature

Chapter Resources

These books, found in your local or school library, can be used to help build math concepts.

- **Numbers**
  by Henry Pluckrose
  Children's Press, 1995
- **"Lester,"** from **Where the Sidewalk Ends**
  by Shel Silverstein
  Harper & Row, 1974

Home-School

Family Letter With Activity
Home-School Connection Booklet

The Family Letter for Chapter 6 introduces the concept of multiplying by drawing an array. A family activity suggests switching roles to allow students to become teachers and family members to become students. A concentration game is also provided to reinforce multiplication facts.

Study Buddies
Home-School Connection Booklet

Study Buddies pages provide reinforcement activities for students to work on with a partner.

- Study Buddies 6A provides practice making arrays to multiply.
- Study Buddies 6B reinforces multiplying three numbers.

Math Backpack
Take-Home Activities

Math Backpack activities provide a link between the classroom and the home. Activity Cards 1–6 can be used with this chapter. Parents and students alike will enjoy using these laminated cards and accompanying manipulatives.

Cross-Curricular Integration

Technology

- Use a calculator, pp. 215, 219.
- Use the Internet to practice multiplication, addition, and subtraction, pp. 227, 231.

Language Arts

- Letters and letter-writing, pp. 220–221.

Social Studies

- Meet a ferry captain, p. 210.
- Investigate different modes of transportation, pp. 210, 215, 219, 226, 229, 231, 232, 237, 241.

Art

- Make your own puzzle, p. 225.

Multiplication Facts

Theme: TRANSPORTATION

Chapter Overview

In this chapter students will learn number patterns and strategies for multiplying by one-digit numbers.

Activating Prior Knowledge

Discuss with students what they already know about multiplication facts. Record responses on the chalkboard.

Baseline Assessment

Ask questions such as:

- **What are some strategies that can help you multiply?** *(Possible responses: Drawing pictures; using counters; using addition)*

- **How are multiplication and addition alike?** *(Both find how many in all.)*

Save student responses for use with the **Ongoing Assessment** section in the chapter Checkpoints on pages 225 and 241.

Multiplication Facts

Chapter Theme: TRANSPORTATION

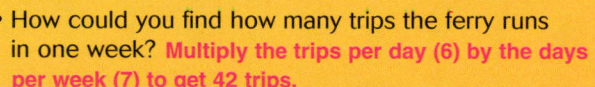

·········Real Facts··········

The Blue & Gold Ferry takes people across San Francisco Bay in California. The chart below shows the 1999-2000 winter ferry weekday schedule. The ferries run between Sausalito and Fisherman's Wharf in San Francisco.

Sausalito–San Francisco Ferry	
Leave Sausalito	**Arrive San Francisco**
11:50 A.M.	12:10 P.M.
1:05 P.M.	1:25 P.M.
2:20 P.M.	2:40 P.M.
3:40 P.M.	4:00 P.M.
5:45 P.M.	6:15 P.M.
8:00 P.M.	8:20 P.M.

- About how long does the trip from Sausalito to Fisherman's Wharf take? **From 20 to 30 minutes**

- How could you find how many trips the ferry runs in one week? **Multiply the trips per day (6) by the days per week (7) to get 42 trips.**

·········Real People··········

Meet Sandy Elles. She is a ferry captain for the Blue & Gold Ferry in San Francisco. She makes sure that the ride is smooth and safe for passengers like those pictured at right.

210

Make a Transportation Chart

 WHOLE CLASS

Materials
- ▶ large piece of posterboard
- ▶ pencils
- ▶ markers
- ▶ yardstick

Here is a project that will help your students learn more about making charts and tables. Specific lessons are referenced to help you work on the project throughout the chapter.

Getting Started

Start the project by telling students they will work as a class to make a chart about transportation. Begin by brainstorming a list of vehicles. Then have students decide what things they will tell about each vehicle. Have them use the brainstorming ideas to help them choose headings for the chart.

- A one-way ferry trip from Sausalito to San Francisco costs $5.50 for an adult and $2.75 for a child (ages 5–11). Round-trip fares are twice the one-way fare.
- The Golden Gate Bridge is 8,981 feet long including approaches. That is about 1.7 miles!

Using the Data

As students review the ferry schedule on page 210, make sure they understand that the first ferry leaves Sausalito at 11:50 A.M. and arrives in San Francisco at 12:10 P.M. Some additional questions you may wish to ask include:

- Suppose you want to be in San Francisco at 3:15 P.M. Which ferry should you take? Explain. *(The 2:20 P.M. ferry which arrives in San Francisco at 2:40 P.M.)*
- The Blue & Gold Fleet runs one less ferry on weekends and holidays than on regular weekdays. How many ferries run on Saturday? on Saturday and Sunday together? *(5 ferries, 10 ferries)*

·········· **Real People** ··········

Sandy Elles started working for San Francisco's Blue & Gold Fleet in 1979. In 1981, she became the fleet's first female ferry captain. As a captain, she is responsible for the safety of the ship, crew, passengers, and cargo. Ask students to discuss how a ferry captain could use math in his or her work.

Building Vocabulary

These key words will be found in this chapter.

square number	multiplication chart
array	skip count

Journal Idea You may wish to have students write about the vocabulary term in their journals at the beginning and end of the chapter.

Project Links

▶ **Lesson 3** Have students work together to make rows and columns for their **transportation chart**. Headings might include: *Type of Vehicle, Number of People It Holds, Where It Is Used,* and *Who Uses It.*

▶ **Lesson 11** Have the class fill in the column showing the maximum number of people that can travel in each vehicle at once. Students **multiply** to find how many people 2, 3, and 4 of each of the vehicles will hold.

Project Wrap-up

Have students work together to fill out and add decorations to the rest of the chart. Then encourage them to take turns asking and answering questions about the chart. For example: *How many people can two buses and three cars carry?* Invite volunteers to use the chart to answer the questions.

Portfolio Students may wish to include their project work in their portfolios.

Lesson Organizer

Objective: Multiply by 4 and 8.

- **NCTM Standards:** 1, 3, 6, 7, 8
- **Manipulatives:** counters (optional)
- **Lesson Resources:**
  Chapter File Folder
      Practice, Reteach, Extend 6-4
  Daily Review 6-4
  Transparency 7

Problem of the Day   6-4

There are 28 seats in the room. Small tables can seat 5. Big tables can seat 6. How many tables of each size are there if all the seats are used? **2 small tables and 3 big tables**

Math Minute

Double the numbers.

4 *(8)*	16 *(32)*	12 *(24)*
6 *(12)*	24 *(48)*	40 *(80)*
9 *(18)*	36 *(72)*	45 *(90)*

It's in the Mail!

Double the 4s facts to help you learn the 8s facts.

Learning About It

Planes bring letters from far-away places. A third-grade class got 8 letters from each of their 5 pen-pal schools. How many letters did they get?

$$5 \times 8 = \blacksquare \quad \text{or} \quad \begin{array}{r} 8 \\ \times\, 5 \\ \hline \end{array}$$

THERE'S ALWAYS A WAY!

- **One way** to find the product is to use doubles.

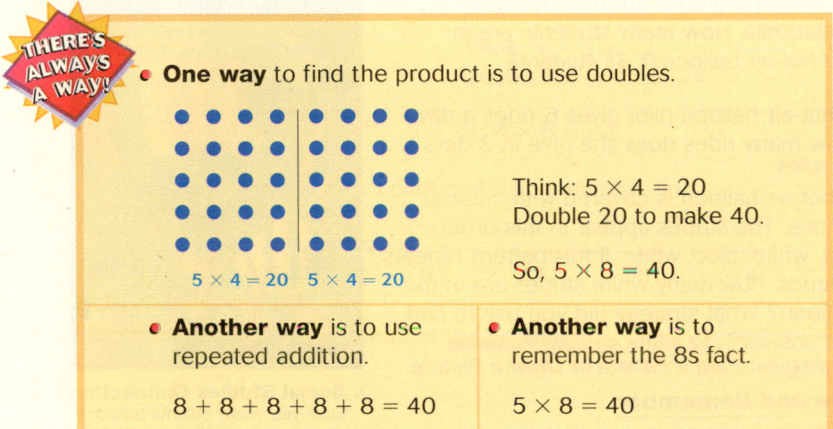

$5 \times 4 = 20 \quad 5 \times 4 = 20$

Think: $5 \times 4 = 20$
Double 20 to make 40.

So, $5 \times 8 = 40$.

- **Another way** is to use repeated addition.	- **Another way** is to remember the 8s fact.
$8 + 8 + 8 + 8 + 8 = 40$	$5 \times 8 = 40$

The third-grade class received 40 letters.

Think and Discuss Which of the above ways do you like best? Tell why. **Answers will vary.**

220

---

① Introduce

Cooperative Activity

KINESTHETIC

 SMALL GROUPS   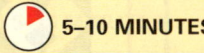 5–10 MINUTES

Materials: counters

1. Students write a 4s fact and make an array with counters to show the multiplication sentence.

2. Students double the number of counters and write an 8s fact.

   - Ask: **How could you use the answer to the 4s fact to write the answer to the 8s fact?** *(Sample answer: Double the product of the 4s fact.)*

② Teach   Pages 220–221

Discuss the ways to find 8s facts shown on page 220.

- Ask: **What 4s fact helps you find 8 × 8?** *(8 × 4 = 32)* **What is the product of 8 × 8?** *(64)*

Critical Thinking   APPLICATION

After Think and Discuss, say: **Suppose that on Tuesday your school received 8 × 3 letters, and on Wednesday it received 8 × 6 letters. How many letters did the school receive on the two days?** *(72 letters)*

Assess Understanding

After Try It Out, say: **Draw a picture that shows how the fact 7 × 4 in Exercise 2 helps you find the second fact, 7 × 8.** *(Sample answer: 7 groups of 4 dots and 7 groups of 4 dots; 56 dots altogether)*

CHALLENGE

The third-grade class has pen pal schools in three cities in Peru. There are four pen pal schools in each city. The third-grade class sent 8 letters to each of its pen pal schools. How many letters did the third-grade class send? *(96)*

Try It Out

Use the first fact to help you multiply the second fact.

1. $8 \times 4 = \blacksquare$ **32**
$8 \times 8 = \blacksquare$ **64**

2. $7 \times 4 = \blacksquare$ **28**
$7 \times 8 = \blacksquare$ **56**

3. $6 \times 4 = \blacksquare$ **24**
$6 \times 8 = \blacksquare$ **48**

4. $9 \times 4 = \blacksquare$ **36**
$9 \times 8 = \blacksquare$ **72**

Practice

Find each product.

5. 8×9 = **72**
6. 8×4 = **32**
7. 8×8 = **64**
8. 2×8 = **16**
9. 3×4 = **12**
10. 7×8 = **56**

11. 4×4 = **16**
12. 6×8 = **48**
13. 8×3 = **24**
14. 4×8 = **32**
15. 7×4 = **28**
16. 9×4 = **36**

Using Algebra Write >, <, or = for each ●.

17. 3×8 **>** 16
18. 3×4 **<** 24
19. 16 **=** 4×4
20. 4×3 **=** 3×4
21. 1×2 **>** 9×0
22. 4×8 **<** 5×8

Problem Solving

23. A class writes letters to a school in Mexico. They write 8 letters each week for 3 weeks. How many letters do they write? **24 letters**

24. **What If?** Suppose the class wrote only 4 letters a week. How many letters would the class have written? **12 letters**

25. **Journal Idea** Write a multiplication word problem that uses either 4 or 8 as a factor. Give it to a classmate to solve. **Check students' word problems.**

26. A student mails 4 envelopes to friends. Each envelope contains 8 pictures. How many pictures did the student send? **32 pictures**

Review and Remember

Choose a Method Use mental math, paper and pencil, or a calculator to find each answer. Tell which method you chose. **Possible methods are given.**

27. $40 + 50$ **Mental math; 90**
28. $590 - 210$ **Paper and pencil; 380**
29. $6,000 - 1,799$ **Calculator; 4,201**
30. $2,385 + 4,000$ **Mental math; 6,385**
31. $4,385 - 2,179$ **Calculator; 2,206**
32. $984 - 206$ **Paper and pencil; 778**

For Extra Practice, see Set C, page 243. **221**

Using Algebra

In Exercises 17–22, students will compare expressions using **numerical relationships**.

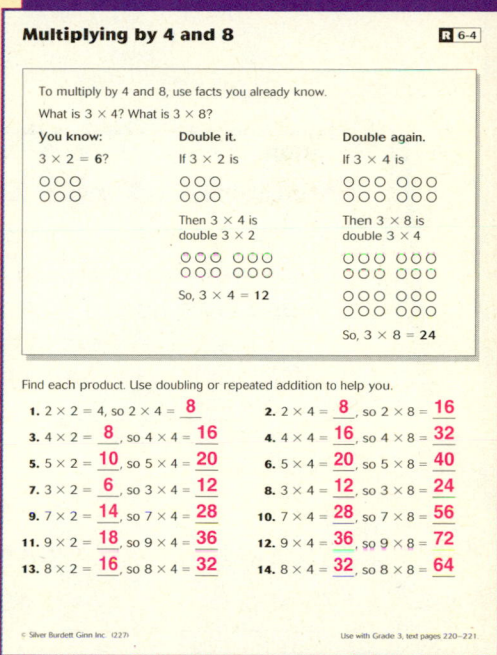
---

3 Wrap-up

Journal Idea To extend the journal idea in Problem 25, ask students to explain why multiplication is the best way to solve their word problem.

Common Error Alert

Watch for students who don't realize that the order of factors does not change the product. Suggest that students create arrays to help them recognize this fact.

Meeting Individual Needs

For Extra Help

Have students use beads to model 4×3. Then have them double the number of groups to model 8×3. Have them model other 4s facts and double for 8s facts.
KINESTHETIC

Acquiring English Proficiency

One partner orally represents Exercise 1 on page 221. The other gives the answers and explains how they were found. Switch roles and repeat for Exercises 2–4.
AUDITORY

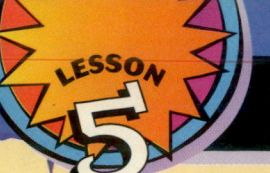

Lesson Organizer

Objective: Decide if there is enough information to solve a problem.

- **NCTM Standards:** 1, 3
- **Lesson Resources:**
  Chapter File Folder
      Practice, Reteach, Extend 6-5
  Daily Review 6-5

Problem of the Day   6-5

Lorena watched an Old West parade. There were 5 floats. Each float held 2 people. Two horses pulled each float. How many feet were in the parade?

60 feet: 40 horse feet and 20 people feet

 Math Minute

Multiply.

9×4 *(36)*	6×4 *(24)*
3×4 *(12)*	3×9 *(27)*
7×4 *(28)*	6×9 *(54)*

Developing Skills for Problem Solving

First read for understanding and then focus on whether there is too much or too little information to solve a problem.

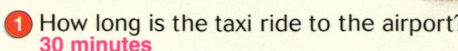

READ FOR UNDERSTANDING

The Cole family is taking a 30-minute taxi ride to the airport. Ed and his mother are going on a trip. Mr. Cole will take a taxi home after saying goodbye to his family. There is a 75¢ toll on the way to the airport. There is no toll on the way home.

1 How long is the taxi ride to the airport?
30 minutes

2 How much is the toll on the way to the airport?
75¢

3 Is there a toll on the way home from the airport?
No

THINK AND DISCUSS

MATH FOCUS

Too Much or Too Little Information
Before you solve a problem, you need to decide whether you have too much or too little information.

Reread the paragraph at the top of the page.

4 Do you have enough information to find the total cost for the toll? Why or why not?
Yes; there is only one toll of 75¢.

5 How much will the taxi ride cost? Is there too much or too little information to solve the problem? **There is too little information given to solve the problem; you need to know the taxi fare for the ride to the airport and the taxi fare for the ride home.**

6 What information in the paragraph is *not* needed to solve Problem 5? What information is needed?
Information not needed: taxi ride lasts 30 minutes.
Information needed: cost of the ride and the cost of the tolls

222

---

1 Introduce

Cooperative Activity
LOGICAL/MATHEMATICAL

 SMALL GROUPS   10–15 MINUTES

1. Write the following on the board: Sara took a ferry trip that lasted 15 minutes. How much did she pay for 3 trips?

   - Ask: **Is it possible to solve the problem if you do not know the cost of one trip?** *(No)*

2. Then ask students to suggest a question that they could answer using the information given. *(Sample answer: How long do 3 trips take?)*

2 Teach   Pages 222–223

Read for Understanding Have students read the paragraph. The questions below it are reading comprehension questions based on information that can be found in the paragraph.

Think and Discuss Discuss the math focus. Ask students if they can tell if they have too much or too little information before they read Questions 4 and 5. *(No, the problem is not yet known.)*

After Question 5, ask students how they could change the story problem to include information that will help them find the total cost of the taxi ride. *(Sample answer: Add the cost of the ride one way.)*

Critical Thinking   APPLICATION

After Think and Discuss, say: **A taxi driver charges $4.00 for a one-way trip to the airport and $8.00 for a round trip. She gives rides to 5 different people. Do you have enough information to find out how much each person paid? Explain.** *(No; it does not say which type of trip each person took.)*

Assess Understanding

Before Show What You Learned, ask students how they can decide if they have too little information to answer a question.

Show What You Learned

Answer each question. Give a reason for your choice.

A taxi driver charges $9 for a trip to the airport. She charges $5 for a trip to the bus station. How much money does she charge for 3 trips to the airport?

1 What information do you *not* need to solve the problem?

a. the number of trips to the airport

b. the charge for one trip to the bus station

c. the charge for one trip to the airport

2 Which number sentence could you use to solve the problem?

a. $9 + $5 = ■

b. 3 × $9 = ■

c. 3 × $5 = ■

A taxi driver gave rides to 60 people on Monday, 48 people on Tuesday, and 54 people on Wednesday. He did not drive the taxi on Thursday or Friday. How many more people rode with him on Monday than on Tuesday?

3 What information do you *not* need to solve the problem?

a. the number of people who rode on Monday

b. the number of people who rode on Tuesday

c. the number of people who rode on Wednesday

4. Yes; since you know the number of people who rode on Monday and on Tuesday, you can find the difference.
60 − 48 = 12 people

4 **Explain** Is there enough information to solve the problem? Why or why not? If not, what else do you need to know to solve the problem? See above.

5 **Explain** Is there enough information to tell how much money the taxi driver collected on Monday and Tuesday? Why or why not? No; you do not know the amount of money charged for each ride.

223

3 Wrap-up

Deanna arrived home from the airport at 8:00 P.M. The taxi ride cost $24. She left the airport at 7:25 P.M. Write a question that cannot be answered with the information in the problem. *(Sample answer: How long was Deanna's flight?)*

Common Error Alert

Watch for students who do not recognize when a problem lacks the necessary information and who try to solve it using the information given.

Meeting Individual Needs

For Early Finishers

Each student writes a story problem and 2 questions that can be answered with the information in the problem. Students trade problems and solve.

LOGICAL/MATHEMATICAL

Inclusion

Tell a story that has too little information. Ask students to tell what is missing so the problem can be solved, then supply the information and solve.

AUDITORY

Checkpoint

······················

Vocabulary Review

You may wish to review this term before students begin the Checkpoint.

square number The product of two equal factors. *Example:* $5 \times 5 = 25$; 25 is a square number.

······················

Using the Page

Purpose To review concepts and skills presented up to this point in Chapter 6

- If necessary, discuss the directions and content of each section of the Checkpoint with the class.

- Page numbers associated with each group of items refer to the pages on which the skill or concept was presented. Those students needing review should turn to the appropriate lessons.

 Using Algebra

In the Critical Thinking Corner, students solve **equations** that contain variables.

Multiplication Facts

Write a multiplication sentence for each array.
(pages 212–215)

1.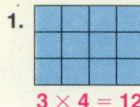
$3 \times 4 = 12$

2.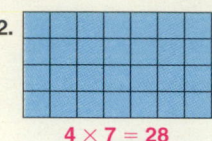
$4 \times 7 = 28$

3.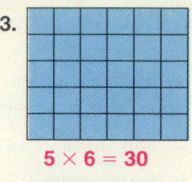
$5 \times 6 = 30$

4. (array)
$4 \times 4 = 16$

5.
$3 \times 8 = 24$

6.
$2 \times 5 = 10$

Use the first fact to help you multiply the second fact.
(pages 216–221)

7. 4×3 **12**
$\quad 4 \times 6$ **24**

8. 5×3 **15**
$\quad 5 \times 6$ **30**

9. 8×3 **24**
$\quad 8 \times 6$ **48**

10. 6×4 **24**
$\quad 6 \times 8$ **48**

11. 9×4 **36**
$\quad 9 \times 8$ **72**

12. 7×4 **28**
$\quad 7 \times 8$ **56**

Find the product. (pages 218–221)

13. $\begin{array}{r}4\\ \times 6\\ \hline 24\end{array}$	14. $\begin{array}{r}6\\ \times 8\\ \hline 48\end{array}$	15. $\begin{array}{r}4\\ \times 2\\ \hline 8\end{array}$	16. $\begin{array}{r}8\\ \times 2\\ \hline 16\end{array}$	17. $\begin{array}{r}4\\ \times 5\\ \hline 20\end{array}$	18. $\begin{array}{r}8\\ \times 5\\ \hline 40\end{array}$
19. $\begin{array}{r}4\\ \times 7\\ \hline 28\end{array}$	20. $\begin{array}{r}0\\ \times 8\\ \hline 0\end{array}$	21. $\begin{array}{r}8\\ \times 7\\ \hline 56\end{array}$	22. $\begin{array}{r}3\\ \times 9\\ \hline 27\end{array}$	23. $\begin{array}{r}6\\ \times 9\\ \hline 54\end{array}$	24. $\begin{array}{r}7\\ \times 3\\ \hline 21\end{array}$
25. $\begin{array}{r}1\\ \times 4\\ \hline 4\end{array}$	26. $\begin{array}{r}7\\ \times 6\\ \hline 42\end{array}$	27. $\begin{array}{r}1\\ \times 8\\ \hline 8\end{array}$	28. $\begin{array}{r}0\\ \times 6\\ \hline 0\end{array}$	29. $\begin{array}{r}4\\ \times 3\\ \hline 12\end{array}$	30. $\begin{array}{r}3\\ \times 8\\ \hline 24\end{array}$
31. $\begin{array}{r}8\\ \times 9\\ \hline 72\end{array}$	32. $\begin{array}{r}5\\ \times 3\\ \hline 15\end{array}$	33. $\begin{array}{r}6\\ \times 5\\ \hline 30\end{array}$	34. $\begin{array}{r}8\\ \times 6\\ \hline 48\end{array}$	35. $\begin{array}{r}9\\ \times 3\\ \hline 27\end{array}$	36. $\begin{array}{r}6\\ \times 7\\ \hline 42\end{array}$

224

Reinforcement and Remediation

 **PAIRS**

- Provide each pair with a spinner (0–9) and counters. Have one student spin a number and multiply it by 3.

- Have the partner multiply the number by 6. Have students compare the products.

- Ask students to repeat the activity by spinning a number and multiplying it by 4 and 8.

- Students can work together to create a table that shows which 3s facts they can use to solve 6s facts. Ask them to make another table for 4s and 8s facts.

- Encourage students to use counters to check if the 3s and 4s facts can help them find the 6s and 8s facts listed.

Problem Solving

37. There are 6 rows in Mel's parking lot. He can park 8 cars in each row. If all the rows are filled, how many cars are parked in his lot? **48 cars**

38. Three skiers fit on one chair of a chair lift. How many skiers can fit on 9 chairs? **27 skiers**

39. Five groups of 8 students take the bus to school. Twice that many students walk to school. How many students walk to school? **80 students**

40. **Analyze** Your father bought 3 packs of amusement ride tickets. There are 6 tickets in each pack. Your brother used half of the tickets. How many tickets are left? **9 tickets**

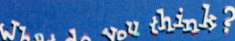

What do you think?
Could you write a multiplication sentence for $6 + 6 + 6 + 3$? Explain why or why not.

No; all the addends are not the same.

 Journal Idea
Explain how knowing $4 \times 5 = 20$ can help you find 8×5. **Students should realize that 8 is the double of 4, so the product of 8×5 is double the product of 4×5. So the product of $8 \times 5 = 40$.**

Critical Thinking Corner

Logical Thinking

Number Puzzler

1. **Using Algebra** In the exercises below, each shape stands for a different number. Find the number for each shape so that all the exercises are correct.

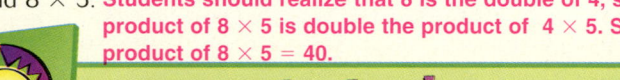

a. $\overset{3}{\bigstar} \times \overset{3}{\bigstar} = 9$ **b.** $\overset{4}{\blacktriangle} \times \overset{3}{\bigstar} = 12$

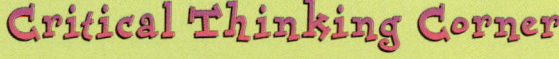

c. $\overset{3}{\bigstar} \times \overset{5}{\blacksquare} = 15$ **d.** $\overset{5}{\blacksquare} \times \overset{4}{\blacktriangle} = 20$

2. **Create Your Own** Make up your own puzzle. Use the same shapes as above or invent your own shapes. Give your puzzle to a friend to solve. **Puzzles may vary.**

225

Critical Thinking Corner

Logical Thinking

- a: **Use arrays to decide which number multiplied by itself equals 9.** *(3)* In all of the sentences the star stands for 3.

- b: **Replace the star with a 3 and solve by creating an array with 3 rows. Find out how many are in each row to total 12.** *(4)* In all of the sentences the triangle stands for 4.

- c: **Replace the star with a 3 and solve by creating an array with 3 rows. Find out how many are in each row to total 15.** *(5)* In all of the sentences the square stands for 5.

- d: **Replace the square with 5 and the triangle with 4.**

Ongoing Assessment

You may want to have students review their responses to the questions presented at the beginning of the chapter. Have students discuss what they have learned so far in this chapter that helps them answer the "What do you think?" question.

What do you think?

Accept reasonable responses. Some students may say no; you can only use repeated addition sentences to write multiplication sentences.

Journal Idea

Encourage students to describe how other 4s facts can help them find 8s facts.

Lesson Organizer

Objective: Multiply by 7.

- **NCTM Standards:** 1, 3, 6, 7, 8
- **Lesson Resources:**
  Chapter File Folder
      Practice, Reteach, Extend 6-6
      Teaching Tool 18
  Daily Review 6-6
  Practice Workbook, p. 27
  Transparencies 7, 16

Problem of the Day   6-6

I am the product of two even numbers. Both of my factors are greater than 3 but less than 10. One of the factors is half the first factor. What number am I? **32**

Math Minute

Multiply.

4 × 6 *(24)*	8 × 9 *(72)*
3 × 4 *(12)*	8 × 3 *(24)*
4 × 9 *(36)*	6 × 5 *(30)*

1 Introduce

Cooperative Activity

KINESTHETIC

SMALL GROUPS   ● **5–10 MINUTES**

Manipulatives: spinner (0–9)

1. One student spins the spinner. Another student adds 7 the number of times shown on the spinner. A third student checks the addition.

2. Students continue spinning and adding 7s until everyone has had a turn.

River Boats

You can multiply by 7 in different ways.

Learning About It

In Brazil, people sometimes ride in boats down the Amazon River. Suppose there are 3 boats on the river and each boat has 7 people in it. How many people are there in all 3 boats?

$3 \times 7 = \blacksquare$ or $\begin{array}{r} 7 \\ \times\ 3 \\ \hline \end{array}$

Amazon River

THERE'S ALWAYS A WAY!

- **One way** to find the product is to skip count by 7s on a number line.

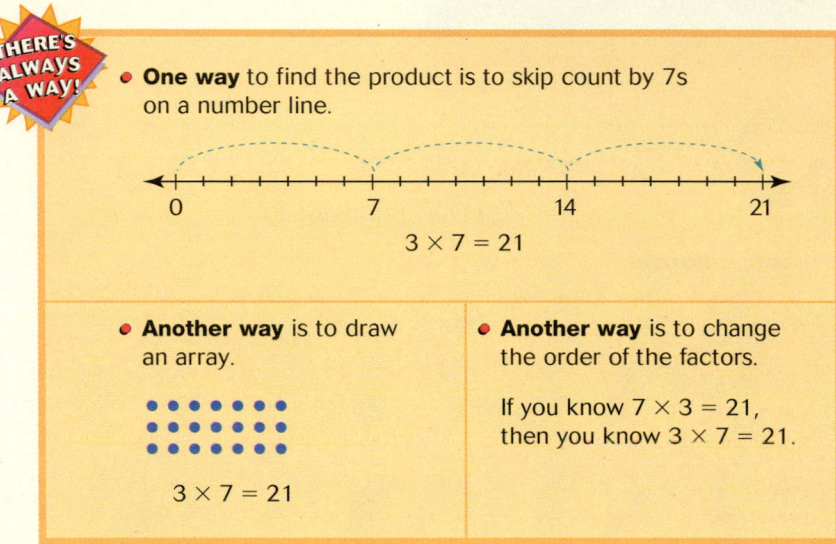

$3 \times 7 = 21$

- **Another way** is to draw an array.

$3 \times 7 = 21$

- **Another way** is to change the order of the factors.

If you know $7 \times 3 = 21$, then you know $3 \times 7 = 21$.

There are 21 people in the boats.

Think and Discuss How would skip counting on a number line be different for 7×3?
There would be 7 jumps showing groups of 3.

226

2 Teach   Pages 226–227

After demonstrating each method described on page 226, encourage volunteers to demonstrate how doubles can be used to find the 7s facts. For example, $3 \times 7 = 21$, so $6 \times 7 = 42$.

Critical Thinking   ANALYSIS

After Think and Discuss, ask: **Does 7 × 4 have the same product as 4 × 7? Explain.** *(Sample answer: Yes; if you make 7 jumps of 4 or 4 jumps of 7 on a number line, you will land on 28.)*

Assess Understanding

After Try It Out, ask three volunteers to demonstrate different ways of finding 5×7.

★ CHALLENGE

Complete.
1. $4 \times 2 \times 5$ *(40)*   4. $7 \times 4 \times 2$ *(56)*
2. $3 \times 4 \times 5$ *(60)*   5. $8 \times 3 \times 2$ *(48)*
3. $6 \times 3 \times 5$ *(90)*   6. $4 \times 4 \times 3$ *(48)*

Try It Out

Use the first fact to help you multiply the second fact.

1. $2 \times 7 = 14$ $7 \times 2 = 14$
2. $5 \times 7 = 35$ $7 \times 5 = 35$
3. $4 \times 7 = 28$ $7 \times 4 = 28$
4. $8 \times 7 = 56$ $7 \times 8 = 56$

Practice

Multiply.

5. $0 \times 7 = 0$
6. $7 \times 1 = 7$
7. $7 \times 3 = 21$
8. $7 \times 7 = 49$
9. $7 \times 4 = 28$
10. $7 \times 6 = 42$

11. $0 \times 7 = 0$
12. $8 \times 7 = 56$
13. $5 \times 7 = 35$
14. $1 \times 7 = 7$
15. $6 \times 7 = 42$
16. $7 \times 9 = 63$

17. $8 \times 9 = 72$
18. $7 \times 4 = 28$
19. $7 \times 9 = 63$
20. $8 \times 5 = 40$

21. $6 \times 8 = 48$
22. $7 \times 7 = 49$
23. $8 \times 3 = 24$
24. $5 \times 9 = 45$

25. $0 \times 7 = 0$
26. $8 \times 7 = 56$
27. $9 \times 5 = 45$
28. $8 \times 8 = 64$

Problem Solving

29. A group of travelers spends 8 weeks exploring the Amazon River. How many days long is their trip? **56 days**

30. **Analyze** Three boats are each 7 feet long. The dock is 4 feet longer than all the boats placed end to end. How long is the dock? **25 feet**

Review and Remember

Using Mental Math Find each answer.

31. $80 - 30$ **50**
32. $5,000 - 2,000$ **3,000**
33. $690 - 30$ **660**
34. $250 - 40$ **210**
35. $300 - 150$ **150**
36. $\$3,000 + \$5,000$ **\$8,000**
37. $470 + 210$ **680**
38. $75 + 25$ **100**

For Extra Practice, see Set D, page 243. **227**

---

3 Wrap-up

How do you find the total number of people if there are 7 people in each of 8 boats? *(Sample answer: Skip count by 7s eight times; 56 people.)*

Common Error Alert

Watch for students who skip count incorrectly. Suggest that they use a number line and repeated addition or arrays to check answers found by skip counting.

Meeting Individual Needs

Gifted and Talented

Students complete the following pattern: 49, 56, 63, 70, ■, 84, ■. *(77, 91)* They create their own pattern, exchange with a partner, and solve.

LOGICAL/MATHEMATICAL

For Early Finishers

Each day a song is Number 1 it earns $7. Students toss a number cube to find the number of days, then multiply to find the total.

LOGICAL/MATHEMATICAL

Internet Activity

www.sbgmath.com

Students will do a multiplication activity based on a Web site about river travel.

Practice

Multiplying by 7   P 6-6

Find each product. Use the letters from your answers to solve the riddle, "What goes up when the rain comes down?"

1. $3 \times 7 = 21$ A
2. $7 \times 1 = 7$ E
3. $7 \times 6 = 42$ U
4. $2 \times 7 = 14$ A
5. $4 \times 7 = 28$ B
6. $0 \times 7 = 0$ M
7. $7 \times 5 = 35$ N
8. $7 \times 7 = 49$ R
9. $9 \times 7 = 63$ L
10. $7 \times 8 = 56$ L

A N   U M B R E L L A
21 35   42 0 28 49 7 63 56 14

Solve.

11. Complete the table.

Weeks	1	2	3	4	5	6
Days	7	14	21	28	35	42

12. It rained for two weeks in November. For how many days did it rain? **14 days**

13. Manny is going to camp for 35 days. Is that more or less than 6 weeks? **less**

14. December is 31 days long. Is this more or less than 4 weeks? **more**

15. Summer vacation is about 9 weeks long. How many days is this? **63 days**

© Silver Burdett Ginn Inc. (232)   Use with Grade 3, text pages 226–227.

Reteach

Multiplying by 7   R 6-6

You can use a number line to find products.

0 7 14 21 28 35 42 49 56 63

$6 \times 7 = ?$

Start at 0.
Count six jumps of 7 each.
Your finger is at 42.
So, $6 \times 7 = 42$.

Use the number line to help you find each product.

0 7 14 21 28 35 42 49 56 63

1. Start at 0. Count 3 jumps. $3 \times 7 = $ **21**
2. Start at 0. Count 2 jumps. $2 \times 7 = $ **14**
3. Start at 0. Count 5 jumps. $5 \times 7 = $ **35**
4. Start at 0. Count 1 jump. $1 \times 7 = $ **7**
5. Start at 0. Count 7 jumps. $7 \times 7 = $ **49**
6. Start at 0. Count 9 jumps. $9 \times 7 = $ **63**
7. Start at 0. Count 0 jumps. $0 \times 7 = $ **0**
8. Start at 0. Count 8 jumps. $8 \times 7 = $ **56**
9. Start at 0. Count 4 jumps. $4 \times 7 = $ **28**

10. $7 \times 5 = $ **35**
11. $1 \times 7 = $ **7**
12. $7 \times 6 = $ **42**
13. $7 \times 8 = $ **56**
14. $9 \times 7 = $ **63**

© Silver Burdett Ginn Inc. (233)   Use with Grade 3, text pages 226–227.

Extend

A-Mazing Facts   E 6-6
NUMBER SENSE

Skip-count by sevens to find multiples of 7.
7 14 21 28 35 42 49 56 63

Help the mouse reach the cheese. First, multiply. Then follow the path where the product is a multiple of 7.

$2 \times 3 = 6$	$5 \times 7 = 35$	$8 \times 4 = 32$	$5 \times 5 = 25$
$7 \times 4 = 28$	$4 \times 9 = 36$	$2 \times 7 = 14$	$8 \times 2 = 16$
$7 \times 9 = 63$	$8 \times 3 = 24$	$0 \times 5 = 0$	$7 \times 3 = 21$	$1 \times 7 = 7$
$9 \times 2 = 18$	$3 \times 7 = 21$	$4 \times 5 = 20$	$5 \times 6 = 30$	$2 \times 4 = 8$
$4 \times 4 = 16$	$8 \times 8 = 64$	$7 \times 8 = 56$	$6 \times 7 = 42$	$4 \times 8 = 32$
$9 \times 5 = 45$	$8 \times 4 = 32$	$6 \times 8 = 48$	$4 \times 5 = 20$	$7 \times 9 = 63$
	$3 \times 3 = 9$	$9 \times 5 = 45$	$7 \times 7 = 49$
	$1 \times 7 = 7$	$8 \times 7 = 56$	$4 \times 6 = 24$

Start

End

What number is part of every fact on your path? **7**

© Silver Burdett Ginn Inc. (234)   Use with Grade 3, text pages 226–227.

Lesson Organizer

Objective: Multiply by 9.

- **NCTM Standards:** 1, 3, 4, 6, 7, 8
- **Lesson Resources:**
  Chapter File Folder
    Practice, Reteach, Extend 6-7
    Teaching Tool 7
  Daily Review 6-7
  Practice Workbook, p. 28
  Transparency 7

Problem of the Day   6-7

Luke walks his dog 3 times on one day, 2 times the next day, 3 times the day after that, and so on. How many times will Luke walk his dog in 2 weeks? **35 times**

Math Minute

Multiply.

3×8 *(24)*	4×8 *(32)*
5×8 *(40)*	6×7 *(42)*
7×8 *(56)*	4×7 *(28)*

Getting Around

The number facts you already know will help you learn the 9s facts.

Learning About It

One of the best seats on a double-decker bus is a window seat on top. On each side of this bus there are 2 rows of windows. Each row has 9 windows. How many windows are there on one side?

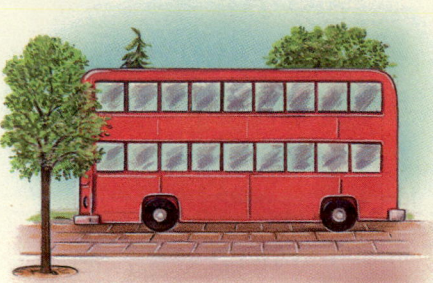

$$2 \times 9 = \blacksquare \quad \text{or} \quad \begin{array}{r} 9 \\ \times\, 2 \\ \hline \end{array}$$

THERE'S ALWAYS A WAY!

- **One way** to find the product is to change the order of the factors.

  If you know $9 \times 2 = 18$, then you know $2 \times 9 = 18$.

- **Another way** is to use a 10s fact. Find 2×10. Then subtract one 2.

  $2 \times 10 = 20$
  $20 - 2 = 18$
  So, $2 \times 9 = 18$

There are 18 windows on one side of the bus.

Think and Discuss Suppose you know that $5 \times 10 = 50$. How can that help you find 5×9? **Subtract one 5 from 50. So $5 \times 9 = 50 - 5$ or 45.**

Try It Out

Use the first fact to help you multiply the second fact.

1. 9×4 **36**	**2.** 9×6 **54**	**3.** 9×1 **9**	**4.** 9×3 **27**
4×9 **36**	6×9 **54**	1×9 **9**	3×9 **27**
5. 9×0 **0**	**6.** 9×7 **63**	**7.** 9×5 **45**	**8.** 9×8 **72**
0×9 **0**	7×9 **63**	5×9 **45**	8×9 **72**

228

---

1 Introduce

Cooperative Activity

AUDITORY

 SMALL GROUPS   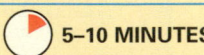 **5–10 MINUTES**

Have students write the numbers you say as you skip count by 9s from 9 to 81.

- Discuss: **What pattern do you notice?** *(Sample answer: One number is odd, the next even.)*

- Discuss: **What do you notice about the sum of the digits of the numbers?** *(The sum is always 9.)*

2 Teach   Pages 228–229

Demonstrate each way to find 2×9. Ask volunteers to demonstrate each way to find 9×3.

Critical Thinking   SYNTHESIS

After Think and Discuss, have students find the products of 1×9, 2×9, 3×9, 4×9, and so on. Ask: **Which way is the easiest way to find each product?** *(Sample answer: One 9 is 9; use doubles for 2×9, 4×9, 8×9; skip count for 5×9; use repeated addition for 3×9; use a fact you know, such as 9×7, for 7×9; and find 9×10 and subtract 9 for 9×9.)*

Assess Understanding

After Try It Out, ask: **If you know that $9 \times 7 = 63$, what 9s fact do you also know?** *($7 \times 9 = 63$)*

 **USING TECHNOLOGY**

Math Blaster® 1, Math Blaster
Multiplication: Level 5
Multiply by 7, 8, 9
With products 1–108

Practice

Find the product.

9. $\begin{array}{r} 9 \\ \times 5 \\ \hline 45 \end{array}$
10. $\begin{array}{r} 9 \\ \times 9 \\ \hline 81 \end{array}$
11. $\begin{array}{r} 6 \\ \times 9 \\ \hline 54 \end{array}$
12. $\begin{array}{r} 0 \\ \times 9 \\ \hline 0 \end{array}$
13. $\begin{array}{r} 8 \\ \times 9 \\ \hline 72 \end{array}$
14. $\begin{array}{r} 9 \\ \times 7 \\ \hline 63 \end{array}$

15. $\begin{array}{r} 9 \\ \times 8 \\ \hline 72 \end{array}$
16. $\begin{array}{r} 9 \\ \times 1 \\ \hline 9 \end{array}$
17. $\begin{array}{r} 2 \\ \times 9 \\ \hline 18 \end{array}$
18. $\begin{array}{r} 9 \\ \times 6 \\ \hline 54 \end{array}$
19. $\begin{array}{r} 7 \\ \times 9 \\ \hline 63 \end{array}$
20. $\begin{array}{r} 9 \\ \times 3 \\ \hline 27 \end{array}$

21. 2×9 **18**   22. 9×3 **27**   23. 4×9 **36**   24. 9×5 **45**

Using Algebra Find the rule. Then complete each table.

25. Rule: **Multiply by 4.**

Input	Output
2	8
26. 9	**36**
27. 7	**28**

28. Rule: **Multiply by 9.**

Input	Output
29. 9	**81**
3	27
30. 6	**54**

31. Rule: **Multiply by 7.**

Input	Output
32. 9	**63**
7	49
33. 6	**42**

Problem Solving

34. Each week you use 6 bus tokens. How many tokens do you use in 9 weeks? **54 tokens**

35. **Analyze** James travels 9 miles to school by bus. How many miles does he travel to school and home again in 2 days? **36 miles**

36. **Explain** The E bus makes 3 stops on its route. The C bus makes 5 stops on its route. If the E bus completes 6 trips and the C bus completes 4 trips, which bus makes more stops? **The C bus makes more stops because 6×4 is greater than 3×5.**

▲ **Social Studies Connection** Double-decker buses can be found in cities around the world. This picture shows a double-decker bus in London.

Review and Remember

Find the total amount of each.

37. 5 pennies
2 dimes
3 quarters
$1.00

38. 10 nickels
2 quarters
4 dollars
$5.00

39. 6 pennies
6 dimes
3 quarters
$1.41

40. 5 dimes
1 quarter
3 dollars
$3.75

For Extra Practice, see Set E, page 243. **229**

For Extra Practice, see Set E, page 243.

Using Algebra

In Exercises 25–33, students use **functions** to complete tables.

3 Wrap-up

Describe how to find the product of 9 × 7.
(Sample answer: Multiply 10 × 7, then subtract 7; 63.)

Journal Idea To find 9 × 8, would you rather add 9 eight times or use 9s facts? Explain.

Common Error Alert

Watch for students who multiply by 10 and subtract 1. Suggest they circle the matching numbers in the multiplication and subtraction sentences.

Meeting Individual Needs

Cooperative Learning

Students toss 2 number cubes labeled 4–9. One student draws an array to find the product. Another skip counts on a number line. Students compare answers.
LOGICAL/MATHEMATICAL

For Extra Help

Students use counters to explore 9s facts by creating arrays. Have students write a multiplication fact for each array they create.
VISUAL/SPATIAL

Practice

Multiplying by 9   P 6-7

Complete the table.

	Fact	Product	Sum of digits in product
1.	1 × 9	9	
2.	2 × 9	18	9
3.	3 × 9	27	9
4.	4 × 9	36	9
5.	5 × 9	45	9
6.	6 × 9	54	9
7.	7 × 9	63	9
8.	8 × 9	72	9
9.	9 × 9	81	9

Use the table to answer the questions.

10. What patterns do you see in the tens digits and in the ones digits in the list of products? **Tens digits increase by 1; ones digits decrease by 1.**

11. Describe the pattern in the sums of the digits. **The sum of the digits is always 9.**

Solve.

12. How many puppies are there if 9 dogs each have 9 puppies? **81 puppies**

13. Jorge must travel 9 miles to get to school and back each day. How many miles does he travel in a 5-day week? **45 miles**

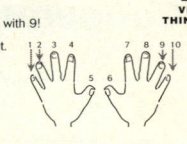

© Silver Burdett Ginn Inc. (235)   Use with Grade 3, text pages 228–229.

Reteach

Multiplying by 9   R 6-7

To multiply by 9:	$4 \times 9 = ?$
First multiply 4 by 10.	$4 \times 10 = 40$
Then subtract 4 from the product.	$40 - 4 = 36$
	So, $4 \times 9 = 36$

Find the products. Multiply by 10 to help you.

1. $2 \times 9 = ?$
$2 \times 10 = $ **20**
20 − 2 = **18**
So, $2 \times 9 = $ **18**

2. $5 \times 9 = ?$
$5 \times 10 = $ **50**
50 − 5 = **45**
So, $5 \times 9 = $ **45**

3. $5 \times 9 = ?$
$5 \times 10 = $ **50**
50 − 5 = **45**
So, $5 \times 9 = $ **45**

4. $7 \times 9 = ?$
$7 \times 10 = $ **70**
70 − 7 = **63**
So, $7 \times 9 = $ **63**

5. $3 \times 9 = ?$
$3 \times 10 = $ **30**
30 − 3 = **27**
So, $3 \times 9 = $ **27**

6. $6 \times 9 = ?$
$6 \times 10 = $ **60**
60 − 6 = **54**
So, $6 \times 9 = $ **54**

7. $8 \times 9 = ?$
$8 \times 10 = $ **80**
80 − 8 = **72**
So, $8 \times 9 = $ **72**

8. $9 \times 9 = ?$
$9 \times 10 = $ **90**
90 − 9 = **81**
So, $9 \times 9 = $ **81**

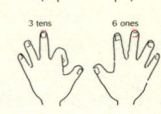
"9 = 10 - 1"

© Silver Burdett Ginn Inc. (236)   Use with Grade 3, text pages 228–229.

Extend

Finger Fun   E 6-7   **VISUAL THINKING**

You can use your fingers to find products with 9!

Hold your hands out with palms facing out. Mentally number your fingers as shown.

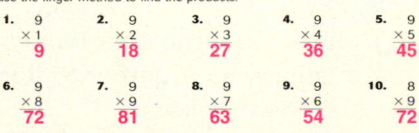

To find the product of 9 × 4, bend your fourth finger. Fingers to the left of the bent finger tell how many tens in the product. Fingers to the right of the bent finger tell how many ones in the product.

Use the finger method to find the products.

1. $\begin{array}{r} 9 \\ \times 1 \\ \hline 9 \end{array}$
2. $\begin{array}{r} 9 \\ \times 2 \\ \hline 18 \end{array}$
3. $\begin{array}{r} 9 \\ \times 3 \\ \hline 27 \end{array}$
4. $\begin{array}{r} 9 \\ \times 4 \\ \hline 36 \end{array}$
5. $\begin{array}{r} 9 \\ \times 5 \\ \hline 45 \end{array}$

6. $\begin{array}{r} 9 \\ \times 8 \\ \hline 72 \end{array}$
7. $\begin{array}{r} 9 \\ \times 9 \\ \hline 81 \end{array}$
8. $\begin{array}{r} 9 \\ \times 7 \\ \hline 63 \end{array}$
9. $\begin{array}{r} 9 \\ \times 6 \\ \hline 54 \end{array}$
10. $\begin{array}{r} 8 \\ \times 9 \\ \hline 72 \end{array}$

11. Describe another pattern to help find products that have 9 as a factor. **Digit in tens place always 1 less than factor multiplied by 9; digit in ones place is difference between 9 and digit in tens place; sum of the digits in tens and ones places always 9.**

© Silver Burdett Ginn Inc. (237)   Use with Grade 3, text pages 228–229.

Lesson Organizer

Objective: Use multiplication strategies.

- **NCTM Standards:** 1, 3, 6, 7, 8
- **Materials:** multiplication chart (optional)
- **Lesson Resources:**
  Chapter File Folder
      Practice, Reteach, Extend 6-8
      Teaching Tool 9
  Daily Review 6-8
  Transparencies 7, 23, 23b

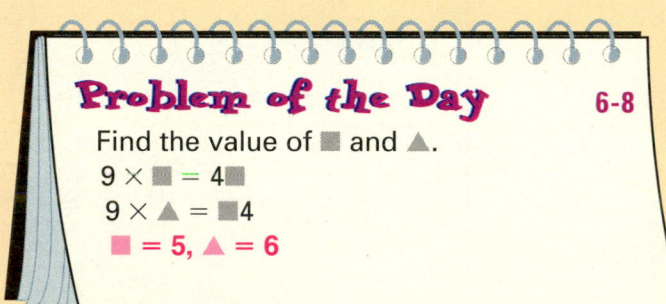

Problem of the Day   6-8

Find the value of ■ and ▲.

$9 \times ■ = 4■$

$9 \times ▲ = ■4$

■ = 5, ▲ = 6

Multiply.

0×3 *(0)*	8×3 *(24)*
9×9 *(81)*	6×7 *(42)*
4×5 *(20)*	2×9 *(18)*

Subways

There are many ways to find a product. The way you do it is up to you.

Learning About It

Subway trains roar in and out of the station. This train has 4 cars. There are 8 people riding in each car. How many people are riding in all?

$4 \times 8 = ■$ or $\begin{array}{r} 8 \\ \times 4 \\ \hline \end{array}$

THERE'S ALWAYS A WAY!

There are many strategies you can use.

- You can **draw an array**.

  $4 \times 8 = 32$

- You can **change the order** of the factors.

  If you know $8 \times 4 = 32$, then you know $4 \times 8 = 32$.

- You can **skip count** by 8s.

  8, 16, 24, 32

- You can use a **multiplication chart**.

x	0	1	2	3	4	5	6	7	8	9
0	0	0	0	0	0	0	0	0	0	0
1	0	1	2	3	4	5	6	7	8	9
2	0	2	4	6	8	10	12	14	16	18
3	0	3	6	9	12	15	18	21	24	27
4	0	4	8	12	16	20	24	28	32	36
5	0	5	10	15	20	25	30	35	40	45
6	0	6	12	18	24	30	36	42	48	54
7	0	7	14	21	28	35	42	49	56	63
8	0	8	16	24	32	40	48	56	64	72
9	0	9	18	27	36	45	54	63	72	81

$4 \times 8 = 32$

There are 32 people in the 4 subway cars.

Think and Discuss Which strategy do you like best? Would you always use the same strategy? Why or why not? *Students should realize that different strategies may work better in different situations.*

230

---

1 Introduce

Cooperative Activity

KINESTHETIC

 PAIRS    5–10 MINUTES

Materials: 2 sets of cards numbered 0–9

1. One student shuffles the cards and places them face down.
2. The partner turns over two cards. Both students work together to find the product of the numbers.
3. Students continue until all cards have been turned over.

   - Discuss: **Which facts did you know by memory?** *(Sample answer: 2s and 3s)*

---

2 Teach   Pages 230–231

Help students practice using a multiplication chart.

- Ask: **How do you find 6 x 8 using a multiplication chart?** *(Sample answer: Put one finger on 6 in the side column and another on 8 in the top row. Move the first finger down and the second finger across until they meet.)*

Critical Thinking   APPLICATION

After Think and Discuss, say: **Suppose a subway train has 16 cars with 9 people in each car. How can you use an 8s fact to find the number of people in 16 cars?** *(Sample answer: Double the product of 8×9.)*

Assess Understanding

After Try It Out, ask: **What strategy did you use to find the answer to Exercise 2?** *(Sample answer: I found 9×10 and subtracted 9.)*

USING TECHNOLOGY

MathProcessor™ Activities
See **Activities 33 and 34** in the MathProcessor™ Activity Cards.

Try It Out

INTERNET ACTIVITY
www.sbgmath.com

Multiply.

1. $\begin{array}{r} 9 \\ \times 2 \\ \hline 18 \end{array}$ 2. $\begin{array}{r} 9 \\ \times 9 \\ \hline 81 \end{array}$ 3. $\begin{array}{r} 3 \\ \times 8 \\ \hline 24 \end{array}$ 4. $\begin{array}{r} 4 \\ \times 7 \\ \hline 28 \end{array}$ 5. $\begin{array}{r} 0 \\ \times 7 \\ \hline 0 \end{array}$ 6. $\begin{array}{r} 8 \\ \times 6 \\ \hline 48 \end{array}$

Practice

Find each product.

7. $\begin{array}{r} 7 \\ \times 5 \\ \hline 35 \end{array}$ 8. $\begin{array}{r} 7 \\ \times 9 \\ \hline 63 \end{array}$ 9. $\begin{array}{r} 0 \\ \times 9 \\ \hline 0 \end{array}$ 10. $\begin{array}{r} 8 \\ \times 7 \\ \hline 56 \end{array}$ 11. $\begin{array}{r} 7 \\ \times 6 \\ \hline 42 \end{array}$ 12. $\begin{array}{r} 3 \\ \times 9 \\ \hline 27 \end{array}$

13. $\begin{array}{r} 5 \\ \times 8 \\ \hline 40 \end{array}$ 14. $\begin{array}{r} 4 \\ \times 9 \\ \hline 36 \end{array}$ 15. $\begin{array}{r} 6 \\ \times 9 \\ \hline 54 \end{array}$ 16. $\begin{array}{r} 7 \\ \times 7 \\ \hline 49 \end{array}$ 17. $\begin{array}{r} 5 \\ \times 9 \\ \hline 45 \end{array}$ 18. $\begin{array}{r} 3 \\ \times 5 \\ \hline 15 \end{array}$

19. 6×5 **30**   20. 3×7 **21**   21. 8×4 **32**   22. 9×8 **72**

23. 7×6 **42**   24. 6×4 **24**   25. 4×9 **36**   26. 8×8 **64**

Problem Solving

27. Sarah takes the subway 6 times a week. How many trips will she take in 7 weeks?
42 trips

28. There are a total of 136 stations in the Moscow subway system. If 24 of the stations are being painted, how many stations are not being painted?
112 stations

29. Seven people get on the train at the first stop. At the second stop, 4 people get on the train and 2 others get off. At the third stop, 5 people get on the train and 3 people get off. How many people are on the train? What strategy did your use?
11 people; Possible strategy: *Act It Out.*

▲ **Social Studies Connection**
The Moscow subway system is the busiest subway system in the world. Over 5 million people ride it every day.

Review and Remember

Using Estimation Estimate by rounding to the greatest place value.

30. $\begin{array}{r} 175 \\ + 432 \\ \hline 600 \end{array}$ 31. $\begin{array}{r} 59 \\ + 67 \\ \hline 130 \end{array}$ 32. $\begin{array}{r} 45 \\ - 17 \\ \hline 30 \end{array}$ 33. $\begin{array}{r} 721 \\ + 819 \\ \hline 1,500 \end{array}$ 34. $\begin{array}{r} 645 \\ - 195 \\ \hline 400 \end{array}$

For Extra Practice, see Set F, page 244. **231**

Internet Activity

www.sbgmath.com

Students review addition and subtraction concepts while visiting a site about Washington, D.C.

Practice

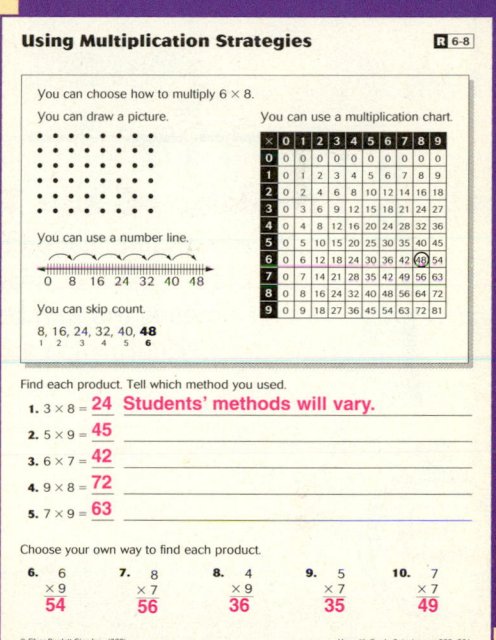

Using Multiplication Strategies P 6-8

Find each product. Color the box red if the product is even. Color the box yellow if the product is odd.

1. $\begin{array}{r} 3 \\ \times 7 \\ \hline 21 \end{array}$ 2. $\begin{array}{r} 4 \\ \times 6 \\ \hline 24 \end{array}$ 3. $\begin{array}{r} 6 \\ \times 7 \\ \hline 42 \end{array}$ 4. $\begin{array}{r} 8 \\ \times 8 \\ \hline 64 \end{array}$ 5. $\begin{array}{r} 7 \\ \times 7 \\ \hline 49 \end{array}$

6. $\begin{array}{r} 2 \\ \times 8 \\ \hline 16 \end{array}$ 7. $\begin{array}{r} 9 \\ \times 7 \\ \hline 63 \end{array}$ 8. $\begin{array}{r} 6 \\ \times 6 \\ \hline 36 \end{array}$ 9. $\begin{array}{r} 5 \\ \times 7 \\ \hline 35 \end{array}$ 10. $\begin{array}{r} 2 \\ \times 6 \\ \hline 12 \end{array}$

11. $\begin{array}{r} 6 \\ \times 8 \\ \hline 48 \end{array}$ 12. $\begin{array}{r} 9 \\ \times 2 \\ \hline 18 \end{array}$ 13. $\begin{array}{r} 9 \\ \times 3 \\ \hline 27 \end{array}$ 14. $\begin{array}{r} 4 \\ \times 7 \\ \hline 28 \end{array}$ 15. $\begin{array}{r} 4 \\ \times 8 \\ \hline 32 \end{array}$

16. $\begin{array}{r} 4 \\ \times 9 \\ \hline 36 \end{array}$ 17. $\begin{array}{r} 9 \\ \times 5 \\ \hline 45 \end{array}$ 18. $\begin{array}{r} 4 \\ \times 4 \\ \hline 16 \end{array}$ 19. $\begin{array}{r} 1 \\ \times 7 \\ \hline 7 \end{array}$ 20. $\begin{array}{r} 8 \\ \times 7 \\ \hline 56 \end{array}$

21. $\begin{array}{r} 7 \\ \times 5 \\ \hline 35 \end{array}$ 22. $\begin{array}{r} 7 \\ \times 8 \\ \hline 56 \end{array}$ 23. $\begin{array}{r} 9 \\ \times 8 \\ \hline 72 \end{array}$ 24. $\begin{array}{r} 8 \\ \times 6 \\ \hline 48 \end{array}$ 25. $\begin{array}{r} 3 \\ \times 9 \\ \hline 27 \end{array}$

26. What shape do you see in the box? **multiplication sign, x**

© Silver Burdett Ginn Inc. (238)   Use with Grade 3, text pages 230–231.

Reteach

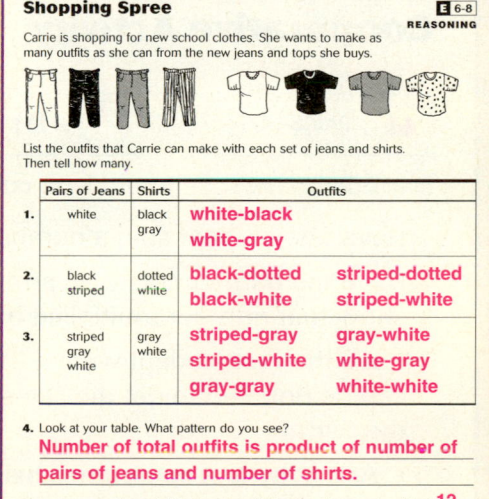

Using Multiplication Strategies R 6-8

You can choose how to multiply 6×8.

You can draw a picture.

You can use a multiplication chart.

×	0	1	2	3	4	5	6	7	8	9
0	0	0	0	0	0	0	0	0	0	0
1	0	1	2	3	4	5	6	7	8	9
2	0	2	4	6	8	10	12	14	16	18
3	0	3	6	9	12	15	18	21	24	27
4	0	4	8	12	16	20	24	28	32	36
5	0	5	10	15	20	25	30	35	40	45
6	0	6	12	18	24	30	36	42	48	54
7	0	7	14	21	28	35	42	49	56	63
8	0	8	16	24	32	40	48	56	64	72
9	0	9	18	27	36	45	54	63	72	81

You can use a number line.

0 8 16 24 32 40 48

You can skip count.

8, 16, 24, 32, 40, **48**

Find each product. Tell which method you used.

1. $3 \times 8 =$ **24** Students' methods will vary.

2. $5 \times 9 =$ **45**

3. $6 \times 7 =$ **42**

4. $9 \times 8 =$ **72**

5. $7 \times 9 =$ **63**

Choose your own way to find each product.

6. $\begin{array}{r} 6 \\ \times 9 \\ \hline 54 \end{array}$ 7. $\begin{array}{r} 8 \\ \times 7 \\ \hline 56 \end{array}$ 8. $\begin{array}{r} 4 \\ \times 9 \\ \hline 36 \end{array}$ 9. $\begin{array}{r} 5 \\ \times 7 \\ \hline 35 \end{array}$ 10. $\begin{array}{r} 7 \\ \times 7 \\ \hline 49 \end{array}$

© Silver Burdett Ginn Inc. (239)   Use with Grade 3, text pages 230–231.

---

3 Wrap-up

Describe different ways to find 7×9. Find the product. *(Sample answer: Use a multiplication chart or skip count; 63.)*

Common Error Alert

Watch for students who use repeated addition and do not use the correct number of addends to find a product. Encourage them to use another strategy.

Meeting Individual Needs

Manipulatives

Give students grid paper and multiplication facts written on index cards. They color an array on the paper to model each fact, then record the fact.
VISUAL/SPATIAL

For Extra Help

Provide pairs with a blank multiplication chart. Students take turns writing in the multiplication facts to complete the chart.

LOGICAL/MATHEMATICAL

Extend

Shopping Spree E 6-8 REASONING

Carrie is shopping for new school clothes. She wants to make as many outfits as she can from the new jeans and tops she buys.

List the outfits that Carrie can make with each set of jeans and shirts. Then tell how many.

	Pairs of Jeans	Shirts	Outfits	
1.	white	black gray	**white-black** **white-gray**	
2.	black striped	dotted white	**black-dotted** **black-white**	**striped-dotted** **striped-white**
3.	striped gray white	gray white	**striped-gray** **striped-white** **gray-gray**	**gray-white** **white-gray** **white-white**

4. Look at your table. What pattern do you see?
Number of total outfits is product of number of pairs of jeans and number of shirts.

5. How many outfits could Carrie make with 3 pairs of jeans and 4 shirts? **12**

6. Tell how many pairs of jeans and how many shirts Carrie might buy if she wanted to have a total of 8 outfits?
2 pairs of jeans, 4 shirts; 4 pairs of jeans, 2 shirts

© Silver Burdett Ginn Inc. (240)   Use with Grade 3, text pages 230–231.

Problem-Solving Strategy: Choose a Strategy

Lesson Organizer

Objective: Choose a strategy to solve problems.

- **NCTM Standards:** 1, 3, 7
- **Lesson Resources:**
  Chapter File Folder
      Practice, Reteach, Extend 6-9
  Daily Review 6-9

Problem of the Day   6-9

Think of a multiplication chart for all products from 0×0 through 9×9. How many times is the number 5 on the chart?
15 times, 13 of which are in products

Math Minute

Multiply.

3×7 *(21)*	4×3 *(12)*
9×4 *(36)*	3×8 *(24)*
6×7 *(42)*	7×4 *(28)*

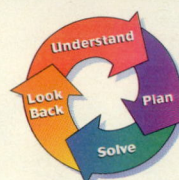

Problem Solving
Choose a Strategy

There is often more than one strategy that can help you solve a problem.

Some students are exploring a streetcar at the transportation museum. They sit in 6 seats. Each seat holds 2 people. How many students are sitting on the streetcar?

▲ **Social Studies Connection**
An electric streetcar from the late 1800s

 UNDERSTAND

What do you need to find?

You need to find the total number of students sitting on the streetcar.

 PLAN

How can you solve the problem?

You can often use more than one strategy to solve a problem. For this problem, you could **draw a picture** or **write a number sentence**.

 SOLVE

Draw a Picture

- Draw 6 lines to stand for the seats.
- Draw 2 Xs on each line. Then count the Xs.

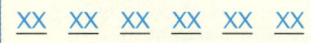

Write a Number Sentence

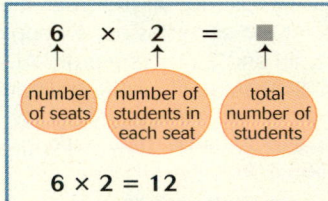

$6 \times 2 = 12$

There are 12 students sitting on the streetcar.

 LOOK BACK

Can you think of another way to solve the problem?
You could write an addition number sentence. $2 + 2 + 2 + 2 + 2 + 2 = 12$

1 Introduce

Cooperative Activity

KINESTHETIC

PAIRS   **5–10 MINUTES**

Manipulatives: spinner (1–4), counters

1. Have one student spin a number.

2. Have the partner create an array to show that number multiplied by six.

3. Have the first student write a 3s fact that can be doubled to get the same product the partner found.

   - Ask: **Why is it sometimes helpful to know different ways to find an answer?**

2 Teach   Pages 232–233

Understand Have students identify the number of seats and how many people fit on each seat.

Plan Help students understand that they can draw a picture if they cannot identify the multiplication fact that could solve the problem.

Solve Encourage students to count by 2s to find the product in the picture.

Look Back Discuss the different ways that students solved the problem.

Critical Thinking GENERALIZATION

After Look Back, ask: **How is drawing a picture similar to acting out the problem?** *(Sample answer: You can visualize the solution as you solve the problem.)*

Assess Understanding

Before Using Strategies, ask: **Which strategy did you find easiest to use?** *(Sample answer: I think that drawing a picture is the easiest strategy to use.)*

Using Strategies

Try these or other strategies to solve each problem.
Tell which strategy you used. Strategies will vary. Possible strategies are given.

Problem Solving Strategies

- *Use Logical Reasoning*
- *Make a Table*
- *Make a List*
- *Work Backwards*
- *Act It Out*
- *Write a Number Sentence*

1 The museum has 5 rows of train pictures and 3 rows of airplane pictures. How many more rows of train pictures are there? *Write a Number Sentence*; 2 rows

2 There are 7 tables where students can make model cars. If 4 students work at each table, how many students can make model cars? *Write a Number Sentence*; 28 students

3 Jim is next in line to ring the bell on the streetcar. Ramón is standing behind Jim but in front of Melody. In what order are the students waiting in line? *Act It Out*; Jim, Ramón, Melody

4 You are putting together 6 model trucks. Each truck needs 6 wheels. How many wheels do you need in order to put together all 6 trucks? *Write a Number Sentence*; 36 wheels

5 Ben, Dan, and Will wrote their names on cards. They put the cards in a hat. Then they each took out one card. No one had his own name. Ben picked Dan. What name did Will pick? *Use Logical Reasoning*; Ben

6 **Analyze** In front of the museum, a model streetcar moves around a tiny town. The streetcar can travel 100 feet in 2 minutes. How long does it take the streetcar to travel 1,000 feet? *Make a Table*; 20 minutes

7 When Nora got to the museum, she looked at cars for an hour. Next, she watched a 30-minute movie about trains. The movie ended at 1:15 P.M. When did Nora get to the museum? *Work Backwards*; 11:45 A.M.

8 You put 14 model train cars down on a track. Your friend picks up 4 cars. You put down 5 cars. Your friend picks up 6 cars. Then you put down 3 cars. How many cars are on the track now? *Act It Out*; 12 cars

233

Wrap-up

How can you find the number of people on 9 train seats if each seat is holding 4 people? (Sample answer: Draw 9 lines, each with four Xs; $9 \times 4 = 36$.)

Journal Idea Describe 3 strategies for solving word problems.

Common Error Alert

Watch for students who do not label their answers correctly. For example, writing *2 trains* instead of *2 rows.* Have students compare their answers with the questions.

Meeting Individual Needs

For Early Finishers

Each student writes a word problem, then trades with a partner. Partners use one of the strategies on page 233 to solve. Students check their answers.

LOGICAL/MATHEMATICAL

Acquiring English Proficiency

Brainstorm with students several definitions for *strategy.* Ask them to choose one definition and write it on a card to keep for reference.

LINGUISTIC

Lesson Organizer

Objective: Multiply 3 numbers.

- **NCTM Standards:** 1, 3, 6, 7, 8
- **Lesson Resources:**
  Chapter File Folder
    Practice, Reteach, Extend 6-10
  Daily Review 6-10
  Practice Workbook, p. 29
  Study Buddies 6B
  Transparency 7

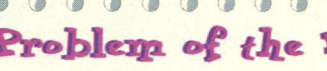

Problem of the Day   6-10

Draw a rectangle. Divide it into 5 sections. Put 1, 2, or 3 dots in each section. Do NOT put the same number of dots in sections that touch. Draw 11 dots in all. **See answer, page 242.**

 Math Minute

Find the product.

1 × 2 *(2)*	8 × 2 *(16)*
2 × 1 *(2)*	2 × 8 *(16)*
5 × 0 *(0)*	9 × 6 *(54)*

 10   **Multiplying Three Numbers**

In-line Numbers

You can multiply 3 numbers in any order.

Learning About It

The race is on! Each of the 3 skaters is wearing 2 skates. There are 4 wheels on each skate. How many wheels are there in all?

$$3 \quad \times \quad 2 \quad \times \quad 4 \quad = \quad \blacksquare$$

skaters   skates on each skater   wheels on each skate   product

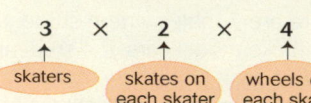 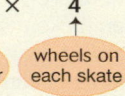

THERE'S ALWAYS A WAY!

- **One way** to find the product is to multiply 3 × 2 first.

$$(3 \times 2) \times 4 = \blacksquare$$
$$6 \quad \times 4 = 24$$

- **Another way** to find the product is to multiply 2 × 4 first.

$$3 \times (2 \times 4) = \blacksquare$$
$$3 \times \quad 8 \quad = 24$$

There are 24 wheels in all.

Think and Discuss What is another way to multiply 3 × 2 × 4? **You could multiply 3 × 4 = 12 and then multiply 12 × 2.**

Try It Out

Using Algebra Find the product. Multiply factors in the parentheses ( ) first.

1. (2 × 3) × 1 = ■ **6**
      2 × (3 × 1) = ■ **6**

2. 4 × (2 × 3) = ■ **24**
      (4 × 2) × 3 = ■ **24**

3. (1 × 4) × 2 = ■ **8**
      1 × (4 × 2) = ■ **8**

4. **Journal Idea** Choosing the right order can make multiplying easier. Look back at Exercise 2. Which way was easier for you? Tell why. **Answers will vary.**

234

---

1 Introduce

Cooperative Activity

KINESTHETIC

 PAIRS   **5–10 MINUTES**

Manipulatives: spinner (0–9), counters

1. One student spins two numbers to make a basic fact.

2. The partner finds the product.

3. The first student changes the order of factors and finds the product.

- Discuss: **Does changing the order of factors change the product?** *(No)*

---

2 Teach   Pages 234–235

- Ask: **Which multiplication facts must you know to find the number of wheels for the three skaters?** *(2s, 3s, and 4s)*

- Ask: **How do you know if the product of 3 × 2 × 4 will be even or odd?** *(When at least one number to be multiplied is even, the product is even.)*

Critical Thinking   ANALYSIS

After Think and Discuss, ask: **Before you multiply 2 × 9 × 2, how do you know the product will be greater than 20?** *(2 × 9 is 18, and the final product will be twice that number.)*

Assess Understanding

After Try It Out, say: **Describe two ways to multiply 2 × 4 × 5.** *(Sample answer: Multiply 2 × 4 first, then 8 × 5, or multiply 4 × 5 first, then 20 × 2.)*

 **USING TECHNOLOGY**

MathProcessor™ Activities
See **Activities 35 and 36** in the MathProcessor™ Activity Cards.

Practice

Using Algebra Multiply in any order.

5. $9 \times 1 \times 7 = \blacksquare$ **63**   6. $2 \times 3 \times 3 = \blacksquare$ **18**   7. $5 \times 6 \times 1 = \blacksquare$ **30**

8. $8 \times 0 \times 9 = \blacksquare$ **0**   9. $3 \times 3 \times 2 = \blacksquare$ **18**   10. $3 \times 2 \times 4 = \blacksquare$ **24**

11. $4 \times 2 \times 3 = \blacksquare$ **24**   12. $1 \times 7 \times 9 = \blacksquare$ **63**   13. $2 \times 1 \times 4 = \blacksquare$ **8**

14. $2 \times 2 \times 4 = \blacksquare$ **16**   15. $1 \times 5 \times 3 = \blacksquare$ **15**   16. $2 \times 6 \times 1 = \blacksquare$ **12**

Using Algebra Write >, <, or = for each ●.

17. $(2 \times 3) \times 2$ ● **<** 14

18. $4 \times (1 \times 5)$ ● **=** 20

19. $(3 \times 3) \times 4$ ● **=** 9×4

20. $2 \times (3 \times 3)$ ● **>** 2×3

Problem Solving

21. A park has 4 skate paths. Each path is 3 miles long. How many miles long are all the paths? **12 miles**

22. Elbow pads are on sale for $5 each. How much would it cost to buy 4 *pairs* of elbow pads? **$40**

23. Your mom, dad, and two grandparents each have a pair of 5-wheel skates. How many wheels is that in all? **40 wheels**

24. Suppose secondhand skates cost $35. You have $29.14. How much more money do you need to buy the skates? **$5.86**

Review and Remember

Write *inches*, *feet*, or *miles*.

25. Your skates might add 2 __?__ to your height. **inches**

26. You might ride your bike for 2 __?__. **miles**

27. You might have grown 4 __?__ since birth. **feet**

28. Your finger might be 2 __?__ long. **inches**

For Extra Practice, see Set G, page 244.   **235**

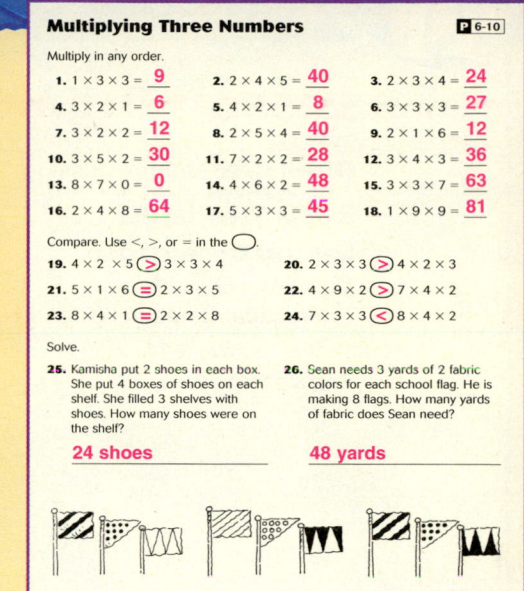
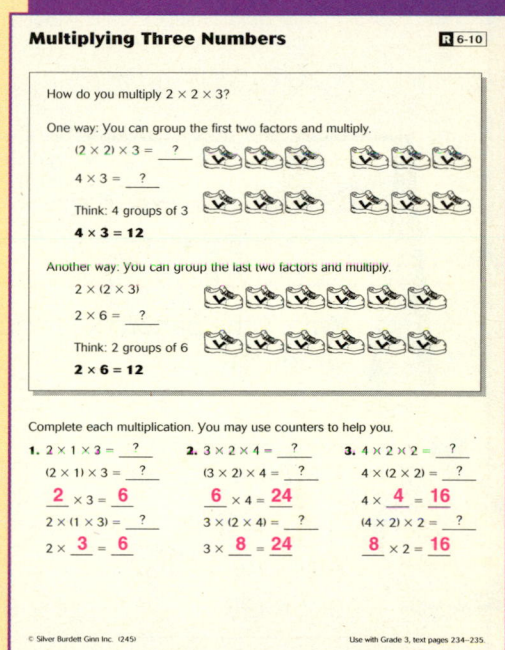
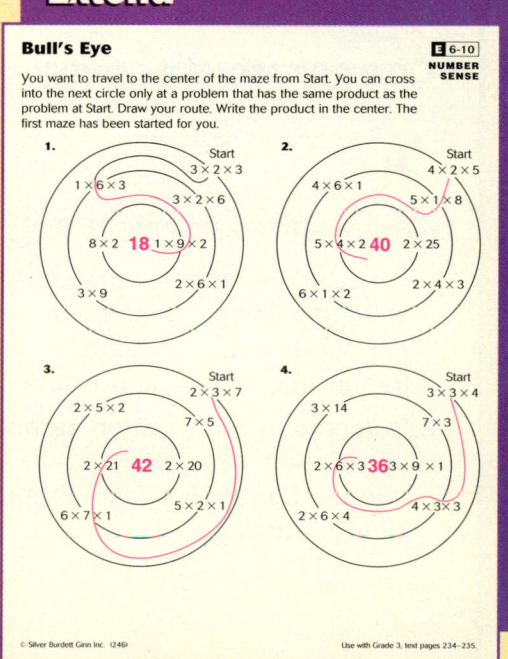
---

3 Wrap-up

Journal Idea Extend the Journal Idea in Exercise 4 by asking students to tell if the product would be the same if they multiplied $(4 \times 3) \times 2$.

Common Error Alert

Watch for students who forget to multiply by the third factor. Suggest that students cross off or write the factors as they multiply.

Meeting Individual Needs

For Early Finishers

One student picks three number cards and reads them to the group. Students write a multiplication sentence, then tell how they found the product.
LINGUISTIC

Cooperative Learning

Provide pairs with sentences such as $3 \times 1 \times 7 = ?$ One student multiplies the first two numbers and records the product. A partner completes the multiplication.
KINESTHETIC

LESSON 10   235

Lesson Organizer

Objective: Identify missing factors.

- **NCTM Standards:** 1, 3, 7, 8
- **Lesson Resources:**
  Chapter File Folder
  Practice, Reteach, Extend 6-11
  Daily Review 6-11
  Transparency 7

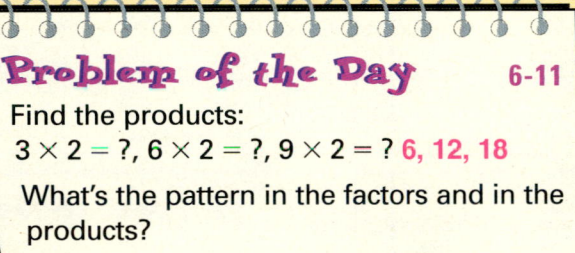

Problem of the Day   6-11

Find the products:
$3 \times 2 = ?, 6 \times 2 = ?, 9 \times 2 = ?$ **6, 12, 18**

What's the pattern in the factors and in the products?

 **Math Minute**

Find the answers.

7×3 *(21)*	6×8 *(48)*
$4 + 2$ *(6)*	$5 + 7$ *(12)*
9×4 *(36)*	4×9 *(36)*

Flying Factors

Using Algebra

Remembering the multiplication facts can help you find a missing factor.

Learning About It

Twenty-eight people wait on the helicopter pad. Seven people can fit in each helicopter. How many helicopters are needed?

Write: $\blacksquare \times 7 = 28$.

Then find the missing factor.

 **THERE'S ALWAYS A WAY!**

One way to find the missing factor is to skip count by 7s until you reach 28. 7, 14, 21, 28 You counted 4 numbers.	**Another way** is to list the 7s facts until you reach 28. $1 \times 7 = 7$ $2 \times 7 = 14$ $3 \times 7 = 21$ $4 \times 7 = 28$

The number 4 is the missing factor.
So 4 helicopters are needed for 28 people.

Think and Discuss How do you know that the missing factor in $4 \times \blacksquare = 12$ is more than 2?
Students should realize that 4×2 is only 8, so the missing factor must be larger.

Try It Out

Find each missing factor.

1. $8 \times \blacksquare = 24$ **3**
2. $\blacksquare \times 7 = 56$ **8**
3. $6 \times \blacksquare = 30$ **5**
4. $5 \times \blacksquare = 25$ **5**
5. $3 \times \blacksquare = 21$ **7**
6. $\blacksquare \times 2 = 18$ **9**

236

---

1 Introduce

Cooperative Activity

LOGICAL/MATHEMATICAL

 SMALL GROUPS   **5–10 MINUTES**

Manipulatives: spinner (1–9)

1. One student spins a number. A second student skip counts aloud 9 times, using the number spun. A third student writes the numbers the second student says.

2. Students use the written numbers to complete this sentence:
   number spun $\times$ 9 = last number said
   (Sample answer: $3 \times 9 = 27$)

2 Teach   Pages 236–237

Suggest that students divide 28 counters into groups of 7.

- Ask: **Could the missing factor in $\blacksquare \times 7 = 28$ be 5 or greater? How do you know?** *(No; 7×5 is more than 28.)*

Critical Thinking   ANALYSIS

After Think and Discuss, ask: **How do you know if the missing factor in $\blacksquare \times 9 = 54$ is even or odd?** *(Since the product is even, the missing factor is even.)*

Problem of the Day: The first factor increases by 3 each time; the second factor is always 2; each product increases by 6.

Assess Understanding

After Try It Out, ask: **Explain why the missing factors are the same in $\blacksquare \times 6 = 24$ and $6 \times \blacksquare = 24$.** *(Changing the order of factors does not affect the product.)*

 **CHALLENGE**

Find the missing factors.
$1 \times 4 \times 3 \times 2 \times \blacksquare = 24$ *(1)*
$2 \times 3 \times 5 \times \blacksquare \times 1 = 120$ *(4)*
$4 \times \blacksquare \times 7 = 56$ *(2)*
$\blacksquare \times 2 \times 5 \times 6 = 240$ *(4)*

Practice

Find each missing factor.

7. $9 \times \blacksquare = 63$ **7** 8. $5 \times \blacksquare = 45$ **9** 9. $\blacksquare \times 4 = 28$ **7**

10. $1 \times \blacksquare = 6$ **6** 11. $2 \times \blacksquare = 12$ **6** 12. $9 \times \blacksquare = 36$ **4**

13. $\blacksquare \times 3 = 27$ **9** 14. $9 \times \blacksquare = 0$ **0** 15. $\blacksquare \times 7 = 35$ **5**

16. $\blacksquare \times 5 = 40$ **8** 17. $\blacksquare \times 9 = 54$ **6** 18. $9 \times \blacksquare = 81$ **9**

Problem Solving

Write a multiplication sentence to solve each problem.

19. A company has 2 pilots for each helicopter it owns. If there are 14 pilots, how many helicopters does the company own?
$2 \times \blacksquare = 14$ or $\blacksquare \times 2 = 14$; **7 helicopters**

20. Suppose each helicopter has 3 passenger seats. How many passengers could ride in 8 helicopters?
$8 \times 3 = \blacksquare$ or $3 \times 8 = \blacksquare$; **24 passengers**

21. Every hour a helicopter pilot gives 4 rides. How many rides does she give in 8 hours?
$8 \times 4 = \blacksquare$ or $4 \times 8 = \blacksquare$; **32 rides**

22. If 3 people can ride in each helicopter, how many helicopters are needed for 15 people?
$3 \times \blacksquare = 15$ or $\blacksquare \times 3 = 15$; **5 helicopters**

Review and Remember

Using Estimation Estimate each answer to the nearest 10.

23. $57 - 32$ **30** 24. $72 + 55$ **130** 25. $79 + 48$ **130** 26. $89 - 76$ **10**

Money $ense

Bag of Coins

1. Suppose you take two coins out of the bag. What could their total worth be? Name all the possible amounts. **2¢, 6¢, 10¢, 11¢, 15¢, 26¢, 30¢, 35¢, 50¢**

2. Suppose you take 3 coins out of the bag. If there is more money outside the bag than inside, what 3 coins could you have taken out?
3 quarters or 2 quarters and any other coin.

For Extra Practice, see Set H, page 244. **237**

Using Algebra

Using Algebra

In this lesson, students solve **equations** by finding missing factors.

Money Sense

Once students are finished, have them find the total value of all the coins in the bag.

Practice

Missing Factors P 6-11

Cut out the missing factor sentence strips below. Paste them next to the correct missing factor number. When you are done, add a missing factor multiplication sentence under each group.

5
$2 \times ? = 10$
$? \times 7 = 35$
$6 \times ? = 30$
$? \times 9 = 45$
Check that sentence has 5 as a factor.

6
$? \times 3 = 18$
$7 \times ? = 42$
$? \times 6 = 36$
$4 \times ? = 24$
Check that sentence has 6 as a factor.

7
$? \times 3 = 21$
$8 \times ? = 56$
$4 \times ? = 28$
$? \times 9 = 63$
Check that sentence has 7 as a factor.

8
$? \times 8 = 64$
$? \times 6 = 48$
$? \times 9 = 72$
$5 \times ? = 40$
Check that sentence has 8 as a factor.

$7 \times ? = 42$	$? \times 3 = 18$	$2 \times ? = 10$	$? \times 9 = 63$
$? \times 8 = 64$	$? \times 3 = 21$	$? \times 7 = 35$	$4 \times ? = 24$
$8 \times ? = 56$	$? \times 6 = 36$	$6 \times ? = 30$	$? \times 9 = 45$
$5 \times ? = 40$	$? \times 9 = 72$	$? \times 6 = 48$	$4 \times ? = 28$

© Silver Burdett Ginn Inc. (247) Use with Grade 3, text pages 236–237.

Reteach

Missing Factors R 6-11

You can use what you know about multiplication facts to help you find a missing factor.

$4 \times ? = 20$

Count and draw groups of 4 until you reach 20.

$4 \times 1 = 4$ ○○○○
$4 \times 2 = 8$ ○○○○ ○○○○
$4 \times 3 = 12$ ○○○○ ○○○○ ○○○○
$4 \times 4 = 16$ ○○○○ ○○○○ ○○○○ ○○○○
$4 \times 5 = 20$ ○○○○ ○○○○ ○○○○ ○○○○ ○○○○
So, $4 \times 5 = 20$.

Check students' pictures.

Find each missing factor. Draw pictures to help. The first one is done for you.

1. $3 \times \underline{2} = 6$ ○○ ○○ ○○ 2. $\underline{1} \times 5 = 5$

3. $2 \times \underline{4} = 8$ 4. $\underline{3} \times 5 = 15$

5. $4 \times \underline{3} = 12$ 6. $3 \times \underline{6} = 18$

7. $6 \times \underline{4} = 24$ 8. $4 \times \underline{5} = 20$

9. $7 \times \underline{2} = 14$ 10. $9 \times \underline{3} = 27$

11. $9 \times \underline{2} = 18$ 12. $3 \times \underline{8} = 24$

13. $7 \times \underline{4} = 28$ 14. $6 \times \underline{5} = 30$

© Silver Burdett Ginn Inc. (249) Use with Grade 3, text pages 236–237.

Extend

Cross Out! E 6-11 REASONING

Look at the number grid. One number in the grid is the secret number. To find out the secret number, you must play Cross Out!

26	27	28	29	30
31	32	33	34	35
36	37	38	39	40
41	42	43	44	45
46	47	48	49	50

A **factor** is one of two numbers that are multiplied together to get a product. For example, 4 and 3 are each factors of 12.

Secret number is 41.

To play Cross Out!, read and follow each direction in order.

1. Put an × on numbers that have 7 as a factor.
2. Put an × on numbers that have 5 as a factor.
3. Put an × on numbers that have 3 as a digit.
4. Put an × on numbers where the sum of the digits is 10 or more.
5. Put an × on the remaining numbers for which the product of the digits is more than 10.
6. What number is left? **41**
7. Check yourself. Look at your answer to 6. The sum of the digits should be 5. The product of the digits should be 4.

Create Your Own

Make your own game of Cross Out! on another sheet of paper. Use these numbers. Write directions for crossing out all but one number. The first direction is done for you.

55	56	57	58	59
60	61	62	63	64
65	66	67	68	69

① Put an × on numbers that have 6 as one of the digits.

© Silver Burdett Ginn Inc. (249) Use with Grade 3, text pages 236–237.

Show Wh...

Use the pict... right to answ...

There are d... cars on the t... pictograph a... some of the ... and how man... there are.

1 Which kin... the great... **The day c...**

3 How man... are there...

Use the pict... the right to a... Problems 5—...

The pictogr... right shows t... of people sitt... section of a ...

5 How man... in Section...

7 Explain ... without c... even or a... people in... altogethe...

9 Analyze ... dining car... A group ... in. They w... which sec... **Section 1 ...**

---

3 Wrap-up

Why would you... graph to stand ...
(Sample answe... items to show a... tures in the grap... a lot of pictures... large numbers.)

Suppose only three people can fit into a small helicopter. If 18 people are waiting for a ride, how can you find the number of times the helicopter should pick up and drop off people? (Sample answer: Skip count by 3s until you reach 18. Then count how many numbers you said.)

Comm...

Watch for st... what numbe... pictograph r... they write a... ture, then ad...

Common Error Alert

Some students might skip count or list facts incorrectly. Remind students to check that each number they say or write increases by the number they are multiplying.

Meeting Individual Needs

For Early Finishers

Students write the 9s facts and look for patterns in the products. (Sample answer: Digits in each product have a sum of 9.)
VISUAL/SPATIAL

Gifted and Talented

Students can create 3 factor problems that have 1 factor missing. They can create shapes to represent the missing factors, keeping the shapes consistent.
LOGICAL/MATHEMATICAL

---

7. By looking... are no partial...

Math Minute

Who

LOGIC

Manip

1. Each
   once
   rolle

2. All st
   is sp

3. Discu
   stude
   the d

Glossary

cup (c) A customary unit used to measure capacity. 1 cup equals 8 ounces. (p. 144)

customary system A measurement system that measures length in inches, feet, yards, and miles; capacity in cups, pints, quarts, and gallons; weight in ounces, pounds, and tons; and temperature in degrees Fahrenheit. See Table of Measures. (p. 488)

cylinder A space figure with two faces that are congruent circles. (p. 386)

D

data Information that is gathered. (p. 252)

decimal A number with one or more places to the right of a decimal point. (p. 420)
Examples: 0.7, 1.8, 2.06

decimal point The dot used to separate dollars from cents and ones from tenths. (p. 420)
Examples: $1.54, 1.3

decimeter (dm) A metric unit used to measure length. 1 decimeter equals 10 centimeters. (p. 152)

degree Celsius (°C) A metric unit used to measure temperature. (p. 160)

degree Fahrenheit (°F) A customary unit used to measure temperature. (p. 148)

denominator The number below the fraction bar in a fraction. (p. 402)
Example: $\frac{2}{5}$ ← denominator

difference The answer in subtraction. (p. 62)
Example: $9 - 4 = 5$
The **difference** is 5.

digit Any of the symbols used to write numbers: 0, 1, 2, 3, 4, 5, 6, 7, 8, and 9. (p. 7)

divide To separate a number of items into groups of equal size. (p. 288)

dividend The number to be divided. (p. 292)
Example: $6\overline{)36}$ or $36 \div 6$
The **dividend** is 36.

divisible A number is divisible by another number if the remainder is 0 after dividing. (p. 466)

division An operation on two numbers that results in a quotient. (p. 288)
Example: $18 \div 2 = 9$

divisor The number by which another number is to be divided. (p. 292)
Example: $7\overline{)28}$ or $28 \div 7$
The **divisor** is 7.

E

edge The segment where two faces of a space figure meet. (p. 386)
Example:

edge

elapsed time The amount of time that has passed. (p. 132)

endpoint A point at the end of a line segment or ray. (p. 366)

equally likely Outcomes that have the same chance of occurring. (p. 272)

equivalent fractions Fractions that name the same number. (p. 404)
Examples: $\frac{1}{2}$ and $\frac{2}{4}$

estimate To give an approximate rather than an exact answer. (p. 82)

even A whole number that is divisible by 2. Even numbers have 0, 2, 4, 6, or 8 in the ones place. (p. 2)

expanded form A number written as the sum of the value of its digits. (p. 6)
Example: $1,000 + 200 + 30 + 4$ is the **expanded form** of 1,234.

F

face A flat surface of a space figure. (p. 386)
Example:
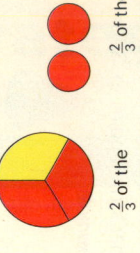
face

fact family Related facts using the same numbers. (p. 66)
Example:
$2 + 3 = 5$ $5 - 2 = 3$
$3 + 2 = 5$ $5 - 3 = 2$
    or
$2 \times 5 = 10$ $10 \div 2 = 5$
$5 \times 2 = 10$ $10 \div 5 = 2$

Glossary

factors The numbers that are multiplied to give a product. (p. 176)
Example: $3 \times 8 = 24$
The **factors** are 3 and 8.

foot (ft) A customary unit used to measure length. 1 foot equals 12 inches. Also an ancient Egyptian unit of measure equal to a human foot. (p. 140)

fraction A number that names part of a region or a part of a group. (p. 402)
Examples: $\frac{1}{2}$ and $\frac{6}{8}$ are **fractions**.

$\frac{2}{3}$ of the region is red.

$\frac{2}{3}$ of the group is red.

front digit The digit in the place with the greatest value, used for front-end estimation. (p. 107)

front-end estimation A method using only the front-end digits to estimate sums, differences, products, and quotients. (p. 107)

G

gallon (gal) A customary unit used to measure capacity. 1 gallon equals 4 quarts. (p. 144)

gram (g) A metric unit used to measure how heavy an object is. 1,000 grams equal 1 kilogram. (p. 158)

490   491

graph A drawing used to show information. (p. 256)

greater than (>) The symbol used to compare two numbers when the greater number is written on the left. (p. 22)

Examples: 7 > 4, 9 > 6

grouping property of addition The way in which addends are grouped does not change the sum. (p. 50)

Example: 2 + (4 + 5) = (2 + 4) + 5

grouping property of multiplication The way in which factors are grouped does not change the product. (p. 234)

Example: 2 × (3 × 5) = (2 × 3) × 5

H

hexagon A plane figure with six sides and six corners. (p. 362)

hour (h) A unit of time equal to 60 minutes. (p. 128)

hour hand The short hand on a clock. The hand on a clock that shows hours. (p. 128)

hundreds Groups of ten tens. (p. 86)

hundredths One or more of one hundred equal parts of a whole. (p. 424)

I

inch (in.) A customary unit used to measure length. 12 inches equal 1 foot. (p. 140)

K

kilogram (kg) A metric unit used to measure how heavy an object is. 1 kilogram equals 1,000 grams. (p. 158)

kilometer (km) A metric unit used to measure length. 1 kilometer equals 1,000 meters. (p. 152)

L

less likely Smaller chance that an event will happen. (p. 272)

less than (<) The symbol used to compare two numbers when the lesser number is written on the left. (p. 22)

Examples: 7 < 10, 4 < 8

line A collection of points along a straight path that goes on and on in opposite directions. A line has no endpoints. (p. 366)

line of symmetry A line on which a figure can be folded so that both sides match. (p. 374)

Example:

line of symmetry

line segment A part of a line between two endpoints. (p. 366)

liter (L) A metric unit used to measure capacity. 1 liter equals 1,000 milliliters. (p. 156)

M

meter (m) A metric unit used to measure length. 1 meter equals 100 centimeters. (p. 152)

metric system A measurement system that measures length in millimeters, centimeters, meters, and kilometers; capacity in milliliters and liters; how heavy an object is in grams and kilograms; and temperature in degrees Celsius. See Table of Measures. (p. 488)

mile (mi) A customary unit used to measure length. 1 mile equals 5,280 feet. (p. 140)

milliliter (mL) A metric unit used to measure capacity. 1,000 milliliters equal 1 liter. (p. 156)

minute A unit of time equal to 60 seconds. (p. 128)

missing addend A number to be added to one or more other numbers to equal a given number. (p. 62)

Example: 5 + ■ = 8

The **missing addend** is 3.

mixed number A number written as a whole number and a fraction. (p. 414)

Example: $3\frac{1}{2}$

month One of the twelve parts into which the year is divided. (p. 136)

more likely Greater chance that an event will happen. (p. 272)

multiplication An operation on two or more numbers, called factors, to find a product. (p. 174)

Example: 4 × 5 = 20

The **product** is 20.

multiplication table A table that organizes multiplication facts. (p. 198 and p. 328)

multiply To find the total number of items in groups of equal size. (p. 174)

N

noon Twelve o'clock in the daytime. (p. 128)

number line A line that shows numbers in order. (p. 10)

Example:

0 1 2 3 4 5 6 7

numerator The number above the fraction bar in a fraction. (p. 402)

Example: $\frac{2}{5}$ ← numerator

O

odd A whole number that is not divisible by 2. Odd numbers have 1, 3, 5, 7, or 9 in the ones place. (p. 2)

order property of addition The order in which addends are added does not change the sum. (p. 48)

Example: 9 + 3 = 3 + 9

Glossary

order property of multiplication The order in which factors are multiplied does not change the product. (p. 179)
Example: $3 \times 2 = 2 \times 3$

ordered pair A pair of numbers that give the location of a point on a map or a graph. (p. 268)

ordinal numbers A number used to tell order or position. (p. 4)
Examples: first, fifth

ounce (oz) A customary unit used to measure weight. 16 ounces equal 1 pound. (p. 146)

outcome A result of a probability experiment. (p. 274)

P

P.M. Used to show time between noon and midnight. (p. 128)

palindrome A number, word, or sentence that reads the same backward or forward. (p. 123)

pentagon A plane figure with five sides and five corners. (p. 362)

perimeter The distance around a figure. (p. 380)

pictograph A graph that shows information by using pictures. (p. 260)

pint (pt) A customary unit used to measure capacity. 1 pint equals 2 cups. (p. 144)

place value The value determined by the position of a digit in a number. (p. 6)
Example: In 562, the digit 5 means 5 hundreds, the digit 6 means 6 tens, the digit 2 means 2 ones.

plane figure A geometric figure whose points are all in one plane. (p. 362)
Examples:

circle   square   triangle

pound (lb) A customary unit used to measure weight. 1 pound equals 16 ounces. (p. 146)

probability The chance that an event will occur. (p. 272)

product The answer in multiplication. (p. 176)
Example: $4 \times 8 = 32$
The **product** is 32.

properties of 1 for division Any number divided by 1 is that number. Any number except 0 divided by itself is 1. (p. 310)
Examples: $6 \div 1 = 6, \ 3 \div 3 = 1$

property of one for multiplication The product of any number and 1 is that number. (p. 196)
Examples: $6 \times 1 = 6$ and $1 \times 6 = 6$

pyramid A space figure whose base is a plane figure and whose faces are triangles with a common corner. (p. 386)
Example:

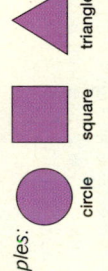

Q

quadrilateral A plane figure with four sides and four corners. (p. 363)

quart (qt) A customary unit used to measure capacity. 1 quart equals 4 cups. (p. 144)

quotient The answer in division. (p. 292)
Example: $24 \div 3 = 8$ or $3\overline{)24}$
The **quotient** is 8.

R

ray A part of a line that has one endpoint and goes on and on in one direction. (p. 366)

rectangle A plane figure with four right angles and four sides. (p. 362)
Example:

rectangular prism A space figure whose faces are all rectangles. (p. 386)
Example:

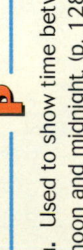

regroup To rename a number by exchanging base-ten materials of one value for base-ten materials that are equal to it. (p. 86)
Examples: 12 can be regrouped as 1 ten 2 ones. 253 can be regrouped as 2 hundreds 5 tens 3 ones.

Glossary

remainder The number that is left after dividing. (p. 346)
Example: $42 \div 8 = 5$ R2
The **remainder** is 2.

right angle An angle that has the shape of a square corner. (p. 366)
Example:

rounding Expressing a number to the nearest ten, hundred, thousand, and so on. (p. 10)
Example: 43 **rounded** to the nearest ten is 40.

S

side A line segment that is part of a plane figure. (p. 362)

similar Figures that have the same shape. They are not necessarily the same size. (p. 372)

space figure A geometric figure whose points are in more than one plane. (p. 386)

sphere A space figure shaped like a round ball. (p. 386)

square A rectangle with four equal sides and four right angles. (p. 362)

square number The product of two equal whole number factors. (p. 212)
Example: $5 \times 5 = 25$
25 is a **square number**.

Glossary

standard form A number written with commas separating groups of three digits. (p. 6)

subtraction An operation on two numbers to find the difference. (p. 56)
Example: 15 − 3 = 12
The **difference** is 12.

sum The answer in addition. (p. 48)
Example: 8 + 7 = 15
The **sum** is 15.

symmetry A plane figure has symmetry if it can be folded along a line so that the two parts match exactly. (p. 374)

T

tally chart A chart used to record data. (p. 252)

tangram A Chinese puzzle that has seven geometric pieces. (p. 365)

tenths One or more of ten equal parts of a whole. (p. 422)

triangle A plane figure with three sides and three corners. (p. 362)

V

Venn Diagram A diagram that uses circles to show the relationships between groups of objects. (p. 263)
Example:

volume The number of cubic units needed to fill a space figure. (p. 390)

W

week A period of seven days. (p. 136)

Y

yard (yd) A customary unit used to measure length. 1 yard equals 3 feet. (p. 140)

year A period of 365 days divided into 12 months. (p. 136)

Z

zero property of addition The sum of any number and 0 is that number. (p. 48)
Example: 3 + 0 = 3

zero property of division 0 divided by any number except 0 is 0. You cannot divide a number by 0. (p. 310)
Example: 0 ÷ 12 = 0

zero property of multiplication The product of any number and 0 is 0. (p. 196)
Example: 5 × 0 = 0 and 0 × 5 = 0

zero properties of subtraction When 0 is subtracted from any number, the difference is that number. When a number is subtracted from itself, the difference is 0. (p. 110)
Examples: 7 − 0 = 7 and 12 − 12 = 0

Index

Credits

Scope and Sequence

GRADE 2	GRADE 3	GRADE 4

Number and Number Theory

GRADE 2

Comparing
two-digit numbers 91–92
three-digit numbers 269–270
using symbols 91–92, 269–270
Counting
by tens 67–68
by hundreds 255–256
to ninety-nine 85–86
to one thousand 272
Even and odd numbers 89–90
Expanded form 264
Fractions
of a region 299–304
of a group 305–306
Names for numbers 67–68, 261–262
Number line 8, 37–38, 93, 271, 273, 279
Number patterns 85, 265–266
Ordering numbers
to one hundred 93–94
to one thousand 271–272
Ordinal numbers
to twentieth 95–96
Place value
tens and ones 69–70, 77–78
hundreds, tens, ones 259–260,
263–264
Regrouping 73–74, 79–80
Rounding numbers 279
Skip counting
by 2s, **3s, 4s,** 5s, 10s 87–88
from any number 88, 103
on and back by 10s, 100s 273
Understanding numbers
to ninety-nine 69–70
to nine hundred ninety-nine 257–258
Writing numbers
to ninety-nine 71–72, 85–86
to nine hundred ninety-nine 259–261

GRADE 3

Babylonian number system 41
Comparing
whole numbers 22–25
fractions 406–407
Decimals 422–427
Even and odd numbers 2–3
Expanded form 6–9, 20–21, 28–29,
422–427
Factors 176–177, 236
Fractions 402–411
Number line 10–13, 184, 186, 190, 192,
218, 226, 290–291, 298, 306, 332,
344
Number patterns 2–3, 216, 444
Mixed numbers 414–415
Ordering
whole numbers 22–25
Ordinal numbers to 99th 4–5
Place value
whole numbers
hundreds 6–9
thousands 18–21
hundred thousands 28–29
decimals
tenths 422–423
hundredths 424–425
greater than one 426–427
Relating
fractions and decimals 420–421
mixed numbers and decimals 426–427
Rounding to the nearest
ten and hundred 10–13
Standard form 6–9, 20–21, 28–29,
422–427
Whole numbers 2–29
Word form 6–9, 20–21, 28–29, 422–427

GRADE 4

Comparing
whole numbers 8–11
decimals 398–401
fractions 352–355
Decimals 390–401
Even and odd numbers 86, 90
Expanded form 4–7, 18–19, 396–397
Factors 94–97
Fractions 338–357
Mixed numbers 356–357
Multiples 94–97
Number line 24–27, 178
Number patterns 94–97, 216–217,
298–299
Ordering
whole numbers 8–11
decimals 398–401
fractions 352–355
Place value
whole numbers
hundred thousands 4–7
millions 16–19
decimals to hundredths 396–397
Prime numbers 129
Relating
fractions and decimals 390–393
mixed numbers and decimals 394–395
Roman number system 37
Rounding
whole numbers 24–27
decimals 406–409
Simplest form 346–349
Standard form 4–7, 18–19, 396–397
Whole numbers 2–27
Word form 4–7, 18–19, 396–397

Blue type indicates introduction of a topic.

Measurement, Money, and Time (continued)

MONEY	Perimeter 380–381	gram, kilogram 280–281

MONEY

Adding money 187–188, 335–336

Comparing sets of coins 115–116

Counting coins
pennies, nickels, dimes 107–112
pennies, nickels, dimes, quarters 113–114
pennies, nickels, dimes, quarters, **half dollars**, 117–118, 121–122
coins and **bills** 131

Dollar 121–122

Enough money 114, 123–124

Half dollar 117–118

Making change 125–126

Matching coins with price 114, 123–126

Money Sense 11B, 39B, 83B, 123B, 141B, 169B, 201B, 243B, 261B, 295B, 337B, 349B

Notation
cent sign 107–126
dollar and decimal point 121–122, 131

Subtracting money 187–188, 335–336

Value of currency 107–126

Ways to show amounts 109–110, 119–120

TIME

Analog clock 203–212, 214

Calendar
day, week, month, **year** 215–216

Digital clock 205–206, 212

Elapsed time 211–214

Estimating time
minutes 199–200
minutes, hours, or **days** 201–202

Reading a schedule 213–214

Telling time
to the half hour 203–204
to five minutes 205–206, 209–210
to quarter hour 207–208

Time Sense 5B, 47B, 91B, 117B, 137B, 185B, 211B, 225B, 287B, 321B, 353B

Perimeter 380–381

Temperature
Celsius 160–161
Fahrenheit 148–149

Weight
ounce, pound 146–147

Volume
counting cubic units 390–391

MONEY

Adding money 82–83, 88–95, 114–115, 432–433

Counting coins and bills 30–31

Five dollar bill 30–31

Making change 32–33

Money Sense 25, 65, 90, 143, 197, 237, 269, 305, 347, 371, 431, 459

Multiplying with 200–201

Notation 30–31

Subtracting money 100–101, 104–111, 114–115, 432–433

Using money 32–33, 114–115, 200–201, 312–313, 432–433, 476–477

TIME

Calendar 136–137

Elapsed Time 132–133

Telling Time
to the quarter hour 128–129
to the minute 130–131

Units of time
minute, hour 128–129
week, month, year 136–137

gram, kilogram 280–281

Perimeter 452–453

Temperature
Celsius 284–285
Fahrenheit 272–273

Weight
ounce, pound, **ton** 268–269

Volume
counting cubic units 462–463
formula for rectangular prism 462–463

MONEY

Adding money 48–49, 72–73

Estimating sums and differences 44–45

Making change 68–69

Money Sense 11, 67, 89, 153, 199, 219, 279, 317, 365, 409, 457, 487

Multiplying with 200–205, 418–419, 492–493

Rounding to the nearest dollar 44–45

Subtracting money 48–49, 72–73, 204–205, 492–493

Using money 72–73, 204–205, 376–377, 418–419, 492–493

TIME

Calendar 258–259

Elapsed Time 252–255

Making a schedule 295

Telling time
to the minute 250–251

Units of Time
second, minute, hour, day 250–251
week, month, year, **leap year, decade, century, millennium** 258–259

Blue type indicates introduction of a topic.

GRADE 2	GRADE 3	GRADE 4

Probability, Statistics, and Graphing

PROBABILITY
Comparing likelihoods 309–310
Experiments 309–310
Predicting 309–310

STATISTICS
Collecting data 45–46
Survey 46, 307–308
Tally 307–308
Using data
   from a graph 45–46, 295–296,
     365–366
   from a picture 123–124
   from a table 157–158

GRAPHING
Bar graphs
   read 45–46, 295–296
   make 46, 295–296, 307–308
Ordered pairs 315
Pictographs
   read and make 365–366

PROBABILITY
Certain event 272–274
Comparing likelihoods 274–277
Experiments 272–275
Fair and unfair games 276–277
Impossible event 272–274
Predicting 274–275

STATISTICS
Collecting data 252–253
Survey 252–253
Tally 252–253
Using data
   from a graph 68–69, 238–239,
     264–265
   from a picture 114–115, 200–201,
     432–433
   from a table 163, 254–255, 265, 377

GRAPHING
Bar graphs
   read and make 256–259
Circle graphs 285
Ordered pairs 268–271
Pictographs
   read and make 260–263

PROBABILITY
Certain event 162–163
Combinations 232–233
Comparing likelihoods 162–163
Experiments 164–165
Fair and unfair games 166–167
Impossible event 162–163
Predicting 162–163
Tree diagrams 232–233

STATISTICS
Average (mean) 322–325
Collecting data 134–137
Median 134–137, 158–159
Mode 134–137, 158–159
Survey 134–137
Using data
   from a graph 28–29, 154–155,
     160–161, 326–327, 120–121
   from a picture 72–73, 204–205,
     418–419, 458–459, 492–493
   from a table 72–73, 154–155,
     236–237, 286–287, 326–327

GRAPHING
Bar graphs
   read and make single 28–29, 138–141,
     154–155, 326–327
Circle graphs 376–377
Choosing the best graph 160–161
Line graphs 146–149, 175
Non-numerical graphs 146–147
Ordered pairs 150–153
Pictographs
   read and make 120, 142
Stem-and-leaf plots 158–159

Algebra

Calculators and patterns 104
Continuing a pattern
   of geometric figures 288
   of numbers 93–94
Creating a pattern 266
Function tables 50, 371
Graphing
   graphing whole numbers 45–46, 295,
     365–366
   making a graph 46, 295
Missing addends 27–28
Missing numbers 20, 85–86, 264,
   265–266, 271–272

Calculators and patterns 215
Continuing a pattern
   of geometric figures 267
   of numbers 8, 29, 81, 83, 187
Creating a pattern 225
Function tables
   find output 49
   find rule 209, 229
   follow rule 191, 229
Graphing
   graphing whole numbers 261
   making a graph 261
   ordered pairs 270–271, 278

Calculators and patterns 53, 485
Continuing a pattern
   of geometric figures 481
   of numbers 11, 59, 119, 178–179,
     216–217, 298–299, 365, 474–475,
     481
Equivalent fractions 344–349
Formulas 452–453, 454–457, 462–463
Function tables
   find rule 117, 316, 343–345
Graphing
   graphing change over time 148–149
   making graphs 138, 139, 140, 142–145

Blue type indicates introduction of a topic.

GRADE 2	GRADE 3	GRADE 4

Algebra *(continued)*

GRADE 2

Number line 93, 103, 271, 279
Ordered pairs 315
Patterns in tables 18, 33, 167, 265–266
Properties of addition
    grouping (associative) 25–26
    order (commutative) 5–6
    zero (identity) 1–2
Properties of multiplication
    order (commutative) 355–356
Special patterns and sequences
    evens and odds 89–90
    patterns in hundreds chart 85–86, 88,
      183
    repeating patterns 258
    skip counting
      by fives 87, 103, 121
      by fours 87, 103
      by hundreds 88, 255–256, 264,
        273–274
      by tens 67–68, 87, 121, 133–134,
        274–275
      by threes 87, 103
      by twenty–fives 113, 121
      by twos 87, 103, 273
Symbols showing relationships (=, >, <)
    91–92, 176, 269–270
Using patterns
    in addition 9–10, 11–12, 42,
      133–134, 135–136, 151–152,
      317–318
    in division 361–362, 363–364
    in mental math 136, 176, 183
    in multiplication 347–348, 349–350,
      351–352, 353–354, 355–356
    to solve problems 354, 357, 358,
      359, 362, 364
    in subtraction 165–166, 167–168,
      181–182, 325–326
    with time 207–208

GRADE 3

Missing factors 236–237, 299, 304
Missing addends 62–63
Missing numbers 9, 77, 97, 107, 109, 137,
    180, 225
Patterns in tables 198–199, 216–217,
    230, 247
Properties of addition
    associative (grouping) 50–51
    commutative (order) 48–49
    identity (zero) 48–49
Properties of multiplication
    associative (grouping) 234–235
    commutative (order) 178–181
    identity (one) 196–197
    0 and 1 as factors 196–197
Special patterns and sequences
    evens and odds 2–3
    skip counting
      by eights 220–221
      by fifties 49
      by fives 25, 49, 133, 186–187,
        306–307
      by fours 25, 49, 192–193, 220–221,
        304–305
      by hundreds 81
      by nines 228–229
      by sevens 226–227
      by sixes 218–219
      by tens 49, 81, 184–185, 296–297
      by threes 25, 190–191, 218–219,
        298–299
      by twos 25
Symbols showing relationships (=, >, <)
    22–25, 46, 47, 101, 106, 197, 221,
    235
Number line 45, 184, 186, 190, 192, 218,
    226, 290–291, 298, 306
Using patterns
    in addition 44–45
    in division 288–289, 290–291,
      296–297, 298–299, 304–305,
      306–307, 310–311, 321
    in multiplication 174–175, 176–177,
      178–181, 184–185, 186–187,
      192–193, 198–199, 212–215,
      218–219, 230–231
    in subtraction 58–59, 62–63
    to solve problems 376–377
Venn diagram 263

GRADE 4

Missing addends 69, 113, 255
Missing factors 107, 113, 190, 230, 255,
    355
Missing numbers 11, 41, 43, 61, 96, 107,
    110, 141, 149, 179, 193, 227, 255,
    259, 283, 355, 413, 484, 485
Missing operations 119
Ordered pairs 150–153
Patterns in tables 94, 129
Properties of addition
    associative (grouping) 40–43
    commutative (order) 40–43
    identity (zero) 40–43
Properties of multiplication
    associative (grouping) 88–89
    commutative (order) 88–89, 94–95
    identity (one) 88–89, 94–95
    0 and 1 as factors 88–89
Special patterns and sequences 52, 198
Symbols showing relationships (=, >, <)
    9–10, 49, 93, 111, 235, 461
Using patterns
    in addition 42, 43, 53
    in division 299, 310
    in mental math 113, 216–217
    in multiplication 61, 179, 216–217, 298,
      474–475
    in subtraction, 42, 53
    to solve problems 22–23, 375
Variable 61
Venn diagram 159

Blue type indicates introduction of a topic.

Patterns, Relations, and Functions

GRADE 2

PATTERNS

Calculators and patterns 104
Continuing a pattern
   of geometric figures 288
   of numbers 93–94
Creating a pattern 266
Patterns in tables 18, 33, 167, 265–266
Special patterns and sequences
   evens and odds 89–90
   patterns in hundreds chart 85–86, 88, 183
   repeating patterns 258
   skip counting
      by fives 87, 103, 121
      by fours 87, 103
      by hundreds 88, 255–256, 264, 273–274
      by tens 67–68, 87, 121, 133–134, 274–275
      by threes 87, 103
      by twenty–fives 113, 121
      by twos 87, 103, 273
Using patterns
   in addition 9–10, 11–12, 42, 133–134, 135–136, 151–152, 317–318
   in division 361–362, 363–364
   in mental math 136, 176, 183
   in multiplication 347–348, 349–350, 351–352, 353–354, 355–356
   to solve problems 354, 357, 358, 359, 362, 364
   in subtraction 165–166, 167–168, 181–182, 325–326
   with time 207–208

RELATIONS AND FUNCTIONS

Function tables 50, 371
Ordered pairs 315
Symbols showing relationships (=, >,<) 91–92, 176, 269–270

GRADE 3

PATTERNS

Calculators and patterns 215
Continuing a pattern
   of geometric figures 267
   of numbers 8, 29, 81, 83, 187
Creating a pattern 225
Patterns in tables 198–199, 216–217, 230, 247
Special patterns and sequences
   evens and odds 2–3
   skip counting
      by eights 220–221
      by fifties 49
      by fives 25, 49, 133, 186–187, 306–307
      by fours 25, 49, 192–193, 220–221, 304–305
      by hundreds 81
      by nines 228–229
      by sevens 226–227
      by sixes 218–219
      by tens 49, 81, 184–185, 296–297
      by threes 25, 190–191, 218–219, 298–299
      by twos 25
Using patterns
   in addition 44–45
   in division 288–289, 290–291, 296–297, 298–299, 304–305, 306–307, 310–311, 321
   in multiplication 174–175, 176–177, 178–181, 184–185, 186–187, 192–193, 198–199, 212–215, 218–219, 230–231
   in subtraction 58–59, 62–63
   to solve problems 376–377

RELATIONS AND FUNCTIONS

Function tables
   find output 49
   find rule 209
   follow rule 191, 229, 303
Graphing
   ordered pairs 270–271, 278
Symbols showing relationships (=, >, <) 22–25, 46, 47, 101, 106, 197, 221, 235

GRADE 4

PATTERNS

Calculators and patterns 53, 485
Continuing a pattern
   of geometric figures 481
   of numbers 11, 59, 119, 178–179, 216–217, 298–299, 365, 474–475, 481
Patterns in tables 94, 129
Special patterns and sequences 52, 198
Using patterns
   in addition 42, 43, 53
   in division 299, 310
   in mental math 113, 216–217
   in multiplication 61, 179, 216–217, 298, 474–475
   in subtraction, 42, 53
   to solve problems 375

RELATIONS AND FUNCTIONS

Function tables
   find rule 117, 316, 343–345
Graphing
   graphing change over time 148–149
   ordered pairs 150–153
Symbols showing relationships (=, >, <) 9–10, 49, 93, 111, 235, 461

Blue type indicates introduction of a topic.

Technology

GRADE 2

Calculator
   money
      adding and subtracting 346
   place value 280
   skip counting 104
   whole number operations 34, 66, 164, 196, 254
Computer
   CD-ROM (MathProcessor™)
      area 316
      arrays 372
      money 132
      time 222

GRADE 3

Calculator
   adding and multiplying 215
   adding greater numbers 112
   adding more than two numbers 94–95
   as a computation method 112, 113
   fractions to decimals 423
   memory 311
   products 215
   showing numbers 9
   skip counting 3
   subtracting greater numbers 108
   using 9, 106, 131, 185, 219, 263, 381, 415, 450, 463
Computer
   CD-ROM (MathProcessor™)
      arrays 181
      base-ten blocks 91
      geometry tool 373
      names for ten 47
      similar triangles 373
   Internet
      databases 327
      exploring space 451
      weather information 149
Using Technology (Teacher's Edition) 8, 12, 24, 30, 46, 48, 50, 58, 64, 80, 90, 102, 106, 108, 110, 128, 136, 142, 148, 154, 160, 174, 180, 184, 196, 198, 214, 218, 228, 230, 234, 252, 258, 262, 272, 288, 294, 296, 304, 306, 326, 328, 330, 340, 346, 364, 372, 380, 382, 388, 402, 406, 410, 414, 420, 430, 450, 456, 462, 470

GRADE 4

Calculator
   adding four- and five-digit numbers 50–53
   as computation method 70–71
   changing values of numbers 7
   dividing by two-digit numbers 490
   division 307
   estimating 477
   finding averages 324
   finding change 427
   finding products 245
   finding square numbers 485
   fractions to decimals 401
   guess and check 477
   multiplying greater numbers 234–235
   multiplying money 200–203
   number patterns 53
   quick changes 7
   subtracting four- and five-digit numbers 58–59
   using, 52, 109, 141, 202, 230, 281, 332, 375, 409, 415, 417, 453, 461, 477
Computer
   CD-ROM (MathProcessor™)
      changing units of measure 267
      large frames 105
      lines and angles 435
      money tools 203
      small frames 231
   Internet
      using a second engine 137
      using Hypertext 369
Using Technology (Teacher's Edition) 6, 18, 26, 42, 52, 60, 66, 84, 88, 96, 104, 110, 118, 136, 140, 144, 152, 166, 178, 190, 198, 202, 216, 224, 230, 254, 258, 266, 272, 278, 284, 298, 300, 306, 316, 324, 342, 348, 354, 364, 368, 374, 392, 400, 408, 414, 430, 434 , 442, 446, 456 , 460, 474, 484, 490

Blue type indicates introduction of a topic.

Becoming a Better Test Taker

You've learned a lot of math skills this year! These skills will help you with your school work and with everyday activities outside of school. How can you show what you've learned in math? One way is by taking tests.

Did you know you could do better on tests just by knowing how to take a test? The test-taking strategies on these pages can help you become a better test taker. They might also help you think of test questions as a fun challenge! When you take a test, try to use these strategies to show all you know.

507

Becoming a Better Test Taker

Becoming a Better Test Taker was designed to help students become more comfortable with test taking in general and to help them develop test-taking strategies for the types of problems commonly found on standardized tests.

The next five pages are devoted to helping students do better on

- **Multiple Choice** problems
- **Multistep** problems
- **Measurement** problems
- **Short-Answer** questions
- **Long-Answer** questions

What kind of help will students find for each type of problem?

- **Example** provides students with a model of the problem.
- **Think It Through** suggests steps for solving the example problem.
- **Try It** provides problems for students to solve on their own or in groups.
- **Testing Tips** provide helpful hints to help students avoid careless mistakes on tests.

Multiple Choice Questions
Know Your ABCs!

Using the Page

Purpose To improve students' performance on multiple-choice problems.

Getting Started

- Remind students that they have seen multiple-choice problems before, and explain that there are some simple things they can do to improve how well they do with this type of problem.

- Provide students with examples of multiple-choice problems and ask what strategies they would use to solve each problem.

- Discuss the example problem and the strategies listed in *Think It Through.*

- Point out *Testing Tips* and ask volunteers to read them aloud. Make sure your students understand how these tips and the strategies can help them do better on multiple choice problems.

- Have students solve the problems under *Try It!* For a group activity, have students tell how they solved the problem, using each of the *Think It Through* strategies.

- For bubble answer sheets to use with multiple-choice tests, see Teaching Tool 1 (1–50) and Teaching Tool 2 (51–100) in the Chapter File Folder or page 57 in the **Assessment Guide.**

Multiple Choice Questions
Know Your ABCs!

For multiple choice questions, you are given several answer choices for a problem. Once you have solved the problem, you need to choose the right answer from the choices that are given.

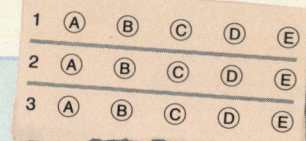

Example

$5 \times 3 = \blacksquare$

A 20   **B** 15   C 8   D 2   E Not Here

Think It Through

Read Did I read the problem carefully?
I need to multiply 5 times 3.

Cross Out Are there any answers that are not reasonable?
If there are five groups of 3, then 2 is too small, so I can cross out answer D.

Solve What is 5×3?
$5 \times 3 = 15$

Check Is there a way that I can check my answer?
I can check using repeated addition.
$3 + 3 + 3 + 3 + 3 = 15$

Choose Which letter is next to my answer?
My answer is 15, and 15 is next to letter B.

Try It!

1 $6 + 10 = \blacksquare$
   A 4   B 7   **C** 16   D 60   E Not Here

2 $24 - 8 = \blacksquare$
   A 6   B 14   **C** 16   D 32   E Not Here

3 $6 \times 3 = \blacksquare$
   A 20   **B** 18   C 12   D 9   E Not Here

Estimate whenever you can before you solve a problem. You can use an estimate to check whether your answer is reasonable, or to identify answer choices that are not reasonable.

Reread the question and check your work before choosing "Not Here."

Make sure you bubble in the letter on the answer sheet that matches your answer.

508

Additional Problems

For additional practice, have students solve these problems. Ask them to follow the *Think It Through* strategies for each problem.

1 $4 \times 2 = \blacksquare$
   A 2   B 6   **C** 8   D 12   E Not Here

2 $16 - 4 = \blacksquare$
   A 20   B 14   **C** 12   D 10   E Not Here

3 $9 + 8 = \blacksquare$
   A 1   **B** 17   C 18   D 20   E Not Here

Multistep Questions
One Step at a Time

Sometimes you need to do more than one step to answer a multiple choice question.

Example

Jen spent $8 on rides and $5 on food at the fair. Then she spent $6 more on souvenirs. If Jen came to the fair with $21, how much money does she have left?

(A) $2   B $3   C $19   D $40   E Not Here

Think It Through

Read Did I read the problem carefully?
I need to find how much money Jen has left.

Cross Out Are there any answers that are not reasonable?
Jen had $21 and spent money, so she can't have $40 now. I can cross out answer D.

Solve How much money does Jen have now?
$8 + $5 + $6 = $19, so Jen spent $19.
$21 − $19 = $2, so Jen has $2 left now.

Check Is there a way that I can check my answer?
I can check by adding all the amounts.
$2 + $8 + $5 + $6 = $21

Choose Which letter is next to my answer?
My answer is $2, and $2 is next to letter A.

Try It!

1. Lou is two years older than Gene. Gene is 3 years older than Deb. Deb is 5. How old is Lou?

   A 6   B 9   (C) 10   D 31   E Not Here

2. Mary is coloring circles in this pattern: red, yellow, green, blue, red, yellow, green, blue. What color will the 14th circle be?

   A Red   (B) Yellow   C Green
   D Blue   E Not Here

Testing Tips

▷ Always look at all of the answer choices that are listed.

▷ Even if you find your answer among the choices, check your work. Answers that come from making common mistakes are usually included in the choices!

▷ If you are having trouble answering a question, go on to the next question and come back to the more difficult question later.

509

Additional Problems

For additional practice, have students solve these problems. Ask them to follow the *Think It Through* strategies for each problem.

1. A nickel is worth 5 cents. How much are 12 nickels and 2 pennies worth?

   A 19¢   B 60¢   (C) 62¢   D 70¢   E Not Here

2. When Anna walked through the park, she saw 10 tricycles and 3 bicycles. How many wheels did she see?

   A 6   B 20   C 30   (D) 36   E Not Here

Multistep Questions
One Step at a Time

Using the Page

Purpose To improve students' performance on enhanced multiple choice problems.

Getting Started

- Remind students that sometimes multiple choice problems require more than one step to find the answer. Students should think through the steps carefully before they try to solve the problem.

- Point out that a successful test taker reads the problem several times to make sure he or she understands what is being asked.

- Discuss the example and the strategies listed in *Think It Through*.

- Read *Testing Tips* together and ask a volunteer to explain why it's important to look at all the answer choices.

- Have students solve the problems under *Try It!* You may wish to model Problem 1 on the board, using the *Think It Through* strategies.

Measurement Questions
Measure Up!

Using the Page

Purpose To improve students' performance on interactive multiple-choice problems using a ruler.

Getting Started

- Remind students that sometimes they will need to use a tool (such as a ruler) or a manipulative (such as pattern blocks) to help them solve a multiple-choice problem.

- Remind students to read the problem several times to make sure they know which side of the ruler they will be using to measure a given object. They may be asked to measure in inches or in centimeters.

- Discuss the example problem and the strategies listed in *Think It Through*.

- Point out the *Testing Tips* and discuss how important it is for the students to know which side of the ruler to use, as well as how important it is to line up the 0 mark on the ruler with one end of the object they are measuring.

- Make sure students understand that they may be asked to measure to the nearest $\frac{1}{4}$ inch or $\frac{1}{2}$ inch, in addition to the nearest inch.

- Have students work through the problem in *Try It!* Encourage students to check each other's measurements for correct precision using the correct units.

Measurement Questions
Measure Up!

Sometimes you will need to use a tool (such as a ruler) or a manipulative (such as pattern blocks) to help you solve a multiple choice question.

Example

Use the inch side of the ruler to solve this problem.

Sara is growing a bean plant. The picture shows the height of the plant after one week. To the nearest inch, how tall is the plant in the picture?

(A) 2 in.　　**B** 3 in.　　**C** 5 in.　　**D** 12 in.

Think It Through

Understand	Did I read the problem carefully? *I need to use the inch side of the ruler.*
Cross Out	Are there any answers that are not reasonable? *I know the plant isn't a foot long (12 in.). I can cross out answer D.*
Solve	What can I do to solve the problem? *I will measure the plant. It measures 2 in.*
Check	Is there a way that I can check my answer? *I can measure again, making sure I line up the 0 mark with the bottom of the plant.*
Choose	Which letter is next to my answer? *The letter A is next to 2 inches.*

Try It!

Use the centimeter side of the ruler to solve this problem.

Measure how far the turtle walked to the nearest centimeter.

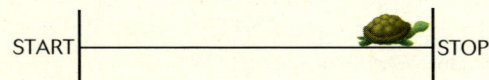

START | ————————————————— | STOP

How many centimeters (cm) did the turtle walk?

A 4 cm　　**B** 5 cm　　**(C)** 7 cm　　**D** 8 cm

510

> Make sure you are using the correct side of the ruler when you are measuring something. You may be asked to measure in inches or in centimeters.

> Make sure you line up the 0 mark on the ruler with one end of the object you are going to measure.

> Check to see how precisely you need to measure the object, such as to the nearest $\frac{1}{2}$ inch or the nearest $\frac{1}{4}$ inch.

Additional Problems

For additional practice, have students solve these problems. Ask them to follow the *Think It Through* strategies for each problem.

1 Use the inch side of the ruler to solve this problem. About how long is a new pencil?
A 4 inches　　**(B)** 7 inches　　**C** 12 inches　　**D** 15 inches

2 Use the centimeter side of the ruler to solve this problem. About how long is a toothpick?
(A) 5 cm　　**B** 8 cm　　**C** 12 cm　　**D** 15 cm

3 Use the inch side of the ruler to solve this problem. About how long is a drinking straw?
A 3 inches　　**(B)** 8 inches　　**C** 12 inches　　**D** 18 inches

Short Answer Questions
The Write Stuff

Sometimes a test question asks you not only to *solve* a problem but to show *how* you solved the problem. For questions like these, you need to be able to write your thoughts on paper.

Miss Jackson's Class's Favorite Ice-Cream Flavors

Example

The bar graph at the right shows the favorite ice-cream flavors of Miss Jackson's class.

Suppose Miss Jackson orders ice cream cups for the class. How many cups should she order in all? How many cups should she order of each flavor?

Think It Through

Read   What am I being asked to write about?
            I need to find how much of each flavor of ice cream should be ordered.

Plan   What can I do to solve the problem?
            I can compare the bars on the graph to find out how many cups of each flavor to order. Then I can add the number of students shown to find how much to order in all.

Solve   What is the answer to the problem?
            Miss Jackson should order 24 cups: 10 chocolate, 8 vanilla, and 6 strawberry.

Explain   How did I get my answer?
            The bar graph shows the number needed of each flavor, and that there are 24 students.
            1. Students' work should show that chocolate is the flavor you would probably see most students eating.

Try It!

Use the graph to answer Questions 1–2. Explain your answers.

1. If you walked into the class, what flavor ice cream would you probably see the most students eating?
   See above.

2. Three students who liked chocolate before like vanilla now. Does this change your answer for Question 1?
   Students' work should show that now vanilla would be the flavor you would probably see most students eating.

TESTING TIPS

▷ Be sure to follow the directions carefully. Sometimes you will be asked to write an explanation in words. Other times you will be asked to show your work in numbers or with drawings.

▷ Be prepared to take more time to answer short answer questions than to answer multiple choice questions.

▷ You can usually get partial credit for an answer. So, even if you can't solve the whole problem, write what you can!

511

Short-Answer Questions
The Write Stuff

Using the Page

Purpose To improve students' performance on short-answer questions.

Getting Started

- Remind students that on some math problems they will be asked to explain the answers. Students should concentrate on making their explanations clear and easy to understand.

- Point out that reading the problem carefully is very important. Encourage students to read the problem several times and to cross out any information that they do not need to solve the problem.

- Read the sample problem together and discuss the strategies in *Think It Through*. Make sure students recognize the importance of the *Plan* step.

- Read *Testing Tips* together and ask a volunteer to explain why short-answer problems take more time to answer than multiple choice problems. Also make sure students understand that they should always make an attempt to answer the question in the problem.

- Have students solve the problems under *Try It!* Model or have a student model solving the first problem on the board. Focus on the *Explain* step.

Additional Problems

For additional practice, have students solve these problems, using the *Think It Through* strategies. Choose examples of clear, concise explanations to share with the class.

For each question, use numbers and drawings or graphs to show your work. Then explain how you got your answers.

1. Tony wants to bake 28 oatmeal cookies. He has one large cookie tray. Can Tony put the cookies in 4 rows on the tray?
   Sample answer: Yes because 28 ÷ 4 = 7.

2. What are the fewest coins that would add up to equal 95 cents?
   Sample answer: 1 half dollar, 1 quarter and 2 dimes.

Rubric:
   2 points = completely correct answer with clear explanations
   1 point = partly correct answer
   0 points = completely incorrect, no answer, or not able to read the answer

Long-Answer Questions
In Your Own Words

Using the Page

Purpose To improve students' performance on long-answer questions.

Getting Started

- Remind students that long-answer problems, just like short-answer problems, require clear responses. Students should take time to think through the answer before beginning to write.

- Explain that sometimes answering a question will involve drawing a picture, showing an answer, and explaining how the problem was solved. Remind students that all three parts are important.

- Ask a volunteer to read the example problem. Discuss the strategies listed in *Think It Through*.

- Read and discuss *Testing Tips*. Emphasize that long-answer problems take time to answer and should not be rushed through.

- Have students solve the problems under *Try It!* Work out one of the problems on the board with the whole class.

1. Answer: Students may draw a bar graph, a tally table, or a pictograph. Check for accuracy and clear explanations.
2. Answer: There are 4 starfish and 3 octopuses. Students should draw a picture that shows the animals. They should show equations $4 \times 5 = 20$, $3 \times 8 = 24$, $3 + 4 = 7$, and $20 + 24 = 44$.

Long Answer Questions
In Your Own Words

Long answer questions are like short answer questions, only they are longer and often have more than one step.

Example

> Sean has 12 buttons. He wants to arrange them in equal rows. What are the different ways he can arrange them? Show your answer in numbers and with a drawing. Then explain your answer.

Think It Through

Read   What am I being asked to write about?
I need to find all the ways Sean can arrange 12 buttons in equal rows.

Plan   What can I do to solve the problem?
I can draw all the different arrangements.

Solve   What is the answer to the problem?
Sean can arrange them in 2 rows of 6, 6 rows of 2, 3 rows of 4, 4 rows of 3, 12 rows of 1, or 1 row of 12.

Explain   How did I get my answer?
I drew all the arrangements and then added to make sure that each one had 12 buttons.

1. No, there are 6 combinations: yellow shirt, black pants; yellow shirt, brown pants; green shirt, black pants; green shirt, brown pants; red shirt, black pants; red shirt, brown pants.

Try It!

For Questions 1 and 2, use numbers and drawings to show your work. Be sure to explain how you got your answers.

1. Jim is going on a trip. He takes 3 shirts: yellow, green, and red. He takes 2 pairs of pants: black and brown. Jim's trip is 8 days long. Will he be able to wear a different combination of shirt and pants each day?
See above.

2. Four friends are in line in order from youngest to oldest. Their ages are 7, 8, 9, and 12. Keesha is before Paul. Derek is after Paul. Ana is between two people, but she is not next to Derek. How much older is Paul than Keesha?
Paul is 2 years older than Keesha.

512

> Remember to explain *how* you got your answer.
>
> When you're finished writing, read the question again to be sure you've answered it completely.
>
> Keep trying! If your first strategy doesn't work, try another one. You might get partial credit even if you can't find an answer.
>
> Long answer questions take longer to answer! Be patient, and take your time.

Additional Problems

For additional practice, have students solve these problems. Ask them to follow the *Think It Through* strategies for each problem.

1. **Mr. Cruz's class took a survey of favorite foods. 5 students like fruit, 8 like tacos, 6 like yogurt, and 10 like pizza. Draw a graph that shows this data. Explain what you did.** See left.

2. **An aquarium has a total of 7 octopuses and starfish. Octopuses have eight arms and starfish have 5. Altogether they have 44 arms. How many octopuses and how many starfish are there?** See left.

Rubric:
- 4 = completely correct answer with clear explanations
- 3 = correct answer with minor flaws due to carelessness
- 2 = partially correct answer, lacks essential understanding
- 1 = incomplete or flawed answer, limited understanding
- 0 = completely incorrect, uninterpretable, or no answer

Puttin' On The Peachtree

Dining in. Atlanta style.

W9-AUY-340

THE JUNIOR LEAGUE OF DEKALB COUNTY, GEORGIA

20th Anniversary Edition

The Junior League of DeKalb County is an organization of women committed to promoting voluntarism, developing the potential of women and improving communities through the effective action and leadership of trained volunteers. Its purpose is exclusively educational and charitable.

Affiliated with the Association of Junior Leagues International, the Junior League of DeKalb County reaches out to women of all races, religions and national origins who demonstrate an interest in and commitment to voluntarism.

The cover design has been donated to the Junior League of DeKalb County by a former League member, Ellen Cavendish Phillips. Ellen graduated with a degree in Art and Biology from Agnes Scott College in Decatur, Ga. After college, Ellen taught art classes and continued to paint and exhibit her own work. Ellen has received innumerable awards and honors, including a commission from the DeKalb Chamber of Commerce to paint a portrait of Hank Aaron commemorating the 25th anniversary of his historic home run. Continuing in the League tradition, Ellen remains very active in her community.

The scene depicted by Ellen Phillips is of the Junior League of DeKalb's headquarters, The Mary Gay House. The house was once the home of a Southern heroine and author, Mary Ann Harris Gay. Her firsthand accounts of the Civil War are chronicled in her book, *Life in Dixie During the War*. They include her dangerous journey through enemy lines to deliver Northern newspapers borrowed from Yankee occupationists and uniforms to the Confederates. The house was built around 1820 and placed on the National Register of Historic Places in 1975. The house is available for rent for special occasions.

Puttin' on the Peachtree. Dining in. Atlanta Style.
The Junior League of DeKalb County, Georgia, Inc.

1st edition	Sept. 1979	20,000	5th edition	Jun. 1986	20,000
2nd edition	Dec. 1980	20,000	6th edition	May 1991	15,000
3rd edition	Apr. 1982	20,000	7th edition	Jan. 1999	15,000
4th edition	Mar. 1984	20,000			

ISBN 0-9618508-2-5

Printed in the USA by

WIMMER
The Wimmer Companies
Memphis
1-800-548-2537

Table of Contents

Original Cookbook Committee 1979

Chair
Elise Griffin

Co-Chair
Barrie Aycock

Committee

Joan Adams
Molly Ahlquist
Susan Barton
Emy Blair
Billie Bothwell
Phyllis Kennedy

Terry Morris
Susan Morley
Jane Nardone
Sandra Pritchett
Julia Ray
Sallie Smith

The success of this cookbook is credited to the support of many dedicated volunteers who have given of their expertise and enthusiasm. To name all these would be impossible. Thus in special mention, we list below the cookbook chairs in order as they have served since the original printing of *Puttin' on the Peachtree* in 1979:

Elise Griffin
Barrie Aycock
Winnie Goodman
Connie Panter
Sandy Jernigan
Terri Goldstein
Marge Carter
Chris Kendrick
Pattie Tuggle
Sally Maloof
Lynne Lock

Susan Roberson
Kathy Mulling
Barbara Williams
Betsy Menneg
Carolyn Yelton
Caroline Miller
Renee Swaim
Cathie Jones
Laurie McDowell
Sandra Smith
Montie Stone

History of the
Junior League of DeKalb County

Every purchase of *Puttin' on the Peachtree* helps the Junior League of DeKalb improve lives, especially for women and children, locally and nationally. Our organization, which started in 1934 with only 16 members, now includes 500 volunteer members contributing 40,000 hours of service annually.

Since its founding, JLD has taken a project-oriented approach to solving the problems of the day. The first project, the Children's Milk Fund, led the way to organizing medical, dental and hearing clinics in the 1940s. The 1950s saw the development of a Children's Emergency Shelter and a hospital for DeKalb County. Historic preservation was a prominent project area in the 1960s and 1970s. In the last two decades, the women of JLD have unflinchingly taken on the sensitive issues of rape and domestic violence.

Today, the Junior League of DeKalb is a strong voice of leadership throughout the state. Through time, money and advocacy, we work to:

- Prevent and lessen the effects of violence against women and children through the establishment of the DeKalb Rape Crisis Center and the International Women's House and support of the DeKalb Children's Emergency Shelter.
- Improve educational and recreational opportunities for children, most recently by awarding Mini-grants to schoolteachers annually.
- Encourage the arts and historic preservation. In addition to our affiliation with the DeKalb Historical Society, JLD has restored the Mary Gay House and helped establish Callanwolde Fine Arts Center and the Spruill Arts Center.
- Aid organizations promoting health care by our current and past volunteer involvement with Egleston Children's Hospital, Scottish Rite Children's Medical Center, Senior Connections and Wesley Woods Geriatric Center. A past project included establishing the DeKalb General Hospital Auxiliary.

With such a rich history of service, our future is limitless. Our members are committed to helping others with enthusiasm and innovative ideas. The Junior League of DeKalb County will continue to be on the forefront, meeting the needs of our communities.

In addition to the rewards of great dining, we hope you will enjoy knowing that you have become a participant in our success. We could not do it without your support.

Thank you—and bon appétit!

Introduction

Our forebearers brought to this country a knowledge of sensible, life-sustaining food. They combined that knowledge with the bounty from the Georgia soil and called it "Southern Cooking".

The native Indians added appreciation of the gifts of woods and waters.

Country folks taught us that good food shared with good friends is reason enough for a celebration.

Shy mountain women proved to us that food speaks clearly of love when the tongue cannot.

City sophisticates helped us find creative expression in cooking for the sheer fun of it.

As Atlanta grew from country crossroad beginnings to become the major city of the New South, people from every corner of the world came to share the spirit of this always new city. Each individual brings a totally unique culinary heritage, whether an exotic ingredient from some faraway place or simply "the way Mama always did it." Formerly foreign words, curry and cumin, pita and pasta, stir-fry and strudel, have become common kitchen vocabulary. We still call it Southern Cooking because the basic Southern components of freshness, abundance and hospitality are always present!

We invite people into our homes to mark special occasions or we simply share the warm companionship of time and food together. Whatever our reasons for entertaining, food shared with friends must be our best; cooked with love, served with style.

Wherever you cook, there's a phrase for it:
In the city, it's puttin' on the ritz.
In the country, it's puttin' on the dog.
In some places in between, it's puttin' on your best bib and
    tucker.
In Atlanta, it's PUTTIN' ON THE PEACHTREE!
It speaks of entertaining people you care about and doing it
    well.
It's Dining In. Atlanta Style.

Menus for all Occasions

No matter what the occasion, every meal can be cause for puttin' on the peachtree. Whether you are preparing an elegant dinner, an outdoor barbeque or a dish for the family reunion, the following menu suggestions will make the event special as well as delicious!

Exceptionally Elegant

In Atlanta, Georgia, where gracious parties and meals have not gone by the wayside, style is almost as important as taste. The perfect menu can turn an ordinary evening into a gala affair.

New Year's Eve Cocktail Buffet
Caviar and Artichokes   p. 6
Quiche Hors D'oeuvres   p. 13
Veggies with Vegetable Party Dip   p. 13
Stuffed Mushrooms   p. 18
Baked Cheese Sandwiches   p. 28
Shrimp Arnaud   p. 25
Ham Biscuits with Mustard Spread   p. 19
Cranberry Nut Muffins   p. 247
Cheese Marmalade Tarts   p. 8

Dinner Club
Kir   p. 34
Artichoke Mixed Salad   p. 190
Tournedos in Puff Pastry   p. 93
Crunchy Asparagus   p. 152
Mushroom Stuffed Tomatoes   p. 176
Devonshire Cream   p. 264

Concert in the Park
Dill Weed Dip for Veggies   p. 12
Bleu Cheese Slaw   p. 200
Baked Ham   p. 118
Chilled Lemon Broccoli   p. 159
Baps   p. 234
Sangria   p. 32
Pecan Tassies   p. 302
Chocolate Macaroons   p. 300

All-Star Southern

In keeping with our Southern heritage, great meals need to include lots of fresh veggies, enjoyed out-of-doors before the big game or as the main event. Some of y'all may not know that we Southerners take football and barbeque as seriously as our food.

A Winning Tailgate Party

Get Your Vegetables

Simply Southern Supper

Just Like Family

Family is the core of Southern culture, and nothing brings the family closer together than the dinner table. After all, who better to enjoy your home cookin' than those you love the most?

Lazy Summer Supper

Vegetable Party Dip with French Bread   p. 13
Summer Pasta   p. 72
Darvish Salad   p. 194
"The" Strawberry Pie   p. 296

Autumn Celebration

Pork Tenderloin Lorraine   p. 113
Easter Potato Casserole   p. 171
"Skinny" Green Beans   p. 155
Apple Cream Pie   p. 294

For Mom on Mother's Day

Banana Bites   p. 4
Grilled Ham Slice   p. 116
The Potato   p. 170
Sliced Tomatoes
Cottage Coconut Pie   p. 292

Dad's Backyard Picnic

Charcoaled Flank Steak   p. 96
Onion Pie   p. 166
Hot Bean Salad   p. 193
Beer Bread   p. 235
Peach Custard Pie   p. 293

Treats (No Tricks) for Grownups

Chips & Guacamole Dip   p. 12
Homestyle "Boursin" and Crackers   p. 5
Asparagus Bites   p. 3
Emergency Tuna Pate   p. 15
Hot Dogs Creole   p. 118
Pumpkin Cheesecake   p. 283
Hot Spiced Wine   p. 33

Wedding Weekend

Although the actual wedding ceremony may only last a few minutes, the events last several days and include many meals. The guests from near and far come to see the nuptials, and the food can often be the center of the celebration.

Showered with Compliments

Fresh fruit with Dip for Fruit   p. 12
Mystery Canapes   p. 15
Shrimp Mold   p. 27
Baked Cheese Sandwiches   p. 28
Ethel Mincey's Punch   p. 31
Chinese Almond Cakes   p. 314
Pineapple Torte   p. 270

Ladies Luncheon

Hot Cheese Puffs   p. 9
Crunchy Pea Salad   p. 198
Crab Stuffed Chicken   p. 124
Tomato Lemon Aspic   p. 185
Sour Cream Rolls   p. 233
Bourbon Slush   p. 29
Sherman Strikes Again   p. 271

The Rehearsal Dinner

Raspberry Apéritif   p. 34
Party Casserole   p. 129
Herb Rice Blend   p. 65
Six Vegetable Medley   p. 179
Chocolate Mousse   p. 281
Irish Coffee   p. 30

Brunch for a Bunch

Sacramento Fruit Bowl   p. 183
Sausage Quiche   p. 58
Blintz Casserole   p. 59
Monterey Fondue Casserole   p. 59
German Butterkuchen   p. 248

The reprint committee would like to thank Susan Barton, Fran Scott, and Carroll Ball for providing the menus.

Guidelines for Healthy Eating

Your favorite recipes can be modified to make them more nutritious or lower in fat by reducing or substituting ingredients that are more acceptable. Test new ways to decrease the amount of fat, calories, sugar and salt in your recipes. Remember that recipes are only guidelines, not rules, for preparing food. Don't be afraid to experiment.

The Food Pyramid. The USDA recommends that Americans eat healthier by using their suggestions for daily servings of the following:

6–11 Servings of grain
3–5 servings of vegetables   2–4 servings of fruit
2–3 servings of dairy products
2–3 servings of meat, fish, eggs, nuts
using sparing amounts of fats, oils and sweets

Calories. To maintain your ideal weight you can estimate the number of calories allowed daily. Simply multiply your ideal weight (be realistic) by 13 if you are moderately active and by 15 if you are very active.

Fat. Only 30 percent of your total daily calories should come from fat. If you take your daily calorie intake, drop the last digit and then divide by 3, and you will have the recommended fat allowance.

Sodium and Cholesterol. The Recommended Daily Dietary Allowances (for healthy adults over 25) are no more than 2,400 mg sodium (this equals about $\frac{1}{2}$ to $1\frac{1}{2}$ teaspoons of salt) and no more than 300 mg cholesterol.

Substitutions

- 2 egg whites or egg substitute = 1 whole egg
- Use graham cracker or chocolate cookie crumb crusts in recipes that call for a higher fat pastry dough crust.
- Instead of chocolate chips or nuts, use raisins.
- Instead of ground beef, use ground round or LEAN ground turkey.
- Use $\frac{1}{2}$ prune or banana puree for butter or margarine in baking and cooking.
- Use corn oil, canola oil and peanut oil. To substitute liquid oil for solid fats, use about $\frac{1}{4}$ less than called for in the recipe.
- To decrease the amount of sodium in your foods, use low sodium or unsalted ingredients in your recipes.
- Reduce sugar by $\frac{1}{4}$ to $\frac{1}{3}$ in baked goods. Substitute flour for the omitted sugar. Adding cardamon, cinnamon, nutmeg or vanilla to your recipes will enhance the impression of sweetness.
- To increase fiber, choose whole grain for part of your ingredients instead of highly refined products using whole wheat flour, oatmeal and whole cornmeal. Whole wheat flour can be substituted for up to $\frac{1}{2}$ of all purpose flour.
- Use plain lowfat or nonfat yogurt instead of sour cream. You can also substitute buttermilk or blended lowfat cottage cheese.
- Use skim milk or 1% milk instead of whole milk or half and half. For extra richness, try evaporated skim milk.

Cooking Techniques

- Cooking methods: Bake, broil, poach, microwave or steam foods instead of frying.
- Seasoning: Use herbs, juices, and vinegar instead of fats for flavoring.
- Saute in water, juice, broth, or use nonstick vegetable spray.
- Make soups, sauces and gravies ahead of time, refrigerate and skim the hardened fat off the top before reheating.
- Thicken sauces, gravies, stews and soups with pureed vegetables. Try cooked winter squash, potatoes, dried beans and peas, carrots and cauliflower.

Healthy Shopping

- Choose skim milk, low fat cheeses, low fat versions of sour cream and mayonnaise.
- Choose leaner cuts of meat (like tenderloin, top round or flank steak) instead of fatty, marbled varieties (like rib roast, T-bone and ground chuck).
- Choose more dark green and dark yellow vegetables.
- Fresh or frozen vegetables have less added salt than canned.

Sources: USDA
           National Institutes of Health
           American Heart Association
           American Diabetes Association

Appetizers and Beverages

Almond Bacon Cheese Spread

½ cup diced almonds
4 strips bacon, crisply cooked
   and crumbled
2 cups grated American
   cheese, packed
4 Tablespoons chopped green
   onion
1 cup mayonnaise
½ teaspoon salt

Mix ingredients thoroughly. Chill to enhance flavors in a covered container. May be prepared the day before serving. 2½ cups

JoAnn P. Whitehead (Mrs. Harry C.)

Antipasto Spread
Serve this as a first course

½ cup butter
12 ounces tomato paste
5 ounces cocktail onions
   and juice
4 ounces sliced canned
   mushrooms, drained
14 ounces tuna, drained
1 chopped dill pickle
8 ounces shrimp, cooked
   and chopped
6 ounces green olives with
   pimientos, sliced
¼ cup dry red wine (Burgundy
   or Bordeaux)
¼ cup beer
1 Tablespoon sugar
Dash crushed basil
Dash paprika
14 ounces cherry peppers,
   seeds removed, chopped

Melt butter. Combine all ingredients and chill several hours. May be served with wheat crackers, melba toast, or as first course on a lettuce bed.

Susan M. Morley

Asparagus Bites

1 (8 ounce) package cream
   cheese, softened
4 ounces blue cheese,
   crumbled
1 egg, well beaten
1 can asparagus spears,
   drained
Thin sliced white bread
2 sticks butter or margarine,
   melted

Mix cream cheese with blue cheese and add egg. Count number of asparagus spears in can; count out same number of slices of bread. Trim crusts from bread. Roll trimmed bread as thin as possible with rolling pin. Spread each slice of bread with cheese and egg mixture. Place asparagus spear on each bread slice and roll up. Cut each rolled slice into thirds. Dip each roll into melted butter. Place close together in shallow baking pan. May be frozen at this stage. Bake at 400° for 15-20 minutes if not frozen. Bake 30 minutes or until browned if frozen. 8-10 servings

Ruth D. Hardy (Mrs. Wallace E.)

Artichoke Spread

1 can artichoke hearts (6-8 in
   can—not marinated)
1 cup mayonnaise
1 cup grated Parmesan cheese
Dash garlic powder

Drain artichoke hearts well; chop. Mix with mayonnaise, cheese and garlic powder. Bake in an oven-proof casserole at 350° for 25 to 30 minutes. Serve with crackers. Ingredients may be mixed ahead and baked later but not frozen.

Joan M. Adams (Mrs. John P., Jr.)

HINT

If substituting fresh herbs for dried, use 3 or 4 times as much. Add herbs at same time as salt and pepper to meats, vegetables, sauces, and soups. In long-cooking foods, such as stews, add herbs during last half hour of cooking time.

Hot Stuffed Avocado

3 large or 4 small avocadoes,
    peeled
Lemon juice to coat
6-8 Tablespoons vinegar or
    lemon juice
6-8 cloves garlic
2 Tablespoons butter
2 Tablespoons flour
1 cup light cream
1 Tablespoon grated onion
¼ teaspoon celery salt
Salt and pepper to taste
2 cups cooked Alaskan crab,
    shrimp, lobster or chicken
½ cup grated sharp cheddar
    cheese

Roll outside of peeled avocado in lemon juice to preserve color. Cut avocados in half. Remove pits and place 1 Tablespoon vinegar or lemon juice and clove of garlic in each half. Let stand 30 minutes. Meanwhile, melt butter and blend in flour. Add cream and stir over heat until thickened. Add grated onion, spices and meat. Pour vinegar and garlic from avocado and fill with meat mixture. Sprinkle with cheese and place in baking dish filled with ½-inch of water. Bake 15 minutes at 350°. 6 servings

Cookbook Committee

Banana Bites

Cut bananas into 1 inch lengths. Dip in thawed lemonade concentrate (undiluted). Roll in fine flake toasted coconut. Serve on toothpicks.

Variation: Omit lemonade and roll slices in wheat germ, coating well. Freeze. Serve frozen on toothpicks.

Agnes Siebert (Mrs. "Sam")

Beer Cheese Dip

½-1 cup beer, boiled and
    cooled
3 (6 ounce) rolls Kraft nippy
    cheese
1¼ ounces Roquefort cheese
2 Tablespoons butter
1 medium onion
2 cloves garlic
1 teaspoon Worcestershire
    sauce
½ teaspoon Tabasco
1 loaf Rye bread (round)

Put all ingredients into a blender (add beer carefully so as not to let mixture be too runny). Blend until smooth. Hollow out a loaf of Rye bread; cut the hollowed out portions into cubes. Cubes may be toasted in oven if desired. Pour dip into Rye loaf. Dip cubes into loaf.
10-12 servings

Judy Scheidt (Mrs. Kenneth A.)

Homestyle "Boursin"

8 ounces whipped butter,
    softened
16 ounces cream cheese,
    softened
2 cloves garlic, mashed or
    pressed
½ teaspoon oregano
¼ teaspoon basil
¼ teaspoon dill weed
¼ teaspoon marjoram
¼ teaspoon black pepper
¼ teaspoon thyme

Mix all ingredients thoroughly in electric mixer. Refrigerate overnight to blend flavors. Serve at room temperature with assorted mild crackers. Keeps well and can be frozen.

Tippi Lassiter

Marinated Broccoli
Beautiful served in a crystal bowl

1 cup cider vinegar
1 Tablespoon sugar
1 Tablespoon dill weed
1 Tablespoon MSG
1 teaspoon salt
1 teaspoon pepper
1 teaspoon garlic salt
1½ cups vegetable oil
3 bunches broccoli, broken
    into flowerettes

Combine ingredients and marinate for 24 hours. 12 servings

Pat W. Engel (Mrs. John D.)

Clara's Crab

2 (6-ounce) packages frozen
    crabmeat, thawed and
    drained
3 hard boiled eggs, chopped
Juice of ½ lemon
1 teaspoon Worcestershire
    sauce
2 green onions, white and
    green parts, chopped
¾ cup (or more) mayonnaise
Salt, and cayenne pepper
    to taste

Break up crabmeat and add seasonings. Toss lightly with mayonnaise. Serve with crackers, or stuffed in tomatoes for a delightful cold appetizer. 2 cups

Nancy Wactor (Mrs. William R.)

Caponata
(Italian Eggplant Relish)

2 medium eggplants (about
  2 pounds)
Salt
½ cup olive oil
1 medium onion, finely
  chopped
2 large stalks celery, thinly
  sliced
½ cup wine vinegar
½ cup tomato purée
1 Tablespoon sugar
½ cup capers
6 large green olives, sliced or
  about 2 Tablespoons sliced
  salad olives
Salt and pepper to taste

Cut off ends of eggplant. Cut unpeeled eggplant into ¾ inch cubes. Place in a colander. Sprinkle with salt and let eggplant remain for about 20 minutes until much of the liquid has been drawn from them. In a non-stick pan, heat olive oil and brown egg-plant cubes lightly. Place in a colander over a bowl to drain. Cook onion and celery in remaining oil in pan over low heat until soft, not brown. Pour wine vinegar over onions and celery and let steam covered a few minutes until liquid evaporates. Return eggplant to pan and combine with onion and celery. Blend sugar, and tomato purée into the eggplant mixture. Add capers, olives, pepper and salt to taste. Let relish heat through. May be frozen. Serve cool as an antipasto, appetizer or main course accompaniment.

Mrs. August J. Nardone

Caviar and Artichokes
Elegant appetizer for a small dinner party

1 can marinated artichoke
  hearts, drained
4 hard boiled eggs
4 green onions
1 small jar black caviar
Mayonnaise

Finely chop artichokes, eggs and onions in separate bowls. In small bowl (1 quart or less) layer in following order: ½ of eggs, artichokes, caviar, onions and mayonnaise. Repeat layer. Chill. Unmold and serve with crackers. Must be prepared the day before serving to allow flavors to blend. 8 servings

Jane G. Skelton (Mrs. Douglas)

Cha Gio
Vietnamese Spring Roll

1 package spring roll skins
    from Oriental grocery store;
    soak in water before use
1½ pounds ground pork
½ pound shrimp, peeled and
    deveined
1 small bundle bean threads
    (cellophane noodles)
1 raw egg
1 bunch green onions
4 cloves garlic
6-8 mushrooms (dried or fresh)
2 carrots, shredded
2 teaspoons fish sauce or soy
    sauce
Peanut or vegetable oil
SAUCE:
Fish sauce or soy sauce to
    taste
Water
Sugar

Finely dice all vegetables except carrots, which have been shredded. Soak noodles until they expand. Mix ingredients together. Place 2 Tablespoons of the mixture on each skin, turn ends up and roll. Fry in vegetable oil until crisp. Dip in sauce to serve.

Sauce: Blend fish sauce or soy sauce, with water and sugar to taste.

Sharon Samford

Champignon Schnitte

2 Tablespoons butter
1 pound fresh mushrooms,
    sliced
2 medium onions, chopped
Salt to taste
1-2 loaves cocktail size rye
    or pumpernickel bread
1 (12-ounce) package grated
    Swiss cheese
1 cup grated Parmesan cheese

Melt butter in large frying pan. Add mushrooms and onion. Cook until onions are soft and mushrooms are beginning to turn brown. Add salt. Remove from heat. Spread mixture on slice of bread using 1 Tablespoon per slice. Arrange in baking pan. Sprinkle Swiss cheese liberally over slices; then sprinkle with Parmesan cheese. Broil until cheese melts and lightly browns. Remove and serve immediately. May be frozen. Thaw and broil. 40 pieces

Camille T. Allen (Mrs. Julian D.)

Cheese Marmalade Tarts

1 (4-ounce) jar Old English
  Cheddar Cheese
1 cup plus 2 Tablespoons
  sifted flour
1 stick margarine
2 Tablespoons cold water
Orange marmalade

Cut margarine and cheese into flour as for pastry. Mix with water and shape into a ball, or place margarine, cheese and flour in food processor and process for 10 seconds; add water and process until a ball is formed. Put in wax paper and refrigerate overnight. Roll dough and cut into 3-inch circles on a floured board (the rim of a can works well for this). Put approximately ½ teaspoon marmalade onto center of each circle and fold over. Dampen edges with water to seal and press down with tines of a fork. Prick a few holes in the top. Bake at 375° for 10 minutes. May be prepared ahead or frozen. Wonderful to pass at cocktail party. 20 servings

Linda D. Bobo (Mrs. W. Earl)

Curried Cheese Ball with Fresh Pears

3 fresh Anjou, Boxc or Comice
  pears
1 (8-ounce) package cream
  cheese, softened
2 Tablespoons powdered sugar
½ teaspoon curry powder
⅓ cup flaked coconut
⅓ cup chopped pecans
Maraschino cherry for garnish

Refrigerate pears. Combine cream cheese, sugar, curry powder, coconut, and half of the pecans. Mix with hands, or in a food processor, process for 15 seconds or until smooth. Wrap in plastic wrap and refrigerate until firm. Press remaining pecans on cheese ball and garnish with a maraschino cherry. To serve, core and slice pears into wedges; use cheese as a spread for wedges; serve as an appetizer or dessert. 8 servings

JoAnn P. Whitehead (Mrs. Harry C.)

Hot Cheese Puffs
An easy cocktail party food

2 egg whites
½ teaspoon baking powder
¼ teaspoon salt
¼ teaspoon paprika
½ cup sharp grated Cheddar
  cheese
Toast rounds, sautéed on
  one side in butter
Bacon, cooked, drained and
  crumbled

Beat egg whites until stiff. Beat in baking powder, salt and paprika. Fold in cheese. Heap onto toast rounds, dry side down. Broil 4 or 5 minutes until brown. Sprinkle with bacon.

Mrs. Ellis H. Taylor

Hot Crab and Cheese Crackers

1 (6½-ounce) can crab, drained
  and checked for shells
1 Tablespoon minced onion
1 cup shredded sharp Cheddar
  cheese
1-2 Tablespoons mayonnaise
Paprika
Melba toast rounds

Mix all ingredients. When ready to serve, spread on melba toast rounds, sprinkle with paprika and broil until bubbly. 6-8 servings

Pat W. Engel (Mrs. John D.)

Crab Meat Hot Dip

3 (8 ounce) packages
  Philadelphia cream cheese
2 (6½ ounce) cans crab meat
  and juice, checked for
  shells
2 cloves garlic, crushed
½ cup mayonnaise
2 teaspoons prepared mustard
½ cup sherry
1 teaspoon onion juice
Lawry's seasoned salt

Heat all ingredients together in a double boiler until well blended and cheese is melted. Refrigerate. Reheat before serving. Serve in a chafing dish or fondue pot. Serve with plain crackers, not salted crackers or chips. 20 servings

Beverly Bibent (Mrs. Maury J.)
Cincinnati, Ohio

Chicken Bites with Sauce
Unusual and delicious

3 whole chicken breasts, boned
Small amount of butter or
** margarine**
1 cup sour cream
½ cup mayonnaise
¼ cup chili sauce
2 Tablespoons horseradish
1 Tablespoon Worcestershire
** sauce**
2 Tablespoons lemon juice
¼ teaspoon Tabasco
1 teaspoon curry powder
2 Tablespoons chutney,
** finely minced**
4 Tablespoons capers
2 Tablespoons chopped parsley

Cut chicken breasts into bite sized pieces and place in a pan with a small amount of butter or margarine. Cover with a sheet of wax paper and place in a 400° oven for 6-8 minutes. They are done if they spring back when pressed with a finger. Combine chicken with all other ingredients. Refrigerate several hours or overnight. To serve, pile in the center of a serving dish surrounded by lettuce leaves. Sprinkle with additional parsley and capers. Serve with toothpicks. 6 servings

Robbin A. Churchill (Mrs. John S.)
Jacksonville, Florida

Chicken Liver Pâté

½ pound chicken livers
1 teaspoon salt
Pinch cayenne pepper
1 stick butter
¼ teaspoon nutmeg
1 teaspoon dry mustard
⅛ teaspoon ground cloves
2 Tablespoons finely minced
** onions**
1 large clove garlic, crushed

Barely cover chicken livers with water and bring to a boil. Reduce heat, cover and simmer 15 to 20 minutes. Drain and put in blender or food processor. Mix with remaining ingredients. Blend well. Pack in crock or jar and refrigerate at least 24 hours before serving. Pâté may be frozen at this point. Serve with crackers or French bread.

Lynn H. Barnes

HINT ■■■■■■■■■■

To mince parsley easily, bunch the leafy tops together and cut with scissors into a measuring cup. Then to mince finer, put scissors in the cup and snip away.

Deviled Clams

¼ pound butter
3 medium onions, chopped
2 green bell peppers, chopped
2 (6½ ounce) cans minced
    clams and juice
1 teaspoon curry powder
Dry bread crumbs
4 slices bacon

Sauté onions and peppers in butter in covered pan until tender. Add clams, juice and curry powder. Stir in enough bread crumbs to thicken. Place in individual baking shells. Top with ½ slice bacon. Pour small amount of water in pan around shells to keep shells from becoming too hot. Bake at 400° until bacon is crisp, about 20 minutes. May be prepared in advance and baked when ready to serve. 6 servings

Mr. H. Malcolm Teare

Curry Dip

½ cup mayonnaise
1 cup sour cream
2 Tablespoons lemon juice
1 teaspoon curry powder
½ teaspoon paprika
2 Tablespoons minced parsley
½ teaspoon tarragon
2 Tablespoons grated onion
2 teaspoons prepared mustard
1 Tablespoon minced chives
Dash Tabasco
Dash salt and pepper

Combine all ingredients in a quart size covered container. Refrigerate at least 24 hours before serving. Will keep for several days in the refrigerator. Serve with carrots, celery, cucumbers, mushrooms, yellow squash or cauliflower. 1 quart

Nancy W. Jones (Mrs. Edmund W.)

Cheese-Ground Beef Dip

½ pound ground beef
½ pound Velveeta cheese
½ pound sharp Cheddar
    cheese
1 roll garlic cheese
1 egg
1 cup green chilies and
    tomatoes, chopped
Tabasco to taste

Brown and drain ground beef. Melt cheeses in top of double boiler. Add all other ingredients. Serve hot with Dorito chips.

Mrs. Gary Hays

Dip for Fruit

1 cup sour cream
1 Tablespoon gelatin
¼ cup sugar
½ teaspoon vanilla
1 cup heavy cream, whipped
Bite size pieces of fruit

In bowl of double boiler over hot water, mix sour cream, gelatin and sugar until gelatin dissolves and sugar melts. Stir in vanilla. Cool mixture. Fold in whipped cream. Refrigerate until ready to use.

Sidney Murphey (Mrs. William)

Guacamole Dip
Delicious in sandwiches
or as a dip with corn chips or fresh vegetables

2 very ripe avocados
½ cup sour cream
Juice of 1 lime
1 clove garlic, crushed
Salt and freshly ground pepper
    to taste
3 Tablespoons Jalapeno relish

Scoop out avocado meat. Mash in a non-metal bowl with remaining ingredients. It should be a very rough puree. Cover closely with plastic wrap and refrigerate until ready to use.

Susan L. Kreitzman
"In Good Taste" School of Cookery

Dill Weed Dip

1 cup sour cream
⅓ cup mayonnaise
1 Tablespoon shredded green
    onion
1 Tablespoon dried parsley
1 teaspoon dill weed
1 teaspoon Beau Monde
    seasoning

Combine ingredients and chill. Serve with chips or vegetables.

Pat Brasher
San Antonio, Texas

MICROWAVE HINT ■■■■■

To separate slices of cold bacon easily, heat package for a few seconds.

Raw Spinach Dip

1 package chopped frozen
   spinach
½ cup dehydrated parsley
   flakes
½ cup chopped green onions
2 Tablespoons Salad Supreme
½ Tablespoon dill seed
1 cup mayonnaise

Thaw spinach and squeeze in cheesecloth. Combine spinach with rest of the ingredients. Refrigerate at least 3 hours; may be prepared 1 or 2 days in advance. Serving suggestions: Serve as a dip with corn chips, fill hollowed-out cherry tomatoes with dip, or place a dollop of dip on a thick slice of tomato and heat.

Vegetable Party Dip

1 cup mayonnaise
1 teaspoon tarragon vinegar
1 teaspoon horseradish
⅛ teaspoon black pepper
1½ teaspoon curry powder

Mix all ingredients together until smooth. Refrigerate one hour before using. Serve with crisp vegetables. 1 cup

Nancy Kirby (Mrs. Jeff D., III)

Quiche Hors D'oeuvres

2 pie shells
Melted butter
2 large onions, thinly sliced
1 (6-ounce) can sliced
   mushrooms
1 pound grated Swiss cheese
2 Tablespoons flour
3 eggs
1¼ cups milk
1 teaspoon salt
½ teaspoon pepper
Dash nutmeg

Prick pie shells. Cook 10 minutes at 375°. Cook the onions until tender in melted butter and divide between the shells. Divide the mushrooms between the shells. Toss grated cheese with flour and sprinkle over each pie. Mix eggs, milk, salt, pepper and nutmeg. Pour over ingredients in pie shells. Bake at 400° for 20 minutes, then at 300° for 25 minutes. Let stand until cool. Cut in small wedges or squares and serve immediately. Can be frozen. 4 dozen

Julia W. Ray (Mrs. Frederick C.)

Escargots a la Bourguignonne

3 dozen canned snails
3 dozen shells
½ pound butter
3 Tablespoons finely chopped
parsley
2 Tablespoons finely chopped
shallots
1 clove garlic, crushed
¼ teaspoon salt
Freshly ground black pepper
French bread

Wash and drain snails. Wash, drain and dry shells. In small mixing bowl, cream butter until soft using a wooden spoon. Add parsley, shallots, garlic, salt and pepper. Mix well. Insert a snail in each shell, pushing it as far as it will go with finger. Fill shell with butter mixture. Place snails in special snail dishes or in flat baking dish with open ends up. Place any leftover butter mixture around snails. Bake at 425° for 10 minutes until hot and bubbly. Serve at once with French bread and white wine. Butter mixture may be made in advance and stuffed into shells just before baking. 6 servings

Kimpy Edge (Mrs. J. Dexter)

Escargots
Serve in shells, in mushroom caps, or on toast rounds

2 dozen snails, drained
2 cups boiling water
2-3 beef bouillon cubes
½ stick butter
1 teaspoon diced onion flakes
2 teaspoons parsley flakes
½ teaspoon liquid garlic or
1 clove garlic, crushed
Salt and pepper to taste

Boil snails in bouillon for 2 minutes. (This step really adds a good flavor.) Drain. Melt butter and add rest of ingredients. Place 1 snail in each shell and cover with butter mixture. Heat in 350° oven until butter sizzles. Serve with warm crusty French bread. May be prepared early in day and refrigerated until ready to cook. 4 servings

Dr. Paul Conner

MICROWAVE HINT ■■■

Melba toast for canapes—Cut thin slices of stale bread into decorative shapes and arrange on a paper towel; cook 2 minutes, let stand 5 minutes.

Eggplant Caviar

2 Tablespoons olive oil
1 small-medium eggplant,
    peeled and diced
1 large green pepper, chopped
    (about ¾ cup)
2 medium onions, chopped
    (1 cup)
2 Tablespoons tomato paste
1 teaspoon sugar
1½ teaspoons salt
¼-½ teaspoon freshly ground
    black pepper
1 Tablespoon lemon juice

Heat oil; add eggplant, green pepper and onions and sauté 20 minutes stirring frequently. Mix in other ingredients except lemon juice and cook 10 minutes over low heat. Remove from heat and add lemon juice. Blend well. This was a recipe from a friend in Florida. Even those who don't care for eggplant or green pepper have raved about this when used as a cold dip with crackers.

Beth Benefield (Mrs. Phillip)

Emergency Tuna Pâté

1 (8-ounce) package cream
    cheese
2 Tablespoons chili sauce
2 Tablespoons chopped
    parsley or 3 Tablespoons
    dried
1 teaspoon minced onion
½ teaspoon bottled hot
    pepper sauce
2 (6½-ounce) cans tuna, drained

Blend cream cheese, chili sauce, parsley, onion and pepper sauce until smooth. Add tuna gradually until all is thoroughly blended. Pack in a 4-cup bowl as a mold. Chill at least 3 hours. Unmold on lettuce and serve with crisp, sesame crackers.
8-10 servings

Tippi Lassiter (Mrs. Robert)

Mystery Canapés

½ cup chopped raw almonds
½ cup mayonnaise
2 Tablespoons catsup
1 cup finely chopped celery
1 cup finely chopped onion
½ teaspoon curry powder
Pinch salt
½ cup pitted chopped dates
Triscuits

Mix all ingredients together and spread on Triscuits. Bake in a 400° oven 1-2 minutes. Mixture will keep in refrigerator up to 2 weeks. 4 cups

Susan N. Barton (Mrs. David L.)

Fried Gyoza
"Pot Stickers"

5 ounces cabbage, chopped
6 ounces ground pork or beef
(or combination of both)
2 Tablespoons Japanese soy
sauce
1 Tablespoon sesame oil
1 teaspoon Mirin (Japanese
rice wine) or sherry
1 green onion, minced
1 teaspoon grated ginger
1 dried black mushroom,
soaked in 2 Tablespoons
water
2-3 Tablespoons peanut oil
¼ cup hot water
1 small package Gyoza skins
(available at Oriental food
stores)
DUNKING SAUCE:
¼ cup Japanese soy sauce
1 teaspoon rice wine vinegar
Dash Rayu or sesame oil

Cook cabbage in a small amount of boiling salted water until tender. Squeeze out all liquid and mince fine. Chop mushroom. Mix soy sauce, sesame oil, Mirin, pork, green onion, ginger, mushroom and cabbage. Refrigerate for 1 hour or more. Place a scant teaspoon of mixture on each gyoza skin. Moisten edges with cornstarch and water, fold over and seal. Crimp edges with a fork. Cover bottom of a large non-stick skillet (electric is good) with oil. Brown the gyoza over medium heat (350°) turning frequently. Add ¼ cup water to skillet, cover and steam on low heat 7 minutes. Stir often to prevent sticking. Remove cover, raise heat and cook for 2 minutes until crisp. Place sauce on table in small, individual bowls. Gyoza may be prepared in advance or frozen. Lay them in a single layer on a greased cookie sheet, and cover with greased paper. Thaw before cooking. "Pot Stickers" are usually served as a first course. They are also excellent as an appetizer.
Suggestion: Egg Drop Soup and "Pot Stickers", followed by Beef with Oyster Sauce a crisp green vegetable and hot Chinese tea.

Cookbook Committee

Curried Meatballs

1 pound lean ground beef
2-3 teaspoons curry powder
Salt and pepper to taste
1 cup herb stuffing mix
¼ cup butter

Mix all ingredients well and shape into walnut size balls. Sauté in skillet in butter or cook in microwave. Serve warm from chafing dish or freeze and reheat. 6-8 servings

Joan King (Mrs. Lewis)

Mushroom Tarts
An hors d'oeuvre, or an entrée with soup or salad

25 thin slices bread
½ stick butter
½ pound fresh mushrooms, chopped
3 Tablespoons chopped green onion
1½ Tablespoons flour
1 cup heavy cream
½ teaspoon salt
Juice of ½ lemon
1½ Tablespoons chopped parsley
1 Tablespoon chives
⅛ teaspoon cayenne
Parmesan cheese

Tart shell: Grease muffin tins using butter. Cut circles out of bread centers using a 4-inch glass. Press gently into tins and bake for 10 minutes at 375°. Shells can be frozen at this point. 25 servings

Filling: Sauté chopped mushrooms and green onions in remaining butter for 20 minutes. Add flour to thicken. Add cream, slowly stirring over heat until bubbles form. Remove from heat and add remaining ingredients except Parmesan cheese. Place tarts on a cookie sheet; fill to top and sprinkle with Parmesan cheese. Cook for 10 minutes at 375°. Filling may be frozen and reheated on stove, or tarts and filling can be frozen already made up.

Martha K. Randolph (Mrs. William H., IV)

To cut fresh bread, heat the serrated knife.

Pickled Mushrooms

Fresh mushrooms
Salt
Marinating solution in these
    proportions:
    ½ cup olive oil
    2 cloves garlic, crushed
    4 Tablespoons white wine
        vinegar
    2 teaspoons grated onion

Trim and wash mushrooms. Measure and place into saucepan with ½ teaspoon salt for every cup of mushrooms. Add no water but simmer them, covered, for 15 minutes. Drain. Mix mushrooms into marinating solution and place into covered container. If you do not have enough oil mixture to cover, make some more. Mushrooms must be covered. Let them age for 3-5 days before using. They will keep for months in refrigerator, if oil layer is on top. Serve with toothpicks on bed of lettuce or parsley. Also can be coarsely chopped, mixed with a little oil sauce and served hot or cold with steaks or hamburgers. Hint: Use a narrow jar to keep for a period of time. Oil layer is thicker in narrow jar.

Emy E. Blair (Mrs. H. Duane)

Stuffed Mushrooms

24 large fresh mushrooms
⅓ cup melted butter or
    margarine
1 (8 ounce) can minced clams,
    drained
3 Tablespoons sliced green
    onion
1 Tablespoon chopped parsley
¼ teaspoon salt
⅛ teaspoon pepper
⅛ teaspoon garlic powder
¾ cup mayonnaise
½ teaspoon prepared mustard

Clean mushrooms with a damp cloth; remove stems, leaving caps intact. Set mushroom caps aside. Chop mushroom stems; sauté in butter 10 minutes. Add clams, onion, parsley, salt, pepper and garlic powder; sauté 5 minutes. Stuff mushroom caps with clam mixture. Place in a lightly greased baking dish; chill. Combine mayonnaise and mustard; top each mushroom cap with mayonnaise mixture. Bake at 350° for 10-15 minutes. 6-8 servings

Billie E. Bothwell (Mrs. Eugene L., Jr.)

Ham Biscuits with Mustard Spread
A big hit at cocktail parties

Biscuits
Swiss cheese
Ham
SPREAD:
2 sticks butter, softened
2 Tablespoons poppy seed
2 small onions or 1 large onion
5 heaping teaspoons prepared
mustard

Blend spread ingredients in blender until smooth. Refrigerate at least 24 hours. Split biscuits, spread with mixture and top with Swiss cheese and thin sliced ham. Seal in foil and bake at 350° until cheese melts, about 5 minutes. For microwave heat 20 small biscuits covered with paper towel for 1 minute. To freeze, make biscuits and spread them ahead of time. Freeze and reheat as needed. Variation: put mix on lengthwise split French bread. Add ham and cheese and take on a picnic.

Mrs. J. W. Mullen

Baked Oysters Beach House

2 Tablespoons butter
¼ cup chopped green onions
⅛ cup chopped white onions
½ cup sliced fresh mushrooms
⅛ cup diced, peeled tomatoes
½ cup flour
2 cups milk, heated
1 cup fish stock
1 cup white wine
1 teaspoon Worcestershire
sauce
1 touch Tabasco sauce
2 bay leaves
1 touch finely chopped garlic
Salt and white pepper
2 egg yolks
½ cup cream
36 Long Island oysters on
the half shell
Hollandaise Sauce (see Index)
Parmesan cheese
Bread crumbs

Melt butter in saucepan, add chopped green and white onions and sliced mushrooms; sauté for about 3 minutes. Add tomatoes and mix well. Stir in flour. Add heated milk, fish stock and white wine, bring to a boil and stir until thick and creamy. Add other seasonings. Mix the egg yolk and cream together and stir into the sauce bringing to another boil. Remove from heat and cool. Remove oysters from shells. Spoon some sauce into empty shells and put oysters on top of the sauce. Bake at 350° for approximately 3-4 minutes. Remove from oven; cover with Hollandaise Sauce and sprinkle with Parmesan cheese and bread crumbs. Broil until browned to perfection. Serve with lemon wedges and Worcestershire sauce. Bon Appetit! 6 servings

The Abbey Restaurant
Atlanta, Georgia

Oysters Lafitte

4 Tablespoons butter
1 cup chopped cooked shrimp
2 cups chopped mushrooms
¼ cup chopped green onion
¼ cup snipped parsley
1 clove garlic, minced
2 dozen fresh oysters
½ teaspoon salt
Dash cayenne
1 cup light cream
¼ cup flour
½ cup dry white wine
24 oyster shells or 8 coquille
    shells
Rock salt
⅓ cup fine bread crumbs
2 Tablespoons butter
⅛ teaspoon paprika

Melt butter; add shrimp, mushrooms, onion, parsley and garlic. Cook 1 minute. Drain oysters and set aside; reserve liquid and add enough water to make ¾ cup. Add liquid, salt and cayenne to shrimp mixture; bring to simmer for 1 minute. Combine cream and flour and add to mixture. Stir in wine. Cook until thickened. Arrange oyster shells in shallow pan on bed of rock salt. Place 1 oyster in each oyster shell or 3 oysters in each coquille shell. Spoon sauce over oysters. Combine bread crumbs and butter and sprinkle over oysters. Sprinkle paprika on top and bake at 450° for 10-12 minutes. May be prepared in advance and refrigerated until baking time. Serve as a first course with a spinach salad and a light wine such as Vouvray or a chenin blanc. 6 servings

Susan M. Morley

What's This?

4 dozen oysters, washed
    and drained
1 cup chili sauce
2 Tablespoons Worcestershire
    sauce
2 Tablespoons chopped
    green pepper
12 slices uncooked bacon,
    chopped and cooked until
    half done
1 cup grated Parmesan cheese

Place oysters in a saucepan and heat. Drain again. Put oysters in casserole dish and cover with sauces and pepper. Bake in oven at 350° until oysters puff, about 20 minutes, and until pepper is soft. Remove from oven and sprinkle with bacon and cheese. Return to oven and cook 10 more minutes or until bacon is done. Serve hot with crackers. May be prepared the day before serving or may be frozen.

Carolyn S. Brooks (Mrs. John L.)

Peppers and Anchovies

8 sweet peppers
20 flat anchovy filets
Salt, ground pepper and
    oregano
3 Tablespoons capers
4 cloves garlic, peeled and
    crushed
Olive oil

Broil peppers until skins swell and are charred on all sides. Peel while still hot. Cut peppers into strips 1½-2 inches wide and remove pulp, core and seeds. Pat dry with towel. Choose a shallow dish (for 4-5 layers). Arrange layer of pepper on bottom, lay 4-5 anchovies over them and a touch of salt, plenty of pepper, and a pinch of oregano; repeat the layers. Add olive oil to top layer. Refrigerate at least 4 hours but bring to room temperature just before serving. Note: If refrigerated for more than 24 hours, remove garlic.
4-6 servings

Decie Nygaard (Mrs. W.F.)

Fresh Stuffed Pepper Strips

1 8-ounce package cream
    cheese, softened
6 ounces blue cheese
¼ cup chopped parsley
¼ cup chopped chives
1 large pimiento, chopped
Salt and pepper to taste
2 Tablespoons soft butter
3 green peppers

Combine cream cheese, blue cheese, parsley, chives, pimiento, butter, salt and pepper. Mix until smooth. Cut peppers in half lengthwise and clean out. Cut in half lengthwise again; fill strips with cheese mixture and chill until firm. Cut in half lengthwise again and serve on relish tray or fresh vegetable platter. 24 servings

Judy L. O'Shea (Mrs. Timothy)

Ripe Olive Pâté

1 medium onion, chopped
1 stick butter
1 cup chopped ripe olives
3 Tablespoons cream cheese
Dash thyme
Black pepper (few turns of
   grinder)

Cook onions in butter until soft. Place in blender or food processor. Add other ingredients and blend until smooth. Transfer to a small, greased mold and chill until firm. Serve with thin slices of French bread or on unsalted crackers. 1 cup

Emy E. Blair (Mrs. H. Duane)

Liver Pâté

1 (1-ounce) package unflavored
   gelatin
1 (10-ounce) can consommé,
   undiluted
1 large (4-ounce) can Liverwurst
1 (8-ounce) package cream
   cheese
1 Tablespoon Worcestershire
   sauce
3 Tablespoons rum
1 Tablespoon lemon juice

Moisten gelatin with a little water. Add to consommé and heat until dissolved. Barely cover bottom of 4-6 cup mold with consommé mixture. Refrigerate until set. Put remaining ingredients in blender. Blend. Pour over set gelatin. Chill until set. Unmold when ready to serve.
8-12 servings

Kenney K. Linton (Mrs. Sidney E.)

Hot Beef Spread

1 package dried beef, chopped
1 (8-ounce) package cream
   cheese, softened
2 teaspoons minced onion
½ teaspoon garlic salt
¼ teaspoon pepper
½ pint sour cream
2 Tablespoons butter, melted
½ teaspoon salt
½ cup chopped pecans

Mix first six ingredients together and spread in a lightly greased 9-inch pie pan or casserole dish. Top with a mixture of melted butter, salt and pecans. Bake at 325° for 20 minutes. Serve warm from a fancy pie server or from chafing dish with plain crackers.

Ann T. McCrory (Mrs. Charles O.)

Sausage Strudel

1 pound sweet Italian sausage
1 pound mushrooms (duxelles)
1 (8-ounce) package cream
   cheese, cut in small pieces
Chopped shallots (optional)
¼ cup butter
1 package frozen strudel or
   filo dough
Melted butter
Dried bread crumbs

Remove sausage from casing; scramble and brown. Drain off all fat. For duxelles: chop mushrooms very fine; sauté in ¼ cup butter slowly until all liquid has evaporated. Add shallots if desired. Prepare strudel dough according to package directions. Use 2 sheets to a strudel roll, each one buttered and bread crumbed. Recipe makes 2 rolls. (Work quickly with filo dough as it dries out very fast). Spread sausage, mushrooms and pieces of cream cheese over two-thirds of the length of the strudel dough. Roll up with empty strudel end on the top. Bake at 350° until lightly browned, about 35 minutes. Cut with sharp knife, 8 pieces per roll for hors d'oeuvres, or 4 per roll for luncheon. May be frozen. Prepare as for cooking and then freeze. May take a few minutes longer to brown from frozen state. This is a spicy dish and goes well with green salad. If used as luncheon main dish, treat as you would any Italian food. It does need a plate and fork when served as an appetizer.

Karen Consolini
New York City

HINT

To keep parsley fresh longer, leave a little moisture on it after washing, and store in a closed jar in the refrigerator.

Salmon Sour Cream Spread

SALMON:
16 ounces chilled poached salmon, flaked, boned and skinned
¼ cup mayonnaise
2 Tablespoons lemon juice
¼ teaspoon garlic salt
¼ teaspoon dried dill weed
¼ teaspoon Worcestershire sauce
⅛ teaspoon cayenne
SPREAD:
1 cup sour cream
½ cup finely chopped zucchini
2 Tablespoons thinly sliced green onion
2 Tablespoons drained capers

Drain salmon; combine with mayonnaise, lemon juice, garlic salt, dill weed, Worcestershire sauce and cayenne. Place in serving dish. Combine sour cream, zucchini, green onion and capers. Place in adjacent serving dish. Chill until ready to serve. To serve, spread salmon mix on crisp bread or water wafer; top with sour cream spread.

Yield; 1¾ cups salmon mixture
1¼ cups sour cream spread

Susan M. Morley

Scallops Seviche

26 ounces scallops
6½ whole limes
6 ounces fresh chopped onion
6 ounces chopped green pepper
2 sprigs parsley, chopped
1 Tablespoon oil
2 teaspoons salt
2 teaspoons pepper

Allow scallops to reach room temperature. Squeeze juice from limes over scallops and allow scallops to marinate for at least 2 hours in lime juice. Drain juice from scallops and add chopped onion, pepper, parsley and oil. Season with salt and pepper. May be used also as an entrée.

The Peasant Restaurants
Atlanta, Georgia

Shrimp Alliade

1 pound peeled cooked shrimp
12-14 walnuts, finely chopped
3 cloves garlic, crushed
¾ cup oil
1 Tablespoon lemon juice
½ teaspoon salt
2 Tablespoons chopped fresh parsley

Blend all ingredients and chill several hours before serving. This may be served on lettuce cups as a first course or used as an appetizer. If serving on lettuce cups, drain oil. 8 servings

Elise M. Griffin

Cold Curried Shrimp

4 Tablespoons butter
1 clove garlic, crushed
¼ cup apple, minced
¼ cup onion, minced
2 Tablespoons flour
1 cup stewed tomatoes
2 teaspoons curry powder
Salt and pepper to taste
Mayonnaise
1 Tablespoon lemon juice
2 pounds shrimp, cooked
    and peeled
Thinly sliced cucumbers for
    garnish
Slivered almonds for garnish

Sauté garlic, apple and onion in butter until onion is golden. Remove garlic. Stir in flour and add tomatoes, curry powder, salt and pepper. Bring sauce to a boil and strain it through a fine sieve. Cool. Measure the sauce and add an equal amount of mayonnaise and the lemon juice. Fold in shrimp and chill for 3 hours. Serve on a glass plate garnished with a ring of cucumber slices and sprinkled with almonds.

This amount of sauce is enough for 4 pounds of shrimp.
6 servings

Pamela T. Marcus

Shrimp Arnaud

6 Tablespoons olive oil
2 Tablespoons wine or
    tarragon vinegar
4 Tablespoons Zatarain's
    Creole mustard
½ teaspoon salt
½ teaspoon white pepper
2 Tablespoons finely chopped
    celery
2 Tablespoons finely chopped
    onion
2 Tablespoons finely chopped
    parsley
Horseradish to taste (optional)
Cooked and peeled shrimp

Mix ingredients and blend well. Marinate cooked and peeled shrimp several hours or overnight in prepared sauce. Add horseradish if desired. Three recipes will make enough sauce for 5 pounds of shrimp.

Josephine C. Fleming (Mrs. Tom)

Shrimp Toast or "Kogi Chunkol"
This is a delicious Phillipino delicacy

5 ounces water chestnuts, drained
1 pound raw shrimp
¼ cup chopped green onion tops
2 teaspoons salt
1 teaspoon sugar
1 egg, beaten
15 slices very thin white bread
Breadcrumbs

Purée water chestnuts, shrimp and onions. Add salt, sugar and egg. Spread paste on one side of each bread slice. Sprinkle with crumbs. Cut each slice into 4 triangles. Heat 1 inch of oil to "hot" (not smoking) and fry each triangle, shrimp side down, then brown on other side, (approximately 2 minutes on each side). Drain. May be frozen before serving; defrost, reheat at 400° for 5 minutes. Yield: 60

Susan Morley

Shrimp Spread

2 cups finely diced shrimp, cooked and deveined
½ cup softened butter
2 Tablespoons lemon juice
1 teaspoon salt
¼ teaspoon paprika
1 teaspoon Worcestershire sauce
½ teaspoon prepared mustard

Mix all ingredients by hand until well blended. Place in small shallow bowl with butter spreader; serve with crackers, toast rounds or bread squares. May be frozen. 2 cups

Josephine D. Weekes (Mrs. John W.)

Shrimp Romanoff
From Armando's Restaurant in Acapulco, Mexico

1 cup mayonnaise
¼ cup catsup
4 teaspoons white wine
¾ teaspoon Maggi liquid seasoning
2 pounds shrimp, cooked and shelled

Place all ingredients in bowl and blend until smooth. Refrigerate. When ready to serve, arrange boiled shrimp (which have been refrigerated) on lettuce on individual plates and spoon sauce liberally over shrimp. Sauce may be prepared several days ahead and refrigerated. 8 servings

Marceline T. May (Mrs. Earle B., Jr.)

Shrimp Mold

1 pound cooked shrimp
2 cups mayonnaise
1 small onion, grated
Juice of one lemon
2 Tablespoons horseradish
2 envelopes unflavored gelatin
½ cup water
Few drops of red food coloring
    to make mixture light pink

Sprinkle gelatin in water and place in double boiler to dissolve. Cool. Combine with remaining ingredients. Pour into mold. Chill. Serve with crackers. Should be prepared the day before serving for best results.

Ann T. McCrory (Mrs. Charles O.)

Shrimp Ernie
From the Olde College Inn in Houston, Texas

2 pounds raw jumbo shrimp,
    shelled and deveined
1 pint salad oil
1 teaspoon salt
1 clove garlic, minced
4 Tablespoons catsup
1 teaspoon paprika

Marinate shrimp in the remaining ingredients overnight. When ready to serve, place shrimp in shallow pan and pour some sauce over (do not cover shrimp). Broil 3-5 minutes each side. Serve from chafing dish as appetizer. 16-20 Shrimp

Elise M. Griffin

Toasted Finger Rolls

1 sliced loaf fresh bread
1 can mushroom soup
1 pound bacon

Remove crust from bread and spread with undiluted soup. Do not use a heavy coat of soup. Roll bread from corner to corner and wrap a piece of bacon (usually half a slice) around each roll, holding in place with a toothpick. Place rolls on ungreased cookie sheet and bake at 325° until golden brown, about 35 minutes. Serve with soup or salad or use as an appetizer. May be frozen. 8 servings

Beth M. Johnston (Mrs. J. Gibson)

Zucchini and Carrot Appetizer

Easy to prepare when done in a food processor
Wonderful for calorie counters

1 medium zucchini
2 Tablespoons oil
1½ teaspoons wine vinegar
or lemon juice
Dash salt
Dash freshly ground pepper
Mixed herbs (optional)
2 medium carrots

Install medium slicer and feed zucchini into tube. Remove sliced zucchini and set aside. Put oil, vinegar or lemon juice, salt, pepper and mixed herbs in work bowl. Peel carrots and cut them into 2½-inch diagonal lengths. Lay flat in feed tube and shred. Toss carrots lightly with dressing. Mound shredded carrots on sliced zucchini and chill. 6 servings

Martha H. Whitehead (Mrs. Richard)

Baked Cheese Sandwiches

2 cups grated sharp cheese
¼ cup butter
¼ cup mayonnaise
¼ cup minced onions
¼ cup chopped pimentos
Dash of tabasco sauce
12 slices sandwich bread
with crust removed

Combine first six ingredients. Spread mixture on one side of bread slices. Roll tightly and place close together on greased baking sheet. Bake at 350° for 10 minutes. Serve hot. Serve with salad for lunch or as a finger food.
Serves 12

Linda Hightower (Mrs. Charles R.)

MICROWAVE HINT ■■■

Dry fresh herbs between 2 layers of paper towel or napkin until they can be crumbled.

Bourbon Slush

2 regular size tea bags
1 cup boiling water
½ cup sugar
3½ cups water
1 (6 ounce) can frozen orange
  juice concentrate, thawed
½ cup bourbon
1 (6 ounce) can frozen
  lemonade concentrate,
  thawed

Steep tea bags in boiling water 2 to 3 minutes; remove tea bags. Stir in sugar. Add remaining ingredients; mix until sugar is dissolved. Pour into freezer trays; freeze until firm. Remove from freezer about 10 minutes before serving. Spoon into cocktail glasses; garnish with lemon wedges if desired. Keep unused portions in freezer. 1½ quarts

Beverly W. Bibent (Mrs. Maury J.)
Cincinnati, Ohio

Strawberry Daiquiri
For strawberry lovers!

1 pound package frozen
  sweetened strawberries
4 ounces light rum
4 ounces (Arrow) strawberry
  liqueur
1 capful lemon juice
  concentrate
Enough ice to fill blender

Put all ingredients in blender. Add ice and blend at high speed. This can be frozen for future use. 4 servings

Sue C. Smith (Mrs. Douglass C.)

Instant Hot Chocolate
Very creamy
Kids love having this available

1 one pound box Nestle's Quik
1 (8-quart) package non-fat dry
  milk
1 (7-ounce) jar powdered
  non-dairy creamer
⅔ cup sifted confectioners
  sugar

Mix all ingredients together and store in jars. To serve, fill cup halfway with mixture and add hot water.

Kimpy Edge (Mrs. J. Dexter, Jr.)

HINT

For large parties, use washing machine to store ice, cool beer, etc.

Café Glacé
(Iced Coffee)

¾ cup sugar
1½ cups milk
1 teaspoon vanilla extract
1½ cups cold coffee
¾ cup heavy cream
Unsweetened whipped cream

Combine sugar and milk in a saucepan and bring to a boil, stirring until sugar is dissolved. Remove from heat; add vanilla extract and let stand until cold. Combine milk mixture, coffee and cream, mixing well; then pour into a metal pan. Freeze until hard. Put in blender or food processor and process until mushy. (Thawing slightly will make this process simpler.) Pour into tall glasses. Top with spirals of whipped cream. Serve immediately. 4-6 servings

Lynn H. Barnes

Mexican Mocha

¼ cup cocoa
3 Tablespoons sugar
⅟₁₆ teaspoon salt
⅓ cup water
3 cups milk
2 Tablespoons kahlua
Whipped cream, flavored with
   dash kahlua

In a saucepan, mix together cocoa, sugar, salt and water. Bring almost to a boil and simmer gently 2 minutes, stirring constantly. Add the milk and immediately lower heat. Keep over low heat, stirring gently until heated through. Take off heat and stir in kahlua. Serve in 4 cups or mugs topped with whipped cream. 4 servings

Sandra R. Pritchett (Mrs. Edwin P.)

Irish Coffee

1½ teaspoons sugar
3 Tablespoons hot coffee
¼ cup Irish whiskey
Hot coffee
3 Tablespoons whipped cream
Nutmeg

Place silver spoon in Irish coffee glass or stemmed glass to absorb heat. Add sugar and 3 Tablespoons hot coffee to glass and stir. Add whiskey and fill glass to within 1 inch of top with hot coffee. Float whipped cream on coffee; sprinkle with nutmeg. 1 serving

Jeanine C. Andrews (Mrs. Edward B.)

Kahlua
Serve as an after dinner liqueur
or over vanilla ice cream with whipped cream, nuts
and shaved chocolate

2 rounded Tablespoons instant
  coffee
1 cup water
3 cups white sugar
1 vanilla bean, finely chopped
1 fifth vodka

Boil coffee, water and sugar. Stir until completely dissolved. Cool completely. Add finely chopped vanilla bean. Add vodka. Cork in airtight vessel. Store in a cool place for 30 days.

Joy K. Tyler (Mrs. John P.)

Lime Cooler
Delicious at a springtime luncheon

2 (6-ounce) cans frozen
  limeade, partially thawed
4 cups water
½ cup lemon juice
1 quart chilled ginger ale or
  club soda
1½ cups Vodka (optional)
Pineapple slices or mint sprigs

Place limeade and water in blender and blend at medium speed until frothy. Stir in lemon juice. Transfer into container and chill at least one hour. When ready to serve, add soda and vodka and shake. Garnish each glass with a mint sprig or a twisted pineapple ring
12 8 ounce servings

Decie Nygaard (Mrs. W. F.)

Ethel Mincey's Punch
A sweet punch especially good in summer

1 gallon water
5 pounds sugar
3 large cans pineapple juice
1 large bottle lemon juice
3 Tablespoons or 2 small
  bottles almond flavoring
2 quart bottles ginger ale

Mix all ingredients except ginger ale which is added just before serving. Fill punch bowl about half full of crushed ice. This will serve 50 (5-ounce) cups. 50 servings

Claire W. Johnson (Mrs. A. Sidney)

HINT

Freeze crystal clear ice block for punch bowl by using a mold and distilled water. Add strawberries, flowers or greenery if desired.

Bees Knees

1 ounce lemon juice
1 ounce honey
1 jigger gin
1 teaspoon cherry juice
Ginger ale

Mix equal parts (1 ounce each) of lemon juice and honey. Shake well. Chill. Add one jigger of gin and one teaspoon of cherry juice to above mixture. Stir well, add ginger ale and crushed ice to fill a 10 or 12 ounce glass. 1 serving

Margaret Westbrook (Mrs. William L.)

Bola
A German punch

2 bottles white wine (Chablis or sauterne)
1 bottle champagne
1 pint strawberries, cleaned and hulled

Marinate strawberries in white wine all day. Add champagne just before serving. 20 servings

Jerry P. Connor (Mrs. Paul)

Sangria

2 peaches or nectarines, sliced
½ pint fresh strawberries, hulled
2 Tablespoons sugar
2 Tablespoons brandy
2 Tablespoons orange flavored liqueur
1 bottle (⅘ quart) rose wine
Mint sprigs if desired

Place peaches, strawberries, sugar, brandy and liqueur in pitcher or bowl. Let stand at room temperature 30 minutes. Stir in wine. Refrigerate covered at least 4 hours. Garnish with mint sprigs. 4 servings

White Sangria

1 large orange, thinly sliced and seeded
1 large lemon, thinly sliced and seeded
1 large lime, thinly sliced and seeded
1 cup Triple Sec or Grand Marnier
½ cup sugar
2 fifths dry white wine, chilled
1 quart club soda, chilled

At least eight hours before serving, mix fruit and Triple Sec in a plastic bag or container. Refrigerate until serving. Before serving, mix fruit and sugar in punch bowl or large pitcher. Add wine and club soda. Do not add ice. 20 servings

Lynn H. Barnes

Hot Cranberry Cheer

1½ quarts cranberry juice
2 quarts unsweetened apple
 juice
½ cup dark brown sugar
½ teaspoon salt
4 cinnamon sticks
1½ teaspoons cloves

Put juices, sugar and salt in coffee pot. Put cinnamon sticks and cloves in top of coffee maker. Juices will brew through spices as beverage perks. Note: All ingredients can be heated slowly in large pot and simmered about 2 hours. 8-10 servings

Wassail
For holiday cheer!

½ gallon apple cider (8 cups)
4 cups cranberry juice
1 (6-ounce) can frozen
 lemonade concentrate
1 (6-ounce) can frozen orange
 juice concentrate
4 sticks cinnamon
1½ teaspoons whole cloves
1½ teaspoons whole allspice

Simmer all ingredients for 1-2 hours. Cinnamon, cloves and allspice can be tied in a cheesecloth bag and removed before serving or the wassail should be strained before serving. Serve hot in mugs. Dark rum or bourbon may be added before serving or pitchers of rum and bourbon could be passed to be added individually.

Wassail can be made 2 or 3 days in advance, stored in refrigerator and heated before serving. 14 servings

Myrick L. King (Mrs. David L.G., Jr.)

Hot Spiced Wine

½ cup sugar
1 cup water
10 cloves
3 cinnamon sticks
¼ teaspoon allspice
1 orange, sliced
1 lemon, sliced
1 (46-ounce) can pineapple
 juice
1 fifth Burgundy

Combine all ingredients except Burgundy in a pot on the stove or a crock pot (3½ quart size or larger). Cover and heat for at least 1 hour, slowly as in a crock pot. Fifteen minutes before serving, add Burgundy. Heat slowly and serve in mugs or other heat proof cups. 12 servings

Barbara R. Schuyler (Mrs. Lambert, Jr.)

Raspberry Apéritif

1 (10-ounce) package frozen
   raspberries
3 ounces orange liqueur
1 bottle champagne, chilled

Purée and strain raspberries, saving juice, discarding seeds. Chill until very cold. Add liqueur and chilled champagne. Serve in chilled, stemmed glasses. For punch, add 1 bottle ginger ale.
4-6 servings

Kir or Chablis Cassis

A French apéritif to substitute for the
"before dinner cocktail"

1 Fifth of California Chablis
2 ounces creme de cassis
   (black currant liqueur)
Lemon peel

From a fifth bottle of California Chablis, remove 1 or 2 ounces of the wine and add 2 ounces of creme de cassis to the bottle. A corkscrew of lemon peel can be added to the bottle or small strip of lemon peel can be added to each glass. Shake the bottle gently and chill. Serve "straight up" or "on the rocks". This can also be served from a punch bowl for a crowd.

Sarah Looper (Mrs. Joseph W.)

Soups

Purée of Asparagus Soup

1½-2 pounds asparagus or
   3 (15-ounce) cans
   asparagus spears
¼ cup butter
½ cup chopped onion
4 cups chicken broth
⅛ teaspoon nutmeg
Salt and pepper, to taste
Sour cream for garnish
Chopped toasted almonds
   (optional)
Chopped shrimp (optional)

If fresh asparagus is used, cut off upper half and cut into ½-inch pieces. Melt butter in large skillet or Dutch oven; add onions and cook 3 minutes. Add asparagus and cook 1 minute. Add 2 cups broth and seasonings. Cover and simmer until tender. Put in blender until smooth. Chill several hours. Add rest of chilled broth. Mix well and serve in chilled bowls topped with a Tablespoon of sour cream. Garnish with chopped toasted almonds or chopped shrimp, if desired. Variation: For an excellent cold dip, add a carton of sour cream to chilled asparagus purée and omit last 2 cups broth. Serve with raw vegetables. 4-6 servings

Sallie B. Smith (Mrs. Tommy W.)

Cauliflower Ham Chowder

2 cups cauliflower, sliced
1¾ cups chicken broth, or
   1 (13-ounce) can
1 cup light cream
1 can cream of potato soup
¼ cup water
2 Tablespoons cornstarch
¼ teaspoon white pepper
2 cups ham, cooked and diced
Parsley for garnish

Cook cauliflower in chicken broth in large covered saucepan until almost tender—about 10 minutes. Do not drain. In a mixing bowl, gradually stir cream into potato soup. Blend water, cornstarch and pepper; stir into potato mixture. Pour over cauliflower and cook, stirring often, until thick and bubbly. Stir in ham; simmer over low heat for 10 minutes. Garnish with parsley. 4-6 servings

Barbara Ender (Mrs. Steven)

Cream of Broccoli Soup

1 small onion, thinly sliced
1 green onion (white portion only) thinly sliced
1 small stalk celery, sliced (no leaves)
1 Tablespoon butter
½ cup water
2 teaspoons salt
Dash cayenne pepper
2 Tablespoons uncooked rice
2 cups chicken broth
2 cups cooked broccoli, coarsely cut (do not salt broccoli while cooking; reserve cooking liquid)
½ cup cream or milk

Place onion, green onion, celery, butter and water in 2-quart saucepan; simmer slowly for about 2 minutes over medium heat. Add salt, cayenne, rice and 1 cup broth, and simmer for 15 minutes. DO NOT BOIL. Pour broth-onion mixture into blender or food processor. Blend until liquified. Return to saucepan. Put cooked broccoli and remaining cup of broth in blender or food processor a little at a time, cover and blend until broccoli is liquified. If mixture becomes too thick to flow, add broccoli cooking liquid to thin. Add broccoli to onion mixture in saucepan. Add cream or milk. Heat (DO NOT BOIL) and serve. May be prepared up to 2 days in advance. 4 servings

Billie E. Bothwell (Mrs. Eugene L., Jr.)

Shrimp Chowder

4 large onions, peeled and sliced
¼ cup margarine
1 cup boiling water
6 medium potatoes, pared and cubed
1 Tablespoon salt
½ teaspoon seasoned pepper
1½ quarts milk
2 cups (½ pound) grated sharp Cheddar cheese
2 pounds raw shrimp, shelled and deveined
3 Tablespoons snipped parsley for garnish

Melt margarine in heavy Dutch oven; sauté onion slices until tender. Add boiling water, potatoes, salt and seasoned pepper. Simmer covered for 20 minutes until potatoes are tender. Do not drain. Meanwhile, heat milk with cheese in saucepan over a very low temperature until cheese has melted and milk is hot. Do not boil. Add shrimp to potatoes and cook until they turn pink—about 3 minutes. Add hot milk and cheese mixture. Heat, but do not boil. Sprinkle with parsley before serving. 8 servings

Pat Adams (Mrs. P. H.)

New England Style Clam Chowder

I researched from 20 to 30 recipes for clam chowder, none of which contained all of the following, but every ingredient below was in at least one. Most did not have green onions, garlic, pimiento, chicken broth, parsley or bacon. I think they add a great deal.

2 slices bacon
3 Tablespoons butter
1 cup chopped onion,
  (½ regular and ½ green onions)
1 cup chopped celery, heart and leaves
1 cup chopped carrots
½ cup chopped green pepper
1 clove garlic, chopped
3 Tablespoons flour
3 cups hot chicken stock, or 3 heaping teaspoons instant bouillon dissolved in 3 cups hot water
1½ cups potatoes, cubed
1 teaspoon salt
¼ teaspoon white pepper
1 (10 ounce) can whole baby clams and juice
2 Tablespoons butter
2 Tablespoons flour
2 cups half and half
1 whole pimiento, chopped
3 Tablespoons fresh parsley (or 1 teaspoon dried)

Chop and fry bacon. Add 3 Tablespoons butter to bacon and grease; add onions, carrots, celery, garlic and green pepper; saute a few minutes. Add 3 Table-spoons flour, stir awhile (this will become very dry), and slowly add hot chicken stock. Cook about 10 minutes; add salt, pepper, potatoes, clams and juice. Cook 10 minutes. In another pot or double boiler, make a roux with 2 Tablespoons butter and 2 Table-spoons flour. Add 2 cups half and half to make a fairly thick cream sauce. Blend in pimiento and parsley. Bring almost to boil; let cool. Combine both mixtures and store overnight in refrigerator. Before serving heat almost to boiling. If too thick, add a little half and half to thin.

Frank B. Roberts

Billy's Seafood Chowder

4 large onions, chopped (2)
5 large potatoes, diced (2)
2 sticks butter (1)
2 pounds filleted trout
    (¾ pound)
4 pounds cooked, peeled
    shrimp (1½ pounds)
4 pints oysters and juice
    (1½ pints)
4 (8-ounce) bottles clam
    juice (2)
2 pints crabmeat (1)
Salt and pepper to taste
4 quarts half and half (1)
6 quarts milk (2; add more later
    if too thick)

The numbers to the side in parentheses make less than 2 gallons.

In large skillet saute onions in one stick butter until clear; add more butter and cook fish until tender. In very large pot, boil potatoes gently until tender but not mushy. Drain. To potatoes add sautéed mixture, oysters, crabmeat, clam juice, cream and milk. Heat slowly on lowest heat until boiling point, (do not let boil) stirring frequently, with wooden spoon. This takes at least 1 hour. This chowder will keep 4-5 days in refrigerator. Reheat on lowest heat and stir frequently. If sticking occurs, change to another pot. It is best made in a large quantity but, since this is very expensive, use the numbers to the side for 1 meal. 4 gallons

Freddie Fleming (Mrs. William T.)

Clam Bisque
Can be doubled easily

1 (7-ounce) can minced clams
2 cups milk
½ teaspoon dill weed
½ teaspoon Beau Monde
    seasoning
1 Tablespoon butter
2½ teaspoons cornstarch
1 Tablespoon cold water

Drain clams, reserving juice. Mix clam juice, milk and dill weed in heavy saucepan. Heat on medium until boiling, add clams, Beau Monde seasoning, butter, and simmer 5 minutes. Mix cornstarch and water, stir into hot bisque, keep warm. Sprinkle with dill weed for garnish when serving. 2-3 servings

Winnie R. Goodman (Mrs. James)

Chicken Soup With Meatballs
This interesting soup freezes beautifully

1 (2 pound) stewing chicken
4 cups water
2½ teaspoons salt
Freshly ground black pepper
¼ teaspoon basil
1 bay leaf
¼ teaspoon mace
1 clove garlic, crushed
½ pound white onions, sliced; or pearl onions
5 small carrots, sliced
1 Tablespoon chopped parsley
1 Tablespoon chopped celery leaves
MEATBALLS:
1 cup ground pork
1 egg
1 slice white bread, crumbled
2½ Tablespoons flour
½ teaspoon salt
Freshly ground black pepper

Simmer chicken 1½ hours in water, salt, pepper, basil, bay leaf, mace and garlic. Remove chicken. Strain broth and skim fat. Bring broth to boil and add onions, carrots, parsley and celery. Simmer gently 10 minutes.

Meatballs: Mix ingredients to form meatballs ¾ inch in diameter. Add to soup and simmer 35 minutes. Meanwhile, skin and bone chicken, returning meat, cut in bite-sized pieces, to soup.
4-6 servings

Joan Roes (Mrs. Hans)

Chicken Velvet Soup
Divinely smooth and rich!

6 Tablespoons butter
6 Tablespoons flour
½ cup milk
½ cup light cream
3 cups chicken broth
1 cup finely chopped cooked chicken
Dash pepper

Melt butter in saucepan. Blend in flour, stirring. Remove from heat and add liquid ingredients. Return to heat and cook, stirring constantly, until mixture thickens and comes to a boil; reduce heat. Stir in chicken and pepper. Return to boiling and serve immediately.
5 servings

Pamela T. Marcus

Green Pea and Crabmeat Soup

1 Tablespoon butter
1 small onion, minced
1 can green pea soup
1 can beef consommé
1 can white crabmeat
1 (3 ounce) can sliced
    mushrooms
⅔ soup can water
⅓ cup sherry
Salt and pepper to taste

Sauté onion in butter. Put onion and remaining ingredients into a saucepan and cook over medium heat for 5-10 minutes. Serve hot. May be prepared the day before serving.

Myrick L. King (Mrs. David L.G., Jr.)

Hangover Soup

3 cans tomatoes, chopped
    drained
1 cup chopped celery
1 large cucumber, chopped
1 green pepper, chopped
1 large onion, chopped
3 cloves garlic, crushed
2 large (46 ounce) cans V-8 juice
½ cup olive oil
½ cup vinegar
1 teaspoon basil
1 teaspoon curry powder
Salt and pepper, to taste
Worcestershire sauce, to taste

Mix ingredients together and taste to adjust seasonings. Keep refrigerated and serve cold. Note: Recipe may be halved.

Jennifer W. Clements (Mrs. Harold A.)

HINT

Too much salt in the soup—add a pinch of brown sugar.

Lentil Soup
Good hearty winter soup

1 pound dried lentils, washed
¼ cup oil
3 cups diced ham
½ pound Polish sausage cut
   in ½ inch slices
2 large onions, chopped
1 clove garlic, crushed
2 cups celery with leaves,
   chopped
1 tomato, peeled and chopped
3 quarts water
½ teaspoon Tabasco sauce
1½ teaspoons salt
1 (10-ounce) package frozen
   chopped spinach, thawed

Soak lentils in water to cover overnight. Heat oil in large soup kettle and sauté ham, sausage, onion and garlic. Add celery, tomato, lentils, water, tabasco and salt. Simmer for 2 hours until lentils are tender. Add spinach and cook for 10 minutes. This soup freezes very well. Serve with a fruit salad and toasted English muffins with cheese. 4 quarts

Mrs. Elsie B. Manry
Tampa, Florida

Navy Bean Soup

1 pound navy beans
1 ham bone with lots of ham,
   fat trimmed off
1 medium onion, chopped
2 ribs celery with leaves,
   chopped
1 bay leaf
1 carrot, finely chopped
3 cups chicken bouillon
8 slices bacon, fried and
   chopped
1 teaspoon seasoned salt
1 teaspoon salt (start with less)
1 potato, peeled and cut into
   ¼ inch cubes
½ cup catsup

Soak beans overnight, or bring to boil for 2 minutes and set aside for 1 hour, covered. Return to heat, add ham bone, onion, celery, carrot, bay leaf and chicken bouillon. Simmer, covered, until beans are done. You may have to add some water. Take out ham bone, trim off all meat, and chop. Purée ½ of soup in blender or food processor and return to pot; add the remaining ingredients and simmer for another 15 minutes. Let cool and refrigerate overnight. If soup is too thick after refrig- eration, add milk to thin after reheating. May be frozen. 8 servings

Frank B. Roberts

Fresh Mushroom Soup

1 pound mushrooms
6 Tablespoons butter
2 cups finely chopped onion
½ teaspoon sugar
¼ cup flour
1 cup water
1¾ cup chicken broth
1 cup dry vermouth
1 teaspoon salt
⅛-¼ teaspoon pepper

Slice ⅓ of the mushrooms and finely chop the rest. Melt butter in a large saucepan. Add onions and sugar; sauté over medium heat, stirring frequently until golden— about 15 minutes. Add sliced and chopped mushrooms and sauté for 5 minutes. Stir in flour until smooth; cook for 2 minutes, stirring constantly. Pour in water and stir until smooth. Add remaining ingredients and heat to boiling, stirring constantly. Reduce heat and simmer uncovered for 10 minutes. May be prepared in advance to this point. Cover; refrigerate. To reheat, heat to boiling, cover and simmer 10 minutes. 6 servings

Carolyn B. Hoose (Mrs. Kenneth A., Jr.)

Brennan's Creole Onion Soup

8 medium onions, chopped
1½ cups butter
1¼ cups all-purpose flour
10 cans beef stock or 12 cups
   homemade beef stock
1 Tablespoon salt
½ teaspoon cayenne pepper
2 Tablespoons cream
1 egg yolk
Buttered croûtons
Parmesan cheese

Melt butter in a large soup pot; add onions and lower heat. Cook until onions are clear. Do not brown. Add flour and cook 10 minutes, stirring. Add salt and cayenne pepper. Blend in beef stock (always stirring) and bring to a full boil. Reduce heat and cook slowly for 20 minutes. Remove from heat. Beat cream and egg yolk together. Add a little hot soup to mixture, blend, then pour back into soup. If soup becomes too thick, add a little more water. To serve: pour into bowls, add croutons and sprinkle with Parmesan cheese. This soup makes a great meal served with a spinach salad and hot French bread. 12 servings or 6 luncheon servings

Nancy Kirby (Mrs. Jeff D., III)

Ertwen Soup
(Pronounced "Air-twin")
A hearty Dutch split pea soup

1 (16 ounce) package split peas
3 quarts water
2 pounds pork neck bones
   or ribs
1½ teaspoons salt
3 leeks, thinly sliced or 2
   medium yellow onions,
   sliced
1 stalk celery, chopped
3 large potatoes, cubed
Leafy tops from 1 bunch celery
2 Polish sausages, or ham, or
   frankfurters

Soak peas in water overnight. Drain and put in water with pork and salt. Simmer over low heat 3 hours. Add leeks, celery, potatoes and celery tops; simmer over low heat another 30 minutes, stirring often. Slice sausage into bite-size rings and add to soup. Simmer 10 minutes more. Serve with buttered pumpernickel bagels. 3 quarts

Joan Roes (Mrs. Hans)

Steak Soup

Leftover steak (1 pound
   approximately)
2 cups cold water
2 beef bouillon cubes
1 large onion, thinly sliced
1 cup sour cream

Cut leftover steak in small cubes; cut away any fat or bones. Cover meat with cold water, add bouillon cubes and onion and cook over low heat for 30-45 minutes. Put in blender or food processor and process until smooth. Return to pan, add sour cream and heat.

Winnie R. Goodman (Mrs. James E.)

HINT ■

To remove excess grease from soups and gravys, drop in several ice cubes; the grease will cling to the cubes and can be removed easily.

Garden Tomato Soup
The wine and spices make this soup especially tasty

6 shallots or green onions,
   peeled and sliced
1½ ounces butter
1 heaping Tablespoon flour
4 pints canned consommé or
   meat stock
1½ cups white wine
12-13 large ripe tomatoes,
   chopped
1 heaping teaspoon thyme
½ teaspoon rosemary
Sour cream or cream for
   garnish

Sauté shallots in butter until soft—about 5 minutes. Stir in flour and cook 2 minutes. Add stock, wine, tomatoes and seasonings. Cover and simmer 1 hour. Remove from heat. Process in blender or food processor until smooth. Strain through sieve or cheesecloth. Return to pan and reheat. Garnish with sour cream and serve immediately. This freezes beautifully and doubles easily. 6 servings

Vivian deKok (Mrs. Peter)

Tomato and Mushroom Soup

4 Tablespoons butter, melted
1 onion, chopped
1 cup fresh sliced mushrooms
   or 1 (4-6-ounce) can sliced
   mushrooms
1 (11-ounce) can cream of
   mushroom soup
1 Tablespoon tomato paste
1 (11 ounce) can beef
   consommé
1 (6-ounce) can Snap-E-Tom
   Tomato Cocktail juice
1 (16-ounce) can whole
   tomatoes in thick purée,
   cut up
½ cup heavy cream
2-3 Tablespoons parsley

Sauté onion in melted butter until transparent. Add sliced mushrooms to onions and sauté another minute. Add mushroom soup, tomato paste, consommé, tomato juice and tomatoes. Bring to boil and cook for a few minutes. Up to this point, the soup can be made the night before. Before serving, add cream and parsley. Add salt if needed. 8 servings

Myrick L. King (Mrs. David L. G., Jr.)

Country French Vegetable Soup

The turnip is the secret ingredient that makes this
vegetarian soup so special

1 stick butter
1½-2 cups sliced onion
1 cup sliced carrots
1 cup sliced turnips
1 cup sliced celery
1 cup sliced potatoes
1 teaspoon salt
4 cups water
1 cup heavy cream

GARNISH:
2 Tablespoons butter
1 small turnip, diced
1 carrot, diced
1 stalk celery, diced

Melt 1 stick butter in deep, heavy pot. In food processor with slicing disk or by hand, slice one vegetable at a time. Place sliced vegetables and salt in pot. Stir in butter. Cover tightly and stew over low heat for 20 minutes. In food processor with steel knife or by hand, chop the cooked vegetables and return to pot. Add water and bring to a boil. Simmer for 20 minutes. With steel knife or by hand, finely dice vegetables for garnish. Melt 2 Tablespoons butter in a saucepan. Add chopped vegetables and brown lightly. Add to soup. Add cream, adjust the seasonings and serve either hot or cold. The vegetables may be varied in quantity and type—using what is available. However onions and the turnip are a necessary part of this soup.

Cookbook Committee

Vegetable Soup with Ground Beef

1 pound lean ground beef
1 cup chopped onion
1 clove garlic, minced
1 (15 ounce) can kidney beans
1 cup sliced carrots
1 cup sliced celery
¼ cup uncooked rice
2 (16 ounce) cans stewed
    tomatoes
3½ cups water
5 beef bouillon cubes
1 Tablespoon chopped parsley
1 teaspoon salt
¼ teaspoon basil
⅛ teaspoon pepper
1 cup frozen or fresh green
    beans

Cook beef in skillet with onion and garlic until browned. Drain off fat. Combine all ingredients except beans (if they are frozen), and place in a soup pot or crock pot. Cover and cook on low heat 2-3 hours on range or 8 hours in crock pot. Add frozen beans during last hour of cooking. Note: If crisper vegetables are desired, cook meat, spices and liquid ingredients adding vegetables toward the end of the cooking time. 8 servings

Pamela T. Marcus

Consommé with Sour Cream
An elegant change of pace for hot weather entertaining

2 cans consommé madrilène
1 cup sour cream
1 Tablespoon lemon juice
2 Tablespoons chives
Lemon twists for garnish

Beat all ingredients except lemon twists with a rotary beater to blend. Chill, covered, 3 hours. Garnish each cup of soup with a lemon twist. 4 servings

Cookbook Committee

Chilled Cucumber Yogurt Soup

3-4 cucumbers
4 cups chicken stock
2 Tablespoons minced scallion
½ cup chopped celery
½ teaspoon dried dillweed
½ teaspoon dried mint leaves
1 teaspoon grated lemon rind
2 cups plain yogurt
Minced parsley

Peel cucumbers, cut into halves and remove seeds. Dice enough to make 3 cups. Bring chicken stock to a boil, add cucumbers, scallion, celery, dill-weed and mint. Simmer for 10 minutes. Cool: mix in a blender or food processor until smooth. Stir in lemon rind and yogurt. Chill for 3-4 hours. Sprinkle each serving with parsley. 6 servings

Cookbook Committee

Carrot Vichyssoise
This beautifully colored soup is from the
Four Seasons Restaurant in New York

3 cups chicken stock
2 cups peeled, diced boiling
    potatoes
1¼ cups sliced carrots
1 leek, sliced (white part only)
1 cup cream
1 teaspoon salt
Dash of white pepper
Dash of nutmeg
Shredded raw carrot for
    garnish

Place stock, potatoes, carrots and leek in a saucepan, bring to a boil and simmer until vegetables are tender, about 25 minutes. In a food processor or blender, purée mixture, half at a time. Pour into a bowl and add cream and seasonings. Chill. Serve cold. Garnish with shredded carrot. 4 servings

Jane S. Boyd (Mrs. Benjamin)

Chilled Strawberry Soup

2 quarts ripe strawberries
Juice of 1 lemon
3 cups water
¾-1 cup sugar
2 Tablespoons minute tapioca
1 cup sweet white wine

Clean and crush strawberries; add lemon juice. Cover with water; add sugar and tapioca. Boil over medium heat 15 minutes. Remove from heat and add wine. Chill thoroughly and serve very cold as a first course. 6-8 servings

Cold Peach Soup

4 large ripe peaches
2 cups dry white wine
1 cup water
3 Tablespoons sugar
¼ teaspoon cinnamon
¼ teaspoon curry powder
3 cloves
Sour cream for garnish
Orange slices for garnish

Drop peaches in boiling water for 1 minute. Peel and halve. Purée in blender or food processor. Put purée in enamel saucepan, add wine, water, sugar and spices. Bring to a boil and simmer 10 minutes, stirring. Remove cloves and chill at least 4 hours. Serve in chilled bowls with a thin slice of orange and a dollop of sour cream.

For use as a dessert soup, 1 pint of heavy cream may be added immediately before serving, eliminating the sour cream. 4 servings

Basic Principles of Egg Cooking

Use a moderate to low temperature with exact timing. When eggs are cooked at too high a temperature or for too long at a low temperature, egg whites shrink and become tough or rubbery, yolks become toughened and their surface may turn grey-green.

Eggs separate better when cold, but beat better at room temperature. Remove from refrigerator about 30 minutes before heating.

One large egg equals approximately 3 tablespoons.

If any of the yolk or any fat gets into egg whites, the white will not beat.

A large egg has about 80 calories, 60 of which come from the yolk.

Contrary to popular opinion, shell color does not affect egg quality or nutritive value. Shell color is determined by the breed of the laying hen. Brown and white eggs are equally good.

Break egg shell by a sharp tap at center with knife blade. Press thumbs into cracks, turning crack down. Pull apart and let egg drop into a bowl. To separate let each half of shell serve as a cup and rock yolk from cup to cup while white pours out.

Cream of tartar added to egg whites increases the stability of meringue. A test to see if meringue has been beaten enough is to rub a little of the meringue between the thumb and forefinger. If you can feel any grains of sugar, the meringue has not been beaten enough. Continue to beat until no grains of sugar can be felt.

When topping a pie with meringue, put meringue on while the filling is still hot and bake at 375°F until the meringue is a light golden brown. This reduces the amount of liquid that collects between the meringue and filling. Spread meringue all the way to the pie crust and make sure the filling is completely sealed to prevent the meringue from shrinking.

When combining beaten egg whites with other heavier mixtures handle carefully so that the air beaten into the whites is not lost. It is best to pour the heavier mixture onto the beaten egg whites. Fold just until there are no streaks remaining in the mixture. Don't stir as this will force air out of the whites.

Never attempt to cook an egg still in the shell in the microwave. Rapid heat applied by the microwave will expand the air inside the egg shell and possibly cause it to explode.

In cooking eggs by microwave, always remember that they continue to cook after they have been removed from the oven. For this reason it is best to remove them while still underdone.

Soft-Cooked Eggs

Put eggs in saucepan and add enough tap water to come at least 1 inch above eggs. Cover; bring rapidly just to boiling. Turn off heat; if necessary, remove pan from burner to prevent further boiling. Let stand in the hot water 1-4 minutes, depending on desired degree of doneness. Cool eggs promptly in cold water for several seconds to prevent further cooking and to make them easier to handle.

To serve: Break shell through middle with a knife. With a teaspoon, scoop egg out of each half shell into individual serving dish. If egg cup is used, slice off large end of egg with knife and eat from shell.

Hard-Cooked Eggs

Put eggs in saucepan and add enough tap water to come at least 1 inch above eggs. Cover; bring rapidly just to boiling. Turn off heat; if necessary, remove pan from burner to prevent further boiling. Let stand in the hot water 15 minutes for large eggs—adjust time up or down by approximately 3 minutes for each size larger or smaller. Cool immediately and thoroughly in cold water. To remove shell: crackle it by tapping gently all over. Roll egg between hands to loosen shell; then peel, starting at large end. Hold egg under running cold water or dip in bowl of water to help ease off the shell.

Poached Eggs

Lightly oil a sauce pan. Add enough water* to make 2 inches deep. Heat to boiling. Reduce heat to hold temperature at simmering. Break eggs, one at a time, into sauce dish; then slip each egg into water, holding dish close to water's surface. Simmer 3-5 minutes, depending on degree of doneness desired. When done, remove eggs with slotted pancake turner or spoon; drain on paper towel and trim edges, if desired.

*Milk or broth may be used instead of water.

Baked (Shirred) Eggs

Break and slip 2 eggs into greased individual shallow baking dish or ramekin. Add 1 tablespoon of milk or light cream, if desired. Season with salt and pepper. Bake in preheated 325°F. oven 12-18 minutes or until desired degree of doneness. Serve in baking dish. Makes 1 serving.

Eggs Sardou

6 large artichokes
1 cup creamed spinach
6 eggs
Hollandaise Sauce
CREAMED SPINACH:
1 package chopped spinach,
 cooked to package
 directions and drained
2 Tablespoons butter, melted
2 Tablespoons flour
1 cup milk
HOLLANDAISE SAUCE:
2 sticks butter
3 egg yolks
Juice of 1 lemon, strained
Salt, pepper and cayenne,
 to taste

Prepare creamed spinach by making a cream sauce with the butter, flour and milk and adding spinach. Boil artichokes in salted water, drain and remove choke and leaves. Fill hearts with creamed spinach. Poach eggs and place 1 on each artichoke heart on top of spinach. Cover with Hollandaise sauce, made as follows: In double boiler, gradually add melted butter to egg yolks and lemon juice, stirring constantly until thick. Season to taste and serve over eggs.

This very rich dish is an excellent brunch or luncheon dish. 4-6 servings

Eggs Hussarde

4 large thin ham slices, grilled
4 Holland Rusks
4 slices grilled tomato
4 soft poached eggs
Marchand de vin sauce
 (see Index)
Hollandaise sauce (see Eggs
 Sardou)
Paprika

Lay a slice of ham across each Holland Rusk and cover with ¼ cup Marchand de vin sauce. Lay slices of tomato on the sauce and place poached eggs on tomato slices. Top with ¼ cup Hollandaise sauce and garnish with a sprinkling of paprika. 4 servings

Scrambled, Chipped Eggs

Excellent breakfast recipe for anything from
a brunch to a camping trip

3 Tablespoons butter
¼ cup finely chopped green
 onion tops
9 eggs
1 cup cottage cheese
4 ounces shredded dried beef
 (1½ cups)
Salt and pepper to taste

Melt butter in skillet; sauté green onions. Beat eggs with cottage cheese and add to skillet with beef. Cook over low heat until scrambled, stirring constantly. Season to taste. 6 servings

Phyllis K. Kennedy (Mrs. Crawford M.)

Egg Foo Yung and Special Sauce
A wonderful light supper

½ pound cooked, chopped
    shrimp
8 eggs, slightly beaten
½ cup chopped green onions
1 teaspoon sugar
2 teaspoons soy sauce
1½ teaspoons salt
4 Tablespoons oil
SAUCE:
1 beef bouillon cube
2 Tablespoons soy sauce
1 cup water
½ teaspoon pepper
1 Tablespoon cornstarch mixed
    with 1 Tablespoon water

Mix shrimp together with eggs, green onions, sugar, soy sauce, and salt. Drop by tablespoons in hot oil and fry as for pancakes. Turn when brown. Keep warm and serve with special sauce.

Sauce: Mix all ingredients together and heat to thicken and blend flavors.

Linda Cohen (Mrs. Larry)

Greybowy Tort
(Mushroom Omelet Pie)

½ pound mushrooms, sliced
½ medium onion, chopped
½ cup butter, melted
4 eggs
1 Tablespoon flour
Salt and pepper, to taste
2 Tablespoons grated
    Parmesan or Romano
    cheese

Sauté mushrooms and onion in butter until golden. Beat eggs, flour, salt and pepper together. Pour this mixture into 2 small buttered skillets and cook until set. Put 1 omelet on a warmed platter; cover with mushrooms and onions. Sprinkle with salt and pepper. Cover with second omelet and sprinkle with grated cheese. Serve with fried potatoes and champagne. 2 servings

Susan M. Morley

HINT ■■■■■■■■■■■■■■■■

Egg yolks will beat better and will combine with hot mixture more easily if you add 1 teaspoon water before beating.

Poached Eggs in Red Wine Sauce

1 egg per person
3 Tablespoons butter
1 small clove garlic
1 white onion, chopped
2 Tablespoons chopped celery
1 small bay leaf
Salt and pepper, to taste
Dash thyme
2 cups dry red wine
½ English muffin per person
1 teaspoon flour creamed with
   2 teaspoons butter

In a heavy saucepan, melt butter, add garlic for a minute, then remove. Add onion and celery and sauté until tender. Add bay leaf, thyme, salt, pepper and wine. Simmer 10 minutes. While sauce is simmering, butter and toast ½ English muffin per person. Keep warm. Slip 1 egg per person into the simmering sauce and poach for 3 minutes or until white is set. Carefully remove and place on muffin halves and keep warm. Strain sauce into another saucepan; whisk in flour and butter mixture, cook until thickened and spoon over eggs.

Cookbook Committee

Oven Omelet
A good, fast and easy breakfast dish for company

8 eggs
1 cup milk
1 (3 ounce) package thin sliced
   corned beef or ham
Cooked bacon or mushrooms
1 cup shredded Cheddar
   cheese or mozzarella
   cheese
1 Tablespoon minced onion

Preheat oven to 350°. Beat eggs and milk. Tear beef or bacon; chop ham or mushrooms and put into egg mixture. Stir in cheese and onion. Pour into a greased 11½ x 7½ x 1½ inch or 8 x 8 x 2 inch baking dish. Bake uncovered 40-45 minutes or until omelet is set and top is golden brown. 4 servings

Lucy C. White (Mrs. Richard A.)

Dan's Eggs

8 slices bacon, chopped
2 slices white bread, cubed
8 eggs
½ cup milk
½ teaspoon salt
Dash pepper

Fry bacon in large skillet until crisp. Remove and drain. Reserve half of drippings for later use. Add bread cubes to remaining grease and cook until crisp and brown. Remove cubes. Wipe skillet to remove overcooked crumbs. Combine eggs, milk, salt and pepper. Beat well. Cook egg mixture in reserved bacon drippings until nearly set. Stir in cooked bacon and bread cubes. Recipe may be expanded many times when cooking for a crowd. 4 servings

Brunch Egg Casserole

2 cups plain croûtons
1 cup shredded Cheddar
   cheese
4 eggs, slightly beaten
2 cups milk
½ teaspoon salt
½ teaspoon prepared mustard
⅛ teaspoon onion powder
Dash pepper
4 slices bacon, cooked and
   crumbled

In bottom of 10 x 6 x 1¾-inch baking dish, combine croûtons and cheese. Combine eggs, milk, salt, mustard, onion powder and pepper. Mix until blended. Pour into baking dish. Sprinkle bacon on top and bake at 325° for 50 minutes or until eggs are set. Garnish with bacon curls, if desired. May be prepared the night before serving except for bacon. Perfect for overnight company breakfast, and brunch. 6 servings

Carolyn S. Brooks (Mrs. John L.)

HINT ████████████████████

If some of the egg yolk falls into the whites when separating them, remove it with a bit of shell or by touching it with a cloth moistened in cold water.

Artichoke Quiche
Outstanding for a luncheon or with cocktails

2 6 oz. jars marinated
   artichokes, drained and
   chopped
8 saltine crackers, crushed
½ pound cheddar cheese,
   grated
4 eggs
1 bunch green onions, finely
   chopped
3 Tablespoons butter
Salt and pepper to taste
Tabasco sauce

Mix artichokes, crackers and cheese together. Sauté onions in butter and add to mixture. Grease 8 x 10-inch baking dish or 9-inch pie pan. Pat artichoke mixture in place. Beat eggs well, season with salt, pepper and Tabasco sauce and pour over top. Bake at 350° for 35 minutes. Cut into small squares for serving. Can be frozen after cooking and allowed to thaw to room temperature, then heated for 20 minutes at 350°. For use as an appetizer, individual quiches may be made in muffin tins. Serves 8 as appetizer or 4 for an entrée

Phyllis K. Kennedy (Mrs. Crawford M., Jr.)

Crab and Shrimp Quiche

1 (9 inch) deep dish pastry
   shell, unbaked
8 ounces Swiss cheese, diced
2 Tablespoons flour
1 cup milk
3 eggs, beaten
½ teaspoon salt
⅛ teaspoon pepper
Dash ground nutmeg
1 (6 ounce) package Wakefield
   frozen crabmeat and
   shrimp, thawed

Prick bottom and sides of pastry shell with fork; bake at 425° for 6-8 minutes. Set aside. Combine cheese and flour; set aside. Combine milk, eggs, salt, pepper and nutmeg; mix well. Stir in crab and shrimp, and cheese-flour mixture. Pour into pie shell; bake at 350° for 50-60 minutes. Cool slightly before serving. Hint: May be frozen. Bake 40 minutes; wrap tightly in foil and freeze. To serve, thaw quiche and bake 15 to 20 minutes at 350°. 6 servings

Mrs. Nell Johnson

Zucchini Eggplant Quiche

½ pound zucchini, thinly sliced diagonally (about 2 small zucchini)
½ pound eggplant, diced in ½ inch cubes (about ½ small eggplant)
1 green onion, sliced
1 medium clove garlic, minced
¼ cup melted butter
½ cup peeled and chopped tomatoes
½ cup chopped green pepper
½ teaspoon salt
⅛ teaspoon pepper
¼ teaspoon basil
¼ teaspoon thyme
1 (9 inch) pastry shell, partially baked
3 eggs
½ cup heavy cream
½ cup Parmesan cheese

Sauté zucchini, eggplant, onion and garlic in butter. Stir in tomatoes, green pepper and spices. Cook over low heat 10-15 minutes until vegetables are tender and liquid evaporated. Spread mixture evenly in pie shell. Beat eggs and cream until mixed, but not frothy. Pour into shell. Sprinkle with Parmesan cheese. Bake in 375° oven 30-35 minutes until set.

Martha H. Whitehead (Mrs. Richard)

Seafood Quiche

2 pie shells, unbaked
6 ounces frozen or canned crabmeat
1½ cups frozen or canned tiny shrimp
1 (8 ounce) package Swiss cheese, chopped
½ cup chopped celery
½ cup chopped scallions or onions
1 cup mayonnaise
2 Tablespoons flour
¾ cup dry white wine
4 eggs, slightly beaten

Thaw crabmeat and shrimp; combine with cheese, onions and celery. Arrange in pie shells. In a food processor or small bowl, mix mayonnaise, flour, wine and eggs. Pour over mixture in pie shells. Bake in a 350° oven for 35-45 minutes, or until silver knife inserted in center comes out clean. May be frozen before cooking; then cook 50-55 minutes at 350°. For a luncheon main dish, each pie will serve 4-6 people. For appetizers, cut each pie into 12 pieces. 2 quiches

Betty Jo Ridley (Mrs. William E.)

Sausage Quiche

1 pie shell, baked
½ pound hot sausage
2 Tablespoons chopped onions
2 eggs, beaten
¾ cup sour cream
1-2 cups grated Swiss cheese
Salt and pepper to taste
¼ teaspoon nutmeg
½ cup grated Cheddar cheese

Cook and drain sausage; in same skillet, brown onions. In a bowl, mix eggs, sour cream and grated Swiss cheese. Add sausage, onion, salt, pepper and nutmeg. Pour into pie shell. Top with grated Cheddar cheese. Bake at 350° for 30 minutes. Freezes well. 6-8 servings

Mrs. T.L. McDougald

Artichoke Cheese Soufflé

⅔ pound mushrooms,
  chopped
2 Tablespoons butter
½ cup sherry
1 cup heavy cream
1 teaspoon salt
Pepper to taste
4 cooked artichoke bottoms
6 Tablespoons butter
⅓ cup flour
1⅓ cup scalded milk
¾ teaspoon salt
Pepper
Dash nutmeg
3 egg yolks
1½ cups grated sharp cheese
4 egg whites

Sauté chopped mushrooms in 2 Tablespoons butter. Add sherry. Cook for 10 minutes until evaporated. Add cream, salt and pepper. Cook 4-5 minutes until thick. Arrange artichoke bottoms on bottom of an 8-inch buttered and floured souffle dish. Mound mushroom mixture over artichokes. Melt 6 Tablespoons butter in a saucepan. Add flour. Cook for 2 minutes. Add scalded milk, ¾ teaspoon salt, pepper and nutmeg. Cook until thick. Transfer to a large bowl. Cool for 5 minutes. Stir in egg yolks and grated cheese. Beat egg whites with a pinch of salt until stiff. Fold into cheese mixture and gently pour over artichoke-mushroom layers. Bake at 400° for 40 minutes. Serve immediately. 6 servings

Patricia Ritchie

Blintz Casserole
Absolutely divine!
Treat your football fans with this for brunch

FILLING:
2 pounds ricotta cheese
2 eggs
¼ cup sugar
⅛ teaspoon salt
1 lemon, juiced or ¼ cup
   lemon juice
8 ounces cream cheese,
   softened
BATTER:
½ pound margarine, melted
½ cup sugar
2 eggs
1 cup sifted flour
3 teaspoons baking powder
⅛ teaspoon salt
¼ cup milk
1 teaspoon vanilla

Place all ingredients for filling in mixer and blend well. Set aside. Mix batter ingredients by hand and spoon ½ of batter into a greased 9 x 13 x 2-inch pan. Top this with filling; spreading, not mixing. Spread remaining batter over filling. Bake at 300° for 1½ hours. Serve with fresh fruit and grilled Canadian bacon. 12 servings

Terry C. Morris (Mrs. Douglas)

Monterey Fondue Casserole

12 slices (or less) stale French
   bread
Soft butter
1 (12-16 ounce) can whole
   kernel corn
2 small cans green chilies,
   seeded and cut in strips
2 cups grated Monterey Jack
   cheese or 1 cup grated
   Monterey Jack and 1 cup
   grated Cheddar cheese
3 cups milk or cream
4 eggs
1 teaspoon salt
Dash Tabasco sauce
Pitted black olives (optional)

The day before serving, spread bread with butter and slice in half; arrange half the slices in bottom of a 3-quart or larger baking dish. Cover with half of corn; arrange half of seeded chili strips over this. Sprinkle half of grated cheese over all. Repeat layers. Combine milk, eggs, salt and Tabasco sauce and pour over casserole, adding more milk if necessary, to reach level of bottom of cheese (depending on shape of dish used). Garnish with pitted black olives if desired. Cover with foil or plastic wrap and refrigerate overnight. Bake uncovered at 350° 40-45 minutes or until puffy and brown. 8 servings

Joan McMahan (Mrs. James P.)

Cheese Soufflé Crêpes

¼ cup butter
¼ scant cup flour
¾ cup milk
½ teaspoon salt
¼ teaspoon Worcestershire
sauce
¼ teaspoon dry mustard
Dash cayenne
1 cup shredded Cheddar or
Swiss cheese
4 eggs, separated
Butter
12 crêpes (see Index)
2 cups shredded Cheddar
cheese

Melt butter and stir in flour. Cook 3 minutes, stirring. Stir in milk and seasonings, stirring until thick. Blend in 1 cup cheese and stir. Remove from heat. Beat in yolks one at a time and fold in stiffly beaten egg whites. Spoon ¼ cup mixture in center of each crêpe. Fold sides in. Place in buttered 9 x 13-inch baking dish and brush with melted butter. Bake at 350° 8-10 minutes. Sprinkle liberally with 2 cups grated cheese and bake 5 minutes more. Crêpes may be assembled 1-2 hours ahead and refrigerated, then reheated. Complement with grilled or sliced tomatoes and bacon curls. 6 servings

Gail Nichols (Mrs. Robert)
Young Harris, Georgia

Cheese Sandwich Pie

1 egg
¾ cup flour
½ teaspoon salt
⅛ teaspoon pepper
1 cup milk
1 cup (4 ounces) shredded
cheese (Cheddar, Swiss,
Muenster, etc. Can use 1
kind or combination)
Ham (optional)
Bacon (optional)
Onions (optional)
Mushrooms (optional)

In small bowl, combine egg, flour, salt, pepper and milk and any optional ingredients. Mix with rotary beater until blended; stir in half of cheese. Pour into well greased pie pan. Bake at 425° for 30 minutes. Pour on remaining cheese. Return to oven about 2 minutes. Serve as an appetizer or a main dish for lunch or a Sunday night supper. 6-8 servings

Ann Mallard (Mrs. William)

Saucy Cheese Soufflé

1 cup milk
3 Tablespoons Quick Tapioca
1 cup grated mild Cheddar
   cheese
3 egg yolks, beaten
½ teaspoon salt
3 egg whites, stiffly beaten
SAUCE: Serves 8
¼ cup butter
¼ cup flour
½ teaspoon salt
¼ teaspoon dry mustard
1 pint milk, scalded
1¼ cups grated mild Cheddar
   cheese
8 slices bacon, crisply cooked

Cook milk and tapioca until thick. Remove from heat. Add grated Cheddar cheese and stir until melted. Stir in egg yolks and salt. Fold in stiffly beaten egg whites. Pour into a well greased square casserole. Place casserole in pan of hot water and bake at 350° for 1 hour. Top should be brown when taken from oven. Cut into squares and place on plates. Pour a generous Tablespoon of Cheese sauce over soufflé and top with 1 or 2 slices of crisp bacon. 4 servings

Cheese Sauce: Melt butter. Add flour, salt and dry mustard. Add milk gradually. Stir constantly until thick. Fold in mild Cheddar cheese. Keep hot in double boiler.

Soufflé does not need to be served immediately as it does not fall quickly.

Sherril H. Williams (Mrs. Wheat, Jr.)

Cottage Cheese Pancakes
For a special Sunday night supper

1 cup heavy cream
4 eggs
½ cup flour (may need more)
¼ teaspoon salt
¼ cup oil
½ cup milk
½ teaspoon vanilla
8 ounces cottage cheese

Place all ingredients except cottage cheese in blender. Mix well. Fold in cottage cheese. Do not blend lumps out. Heat frying pan and fry as you would any pancake. Try them with pork links rolled inside, with blueberries over the top or with any fruit sauce spooned over the pancakes.
4 servings

Cookbook Committee

Roquefort Soufflé
An excellent appetizer

3 Tablespoons butter
¼ cup flour
½ teaspoon salt
Dash pepper
1½ cups milk
6 ounces Roquefort cheese,
    crumbled
6 egg yolks
6 egg whites

Melt butter. Blend in flour, salt and pepper. Stir in milk and bring to boil, stirring constantly. Cook 5 minutes. Add Roquefort cheese. Add egg yolks, one at a time, beating hard after each addition. Cool. Recipe may be prepared in advance to this point. Beat egg whites until stiff, but not dry. Add about ⅓ of whites to cheese mixture, blending well. Then very gently fold in remaining whites. Turn into buttered and floured 2-quart soufflé dish and bake in a 375° oven for 30-40 minutes. 4 servings

Emy E. Blair (Mrs. H. Duane)

Garlic Cheese Grits

5 cups boiling water
1 teaspoon salt
1 cup grits
1 roll garlic cheese, cut up
1 stick margarine
3 egg whites, stiffly beaten

Stir grits into boiling, salted water and simmer slowly for 25 minutes stirring often. Remove from heat and add cheese and margarine. Cover and let sit until cool. May be prepared ahead to this point. Fold in egg whites; put in greased casserole and bake for 25 minutes at 350°. 8 servings

Lee Shelnut (Mrs. M.T.)

Bulgur-Nut Pilaf

1 cup bulgur (cracked wheat)
3 Tablespoons butter
2 cups beef or chicken broth
2 medium carrots, shredded
½ to ¾ teaspoon salt
½ cup chopped walnuts,
    pecans or almonds

In large ovenproof skillet or flameproof casserole, sauté bulgur in butter about 5 minutes to brown lightly, stirring occasionally. Stir in broth, carrots and salt; bring to boil. Cover and bake in 350° oven for 25 minutes or until broth is absorbed, stirring occasionally. Stir in walnuts. Good with lamb or poultry. 4-6 servings

Barley and Mushrooms

4 Tablespoons butter
1 large onion, minced
¼ pound mushrooms, sliced
1 cup barley
4 chicken bouillon cubes or
  envelopes
1 teaspoon salt
3 cups water

In large skillet over medium heat, melt butter and sauté onions and mushrooms until tender, stirring occasionally, for about 5 minutes. Remove from skillet. In same skillet, in remaining butter, lightly brown barley, stirring constantly. Stir in bouillon granules or bouillon cubes, onions, mushrooms and water. Heat to boiling. Reduce heat to low. Cover and simmer 35-40 minutes until tender, stirring occasionally until barley is tender and all liquid is absorbed. 8-12 servings

Pat Adams (Mrs. P.H.)

Cheese and Rice Casserole

¼ pound butter or margarine
1 large onion, chopped
1¾ cups uncooked rice
2 cans consommé
1 cup blanched, slivered
  almonds
1 small can mushrooms,
  drained
¾ pound grated Cheddar
  cheese

Sauté onion in butter. Mix all ingredients together in a 9 x 13-inch casserole. Bake uncovered 1 hour and 15 minutes at 300°. Stir occasionally. May be prepared for baking early in day. 10-12 servings

Fruited Rice Curry

Prepared in advance and kept in an airtight container this makes a very nice gift at holiday time

1 cup long grain rice
2 teaspoons curry powder
2 beef bouillon cubes
¼ cup chopped mixed dried
  fruits
¼ cup blanched slivered
  almonds
1 Tablespoon instant minced
onion
½ teaspoon salt
2 Tablespoons light raisins

Combine all ingredients. Package in an airtight container.
To prepare Rice Curry: Combine rice mix with 2½ cups water and 2 Tablespoons butter or margarine in saucepan. Cover tightly. Bring to a boil; reduce heat. Simmer for 20 minutes. Do not lift cover. 4 cups

Lucia H. Sizemore (Mrs. Thomas A., III)

Fried Rice

4 strips bacon
1 bunch green onions,
    chopped or 1 large onion,
    chopped
2 eggs, well beaten
2-3 cups cooked, day-old rice,
    cooled
¼ cup Japanese soy sauce
    or more, as desired
OPTIONAL:
Water chestnuts, sliced
Bamboo shoots
Mushrooms, sliced and
    sautéed
Leftover pork, chicken or
    shrimp, chopped

Cook bacon in a large skillet or wok until crisp. Drain on paper towels and crumble, leaving bacon grease in pan. Sauté onions in grease over medium heat until translucent. Add eggs. Scramble until thoroughly cooked and eggs can be broken into very tiny bits. Add rice; stir to combine. Add bacon, water chestnuts, bamboo shoots, mushrooms and chopped pork, chicken or shrimp, as desired. Sprinkle in soy sauce to taste and stir over low heat until mixture is thoroughly combined and warm.

Exotic Rice

1 can beef consommé
1 can onion soup
1 (8 ounce) can water
    chestnuts, drained and
    sliced
1 (3 ounce) can sliced Broiled
    in Butter mushrooms,
    drained
1 cup uncooked rice
½ teaspoon salt
½ stick butter

Put first 6 ingredients together in a 1½-quart casserole and mix well. Dot with butter. Cover and cook in a 325° oven for 1 hour and 45 minutes. 6-8 servings

Alice C. Shinall (Mrs. Robert P.)

Green Rice with Cheese

⅓ cup melted butter
2 Tablespoons chopped onion
2 eggs, beaten
2 cups milk
1 cup minute rice, uncooked
½ pound Cheddar cheese,
    grated
½ (10 ounce) package frozen
    spinach, thawed
½ teaspoon salt
¼ teaspoon garlic salt

Brown onions in melted butter. Mix remaining ingredients together. Add onions. Mix well. Place in ungreased baking dish. Bake 1 hour at 325°. May be frozen before baking. 6-8 servings

Diane J. Pitts

Green Rice

2 cups uncooked rice
⅔ cup finely chopped green
   peppers
1 cup sliced green onions
⅓ cup chopped parsley
¼ cup olive oil
1½ Tablespoons
   Worcestershire sauce
1 teaspoon salt
¼ teaspoon cayenne pepper
1 quart beef broth

Preheat oven to 350°. Grease 2-quart casserole. Combine all ingredients. Pour into casserole. Cover and bake for 45 minutes. After cooking, toss rice and serve. May be prepared in advance. 12 servings

Dunja S. Awbrey (Mrs. James J.)

Herb Rice Blend

A perfect mixture of uncooked rice and assorted dried herbs,
that makes a nice holiday remembrance

1 cup uncooked rice
2 beef bouillon cubes
½ teaspoon salt
½ teaspoon rosemary
½ teaspoon marjoram leaves
½ teaspoon thyme leaves
1 teaspoon dried green onion
   flakes

Mix all ingredients. Put in a plastic bag or container. Attach these cooking directions to the package: Combine rice mixture, 2 cups cold water and 1 Tablespoon butter in heavy saucepan. Cook over high heat. When mixture boils, reduce heat to medium-low. Stir once with fork. Cover tightly and simmer 12-14 minutes, or until all liquid is absorbed.

Wild Rice Paprika

2 cups wild rice, cooked
2 eggs
½ cup salad oil
1 medium onion, chopped
1 cup fresh chopped parsley
1½ cups grated Cheddar
   cheese
1 cup milk
1½ teaspoons salt
2 teaspoons paprika

Cook wild rice according to directions on box. Beat eggs; add oil slowly, then onion and parsley. Put in cheese, cooked rice, milk and salt. Add paprika and mix well. Sprinkle top of casserole generously with paprika. Bake for 45 minutes at 350°. 12 servings

Marijo Culwell

Indian Pilaf with Carrots and Raisins

¼ cup sugar
2 Tablespoons water
3 cups hot chicken bouillon
1¼ cups diced, pared carrots
2 tablespoons raisins
3 Tablespoons butter
1½ cups uncooked long-grain rice
½ teaspoon salt
¼ teaspoon ground cardamon
¼ teaspoon ground cinnamon
¼ teaspoon ground nutmeg

Mix sugar and water in medium size saucepan. Heat to boiling; reduce heat; simmer uncovered until golden; remove from heat. Add bouillon, stirring until sugar is dissolved. Return to heat; cook 2-3 minutes; reserve. Sauté carrots and raisins in butter in 2 quart saucepan, covered, 10 minutes. Add rice to carrot mixture; stir until coated with butter. Stir in reserved bouillon mixture and remaining ingredients. Heat to boiling; reduce heat. Simmer covered until bouillon is absorbed, 25-30 minutes. Transfer to serving dish. Sprinkle with freshly grated nutmeg, if desired. 6-8 servings

Cookbook Committee

Sausage and Wild Rice Casserole

1 pound bulk sausage
2 medium onions, chopped
2 (3 ounce) cans mushrooms, drained (whole, button or sliced)
2 cups wild rice, washed
¼ cup flour
½ cup heavy cream
2½ cups chicken broth
1 teaspoon MSG
Pinch oregano
Pinch thyme
Pinch marjoram
1 teaspoon salt
⅛ teaspoon pepper
½ cup toasted slivered almonds

Sauté sausage; drain on paper towels. Sauté onions in fat left in pan. Add mushrooms and cooked sausage. Meanwhile cook 2 cups thoroughly washed wild rice according to directions on box. Drain. Mix flour with heavy cream until smooth. Add condensed chicken broth and cook until thickened. Add seasonings and toss well. Pour into greased 9 x 13-inch casserole. Bake 25-30 minutes at 350°. Sprinkle with toasted almonds when ready to serve. Freezes beautifully and can serve a crowd. Hint: To soften the cost, use ½ wild rice and ½ white; cook separately; white rice cooks more quickly than wild rice and must not be cooked in the same pot. 10-12 servings

Decie Nygaard (Mrs. W.F.)

Spiced Brown Rice
What a surprise this dish is!
Especially good with pork

1 cup thinly sliced onion
⅓ cup chopped pitted prunes
2 Tablespoons melted butter
2 Tablespoons sugar
1 teaspoon ground cinnamon
¼ teaspoon ground cloves
⅛ teaspoon curry powder
1 cup washed and uncooked
    brown rice
3 cups chicken bouillon
¼ cup pine nuts
2 teaspoons melted butter
Salt and pepper, to taste
Sliced spiced peaches for
    garnish

Sauté onion and prunes in 2 Tablespoons melted butter in heavy 3-quart ovenproof saucepan over medium heat, stirring constantly for 3 minutes. Reduce heat; add sugar; simmer covered until onion is very soft and sugar is caramelized, about 10 minutes. Preheat oven to 350°. Add cinnamon, cloves and curry powder to onion mixture; cook 1 minute. Stir in rice; cook until hot and well coated with sugar. Add bouillon. Heat to boiling; remove from heat; cover and place in center of oven. Bake until rice is tender and liquid is absorbed, about 1 hour. Sauté pine nuts in 2 Tablespoons melted butter in small skillet, stirring constantly, until golden, about 3 minutes. When rice is cooked, add pine nuts, tossing with 2 forks to fluff rice. Add salt and pepper. Transfer to serving dish; garnish with sliced spiced peaches, if desired. May be prepared in advance and reheated in oven or microwave oven. 6 servings

Rice Stuffing with Grapes

1 (6-ounce) package long grain
    and wild rice
2½ cups water
1 Tablespoon butter
1 teaspoon chicken seasoned
    stock base
1 cup sliced mushrooms
1 cup chopped celery
1 cup halved green grapes
1 (2-ounce) jar chopped
    pimientos, drained

Combine rice, water, butter and stock base in saucepan; bring to boil. Cover tightly and cook over low heat for 15 minutes. Remove from heat; stir in remaining ingredients. Mixture will be moist. Makes enough stuffing for a 10 pound goose. Or serve as a side dish with any wild game, grilled shrimp or scallops.
6-8 servings

Dorothy W. Smith (Mrs. William P., III)

Syrian Rice

Small amount (approximately
    6-8 pieces) spaghetti,
    broken into 1-inch pieces
1 small onion, minced
3-4 Tablespoons olive oil
2½ cups water
2 bouillon cubes (chicken
    or beef)
1 teaspoon salt
½ teaspoon MSG
⅛ teaspoon garlic powder
1 cup uncooked long grain rice

In saucepan soak onion and spaghetti in olive oil for about 5 minutes. Simmer until onions are soft and spaghetti is lightly browned; then add water, all seasonings and bring to a boil. Slowly stir in rice; mix well. Bring to a rolling boil, cover, reduce heat to low and cook until all water is absorbed. Do not stir. Note: The recipe does not call for it, but I wash rice once in cold water before cooking. 8 servings

Constance D. Wilson (Mrs. Alexander E., Jr.)

Rice Pilaf

2 cups uncooked rice
⅔ cup butter
4 cups chicken stock
¾ cup chopped celery
¾ cup shredded carrots
¾ cup chopped parsley
½ cup chopped green onion
1 cup chopped pecans
Salt to taste

Sauté rice in butter until lightly browned. Add stock and place in a casserole. Bake covered at 350° for 30 minutes. Add celery, carrots, parsley, green onions, pecans and salt. Return to oven for 30 minutes. Excellent with chicken, ham or roasts. 6-8 servings

Elise M. Griffin

Parsleyed Rice
A new way with rice—delicious!

1 egg, beaten
1 cup milk
1 cup chopped fresh parsley
1 onion, minced
2 cups cooked rice
½ cup grated sharp cheese
2 Tablespoons butter
Salt and pepper

Combine all ingredients and pour into a buttered baking dish. Bake uncovered at 350° for 30 minutes. 8 servings

JoAnn P. Whitehead (Mrs. Harry C.)

Fettuccine with Zucchini and Mushrooms

½ pound mushrooms, trimmed
  and thinly sliced
1½ sticks butter
1¼ pounds zucchini, scrubbed
  and cut into julienne strips
1 cup heavy cream
7 quarts water
2 Tablespoons salt
1 Tablespoon olive oil
1 pound fettuccine
¾ cup freshly grated
  Parmesan cheese
½ cup chopped parsley
Salt and pepper to taste

In a large deep skillet, sauté mushrooms in ½ stick melted butter over moderately high heat for 2 minutes. Add zucchini, heavy cream and 1 stick butter cut into bits. Bring liquid to a boil and simmer mixture for 3 minutes. Bring 7 quarts water to boil in a large kettle; add 2 Tablespoons salt and olive oil. Add fettuccine and boil until al dente. Drain pasta in a large colander; add it to skillet with grated Parmesan cheese and parsley. Toss mixture, lifting the pasta and combining well. Transfer mixture to a heated platter and serve with additional Parmesan cheese, salt and pepper. 6 servings

Joe Nardone

Fettuccine Milano

1 pound mild Italian sausage
3 cups fresh sliced
  mushrooms
2 cloves garlic, minced
1 large green pepper, seeded
  and cut in chunks
1 cup chopped green onion
1 cup chopped parsley
1 teaspoon crumbled sweet
  basil
½ teaspoon crumbled oregano
¼ teaspoon crumbled rosemary
½ cup olive oil
½ cup melted butter
1 pound hot, cooked fettuccine
  or linguine noodles
Grated Parmesan cheese

Remove sausage from casings. Crumble and brown. Remove from pan and drain. Sauté mushrooms, garlic, green pepper, onion, parsley and seasonings in olive oil and butter until green pepper is soft. Remove from heat. Stir in sausage. Toss with hot fettuccine. Sprinkle generously with Parmesan cheese. Serve with crusty Italian bread. 6 servings

Alicia LaRocco

Noodle Kugel

This is a "sweet starch" and can be used in place
of potatoes or rice

8 ounces cottage cheese (do
   not use "low fat" or
   "dry curd")
1 (1 pound 4 ounce) can
   crushed pineapple with
   juice
12 ounces flat noodles, cooked
4 eggs, beaten
½ cup margarine, melted
½ cup pre-mixed sugar and
   cinnamon
½ pint sour cream
½ cup raisins (optional)

Mix all ingredients and fold
in beaten eggs. Sprinkle with
extra sugar and cinnamon. Bake
in 9 x 13-inch pan at 350° for
1 hour or until knife comes out
clean.

Mrs. Harvey Cook

Paglia E Fieno Papalina

(Straw and Hay)

4-6 Tablespoons butter
1 clove garlic
1 pound fresh mushrooms,
   sliced
Salt
½ pound Prosciutto, minced
   (Canadian bacon may be
   used if necessary)
1 cup light cream
8 ounces egg noodles
8 ounces green spinach
   noodles
¼ cup grated Parmesan
   cheese

Heat half of the butter in deep
frying pan; add garlic clove, sauté
until brown. Remove garlic and
add sliced mushrooms. Sprinkle
lightly with salt and sauté for 10
minutes.

In another pan, melt rest of
butter and fry prosciutto until
browned. Heat cream; keep all the
above warm.

In 2 separate pots of boiling,
salted water, cook both noodles
until tender. Drain. Combine on a
heated serving platter; toss
together with mushrooms,
prosciutto, cream and grated
cheese. Serve immediately.
6 servings

Baked Manicotti

PASTA DOUGH:
1 cup flour
1 cup water
¼ teaspoon salt
4 eggs
FILLING:
2 eggs
1½ pounds ricotta cheese
**½ pound mozzarella cheese,
    cubed, grated or in slivers**
**½ cup grated Parmesan
    cheese**
1-2 Tablespoons parsley flakes
½ teaspoon salt
SAUCE:
**3-4 cups of your favorite
    marinara or spaghetti meat
    sauce**

To make pasta stir flour, water and salt in a bowl until smooth. Beat in eggs 1 at a time. Put about 3 Tablespoons of batter in hot, greased 5-6 inch skillet. Cook until firm but not brown to form a crêpe the size of pan. Turn and cook lightly on the other side. Stack crêpes on a plate with waxed paper between each crêpe until ready to fill. Can be frozen at this point for future use. Combine all filling ingredients. Spread a little of the marinara or meat sauce on the bottom of a 13 x 9 x 1½-inch oblong baking dish. Place about 2-3 Tablespoons cheese mixture on each crêpe. Gently roll pasta around cheese mixture and place each manicotti seam side down in a single layer in the baking dish. Top with additional marinara or meat sauce. Sprinkle with grated cheese. Bake manicotti about 20 minutes or more at 375° until the filling is set and the sauce bubbles. Serve with additional sauce and grated cheese. 6 servings

Mrs. August J. Nardone

Dunbar Macaroni
Serve with a cold meat at an informal dinner

**1 (32-ounce) can tomatoes,
    mashed**
Salt and pepper to taste
1 medium onion, chopped
2 Tablespoons sugar
**1 (8-ounce) package macaroni,
    cooked and drained**
¼ cup margarine
1 can mushroom soup
1 can chicken broth
**1 pound sharp Cheddar
    cheese, grated**

Combine tomatoes, salt, pepper, onion and sugar. Cook gently. Add to macaroni. Combine margarine, soups and cheese; add to tomato-macaroni mixture. Cook in an uncovered casserole at 400° for 25-30 minutes. Allow to stand 5-10 minutes before serving. May be prepared in advance. 12 servings

Ann T. McCrory (Mrs. Charles O.)

Linguine with Artichokes

¼ cup olive oil
½ stick butter
1 teaspoon flour
1 cup chicken broth
1 garlic clove, crushed
1 Tablespoon lemon juice
2 teaspoons parsley flakes
½ teaspoon salt
$\frac{1}{8}$ teaspoon pepper
1 can artichoke hearts,
    drained and halved
2 Tablespoons Parmesan
    cheese
1-2 teaspoons capers, drained
1 pound linguine
6 quarts water
2 Tablespoons olive oil
1 Tablespoon Parmesan
    cheese
1 Tablespoon softened butter
¼ teaspoon salt

In a large, heavy saucepan, heat ¼ cup olive oil over medium low heat. Add ½ stick butter and melt it; add flour. Cook mixture, stirring for 3 minutes. Stir in chicken broth. Increase heat to moderately high and cook 1 minute. Add crushed garlic clove, lemon juice, parsley flakes, the ½ teaspoon salt and pepper. Cook over moderate/low heat stirring for 5 minutes. Add artichokes, 2 Tablespoons Parmesan cheese and capers. Cook sauce covered, basting artichokes with sauce several times, for 8 minutes. Cook linguine in water approximately 10 minutes or until tender. Drain. In the linguine kettle, combine 2 Tablespoons olive oil, 1 Table-spoon Parmesan cheese, softened butter and ¼ teaspoon salt. Return drained linguine to kettle and toss with cheese mixture. Pour artichoke mixture over pasta, toss and serve on a heated platter with extra Parmesan cheese to sprinkle on top. Sauce may be prepared in advance. 6 servings

Joe Nardone

Summer Pasta

4 fresh tomatoes, peeled,
    seeded and chopped
1 pound mozzarella cheese,
    diced
¼ cup fresh minced basil or
    2 Tablespoons dry basil
1-2 cloves garlic, crushed
1 cup olive oil
Salt and pepper to taste
1 pound spaghetti, cooked
Grated Parmesan cheese

Combine all ingredients except the spaghetti. Let stand at room temperature. Toss with 1 pound hot cooked spaghetti. Serve immediately with grated Parmesan cheese. 4-6 servings

Carol Olsen (Mrs. Donald)

Fish and Shellfish

Rainbow Trout with Mushroom Herb Stuffing

6 pan-dressed rainbow trout
1½ teaspoon salt
4 cups soft bread cubes
½ cup butter
1 cup sliced fresh mushrooms
½ cup sliced green onions (or more)
½ teaspoon salt
½ cup chopped parsley
1 (2-ounce) jar chopped pimientos
1½ Tablespoons lemon juice
½ teaspoon thyme (or more)
2 Tablespoons butter, melted

Sprinkle 1½ teaspoons salt evenly over inside and outside of fish. Sauté bread crumbs in butter until lightly browned, stirring frequently. Add mushrooms and onions, and cook until mushrooms are tender. Add ½ teaspoon salt, parsley, pimientos, lemon juice and thyme, and toss lightly. Stuff fish with dressing, and arrange in a well-oiled baking pan. Brush with melted butter. Bake at 350° for 25-30 minutes, or until fish flakes easily with a fork. 6 servings

Cookbook Committee

Foil Baked Fish For Grill

3 pounds fish fillet, ½ inch thick (any firm-flesh fish)
5 slices bacon, minced
1 large green pepper, minced
1 large red pepper, minced
1 large onion, minced
1 cup sour cream
1 teaspoon salt
¼ teaspoon pepper
¼ teaspoon paprika
¼ cup butter, melted
Aluminum foil

Cut fish into serving pieces. Cook bacon just enough to render fat; remove and drain. Sauté peppers and onions in bacon fat until soft. Stir in sour cream and add bacon. Sprinkle fish with salt, pepper and paprika. Grease a large sheet of aluminum foil with butter. Spread some of the sour cream mixture on the foil, and top with the fish. Spread remaining sauce on top. Bring foil up over fish, and seal ends tightly. Grill 20-25 minutes almost directly on coals. 6 servings

Cookbook Committee

HINT ■■■■■■■■■■■■■

Put lemon on fish after cooking, never before, to keep from getting mushy.

Grilled Red Snapper

6 snapper fillets (or similar
   fish)
Salt and pepper to taste
1-2 cloves garlic, minced
2-3 lemons, very thinly sliced
½ cup butter
Hickory chips, soaked in water

Season fillets with salt and pepper. In a saucepan, melt butter, add garlic and cook 1-2 minutes. Arrange half the lemon slices in a shallow baking dish, add fish in a single layer and put remaining lemon slices on top. Pour butter over fish. Add hickory chips to slow coals, place dish on heavy-duty foil atop grill and close hood (make a tent with foil if you do not have a covered grill). Cook until fish flakes easily with a fork, 15-20 minutes. Baste occasionally with butter. 6 servings

Barrie C. Aycock (Mrs. Robert R.)

Shrimp Rolled Fillets
Simple to prepare but elegant enough for
your most important guests

¼ cup butter
1 clove garlic, minced
1 small onion, minced
¼ cup minced green pepper
12 large shrimp, cooked,
   shelled and deveined
¼ cup day old bread crumbs
1 Tablespoon parsley
½ teaspoon salt
⅛ teaspoon pepper
4 fillets of sole or flounder
   (1¼ pounds)
BLENDER HOLLANDAISE:
½ cup butter
3 egg yolks
2 Tablespoons lemon juice
Dash cayenne pepper
½ teaspoon salt

Melt 2 Tablespoons butter in a skillet. Sauté garlic, onion and pepper until soft. Dice 8 shrimp and add to sautéed mixture with bread crumbs, parsley, salt and pepper. Remove from heat. Spread 2 Tablespoons of shrimp mixture onto boned side of each fillet, and roll up, lengthwise. Refrigerate on a cookie sheet until ready to bake. Melt the remaining 2 Tablespoons butter. Arrange the fillets in a 10 x 6-inch baking dish, and brush with melted butter. Bake at 350° for 25-30 minutes, or until fish flakes easily with a fork. Pour Hollandaise sauce over fish and garnish with remaining shrimp. 4 servings

Hollandaise: Heat butter until bubbling. Put rest of ingredients in blender and mix on low speed. With motor running, pour bubbling butter into blender in a slow, steady stream; blending until sauce thickens.

Elise M. Griffin

Hill's Broiled Red Snapper
Outstandingly simple and delicious

4 red snapper fillets
Salad oil
½ cup butter, melted
Juice of ½ lemon
¼ cup Worcestershire sauce
Lemon slices (for garnish)
¼ cup chopped parsley (for garnish)

Line a baking pan with aluminum foil and oil lightly. Place fillets on foil, skin side down. Brush top sides of fillets with oil. Place 4 inches below broiler heat and cook 15-20 minutes or until fish flakes easily with a fork. Meanwhile make a heated sauce of the butter, lemon and Worcestershire sauce. Place fillets on serving plate and pour hot sauce over. Garnish with parsley and lemon slices. Serve immediately. 4 servings

Scalloped Haddock

2 pounds Haddock
1 can cream of mushroom soup
1 (5.33 fluid ounce) can evaporated milk
½ cup sherry
1 teaspoon Worcestershire sauce
Liquid from 1 (3 ounce) can sliced mushrooms
2-3 Tablespoons butter
¼ cup diced onions
½ cup finely chopped green pepper
1 cup finely chopped celery
4 Tablespoons flour
½ cup mayonnaise
½ pound cooked shrimp, cut in bite sized pieces
½ cup thinly sliced water chestnuts
1 can sliced mushrooms (from which liquid was drained earlier)
Salt to taste
Buttered breadcrumbs
Paprika

Rinse Haddock quickly under cold water, remove all bones and place in a single layer in a baking dish. Heat cream of mushroom soup, evaporated milk, sherry, Worcestershire sauce and liquid from mushrooms. Pour over fish. Bake 15 minutes at 400°. While fish is baking, sauté onions, green pepper and celery in butter. Add flour, stir until well blended. Add liquid in which fish was cooked. (Set fish aside.) Add mayonnaise, shrimp, water chestnuts, mushrooms and salt. Add more sherry, if desired. Break fish into pieces. Add very carefully to the sauce. Pour in casserole (about 3-quart). Top with buttered bread-crumbs and paprika. Bake 20-30 minutes at 400°. Freezes well. 8-10 servings

Virginia P. Rick (Mrs. James, III)

Flounder with Cheese Sauce

1½ pounds flounder fillets
¼ cup evaporated milk
¼ cup milk, approximate
¾ teaspoon salt
2 Tablespoons margarine
2 Tablespoons flour
¼ cup diced Cheddar cheese
2 Tablespoons sherry, or to
   taste

Arrange fish fillets in single layer in baking dish. Salt and barely cover with milk. Bake at 400° for 5-10 minutes, until fish flakes easily with a fork. In the meantime, mix margarine and flour in saucepan over low heat. Remove from heat and add cheese. When fish is done, lift out of pan carefully. Set aside. Add liquid from fish to cheese mixture. Heat until cheese is melted and mixture is bubbly. Add sherry to taste. Put fish back in baking dish. Pour cheese mixture over fish. Brown under broiler just before serving. 4 servings

Virginia P. Rick (Mrs. James, III)

Salmon Loaf with Dill Sauce

SALMON LOAF:
2 Tablespoons salad oil
¾ cup finely chopped celery
½ cup chopped onion
1 (7¾ ounce) can salmon
1 egg, slightly beaten
1 (5.3 ounce) can evaporated
   milk
1 cup fine bread crumbs
1 teaspoon salt
¼ teaspoon pepper
DILL SAUCE:
½ cup mayonnaise
¼ cup sour cream
1 Tablespoon lemon juice
1 Tablespoon milk
2 teaspoons dill weed
½ teaspoon sugar
½ teaspoon salt

Prepare at least 1½ hours before serving. Put oil in 2-quart saucepan. Sauté celery and onion over medium heat, about 10 minutes, until tender. Remove from heat; add salmon and salmon liquid, milk, breadcrumbs, salt and pepper. Mix until smooth. Grease 6 x 3½-inch loaf pan and spoon mixture into pan. Bake at 350° for 50 minutes. Remove loaf from pan. Serve either hot or cold with Dill Sauce. 4 servings

Dill Sauce: Combine all ingredients and refrigerate.

Susan M. Morley

Frog Legs

4 pairs frog legs, cleaned
  and skinned
1 small onion, sliced
2 cloves garlic, mashed in 1
  Tablespoon salt
1 cup white vinegar (or more)
1 lemon, sliced
BATTER:
1 cup flour
1 egg
1 teaspoon salt
1 teaspoon black pepper
¼ teaspoon cayenne pepper
½ cup milk

Place frog legs on a flat dish or pan and cover with vinegar. Sprinkle onions and garlic salt over top. Marinate for 2 hours. Drain. Boil in salted water with lemon for 20 minutes. Remove and drain.

Mix all batter ingredients together. Dip frog legs in batter and fry quickly in hot fat.
4 servings

Terry Morris (Mrs. Douglas)

Shrimp Elégante

½ cup butter
½ cup margarine
8 Tablespoons all-purpose
  flour
2 pints half and half
3 (3-ounce) cans chopped
  mushrooms with liquid
6 green onions, finely chopped
½ teaspoon tarragon
½ teaspoon rosemary
¼ teaspoon cayenne pepper
1 Tablespoon celery seed
4 bay leaves
5 cloves garlic, crushed
Salt to taste
4 pounds shrimp, cooked
  and peeled
½ cup sherry
Toast cups:
3-4 loaves white sandwich
  bread
1 cup butter

Melt butter and margarine in a saucepan; add flour. Add cream and cook over medium heat until well blended, stirring constantly. Add mushrooms and liquid. Add green onions, tarragon, rosemary, cayenne pepper, celery seed, bay leaves, garlic and salt. Cook slowly for 15 minutes, do not boil. Add shrimp and sherry, and simmer 10 minutes. For luncheon or dinner, serve over rice. For a cocktail party, serve in toast cups.

Toast cups: Using a ½ inch cookie cutter, cut out bread (3 rounds per slice of bread). Brush melted butter on both sides of bread and press into small muffin tins. Bake at 300° for about 20 minutes, or until light brown and crusty. These can be placed in plastic bags and frozen until party time. 12 servings or 50 cocktail servings

Nancy Kirby (Mrs. Jeff D., III)

Shrimp with Tarragon

1 clove garlic, finely minced
½ teaspoon salt
½ cup butter, room
temperature
2 teaspoons finely chopped
parsley
1 teaspoon minced fresh or
dried tarragon
¾ cup soft bread crumbs
3 Tablespoons sherry
1 pound cooked, shelled
shrimp (2 pounds fresh
shrimp before shelling)

Crush garlic and salt together with back of a spoon until it is almost a purée. Cream the purée with butter, parsley, tarragon, bread crumbs and sherry. Spread half of mixture in bottom of individual ramekins. Arrange an equal portion of shrimp in each ramekin. Spread remaining butter mixture over shrimp. Bake at 400° until shrimp are done and until bread crumbs are brown, about 10 minutes depending on size of shrimp. 4 servings or 8 appetizer servings

Jane Acker (Mrs. Reynolds B.)
Westport, Connecticut

Shrimp Asopao

A Puerto Rican peasant stew usually served as a main course

¼ cup olive oil
1½ cups finely chopped onion
1½ cups finely chopped green
pepper
¼ pound bacon, chopped
¼ pound piece salt pork
6 cans condensed chicken
broth
2 cups uncooked converted
white rice
3 pounds large raw shrimp,
shelled and deveined
1 (10 ounce) package frozen
green peas
½ cup capers, drained
½ cup sliced stuffed green
olives
2 pimientos, sliced
4 tomatoes, peeled, seeded
and chopped

Heat oil in 6-8 quart kettle. Add onion, pepper, bacon and pork; cook covered over low heat 10 minutes. Add broth and 6 soup cans water. Bring to boil; add rice; return to boil; reduce heat; cook covered, stirring occasionally, 30 minutes. Add shrimp; bring to boil; reduce heat and simmer 15 minutes. Add frozen peas, capers, olives and pimientos. Return to boiling; reduce heat and cook 5 minutes or until peas are tender. Discard salt pork. Serve in deep soup plates with crusty bread and a fruit salad. 5 quarts 10-12 servings

Pamela T. Marcus

Shrimp Jekyll
A good way to make shrimp go a long way!

1½ sticks butter
8 ounces fresh mushrooms, sliced
1 cup chopped onions
2 pounds small shrimp, cleaned and deveined
1 teaspoon seasoned salt
½ teaspoon lemon pepper
2 Tablespoons chopped parsley
1 Tablespoon Worcestershire sauce
½ cup grated Romano cheese
4 ounces chopped ripe olives (optional)
12 ounces thin spaghetti (Vermicelli) broken into thirds

Melt ¾ stick butter over moderate heat. Sauté mushrooms and onions in butter about 5-8 minutes. Transfer to mixing bowl. Melt ¾ stick butter in same pan and quickly cook shrimp until just pink. Transfer shrimp and liquid to same mixing bowl. Add salt, lemon pepper, parsley, Worcestershire, ¼ cup cheese and olives to shrimp-mushroom mixture. While preparing above, cook vermicelli al dente (about 9 minutes). Drain. Add to other ingredients while warm. Place in baking dish and top with remaining ¼ cup cheese. Bake at 350° for 20-30 minutes or until warmed through. This dish is best if made a few hours in advance to allow the flavors to blend. 6-8 servings

Emy Blair (Mrs. Duane)

Shrimp With Fresh Mushrooms

¼ cup butter
1 pound fresh shrimp, peeled and deveined
2 Tablespoons shallots or green onions, minced
½ pound fresh mushrooms, sliced
1 Tablespoon flour
½ teaspoon salt
Freshly ground black pepper
3 Tablespoons sherry
1½ cups sour cream

Melt butter in a large skillet; add shrimp and shallots, and sauté until shrimp turn pink. Add mushroom slices and cook 5 minutes. Mix flour, salt and pepper. Sprinkle over ingredients in pan. Add sherry and sour cream, blending well; and continue heating gently. Adjust seasonings. Serve with steamed rice in a separate bowl, or spoon mixture into patty shells. 4 servings

Joan McMahan (Mrs. James P.)

Shrimp Curry
An outstanding curry!

Shrimp:
2 pounds raw shrimp, (18-20 count per pound)
1 Tablespoon salt
1 small onion, sliced
½ lemon, sliced
5 whole black peppercorns
CURRY SAUCE:
3 Tablespoons butter
1 cup finely chopped onion
1 cup finely chopped, pared apple
1 clove garlic, crushed
2-3 teaspoons Madras curry powder
¼ cup unsifted flour
1 teaspoon salt
1 teaspoon grated fresh ginger, (or ¼ teaspoon ground ginger)
¼ teaspoon ground cardamon
¼ teaspoon pepper
22 ounces chicken broth (undiluted)
2 Tablespoons fresh lime juice
2 teaspoons grated lime peel
¼ cup chopped chutney

Rinse shrimp under cold water. Combine 1 quart water, salt, onions, lemon and pepper. Bring to a boil and add shrimp. Reduce heat and simmer 5 minutes, or until shrimp turn pink. Remove from liquid, peel and devein. Refrigerate until needed.

In a large saucepan, melt butter, and stir in curry powder. Add onions, apple, and garlic, and sauté until soft, about 5 minutes. Remove pan from heat; stir in flour and other spices. Gradually add broth, lime juice and peel. Return to heat and bring mixture to a boil, stirring constantly. Reduce heat and simmer sauce for 20 minutes. Stir occasionally. Mixture may be prepared several hours in advance, and refrigerated until serving time. Before serving, heat sauce, add shrimp and chutney. Serve hot with rice, and your choice of condiments. 6 servings Condiment suggestions: chopped peanuts, tomatoes, raisins, coconut, chopped hard-cooked eggs, green pepper.

Susan M. Morley

Steamed Shrimp

1 pound raw shrimp, unpeeled
½ cup sweet pickle juice
¾ cup cider vinegar
3 Tablespoons pickling spice
Dash garlic salt
2 teaspoons salt

Place shrimp in bottom of a heavy pot. Pour sweet pickle juice and cider vinegar over shrimp. Cook over high heat until shrimp begin to turn pink. Add pickling spice, garlic salt and salt. Stir until very pink, about 3-4 minutes. Pour into bowl with juices. Cool, peel and serve. Shrimp may be prepared ahead and used as an appetizer or in a salad.
2-4 servings

Mary Lib Dillard (Mrs. George P.)

Shrimp in Puff Pastry

20-24 large shrimp
Lemon juice
Salt and pepper
Worcestershire sauce
Butter
1 large onion, finely chopped
2 cloves garlic, crushed
4-5 green onions, finely
    chopped
6-8 mushrooms, thinly sliced
1 large tomato, peeled and
    diced
1 Tablespoon chives
1 bunch parsley, finely
    chopped
Salt and pepper to taste
1 sheet of puff pastry cut in
    5 x 5-inch squares
Slightly beaten egg
Sauce Bernaise

Peel and devein shrimp, and marinate in lemon juice, salt, pepper, and Worcestershire sauce in refrigerator. Melt butter in skillet large enough to hold all herbs and vegetables. Sauté onions, crushed garlic, green onions, mushrooms, tomatoes, chives and parsley, and season with salt and pepper. This should not take longer than 5 minutes. Take off stove and cool. Take about 5-6 shrimp and place on pastry squares and top with mixture divided equally among the 4 servings. Fold opposite edges of pastry and brush with egg. Bake at 400° until pastry is done. Serve topped with Sauce Bérnaise, with assorted vegetables on the side. 4 servings

Yvette Greune
Old Vinings Inn
Atlanta, Georgia

Barbequed Shrimp

Give everyone a damp hot towel afterwards
Spicy and messy, but fun!

2 pounds (16-20 per pound)
    shrimp, unpeeled
6 cloves garlic, crushed
2 bay leaves
1 teaspoon rosemary
1 teaspoon oregano
1 teaspoon whole peppercorns,
    crushed
1 Tablespoon salt
2 Tablespoons Sauterne wine
4 Tablespoons olive oil

Heat oil in frying pan. Add shrimp and spices. Sauté 20 minutes. Add sauterne and simmer 5 minutes. Peel shrimp at table and dunk in sauce. Serve with hot crisp bread, also good for dunking into sauce.
4-6 servings

Elise M. Griffin

HINT

When handling freshly caught fish, coat hands with salt for easier gripping.

Sweet and Sour Shrimp

1 onion, sliced thin
1 green pepper, sliced or
    chopped
¼ cup butter, melted
½ cup sugar
1 (8½ ounce) can pineapple
    chunks, undrained
2 Tablespoons cornstarch
½ teaspoon dry mustard
¼ teaspoon salt
½ cup white vinegar
1 Tablespoon soy sauce
1 cup cherry tomatoes
1 pound shrimp, boiled,
    shelled and deveined
1 cup fresh Chinese snow
    peas or 1 package frozen
    peas
1 cup toasted slivered almonds
    (optional)

Sauté onion and green pepper in butter. Mix sugar, pineapple syrup, cornstarch, dry mustard, salt, vinegar and soy sauce, and add to the sautéed vegetables. Simmer for 10 minutes. Before serving, add tomatoes, shrimp, snow peas and pineapple. Cook for an additional 5-10 minutes. Serve on rice. Garnish with toasted almonds if desired. 6-8 servings

Cile M. Davidson (Mrs. Charles, Jr.)

Shrimp and Wild Rice

2 (6 ounce) packages long
    grain and wild rice, cooked
2 Tablespoons butter
1 cup bias-cut celery
½ cup chopped green onions
2 (2½ ounce) jars sliced
    mushrooms, drained
2 Tablespoons chopped
    pimiento
2 cups cooked and peeled
    shrimp (more if desired)
Salt and pepper to taste
TOPPING:
1 can cream of mushroom soup
1⅓ cups sour cream
⅔ cup dry bread crumbs
2 Tablespoons chopped parsley

Melt butter and sauté celery, green onions, pimiento and mushrooms until tender. Add shrimp, salt and pepper. Add rice. Spoon mixture into a greased 2-quart casserole. Mix soup and sour cream. Spread over rice mixture. Top with bread crumbs and parsley. Bake 30 minutes at 325°. May be prepared in advance. 8 servings

Mrs. Kirk Scruggs

Crabmeat Soufflé

1½ **cups fresh or frozen crabmeat, drained and flaked**
¼ **cup butter or margarine**
¼ **cup flour**
1 **cup milk**
½ **teaspoon salt**
1 **cup shredded sharp Cheddar cheese**
4 **eggs, separated**

Preheat oven to 300°. Place crabmeat in bottom of a 5-cup soufflé dish. Make a white sauce with butter, flour, milk and salt. Add cheese and stir until melted. Remove from heat. Add slightly beaten egg yolks, and cool. Beat egg whites until stiff, and fold lightly into sauce. Pour sauce over crabmeat in dish. With tip of spoon, make a slight indentation or "track" around top of soufflé, 1 inch from edge to form a top hat. Bake at 300° for 60-65 minutes, or until browned and set. Serve immediately. 4 servings

Jeanine C. Andrews (Mrs. Edward B.)

Crab Imperial

This receives rave reviews in Tidewater, Virginia
where folks enjoy their seafood

2 **cups backfin crabmeat**
4 **Tablespoons butter, melted**
1 **teaspoon grated onion**
2 **Tablespoons chopped pimiento**
4 **Tablespoons mayonnaise**
2 **Tablespoons cream**
1 **teaspoon Worcestershire sauce**
½ **cup finely chopped green pepper**
Salt and pepper to taste
Ritz cracker crumbs

Combine all ingredients except cracker crumbs. Fill individual baking shells or 1-quart casserole. Spread top with additional mayonnaise and sprinkle with rolled Ritz cracker crumbs. Bake 30 minutes in a 350° oven. 4 servings

Mrs. Alfred J. Westcott
Norfolk, Virginia

Crab Continental

4 Tablespoons butter
4 Tablespoons flour
Dash pepper
1 teaspoon salt
⅛ teaspoon paprika
2 cups milk
½ pound sharp yellow cheese, grated
6 hard-boiled eggs, chopped
2 Tablespoons Worcestershire sauce
1 cup stuffed olives, sliced
1 (12 ounce) can mushrooms, or fresh if desired
1 cup slivered almonds
3 cans (6 to 8 ounces) crabmeat
4 Tablespoons sherry (optional)
Parmesan cheese

Melt butter. Add flour and salt and cook until bubbly. Add heated milk gradually stirring until sauce is slightly thickened. Add paprika and pepper. Add cheese and let melt. Pour in large baking pan and add remaining ingredients. Top with Parmesan cheese. Bake 30 to 40 minutes at 350°. May also be baked and then used as a filing for patty shells. 6 servings

Beth Johnston (Mrs. J. Gibson)

Eggplant Stuffed with Crab and Shrimp

6 medium eggplant
3 Tablespoons butter
4 green peppers, finely chopped
4 medium carrots, finely chopped
½ cup chopped parsley
½ cup finely chopped celery
3 cloves garlic, minced
1 pound white lump crabmeat
1 pound small shrimp, shelled
Salt and pepper to taste
Cup bread crumbs
Paprika
1 cup butter, melted

Boil eggplants until soft, cut in halves (or cook in microwave—place halves on tray 1 inch apart, cook 2 minutes, rotate and cook 2-3 minutes more until tender). Scoop out meat, reserve shells. Sauté vegetables in 3 Tablespoons butter until tender. Add eggplant and cook over medium heat until most of liquid has evaporated. Add shrimp and cook 15 minutes. Add crabmeat and bread crumbs, cook 3-5 minutes, and season with salt and pepper. Stuff shells with mixture, and sprinkle with paprika. Pour melted butter over, and heat in a 350° oven until thoroughly warmed. 12 Servings

Lucy Dyer

Baked Crab

This Gulf coast specialty is the favorite of our cover artist.
It's his mother's recipe.

1 cup finely chopped celery
½ cup finely chopped parsley
1 cup finely chopped green
   pepper
1 cup finely chopped onion
3 Tablespoons bacon grease
1 pound fresh lump crabmeat
1 pound fresh claw crabmeat
2 cups milk
2 eggs, beaten
2 cups fresh bread crumbs
½ cup butter, melted
½ cup buttered bread crumbs
   for topping

In a large skillet, sauté vegetables in bacon grease until soft. Combine remaining ingredients and mix well; add sautéed vegetables. Place in a 2-quart baking dish, sprinkle with buttered crumbs and bake in 350° oven for 30-45 minutes until bubbling and nicely browned. Serve with a colorful fruit salad, a green vegetable, and a dry white wine. 8-10 servings

Mrs. T.S. Morton, Jr.
Gulfport, Miss.

Broiled Soft Shell Crabs

8 soft shelled crabs
½ pound butter, melted
4 garlic cloves, minced
6-8 green onions, chopped
1 teaspoon salt
Pepper
Paprika

Wash crabs and drain well. Place in single layer in baking pan; use earthen-ware if possible. Mix remaining ingredients and use to brush crabs. Broil under high heat until claws are crisp. Serve with slaw and hot French bread. 4 servings

Terry C. Morris (Mrs. Douglas)

Baked Scallops

1 pound scallops (if large, cut
   in 4 pieces)
Fresh bread crumbs (about 6
   slices), buttered
2 eggs, lightly beaten with
   pinch of salt
⅓ cup melted butter or
   margarine (approximate,
   add more if necessary)

Dip scallops in egg and then in crumbs. Put in shallow baking dish in single layer. Drizzle with melted butter. Can be done earlier in the day to this point and refrigerated until time to cook. Bake in 450° oven for 15-20 minutes, until brown and crisp. Serve with tartare sauce. 3-4 servings

Virginia P. Rick (Mrs. James, III.)

Seafood Casserole
Excellent for a buffet supper

2 (6-ounce) packages wild and long grain rice mix
1 pound lump crab meat, cooked and cleaned or 3 (6 ounce) cans white crab meat
1 pound fresh shrimp, cooked or 4 (4½ ounce) cans shrimp, drained
3 cans cream of mushroom soup
½ onion, grated
1 cup chopped green pepper
1 cup chopped celery
1 (14-ounce) jar pimiento, chopped
2 Tablespoons lemon juice
1 (8-ounce) can button mushrooms
1 (14-ounce) can artichoke hearts, drained well

Cook rice as label directs. Remove any cartilage from crab. Rinse shrimp in cold water and drain well. Preheat oven to 325°. Mix all ingredients and place in a greased 4-quart casserole. Bake for 1½ hours or, use two 2-quart dishes and bake for 45 minutes. 14 servings

Constance D. Wilson (Mrs. A.E., Jr.)

Scallop Kabobs
A low calorie meal

1½ pounds sea scallops
2 cups canned pineapple chunks
2 cups small, whole mushroom caps
1 medium green pepper, cut into 1-inch squares
¼ cup soy sauce
¼ cup lemon juice
¼ cup chopped fresh parsley
½ teaspoon salt
Dash pepper
½ teaspoon grated fresh ginger (optional)

Combine all ingredients in a large bowl; toss lightly but thoroughly. Let stand 30 minutes, stirring occasionally. Drain ingredients; reserve marinade and keep warm. Thread scallops, pineapple, mushrooms and green pepper, evenly divided, on each of eight 12-inch skewers. Broil on grill about 4 inches from heat source for about 5 minutes. Turn and cook 5 minutes longer. May be prepared earlier in day and refrigerated until ready to cook. 4 servings

Dot W. Smith (Mrs. William P., III)

Scallop Sauté

¼ cup butter
½ teaspoon salt
⅛ teaspoon pepper
1 clove garlic, minced
½ teaspoon paprika
1 pound bay scallops
3 Tablespoons lemon juice
1 Tablespoon parsley

In a large skillet, heat ½ of the butter with the garlic and seasonings. Add scallops to cover bottom of skillet without crowding. Cook quickly on high heat, stirring occasionally until golden, about 5-7 minutes. Repeat until all scallops are cooked, keeping the cooked ones warm. In same skillet, place parsley, lemon juice and remaining butter. Pour sauce over scallops. 4 servings

Cookbook Committee

Oysters Pan Roast

½ cup butter
2 slices bacon, cut in ½ inch pieces
1 bunch shallots or green onions, finely chopped
1 bunch parsley, finely chopped
1-2 cloves garlic, finely chopped
½ cup flour (or more if a thick sauce is desired)
1 quart oysters (select), undrained
¼ teaspoon seasoned pepper
½ teaspoon salt
4 Tablespoons Worcestershire sauce
¼ cup vermouth
1-2 dashes Tabasco sauce
1 cup Italian bread crumbs

Melt butter in saucepan. Sauté bacon, shallots, parsley and garlic 5 minutes over medium heat. Remove pan from heat, and stir in flour. Meanwhile, heat oysters in their liquid until the edges curl. Drain, and pour the oyster liquid gradually into the flour mixture, stirring rapidly until blended. Return to heat and cook, stirring constantly, until sauce becomes thick. Add seasoned pepper, salt, Worcestershire, vermouth and Tabasco. Taste and adjust seasoning as desired. Gently stir in oysters. Pour into buttered casserole dish and sprinkle bread crumbs on top, or use 4 individual ramekins. Bake 20 minutes at 475°. Entire dish may be made in advance and baked at the last minute. A green salad, French bread and a special dessert make this a wonderful company dish for oyster lovers. 4 servings

Elise M. Griffin

Deviled Oysters

1 pint oysters with liquid
¼ cup butter, melted
1 cup oyster cracker crumbs
1 medium green pepper,
    seeded and finely chopped
¼ cup finely chopped parsley
1 medium onion, grated
2 teaspoons Worcestershire
    sauce
2 hard-cooked eggs, chopped
3 eggs, slightly beaten
½ cup light cream
1 teaspoon Dijon mustard
⅛ teaspoon cayenne pepper
½ teaspoon salt

Combine all ingredients and toss to mix well. Turn into a buttered 5-6 cup soufflé dish or casserole. Bake 30 minutes at 375° until set and lightly browned. For individual servings, spoon mixture into buttered ramekins or scallop shells and bake for 15 minutes. To serve as hors d'oeuvres, bake in buttered oyster or clam shells for 10 minutes or until set. 6 servings

Peggy Weitnauer (Mrs. John)

Lobster Supreme
For a special party

8 lobster tails, split
¼ pound butter
4 Tablespoons flour
1 teaspoon salt
1 teaspoon paprika
Dash cayenne
2 cups half and half
2 teaspoons lemon juice
TOPPING:
¼ cup cracker crumbs
¼ cup grated Parmesan
    cheese
1 Tablespoon butter, melted

Boil lobster tails in salted water. Cut meat out and dice. Sauté meat in butter, remove, blend in flour, salt, paprika, and cayenne. Slowly stir in cream, cook until thick—boil one minute. Stir in lemon juice. Spoon into shells and add topping. Bake at 450°, approximately 10-12 minutes. May be refrigerated before the last cooking. Goes well with fresh asparagus topped with lemon juice, butter and toasted sesame seeds. 4 servings

Lynn Herring (Mrs. Roy P.)

Lobster Thermidor

4 boxes rock lobster tails
½ pound fresh mushrooms,
   sliced
4 Tablespoons butter
4 Tablespoons flour
Salt and pepper to taste
⅛ teaspoon Tabasco sauce
1 teaspoon Worcestershire
   sauce
1 pint half and half
½ cup grated Parmesan
   cheese
1 cup soft bread crumbs
1 cup grated Cheddar cheese
4 Tablespoons butter

Follow package directions for boiling lobster tails. Remove from water and allow to cool. Remove lobster from shells; cut into bite-size pieces. Reserve shells for serving if desired. Melt butter in large skillet; add mushrooms and sauté over low heat. Add flour, salt and pepper, Tabasco and Worcestershire sauce. Remove from heat and add cream slowly, stirring constantly. Simmer sauce over low heat until sauce thickens. Add lobster and Parmesan cheese. Flatten lobster shells. Fill shells with mixture. Sprinkle tops with bread crumbs and grated Cheddar cheese. Dot with butter. Broil 3 minutes or until lightly browned.
4 servings

White Clam Sauce for Spaghetti
A superb quickie—elegant and easy

1 onion chopped
1 bunch green onions and
   some tops, chopped
¼ cup olive oil (Berio brand)
2 cans Buitoni white clam
   spaghetti sauce
1 pound shrimp or lobster
¼ cup dry vermouth
1 Tablespoon Worcestershire
   sauce
Salt and pepper to taste
½ teaspoon sugar
Juice of ½ lemon
1 (8 ounce) package spinach
   noodles or vermicelli,
   cooked according to
   directions

Sauté onions gently in olive oil. Add clams, seafood and seasonings. Simmer slowly for a few minutes. Spoon over cooked spinach noodles or vermicelli.
4 servings

George Pendley

Meats

How to Stir-Fry Successfully

Three rules—cut bite-size, cook quickly, and serve immediately.

Preparation

Meats and vegetables which are cooked together should be of equal size and thickness so cooking times will be the same.

Cut meats across the grain into thin strips. Meat will slice easier if partially frozen.

Cut celery, asparagus, and less tender vegetables diagonally to expose more surface and allow quicker cooking.

Types of Oil

Any vegetable oil which does not have a strong flavor is acceptable for stir-frying. Peanut oil is best; it has a good flavor and does not burn easily. The Chinese prefer to use lard which gives a rich flavor and clear color, but we do not recommend its high cholesterol content. Butter, margarine, olive oil and solid shortenings are not suitable. Chicken fat gives a good flavor to certain vegetable dishes, especially Chinese cabbage.

The oil may be flavored by adding a clove of garlic and 1-2 slices of fresh ginger. Brown them in the oil, then remove before adding other ingredients.

Method

Always stir-fry the minimum amount of time necessary. Meats will become tough if over-cooked; vegetables should remain crisp to retain color and nutrients.

Have all ingredients prepared and within reach before beginning to cook. Heat wok or large skillet over high heat, add 1-2 Tablespoons oil. Cook ingredients in small batches, over medium-high to high heat, stirring constantly adding more oil as needed for each batch. Meats and vegetables are usually cooked separately. Drain on a rack or on paper towels. If a sauce is desired, return all ingredients to the pan and add cornstarch dissolved in water, broth, or soy sauce. Use 1 Tablespoon cornstarch to 2-3 Tablespoons liquid. Additional soy sauce, sesame oil, salt and pepper, MSG and wine may be added as desired for flavor. If a marinade is used for the meat, dissolve cornstarch in marinade and add to the pan. Cook just until thickened.

A good basic marinade for beef: To 1 pound sirloin or round steak, thinly sliced, add 3 Tablespoons soy sauce, 1 Tablespoon dry sherry or Mirin, 1 teaspoon sugar and ¼ teaspoon MSG. Marinate at least 30 minutes.

Soy Sauce

Imported Japanese soy sauce is a good all-purpose sauce to use. For variety, try experimenting with good Chinese imports; the dark variety is thick and black, the light variety is thin and more salty.

Tournedos Sautés Aux Champignons

2 Tablespoons butter
3 Tablespoons minced shallots
½ pound mushrooms, sliced
2 Tablespoons chopped chives
1 teaspoon marjoram
Salt and pepper to taste
½ cup dry white wine
6 fillet steaks, 1 inch thick
    or 1 (3½-4 pound) tender-
    loin roast
¼ cup brandy

In skillet melt butter, stir in shallots and cook slowly 1 minute. Add mushrooms and cook 1 minute. Stir in herbs, seasonings and white wine. Cook over moderately high heat for 3 minutes. In a separate pan, sauté steaks in butter until cooked to your preference. (May be grilled if desired.) Cook the roast, uncovered, at 325° for approximately 1 hour, and cut in ¾ inch slices. Pour sauce over meat. Heat brandy, ignite and pour over meat; serve immediately. Sauce may be prepared in advance. 6 servings

Sandy L. Carley (Mrs. George H.)

Tournedos in Puff Pastry

This elegant entrée may be prepared early in the day
and refrigerated until cooking time

6 tournedos (filet mignon)
5 Tablespoons butter
Salt and pepper to taste
½ pound fresh mushrooms,
    chopped
½ cup liver pâté (homemade
    or liverwurst)
3 Tablespoons sherry
6 frozen Pepperidge Farm
    Patty Shells, thawed
1 egg, separated

Sauté tournedos in 3 Tablespoons butter for 3 minutes on each side. Season and cool. Sauté mushrooms in remaining 2 Tablespoons butter; add pâté and sauté until brown. Add enough sherry to bind mixture. Spread a thin layer of pâté mixture on top of each tournedo. Cool again. Remove center portion of patty shells, and roll each into a thin round; roll out shells in the same manner. Place each of the 6 tournedos on the smaller rounds and cover with the large rounds. Paint edges with slightly beaten egg yolk and seal. Bake 10 minutes in a 400° oven until pastry is golden. Serve with Madeira Sauce (see Index). 6 servings

Ann T. McCrory (Mrs. Charles O.)

Helen Corbitt's Tenderloin of Beef with Lobster

3 lobster tails
½ cup imported soy sauce
1 3-4 pound tenderloin, oven-
    ready*
2 Tablespoons grated fresh
    ginger
1 medium onion, sliced
¾ cup dry sherry
4 Tablespoons butter, melted
Chopped parsley
*An oven ready tenderloin has
    had all excess fat and
    membrane trimmed away.

Preheat oven to 350°. Split lobster tails, loosen meat. Rub with soy sauce. Bake for 10 minutes. Remove meat from shells. Preheat oven to 450°. Rub the tenderloin with soy sauce and grated ginger. Place on top of sliced onions in a broiler pan and bake for 25 minutes at 450°. Baste with half of the sherry. Split tenderloin ¾-inch deep, stuff lobster into cavity. Place under broiler just long enough to heat, basting with a mixture of the remaining soy sauce and sherry, or heat briefly in a 350° oven. Sprinkle with melted butter and chopped parsley before serving.
6 servings

Mongolian Beef

1½ pounds beef (preferably
    sirloin), cut in thin strips
½ teaspoon MSG
¼ cup peanut oil
1 cup beef bouillon
½ teaspoon sugar
¼ teaspoon grated ginger root
1 teaspoon Japanese soy sauce
2 large ribs celery, cut bite size
2 green peppers, cut bite size
1 large onion, cut bite size
2 large tomatoes, cut in 8
    sections
2 teaspoons cornstarch
2 Tablespoons water

Sprinkle beef with MSG. Brown quickly in hot oil in a skillet or wok. Add bouillon, sugar, ginger, and soy sauce. Bring to a boil and simmer 15 minutes. Add vegetables and cook 5 minutes longer. Combine cornstarch and water, add to beef and stir until it thickens. Serve over rice.
4 servings

Pamela T. Marcus

Beef and Oyster Sauce
A Chinese "stir-fry" dish

4 Tablespoons bottled oyster
    sauce (found in gourmet or
    oriental food stores)
1 teaspoon sugar
Dash pepper
1 cup beef broth
4 Tablespoons cornstarch
¼ cup Japanese soy sauce
4 Tablespoons water
2 Tablespoons peanut oil
1 onion, chopped
1 clove garlic, minced
1 teaspoon fresh ginger
1 pound sirloin or round steak,
    thinly sliced

Combine oyster sauce, sugar, pepper and broth. In another bowl, blend cornstarch, water and soy sauce to a paste. Put oil in wok or large fry pan and bring to high heat. Stir-fry onion, garlic and ginger for 30 seconds. Add beef and stir-fry until it loses its redness. Add oyster sauce mixture, heat thoroughly, and cook covered for one minute. Add cornstarch mixture to thicken. Stir well; turn on low to keep warm. Serve with steamed rice. 4 servings

Decie Nygaard (Mrs. W.F.)

Blackbirds

3 pounds top round steak,
    1" thick
1 pound bacon
Salt & pepper
Celery salt
8 medium onions

Cut steak in strips ¼" wide. Lay flat and place slice of bacon on top. Roll bacon inside and insert toothpicks to hold. Place in frying pan and sear top, bottom and sides. Remove. Chop 8 onions and brown in same pan. Remove onions. Replace blackbirds and pour onions on top. Add salts, pepper and enough water to cover ⅔ of meat (about 1 cup). Cover tightly and simmer for 2 hours 15 minutes. Remove grease from top and serve. 8 servings

Mrs. William J. Patterson

Pic-L-Nic Beef Roll
Great for a tailgate picnic

1 (2½ pound) flank steak
Prepared mustard
Seasoned salt, and pepper
6 dill pickles, quartered
   lengthwise
6 carrots, quartered lengthwise
6 scallions
Shortening
1 beef bouillon cube
¼ cup vinegar
2 cups water
1 cup dry red wine
1 Tablespoon whole black
   peppercorns
2 bay leaves
2 stalks celery
Parsley

Spread mustard thinly on steak and sprinkle with salt and pepper. Starting at narrow side, alternate rows of pickles, carrots and scallions on top of steak. Roll up in jelly roll fashion and tie securely with string at 1-inch intervals. Brown steak on all sides in hot oil. Pour off drippings. Add water, bouillon cube, vinegar, wine, peppercorns, bay leaf and celery. Cover and cook for 3 hours. Allow to cool in liquid and chill overnight. To serve, remove from liquid and slice diagonally ¼ inch thick. Serve cold; garnished with parsley. 6 servings

Susan M. Morley

Charcoaled Flank Steak

2 flank steaks (about 2½
   pounds)
½ cup soy sauce
½ cup salad oil
3 Tablespoons wine vinegar
2 Tablespoons instant minced
   onion
¼ teaspoon garlic powder
½ teaspoon MSG
1 Tablespoon liquid smoke
2-3 Tablespoons barbecue
   sauce
2-3 Tablespoons A-1 steak
   sauce
½ cup red wine (optional)

Select top quality flank steaks. Combine all other ingredients and pour over steaks in a shallow pan. Marinate in the refrigerator for 8 to 10 hours, turning meat occasionally. Cook on a charcoal grill over a medium to high fire. Steaks should be cooked rare or medium. If cooked well done, it could be tough. To serve, carve in very thin slices (electric knife helpful) across the grain. 5-6 servings

Mary M. Joines (Mrs. I.W.)

Marinated London Broil

1 (2½-3 pound) London broil
MARINADE:
1 can beer
½ cup peanut oil
1 teaspoon dry mustard
1 teaspoon ginger
1 teaspoon Worcestershire
    sauce
1 Tablespoon sugar
2 Tablespoons orange
    marmalade
1 teaspoon garlic powder
Salt and freshly ground pepper

Mix all marinade ingredients together and pour into oblong glass casserole. Place meat in mixture and spoon marinade over top and sides of meat. Cover and place in refrigerator for 24 hours. Turn meat at least twice. Barbecue to personal taste, brushing with marinade. 4-6 servings

Helen W. Ward (Mrs. William T., Jr.)

Braised Sirloin Tips

1 pound fresh mushrooms,
    sliced
¼ cup butter, melted
1 Tablespoon salad oil
1 (3 pound) sirloin tip steak,
    cut in 1 inch cubes
¾ cup beef bouillon
¾ cup red wine
2 Tablespoons soy sauce
2 cloves garlic, minced
½ onion, grated
2 Tablespoons cornstarch
⅓ cup beef bouillon
½ (10¾ ounce) can cream of
    mushroom soup, undiluted
Salt to taste

Sauté mushrooms in 2 Tablespoons butter and spoon into 3-quart casserole. Add remaining butter and salad oil to skillet; add meat and brown. Spoon over mushrooms. Combine bouillon, wine, soy sauce, garlic and onion; add to skillet, scraping bottom to salvage all particles. Blend cornstarch with remaining ⅓ cup bouillon and stir into wine mixture. Cook, stirring constantly, until smooth and thickened. Spoon over meat, stirring gently to mix. Cover and bake at 275° for 1 hour. Add soup and season with salt. Return to oven; bake approximately 1 hour, or until tender. Serve over rice. May be frozen or prepared in advance. 6-8 servings

Mrs. John Stroop

Beef with Artichokes

2 pounds top sirloin, cubed
⅓ cup flour
Salt and pepper
2 Tablespoons salad oil
2 (8 ounce) cans tomato sauce
1 clove garlic, crushed
1 cup dry red wine
2 beef bouillon cubes
½ teaspoon dill weed
1 can artichoke hearts, drained
1 (1 pound) can small white
    onions, drained
1 (4 ounce) can mushrooms,
    drained

Dredge meat with flour, seasoned with salt and pepper, and brown in oil; set meat aside. Add tomato sauce, garlic, wine, bouillon cubes and dill weed to skillet and mix well. Return meat to pan and simmer for 90 minutes. Add vegetables and heat 30 minutes longer. Serve with rice. 4 servings

Helen W. Ward (Mrs. William T., Jr.)

Carbonnade of Beef
This is a national dish of Belgium

1 (2½ pound) round steak,
    ¼ inch thick
½ cup all purpose flour
½ cup butter or margarine
8 large onions, sliced
2 garlic cloves, minced
1 beef bouillon cube
1 teaspoon thyme leaves
2 teaspoons salt
¼ teaspoon pepper
1 (12 ounce) can beer

Cut round steak into 8 pieces. Using a meat mallet or the side of a saucer, pound ¼ cup flour into one side of steak. Repeat on the other side using remaining flour. Melt ¼ cup butter or margarine in a large skillet. Cook onions over medium heat in melted fat until golden. Drain. In the same skillet, melt remaining fat, and brown meat well on both sides, a few pieces at a time. Return meat and onions to the skillet. Add remaining ingredients. Cover and cook over low heat for 1 to 2 hours until meat is fork tender. 8 servings

Sandra R. Pritchett (Mrs. Edwin P.)

Swiss Steak Supreme

½ Tablespoon butter
2 pounds round steak, sliced thin
1 package onion soup mix
½ pound fresh mushrooms, sliced
½ green pepper, sliced
Fresh ground black pepper
1 (16 ounce) can tomatoes, drained and chopped, reserve juice
¼ teaspoon salt
1 Tablespoon A-1 sauce
1 Tablespoon cornstarch
1 Tablespoon chopped parsley

Butter large 10-inch casserole. Arrange strips of meat in casserole, overlapping each piece. Sprinkle with soup mix, mushrooms, green pepper, black pepper, tomatoes and salt. Mix A-1 sauce and cornstarch in ½ cup tomato juice. Pour over meat. Cover casserole with foil and seal tightly. Bake at 375° for 2 hours. Sprinkle with parsley and serve with buttered noodles. 4 servings

Dunja S. Awbrey (Mrs. James J.)

Beef Rouladen I

2 round steaks, cut ¼ inch thick
Prepared mustard
Salt and pepper
1 large onion, chopped
4 strips bacon, cut into small pieces
1 dill pickle, finely chopped
3 Tablespoons oil
Red wine
½ cup sour cream
2 Tablespoons flour

Cut each steak in half, and pound to tenderize. Spread each piece with mustard, and sprinkle with salt and pepper. Place bacon, onion, and dill pickle on top. Roll each piece and secure with toothpicks. Heat oil in a Dutch oven, and brown meat on all sides. Cover rolls with wine, cover pot and simmer about 1½ hours, until rolls are tender. Combine 2 Tablespoons flour with ¼ cup water; add to stock and simmer until thickened. Add sour cream, and heat through. 4 servings

Barbara Johnson (Mrs. Larry)

Beef Rouladen II
A traditional German dish

3 pounds sirloin tip roast,
   sliced ¼ inch thick
2 large onions, finely chopped
1¼ cups butter
1½ pounds fresh mushrooms,
   finely chopped (save a few
   small ones for the sauce)
¾ pound cooked ham,
   julienned in strips ½ inch
   long and ⅛ inch wide
¾ cup grated Parmesan
   cheese
1 cup dry white wine
1 cup beef broth, full strength
1 teaspoon salt
Freshly ground black pepper
2 Tablespoons cornstarch
2 Tablespoons water
2 Tablespoons finely chopped
   parsley

Pound meat slices to about $\frac{1}{16}$ inch thickness. Melt 2 Tablespoons butter in a skillet and saute onions about 5 minutes until soft. Transfer onions to a bowl, and sauté mushrooms 5 minutes in 2 more Tablespoons butter. Add mushrooms, ham and grated cheese to onions; mix well. Place 1 heaping Tablespoon or more of this filling on each meat slice and roll up, securing with toothpicks. In a skillet, melt 2-4 Tablespoons butter. Brown meat rolls on all sides (You may need two pans). Pour in wine and broth. Season to taste with salt and pepper. Cover and simmer for 10-15 minutes. Remove toothpicks and transfer meat to an ovenproof serving dish. Into the remaining juices and wine, stir cornstarch blended with water, and cook over medium heat until thickened. Toss reserved whole mushrooms in melted butter, and add to the sauce. Pour sauce over meat rolls on a serving plate and cover until serving time. Rolls may be prepared in advance and refrigerated at this point. Before serving, heat thoroughly, covered, in a 375° oven for 20 minutes; or for 45 minutes, if refrigerated. Garnish with parsley. This is traditionally served with potato pancakes and a Moselle wine. 8-10 servings

Susan Morley

Marinated Sirloin Tip Roast

1 5-6 pound sirloin tip roast
1 Tablespoon salt
½ teaspoon pepper
Enough beef suet to cover top
 of roast
MARINADE:
1 cup thinly sliced onions
1 cup thinly sliced carrots
1 cup sliced celery stalks
 and leaves
2 cloves garlic, halved
2 bay leaves
1 Tablespoon thyme leaves
¼ cup minced parsley
5 cups burgundy
¼ cup brandy
½ cup olive or vegetable oil
Flour for thickening gravy, if
 desired

Place half the vegetables and herbs in the bottom of a large bowl. Rub the roast with salt and pepper, and place over the vegetables. Top with the rest of the vegetables and herbs. Add wine, brandy and oil; cover and marinate for 6-24 hours. Turn and baste several times. Remove meat. Put marinade in a saucepan and boil to reduce in volume by ½. Arrange suet on top of meat. Roast in a 350° oven or on a covered grill over slow coals. If gravy is desired, place roast in an ovenproof skillet or baking dish. Cook for about 20 minutes per pound for medium rare. A meat thermometer may be used. To make gravy, add water and some of the marinade to pan juices, and thicken with flour.
10-12 servings

Cookbook Committee

Carl's Roast

1 (2½-3 pound) shoulder roast
1-2 cloves garlic
1-2 red peppers
2 bunches green onions
Salt and pepper
1 brown-in-bag
1 cup sauterne
1 Tablespoon Worcestershire
 sauce
Vegetables: mushrooms,
 potatoes, carrots, onions,
 celery, as desired

With a sharp knife, make slits over surface of roast at 1-inch intervals. Insert a small sliver of garlic and red pepper, and 1 green onion top into each slit. Salt and pepper roast. Prepare bag according to manufacturer's directions and insert roast and vegetables. Mix wine and Worcestershire and pour over roast. Bake at 350° for 2½-3 hours. Thicken gravy if desired.
4-6 servings

Carl Veal

Chinese Pot Roast

4 pounds chuck roast
2 Tablespoons fat
1 teaspoon garlic salt
½ teaspoon dry mustard
¼ teaspoon pepper
¼ cup soy sauce
1 Tablespoon honey
1 Tablespoon vinegar
1 teaspoon celery seed
½ teaspoon ground ginger
2 Tablespoons cornstarch
¾ cup water

Brown meat in fat until browned on all sides. Mix remaining ingredients, and pour over meat. Simmer approximately 2 hours or until meat is tender. 4-6 servings

Linda D. Bobo (Mrs. Earl)

Pennsylvania Pot Roast

1 (3-5 pound) chuck roast, 2 inches thick
Salt
Pepper
Paprika
Flour
½ pound bacon, diced
1 cup sweet pickles, sliced
1 large onion, sliced
1 (8 ounce) can tomato sauce
1 cup water
½ cup sour cream

Rub roast with seasonings and flour. Fry bacon until crisp, drain and reserve fat. Brown roast in fat. Add all other ingredients except sour cream and bacon bits. Cover and cook at 350° for 2-3 hours. Add more water if necessary. Remove meat and thicken gravy. Add bacon bits and sour cream. Blend well. Serve with noodles. 6-8 servings

Spicy Corned Beef

Leftovers make sandwiches that rival "Deli" corned beef

3-4 pounds corned beef brisket (with spices in bag if possible)
1 orange, sliced
1 large onion, quartered
2 stalks celery, cut in half
2 cloves garlic
1 teaspoon dill weed
1 teaspoon rosemary
6 whole cloves
3 inch stick cinnamon
1 bay leaf
Light corn syrup for glaze

Remove meat from package and place in a large, heavy pot or Dutch oven. Add enough water to barely cover meat. Add remaining ingredients, except syrup. Cover and simmer for 1 hour per pound, or until tender. Remove meat from pot and glaze with corn syrup while still hot. To serve, cool slightly, and cut into thin slices. 10-12 servings

Elise M. Griffin

Stifado
(Greek Stew)

3 pounds lean beef stew meat,
  cut into 1½-inch cubes
5 Tablespoons butter
Salt and pepper
1 medium onion, chopped
½ (6-ounce) can tomato paste
1½ cups water
2 Tablespoons red wine
  vinegar
1 clove garlic, minced or
  mashed
1 bay leaf
2 pounds small onions, peeled
¾ cup walnut halves
½ pound feta, Monterey Jack,
  or Gouda cheese

In a Dutch oven or heavy kettle with cover, brown meat over medium heat in butter; season lightly with salt and pepper. Add chopped onion and sauté until limp. Mix tomato paste, ½ cup water, vinegar and garlic; pour over meat. Add bay leaf. Cover kettle and simmer 1 hour; add remaining water, a little at a time, as necessary during cooking. Add onions, cover and simmer 1 hour or longer, or until onions and meat are tender. Add walnuts and feta cheese, cover and simmer 5 minutes. 6 servings

Elise M. Griffin

Buffet Beef Cacciatore
Red pepper gives this dish a spicy flavor

Olive or salad oil
2 medium onions, chopped
3 pounds lean beef, cubed
Flour
2 medium cloves garlic, minced
2 teaspoons salt
½ teaspoon oregano
½ teaspoon red pepper
1 can beef consommé
½ cup red wine
1 (16 ounce) can tomatoes
2 green peppers, cut in strips
12 ounces noodles, cooked

Lightly brown onions in oil, and remove to a bowl. Dredge beef in flour, and brown in same oil. Add onions, garlic, salt, oregano, red pepper and 1 cup of consommé. Cover and simmer on top of stove, or bake in an oven-proof dish at 350° for 2 hours, or until beef is almost tender. Add the rest of the consommé, wine and tomatoes, and simmer 10 minutes more. Stir in green pepper, and cook uncovered an additional 15 minutes. Stir in cooked noodles. Can be made ahead and reheated over low-medium heat. Add a little water if needed. 8 servings

Edna K. Jennings (Mrs. E. Paul, Jr.)

Oriental Beef Stew

2 pounds lean beef stew meat
⅛ teaspoon pepper
1 Tablespoon oil
1 can golden mushroom soup
1¼ cups water
1 medium onion, thinly sliced
2 Tablespoons soy sauce
1 small head cabbage, cut in
    1-inch strips
1 (5 ounce) can bamboo shoots,
    drained
1 (7 ounce) can water
    chestnuts, drained and
    sliced

Brown meat in hot oil in skillet. Add seasonings, water, onions and soy sauce. Cover and simmer 1½-2 hours until meat is tender. Add remaining ingredients. Simmer 10-30 minutes. Serve in soup bowls. 4-6 servings

Diane Douglas (Mrs. Robert)

Lasagne di Carnevale

TOMATO SAUCE:
¼ cup butter
½ pound ground beef
½ pound ground pork (or
    pork sausage)
1 cup chopped onion
1 clove garlic, minced
3¼ cups (1 pound-12 ounce
    can) tomatoes
2 cups tomato paste (3-6
    ounce cans)
2 cups water
2½ teaspoons salt
1 teaspoon pepper
1 teaspoon oregano
LASAGNA:
1 pound broad lasagna noodles
2 pounds Ricotta or cottage
    cheese
6 cups (1½ pounds) shredded
    Mozzarella cheese
1½ cups (6 ounces) grated
    Parmesan cheese
Paprika

Melt butter in a large skillet. Add meat and brown slowly. Add onion and garlic and saute until tender. Stir in remaining sauce ingredients. Simmer over low heat for 45-60 minutes. Preheat oven to 375°. Cook noodles according to package directions and drain well. Handle noodles carefully to prevent them from tearing. Place a layer of noodles in bottom of one 9 x 13-inch or two 8 inch buttered baking dishes. Top with a layer of tomato sauce. Sprinkle over the sauce, one-half each of the Ricotta, Mozzarella and Parmesan cheeses; repeat layers one more time, reserving a small amount of sauce to spread in center of top layer of cheese. Sprinkle with paprika. Bake approximately 30 minutes. Allow to set 10-15 minutes before cutting into squares for serving. Lasagna freezes beautifully before and after cooking. 12 servings

Lucia Sizemore (Mrs. Thomas A., III)

Moussaka
Light, with a quiche-like texture

3 large eggplants, peeled
   and sliced
½ pound potatoes, peeled
   and sliced
Flour
½ pound ground beef
1 large onion, chopped
Salt
Pepper
1 teaspoon oregano
1 Tablespoon tomato sauce
Parmesan cheese (about ½
   cup)
1 quart milk
1 cup flour
½ pound butter
4 eggs

Flour sliced eggplant and
potatoes lightly, and fry in deep
fat until golden brown. Drain on
paper towels. Place ground beef
in skillet with 1-2 Tablespoons
water, salt and pepper to taste,
and sprinkle chopped onion over
top. Saute until meat is browned.
Add oregano and tomato sauce
and simmer until well blended.
Sprinkle parmesan liberally over
the bottom of a 9 x 13-inch baking
dish. Layer potatoes, eggplant and
meat mixture in dish.

   Sauce: Heat milk. Heat butter
and flour together and add milk,
stirring over low heat. Beat eggs
well; remove milk mixture from
heat and add to eggs. Beat well,
until mixture is thick and creamy
(a thin pudding consistency). Pour
sauce over vegetables and meat
in baking dish and shake down.
Bake at 350° for approximately
45 minutes or until dish is light
brown on top. 8-10 servings

Athens Pizza
Decatur, Georgia

Lemon Barbeque Meat Loaves

1½ pounds ground beef
4 slices day old bread, cubed
¼ cup lemon juice
¼ cup minced onion
1 egg, slightly beaten
2 teaspoons seasoned salt
SAUCE:
½ cup catsup
⅓ cup brown sugar
1 teaspoon dry mustard
¼ teaspoon allspice
¼ teaspoon ground cloves
GARNISH:
6 thin lemon slices

Preheat oven at 350°. In a
large bowl, combine ground beef,
bread, lemon juice, onion, egg
and salt. Mix well. Shape into 6
small individual loaves and place
in a baking pan. Bake 15 minutes.
In a small bowl, combine sauce
ingredients. Cover loaves with
sauce and top each with lemon
slices. Bake 30 minutes longer,
basting occasionally with sauce
from pan. Serve sauce over
loaves. 6 servings

Pat Adams (Mrs. P.H.)

Indian Beef Curry

3 pounds chuck or stew beef,
   cut in ½-inch cubes
3-4 Tablespoons olive oil
1 cup seedless raisins
2 sticks cinnamon
3-4 bay leaves
SAUCE:
3 onions chopped
3-4 Tablespoons olive oil
3-4 Tablespoons curry powder
1 teaspoon powdered
   cardamon
2 teaspoons salt
1 Tablespoon brown sugar
1 quart buttermilk

In a large Dutch oven, brown meat in olive oil. Add raisins, cinnamon and bay leaves. Cover and simmer over very low heat while preparing sauce. Cook onions in olive oil until tender. Add spices and simmer gently 5-6 minutes; then add half of the buttermilk. Cover and simmer over very low heat until sauce is well blended. Watch carefully to avoid scorching! Add sauce to meat and simmer for about 3 hours. Add last half of buttermilk as needed to make a moderately liquid sauce. Serve the curry over steamed rice and let each guest serve himself from a tray of the following condiments:
chopped peanuts
4-5 chopped hard-boiled eggs
1-2 chopped green peppers
2 chopped cucumbers
2 bunches chopped green onions
1 can shredded coconut, toasted
2 (14 ounce) cans crushed
   pineapple, drained
1 large bottle good quality chutney
Hint: Curry may be prepared in advance and reheated, or may be frozen. 6 servings

Mrs. Joann Forney

Keep fresh ginger root in a plastic bag in the freezer. Peel and slice or grate as needed, no need to thaw. Another method is to keep small pieces covered with dry sherry or rice wine in a jar in the refrigerator. The ginger adds a delicious flavor to the wine.

Zucchini Lasagna
A delicious variation!

1 pound lean ground beef
1 onion, chopped
1 Tablespoon chopped green
   pepper (optional)
1 teaspoon salt
¼ teaspoon pepper
1 small can tomato paste
2 small cans water
1 can tomato soup
½ teaspoon oregano
3 medium zucchini squash
12 ounce container small curd
   cottage cheese (can be low
   calorie)
½ cup Parmesan cheese
1 Tablespoon parsley flakes
2 eggs, beaten
1½ teaspoons salt
½ teaspoon pepper
12 ounces mozzarella cheese,
   thinly sliced

Brown meat; spoon off any excess grease. Add onions and green peppers, salt and pepper. Cook until onions are tender. Add tomato paste, water and soup. Cook slowly about 30-45 minutes. Add oregano last. Slice zucchini lengthwise after trimming ends. Lightly skim peeling off opposite sides of zucchini so that zucchini lies flat. Layer sliced zucchini as you would lasagna noodles in 13 x 9 x 2-inch baking dish. Mix cottage cheese, Parmesan cheese, parsley flakes, eggs, salt and pepper together. Spread half of this mixture over zucchini slices. Add half of mozarella cheese and top with half of meat sauce. Repeat layers. Bake at 350° about 40-45 minutes. Let stand 10 minutes before cutting into squares. For microwaves, bake 15 minutes on medium-high setting. Cover with plastic wrap and let stand 5 minutes. May be prepared in advance and refrigerated for a couple of days. Freezes well.
8 servings

Beth C. Benefield (Mrs. Phillip D.)

HINT

To peel garlic easily, strike clove with the flat side of a knife.

Chili

2 pounds ground round or
  chuck
1 pound ground pork
3 medium onions, chopped
4 cloves garlic, chopped
4-6 Tablespoons chili powder
1 Tablespoon flour
2 small cans chopped green
  chilis
3 (16 ounce) cans tomatoes,
  crushed
3 bay leaves
1 Tablespoon salt
1 Tablespoon oregano
1 Tablespoon red wine vinegar
1 Tablespoon brown sugar
3 (16 ounce) cans pinto beans

Brown meat, onions and garlic
in a large heavy pot. Drain off fat.
Add flour and chili powder, stirring
to coat well. Add chilis, tomatoes,
bay leaves, salt, oregano, vinegar
and brown sugar. Cover and cook
slowly for 2 hours. Add beans
and cook uncovered 30 minutes
more. Serving Suggestion: pass
bowls of crushed corn chips,
shredded sharp cheese and
shredded lettuce. Let each guest
add these to his bowl of chili.
12 servings

Barrie C. Aycock (Mrs. Robert R.)

Taco Casserole

1 medium onion, chopped
1 large clove garlic, crushed
1½ pounds lean ground beef
1 (8 ounce) can tomato sauce
⅓ cup water
1 Tablespoon or more chili
  powder
1 teaspoon oregano
⅛ teaspoon ground cloves
1 (8 ounce) package corn chips
1 (16 ounce) can kidney beans
  (optional)
TOPPING:
2 cups finely shredded lettuce
1 cup grated Cheddar or
  Monterey Jack cheese
1 red onion, sliced and
  separated into rings
Diced tomatoes (optional)

Sauté onion and garlic in a
small amount of oil until golden.
Add beef and brown quickly. Drain
off fat. Reduce heat and add
tomato sauce and water. Stir in
seasoning and kidney beans. Place
half the corn chips in a buttered
2-quart baking dish. Spoon half
the meat mixture over chips.
Repeat, ending with meat. Bake in
a 325° oven for 20 minutes until
heated thoroughly. Remove from
oven and garnish with shredded
lettuce, grated cheese and onion
rings. Diced tomatoes may be
added if desired. 6 servings

Patricia H. Adams (Mrs. P.H.)

Meat Sauce for Pasta

2 Tablespoons olive oil
1 cup diced onion
2 garlic cloves, minced
1½ cups grated carrots
1 pound lean ground beef
1 (28 ounce) can tomato purée
  or Italian plum tomatoes
1 (8 ounce) jar marinara sauce
  (seasoned herb tomato
  sauce may be used)
1 (6 ounce) can tomato paste
½ pound mushrooms, thinly
  sliced
½ cup diced green pepper
1 Tablespoon chopped parsley
1 teaspoon salt
1 teaspoon dried oregano
1 teaspoon dried basil
1 bay leaf
½ teaspoon white pepper
½ teaspoon allspice
⅛ teaspoon crushed red pepper
½ cup dry red wine

Heat oil in 4-5 quart saucepan over medium-high heat. Add onion and garlic. Sauté, stirring constantly, until lightly browned. Reduce heat to medium, add carrots and cook, stirring, until softened. Add meat and cook, stirring, until crumbly and all liquid has evaporated. Reduce heat to low. Add all remaining ingredients except wine and simmer uncovered 1½ hours, stirring occasionally. Blend in wine and simmer ½ hour more. Adjust seasonings, if necessary. Serve over green spinach noodles or pasta of your choice. Sauce may be refrigerated up to 5 days or frozen up to 4 months.

Jane H. Nardone (Mrs. Joseph A.)

Pita Sandwiches

1 pound ground lean beef
1 large onion, chopped
2 cloves garlic, minced
1 Tablespoon vegetable oil
1 (16 ounce) can tomatoes
½ cup sliced stuffed olives
2 Tablespoons chopped
  almonds
1 teaspoon capers
½ teaspoon chili powder
¼ teaspoon salt
⅛ teaspoon pepper
4 pita bread (Middle Eastern
  pocket bread found in most
  supermarkets, or see index)

In large skillet, cook and stir beef, onion and garlic in oil until meat loses its color. Add remaining ingredients except pita bread. Reduce heat and simmer 30 minutes, stirring occasionally. Cut a large slit in side of pita breads; fill with meat mixture. 4 servings

Trina Graham
Atlanta Gas Light Company

Pizza Casserole

1 (4 ounce) package sliced
   pepperoni
1 medium onion, chopped
2 (8 ounce) cans tomato sauce
⅓ cup melted butter
6 ounces thin spaghetti,
   cooked
1 cup (4 ounces) grated
   Swiss cheese
1 pound mozzarella cheese,
   sliced
1 (4 ounce) can mushroom
   stems and pieces, drained
½ teaspoon oregano
½ teaspoon basil

Boil pepperoni for 5 minutes in water to cover; drain well. Sauté onion in 1⅓ Tablespoons butter until golden brown. Pour remaining ¼ cup butter into 11 x 7 x 2-inch baking dish. Toss spaghetti in buttered dish. Cover with 1 can tomato sauce. Add half of the Swiss cheese, pepperoni and mozzarella cheese, and all of the mushrooms and onions. Sprinkle with oregano and basil. Top with remaining Swiss cheese, pepperoni, tomato sauce and mozzarella cheese. Bake at 350° for 20-25 minutes or until casserole bubbles. 8 servings

Margaret Newsome (Mrs. James L.)

Pizza By The Yard
Wonderful for a crowd of hungry teenagers

1 (18-inch loaf) French bread
1 pound lean ground beef
⅓ cup grated Parmesan
   cheese
¼ cup finely chopped onion
¼ cup finely chopped olives
1 teaspoon oregano
Salt and pepper to taste
1 (6 ounce) can tomato paste
3 tomatoes, sliced
Sliced mozzarella cheese

Split French bread in half lengthwise. Mix next 7 ingredients and spread on both halves of bread, covering edges well (so they will not burn). Broil 12 minutes. Arrange alternate and overlappng slices of cheese and tomato on top of meat, and broil 2 minutes more. Slice in serving size portions and feed to a hungry crowd. The entire loaf may be frozen without the cheese and tomato. Thaw completely before broiling. 8 servings

Cookbook Committee

Pizza Popover

Serve with beer for a post-football supper

1 pound ground beef or pork
1 medium onion, chopped
16 ounces good marinara
  sauce or spaghetti sauce
6 ounces Mozzarella cheese,
  sliced
POPOVER BATTER:
2 eggs, beaten
1 cup milk
1 Tablespoon oil
1 cup flour
½ teaspoon salt
TOPPING:
½ cup grated Parmesan
  cheese

Brown meat and onion. Combine with sauce and simmer 12 minutes. Spoon meat sauce into a greased 13 x 9½ x 2-inch baking pan and top with Mozzarella cheese. Bake at 400° for 10 minutes. Combine eggs, milk and oil in small bowl; add flour and salt, mixing well. Yield is about 2 cups. Remove meat mixture from oven; pour popover batter over top, and sprinkle with Parmesan cheese. Bake at 400° for an additional 30 minutes. May prepare batter and meat sauce separately; then combine right before baking. 6-8 servings

Susan M. Morley

Marinated Roast Leg O' Lamb

5 cups red wine
½ cup gin
¼ cup olive oil
2 Tablespoons dried thyme
3 whole cloves
2-3 small cloves garlic, crushed
1 (5 pound) leg of lamb
10 peppercorns, crushed
1 Brown-In-Bag

Prepare marinade by combining wine, gin, oil and spices in a saucepan. Bring to a boil. Lower temperature and simmer 5 minutes. Cool. Place lamb in an oven bag. Pour cooled marinade over meat. Seal and refrigerate 5 days, turning over meat each day. Place bag in a shallow roasting pan, make slits in top according to manufacturer's directions. Roast at 325° for 35 minutes per pound if desired well-done, reduce cooking time for a more rare roast. Meat thermometer may be used. 6-8 servings

Susan M. Morley

Portuguese Roast Lamb

6-8 pound leg of lamb
½ cup chopped parsley
3 Tablespoons chopped
    rosemary
4 cloves garlic, minced
½ teaspoon ground cardamon
1 Tablespoon olive oil
Salt and pepper to taste
BASTING SAUCE:
1 cup white wine
3 Tablespoons olive oil

Slash lamb in several places with a knife and stuff slashes with herbs mixed with oil. Sprinkle lamb with salt and pepper to taste. Roast at 450° for 15 minutes. Reduce heat to 300° and roast 4 hours, basting with sauce occasionally. 8 servings

Mrs. Elsie B. Manry
Tampa, Florida

Lamb Shoulder Chops, Family Style

Using shoulder chops is an economical way to serve lamb

Lamb shoulder chops
1 clove garlic, crushed
Olive oil
Lemon pepper seasoning
Butter

Rub chops well with crushed garlic, coat generously with olive oil and sprinkle with lemon pepper seasoning. Cover and marinate at room temperature for 1 hour. Broil 4 inches from heat 5 minutes per side, place a pat of butter on each chop and serve immediately. Simple and delicious.

Decie Nygaard (Mrs. William)

Pork Chops in Cream Sauce

4 medium pork chops
Salt and pepper
2 Tablespoons salad oil
1 can beef broth
1 cup heavy cream
2 Tablespoons spicy brown
    mustard

Season chops with salt and pepper. Brown in oil; add broth and cook until tender. Just before serving, combine mustard and cream and pour over chops in pan. Heat. Serve with rice. 4 servings

Patricia King
Cairo, Georgia

Pork Tenderloin Lorraine

1 (1½-2 pound) pork tenderloin
2 Tablespoons butter
Fine bread crumbs to cover
   tenderloin
1 medium onion
1 shallot
1 clove garlic
2-3 sprigs parsley
1 cup stock (beef or chicken)
1 Tablespoon wine vinegar

In a small roasting pan on top of stove, brown meat on all sides in butter. Cover with a generous layer of fine bread crumbs that have been mixed with salt and pepper. Mince onion, shallot, garlic and parsley and sprinkle on meat. Hint: Make fresh bread crumbs in your food processor. Add the onion, shallot, garlic and parsley. Process for 60 seconds and check to see if all is chopped well. Sprinkle this on the meat and brown. Add salt and pepper. Put roast in a 500° oven to brown the layer of bread crumbs, basting several times with the melted butter. Once the crumbs are brown, lower the oven temperature to 350°. Add 1 cup of stock to pan. Cover roast and cook until done, about 50 minutes. Uncover and raise temperature; brown crumbs for 10 minutes. Put on a hot platter and stir 1 Tablespoon of wine vinegar into sauce before serving.
4-6 servings

Kathy Messer (Mrs. Thomas)

Stuffed Pork Loin with Savory Gravy

¾ cup sauerkraut, drained
½ medium onion, chopped
¼ cup or more brown sugar
   to taste
1 (4 pound) pork loin
GRAVY:
Pork drippings
½ onion, sliced
1 teaspoon caraway seed
½ cup water
1 can cream of celery soup
1-2 Tablespoons horseradish
½-1 teaspoon Dijon mustard

In a mixing bowl, combine sauerkraut, onion and sugar. Make 8 slits in roast almost to the bone. Spoon 2 Tablespoons of mixture into each slit. Tie together with string at 2-inch intervals. Roast fat side up at 325-350° for 2½ hours (35-40 minutes per pound). After roasting, transfer meat to a warm platter and combine ingredients for gravy. Serve with a chilled Rhine wine. 6-8 servings

Susan M. Morley

Chinese Pork Rolls
Serve with other Chinese entrées or alone with rice

1 pound pork loin, cut into
  ¾ inch slices
2 Tablespoons soy sauce
1 Tablespoon dry white wine
2 Tablespoons safflower oil
1 cup fresh green beans,
  French cut
½-¾ cup fresh carrots, cut
  same size and shape as
  beans
1½-2 cups shredded cabbage
1 teaspoon salt
1 teaspoon MSG
1 teaspoon lemon juice
SAUCE:
5 Tablespoons sugar
5 Tablespoons vinegar
1 teaspoon soy sauce
1 cup hot water
3 Tablespoons cornstarch

Pound pork slices on both sides, both ways with back of cleaver until very thin (⅛ inch thick). Marinate slices in soy sauce and wine on plate; turn and move pieces around so they are covered at least 10 minutes or up to several hours. Heat oil in pan; sauté beans, carrots and cabbage until limp; add salt, MSG and lemon juice while cooking. Reserve juices in pan. Arrange cooked vegetables on pork and roll up, securing with a toothpick. Prepare sauce in pan in which vegetables were cooked: combine sugar, vinegar, soy sauce, hot water and cornstarch (mix cornstarch with cold liquids until dissolved). Pour over pork rolls. Bake 20 minutes at 450° uncovered. Remove toothpicks and cut in bite size pieces. 4 servings

Barbara R. Schuyler (Mrs. Lambert, Jr.)

Pork Chop Scallop

12 rib pork chops, thin cut
Salt and pepper
4 Tablespoons butter
3 onions, thinly sliced
4 medium potatoes, thinly
  sliced
3 cups beef bouillon
½ cup white wine
2 cloves garlic, crushed
¼ teaspoon thyme leaves
1 bay leaf
1 sprig parsley

Sauté onions in 2 Tablespoons butter until soft. Add garlic and potatoes; season with salt and thyme, toss well and set aside. Season chops with salt and pepper and brown lightly in 2 Tablespoons butter. Remove chops from pan. Add bouillon and wine to pan drippings and scrape browned bits from bottom of pan. Add bay leaf and parsley and cook for a few minutes, until liquid is reduced slightly. Remove herbs. In a 2-quart casserole, alternately layer chops and potatoes. Pour broth over, and bake at 375° for 45 minutes. 6 servings

Helen Ward (Mrs. William T.)

Noisettes de Porc Aux Pruneaux

8 (3 ounce) noisettes of pork
   tenderloin (boned pork-
   chops or slices of
   tenderloin)
1 pound large California prunes
½ bottle dry white wine
2 Tablespoons flour
4 Tablespoons butter
Salt and fresh ground pepper
1 Tablespoon red currant jelly
1 Tablespoon lemon juice
1 cup heavy cream

Soak prunes in wine overnight. Remove 3 Tablespoons liquid from prunes and reserve. Cover pan of prunes and place in a 250° oven for 1 hour or more. Season and flour pork. Saute in butter, being careful not to allow butter to brown. Add 3 Tablespoons reserved prune liquid, cover pan and simmer meat for 20-40 minutes or until fork tender. Pour juice from prunes over meat and bring to a boil for 3-4 minutes. Put pork and prunes on a warm platter to keep hot. Add currant jelly to wine sauce; stir well. Add lemon juice, blend, and add cream very slowly to thicken. Pour over meat and serve. 4 servings

Cookbook Committee

Rio Grande Pork Roast

1 (4-5 pound) boneless rolled
   pork loin roast
½ teaspoon salt
½ teaspoon garlic salt
½ teaspoon chili powder
½ cup apple jelly
½ cup catsup
1 Tablespoon vinegar
½ teaspoon chili powder
1 cup corn chips, crushed

Place pork, fat side up, on rack in shallow roasting pan. Combine the salts and ½ teaspoon chili powder; rub into roast. Roast in a 320° oven for 2-2½ hours or until meat thermometer registers 165°. In a small saucepan, combine jelly, catsup, vinegar and the remaining chili powder. Bring to a boil; reduce heat and simmer, uncovered, for 2 minutes. Brush roast with glaze; sprinkle top with corn chips. Continue roasting 10-15 minutes more or until thermometer registers 170° Remove roast from oven. Let stand 10 minutes. Measure pan drippings, including any corn chips. Add water to make 1 cup. Heat to boiling and pass with meat. Serve with Bean and Avocado Boat Salad. (see Index) 6-8 servings

June L. Wagner (Mrs. James)

Baked Barbecue Spareribs

Sauce may also be used for chicken and pork chops

3-4 pounds spareribs
Salt
1 large onion, thinly sliced
1 lemon, thinly sliced
1 cup catsup
⅓ cup Worcestershire sauce
1 teaspoon chili powder
1 teaspoon salt
⅛ teaspoon Tabasco sauce
1½ cups water

Salt ribs. Place in shallow roasting pan, meat side up. Roast at 450° for 30 minutes. Drain fat. Top each piece with a slice of onion and a slice of lemon. Combine remaining ingredients in a saucepan and bring to a boil. Pour over ribs. Lower oven to 350° and bake 1½ hours. Baste every 15 minutes. 4 servings

Jerry P. Connor (Mrs. Paul)

Oriental Ribs

½ Tablespoon salt
2 Tablespoons vinegar
3 pounds lean pork ribs or backbone
⅓ cup catsup
⅓ cup vinegar
2 or more Tablespoons soy sauce
Dash of pepper sauce
½ cup brown sugar
¼ cup peach preserves
1 teaspoon grated fresh ginger
1 teaspoon salt
Dash coarsely ground black pepper

Place ribs in a large pot and cover them with water. Add ½ Tablespoon salt, 2 Tablespoons vinegar and parboil for 30 minutes. Combine remaining ingredients in a saucepan and simmer for 10 minutes. Dip ribs in sauce, coating well. Grill over slow coals 20-30 minutes, or bake at 350° for 30 minutes. Baste frequently with sauce; turn once. Hint: Ribs may be parboiled or microwaved in advance. Refrigerate until cooking time; reheat sauce and complete cooking on grill or in oven. 4 servings

Barrie C. Aycock (Mrs. Robert R.)

Grilled Ham Slice

1 ham slice, 2 inches thick
2 Tablespoons brown sugar
Gingerale

Cook ham on grill basting with sauce made of brown sugar and gingerale. 4 servings

Ned Stuart

Glazed Ham Loaves
The cold sauce makes this different

2 pounds lean ham, ground
2 pounds lean pork, ground
1½ cups cracker crumbs
1⅓ cups chopped onion
3 eggs, well beaten
1½ teaspoons salt
2 cups milk
2 teaspoons parsley
¼ teaspoon pepper
GLAZE:
1 cup brown sugar
⅓ cup cider vinegar
1 Tablespoon dry mustard
Boil 1 minute.
COLD SAUCE:
½ cup mayonnaise
½ cup sour cream
¼ cup prepared mustard
1 Tablespoon chives
1½ Tablespoons horseradish
Add salt and lemon juice to
    taste

Mix together by hand or in a food processor. Bake in 2 loaf pans at 350° for 30 minutes. Freeze 1 loaf if desired. Pour glaze mixture over loaf and bake 1 hour longer. Serve with Cold Sauce. 12-14 servings

Sallie Smith (Mrs. Tommy W.)
Dede Slappey (Mrs. George N.)

Stuffed Ham Slices
Great for picnics!

1 loaf unsliced French/Italian
    bread
¼ cup mayonnaise
⅓ cup chopped parsley
1 (8 ounce) package cream
    cheese
¾ cup finely chopped celery
½ cup shredded Cheddar
    cheese
2 Tablespoons finely chopped
    onion
¼ teaspoon salt
1 teaspoon lemon juice
1 Tablespoon Worcestershire
8 slices boiled ham
Dill pickle, sliced lengthwise

Slice bread in half, Hollow out each half with fork leaving ½ inch thick shell (save inside for crumbs). Spread hollow with mayonnaise. Sprinkle with parsley. Blend cream cheese, celery, Cheddar cheese, onion, salt, lemon, and Worcestershire; spoon into halves and pack down, leaving ridge in center. Roll pickles in ham slices. Place rolls end to end down center of loaf. Put bread halves together. Wrap and chill. Before serving, slice in sandwich-size portions. 6 servings

Diane Mahaffey (Mrs. Randy)

Baked Ham

1 (5-6 pound) butt end ham
Cavender's Greek seasoning or
   your favorite (lemon pepper
   or other dry seasonings)

Rub ham all over with seasoning. Place in brown grocery bag. Turn edges over several times and staple shut. Place in a roasting pan. Bake 3 hours at 350°. Ham may be glazed in a warm oven after removing from bag. 10-12 servings

Mildred Hodsdon (Mrs. Nicholas)

Hot Dogs Creole

2 Tablespoons margarine
¼ cup chopped onion
¼ cup chopped celery
⅓ cup Madeira
2 teaspoons Dijon mustard
1 Tablespoon Worcestershire
   sauce
½ cup chili sauce
1 Tablespoon brown sugar
⅛ teaspoon cayenne pepper
Dash Tabasco Sauce
8 frankfurters
8 buns

In a skillet, sauté onion and celery in margarine until lightly browned. Add remaining sauce ingredients and simmer 5 minutes. Prick the skins of frankfurters, place them in the sauce, cover and simmer slowly about 15 minutes until thoroughly heated. Lightly butter buns and warm in moderate oven. Place frankfurters in buns and spoon on sauce. 8 servings

Barrie C. Aycock (Mrs. Robert R.)

Sherried Veal

1 pound veal cutlets
Salt and pepper to taste
1 egg, beaten
½ cup dry bread crumbs
3 Tablespoons olive oil
Juice of ½ lemon
1½ cups chicken broth
1 small can sliced mushrooms
   plus liquid
¼ cup dry sherry

Pound veal thin between two sheets of wax paper, and cut into serving-sized pieces. Dip in egg and coat with bread crumbs. Brown quickly in hot olive oil. Add lemon juice, half of broth and mushroom liquid. Reduce heat, cover and simmer until sauce thickens. Add rest of broth and simmer 5 to 10 minutes. Add mushrooms and wine and serve hot. Sprinkle with Parmesan cheese, if desired. 6 servings

Mrs. Elsie B. Manry
Tampa, Florida

Escalopes of Veal Italienne
A favorite of students at Rich's Cooking School

4-8 veal escalopes (about
   1½ pounds)*
¼ cup oil and butter, mixed
1 onion, finely chopped
¼ cup Marsala or sherry
1 Tablespoon flour
1½ cups beef stock or bouillon
1½ teaspoons tomato paste
1 bay leaf
Salt and pepper
FOR GARNISH:
1½ pounds fresh or 2
   packages frozen spinach
1 Tablespoon butter
2 tomatoes, peeled, seeded,
   and sliced
1 clove of garlic, crushed
5-6 Tablespoons heavy cream
4 large slices of Gruyere or
   Muenster cheese
*Boned chicken breasts may
  be used instead of veal;
  flatten slightly with handle
  of a knife.

In a skillet heat the oil and butter, sauté escalopes quickly, about 1-2 minutes on each side until golden brown and remove. Add the onion and cook until soft. Replace escalopes, pour over Marsala or sherry and flame. Take out the escalopes again, boil liquid to reduce slightly, then stir in flour and add stock, tomato paste, bay leaf and seasoning. Bring to a boil stirring, put back escalopes, cover and simmer gently for 7-10 minutes, or until tender. To prepare the garnish: cook fresh spinach in plenty of boiling salted water for 5 minutes or until just tender; defrost the frozen spinach. Drain well, pressing between 2 stacked plates to remove excess water. Melt butter in a frying pan, add tomatoes with garlic and seasoning, sauté briskly for 1-2 minutes or until just cooked. Put the spinach in a pan with cream, reheat well, stirring, and arrange down center of a long ovenproof platter. Drain the escalopes, arrange them, overlapping, on top of the spinach, with a slice of cheese (halving slices if escalopes are small) and 1-2 tomato slices on top of each escalope and brown under the broiler. Reheat sauce, strain, pour a little around the dish and serve the rest separately. 4-6 servings

Nathalie Dupree
Rich's Cooking School

Veal Scaloppine Al Limone

1½ pounds veal scallops
Salt and freshly ground pepper
¼ cup flour
4 Tablespoons butter, divided
3 Tablespoons olive oil
¾ cup beef bouillon
6 lemon slices, cut paper thin
1 Tablespoon lemon juice

Pound veal slightly, season and coat with flour. Sauté veal in mixture of 2 Tablespoons butter and olive oil until golden. Remove veal. Drain most of fat. Add ½ cup bouillon and boil, scraping browned bits from bottom of pan. Return veal to skillet with lemon slices on top. Cover and simmer 10 minutes or until veal is tender. To serve, arrange veal and lemon slices on a heated platter. Add ¼ cup bouillon to juices in skillet and boil until reduced to a syrupy glaze. Add lemon juice and cook, stirring for 1 minute. Remove from heat, stir in remaining butter and pour sauce over veal. 4 servings

Barbara H. Stuart (Mrs. Edward)

Venison Roast

1 Venison roast (about 3 pounds)
½ cup vinegar
1 Tablespoon black pepper
1 clove-garlic, mashed (optional)
1 cup red wine (optional)
12-15 small whole onions, peeled
1 pod red pepper (optional)
Aluminum foil

Place roast in a container with cover. Add vinegar and pepper, garlic and wine (optional), and enough water to cover meat. Marinate covered for 6 hours or overnight. Remove roast from marinade. If desired, brown roast in a skillet with a little fat added. Place meat on a large sheet of aluminum foil, add onion and red pepper, wrap tightly and place in a 300° oven. Cook for 4-5 hours, or until fork tender. 6 servings

Grace Acree (Mrs. Charles)
Dalton, Georgia

Venison Steaks
For all deer hunters

4 venison steaks
MSG
½ cup salad oil
¼ cup cider vinegar
¼ cup chopped onion
2 teaspoons Worcestershire
   sauce

The night before serving, remove all fat from steaks. Sprinkle steaks with MSG and pound well on both sides. Combine salad oil, cider vinegar, chopped onion and Worcestershire sauce. Pour sauce over steaks and marinate overnight. Grill over coals, basting often with marinade until meat is cooked to your preference. 4 servings

Barbara R. Johnson (Mrs. Larry)

Old #7
Popular at a downtown tea room

Sliced French bread
Thinly sliced ham
Thinly sliced turkey
Sliced swiss cheese
Shredded lettuce
Butter
Anchovie paste (optional)
Tomato wedges
Sliced hard cooked eggs
Olives
RUSSIAN DRESSING:
2½ cups real mayonnaise
2 cups finely diced celery
¼ cup finely chopped green
   pepper
¼ cup chili sauce
2 Tablespoons catsup
Dash Worcestershire sauce
½ teaspoon cider vinegar

Mix all dressing ingredients together and chill until ready to serve.

   Spread slices of bread with mixture of butter and anchovie paste (be sparing with the paste as it is strong in flavor). Place sliced ham, turkey, and cheese on each bread slice (about 2 slices per person). Cover completely with shredded lettuce. Pour liberal amount of dressing over sandwich. Garnish plate with tomatoes, sliced eggs and olives.

   This is a complete meal. Only a beverage and dessert is needed to finish the meal.

Mrs. Edward L. Traylor

Tourtière
Traditionally served in French-Canadian homes
after the Christmas Eve midnight Mass
Pass around a good mushroom gravy with this dish

1 pound lean ground beef
½ pound lean ground pork
   and/or veal
1 cup diced onion
½ cup grated carrot
½ teaspoon dry mustard
½ teaspoon thyme
¼ teaspoon sage
1 teaspoon salt
⅛ teaspoon ground cloves
½ cup water
1 recipe, double crust pie
   pastry

Place all ingredients in a frying pan and cook together slowly until pink of meat disappears. Continue to simmer for 20 minutes. Remove all grease. Allow mixture to cool. Place in an uncooked pie crust shell; cover with top crust, and cut vents in top in the shape of a star. Bake at 400° for 25-30 minutes. Cut pie in wedges to serve. May be frozen after cooking completely. Should be frozen if prepared more than a day in advance. 6-8 servings

Judith O'Shea (Mrs. Timothy)

Brunswick Stew

6 pounds chicken
3 pounds lean pork roast (loin)
3 pounds lean beef roast
3 (16 ounce) cans creamed
   corn
2 (28 ounce) cans whole
   tomatoes
1 (14 ounce) bottle catsup
1 (5 ounce) bottle
   Worcestershire sauce
2 lemons, thinly sliced,
   seeds removed
1 cup chopped onions
1 stick butter
1 teaspoon tabasco sauce
   (or to taste)
1 Tablespoon salt (or to taste)
1 Tablespoon sugar
½ teaspoon black pepper

Simmer meat in water or stock until meat falls off bones. Several large pots will be needed to do this. Shred the meat, discarding all waste (this amount requires approximately one hour to shred—can be done ahead of time). Add remaining ingredients to meat. Cook slowly 2 to 3 hours, stirring frequently to keep from sticking. Makes approximately 6 quarts of stew. Serve alone or with barbecue, ribs, cole slaw, bread and pickles. Freezes well. 18-20 servings

Emy Blair (Mrs. H. Duane)

Poultry

Crab Stuffed Chicken

4 large chicken breasts (12
    ounces each), halved,
    skinned and boned
3 Tablespoons butter or
    margarine
¼ cup all-purpose flour
¾ cup milk
¾ cup chicken broth
⅓ cup dry white wine
¼ cup chopped onion
1 Tablespoon butter or
    margarine
1 (7½ ounce) can crab meat,
    drained, flaked and
    cartilage removed
1 (3 ounce) can chopped
    mushrooms, drained
½ cup coarsely crumbled
    saltine crackers
2 Tablespoons snipped parsley
½ teaspoon salt
Dash pepper
1 cup shredded Swiss cheese
½ teaspoon paprika

Place 1 chicken piece, boned side up, between 2 pieces of waxed paper. Working from center out, pound chicken lightly with meat mallet to make a cutlet about ⅛-inch thick (8 x 5 inches). Repeat with remaining chicken. Set aside. In saucepan, melt 3 Tablespoons butter or margarine; blend in flour. Add milk, chicken broth and wine all at once; cook and stir until mixture thickens and bubbles; set aside. In skillet, cook onion in 1 Tablespoon butter until tender, not browned. Stir in crab, mushrooms, cracker crumbs, parsley, salt and pepper. Stir in 2 Tablespoons of the sauce. Top each chicken piece with about ¼ cup crab mixture. Fold sides in; roll up. Place seam side down in 12 x 7½ x 2-inch baking dish. Thin sauce slightly with extra broth, if necessary. Pour remaining sauce over all. Bake, covered, in a 350° oven for 1 hour or until chicken is tender. Uncover; sprinkle with cheese and paprika. Bake 2 minutes longer or until cheese melts. Serve with rice and spoon sauce over. 8 servings

Malinda Steed (Mrs. Richard)

Use dental floss to truss the turkey for roasting.

Phoenix Emperor Chicken

6 boneless chicken breasts,
   skinned
4 Tablespoons soy sauce
3 slices ham (boiled
   Danish style)
1½ cups flour
1 cup water
1 egg
1 teaspoon baking powder
½ teaspoon salt
2 packages frozen leaf spinach,
   thawed and drained
   thoroughly
1 small can pineapple chunks
1 package almond slices
¾ cup oyster sauce
½ pound fresh or frozen pea
   pods
1 quart peanut oil

Spread inside of chicken breasts with soy sauce. Place ½ slice of ham inside chicken and roll chicken around ham. Refrigerate for 2 hours. Make a batter with flour, water, eggs, baking powder and salt. Refrigerate at least 1 hour. Heat oil in a pot which is large enough to hold 3 chickens. Bring oil to 375°. (Do not let the oil get hotter than this or it will burn. Try to keep it above 350° so that the coating will not get soggy or greasy.) With a pair of tongs carefully dip rolled chicken in batter until completely coated. Then place in hot oil. You may cook as many at a time as the pan will hold provided the oil stays above 350°. When the coating has turned golden brown place in oven (350°) to finish cooking and to keep warm until ready to serve. While chickens are cooking, fill a saucepan ½ full of water and bring to a boil. Place spinach in a wire strainer and dip into boiling water. Cook spinach just a few minutes until it is hot. Drain water out by pressing with a large spoon. Have serving plates ready. Have pineapple can opened and drained, almonds and oyster sauce at hand. Put fresh pea pods in boiling water for about 1 minute, until they turn bright green. 6 servings

To assemble plates: Work fast to keep food warm. Make a bed of hot spinach on each plate. Then put chicken down and slice 3 times ¾ way through on 45° angle. Place pea pods in these slits so they stand up out of top of chicken rolls. Pour a line of oyster sauce on top of chicken and pea pods. Garnish chicken with almonds and pineapple chunks and serve immediately.

Sidney's Just South Restaurant
Atlanta, Georgia

Chilled Chicken Breasts with Green Peppercorn Sauce

Delicious for a summer luncheon; serve with
Chilled Lemon Broccoli (see Index)

CHICKEN:
3 whole chicken breasts, skinned, boned and halved
¾ cup white wine
1 bay leaf
3 Tablespoons butter
6 whole peppercorns
6 Tablespoons chopped fresh parsley
Water to cover
GREEN PEPPERCORN SAUCE:
2 Tablespoons Dijon mustard
2 Tablespoons white wine
2 teaspoons sugar
½ teaspoon salt
¼ teaspoon white pepper
2 egg yolks
2 Tablespoons green peppercorns, rinsed and drained (available in gourmet food stores)
1 Tablespoon butter
½ cup heavy cream

Place wine, bay leaf, butter, peppercorns and parsley in a large skillet; add chicken, and water to barely cover chicken. Simmer 7 to 10 minutes, just until breasts are no longer pink (further cooking toughens the meat and spoils the texture). Test for doneness by inserting a knife in the center of the breast, meat should be white, not pink. Remove chicken from liquid, cover, and chill thoroughly. Serve with Green Peppercorn Sauce spooned over each breast. 3-6 servings

Sauce: Place mustard, wine, sugar, salt, pepper and egg yolks in top of double boiler. Cook over hot, not boiling water, stirring constantly with a whisk, until mixture has thickened, about 5 minutes. Remove from heat and stir in green peppercorns and butter. Whip cream until stiff and fold into mustard mixture. Cover and chill at least 8 hours. Sauce will keep about a week in refrigerator. 1½ cups

Elise M. Griffin

Chicken With Apples

2-3 apples, sliced
¼ cup raisins
2 Tablespoons sugar
¼ teaspoon cinnamon
1½ pounds chicken breasts
Seasoned salt to taste
GLAZE:
¼ cup white wine
2 Tablespoons sugar
Juice and grated rind of ½ orange

In buttered casserole place apples, raisins, sugar and cinnamon. Season chicken breasts with seasoned salt and let dry 30 minutes. Place chicken on top of apples. Bake uncovered for 1 hour at 325°. 6 servings

Glaze: Simmer glaze ingredients together for 15 minutes. Glaze chicken. Bake 30 minutes longer.

Martha H. Whitehead (Mrs. Richard K.)

Chicken and Snow Peas

1½ pounds chicken breasts
1 teaspoon ginger
2 teaspoons sugar
1 Tablespoon cornstarch
6 Tablespoons soy sauce
  (imported)
⅓ cup sherry
2 6 ounce packages frozen
  snow peas
¼ cup oil
¾ cup whole blanched
  almonds
Sliced fresh mushrooms
  (optional)

Skin, bone and cut chicken into ½ inch cubes. In bowl, mix ginger, sugar, cornstarch, soy sauce and sherry. Thaw snow peas. In a wok or large skillet heat oil over medium heat. Add almonds. Stir and cook about 3 minutes. Add chicken and cook just until meat turns white. Drain. Pour in sherry mixture. Cook until sauce thickens. Add pea pods and mushrooms; stir fry until hot and glazed. Serve at once.
4 servings

Joe Nardone

Abu Faruque's Homestyle Chicken Curry
This is a mild curry which may be spiced up according to taste

9-12 pieces chicken, skinned
1 jumbo yellow onion, slivered
1½ ginger root, freshly
  grated
2-3 garlic cloves, crushed
1 Tablespoon ground turmeric
½ Tablespoon chili powder
1½ Tablespoons cumin powder
½ Tablespoon coriander
1 cinnamon stick
5-6 whole cardamon pods
½ cup vegetable oil (pure
  mustard oil or ghee—
  clarified butter—is best)
2½ cups water
1 teaspoon salt

Heat oil in Dutch oven until very hot, but not smoking. Add onions and cook until translucent, stirring constantly. Add all the spices and ½ cup water. Cook 12-15 minutes over medium-high heat, stirring constantly, until mixture becomes thick, almost dry. Stir chicken, salt, and 2 cups water into onion mixture. Bring to a boil and cover. Cook over high heat, stirring occasionally, until thickest pieces are tender— about 15-20 minutes. Spoon chicken and sauce into a warm serving dish. 6 servings

Variation: ¼ head of cabbage, sliced, may be added to chicken for last 5-7 minutes to make the sauce milder.

This dish may be made with lamb, beef or pork—only the cooking time of the meats would differ.

ANARKALI Indian Restaurant
Decatur, Georgia

Chicken Rococo

1 (10 ounce) stick medium
    Cheddar cheese
4 chicken breasts, boned
    and skinned
2 eggs, beaten
¾ cup dry bread crumbs
4 Tablespoons margarine
1 chicken bouillon cube
1 cup boiling water
½ cup chopped onion
½ cup sliced fresh mushrooms
½ cup chopped green pepper
⅓ cup margarine
2 Tablespoons flour
1 teaspoon salt
¼ teaspoon pepper
2 cups white rice, cooked
1 cup wild rice, cooked

Heat oven to 400°. Cut cheese into 8 equal lengthwise sticks. Cut chicken breasts in half; flatten each to ¼ inch thickness. Roll each piece around stick of cheese. Secure with toothpicks. Dip in eggs, then in bread crumbs. Cook in margarine until brown and test for doneness. Dissolve bouillon cube in water. Cook onions, mushrooms and green pepper in ⅓ cup margarine until tender. Add flour, seasonings and bouillon. Cook until thickened. Add rices and pour into a 10 x 8-inch baking dish. Top with chicken. Bake at 400° for 20 minutes. Can be prepared in advance and baked at the last minute. Serve with a green vegetable and fresh avocado or fruit salad. 8 servings

Jeanine C. Andrews (Mrs. Edward B.)

Curried Orange Chicken

6 chicken breasts, boned
1-2 Tablespoons curry powder
½ cup orange juice
¼ cup honey
2 Tablespoons mustard
2 teaspoons cornstarch
2 Tablespoons water
Salt to taste

Sprinkle curry powder onto chicken breasts and rub in well. Arrange chicken breasts in a flat baking dish. Combine orange juice, mustard, and honey. Pour over chicken. Bake uncovered at 375° for 1 hour, basting several times while cooking. Combine cornstarch and water, blending well. Drain pan juices, add to sauce, and cook over low heat until thickened. Add salt, if necessary. Pour over chicken when ready to serve. 4-6 servings

Cheryl I. Fletcher (Mrs. John S., Jr.)

Party Casserole
A wonderful answer for a large dinner party

8 whole chicken breasts, cooked and cut into large cubes
4 pounds shrimp in shell, boiled and peeled or 2 pounds cooked shrimp
3 (14 ounce) cans plain artichoke hearts, quartered
3 pounds fresh mushrooms, sauteed in butter
6 cups medium white sauce (see Index)
2 Tablespoons Worcestershire sauce
1 cup sherry or white wine
½ cup freshly grated Parmesan cheese

Divide chicken, shrimp, artichokes, and mushrooms equally in two greased 3-quart (9 x 13-inch) casseroles. Prepare white sauce adding Worcestershire sauce and wine. Pour over casseroles. Top with cheese. Bake uncovered at 375° for 40 minutes until bubbly. The chicken and shrimp can be prepared in advance. Assemble day of party. Refrigerate and allow extra cooking time. 18-20 servings

Carolyn B. Hoose (Mrs. Kenneth A.)

Honolulu Kabobs

MARINADE:
Liquid from 1 (1 pound) can pineapple chunks
½ cup soy sauce (Kikkoman)
¼ cup cooking oil
1 teaspoon dry mustard
1 Tablespoon brown sugar
2 teaspoons ground ginger
1 teaspoon garlic salt
¼ teaspoon pepper
6 chicken breasts, boned and cut in 1 inch cubes
Sliced green pepper
1 can water chestnuts
Cherry tomatoes
Fresh mushrooms
Pineapple chunks

For 1¼ cups marinade: Combine in saucepan, ½ cup pineapple juice (drained from can of chunks), soy sauce, oil, dry mustard, brown sugar, ginger, garlic salt and pepper. Simmer for 5 minutes. Cool. Marinate chunks of chicken for 1 hour.

Thread chicken, pineapple chunks, green pepper slices, water chestnuts, cherry tomatoes and mushrooms on skewers. Grill for 20 minutes, turning often on low gas setting or on upper rack, basting with remaining sauce. Serve with stir-fried rice. 4-6 servings

Jane H. Nardone (Mrs. A. Joseph, Jr.)

Chinese Chicken & Cashews
A Chinese "Amah" (friend) offers this to be eaten with chop sticks

3 whole chicken breasts
5 Tablespoons soy sauce
1 Tablespoon dry white wine
   or sherry
1½ Tablespoons cornstarch
¾ Tablespoon sugar
⅛ teaspoon MSG
1 clove garlic, crushed
¾ cup raw cashews (can use
   regular cashews; not dry
   roasted)
3 green peppers, cut bite-size
1 medium onion, cut bite-size
6 Tablespoons safflower oil
½ teaspoon salt

Skin, bone and cut the chicken into ¾ inch cubes. Marinate for one to two hours in the refrigerator in soy sauce, wine, cornstarch, sugar, MSG and garlic. Boil raw nuts in water 10-15 minutes. Drain. Heat 2 Tablespoons oil in wok or frying pan. Cook cashews until golden, about 10 minutes. If using regular cashews cook 1 to 2 minutes only. Wipe pan and add 3 Tablespoons oil; add chicken and marinade, and stir-fry over high heat until meat is no longer pink, about 5 minutes. Remove chicken onto plate. Wipe pan and heat 1 Tablespoon oil—cook green pepper and onion about 3 minutes. Add chicken and cashews and stir quickly until all is very hot. Arrange on a platter and serve immediately. Ingredients should be prepared in advance and cooked at the last minute.
4 servings

Barbara R. Schuyler (Mrs. Lambert, Jr.)

Lemon Barbecued Chicken
Outstanding for summertime entertaining

Meaty pieces of 2 chickens,
   skinned (or breasts only)
1 cup salad oil
½ cup fresh lemon juice
1 Tablespoon salt
1 teaspoon paprika
2 teaspoons onion powder
2 teaspoons basil
½ teaspoon thyme
½ teaspoon garlic powder

Place chicken in shallow pan. Pour marinade over. Cover and refrigerate overnight. Remove to room temperature 1 hour before grilling. Grill 10-12 minutes per side, basting often. 6 servings

Cookbook Committee

Chicken Sari
The use of Hungarian paprika is the secret

6 large chicken breasts, skinned, boned and halved
¾ cup flour
1½ teaspoons salt
1½ teaspoons Hungarian paprika (found in gourmet shops or gourmet sections of super market)
¼ cup finely chopped onions
2 Tablespoons butter
SAUCE:
2 Tablespoons butter
2 Tablespoons flour
1 cup good quality chicken stock (preferably homemade)
⅔ cup milk
1½ Tablespoons Hungarian paprika
1½ cups sour cream

Coat chicken breasts with mixture of flour, salt and paprika. Sauté onion in 2 Tablespoons butter until transparent. Remove onions. Brown chicken breasts lightly. Meanwhile make sauce in saucepan: melt butter and stir in flour; cook until mixture bubbles, stirring constantly. Remove from heat and gradually add chicken stock. Return to heat, bring to boil and cook 1-2 minutes; add the milk and paprika, stirring constantly; when warmed remove from heat; beat with wire whisk and blend in sour cream. Stir in onion and pour sauce over chicken in pan. Cook over low heat, stirring, 3-5 minutes. Do not boil. Cover skillet tightly, turn off heat and let stand 1 hour. Reheat before serving. 12 servings

Ron Cohn
Hal's Restaurant
Atlanta, Georgia

Sautéed Chicken with Wine and Brandy Sauce

1 fryer, cut up
Salt and pepper to taste
1½ Tablespoons butter
1½ Tablespoons oil
¼ pound mushrooms, sliced
¼ teaspoon marjoram
¼ teaspoon thyme
2 fresh tomatoes, peeled and cut in quarters
½ cup dry white wine
½ cup chicken broth
1 Tablespoon finely chopped parsley
2 Tablespoons minced onion
1 ounce brandy

Rub chicken pieces with salt and pepper; brown chicken in butter and oil over medium high heat, turning frequently. Add mushrooms, marjoram, thyme and tomatoes. Simmer for 5 minutes. Add wine and broth. Season with salt and pepper; cook slowly until tender, about 30 minutes. Remove chicken to a warm platter while preparing sauce. Add finely chopped parsley and minced onion to the liquid in the pan. Cook slowly for 10 minutes. Remove from heat and add brandy. Stir well and pour sauce over chicken. Serve with rice. 4 servings

Barrie C. Aycock (Mrs. Robert R.)

Pollo Alla Cacciatora

1 (3 pound) frying chicken,
　cut up
3 Tablespoons olive oil or
　vegetable oil
2 bay leaves
1 cup dry white wine
1 chicken bouillon cube
1-1½ teaspoons salt
Freshly ground pepper
BATTUTO:
1 Tablespoon fresh parsley
1½ celery stalks with leaves
1 clove garlic

Finely mince battuto ingredients almost to a paste. Brown chicken pieces in olive oil over high heat. Add the battuto and cook over medium-high heat until well browned, turning frequently to keep ingredients from sticking and burning. Add bay leaves, wine and chicken bouillon cube and cook over high heat until wine is almost evaporated. With a wooden spoon, scrape all the browned bits from the bottom and sides of the pan. Add salt and pepper. Simmer for 20 minutes until chicken is tender. Serve with Italian Bread which is delicious dipped into the sauce. 4 servings

Barrie C. Aycock (Mrs. Robert R)

Chicken Paulette

6 pieces of chicken (one per
　person)
Oil
1 small onion or 8 spring
　onions (white part only)
1 carrot
3 mushrooms
Pinch of ginger
Pinch of mace
Salt & pepper to taste
3 ounces of sherry
5 ounces chicken stock
2 Tablespoons Dijon mustard
5 ounces heavy cream
Cornstarch

Brown chicken pieces in hot oil in large casserole. Take out and set aside. Finely chop the onion, carrot and mushrooms; add to casserole, cover and cook gently for a few minutes. Replace chicken, add spices, sherry and stock. Cover and cook gently for 40 minutes. Remove chicken. Reduce sauce a little by boiling. Add mustard and cream. Bring to boil and thicken with cornstarch mixed with water. The sauce should be thick enough to cling nicely to chicken. Spoon sauce over chicken. Serve with saffron rice. 6 servings

Matte Campbell (Mrs. Gilbert R., Jr.)

Chicken Paprikas with Spatzle

CHICKEN:
1 large onion, sliced in rings
5 Tablespoons butter
1½ Tablespoons Hungarian
  paprika
1 small chicken (about 2½
  pounds), cut into serving
  pieces
1 green pepper, sliced
1 tomato, sliced
¼ pound mushrooms (optional)
½ cup sour cream (optional)
SPATZLE:
2¼ cups flour
1 teaspoon salt
1 Tablespoon cream of wheat
2 eggs
1 cup water
1 Tablespoon butter, melted

Sauté onion rings in butter in Dutch oven until transparent. Remove from heat; add paprika, chicken, half of green pepper and half of tomato. Stir to coat chicken. Cover and simmer slowly for 1½ hours turning pieces occasionally to cook evenly. Add small amounts of water if necessary. If mushrooms are used, add during last 15 minutes. When meat is tender, transfer to baking dish; add a little water to pan, scraping onion from pan. Pour over chicken. Garnish with remaining tomato and pepper. Cover with foil and keep warm in oven at low heat. Sour cream may be added to gravy if you prefer. Serve with Spatzle.

Spatzle: Put flour, salt and cream of wheat in a bowl. Make a well in middle and add eggs, water and butter. Stir until batter is smooth. Drop by teaspoons into 8 cups boiling water with 2 teaspoons salt. Avoid crowding. Stir bottom so dumplings will rise to top. After they rise to top, cook gently 1-2 minutes. Remove with slotted spoon. Lightly toss with 4 Tablespoons melted butter. Sauce from chicken may be poured over spatzle.

Spicy Chicken

1 cup orange juice
1 Tablespoon vinegar
2 Tablespoons brown sugar
½ teaspoon nutmeg
½ teaspoon basil
1 clove garlic, whole
¼ cup flour
1 teaspoon salt
⅛ teaspoon pepper
1 frying chicken, cut up
¼ cup shortening
1 orange, sectioned

In a saucepan mix orange juice, vinegar, brown sugar, nutmeg and basil. Add garlic. Bring to a boil and simmer 10 minutes. Remove garlic. Mix flour, salt and pepper in paper bag. Add chicken pieces and shake well. In a skillet brown chicken on both sides in shortening. Pour off drippings. Pour sauce over chicken. Cover and simmer 20-30 minutes or until chicken is tender. Add orange sections and cover. Simmer another 5 minutes. May be prepared in advance. Serve with rice. 4 servings

Alice D. Remigailo (Mrs. Richard)

Chicken Enchiladas with Sour Cream Sauce

2 whole chicken breasts or
    1 whole chicken, cut up
1 medium onion, chopped
1 green pepper, chopped
½ teaspoon chili powder
¼ teaspoon garlic powder
1 (12 ounce) bottle chili sauce
1 dozen tortillas
SOUR CREAM SAUCE:
2 Tablespoons butter
3 Tablespoons flour
Hot water
1 cup milk
2 cups sour cream
3 Tablespoons chives
Salt to taste
¼ pound Monterey Jack
    cheese, grated

Boil chicken in a very small amount of water. When tender, take chicken off bone. Add onion and pepper to stock; cut up chicken and return to stock. Cook until juice is evaporated. Add chili powder and garlic powder. Add chili sauce (¾ of bottle may be enough). Simmer; sauce should be thick.
Sour Cream Sauce: Melt butter; add flour. Mix. Add enough hot water to make thin. Add milk. Cook until sauce begins to thicken. Add sour cream, chives and salt. Roll chicken mixture in uncooked tortillas. Place in oven proof 9 x 13-inch pan, seam side down. Pour sour cream sauce over and top with grated Monterey Jack cheese. Warm in oven or if chicken mixture is already warm, just melt cheese under broiler. Note: Soften tortillas in damp cloth to prevent cracking. 4 servings

Judy George (Mrs. Graham W., Jr.)

Chicken-Shrimp Tetrazzini

2 whole chicken breasts
6 ounces vermicelli
½ cup chopped onion
1 clove garlic, chopped
⅓ cup chopped green pepper
1 cup chopped celery
¼ cup butter or margarine
1 teaspoon snipped parsley
1 Tablespoon Worcestershire
  sauce
1 (4½ ounce) can shrimp,
  drained
1 can cream of mushroom soup
1 (8 ounce) can tomato sauce
Shredded sharp Cheddar
  cheese

Simmer chicken in water until tender, seasoning with salt to taste; cool. Remove meat from bones and cut into bite size pieces. Cook vermicelli according to package directions. Over low heat sauté onion, garlic, green pepper and celery in butter. Add parsley and Worcestershire sauce; stir in chicken, vermicelli, shrimp, soup and tomato sauce. Turn into greased shallow 2½-quart casserole; top with cheese. Bake in 350° oven 45-50 minutes. 4-6 servings

Trina Graham
Atlanta Gas Light Company

Chicken in a Ring with Mushroom Sauce
A nice company dish for a small group

½ cup chopped onion
¼ cup chopped celery
¼ cup butter, melted
¾ cup sliced mushrooms
1 Tablespoon lemon juice
2 cups cooked, diced chicken
¼ cup mushroom soup
½ teaspoon garlic salt
¼ teaspoon black pepper
DOUGH:
2 cups biscuit mix
½ cup milk
1 egg
1 Tablespoon water
SAUCE:
1½ cups sliced mushrooms
2 Tablespoons butter
½ cup mushroom soup
2 Tablespoons chopped
  parsley
2 Tablespoons lemon juice

Sauté onion and celery in butter. Add mushrooms and lemon juice and sauté 2-3 minutes. Combine with chicken, mushroom soup, garlic salt and pepper. Cover and chill 1 hour.

Dough: Make dough by combining mix with milk. Knead 8-10 times on a floured board. Roll into an 18 x 7-inch rectangle. Spread chicken mix evenly over dough. Roll up jelly-roll fashion. Press seam to seal. Moisten ends and shape into a ring, pinching ends to seal. Cut 12 slits around ring. Brush with the egg beaten with water. Slide onto a greased baking sheet. Bake 20-25 minutes at 400°.

Sauce: Make sauce by sauteing mushrooms in butter for 2-3 minutes. Add mushroom soup, parsley and lemon juice. Stir constantly but do not boil. Serve sauce separately. 6 servings

Lucia Sizemore (Mrs. Thomas A., III)

Chicken with Wild Rice

2 (3 pound) whole fryer
  chickens
1 cup water
1 cup dry sherry
1½ teaspoons salt
½ teaspoon curry powder
1 medium onion, sliced
½ cup sliced celery
1 pound fresh mushrooms
¼ cup butter or margarine
2 (6 ounce) packages long
  grain and wild rice with
  seasonings
1 cup sour cream
1 can cream of mushroom
  soup

Place chickens in a deep kettle; add water, sherry, salt, curry powder, onion and celery. Cover and bring to a boil; reduce heat and simmer for 1 hour. Remove from heat; strain broth. Refrigerate chicken and broth at once, without cooling first. When chicken is cool, remove meat from bones and cut meat into bite-size pieces. Rinse mushrooms and pat dry; slice and saute in butter until golden, about 5 minutes, stirring constantly. (Reserve enough whole caps to garnish top of casserole; they may be sauteed along with sliced mushrooms.) Measure chicken broth; use as part of the liquid for cooking rice, following directions for firm rice on the package. Combine chicken, mushrooms and rice in a 3½ or 4 quart casserole dish. Blend in sour cream and mushroom soup and toss with the chicken and rice mixture. Arrange reserved mushroom caps in a circle over the top of the casserole. Cover; refrigerate overnight if desired. To heat, bake, covered, at 350° for 1 hour. The casserole may be completely prepared and frozen ahead of time. 8-10 servings

Mrs. William F. Bell, II

When barbecuing poultry and pork, longer cooking over a low fire means less shrinkage and more tender meat. Let your fire burn down to glowing coals before you begin cooking.

Chick'N Puffs

Good luncheon main dish or use as
an interesting appetizer

⅓ cup crushed seasoned
croûtons
¼ cup finely chopped pecans
1 (3 ounce) package cream
cheese
2 Tablespoons butter, softened
½ teaspoon lemon-pepper
seasoning
1 cup cooked chicken, finely
chopped
⅓ cup (2 ounce can)
mushrooms, drained and
finely chopped
1 can Pillsbury Refrigerated
Crescent Dinner rolls*
3 Tablespoons melted butter
*Substitute 1 (10 ounce)
package Pepperidge Farm
Patty Shells for Crescent
Rolls, if desired.
(see variation)

Place croûtons and pecans in small bowl; set aside. In medium bowl, combine cream cheese, 2 Tablespoons butter and seasonings; stir in chicken and mushrooms. Separate crescent dough into 8 triangles; place 2 heaping Tablespoons mixture on triangles. Roll up starting at shortest side of triangle and roll to opposite point. Tuck sides and point under to seal completely. Dip rolls in melted butter; coat with crumb-nut mixture. For use as an appetizer, cut rolls in half crosswise. Bake on ungreased cookie sheet at 375° for 15-20 minutes until golden brown. May be prepared up to 2 hours before serving; prepare, cover and refrigerate, bake 20-25 minutes. 8 servings.

Variation using Pepperidge Farm Patty Shells: Can be frozen. Double quantity of filling in recipe. Thaw patty shells slightly. Dust with a small amount of flour and roll into approximate 6 inch circles. Place ⅓-½ cup filling on each circle, fold over and seal edges. Dip in melted butter, and coat with crumb-nut mixture. Follow preceding directions for baking, or freeze on cookie sheet and transfer to plastic bag. Thaw before cooking.

Jeanette James (Mrs. T. Allen)

Chicken Crêpes

1 recipe Crêpes (see Index)
¼ cup butter or margarine
¼ cup flour
½ teaspoon salt
½ teaspoon pepper
1¾ cup milk
1 (5 ounce) can boned chicken, cut up
1 (2½ ounce) jar mushrooms, drained and chopped
3 Tablespoons sherry
1 cup grated sharp Cheddar cheese
1 (15 ounce) can extra long green asparagus spears, drained

In medium saucepan melt butter; stir in flour, salt and pepper until smooth. Stirring constantly, slowly add milk and cook over medium heat until thickened. Add chicken, mushrooms, sherry and ¾ cup cheese; cook until cheese is melted. Place 2 asparagus spears atop each crêpe; top with 2-3 Tablespoons sauce. Roll up and place seam side down, in shallow 3-quart baking dish. Top with remaining sauce and cheese. Bake in 350° degree oven 10-15 minutes, or until heated through. 4-6 servings

Trina Graham
Atlanta Gas Light Co.

Stuffed Roast Chicken
The stuffing goes between the skin and the meat

½ cup butter
2 small cloves garlic, minced
3 green onions, minced
1 Tablespoon parsley
¼ teaspoon dried chives
¼ teaspoon dried chervil
¼ teaspoon thyme
1¼ cups bread crumbs
3-4 pound chicken, whole
3 Tablespoons butter, melted
½ cup white wine
2 Tablespoons butter

In food processor, cream butter with garlic, green onions and herbs. Add bread crumbs. Loosen skin around breast of chicken and fill with stuffing. You must use your fingers to place stuffing between skin and meat. Fill cavity with remaining stuffing. Truss chicken. Brown on all sides in 3 Tablespoons butter. Roast in covered pan small enough to crowd chicken at 350° for 1 hour. Remove chicken from pan. To deglaze pan juices, place pan over direct heat, add wine, scrape browned bits and let juices boil 1 minute. Swirl in 2 Tablespoons butter. 2-4 servings

Sylvia Dorough (Mrs. Don)

Chicken Kiev

8 whole chicken breasts,
   boned, skinned and halved
1 cup unsifted flour
2 cups dry bread crumbs
4 eggs, well beaten
Oil for deep frying
HERB BUTTER:
1⅓ cups soft butter
2⅔ Tablespoons chopped
   fresh parsley
2 teaspoons dried tarragon
⅛ teaspoon garlic powder
1 teaspoon salt
¼ teaspoon pepper
1 Tablespoon chives
1 teaspoon rosemary

Herb Butter: Combine all ingredients and whip. Spread out in bottom of square pan. Chill until firm and cut into 16 pieces.

Chicken: Pound breasts to ¼ inch thickness. Place pat of butter in center of each piece of chicken. Fold and fasten with a toothpick so that butter is completely enclosed. Roll each breast in the flour, dip in beaten egg and roll in crumbs. Refrigerate at least 1 hour or overnight. Heat oil (1-2 inches deep) to 360°. Add chicken. Fry, turning with tongs, until brown. Keep warm in 200° oven for no more than 15 minutes.

To Freeze and Serve Later: Fry, as above, and cool. Wrap in freezer wrap and freeze. To serve, unwrap, but do not defrost. Bake, uncovered, 35 minutes at 350° Fry a little less time if you plan to freeze. 16 servings

Betty Jo Ridley (Mrs. William E.)

Chicken Parmigiana

3 whole chicken breasts (about
   12 ounces each), split,
   skinned and boned
2 eggs, slightly beaten
1 teaspoon salt
⅛ teaspoon pepper
¾ cup fine dry bread crumbs
½ cup salad oil
2 cups tomato sauce
¼ teaspoon basil
⅛ teaspoon garlic powder
1 Tablespoon margarine
½ cup grated Parmesan cheese
8 ounces Mozzarella cheese,
   sliced and cut in triangles

Place chicken breasts on cutting board; pound lightly with side of heavy knife until about ¼ inch thick. Combine eggs, salt and pepper. Dip chicken into egg mixture, then crumbs. Heat oil in frying pan to 350°. Brown chicken on both sides, remove to shallow baking dish. Pour excess oil from frying pan, then add tomato sauce, basil, and garlic powder. Heat to boiling; simmer for 10 minutes or until thickened. Stir in margarine. Pour over chicken; sprinkle with Parmesan cheese. cover. Bake at 350° for 30 minutes; uncover. Place mozzarella cheese over chicken. Bake 10 minutes longer or until cheese melts. 6 servings

Trina Graham
Atlanta Gas Light Company

Boneless Chicken Breasts, Italian Style
Good to prepare ahead for a crowd

6 whole chicken breasts,
　　boned, skinned and halved
Salt and pepper
4 cloves garlic, crushed
½ cup flour
3 Tablespoons butter
3 Tablespoons oil
½ teaspoon dry tarragon
1½ cups chicken broth
½ cup dry white wine
12 slices boiled ham
12 thin slices mozzarella
　　cheese

Season chicken with salt and pepper and spread with crushed garlic. Flour and sauté in oil and butter until light brown. Place in shallow casserole and sprinkle with tarragon. Add broth to skillet and heat while scraping brown particles from bottom of pan. Add wine and pour over chicken. Cover and bake at 350° for 30 minutes. Uncover and top each breast with ham slice. Bake 20 minutes, add cheese 5 minutes before serving and bake uncovered until cheese melts. To freeze: after adding the wine mixture to chicken, cover and freeze. Allow casserole to thaw 1-2 hours, then bake, covered 1 hour. Finish as directed. 12 servings

Elise M. Griffin

Chicken and Lobster in Madeira Sauce

SAUCE:
1 cup butter
2 Tablespoons chopped onion
2 Tablespoons chopped celery
1 cup flour
¼ teaspoon thyme
¼ teaspoon rosemary
2 small bay leaves
2 cloves garlic, minced
2 Tablespoons tomato puree
6 cups beef bouillon
2 Tablespoons orange juice
2 Tablespoons sugar
½ cup Madeira wine
4 cups cooked lobster meat
4 cups cooked chicken, boned
　　and cut in large pieces

Melt butter in a skillet until it foams. Add onion and celery and sauté 5 minutes. Stir in flour, spices and tomato purée; cook slowly 5 minutes stirring. Add bouillon, cover and bring to a boil, simmer slowly 1 hour. Strain sauce. Cook orange juice and sugar until caramel colored. Add wine and cook until sugar dissolves. Add lobster and chicken and strained sauce, and heat all together. 8 servings

Helen Ward (Mrs. William T.)

Chicken with Green Noodles

¼ pound butter
¼ pound fresh mushrooms
1 pint heavy cream
1 Tablespoon sherry
1 Tablespoon dry white wine
2 chickens, cooked and diced
2 Tablespoons flour
2 Tablespoons butter
½ package green noodles,
    cooked and drained
Parmesan cheese

Melt butter. Sauté mushrooms. Add cream, sherry, wine and chicken. Make a paste of the butter and flour and stir into chicken mixture. Put noodles into bottom of a greased 2½-quart casserole. Put chicken mixture on top. Sprinkle with Parmesan cheese. Bake at 350° for 30 minutes. 4-6 servings

Kenney K. Linton (Mrs. Sidney E.)

Chicken Spaghetti
This gets better every time it is reheated

2 fryer hens
2 large onions, chopped fine
4 ribs celery, chopped
1 green pepper, chopped
½ stick butter, melted
1 (6 ounce) package vermicelli
2 Tablespoons chili powder
2 Tablespoons chopped parsley
1 small jar pimiento, chopped
    fine
2 cans cream of mushroom
    soup
1 small can mushrooms,
    drained
½ pound Cheddar cheese,
    grated

Boil chicken, debone and save chicken stock. In a skillet, sauté onions, pepper and celery until tender in butter. In another saucepan, boil vermicelli in chicken stock following cooking directions on vermicelli package. Drain. In a large pan, combine chicken, sautéed onions, pepper and celery with vermicelli. Combine chili powder, parsley, pimiento, soup and mushrooms. Mix thoroughly. Cover and refrigerate 24 hours. Place in a large buttered casserole. Sprinkle cheese on top. Bake at 350° for 1 hour. May be frozen. 6 servings

Karen V. Shinall (Mrs. Myrick C.)

Tina's Chicken Divan

3 cups cooked chicken
2 (10 ounce) packages broccoli
   cooked and drained
2 Tablespoons butter
Salt and pepper
1 can mushroom soup
½ cup cream
½ cup white wine
2 cups grated sharp cheese
1 teaspoon lemon juice
½ cup mayonnaise
Parmesan cheese

Butter casserole; layer chicken and broccoli; dot with butter; sprinkle with salt and pepper. Heat soup and cream; when hot, add wine, cheese, and lemon juice; add mayonnaise after cheese melts; pour over chicken and broccoli; sprinkle with Parmesan cheese. Bake at 350° until sauce bubbles, approximately 25 minutes. Casserole may be assembled ahead of time.
6 servings

Joan M. Adams (Mrs. John P., Jr.)

Chicken Livers with Poppy Seeds
A divine dish

4 medium onions, sliced
6 Tablespoons butter
1½ teaspoons marjoram
¼ teaspoon salt
1 pound chicken livers
1 Tablespoon poppy seeds
2 cloves garlic, minced
3 Tablespoons flour
½ teaspoon freshly ground
   pepper
1 teaspoon paprika
⅔ cup dry sherry

In a skillet with cover, sauté onions in 3 Tablespoons butter for 10 minutes. Add 1 teaspoon marjoram and ¼ teaspoon salt. Stir, cover and keep warm. Wipe livers with damp cloth and leave whole. Bruise poppy seeds. Heat remaining 3 Tablespoons butter in a second skillet. Add livers, poppy seeds, garlic, and remaining ½ teaspoon marjoram. Stir well and cook for 5 minutes at high heat. Stir often. Sift in flour, pepper and paprika. Stir and cook for 5 minutes longer. Add salt if needed. Lift out livers. Place atop onions. To the liver skillet, add the sherry and heat to boiling, stirring to loosen and blend the residue from the frying pan. When boiling, pour over the livers and onions, cover the skillet and cook at low heat for 30 minutes, leaving the cover off part of the time so the wine reduces slightly. Do not stir. 4 servings

Cookbook Committee

Cornish Hen with Rice and Curry

2 Rock Cornish hens
¼ cup butter, melted
1 (6 ounce) package curry rice
SAUCE:
1 (1 pound, 1 ounce) can
apricots
¼ cup butter
½ cup sliced onion
½ cup sliced celery
2 Tablespoons flour
1 teaspoon curry powder
1 cup water
½ cup apricot syrup from fruit
2 chicken bouillon cubes
¼ cup medium size pitted
ripe olives
Parsley for garnish

If hens are frozen, thaw and remove giblets. Split hens. Place in 13 x 9-inch baking pan, skin side up. Brush with butter. Bake at 350° for 1-1¼ hours, basting occasionally with remaining butter, until fork tender. While hens are baking, bake rice in a 1½-quart covered casserole according to directions on package.

Sauce: Drain apricots, reserving syrup. In saucepan, melt butter. Sauté onion and celery until almost tender. Stir in flour and curry powder. Remove from heat. Gradually stir in water and ½ cup reserved syrup; add bouillon cubes. Cook, stirring constantly, until mixture thickens and cubes melt. Cook 2 additional minutes. Add drained apricots and olives. Heat to serving temperature. To serve: On heated platter, arrange rice, Cornish hens, apricots and olives. Garnish with parsley. Accompany with remaining sauce. Delicious! 4 servings

Joartis Sims
Fort Worth, Texas

Cornish Hens Andalusia

2 Rock Cornish hens, split
   in two
2 Tablespoons minced parsley
¼ cup minced onion
½ teaspoon minced garlic
2 cups orange juice
Melted butter
¼ cup butter
1 Tablespoon cornstarch
¼ cup raisins
¼ cup slivered almonds
Warmed orange sections
Ripe olives

Marinate Cornish hens for 1 hour in mixture of parsley, onion, garlic and orange juice. Wipe hens dry, baste with butter and roast in uncovered baking pan in 300° oven for 30 minutes. In a small skillet melt ¼ cup butter, add cornstarch and cook 2-3 minutes stirring. Add marinade to this. Pour sauce over hens; sprinkle with raisins and slivered almonds. Bake covered in a 350° oven for 30 minutes. Remove cover and brown under broiler. Garnish with warmed orange sections and ripe olives. Serve over rice. 2-4 servings

Rachel Greenland

Smoked Turkey on a Weber Grill

1 (16-18 pound) butterball
   turkey
Salt
Black pepper
1 (10 pound) bag charcoal
1 bag hickory chips soaked in
   water

Thaw turkey. Remove giblets. Dry bird thoroughly with paper towels. Rub well with salt and pepper, inside and out. Insert meat thermometer. Start charcoal fire using about 40 briquets. When coals are very hot and white, about 30 minutes, rake ½ of coals to each side of grill. Add a generous handful of hickory chips to coals. Place turkey in a large iron skillet or similar pan. Put pan in center of grill. Cover grill. Every 30 minutes, baste turkey with pan juices; add more hickory (for first 2 hours) and add more charcoal as needed. Don't be stingy with the hickory if a good smoked flavor is desired. Cook approximately 20 minutes per pound or until meat thermometer registers proper temperature.

Joe Scroggs

Fillet of Turkey with Olive Sauce
An old family recipe that makes an unusual Thanksgiving dinner

TURKEY:
6 slices uncooked turkey
  breast
1 egg, beaten
½ cup flour
Salt and pepper
2 Tablespoons cooking oil
OLIVE SAUCE:
5 Tablespoons butter
4 Tablespoons flour
2 cups milk
½ teaspoon salt
Dash of pepper
½ teaspoon dry mustard
1 egg yolk, beaten
½ cup sliced olives

Turkey: Cut turkey breast in slices ⅓ inch thick. Dip in egg; then coat with flour that has been mixed with salt and pepper. Sauté in hot oil until golden brown. Place slices on toast or rice and pour Olive Sauce over all.

Olive Sauce: Melt butter in top of double boiler. Blend in flour. Add milk slowly and stir until blended. Add salt, pepper and mustard and cook over hot water until thickened. Pour egg yolk slowly into hot mixture, stirring constantly. Cook for 1 minute longer. Stir in olives. 6 servings

Martha Herod (Mrs. James V.)

Baked Turkey Croquettes

2 Tablespoons butter
1 Tablespoon finely chopped
  onion
¼ cup all-purpose flour
½ Tablespoon salt
⅛ teaspoon pepper
1 cup milk
2 cups finely chopped
  cooked turkey
2 Tablespoons minced parsley
1 package seasoned coating
  mix for chicken
1 cup medium white sauce
  (see Index)
1 Tablespoon chopped green
  pepper
1 Tablespoon minced onion
1 Tablespoon chopped
  pimiento

Melt butter in a skillet; sauté onions until clear. Remove from heat. Add flour, salt, pepper and milk all at once. Return to medium heat and cook until thick, stirring continuously, approximately 1 minute. Add turkey and parsley. Pour mixture into greased 8 x 8 x 2-inch pan. Chill several hours. Shape mixture into balls and brush lightly with milk. Roll the balls in coating mix and place them on a wire rack to dry. Chill for 1 hour. Bake in greased shallow pan at 400° for 20 minutes. Turn and bake 10 minutes longer. Serve with 1 cup medium white sauce (see Index) to which the green pepper, onion and pimiento have been added. 4-6 servings

Susan M. Morley

Turkey Casserole
A noble way to fix leftovers

1 (8 ounce) package egg
  noodles
3 cups cooked turkey or
  chicken, cut up
2 cans cream of chicken soup
2 cups sour cream
1 teaspoon thyme
1 cup buttered dry bread
  crumbs
2 Tablespoons poppy seeds

Cook noodles as directed. Add meat to soup, sour cream and thyme. Stir in noodles. Turn into a large shallow pan that has been buttered. Sprinkle with buttered bread crumbs and then poppy seeds. Bake uncovered for 30 minutes at 350°. This is lovely served with Peach Aspic (see Index). 8 servings

Mickey Hutchinson (Mrs. James)

Roast Duckling with Honey Sauce

1 (5 pound) duckling, quartered
Honey for glazing
SAUCE:
4 Tablespoons lemon juice
3 Tablespoons honey
2 Tablespoons Japanese soy
  sauce
2 Tablespoons butter, melted
2 Tablespoons dry sherry
1 clove garlic, crushed

Blend sauce ingredients and let stand 1 hour. Roast quartered duckling in shallow pan at 325° for 1 hour piercing the skin frequently and basting with sauce. Turn on broiler and brown, basting with sauce, for 5 minutes on each side. Brush with honey, skin side up, and brown 1 minute more. Spoon remaining sauce over duck and serve. 4 servings

Elise M. Griffin

MICROWAVE HINT ▰▰▰▰▰▰▰▰▰▰▰

Approximate conversion table for microwave cooking
Conventional cooking time ÷ 4 less 2
Example: 60 minutes ÷ 4 = 15 minutes, less 2 minutes = 13 minutes

Peking Duck with Mandarin Pancakes

One of the most famous of all Chinese banquet dishes;
Our version is a little different, but we think it's a dish that's
well worth trying.

1 (4-5 pound) duck (the larger
  the better)
1 Tablespoon water
5 Tablespoons dark brown
  sugar
2 Tablespoons salt
2½ Tablespoons black pepper

MANDARIN PANCAKES:
1¾-2 cups all-purpose flour
¾ cup boiling water
2 teaspoons sesame oil
Non-stick 8-10 inch skillet
Hoisin sauce (available at
  Oriental food stores)
12 green onions

**DIRECTIONS FOR GREEN
ONION BRUSHES:**
  **With a paring knife, cut the
white bulb of the onion into
fine bristles. Trim off green
so total brush length is
2 inches.**

To serve: When duck is ready,
allow to cool enough to handle.
Pull meat off bones. Tear skin
into small pieces. Using a green
onion brush, spread 1 Tablespoon
Hoisin onto a pancake, top with
some of the meat and skin. Place
brush on top and roll up like a
crêpe. Serve immediately.
Makes 12 pancakes

Preheat oven to 350°. Prepare
the duck: Pull off excess fat and
neck skin. Remove giblets. Snip
off top half of wings. Dry duck
well. Make a thick paste of water,
sugar, salt and pepper. Put 1
Tablespoon paste in duck cavity.
Place duck breast side up on tray
of roasting pan. Using a pastry
brush, paint top side well with
paste. Turn duck over and paint
backside. Place, backside up, in
350° oven. After 45 minutes, baste
again. Cook 45 minutes more,
baste and turn duck over. Repeat
process. Total cooking time:
3 hours.

Mix 1¾ cups flour and water
in bowl. As soon as hands can
stand the heat, knead dough
together. Add other ¼ cup flour
if needed to make a smooth
dough. Continue kneading for
about 5 minutes until smooth and
elastic. Cover with damp towel
and let rest for at least ½ hour.
On floured surface, roll dough ¼
inch thick. Cut into 2 inch circles.
Brush 1 side with sesame oil and
sandwich 2 circles together (oiled
sides together). Carefully roll out
sandwiches to 6 inch circles; turn
over often; try to keep top and
bottom circles even. Heat skillet
on high for 30 seconds. Reduce
heat to moderate. Cook each
pancake until light brown spots
appear: about 1 minute per side.
Remove from pan and gently
separate halves. Cool slightly;
serve warm. May be refrigerated
or frozen. Heat in foil in oven for
10 minutes at 350°.

Cookbook Committee

HINT

Tie turkey legs with rolled gauze bandage.

Smoked Wild Duck

Wild ducks
Hickory
SAUCE:
½ stick butter
¾ cup vinegar
¼ cup water
1½ Tablespoons salt
2 Tablespoons sugar
1¼ teaspoons Tabasco

Cut ducks in half down backbone. Simmer in water for 2 hours or until tender. Soak hickory chips in water for an hour. Place wet chips on low charcoal fire. Barbecue ducks over low fire (covered) and baste with sauce frequently. Be sure to keep fire low and chips wet so the ducks have smoked taste. Grill for 1 hour or until dark.

DeDe T. Slappey (Mrs. George N.)

Quail with Green Grapes

4 quail
Salt, pepper and flour
¼ cup butter
½ cup water
½ cup seedless green grapes
2 Tablespoons toasted
    almonds, sliced or slivered
1 Tablespoon lemon juice
4 toast slices, buttered

Sprinkle quail inside and out with salt, pepper and flour. Melt butter in skillet; add quail and brown on all sides. Add water. Cover and cook over low heat 15 minutes or until tender. Add grapes and cook 3 minutes longer. Stir in nuts and lemon juice. Serve quail on buttered toast with pan sauce. 4 servings

Judy Carlsen (Mrs. Alfred M., III)

Quail and Oysters

Quail
3 oysters per quail
Melted butter
Corn meal
Flour
Butter
Salt and pepper
Bacon

Wipe birds inside and out with damp cloth. Dip oysters in melted butter, then in cornmeal and place inside bird. Make flour and butter into a paste and rub breasts well with the paste. Put birds in baking dish with a strip of bacon across each bird. Bake for 30 minutes, basting well with butter. Serve on toast or wild rice with a green vegetable.

Judy Carlsen (Mrs. Alfred M.)

Quail Normande

6-8 quail
Flour, seasoned with salt
  and pepper
2 or more Tablespoons butter
4 shallots, chopped
1 wine glass Calvados (apple
  Brandy), warmed
3 apples, peeled, cored, and
  sliced
Salt and pepper to taste
½ pint chicken stock
Bouquet garni
2 Tablespoons whipping
  cream, warmed

Coat quail well with seasoned flour and brown in melted butter in a skillet, adding more butter if needed. Reduce heat, add shallots and cook until golden. Pour warm Calvados over quail and ignite. Add the apples and bouquet garni, and season with salt and pepper. Bring to a boil, then cover and cook over low heat for 30-40 minutes until tender. Remove quail to a heated platter. Strain pan juices, add cream and pour over quail. Serve with wild rice.
3-4 servings

Southern Plantation Cookbook
Corinne Carlton Geer

Wild Duck and Oyster Gumbo

1 wild duck (domestic may be
  used)
2 Tablespoons shortening
2 Tablespoons flour
1 cup chopped onion
2 dozen oysters with liquid
2 quarts hot water
1 teaspoon garlic salt
¼ cup fresh parsley, minced
¼ cup green onion tops,
  minced

Cut duck into 4-6 pieces and season with salt and pepper. Brown in shortening. Remove duck from pan and pour off all but 2 Tablespoons fat. Add flour to fat and mix well. Add onions and cook until tender. Add duck, hot water and garlic salt. Simmer slowly until duck is tender, about 2 hours. Add oysters and liquid, making sure both are free of grit and shell. Add parsley and green onion tops. Season to taste. If oysters are preferred nearly raw, and parsley and onion tops, crisp, then serve immediately; or keep warm until needed. Serve over rice. 4-6 servings

Mrs. Alma DuPont

Doves in Wine Sauce
Outstanding with hot curried fruit, wild rice,
a green vegetable and red wine

4 Tablespoons butter
1 medium onion, chopped
16 dove breasts
1 teaspoon salt
1 teaspoon pepper
2 teaspoons parsley, fresh or
dried
2 teaspoons Worcestershire
sauce
¼ teaspoon thyme
½ cup dry red wine
1 beef bouillon cube, dissolved
in 1 cup boiling water
2 Tablespoons butter, softened
2 Tablespoons flour

In large skillet, melt butter and sauté onions until tender, about 5 minutes. Remove onions and lightly brown doves in same skillet. Reduce heat to simmer. Arrange doves, meat side up. Return onions to skillet. Add salt, pepper, parsley, Worcestershire sauce, thyme, and wine. Simmer uncovered for 15 minutes. Add bouillon; cover and simmer 1-1½ hours until meat is tender.

Remove doves to a warm platter. Mix flour and soft butter to form a roux. Add to the liquid in pan and cook until smooth. Pour thickened sauce over doves. Serves 4-6

Molly Ahlquist (Mrs. Ernest, Jr.)

Smothered Georgia Doves

Doves
Flour
Salt
Pepper
Crisco
Water
Sugar
Kitchen Bouquet

Roll doves in flour, sprinkle with salt and pepper and fry in Crisco until light brown. Remove doves to Dutch oven or electric skillet. Add water to almost cover birds. Add 1 teaspoon Kitchen Bouquet, salt, pepper and sugar to taste. If necessary thicken gravy with cornstarch and water. Cover and simmer in gravy for several hours. Serve over wild rice.

DeDe T. Slappey (Mrs. George N.)

Vegetables

Asparagus Supreme Casserole

3 hard boiled eggs, sliced
2 (14½ ounce) cans green
   asparagus spears
1 (8 ounce) can water
   chestnuts, thinly sliced
6 Tablespoons flour
½ cup whole milk
¼ cup butter
½ teaspoon salt
¼ teaspoon black pepper
1 cup grated sharp Cheddar
   cheese
2 Tablespoons diced pimiento
1 cup seasoned bread crumbs

Drain asparagus and water chestnuts, saving 1½ cups of combined liquids. Mix flour and milk until smooth. Combine with vegetable liquids, butter, seasonings and cheese. Cook over medium heat, stirring constantly, until thickened. Add pimiento. Arrange asparagus in oblong shallow casserole. Top with water chestnuts; then cover with egg slices. Pour sauce over all. Sprinkle with crumbs. Bake in a 375° oven for ½ hour or until top is lightly browned and sauce is bubbly. May be prepared in advance. 8 servings

Constance D. Wilson (Mrs. A.E., Jr.)

Crunchy Asparagus

Fresh asparagus spears
4 Tablespoons oil
SEASONINGS:
1-2 teaspoons accent or salt,
   freshly ground black
   pepper, and oregano to
   taste

Slice asparagus diagonally into ½-1 inch lengths. Place oil in fry pan and heat slightly. Add asparagus, and your choice of seasonings to pan. Cover and shake over medium high heat until asparagus are crispy, about 7 minutes.

Dr. Ruth Kalish

MICROWAVE HINT

Standing time is essential in microwave cooking. Allow all foods to stand from 2 to 10 minutes after cooking. Wrap in a towel to keep warm. Length of standing time depends on the volume of food cooked. For example: a baked potato—2 minutes, a large casserole—10 minutes.

Winter Artichokes

This rich Cuban dish goes well with a light meal

4 large artichokes
¼ cup dried bread crumbs
¼ cup grated Parmesan
cheese
½ cup chopped parsley
¼ cup chopped chives
1 Tablespoon grated onion
½ clove garlic, grated
4 Tablespoons melted butter
Olive oil (about ⅓ cup)

Wash and trim artichokes. Mix bread crumbs, Parmesan cheese, parsley, chives, onion, garlic and butter to make a stuffing. Press stuffing mixture well down into leaves of artichokes and into and across tops. Stand in earthenware casserole with about ½ inch water in bottom. Dribble oil over artichokes. Cover and bake at 325° for 1½ hours or until thoroughly tender and leaves pull away easily. Serve warm with melted butter as a first course. May be cooked ahead and reheated. 4 servings

Cookbook Committee

Bill's Banana Pepper Bake

10 banana peppers
½ cup or more corn oil
6 American cheese slices
½ small package Pepperidge
Farm herb dressing mix
(approximately)

Cut tops from peppers. Cut down one side and remove seeds. Pour oil in glass 8 x 8-inch baking dish. Add peppers turning to coat. (You may need more oil.) Cover peppers with cheese slices. Sprinkle with dressing mix until well covered. Bake at 350° for 30-40 minutes until peppers are soft.

Caroline McPheeters (Mrs. Hal)

MICROWAVE HINT

Always prick foods which are covered by a skin or membrane, such as sausages, baking potatoes, squash, egg yolks and chicken livers, to keep them from bursting.

MICROWAVE HINT

To clarify butter, heat until bubbling and pour off clear liquid, discard residue.

Green Beans Horseradish

2 cans whole green beans
1 large onion, sliced
Several bits of bacon
1 cup mayonnaise
2 hard boiled eggs, chopped
1 heaping Tablespoon
  horseradish
1 teaspoon Worcestershire
  sauce
Salt and pepper to taste
Garlic salt to taste
Celery salt to taste
1½ teaspoon chopped parsley
Juice of 1 lemon

Cook beans with bacon and onion for ½ hour. Blend rest of ingredients and allow to come to room temperature. When ready to serve, drain beans and add horseradish sauce to beans. May be prepared ahead. Do not freeze. 6-8 servings

Jane G. Skelton (Mrs. W. Douglas)

Green Beans with Salted Peanuts

2 slices bacon, diced
⅔ cup sliced onions
4 cups cooked green beans
2 Tablespoons wine vinegar
¼ teaspoon pepper
1½ teaspoons salt
½ cup salted peanuts

Fry bacon and remove from pan. Saute onions in bacon grease until golden. Add cooked green beans, vinegar, salt and pepper. Simmer 12 minutes. Add peanuts and cook 5 minutes longer. Serve with crisp bacon bits on top. 8 servings

Julia W. Ray (Mrs. Frederick C., Jr.)

HINT ▄

Tomatoes have a better flavor if not refrigerated. Even the super-market variety will improve in color and texture if allowed to sit in a sunny window for a day or two.

"Skinny" Green Beans
A "non fattening" favorite—no grease

4 cups water
2 beef bouillon cubes
1 teaspoon sugar
2 pounds fresh green beans,
    washed, strings removed.
Dash Tabasco sauce
Dash freshly ground black
    pepper

Place bouillon cubes in water and bring to boil. Add sugar and beans to bouillon. Cover and cook until tender over medium heat, about 1 hour. Check bouillon and add more water if necessary. During last 15 minutes add Tabasco sauce and pepper. Hint: Use leftovers in vegetable salads. 6-8 servings

Jeanine C. Andrews (Mrs. Edward B.)

Green Beans Tivoli
Wonderful to take on a Stone Mountain picnic

1 pound crisp young green
    beans
¼ cup minced green onions
1 Tablespoon cider vinegar
2 Tablespoons lemon juice
2 teaspoons sugar
2 Tablespoons Dijon mustard
⅓ cup olive oil
1 Tablespoon chopped parsley
3 Tablespoons fresh or dried
    dillweed
Salt
¼ teaspoon fresh ground
    pepper
GARNISH:
⅓ cup sliced radishes
⅓ cup coarsely chopped
    walnuts

Snap ends of beans and cook 5-7 minutes or until just tender. Drain and cool under cold water. Mix all ingredients except radishes and walnuts and pour over vegetables. Refrigerate at least 2 hours. Before serving, stir in radishes and walnuts. Note: Red on radishes will bleed if stirred into beans more than 1-2 hours in advance. Wonderful leftovers if you don't mind red radish slices.

4-6 servings

Cookbook Committee

Jim's Favorite Beans

¾ cup sliced apples
½ cup chopped onion
1 (31 ounce) can or 2 (16 ounce) cans pork and beans
6 ounces smoked sausage links, thinly sliced
¼ cup raisins
2 Tablespoons catsup
2 teaspoons prepared mustard
¼ teaspoon ground cinnamon
Dash cayenne

Cook apples and onion in small amount of water until crisp and tender, about 5 minutes, and drain. Mix with all other ingredients and turn into bean pot or casserole. Bake, uncovered, in a 375° oven (or less) for 1-1¼ hours STIRRING ONCE. Serve with corn muffins. 8-10 servings

Joan McMahan (Mrs. James P.)

Black Beans and Rice

1 pound dried black beans
10 cups water
1 green pepper, diced
⅔ cup olive oil
1 large onion, chopped
Garlic salt to taste
¼ pound bacon, diced
1 green pepper, diced
4 teaspoons salt
½ teaspoon pepper
2 Tablespoons olive oil
WHITE RICE:
3 Tablespoons oil
3 cups water
1 Tablespoon salt
1 pound rice
1 pint sour cream (optional)

Wash beans and soak with 1 diced green pepper in water 6-8 hours or overnight. Boil beans in this water for 45 minutes or until tender. Heat olive oil in skillet; add onion, green pepper, garlic salt and bacon; cook until light brown. Pour mixture into beans; add salt and pepper. Cook 1 hour longer. Add 2 Tablespoons olive oil when ready to serve.

To cook rice, combine water, oil and salt; bring to a full boil. Add rice. When it comes to a boil, reduce heat to simmer and cook 30 minutes or until done. Serve black beans over rice with chopped raw onions and a dollop of sour cream (optional) on top. Can be a main dish or an accompaniment to pork roast. Add more liquid to make black bean soup. 8 servings

Patricia Barton (Mrs. William L.)

Red Beans and Rice

6 cups water
1 pound dried small red beans
   or 1 pound dried red kidney
   beans
4 Tablespoons butter
1 cup finely chopped green
onions, divided
½ cup finely chopped onions
1 teaspoon finely chopped
garlic
2 (1 pound) smoked ham hocks
or ham bones with meat
1 teaspoon salt
½ teaspoon black pepper
6-8 cups cooked long grain
   rice

Rinse beans in cold water. In 3-4 quart saucepan, bring 6 cups water to boil. Drop beans in and boil briskly for 2 minutes. Turn off heat and let beans soak for 1 hour. Drain beans; save liquid; add more water to make 4 cups. Melt butter in heavy 4-5 quart kettle. Sauté ½ cup of the green onions, onions and garlic for about 5 minutes until they are soft and translucent. Stir in beans, their liquid, ham hocks, salt and pepper. Bring mixture to a boil, reduce heat to low and simmer about 3 hours, covered, or until beans are very soft. Check pot from time to time, adding more water (up to 1 cup) if beans seem too dry. During last 30 minutes, stir frequently and crush beans against the sides of pan to form a thick sauce. Remove ham bones to cutting board; cut meat from bone into bite size chunks. Return ham to beans. Discard bones. Serve mixture over rice with ½ cup green onions sprinkled on top. May be prepared in advance.
6 servings

Jane H. Nardone (Mrs. A. Joseph, Jr.)

HINT

Add ½ teaspoon sugar to vegetables such as corn, peas or carrots, when cooking, to help bring out the flavor.

Kidney Bean Casserole

A must for an outdoor cookout

2 (15 ounce) cans kidney
  beans, partially drained
1 green pepper, coarsely
  chopped
2 small onions, coarsely
  chopped
2 tomatoes, cut into small
  chunks
1 strip raw bacon, finely
  chopped
½ cup brown sugar
½ (14 ounce) bottle catsup or
  chili sauce

Combine all ingredients in casserole dish and bake, covered, for 2 hours at 325°. May be prepared in advance, and is good reheated. 6 servings

Judy L. O'Shea (Mrs. Timothy)

Southern Baked Beans

1 pound dried navy beans
6 cups water
2 minced garlic cloves
2 large onions, sliced
1 dried hot red pepper, small
1 bay leaf
¾ pound sliced salt pork or
  4 strips bacon
3 Tablespoons molasses
¼ cup catsup
1 teaspoon dry mustard
½ teaspoon ground ginger
1½ teaspoons Worcestershire
½ teaspoon salt
¼ cup brown sugar, firmly
  packed

Cover beans with water and bring to a boil, boiling for 2 minutes. Cover and let stand one hour. Add next 5 ingredients and cook until beans are tender. Drain, save liquid. Add remaining ingredients, except sugar, to two cups of liquid. Place beans in a shallow 2-quart baking dish. Arrange slices of pork on top and add liquid. Sprinkle with brown sugar. Bake at 400° for 1 hour.

June Parker (Mrs. Charles)

Stir Fried Broccoli

2 pounds fresh broccoli
2 Tablespoons oil
2 Tablespoons chicken stock
1 teaspoon salt
½ teaspoon sugar
1 teaspoon cornstarch
   dissolved in 1 Tablespoon
   stock

Divide broccoli into florets; Peel stems. Heat oil and stir fry broccoli about 1 minute. Add chicken stock, salt and sugar. Cover and cook 3-4 minutes. Lower heat and add cornstarch dissolved in stock; stir briefly to thicken. Serve immediately. Will hold warm for a few minutes. 6 servings

Pamela T. Marcus

Sesame Broccoli

2 pounds fresh broccoli, cut
   into 2-inch pieces
2½ Tablespoons sugar
2 Tablespoons sesame seeds,
   toasted
2 Tablespoons oil
2 Tablespoons vinegar
2-3 Tablespoons Japanese soy
   sauce

Cook broccoli in small amount of boiling, salted water until tender—about 7 minutes. Drain and keep warm. Combine remaining ingredients in small pan and bring to boil over medium heat. Pour over broccoli, coating well. Serve immediately. Serves 6

Cookbook Committee

Chilled Lemon Broccoli
An excellent summertime vegetable

1 bunch fresh broccoli
Juice of 1 lemon
3 Tablespoons olive oil
Salt to taste
¼ cup pine nuts or sliced
   almonds

Divide broccoli into florets. Steam over boiling water 5 minutes only. Drain. Pour several changes of ice water and ice cubes on broccoli to retain color. Chill. Mix lemon juice, oil and salt. Pour over broccoli. When ready to serve, sprinkle with pine nuts (or almonds). Recipe can be doubled easily. 4 servings

Elise M. Griffin

Broccoli Rice Casserole

1 medium onion, chopped
¼ cup chopped celery
½ stick butter
1 (10 ounce) package frozen
   chopped broccoli, or 1
   bunch fresh broccoli
   (chopped), cooked and
   drained well
2½ cups cooked rice
1 can condensed cream of
   chicken soup
4 ounces Cheese Whiz
Dash Tabasco
Pepper to taste

Sauté onion and celery in butter until tender. Combine with other ingredients. Pour into greased 1½-quart baking dish. Bake at 350° until bubbly; about about 30-35 minutes. May be frozen. Best when prepared a day ahead. 6 servings

Lachlan M. Fiveash (Mrs. Charles)

Brandied Carrots

Enough slender carrots to
   serve 4-6 people
½ stick butter (approximately)
Brown sugar
⅓ cup brandy

Scrape carrots and cut in thirds. Layer carrots in a buttered baking dish. Dot each layer with butter and sprinkle with brown sugar. Pour brandy over top. Cover dish and bake at 350° about 1 hour. 4-6 servings

Gingered Carrots

1 pound carrots
½ cup water
Salt
1 teaspoon ground ginger
1 Tablespoon brown sugar
2 Tablespoons butter

Cut carrots in lengthwise strips or crosswise circles. Cook in water seasoned with salt for 10 minutes or until tender; drain. In skillet melt butter; add ginger and sugar and cook 2-3 minutes turning carrots several times until well glazed. 4 servings

Cookbook Committee

Carrot Mold with French Peas

A rich and delicious way to serve carrots
The cake-like texture of the mold eliminates the need to serve bread

CARROT MOLD:
1½ sticks butter, softened
½ cup brown sugar, firmly
packed
2 eggs, separated
1½ cups finely grated raw
carrots (approximately
½ pound)
1 Tablespoon cold water
1 Tablespoon lemon juice
1 cup plain flour
½ teaspoon baking soda
1 teaspoon baking powder
½ teaspoon salt
Breadcrumbs
FRENCH PEAS:
3 Tablespoons butter
¼ cup lettuce, finely chopped
1 box frozen green peas (top
quality)
¼ cup minced shallots or
green onions
1 large sprig parsley
2 teaspoons sugar
½ teaspoon salt
Dash of white pepper

Preheat oven to 350°. In mixer, cream butter and brown sugar. Add egg yolks and beat until thick. Add carrots, water, lemon juice, flour, soda, baking powder and salt. Mix thoroughly.*
Beat egg whites until stiff peaks form and fold into carrot mixture. Generously oil 1½ quart ring mold and dust with breadcrumbs. Turn mixture into mold. Bake for 45 minutes or until firm. Turn onto serving dish. Fill with French peas.
*May be prepared ahead to this point.

Melt butter in saucepan. Place lettuce on top of butter. Add remaining ingredients. Simmer covered 5-7 minutes, stirring occasionally until peas are tender. Remove parsley. Serves 4

Cookbook Committee

Dressed-Up Cabbage

1 head cabbage, cut in bite
size pieces
1 cup thick white sauce (see
Index)
2 Tablespoons catsup or chili
sauce
½ cup grated Cheddar cheese
½ cup mayonnaise or salad
dressing
½ small green pepper, minced
½ small onion, minced

Cook cabbage in boiling salted water until barely tender, about 8 minutes. Drain and put in buttered casserole. Make a thick white sauce and pour over cabbage. Bake covered for 30 minutes. Cover with a mixture of chili sauce, cheese, mayonnaise, pepper and onion. Serve immediately. Serves 6-8

Doris Dixon
Tampa, Florida

Cauliflower-Cheese Fritters
A deliciously different fritter; great with ham

1 large head cauliflower
  or 1 (20 ounce) bag frozen
  cauliflower
¾ teaspoon salt
3 cups grated sharp Cheddar
  cheese
2 eggs, slightly beaten
½ teaspoon baking powder
BATTER:
4 eggs, separated
12 ounces beer
2 cups sifted flour
1½ teaspoons salt
¼ teaspoon pepper
2 ounces butter, melted
4 cups cooking oil

Several hours before serving, remove core from fresh cauliflower and separate into florets. Cook cauliflower in boiling salted water until tender; crush into small pieces. Add cheese, eggs and baking powder. Spread mixture onto a pie plate and refrigerate several hours.

Prepare Batter: Beat egg yolks until light. Add beer and flour. Add salt, pepper and butter. Let stand at least 1½ hours. Twenty minutes before serving time, beat egg whites until stiff. Gently fold into batter.

Heat oil in a large pan to 375° Shape cauliflower mixture into 1-inch balls, dip in batter and fry in hot fat until brown. Serve immediately. Variation: Substitute eggplant or minced mushrooms for cauliflower.

Laura G. Ward (Mrs. Peter C.)

Sesame Cauliflower

1 medium head cauliflower
Salt and pepper to taste
1 cup sour cream at room
  temperature
1 cup (¼ pound) shredded
  Cheddar cheese
2 teaspoons toasted sesame
  seeds

Rinse cauliflower and separate into small florets. Cook in 2-quart covered saucepan in 1-inch boiling salted water 8-10 minutes or until tender; drain well. Place half of cauliflower in a 1-quart casserole; sprinkle with salt and pepper. Spread half of sour cream over cauliflower; sprinkle half of grated cheese over sour cream and top with 1 teaspoon sesame seeds. Repeat layers. Bake at 375° for 15 minutes or until heated through. May be prepared in advance. If refrigerated, heat for about 20 minutes. 6 servings

Joan M. Adams (Mrs. John P., Jr.)

Microwave Corn on the Cob

This American summertime favorite is spectacular
cooked in the microwave

Carefully strip back the husks of each ear of corn and remove the silks, brush corn generously with melted butter and pull the husks back into place. Tie with string around the tip of each ear. When cooking more than 4 ears, remove silks and husks and place in a 3-quart casserole dish. Cover and cook. Allow corn to stand covered 3-5 minutes after cooking.

No. of Ears	Cooking Time in Minutes
1	3-4
2	5-6
3	8-10
4	12-14
5	15-18

Cookbook Committee

Eggplant, Peppers, and Onions

1 eggplant, peeled and sliced
½ teaspoon salt
3 Tablespoons olive oil
2 small onions, chopped
½ pound ripe tomatoes,
   seeded and chopped
Seasoned salt
Freshly ground black pepper
3 large green peppers, or 6
   large banana peppers,
   chopped
2 sprigs fresh basil, or ½
   teaspoon dried basil
½ teaspoon sugar

Sprinkle eggplant with salt and let drain in a colander for 1 hour. Rinse, dry and chop eggplant. Heat oil in a heavy pan and sauté onions until soft. Add tomatoes and season with salt and pepper. Add peppers and eggplant, and sauté for about 5 minutes. Add basil and sugar, and check seasonings. Stir well and cook, covered, over low heat for 30 minutes. 4 servings

Decie Nygaard (Mrs. W.F.)

MICROWAVE HINT

A round cooking dish is best for cooking chicken, meatballs, whole vegetables, etc. Arrange foods of uniform size in a circle, leaving the center empty.

Fried Eggplant Strips

1 medium eggplant, peeled
   and cut into finger-sized
   strips
1½ teaspoons salt, divided
1 cup all-purpose flour
1 egg, slightly beaten
1 cup milk
1 Tablespoon salad oil
Salad oil for frying

Sprinkle eggplant strips with
1 teaspoon salt. Place in a bowl,
cover with cold water and let
stand for 1 hour. Drain and pat
dry with paper towels. Meanwhile,
combine flour and ½ teaspoon
salt in a mixing bowl. Add egg,
milk and 1 Tablespoon salad oil,
beat until smooth. Dip eggplant
strips in batter and deep fry in hot
oil until golden brown. Drain well
on paper towels. 6 servings

Pamela T. Marcus

Fresh Mushroom Casserole

8 slices white bread, cubed
4 Tablespoons margarine
1 pound fresh mushrooms,
   sliced
½ cup chopped onion
½ cup chopped green pepper
½ cup mayonnaise
2 beaten eggs
1 cup mushroom soup
1½ cups milk
¾ teaspoon salt
Grated sharp cheese

Cut bread into cubes (may
trim edges). Sauté mushrooms,
onion and green pepper in
margarine. Mix mayonnaise, eggs,
soup, milk and salt. Grease a 2-
quart casserole. Put bread cubes
in bottom and up sides. Mix other
ingredients together, pour over
bread and mix gently but
thoroughly. Let stand overnight in
refrigerator. Cook uncovered at
350° for 40 minutes. Remove and
cover with sharp grated cheese;
return to oven and cook 10
minutes longer. 8 servings

Eleanor R. McCormack (Mrs. T. Wayne)

Mushroom Pie

2 medium onions, chopped
or sliced
⅓ cup butter
1 pound mushrooms, cleaned
and thinly sliced
1 Tablespoon flour
½ cup half and half
1 Tablespoon sherry
Salt and pepper to taste
Double pie crust

Sauté onions in butter until golden, stirring often. Add mushrooms and cook 1-2 minutes, stirring occasionally. Add flour and toss mixture until blended. Add cream and bring to boil. Stir to thicken, adding more flour if needed. Add sherry and seasonings. Cool. Fill pastry lined pie plate with mushroom mixture. Lace top of pie with ½ inch strips. Flute edges. Bake on lower rack at 450° for 20 minutes. May be prepared in advance. 6-8 servings

Dona B. Ansley (Mrs. Wiley S.)

Mushrooms Polonaise

½ cup butter
1½ pounds fresh mushrooms,
sliced
¼ cup sherry (optional)
1 medium onion, minced
2 Tablespoons flour
1 cup sour cream
¼ cup heavy cream
Salt and pepper to taste
¼ teaspoon nutmeg
2 Tablespoons chopped fresh
parsley
¼ cup soft bread crumbs,
tossed in ¼ cup melted
butter

Melt butter in heavy skillet;* add mushrooms and sauté until browned slightly and liquid is evaporated. Add onion and sauté until soft. Stir in flour; cook 5 minutes over low heat, stirring constantly. Blend in sour cream and cream. Add salt, pepper and nutmeg and cook until thickened. Stir in parsley. Pour into buttered casserole and sprinkle with bread crumbs. Bake in a 325° oven for 35 minutes or until lightly browned. 6 servings
*¼ cup sherry may be added to the butter when sautéing mushrooms, if desired.

Betty Jo Ridley (Mrs. William E.)

Southern Okra and Tomatoes

1 cup okra, cut in ½ inch
  slices
½ cup chopped onion
¼ cup chopped green pepper
3 Tablespoons margarine or
  bacon fat
4 quartered tomatoes (peeled
  if desired)
1 teaspoon salt
¼ teaspoon pepper
1 cup fresh corn (optional)

Sauté okra, onion and green pepper in margarine or bacon fat over low heat. Add tomatoes and seasonings. Cook until tender, stirring as little as possible. One cup fresh corn cut from cob may be added. May be prepared in advance. 4 servings

Jeanine C. Andrews (Mrs. Edward B.)

Onion Pie
Absolutely delicious!

1 cup finely crumbled Ritz
  cracker crumbs
½ stick butter, melted
2 cups yellow onions, thinly
  sliced (Vidalia's are best)
2 Tablespoons butter
2 eggs
¾ cup milk
¾ teaspoon salt
Dash pepper
¼ cup grated sharp Cheddar
  cheese
Paprika
Parsley

Mix cracker crumbs with melted butter; press into 8-inch pie plate. Sauté onions in 2 Table-spoons butter until clear, but not brown. Spoon into crust. Beat eggs together with milk, salt, pepper and pour over onions. Sprinkle with cheese and paprika. Bake at 350° for 30 minutes, or until a knife inserted in the center comes out clean. Sprinkle with parsley before serving. Serves 6-8

Fran Scott (Mrs. Romney E.)

HINT ■■■■■■■■■

To remove skins easily from tomatoes, place in a brown paper bag in the sink, make a cuff around top of bag and fill it with boiling water. The bag generally splits after 15 to 20 seconds. After draining, refrigerate tomatoes. They are ready to skin. Cherry tomatoes can be fixed this way for marinating.

Fabulous Fried Onion Rings

1½ cups all-purpose flour
1½ cups beer (active or flat;
   cold or room temperature)
1 teaspoon salt
3 large yellow onions
3-4 cups shortening or
   vegetable oil

Combine flour, beer and salt in large bowl using a whisk. Cover bowl and allow batter to sit at room temperature for no less than 3 hours. Twenty minutes before batter is ready, preheat oven to 200°. Place brown paper bag or layer of paper toweling on a cookie sheet. Peel onions and cut into ¼ inch thick slices. Separate slices into rings. On top of stove, melt shortening in a 10-inch skillet to a depth of 2 inches. Heat shortening to 375°. With metal tongs, dip a few onion rings into batter. Carefully place in hot fat. Fry rings, turning once or twice, until evenly browned. Transfer to brown paper in pan and place on middle shelf in oven. Keep in oven until all rings are fried. To freeze, fry rings and drain on brown paper. Let rings reach room temperature. Arrange on cookie sheet and freeze. When frozen, place in plastic bags and return to freezer. Reheat on cookie sheet in a 400° oven for 4-6 minutes. 6 servings

Jeanine C. Andrews (Mrs. Edward B.)

HINT ▬▬▬▬▬▬▬▬▬▬▬▬▬▬▬▬▬

To keep sweet white onions such as Vidalias fresh longer, tie them in a stocking with a knot between each onion so they do not touch, and hang from a hook.

Onion Ring Casserole
A good recipe for your outdoor gas grill

1 pound onions
Salt and pepper
⅓ cup water
2 Tablespoons butter or
  margarine
½ cup milk
1 egg, well beaten
½ cup shredded sharp
  Cheddar cheese
Paprika

Peel and slice onions ¾ inch thick; separate into rings. Place onion rings in 9-inch foil pan; season to taste with salt and pepper. Add water. Cover snugly with foil. Preheat grill. With cover down, cook on low setting 20 minutes, or until onions are tender. Uncover; dot with butter, stirring as butter melts. Combine milk and egg; pour over onions. Top with cheese, then sprinkle with paprika. Replace foil. With cover down, cook on low setting 10 minutes, or until "set". To cook in oven, cook in a covered casserole dish at 350° for 1 hour. 4 servings

Trina Graham
Atlanta Gas Light Company

Chinese Pea Pods

1 (6 ounce) package Chinese
  pea pods, plain or with
  water chestnuts
⅓ cup diced green onion
  (with tops)
1 (3 ounce) can (or smaller)
  mushrooms and juice
2 Tablespoons butter
¾ cup chicken broth
2 teaspoons cornstarch
2 Tablespoons pale or medium
  sherry
1 teaspoon sugar
1 Tablespoon Japanese soy
  sauce
⅛ teaspoon garlic powder
2 Tablespoons toasted almonds

Thaw pea pods and drain off all water. Sauté onions and mushrooms in butter and small amount (¼ cup) chicken broth for 10 minutes. Add all other ingredients except pea pods and almonds. Cook for 5 minutes until sauce thickens slightly. Add pea pods and cook for 3 minutes (do not boil). Serve immediately with almonds sprinkled on top. Note: Sauce can be cooked ahead of time and chilled. Diced cooked pork or chicken can be added to this sauce for a main dish. 4 servings

Jerry P. Connor (Mrs. Paul)

French Peas in Cream

1 cup fresh sliced mushrooms
2 Tablespoons melted butter
4 slices chopped bacon
1 Tablespoon chopped onion
1 Tablespoon all-purpose flour
1 cup half and half
1 (17 ounce) can green peas, drained
Salt and pepper to taste

Sauté mushrooms in butter about 1 minute. Cook bacon in large saucepan until bacon starts to brown. Add onions and sauté until tender. Bacon bits should be crisp. Blend in flour and cook until mixture bubbles. Gradually add half and half; cook until smooth and thick, stirring constantly. Add mushrooms, peas and salt and pepper. May be prepared earlier and reheated at serving time.
6 servings

Pea Puff

An unusual dish to complement ham or barbeque

2½ cups cooked, drained blackeyed peas
¼ cup bacon drippings
1 egg, beaten
1½ cups shredded sharp Cheddar cheese
1 medium onion, chopped
½ cup chopped green pepper
½ teaspoon pepper
1 teaspoon salt
1 teaspoon garlic powder
TOPPING:
½ cup shredded Cheddar cheese
Several rings of green pepper and onion

Purée peas in blender or food processor (add pea liquid if needed to purée). Combine remaining ingredients with peas and spoon into well greased 1-quart casserole. Bake at 300° for 40-60 minutes. top with onion and pepper rings and cheese. Brown briefly under broiler.
1 quart

Susan M. Morley

The Potato
Variation on a theme

4 russett potatoes, cleaned
1 stick butter or margarine
2 medium Vidalia onions,
    sliced thin (or other sweet
    yellow onions)
Salt and pepper to taste
Aluminum foil

Preheat oven to 350°. Cut each potato into ½-inch thick slices, butter each slice generously on both sides, and sprinkle with salt and pepper. Place one onion slice (all rings together) between each slice of potato, forming potato back together. Wrap each potato in aluminum foil and bake for 1 hour. Great for barbeque: can be cooked on the grill.

Terry C. Morris (Mrs. Douglas)

Stuffed Baked Potatoes

6 baking potatoes
½ stick butter or margarine,
    softened
3 ounces cream cheese,
    softened
¼ cup Parmesan cheese
½ cup sour cream
½ cup grated Cheddar cheese
Milk, if needed
Salt to taste

Scrub, dry, (and grease, if desired) 6 potatoes and bake at 400°-425° until done, approximately 1-1¼ hours. Immediately remove from oven and using oven mits or potholders to prevent burning hands, slice potato lengthwise about ¼ inch from top. Carefully, scoop out potato meat and put in a mixing bowl. Save shells. Add butter, cream cheese, Parmesan cheese and sour cream. Cream thoroughly. Add a small amount of milk if mixture is too stiff. Add salt to taste. Fill potato shells with mixture and top with grated Cheddar cheese. Heat 10-15 minutes at 400°. This freezes well. Prepare early in the day or well in advance and freeze. Thaw before heating. 6 servings

Jeanette G. James (Mrs. T. Allen)

Easter Potato Casserole

6 medium potatoes
¼ cup butter
1 pint sour cream
1 can cream of chicken soup
⅓ cup chopped green onions
1 cup shredded sharp Cheddar
  cheese
Paprika

Note: It is important to boil the potatoes a day before preparing and leave them in the refrigerator overnight. Shred potatoes into a greased 9 x 13-inch casserole dish. Melt butter in a saucepan. Add sour cream, cream of chicken soup, onions and cheese. Stir until cheese is melted. Spread evenly over potatoes and mix well with a fork. Sprinkle top with paprika and bake at 350° for about 45 minutes. 10 servings

Melva Jansen (Mrs. Klaus)

Plantation Sweet Potato Pone

2 cups finely grated raw sweet
  potatoes
1 cup (1½ small cans)
  evaporated milk
2 eggs, well beaten
¾ cup dark Karo syrup
¼ cup melted butter
1 teaspoon grated lemon rind
2 teaspoons lemon juice
½ teaspoon salt
½ teaspoon nutmeg
½ teaspoon cinnamon
½ cup brown sugar

Grate potatoes into bowl of milk so they will not darken. Mix ingredients in order given. Pour into a greased shallow baking pan. Bake in a 350° oven for 30 minutes; then stir with fork. Bake 15 minutes longer or until brown and crusty on top. 6-8 servings

Lucy C. White (Mrs. Richard A.)

Senator Russell's Potatoes

3 cups cooked, mashed sweet
   potatoes
1 cup sugar
2 eggs
1 Tablespoon vanilla
½ cup butter
TOPPING:
1 cup light brown sugar,
   packed
⅓ cup flour
1 cup chopped pecans
⅓ cup butter

Combine potatoes, sugar, eggs, vanilla and butter. Beat with electric mixer for 2 minutes and pour into a buttered casserole.
   Topping: Mix topping ingredients with fork and sprinkle on top of potatoes. Bake in a 350° oven for about 30 minutes. May be prepared in advance.
4 servings

Beth M. Johnston (Mrs. J. Gibson)

Italian Spinach Pie

1 (9 inch) pastry shell, uncooked
1 10 ounce package chopped
   spinach, cooked and drained
4 Tablespoons butter
Salt and pepper to taste
½ pound Ricotta cheese
3 eggs, slightly beaten
½ cup finely grated Parmesan
   cheese
½ cup heavy cream (or milk)
Dash of nutmeg

Prick pastry shell and bake for 10 minutes at 450°. Cool. Mix cooked spinach with other ingredients. Pour into shell and bake at 375° for 30 minutes or until custard has set. Serves 8

Susan Cuda
Tucson, Arizona

Creamed Spinach and Artichokes

1 small jar marinated artichoke
   hearts, drained
1 small onion, finely chopped
2 Tablespoons butter
2 packages frozen creamed
   spinach, cooked
½ cup freshly grated
   Parmesan cheese
¼ teaspoon nutmeg

Place artichoke hearts in bottom of a casserole. Sauté onion in butter until transparent. Season spinach with onion, ¼ cup cheese and nutmeg; pour over artichoke hearts. Sprinkle remaining ¼ cup cheese on top. Bake at 350° until hot, about 15 minutes. May be prepared in advance. 6-8 servings

Lynn H. Barnes

Spinach Soufflé

3 eggs, beaten
3 Tablespoons flour
1 (9 ounce) package frozen
  chopped spinach, defrosted
  but not drained
1 cup creamy cottage cheese,
  small curd
⅓ pound Cheddar or Colby
  cheese, grated
⅓ cup melted butter
1 teaspoon lemon juice
Dash nutmeg
Salt and pepper to taste

Beat eggs with flour. Add defrosted spinach, cottage cheese, grated cheese, butter, nutmeg, salt and pepper. Put in 1½-quart greased casserole. Bake at 350° 55-60 minutes or until set. During last 10 minutes of baking add additional grated cheese. To freeze, cook for ½ hour, cool, freeze; later bake at 350° 50-60 minutes to serve. May also be prepared in advance, refrigerated and heated through to serve. Note: Do not squeeze moisture from spinach and do not overcook. 8 servings

Carolyn B. Hoose (Mrs. Kenneth)

Spinach with Olives and Raisins
A deliciously different vegetable combination

2 pounds fresh spinach or 2
  packages chopped frozen
  spinach
1 teaspoon salt
¼ cup oil (olive oil or half
  olive, half vegetable oil)
3 Tablespoons sliced almonds
  or pine nuts
¼ cup sliced pimiento stuffed
  green olives
¼ cup sliced ripe olives
1 Tablespoon capers, drained
3 Tablespoons seedless raisins

Wash and drain spinach. Place in skillet, sprinkle with salt, cover and cook 5 minutes (only until spinach wilts). If frozen spinach is used, cook 1 minute less than package directs. Drain cooked spinach and chop if leaf spinach is used. Heat oil in skillet; stir in nuts and sauté until golden. Add the olives, capers and raisins, mixing until heated. Add the spinach, stir until heated through. Serve warm. Note: Spinach must not be overcooked. These various flavors and textures are best complemented by a roasted meat. 6 servings

Phyllis K. Kennedy

Baked Yellow Squash

2 Tablespoons butter, melted
Juice of ½ lemon
¾ teaspoon thyme
¼ teaspoon salt
⅛ teaspoon pepper
4-5 medium yellow squash,
    halved lengthwise

Pour melted butter into a 9-inch pan or baking dish. Add lemon juice, thyme, and salt and pepper to the butter; stir with a fork until mixed. Place squash in pan, cut side down. Cover and bake at 350° for 30 minutes or until squash is tender. Or microwave in a pyrex dish for about 8 minutes, turn once. This is especially attractive when served around a carved roast.

Cookbook Committee

Microwave Squash Casserole

2 Tablespoons butter
½ cup Ritz Cracker crumbs
    or ¼ cup chopped pecans
    and ¼ cup crumbs
¼ cup water
½ teaspoon salt
1 pound yellow squash, sliced
¼ cup mayonnaise
1 egg, beaten
½ cup grated Cheddar cheese
2 Tablespoons butter, melted
1 teaspoon sugar
¼ - ½ teaspoon instant minced
    onion
½ - 1 teaspoon horseradish

In a 1-quart casserole, melt butter on high temperature ½-1 minute until melted; add crumbs and cook on high 2 minutes. Stir after 1 minute. Place on wax paper and set aside. Place water, salt and squash in casserole, cover. Cook on high 8-10 minutes or until tender. Stir after 4 minutes; drain squash. Mix remaining ingredients in casserole, add squash and cook uncovered at medium temperature for 4 minutes. Add crumb topping. Cook 2-4 minutes more until center is set. Let stand 5 minutes before serving.
4 servings

Cookbook Committee

Acorn Squash in the Microwave

1 (1½ pound) acorn squash
1 Tablespoon brown sugar
1 Tablespoon butter

Pierce squash with fork. Place on paper plate in microwave and cook 4 minutes. Give ½ turn, cook 4 minutes more. Remove from oven and let stand 2 minutes. Cut in half and remove seeds. Mix butter and brown sugar and fill each cavity with mixture. Cook 2 to 4 minutes more. Total cooking time 8 to 10 minutes. 2 servings

Georgia Power Company
Home Economist

Crusty Tomato Scallop

2½ cups canned tomatoes
1 cup dry bread cubes
1 Tablespoon minced onion
¼ cup butter
1 Tablespoon flour
1 teaspoon salt
¼ teaspoon pepper
1 Tablespoon sugar
1 teaspoon prepared mustard
2 slices bread, buttered and
 cubed

Combine tomatoes, dry bread cubes and onion. In a saucepan, melt butter, add flour, seasonings and mustard and cook over low heat until smooth. Add tomato mixture and pour into greased 1½-quart baking dish. Sprinkle buttered, cubed bread over tomatoes. Bake in a 400° oven for 30 minutes. May be prepared in advance. 6 servings

Jeneal L. Benton (Mrs. Gene R.)

Tomato Pie

2 ripe tomatoes
¾ cup chopped green pepper
1 onion, chopped
1 cup shredded Mozzarella or
 Swiss cheese
⅔ cup mayonnaise
1 large can refrigerator
 biscuits

Butter 8 or 9-inch pie pan. Pat canned biscuits out to form crust. Slice tomatoes to cover biscuits. Sauté green pepper and onion in butter. Spread over tomatoes. Mix cheese and mayonnaise together. Add more mayonnaise if mixture is too thick. Spread over top of pie. Bake at 350° for 40-45 minutes. Allow to cool and set for about 30 minutes before serving. 8 servings

Barbara Withers (Mrs. David)

Mushroom Stuffed Tomatoes

6 tomatoes, red, but very firm
Salt
Pepper
Sugar
1 bunch green onions,
  chopped
3 Tablespoons butter
¾ pound mushrooms, sliced
Juice of ½ lemon
1 teaspoon paprika
¾ cup heavy cream
¼ pound freshly grated
  Parmesan cheese
¼ pound Gruyère cheese,
  grated

Cut ½ inch from top of tomatoes and scoop out shell. Chop pulp and drain. Sprinkle pulp and inside of shells with salt, pepper and sugar. Invert shells on paper towels and drain at least 30 minutes. Arrange shells in lightly buttered baking dish, top side up, and bake at 350° for 15 minutes. Drain any liquid that accumulates. In a large skillet, sauté chopped onions in butter until soft. Add mushrooms and sauté until golden. Add tomato pulp, lemon juice, paprika, salt and pepper. Sauté for 2 minutes. Increase heat to high, add cream and stir until mixture is thickened. Fill tomatoes with mushroom mixture and top with 2 teaspoons each of grated Parmesan and Gruyère cheese. Bake at 400° for 10 minutes and serve hot. Mushroom mixture and first baking of tomatoes may be done in advance. Tomatoes will get soggy if filled too far in advance. 6 servings

Phyllis K. Kennedy

Scalloped Tomatoes and Artichoke Hearts
Great winter vegetable

1 (2 pound 3 ounce) can
  whole plum tomatoes
1 (14 ounce) can artichoke
  hearts
½ cup finely chopped onion
1 clove garlic or 2 Tablespoons
  finely chopped shallots
1 stick butter, melted
½ teaspoon basil
2 Tablespoons sugar
Salt and pepper to taste

Preheat oven to 325°. Grease shallow ovenproof casserole; drain tomatoes and artichokes; rinse and quarter artichokes. Sauté onions and garlic (or shallots) until tender in melted butter. Add tomatoes, artichokes and basil; heat 2-3 minutes. Season with sugar, salt and pepper. Bake in prepared casserole 10-15 minutes or until hot. 4 servings

Vera Cruz Tomatoes
Especially pretty at Christmas around sliced roast beef or turkey

3 strips bacon
¼ cup chopped onion
8 ounces fresh spinach or frozen chopped spinach
1 cup sour cream
Pepper to taste
4 tomatoes
Shredded cheese

Cook bacon until crisp. Drain, reserving 2 Tablespoons of bacon grease. Crumble bacon and set aside. Cook onion in reserved drippings until tender. Stir in spinach. Cook covered until tender, about 3-5 minutes. Remove from heat and stir in sour cream, bacon and pepper. Cut tops from tomatoes; remove centers leaving shells. Drain. Salt shells and fill with spinach mixture. Place in 8 x 8 x 2-inch baking pan. Bake in a 375° oven for 20-25 minutes. Top with shredded cheese and return to oven for 2-3 minutes. May be prepared early on the day it is to be served. 4 servings

Myrick L. King (Mrs. David L.G., Jr.)

Zucchini and Tomatoes Parmesan

¼ cup butter
3 small zucchini, sliced (not peeled)
1 bunch green onions, chopped
2 medium tomatoes, sliced
Salt and pepper to taste
⅓ - ½ cup Parmesan cheese

Melt butter in a skillet and sauté zucchini and onions for 5 minutes, add tomatoes and cook 2 minutes more. Stir ½ of cheese into vegetables, and pour into an ovenproof casserole. Sprinkle remaining cheese on top. Cover and bake at 250° for 30 minutes. 4 servings

Nancy Wactor (Mrs. William R.)

Ethiopian Vegetable Sauté

3 potatoes, cut in ⅓ inch-slices
¼ cup olive oil or vegetable oil
2 onions, minced
2 cups fresh green beans,
    broken into 1-inch pieces
1½ teaspoons tumeric
2 tomatoes, peeled and
    chopped
⅓ cup water
2 garlic cloves, minced
Salt and pepper to taste

Peel potatoes and cut into ⅓-inch slices; place in cold water to soak. In a skillet heat oil and sauté onions until golden. Add beans and tumeric and sauté for 10 minutes. Add tomatoes; saute 2 minutes over moderately high heat. Add drained potatoes, water and garlic cloves. Simmer, covered, for 15-20 minutes or until potatoes are tender, stirring occasionally. Season with salt and pepper. Can be prepared in advance and reheated at serving time.
4 servings

Phyllis K. Kennedy

Jeanine's Vegetable Casserole
A good casserole to take to new neighbors

2 large cans green asparagus,
    reserve juice
2 small cans hearts of
    artichokes, reserve juice
2 small cans water chestnuts,
    reserve juice
½ pound butter
1 cup flour
2 cups grated New York sharp
    cheese
½ cup sherry
Salt and pepper to taste
MSG to taste
Sliced almonds

Melt butter; brown flour slowly in butter. Add juice from vegetables. If needed, add a little water, sauce should be thick. Add grated cheese and sherry. Season with salt, pepper and MSG. Layer ingredients in casserole dish, ending with sauce on top. Sprinkle with almonds. Bake at 350° for 30-35 minutes or until bubbly. May be frozen or prepared in advance. 8 servings

Judy R. Carlsen (Mrs. Alfred M., III)

Six Vegetable Medley

6-8 carrots, cut in 2-inch lengths
2 cups fresh broccoli
florets
½ green pepper, cut in 1 inch
strips
1 medium onion, thinly sliced
2 stalks celery, sliced
10 medium mushrooms,
quartered
Salt and pepper to taste
2 Tablespoons chopped parsley

Steam carrots and broccoli separately until crisp and tender. Sauté onion, green pepper and celery in butter until soft. Cover for a few minutes. Remove cover, add mushrooms and stir-fry until crisp and tender. Add carrots and broccoli, stir until warm, sprinkle with salt, pepper and parsley. 6 servings

Sylvia Dorough (Mrs. Donald)

Two Beans and a Pea

1 box frozen green beans
(French-cut)
1 box frozen green peas
1 box frozen lima beans
SAUCE:
2 cups mayonnaise
4 hard-boiled eggs, chopped
1 grated onion
1 Tablespoon prepared mustard
1 teaspoon Worcestershire
sauce
2 Tablespoons salad oil

Cook vegetables separately, as directed on packages; layer in deep casserole. Dot with butter, salt and pepper to taste.
Mix all sauce ingredients together and refrigerate. When ready to serve, pour sauce on top of hot vegetables. 10 servings

Betty Jensen (Mrs. Peter A.)

Luncheon Vegetables
A breeze in the microwave

1 package frozen artichoke
hearts
1 package frozen green beans
1 package frozen baby lima
beans
4 Tablespoons melted butter
½ cup lemon juice

Cook frozen vegetables separately according to package directions, drain and mix. Combine butter and lemon juice and pour over vegetables. Other combinations of frozen vegetables may be used including peas, Brussels sprouts, broccoli or asparagus. 8 servings

Doris Dixon
Tampa, Florida

Sherried Fruit Casserole
Excellent with ham as a buffet dish for brunch or dinner

12 coconut macaroons
1 (1 pound 13 ounce) can
peach slices
1 (1 pound 13 ounce) can pear
halves, chunked
1 (1 pound 4 ounce) can
pineapple chunks
1 (1 pound) can whole apricots,
pitted and halved
2 (8¼ ounce) cans green grapes
½ stick butter
⅓ cup dark brown sugar
½ cup sherry
Slivered almonds

Drain juices from fruit. Crumble half of the macaroons on bottom of a buttered 2-quart casserole. Arrange fruit on top; melt butter with brown sugar and sherry; pour over fruit. Top with crumbled macaroons. Bake 30 minutes at 350°; sprinkle with almonds and bake 5 minutes more. 12 servings

Jeneal L. Benton (Mrs. Gene R.)

Peppered Oranges
An unusual accompaniment for meat

2 navel oranges
2-4 teaspoons freshly ground
black pepper
½ cup olive oil (Berio or
similar brand)
Parsley or green grapes for
garnish

Trim off and discard a slice from the ends of each orange. Cut oranges into ⅛-inch slices, place in bowl, and sprinkle generously with pepper. Pour olive oil over, and marinate for 1 hour or more. Drain and arrange slices in an overlapping pattern in a serving dish, or around a platter of meat. Garnish with parsley or green grapes. Excellent with roast beef, pork, or chicken. 6 servings

Jeanine Andrews (Mrs. Edward B.)

Grilled Pineapple Slices
Wonderful with ham—a little different, and easy

Fresh pineappple, sliced
Sugar
Butter

Melt butter in skillet. Dip pineapple slices in sugar and sauté in butter. Hint: Pluck a leaf from the pineapple's crown. If it pulls out easily, the fruit is ripe. 4-6 servings

Jeanine C. Andrews (Mrs. Edward B.)

Salads and Dressings

Holiday Ambrosia

1 cup seedless grapes
1½ cups mandarin orange
   sections (or fresh orange
   sections)
1 cup pineapple chunks
2 medium apples, unpeeled,
   cored and cubed
1 cup halved maraschino
   cherries
1 Tablespoon sugar
½ cup flaked coconut, toasted
1 cup sour cream
2 Tablespoons mayonnaise
1 Tablespoon light cream
Lettuce
½ cup sliced almonds, toasted

Combine fruits, sprinkle with sugar, add coconut and toss lightly. Mix sour cream, mayonnaise and cream; then fold into fruit. Serve on lettuce cups and garnish with almonds. Do not add dressing until serving time. Variation: Leave out sour cream mix and saturate fruit with sherry. 6 servings

Cookbook Committee

Apple Cheese Salad
An excellent salad for fall and winter months
when there is a shortage of good produce for salad

2-3 tart red apples (Stayman,
   Rome)
1 cup thinly sliced celery
¾ cup pineapple chunks,
   drained (crushed may be
   used if well drained)
½ cup diced medium Cheddar
   cheese
¼ cup mayonnaise
¼ cup sour cream
1 teaspoon vinegar
Dash tarragon
1 Tablespoon prepared
   horseradish
Salad greens

Core and dice apples, or slice in food processor. Mix with celery, pineapple and cheese. Blend mayonnaise, sour cream, vinegar, tarragon and horseradish to make dressing and toss well with first mixture. Chill. Salad may be served on greens, or 1 cup of broken iceberg lettuce may be tossed with salad at serving time. 4-6 servings

Phyllis K. Kennedy

Apple Cider Salad

1 (6 ounce) package orange
    flavored gelatin
3 cups hot cider or apple juice
1 cup crushed ice
1 (1 pound) can apricot halves,
    drained
2 bananas, sliced
1 small apple, unpeeled and
    diced (optional)

Add gelatin to the hot cider, and stir to dissolve gelatin. Add the ice, and stir until it melts. Add fruit. Pour into a 3-quart mold. Chill until firm. 8 servings

Frozen Yogurt Fruit Salad

1 (8 ounce) carton peach yogurt
1 (8 ounce) carton sour cream
¾ cup sugar
Juice of large lemon
2 bananas, sliced
1 (8¼ ounce) can crushed
    pineapple, drained
¼ cup maraschino cherries,
    sliced
Dash salt
¼ cup chopped nuts (optional)

Mix yogurt, sour cream and sugar together. Add other ingredients and stir well. Pour into oiled mold (individual or other) and freeze. Take out of freezer and let stand at room temperature 30-45 minutes. Slice and serve on lettuce with mayonnaise as a topping. Will keep in freezer for 1 month. 8-10 servings

Sacramento Fruit Bowl
In-season fruit may be substituted
The interest lies in the syrup

2 cups water
1½ cups granulated sugar
3 Tablespoons lemon juice
2 Tablespoons anise flavoring
½ teaspoon salt
1 small pineapple
1 small honeydew melon
1 small cantaloupe
2 oranges
2 nectarines or 4 apricots
2 purple plums
1 cup seedless green grapes
1 lime, sliced

In medium saucepan, combine 2 cups water with sugar, lemon juice, anise and salt. Cook over medium heat 15 minutes until mixture reaches light syrup consistency; chill 6 hours or overnight. Peel pineapple, melon, cantaloupe and oranges, and cut into bite-size chunks. Slice nectarines and plums into wedges. In large bowl combine cut up fruits with grapes and lime slices. Pour chilled syrup over fruits. Refrigerate, stirring occasionally, until chilled. 10 servings

Penny P. Jennings (Mrs. H. Todd)

Cherry Almond Salad

¼ pound almonds
1 (16 ounce) can or 2 (8¾
    ounce) cans white cherries,
    drained
1 (1 pound 4 ounce) can
    sliced pineapple, drained
1 cup mayonnaise
1 envelope unflavored gelatin
¼ cup cold water
1 cup boiling water or juice
    from fruits
½ pint heavy cream, whipped

Blanch almonds and cut in pieces. Stone cherries, keeping as whole as possible; cut up pineapple. Mix fruit and mayonnaise. Soak gelatin in cold water then dissolve in 1 cup boiling water or juice. Strain into fruit mixture; cool. Add whipped cream. Pour into mold and refrigerate until firm. Make day before serving.
8-10 servings

Mrs. Fran A. Spencer

Carrot Salad

1 (3 ounce) package lemon
    flavored gelatin
1 (3 ounce) package orange
    flavored gelatin
1 cup boiling water
1 (1 pound, 12 ounce) can
    crushed pineapple and
    juice (3½ cups)
1 cup diced celery
1 cup grated carrots
¾ cup chopped nuts
2 cups cottage cheese
1 cup heavy cream, whipped
½ cup mayonnaise

In a large bowl, dissolve gelatins in boiling water; add pineapple, celery, carrots, nuts and cottage cheese; fold in whipped cream and mayonnaise. Pour into a 3-quart mold. Refrigerate for 24 hours. If a firmer salad is desired, pineapple may be drained. Serve on lettuce with additional mayonnaise on top. This makes a pretty luncheon plate served with chicken salad. 16 servings

Sarah Looper (Mrs. Joseph W.)

Emerald Isle Mousse

1 (3 ounce) package lime
    flavored gelatin
1 cup boiling water
1 (8¼ ounce) can crushed
    pineapple in syrup
2 Tablespoons green crème
    de menthe
1 cup heavy cream, whipped ·

Dissolve gelatin in boiling water; add pineapple with syrup and crème de menthe. Chill until thickened, stirring often. Fold in whipped cream and spoon into a 1 quart mold or 6 individual molds. Chill. Serve on a bed of crisp lettuce. 6 servings

Dr. Carol Marie Thigpen

Apricot Congealed Salad

2 (3 ounce) packages apricot
　or orange flavored gelatin
1 package unflavored gelatin
2 (1 pound) cans apricots,
　drained; reserve syrup
1 (1 pound 4 ounce) can
　crushed pineapple, drained;
　reserve syrup
1 pint sour cream
1 cup chopped nuts

To syrup from fruit, add water to make 3 cups, and heat. Dissolve gelatins in syrup. Mash apricots and mix with pineapple and sour cream. Add nuts. Refrigerate until firm. 8 servings

Constance Wilson (Mrs. A.E., Jr.)

Cranberry-Raspberry Salad

This is a good accompaniment to any holiday dinner
or use it to make an everyday dinner special.

1 (3 ounce) package raspberry
　flavored gelatin
1 (3 ounce) package lemon
　flavored gelatin
1½ cups boiling water
1 (10 ounce) package frozen
　raspberries
1 (16 ounce) can jellied
　cranberry sauce
1 (7 ounce) bottle lemon-lime
　carbonated beverage

Dissolve gelatins in boiling water. Stir in frozen berries, breaking up large pieces. Break up cranberry sauce with fork. Stir into mixture. Chill until partially set. Carefully pour in soda, stirring gently. Turn into 6-cup mold. Chill 5-6 hours or overnight. Unmold onto crisp greens. Garnish with a poached sliced apple.
8-10 servings

Maddy S. Kligora (Mrs. H. John)

Tomato Lemon Aspic

1 can stewed tomatoes
1 (3 ounce) package lemon
　flavored gelatin
¾ cup mayonnaise
½ cup diced green pepper
1 cup diced celery
1 medium onion, diced

Boil tomatoes; add gelatin straight from package. Stir and cool. Do not boil gelatin. Add mayonnaise, pepper, onion and celery. Pour into a suitable container. Refrigerate until firm.
8-10 servings

Angela Waller (Mrs. Jerry M.)

Georgia Peach Aspic

1 envelope unflavored gelatin
¼ cup cold water
2 (3 ounce) packages peach
   flavored gelatin
1¼ cups boiling water
1 cup orange juice
Grated rind of 1 lemon
3 Tablespoons lemon juice
1½ cups puréed fresh Georgia
   peaches
¼ cup sugar, if necessary
CREAM CHEESE DRESSING:
1 (3 ounce) package cream
   cheese
1 Tablespoon mayonnaise
1 peach, puréed

Soften plain gelatin in ¼ cup cold water. Dissolve both unflavored and peach gelatins in 1¼ cups boiling water. Add orange juice, rind of lemon and lemon juice. Add puréed peaches; sweeten, if necessary. Pour into 1½ quart mold and chill until set. Serve with Cream Cheese Dressing.

Dressing: Cream the cream cheese until smooth. Add mayonnaise, blending well. Add puréed peach; mix. 8 servings

Joan M. Adams (Mrs. John P., Jr.)

Pineapple Cream Salad
Light and fluffy

1 cup evaporated milk
1 (1 pound 4 ounce) can
   crushed pineapple,
   undrained
½ cup sugar
1 (3 ounce) package lemon
   flavored gelatin
1 (3 ounce) package cream
   cheese
DRESSING:
1 cup sugar
1 egg
⅓ cup orange juice
2 Tablespoons lemon juice

Place evaporated milk in freezer until partially frozen. Bring pineapple and sugar to a boil; add lemon gelatin and cream cheese; let melt. Stir until smooth. Cool. Whip milk until very thick; fold into gelatin mixture. Pour into a 1½ quart mold and refrigerate.

Dressing: Combine sugar, egg, orange juice and lemon juice and place in a saucepan. Let come to a hard boil, stirring well. When cool, refrigerate and serve over salad. 8-10 servings

Agnes Seibert (Mrs. "Sam")

Green Bean Salad Mold

1½ packages frozen French
   green beans
2 cups green bean liquid and
   water
1 (3 ounce) package lemon
   flavored gelatin
1 (3 ounce) package lime
   flavored gelatin
½ cup chopped onion
2 Tablespoons lemon juice
1 Tablespoon vinegar
1 cup chopped celery
1 cup chopped nuts (optional)
1 small jar pimiento, drained
Salt and pepper to taste
SAUCE:
½ cup mayonnaise
2 teaspoons horseradish
2 Tablespoons lemon juice

Cook frozen French green beans. Save liquid; add water to make 2 cups. Heat this liquid and use to dissolve both packages of gelatin. Add chopped onion, lemon juice, vinegar, celery, nuts, pimientos, and salt and pepper. Chill. Serve with sauce.
8 servings

Mary Anna Hunter (Mrs. Jack D., Jr.)

Spinach Salad Mold

1 Tablespoon unflavored gelatin
¼ cup water
1 (3 ounce) package lime
   flavored gelatin
1 cup boiling water
1½ cups cottage cheese
½ cup mayonnaise
1 small cucumber, chopped
1 small onion, chopped
2 stalks celery, chopped
1 teaspoon salt
1 package frozen spinach,
   thawed and drained well

Soften unflavored gelatin in ¼ cup water. Dissolve lime and unflavored gelatins in 1 cup boiling water. Cool. Add cottage cheese and mayonnaise. Add cucumber, onion, celery and salt. Squeeze spinach between 2 stacked plates to drain very well. Add to above and pour into a mold prepared with either oil or a non stick spray. Refrigerate until firm. 6 servings

Jane H. Thrash (Mrs. Elmore C., Jr.)

African Salad
An interesting combination of greens and fruit

4 medium apples, peeled
  and diced
1 medium grapefruit, sectioned
1 (1 pound 4 ounce) can
  pineapple chunks, drained
1 teaspoon ground coriander
  (optional)
½ cup raisins
¼ cup sunflower seed kernels
2 cups (approximately) fresh
  greens: spinach, romaine,
  iceberg lettuce
DRESSING:
1 Tablespoon honey
1 Tablespoon lemon juice
2 Tablespoons vegetable oil
1 Tablespoon vinegar
1 Tablespoon grated lemon rind
½ teaspoon white pepper
1 teaspoon salt

Mix apples, grapefruit, pineapple, coriander, raisins, sunflower seeds, and greens together in a salad bowl. Then mix remaining ingredients to make salad dressing. Note: Salad dressing ingredients may need to be doubled depending on amount of greens used.
8-10 servings

Carol Stallings

Jackson Salad

Iceberg lettuce
Romaine
6 hard cooked eggs, sliced
2 avocados, sliced
6 slices bacon, cooked
  and crumbled
DRESSING FOR 6 SALADS:
6 Tablespoons olive oil
3 Tablespoons wine vinegar
3 teaspoons dry mustard
Salt and pepper to taste

Fill large bowl with torn lettuce, Romaine, bacon, egg and avocado. Pour some dressing on salad and toss. Serve other dressings "on the side".
6 servings

Terry C. Morris (Mrs. Douglas)

Esquire Salad

Your choice, mixed greens to equal 2 large heads (iceberg lettuce, fresh spinach, Boston lettuce, etc.)
3 tomatoes, cut in eighths
1 pound mushrooms, thinly sliced
1 can hearts of palm, diced
6 slices bacon, crisply cooked and crumbled
1 (15½ ounce) can garbanzo beans (Pour water off garbanzos and refill can with vinegar; let sit in refrigerator overnight. Drain before mixing.)
SALAD DRESSING:
1 cup oil
½ cup wine vinegar
Juice of ½ lemon
2 cloves garlic, minced
½ teaspoon Worcestershire sauce
2 Tablespoons chili sauce
1 teaspoon prepared mustard
4 Tablespoons Parmesan cheese
Dash oregano
Salt and pepper to taste

Mix all salad ingredients. Mix dressing together in jar, and pour over salad. Toss lightly.
12 servings

Pennsylvania-Dutch Wilted Lettuce

5 slices uncooked bacon, diced
5 slices bacon, cooked and crumbled
1 beaten egg
¼ cup minced onion
¼ cup sugar
½ teaspoon salt
⅓ cup vinegar
1/16 teaspoon white pepper
1 bunch leaf lettuce
2 medium heads Boston lettuce, washed, dried and crisped

Cook diced bacon in a skillet until crisp. Combine other ingredients except lettuce; add to bacon. Heat just to boiling, stirring constantly. Tear lettuce into bowl, pour hot dressing over and toss lightly. Put on salad plates and sprinkle with extra crumbled bacon. Serve immediately.
6-8 servings

Carolyn B. Hoose (Mrs. Kenneth A., Jr.)

Artichoke Mixed Salad

Serve this salad as a separate course so guests
can appreciate the flavors.

2 packages frozen artichoke
   hearts
½ cup dry white wine
½ cup water
2½ cups thinly sliced raw
   mushrooms
2 avocados, diced
1 can filets of anchovy, drained
French Dressing (see below)
Salt and freshly ground black
   pepper to taste
Watercress and romaine
Mayonnaise thinned with
   lemon juice
FRENCH DRESSING: 2 cups
½ cup fresh lemon juice
1½ cups olive oil
2 teaspoons salt
¼ teaspoon pepper
1 teaspoon dry mustard
Dash cayenne
2 garlic cloves, crushed

Cook artichoke hearts in white wine and water until fork tender. Drain and cut into ½ inch slices and marinate with mushrooms in French Dressing. Artichokes and mushrooms should marinate for at least 30 minutes. Dice avocados and sprinkle them very well with lemon juice to keep them from turning dark. Drain anchovies and cut into very small pieces. Drain artichokes and mushrooms and add the avocado and anchovies. Season with salt and pepper. Line a salad bowl with watercress and romaine. Arrange the vegetables in the middle to form a dome. Serve mayonnaise separately. 8 servings

French Dressing: Mix all ingredients in a 1 quart jar; cover tightly and shake until thoroughly blended.

Artichoke Asparagus Tossed Salad

1 head lettuce
1 large can cut-up asparagus,
   drained
1 jar Cara Mia marinated
   artichoke hearts, drained
Croutons, seasoned type
Italian Dressing

Combine lettuce, asparagus, artichoke hearts and croûtons. Toss with prepared Italian dressing. 4-6 servings

Diane D. Mahaffey (Mrs. Randy)

Stuffed Lettuce Salad

2 medium heads lettuce
2 Tablespoons bleu cheese
1 Tablespoon minced green
  pepper
1 Tablespoon minced green
  onion and stems
1 (3 ounce) package cream
  cheese
2 Tablespoons grated carrot
2 Tablespoons diced tomato
⅛ teaspoon pepper
½ teaspoon salt
DRESSING:
1 Tablespoon sugar
1 teaspoon paprika
¼ teaspoon pepper
¾ cup salad oil
1 teaspoon salt
1 teaspoon dry mustard
¼ cup vinegar

Core lettuce; wash and drain well. Mix all stuffing ingredients; cheeses first, tomatoes, last. Stuff lettuce ahead of time. May be done the day before and wrapped tightly in plastic wrap. Store in refrigerator. Quarter lettuce and serve with dressing on table. 8 servings

Dressing: Mix dressing ahead of time and store unrefrigerated in cool place. Keep tightly covered. Serves 8-10. Dressing may be used on tossed salads later.

Betty Jo Ridley (Mrs. William E.)

Avocado Halves, California Style

2 Tablespoons chili sauce
2 Tablespoons catsup
1 Tablespoon vinegar
1 Tablespoon sugar
½ teaspoon Worcestershire
  sauce
6 dashes Tabasco
5 Tablespoons lemon juice
4 medium-sized, ripe avocados,
  chilled and sliced
3 pink grapefruit, peeled and
  sectioned

Sauce: Combine chili sauce, catsup, vinegar, sugar, Worcestershire sauce, Tabasco and 2 Tablespoons lemon juice; mix well. Refrigerate several hours.

Salad: Pit avocados and slice. Brush with remaining lemon juice. Arrange avocado slices with grapefruit. Spoon on sauce. May be served as a first course. 8 servings

Susan M. Morley

Garden Party Salad
Lovely served in a clear crystal bowl so that
the layers show through

1 head lettuce, torn into bite
    size pieces
3 carrots, thinly sliced
½ head purple cabbage,
    shredded
1 (10 ounce) package frozen
    English peas (1 can may be
    used, but frozen is better)
3 yellow squash, thinly sliced
½ cup diced celery
½ cup diced onion
½ cup chopped green pepper
3 hard cooked eggs, sliced
6 slices bacon, cooked and
    crumbled
TOPPING:
3 cups mayonnaise
1½ cups grated cheese
    (Parmesan or Cheddar)

Layer in large bowl in order of listing. Seal with 3 cups mayonnaise spread over entire top. Top with grated cheese. Cover with plastic wrap. Refrigerate overnight. May be prepared 2 days ahead. Note: Amount of mayonnaise and grated cheese may vary according to individual taste and size of ingredients used. 8-12 servings

Edna K. Jennings (Mrs. E. Paul, Jr.)

Spinach Salad and Dressing
A delightful change for spinach salad

DRESSING:
½ cup soy sauce
1 ounce fresh lemon juice
½-¾ teaspoon freshly ground
    black pepper
1½ teaspoons sugar
1 Tablespoon minced onion
1½ teaspoons sesame seeds
1 cup peanut oil
SALAD:
3 cups mixed Romaine and
    Bibb lettuce
3 cups fresh spinach, torn in
    bite sized pieces
½ cup sliced water chestnuts
½ cup sliced mushrooms
½ cup bean sprouts

Blend first 6 ingredients in blender until smooth. Add peanut oil and blend again. Toss with spinach salad and serve.
12 servings

Roswell Public House
Roswell, Georgia

Bean Sprout Salad
An authentic Chinese recipe

1 pound fresh raw bean
   sprouts
4 ounces fresh snow peas
   (Chinese pea pods), thinly
   sliced (can be omitted if
   not available)
2 Tablespoons good quality
   soy sauce
1 teaspoon sesame seed oil
¼ teaspoon MSG
EGG GARNISH: (optional)
2 eggs
½ teaspoon salt
½ teaspoon dry sherry
¼ teaspoon MSG
2 teaspoons peanut oil

Add bean sprouts to 10 cups boiling water in a large saucepan over high heat. Before water boils again, remove pan from heat and drain sprouts in a colander. Soak sprouts in cold water until thoroughly cold; drain well. Remove strings from snow peas; parboil peas in salted water 2-3 minutes; remove and drain. Cut into thin strips, lengthwise. Mix soy sauce, sesame oil and MSG; set aside. 6 servings

Egg Garnish: Beat eggs with salt, sherry and MSG. Put 1 teaspoon oil in hot non-stick skillet over medium heat; remove excess oil with paper towel. Pour in half of beaten egg and tilt to cover bottom of pan. Cook until edge is lightly brown and lifts out easily; remove to cutting board and cut into 4 even strips. Stack strips and cut into fine slivers. Repeat with other half of egg mixture. Place snow peas, bean sprouts and egg garnish in large salad bowl; chill thoroughly. Add soy sauce mixture immediately before serving and toss well.

Cookbook Committee

Hot Bean Salad
Good for a "cook out"

½ pound bacon
1 medium onion, diced
1 can green beans, drained
1 can wax beans, drained
1 can red kidney beans,
   drained
1 can pork and beans
1 cup brown sugar
1 teaspoon salt

Fry bacon until crisp; drain and crumble. Sauté onion in hot bacon drippings. Add drained green beans, wax beans and kidney beans. Add pork and beans (do not drain), brown sugar and salt. Heat through. Sprinkle with crumbled bacon. May be served immediately or may be frozen. 12 servings

Barbara M. Hett (Mrs. Richard E.)

Bean and Avocado Boats

¼ cup salad oil
2 Tablespoons vinegar
2 Tablespoons lemon juice
1 Tablespoon sugar
½ teaspoon chili powder
¼ teaspoon salt
Dash garlic salt
Dash pepper
1 (15 ounce) can garbanzo
    beans, drained
1 (8 ounce) can kidney beans,
    drained
2 Tablespoons sliced green
    onions
2 avocados, halved lengthwise
    and seeded

Combine first 8 ingredients and pour over garbanzo beans, kidney beans and sliced green onion. Chill thoroughly, stirring occasionally. At serving time, spoon beans into avocados. 4 servings   Serve with Rio Grande Pork Roast. (see Index)

June L. Wagner (Mrs. James R.)

Darvish Salad
"Darvish"is a Persian word for gypsy

4 medium cucumbers
Salt to taste
1 clove garlic, split
1 Tablespoon white vinegar
1 cup plain yogurt
1 teaspoon chopped fresh dill
2 Tablespoons olive oil
1 Tablespoon chopped fresh
    mint (optional)

Peel cucumbers. Cut into halves lengthwise and remove seeds; then cut into ¼ inch slices. Sprinkle with salt, set aside. Rub a salad bowl with garlic. Sprinkle white vinegar on salad bowl and roll around in bowl to collect garlic flavor. Add yogurt and fresh dill and mix well. Drain cucumbers, sprinkle with olive oil, and add to bowl. Garnish with fresh mint. May be prepared in advance. This Middle Eastern dish complements any heavily flavored meat dish or strong fish such as salmon. 6-8 servings

Broccoli Salad

1 large bunch broccoli (Use
   only the florets)
1 pint cherry tomatoes, cut
   into halves
4 green onions, chopped
½ pound bacon, fried and
   crumbled
DRESSING:
1 bottle Green Goddess
   dressing
Juice of half a lemon
Garlic powder to taste

Pour dressing over salad
ingredients and toss.
4-6 servings

Nancy H. Kelley (Mrs. James E.)

Cauliflower Salad

1 head cauliflower, broken into
   florets
1 Tablespoon minced onion
½ cup sliced black olives
4 Tablespoons mayonnaise
1 teaspoon salt

Soak cauliflower in salted
water in the refrigerator for 1 hour.
Rinse cauliflower and pat or spin
dry. In bowl combine with onion,
olives, mayonnaise and salt. Chill
well before serving. Amounts of
ingredients may vary according to
size of cauliflower. The crunchy
texture of this sald makes it a
good accompaniment for many
main dishes. 6 servings

Molly L. Ahlquist (Mrs. Ernest, Jr.)

Cheese Dressed Tomatoes
Good on baked potatoes with bacon bits and chives

8 ounces small curd cottage
   cheese
½ medium onion, grated
2 shakes Tabasco sauce
2-3 teaspoons mayonnaise
½ teaspoon salt
Juice of 2 lemons

Mix all ingredients in blender
or food processor. Chill. Serve on
½ tomato or on tomato slices for
salad. Serves 4-6

Mrs. Grace C. Griffin
Scott, Georgia

Home Garden Marinade

¾ cup fresh lime juice*
6 Tablespoons good quality
   olive oil or salad oil
1 clove garlic, crushed
1 Tablespoon sugar
1½ teaspoons salt
½ teaspoon pepper
1 teaspoon Angostura Bitters*
*These 2 ingredients are
   essential. Although ½ part
   fresh lemon juice may be
   used, lime is better.
Sliced vegetables

Combine ingredients in a jar and shake well. Arrange on a platter, a selection of sliced vegetables: garden lettuce, tomatoes, mild onions, cucumbers, radishes, green pepper, avocado, etc. Pour marinade over and marinate for 1 hour before serving. Baste occasionally. Pour off excess before serving. Marinade may be saved and used again.
6 servings

Phyllis K. Kennedy

Cucumber Salad
Serve with pork or as a relish with any type meal

3 large cucumbers, peeled and
   thinly sliced
1 cup white vinegar
¾ cup water
¾ cup sugar
1 teaspoon salt
Dash red hot pepper
Dash dried parsley
Dash black pepper
Dash basil

Combine all ingredients except cucumbers and heat until sugar melts. Pour over cucumbers. Store in refrigerator in an airtight container. Keeps well for several days. 6-8 servings

Winnie R. Goodman (Mrs. James E.)

Lemon Marinated Mushrooms

1 pound fresh mushrooms
½ cup salad or olive oil
3 Tablespoons lemon juice
1 Tablespoon Dijon mustard
½ teaspoon salt
¼ teaspoon freshly ground
   pepper

Cut mushrooms in ⅛ inch slices. In screwtop jar combine oil, lemon juice, mustard, salt and pepper. Cover jar and shake well. Pour mixture over mushrooms tossing gently to coat. Let mixture stand at room temperature 1 hour, stirring occasionally. Serve mushrooms on lettuce leaves.
3-4 servings

Joan M. Adams (Mrs. John P., Jr.)

Hot Mushroom Salad

1 green pepper, cut in thin
    strips
1 small onion, thinly sliced
1 pound fresh mushrooms,
    sliced
1 Tablespoon margarine or
    butter, melted
1-1½ Tablespoons soy sauce
1-1½ Tablespoons Teriyaki
    sauce
Lettuce
3 slices bacon, cooked
    and crumbled

Combine all ingredients except
lettuce and bacon in a skillet.
Cook, stirring frequently, until
mushrooms and onions are tender.
Spoon onto lettuce; garnish with
bacon. Serve immediately.
Vegetables may be sliced ahead
and refrigerated. 3-4 servings

Joan M. Adams (Mrs. John P., Jr.)

Chilled Lima Bean Salad
Great salad for picnics and large parties

3 cups cooked lima beans (tiny
    green limas), drained
1 cup diced celery
¼ cup minced parsley
¼ cup chives
2 teaspoons dill seed
½ cup mayonnaise
½ cup sour cream
1 teaspoon lemon juice
Salt, pepper and paprika to
    taste

Combine lima beans, celery,
parsley, chives and dill seed.
Make a dressing with mayonnaise,
sour cream and lemon juice.
Carefully fold in lima bean mixture.
Add salt and pepper. Sprinkle with
paprika. May be prepared the
night before serving. 6-8 servings

Diane D. Mahaffey (Mrs. Randy)
Nancy D. Mahaffey (Mrs. G.T.)

HINT ▬▬▬▬▬▬▬▬▬▬▬▬▬▬▬▬▬▬▬▬▬▬

To prepare lettuce and spinach for salads, rinse thoroughly and
place in a dish towel or large piece of cheesecloth. Hold cloth by the 4
corners, take outside and, holding cloth in one hand, sling off moisture
by swinging cloth in a circular motion.

Crunchy Pea Salad

1 (10 ounce) package frozen
   green peas
1 can water chestnuts, drained
   and sliced
1 cup shredded carrots
2-3 stalks celery, sliced
3-4 green onions, sliced
2 Tablespoons salad oil
2 Tablespoons wine vinegar
1 Tablespoon soy sauce
1 teaspoon sugar
1 teaspoon paprika
2-3 teaspoons dry mustard
½ teaspoon salt
1 small clove garlic, crushed

Put frozen green peas in a strainer and run hot water over to thaw. Drain. Combine in a bowl with water chestnuts, shredded carrots, celery and green onions. Mix the marinade by combining salad oil, vinegar, soy sauce, sugar, paprika, dry mustard, salt and garlic. Pour marinade over vegetables. Chill at least 1 hour before serving. Note: This should not be prepared more than 1 day in advance since the water chestnuts change color.
8 servings

Elise Nardone Yates
Haleiwa, Hawaii

Dublin Potato Salad

An interesting combination of potato salad and slaw

2 Tablespoons cider or wine
   vinegar
1 teaspoon celery seed
1 teaspoon mustard seed
3 pounds potatoes
2 teaspoons sugar
½ teaspoon salt
2 cups cabbage, shredded
¼ cup chopped dill pickle
¼ cup chopped green onions
1 cup mayonnaise
¼ cup milk
½ teaspoon salt
1 (12 ounce) can corned beef,
   cubed (optional)

Combine first 3 ingredients; set aside. Peel and cook potatoes until barely done; don't overcook. Drain, cube and drizzle with vinegar mixture. Add sugar and salt. Combine remaining ingredients and toss with potato mixture. Chill until serving time.
8-10 servings

Marcia Scroggs (Mrs. Joe D.)

Pepperoni Potato Salad
This unusual salad is good for picnics and casual dinners

10 medium potatoes (red preferred)
4 slices bacon, cooked and crumbled
1 stick pepperoni sausage, sliced and cubed
1 large onion, chopped
 3 hard boiled eggs, sliced (optional)
1 Tablespoon dill pickle cubes
½-¾ cup mayonnaise
1 Tablespoon mustard
Salt, pepper, garlic salt to taste
½ green pepper, sliced (optional)
¼ cup sliced green olives (optional)

Boil and slice potatoes while hot. Leave peelings on potatoes if desired. Sauté chopped pepperoni and onion in bacon drippings over medium heat for 2-3 minutes or until onion is softened. Pour hot pepperoni, onion and drippings over potatoes. Toss gently. Add remaining ingredients. Serve immediately or refrigerate until thoroughly chilled and serve. 8 servings

Lachlan M. Fiveash (Mrs. Charlie B.)

Italian Rice Salad

2 cups long grain rice
2 hard boiled eggs, chopped
½ cup olives, black, green or mixture of both
2 Tablespoons capers
1 (6½ ounce) can tuna
⅓-½ cup olive oil
Juice of 2 lemons
Salt
Black pepper, freshly ground
OPTIONAL:
2 stalks celery, finely chopped
1 small onion, finely chopped
½ green pepper, finely chopped
Radishes, finely chopped
Small jar pimiento, chopped
Cucumber, finely chopped
1 small jar marinated artichoke hearts, drained
1 (8½) ounce can tiny green peas, drained

Cook rice in boiling, salted water until just done. Do not overcook. Grains must not stick together. Add eggs, olives, capers and tuna to cooked, cooled rice, and choose from optional ingredients to suit your taste: any or all of them. Add olive oil, lemon juice, salt and pepper to taste. Chill before serving. 6-8 servings

Barrie C. Aycock (Mrs. Robert R.)

Scandinavian Salad

1 (16 ounce) can French green
   beans, drained
1 small can pitted black
   olives, drained
1 (16 ounce) can tiny green
   peas, drained
1 (2 ounce) jar pimiento,
   drained and chopped
1 medium onion, sliced and
   separated into rings
1½ cups chopped celery
1 (8 ounce) can water
   chestnuts, drained and
   sliced
1 (16 ounce) can bean sprouts,
   drained
DRESSING:
1 teaspoon salt
1 cup vinegar
⅓ cup vegetable oil
1⅓ cups sugar
Dash paprika

Mix dressing and pour over vegetables. Refrigerate for at least 24 hours. Will keep in refrigerator covered 1 week. 10-12 servings

Carolyn Hoose (Mrs. Kenneth A., Jr.)

Bleu Cheese Slaw
Change of pace in slaws

¾ cup corn oil
⅓ cup vinegar
¼ cup sugar
1 Tablespoon grated onion
1½ teaspoons salt
½ teaspoon celery seed
2 quarts (1 head) white
   cabbage, prepared for slaw
1 quart (½ head) red cabbage,
   prepared for slaw
2 (4 ounce) packages bleu
   cheese, crumbled

Mix oil, vinegar, sugar, onion, salt and celery seed. Chill several hours (up to 24 hours). Toss with cabbage and bleu cheese at serving time. 8 servings

Beverly Bibent (Mrs. Maury J.)

Marinated Tomatoes and Green Peppers
Maggi seasoning makes this garden fresh salad different

2 large ripe tomatoes, thinly
   sliced
1-2 green peppers, sliced
MARINADE:
4 Tablespoons red wine
   vinegar
½ teaspoon Dijon mustard
½ teaspoon salt
½ teaspoon chopped frozen
   chives
4-5 dashes Maggi (liquid)
   seasoning
Ground pepper to taste
3 Tablespoons salad oil

Alternate tomatoes and peppers in a shallow dish. Mix marinade ingredients well, adding oil last. Pour over tomatoes and peppers and refrigerate 1-2 hours.
4-6 servings

Dunja S. Awbrey (Mrs. James J.)

Insalata Marinata

1 cup diagonally sliced raw
   carrots
1 cup cauliflower broken into
   small pieces
1 medium green pepper, cut
   in bite-sized pieces
1 package frozen artichoke
   hearts, cooked and drained
1 cup thickly sliced fresh
   mushrooms
½ cup ripe olives
4 slices (2 ounces) proscuitto,
   cut in quarters
6 slices (2 ounces) hard salami,
   cut in quarters
¾ cup prepared Italian dressing

In saucepan cook carrots, cauliflower and green pepper in boiling water until just tender, approximately 5 minutes. Drain. Combine with remaining ingredients. Chill for 6 hours or more, stirring occasionally. Makes about 6 cups. Keeps well for several days. Serve with a cup of light soup and bread sticks.
4 servings

Cookbook Committee

Marinated Vegetable Salad

½ pound mushrooms
1 (14 ounce) can artichoke
    hearts, drained and cut
1 (7 ounce) can baby carrots,
    drained
¼ cup pimientos, chopped
1 cup pitted black olives
DRESSING:
⅔ cup white vinegar
⅔ cup olive oil
¼ cup chopped onions
2 cloves garlic, crushed
1 teaspoon salt
1 teaspoon sugar
1 teaspoon dried oregano
1 teaspoon basil
¼ teaspoon pepper

In salad bowl layer all ingredients starting with mushrooms and ending with olives. Combine dressing ingredients; bring to boil. Remove from heat and cool for 10 minutes. Pour cooked dressing over vegetables. Refrigerate several hours. Toss before serving. Serve on a bed of lettuce. 6-8 servings

Nancy H. Kelley (Mrs. James E.)

Marinated Slaw

1 medium cabbage, prepared
    for slaw
2 large onions, thinly sliced
    and separated into rings
⅞ cup sugar
1 cup vinegar
¾ cup cooking oil
2 Tablespoons sugar
1 teaspoon salt
1 teaspoon celery seed

In a bowl place cabbage alternating with onions. Top with ⅞ cup sugar. Do not stir. Heat vinegar, oil, 2 Tablespoons sugar, salt and celery seed. Let boil. Pour over cabbage and onions. Refrigerate at least 12 hours before serving. Drain before serving. May be prepared 2 days in advance. Nice to serve with fish or barbeque. 6 servings

Nancy W. Jones (Mrs. Edmund W.)

Cobb Salad
A summer meal

DRESSING:
¼ cup water
¼ cup red wine vinegar
¼ teaspoon sugar
Dash lemon juice
2 teaspoons salt
¾ teaspoon black pepper
1 scant teaspoon
 Worcestershire sauce
1 scant teaspoon Dijon
 mustard
½ clove garlic, crushed
¼ cup olive oil
¾ cup salad oil
SALAD:
Greens—mixture of lettuce,
 watercress, chicory,
 Romaine
2 tomatoes, cut in wedges
2 chicken breasts, cooked
 and chopped
6 strips crisp bacon
1 avocado, sliced
3 hard cooked eggs, chopped
2 Tablespoons chopped chives
½ cup crumbled Roquefort
 cheese

Dressing: Blend all ingredients except oil. Add oil slowly to blender. Chill. Shake before serving.

Salad: Arrange tomatoes, chicken, bacon and avocado decoratively on greens. Sprinkle chopped eggs, cheese and chives on top. Pour dressing and toss just before serving. 6-8 servings

Marty D. Halyburton (Mrs. Porter)

Chicken Salad Supreme

2½ cups diced, cooked
 chicken
1 cup finely chopped celery
1 cup halved seedless grapes
½ cup slivered toasted
 almonds
2 Tablespoons minced parsley
1 teaspoon salt
1 cup mayonnaise
½ cup heavy cream, whipped

Gently combine all ingredients. Serve on crisp lettuce. Garnish with thin slices of chicken over top and either sliced ripe or stuffed green olives around the salad. Serve this at a luncheon with a tomato aspic, Asparagus Vinaigrette, and Herbed Potato Rolls (see Index). 8 servings

Curried Turkey Salad

8 cups cooked, diced turkey
(2½-3 pound size)
20 ounces water chestnuts,
drained and sliced
2 pounds seedless grapes
2 cups sliced celery
2-3 cups slivered almonds,
toasted
3 cups mayonnaise
1 Tablespoon curry powder
2 Tablespoons soy sauce
2 Tablespoons lemon juice
1 pound pineapple chunks or
2 (11 ounce) cans lychee
nuts, drained
Boston-Bibb lettuce

Combine all but lettuce and chill for several hours. Serve on bed of fresh lettuce. 12 servings

Cookbook Committee

Crab Aspic

1 pound frozen Alaskan King
crab
1¼ cups boiling water
1 envelope unflavored gelatin,
softened in ¼ cup water
1 (3 ounce) package lemon
flavored gelatin
2 cups tomato juice
1 Tablespoon vinegar
1 Tablespoon Worcestershire
sauce
½ teaspoon salt
1 teaspoon grated onion
4 drops Tabasco
¾ cup chopped celery
⅔ cup chopped cucumber
¼ cup chopped green pepper

Drain thawed crab meat. Reserve some large pieces for garnish. Finely slice the rest. Add boiling water to gelatins, stirring until dissolved. Add tomato juice, vinegar, Worcestershire sauce, salt, onion and Tabasco. Chill until mixture is consistency of egg whites. Add vegetables and crab meat. Pour into greased mold and chill. Garnish with crab pieces and deviled eggs.

Mrs. John Hellriegel

Tuna Salad Surprise

2 large cans tuna, drained
1 cup minced celery
1 medium onion, minced
1 teaspoon lemon juice
1 teaspoon curry powder
1 package small frozen peas
    or canned peas, drained
1 teaspoon soy sauce (or more
    if desired)
¾ cup mayonnaise
1 can chow mein noodles

Combine all ingredients except noodles the night before serving. Add noodles and toss just before serving. Serve on lettuce cups with tomato wedges. 8 servings

Maureen T. Vandiver (Mrs. Roy W.)

Salmon Sour Cream Mold

1 envelope unflavored gelatin
½ cup cold water
1 envelope sour cream sauce
    mix
½ cup mayonnaise or salad
    dressing
2 teaspoons lemon juice
¼ teaspoon dried dill weed or
    ½ teaspoon dill seed
1 (16 ounce) can red salmon
½ cup diced celery
4 green onions including
    green tops, diced
2-3 drops red food coloring
    (optional)
Carrot curls to garnish, if
    if desired

Soften gelatin in cold water. Stir over boiling water until gelatin dissolves. Cool. Prepare sour cream sauce mix according to package directions. Blend in mayonnaise, lemon juice and dill weed. Gradually stir into gelatin. Drain salmon, discarding skin and large bones; flake. Fold salmon, celery, and onions into sour cream mixture; blend in red food coloring, if desired. Turn into greased 3 cup mold. Chill until set 4-5 hours; unmold and garnish with carrot curls, if desired. May be prepared a day in advance. 6 servings

Carol Ann Neal (Mrs. Michael M.)

Shrimp and Rice Salad
A good light supper or luncheon dish

¾ pound fresh mushrooms,
  coarsely chopped
2 Tablespoons salad oil
2 Tablespoons lemon juice
1 teaspoon salt
3¼ cups cooked rice (half
  white, half wild)
2 hard cooked eggs, coarsely
  chopped
1 green pepper, coarsely
  chopped
1½ pounds shrimp, cleaned
  and cooked
GARLIC MAYONNAISE:
1 clove garlic
¼ teaspoon paprika
½ teaspoon dry mustard
⅛ teaspoon pepper
1 teaspoon warm water
¾ cup mayonnaise

Sauté mushrooms in oil. Add lemon juice and salt, and cook until tender (about 10 minutes). Mix rice, eggs, green pepper, mushrooms and shrimp together. Refrigerate overnight. Toss with Garlic Mayonnaise before serving. 10 servings

Garlic Mayonnaise: Blend all ingredients together well.

Sandra R. Pritchett (Mrs. Edwin P.)

Shrimp and Cabbage Collage
Good with buttered pumpernickel

½ cup sour cream or plain
  yogurt
½ cup mayonnaise
4 teaspoons prepared mustard
1 Tablespoon white vinegar
½ teaspoon salt
¼ teaspoon pepper
1 Tablespoon sugar
12 ounces shrimp, cooked
  and chopped
1 small head green cabbage,
  coarsely shredded
2 green onions, thinly sliced

Combine sour cream, mayonnaise, mustard and spices. Fold in the shrimp. Arrange cabbage in salad bowl, mound shrimp in center and sprinkle with green onions. 4 servings

Susan M. Morley

Taco Salad

1 pound lean ground beef
½ bell pepper, chopped
1 cup chopped onion
1 Tablespoon chili powder
¼-½ teaspoons cumin
Salt and pepper to taste
1 head iceberg lettuce,
    shredded
2 medium tomatoes, chopped
6-8 ounces tortilla chips,
    coarsely crushed
1 small purple onion, chopped
1 avocado, sliced
6-8 ounces Cheddar cheese,
    grated

Brown beef with onions and pepper. Drain off fat. Season with chili powder, cumin, salt and pepper. Keep warm. Mix all other ingredients except cheese. Add warm meat mixture and cover with cheese. Let stand a few minutes to melt cheese slightly. Toss and serve immediately.
6-8 servings

Jerry P. Connor (Mrs. Paul)

Winter Salad
Delicious with baked ham, ham sandwiches or hot dogs

½ cup vinegar
½ cup sugar
¼ cup oil
1 Tablespoon salt
½ teaspoon pepper
1 (16 ounce) can sauerkraut
1 medium onion, chopped
1 green pepper, chopped
2 pimientos, chopped
½ teaspoon garlic salt
1 teaspoon celery seed

Combine vinegar, sugar, salt, oil, and pepper and boil, stirring to dissolve sugar. Rinse and drain sauerkraut. Pour sauce over sauerkraut and add remaining ingredients. Mix and allow to cool slightly. Cover and chill at least 4 hours. Best when chilled for 24 hours. 8 servings

Alicia LaRocco

HINT

To dry large quantities of lettuce or spinach, put in pillow case, tie with twistie, place in washing machine and spin dry.

Cole Slaw Dressing

2 eggs
½ cup sugar
¼ cup vinegar
½ Tablespoon butter
1 teaspoon mustard
¼ teaspoon salt
¼ teaspoon pepper

Beat eggs well with sugar. Add remaining ingredients. Cook in a double boiler until thick, stirring constantly. Store in refrigerator. Thin with cream if too thick.

Prepare ahead and toss with shredded cabbage before serving. 1 cup

Dorothy M. Martens (Mrs. G.H.)

Creamy Fruit Topping

1 cup heavy cream
1 teaspoon unflavored gelatin
¼ cup sugar
1 cup sour cream
1 teaspoon vanilla

Combine heavy cream, unflavored gelatin and sugar in a saucepan. Heat gently until gelatin and sugar are dissolved. Chill. Fold in sour cream and vanilla, chill and serve over fresh fruit. 8-12 servings

Dannie Martin (Mrs. H. Fielder)

Tarragon Dressing

Especially good on a salad containing Bleu or Roquefort cheese

1½ cups salad oil
⅓ cup tarragon vinegar
1 teaspoon lemon juice
½ teaspoon soy sauce
½ teaspoon sugar
1 teaspoon garlic powder
2 teaspoons salt
2 teaspoons coarsely ground
    black pepper
1 teaspoon dry mustard

Mix all ingredients in order listed and store in the refrigerator in a covered container. 2 cups

Julia W. Ray (Mrs. Frederick C., Jr.)

Danish Feta Cheese Dressing

1 cup finely crumbled Feta
    cheese
½ cup mayonnaise
½ cup sour cream
3 Tablespoons buttermilk
1 Tablespoon fresh lemon
    juice
1 clove garlic, pressed
1 teaspoon grated onion
1 teaspoon Worcestershire
    sauce
½ teaspoon dried mixed salad
    herbs
Freshly ground black pepper
    to taste
Black olives for garnish
Chopped green onion for
    garnish

Combine all ingredients except black olives and green onion, blending well. Cover and chill at least 1 hour to allow flavors to blend. Serve over crisp greens. 1½ cups

Joan M. Adams (Mrs. John P., Jr.)

Famous Mustard Vinaigrette

⅓ cup red wine vinegar or
    tarragon vinegar
2 Tablespoons Dijon mustard
1 cup olive oil (or ½ vegetable
    oil and ½ olive oil)
1½ teaspoons dried thyme
1½ teaspoons dried tarragon
    or less
½ teaspoon salt
¼ teaspoon freshly ground
    black pepper
½ teaspoon sugar

Mix wine vinegar and mustard in medium bowl. Add oil in a very slow stream using a small whisk to incorporate oil as it is added. This step should take several minutes and will result in a dressing that does not separate later. Add other ingredients and chill. Do not use a food processor as it will change the consistency. Serve over green salads, and in potato salads. 1½ cups

Elise M. Griffin

Italian Salad Dressing, Il Giardino

4 egg yolks
1 cup olive oil
½ cup freshly grated Romano
　or Parmesan cheese
1 Tablespoon vinegar
1 teaspoon crushed garlic
Juice of 1 lemon
2 teaspoons fresh basil or
　1 teaspoon dried
1 teaspoon coarsely ground
　black pepper

Beat yolks with fork or whisk. Gradually add oil until yolks will hold no more. Blend in remaining ingredients. Store covered and chilled. Do not use blender or food processor; it changes the consistency. 1½ cups

Il Giardino
Charleston, South Carolina

Special French Dressing

1 cup powdered sugar
½ cup cider vinegar
Juice of 1 lemon
8 Tablespoons catsup
½ cup salad oil
Salt and pepper to taste
1 Tablespoon finely minced
　onion
1 garlic clove, pressed or
　finely minced

In blender, or with mixer, blend powdered sugar, vinegar and lemon juice. Add catsup and blend well. Add oil and blend; add onion and spices and blend thoroughly. Cover tightly and refrigerate for at least 24 hours before use. This dressing will keep 3-4 weeks under refrigeration. 1½ cups

Ruth Hardy (Mrs. Wallace E.)

Roquefort Dressing
Very mild—vary by adding more or less cheese

1 (2-3 ounce) wedge Roquefort
　cheese
1 package Cheese Garlic Salad
　Dressing mix
1 pint good quality mayonnaise
2 cups buttermilk
　(approximately)
Juice of ½ lemon

Crumble cheese into a 1 quart container; add dressing mix and mayonnaise; add buttermilk to equal 1 quart. Season with lemon juice. Shake well. This dressing will keep for 2-3 weeks in the refrigerator. 1 quart

Nancy Wactor (Mrs. W. Ray)

Poppy Seed Dressing
A very versatile dressing

⅔ **cup vinegar**
¼ **cup lemon juice**
1½ **cups sugar**
2 **teaspoons salt**
3 **Tablespoons poppy seed**
2 **teaspoons dry mustard**
1 **teaspoon paprika**
1 **small onion, cut in quarters**
2 **cups vegetable oil**

Heat vinegar, lemon juice, sugar and salt until sugar dissolves. Blend poppy seed, mustard, paprika, onion and hot liquids 30 seconds on high. Turn to low speed. Slowly add oil to the rest of the mixture in the blender and blend on low 10 more seconds. Can be stored at least 4 weeks in refrigerator in a covered container. Use over fresh fruit or over spinach salad as a dressing. Marinate chicken in dressing before grilling. Add to barbecue sauce for a sweet and sour taste. Mix with mayonnaise, half and half, and use on cole slaw. 1 quart

Sandy L. Carley (Mrs. George H.)

Mayfair Dressing
From the Mayfair Hotel in St. Louis

1 **cup mayonnaise**
½ **cup sour cream**
1 **(2 ounce) can anchovy fillets**
¼ **cup minced parsley**
3 **Tablespoons chopped green onion**
2 **Tablespoon tarragon vinegar**
2 **Tablespoons lemon juice**
¼ **clove garlic**
½ **teaspoon salt**

Combine ingredients and process in blender or food processor. Store in a covered container.

Pamela T. Marcus

Honey Dressing for Fruit
Good on any frozen or fresh fruit salad

½ cup wine vinegar
¼ cup sugar
¼ cup honey
1 teaspoon dry mustard
1 teaspoon paprika
1 teaspoon celery seed
1 teaspoon celery salt
1 teaspoon grated onion
1 cup vegetable oil

Mix vinegar, sugar, honey, mustard, and paprika; boil for 3 minutes and cool. Add celery seed, salt, onion and oil; pour into 1 pint container and shake vigorously. Store in refrigerator but let come to room temperature before serving. Keeps indefinitely. 1 pint

Barrie C. Aycock (Mrs. Robert R.)

Sour Cream Dressing

½ small onion
4 heaping Tablespoons sour cream
6 Tablespoons oil
1 Tablespoon vinegar
1½ Tablespoons milk
1½ Tablespoons sugar
Salt and pepper to taste

Grate onion or chop fine. Add sour cream, oil, vinegar and milk. Stir until smooth and creamy. Mix in the sugar, salt and pepper. Let stand in the refrigerator at least ½ hour before serving. Best served over Boston or Bibb lettuce, plain, or with tomato. 1 cup

Melva Jansen (Mrs. Klaus)

Tropical Fruit Topping
Good on fruit crêpes too!

1 cup sugar
2 Tablespoons flour
¼ teaspoon salt
2 eggs, well beaten
Juice of 1 lemon
1 cup pineapple juice
1 heaping teaspoon butter
1 cup heavy cream

Mix dry ingredients. Add eggs, then juice. Cook slowly until thick. Add butter. Let mixture cool. Whip cream and fold into cooled mixture. Will keep in the refrigerator for a week. Serve on a fresh fruit salad, or on a fruit crêpe. 2½ cups

Sauces for Meats and Vegetables

Flavored Butters for Meats

**GREEN PEPPERCORN
   BUTTER:**
**1½ Tablespoons green
   peppercorns, drained
   (found in gourmet shops)**
1 stick soft butter
⅛ cup dry white wine
½ Tablespoon tarragon
Juice of ¼ lemon or to taste
⅛ teaspoon salt or to taste

Green Peppercorn Butter:
Blend all ingredients by hand.
Store covered in refrigerator.
Serve with chicken, duck or
broiled meats.

MUSTARD BUTTER:
1 stick soft butter
1-2 Tablespoons Dijon mustard
**2 Tablespoons minced fresh
   parsley or mixed herbs**

Mustard Butter: Blend all
ingredients by hand, blender or
food processor. Store in
refrigerator. Serve with kidneys,
liver, steaks, broiled fish or use to
enrich sauces or soups.

TARRAGON BUTTER:
1 stick soft butter
1 Tablespoon lemon juice
**2-3 Tablespoons fresh tarragon
   (dry if fresh is not available)**

Tarragon Butter: Blend all
ingredients by hand, blender or
food processor. Store in
refrigerator. Serve with broiled
meats and fish or use to enrich
sauces or soups.

Cookbook Committee

Marchand de Vin Sauce

¾ cup butter
⅓ cup sliced mushrooms
½ cup minced ham
⅓ cup chopped green onions
**½ cup finely chopped white
   onion**
**2 Tablespoons garlic, mashed
   with ½ teaspoon salt**
2 Tablespoons flour
⅛ teaspoon pepper
Dash of cayenne
¾ cup beef stock
½ cup red wine

Melt butter and lightly sauté
mushrooms, ham, green onions,
white onion and garlic/salt paste.
When onion is clear, add flour,
pepper and cayenne, continually
stirring. Brown flour well over
medium heat. This should take
10 minutes or so. Remove from
heat and add stock all at once.
Add wine and return to heat,
blending well. Simmer 35-45
minutes. If not for immediate use,
place pan in a pan of water and
leave on low heat. 2 cups

Terry Morris (Mrs. Douglas)

Madeira Sauce

1½ Tablespoons butter
1½ Tablespoons flour
2 cups dark beef stock
⅓ cup Madeira wine

Melt butter in heavy saucepan, add flour and stir and cook until brown in color. Add beef stock, simmer for 30 minutes. Add wine and bring to boil. Serve hot over steak, standing rib roast or Beef Wellington. 2 cups

Mustard Sauce for Ham

1 Tablespoon salad oil
1 Tablespoon prepared mustard
¼ cup granulated sugar
5 Tablespoons catsup
3 Tablespoons vinegar

Mix all ingredients and simmer until well blended. May be prepared 1-2 days in advance. Excellent on sliced ham. 1½ cups

Myrick L. King (Mrs. David L.G., Jr.)

Orange Sauce for Pork

1¼ cups sugar
2 Tablespoons cornstarch
¾ teaspoon salt
1 teaspoon cinnamon
1 Tablespoon whole cloves
3 Tablespoons grated orange
   rind
1 cup fresh orange juice

Mix ingredients and cook until thick and clear. Serve with pork roast or chops. 2 cups

Decie Nygaard (Mrs. W.F.)

HINT

Always use a dry wine, never a sweet one for cooking, unless specifically requested in the recipe. Dry vermouth is a good substitute for white wine. Dry sherry or Mirin (Japanese rice wine) is best for Oriental dishes.

Famous Barbecue Sauce
An original family recipe worked out after years of testing

1 pint tomato juice
1 bottle Heinz meat sauce
½ bottle Worcestershire sauce
Juice of 2 lemons
¾ stick butter
3-4 bay leaves
½ jar horseradish
20 peppercorns
½ can chili powder
1 cup water
Salt and pepper

Simmer all ingredients for 20 minutes. This makes a thin old-fashioned barbecue sauce which is delicious on chicken or ribs. The ingredients may vary depending upon individual tastes. Sauce may be frozen.

Elsie B. Manry
Tampa, Florida

Sauce for Duckling

4 Tablespoons lemon juice
3 Tablespoons honey
2 Tablespoons soy sauce
2 Tablespoons melted butter
1 Tablespoon sherry
1 crushed garlic clove

Blend all ingredients together and let stand 1 hour before using.
Roast quartered duckling in shallow pan at 325° for 1 hour, piercing skin frequently. Baste with sauce frequently. Brown under broiler, basting, for 5 minutes on each side. Brush with honey for one minute.

Marinade for Beef or Chicken

2 cups salad oil
¾ cup soy sauce
¼ cup Worcestershire sauce
2 Tablespoons dry mustard
2½ Tablespoons salt
1 Tablespoon pepper
½ cup wine vinegar
1½ teaspoons parsley
⅓ cup lemon juice
½ cup sherry or Burgundy

Mix ingredients together in a quart jar with a tight lid. Store in refrigerator. This can be used over and over, if used only on beef. It will keep in refrigerator for 4 months and will marinate 5 pounds of meat. Note: If used for chicken, discard after using.
1 quart

Linda Chambliss (Mrs. Harold W.)

Barbeque Sauce for Chicken

1 pint vinegar
½ pint vegetable oil
5 teaspoons black pepper
5 teaspoons poultry seasoning
5 Tablespoons salt
½ stick butter

Mix ingredients in a saucepan and heat to blend flavors. Use to baste chicken while cooking on grill. This recipe makes enough sauce for 5 chickens. Refrigerate in an airtight container.

Claire W. Johnson (Mrs. A. Sidney)

Tartare Sauce

1 cup mayonnaise
1 teaspoon Dijon mustard
1 Tablespoon minced dill pickle
¼ cup chopped green onion
1 teaspoon minced parsley
1 Tablespoon capers

Combine ingredients and chill. Serve with broiled or fried seafood. 1¼ cups

Florence M. Werden

Jezebel Sauce

1 (10 ounce) jar pineapple
  preserves
1 (10 ounce) jar apple jelly
1 (4 ounce) jar Coleman's
  mustard
6 Tablespoons horseradish

At least 24 hours before using, mix all ingredients together with a spoon. Refrigerate. Will keep in refrigerator for 2 weeks. Serve with platters of cold turkey or roast beef; use in place of mayonnaise or mustard. Also fantastic as a topping for cream cheese, served with crackers. 3 cups

Virginia S. Corley (Mrs. Charles C., Jr.)

Shrimp Romanoff Sauce

1 cup mayonnaise
¼ cup catsup
4 teaspoons white wine
¾ teaspoon Maggi Seasoning

Place all ingredients in bowl and blend until smooth. Refrigerate. When ready to serve, arrange boiled shrimp (which have been shelled and refrigerated) on lettuce on individual plates and spoon sauce liberally over shrimp. Serves 8

Mrs. Earle B. May, Jr.

Sauce for Artichokes
Serve with hot or cold artichokes as an appetizer or a vegetable

1 package Good Seasons
    Garlic salad dressing
3 ounces blue cheese
Vinegar
Oil

Note: Deviate from package instructions slightly. Add mix first; then fill to vinegar line on Good Seasons' bottle. Add water and oil as shown on bottle. Put in blender. Add blue cheese and blend; add more or less cheese for personal taste. Chill before serving. Sauce should cling to artichoke leaf when dipped. Will keep several weeks in the refrigerator. 8 servings

Anne M. Shearer (Mrs. William B.)

Hot Sauce for Avocado

3 Tablespoons butter
3 Tablespoons brown sugar
3 Tablespoons vinegar
3 Tablespoons Worcestershire
3 Tablespoons ketchup
⅓ teaspoon salt

Combine all ingredients and cook for 20 minutes in double boiler. Cut avocado in half, remove pit, and fill with hot sauce. Delicious served with chicken salad or barbequed chicken.

Josephine Fleming (Mrs. Tom)

F & W's Basic Mayonnaise with Mustard

3 egg yolks
½ teaspoon Dijon mustard
½ teaspoon salt
¼ teaspoon white pepper
1 Tablespoon lemon juice
1 cup oil (½ olive; ½ vegetable)
Cayenne pepper
Variation: summer mayonnaise;
   add chopped cucumbers,
   lots of freshly chopped
   dillweed and chopped red
   pepper.

Using electric mixer (or blender, food processor or hand whisk) beat first 4 ingredients and 1 teaspoon lemon juice until light and fluffy. Drop by drop add oil beating after each addition until the oil is absorbed. When the mayonnaise begins to thicken, add the oil in spoonfuls as you beat, and then pour very slowly until the entire cup has been incorporated. This should take at least 3 minutes, beating steadily. Add the rest of the lemon juice and Cayenne pepper to taste. Correct the seasoning with more salt, pepper and additional mayonnaise and lemon juice. 1¼ cups

The Editors
The International Review of Food and Wine

Blender Mayonnaise

1 egg
1 teaspoon salt
1 teaspoon sugar
1 teaspoon dry mustard
½ teaspoon paprika
3 Tablespoons lemon juice
1½ cups salad oil

Combine egg, salt, sugar, dry mustard, paprika, lemon juice and ¼ cup salad oil in blender or food processor (use steel blade). Cover and blend a few seconds. With cover on and motor still running, gradually add 1¼ cups salad oil. Blend until thick and smooth. Yield: 1 pint

Flawless Hollandaise

4 egg yolks
½ teaspoon salt
1 Tablespoon lemon juice
Dash tabasco
¼ pound butter, melted

Place egg yolks in blender or food processor with salt, lemon juice and tabasco. Blend briefly. Have melted butter ready, heated to a bubbling stage. Turn blender or food processor on and pour butter in a steady stream until mixture is completely emulsified. Yield: ¾ cup.

White Sauces

THIN WHITE SAUCE:
1½ Tablespoons butter
1½ Tablespoons flour
½ teaspoon salt
Dash white pepper
Dash nutmeg
1 cup milk

MEDIUM WHITE SAUCE:
2½ Tablespoons butter
2½ Tablespoons flour
Repeat ingredients above
starting with salt

THICK WHITE SAUCE:
4 Tablespoons butter
4 Tablespoons flour
Repeat ingredients above
starting with salt

Melt butter in a saucepan over low heat. Stir in the flour and use a whisk to blend thoroughly. Add milk and seasonings and cook, stirring constantly until sauce is thick and smooth. 1 cup

Decie Nygaard (Mrs. W.F.)

Mustard Sauce for Vegetables

3 egg yolks
1 Tablespoon lemon juice
2 teaspoons Dijon mustard
¼ teaspoon salt
½ cup butter

In blender or food processor, combine egg yolks, lemon juice, mustard and salt. Cover and blend. In small saucepan heat butter over low heat until it begins to bubble. With blender on high, slowly add bubbling butter. Blend or process until smooth. Serve at once with hot fresh asparagus or broccoli. 1 cup

Jeanine C. Andrews (Mrs. Edward B.)

Pickles, Relishes, Preserves

Fourteen Day Pickles

1 gallon water
Salt to float an egg
   (3 Tablespoons to 1 box)
16 pounds whole pickling
   cucumbers
1 gallon water
½ box alum
1 gallon white vinegar
1 box pickling spice
10 pounds sugar

Make brine with 1 gallon water and enough salt to make an egg float in the water. Place brine and whole cucumbers in a large stone crock and let soak 14 days. Remove cucumbers, discard brine, wash cucumbers well and slice. Soak slices overnight in 1 gallon water mixed with ½ box alum. The next morning rinse and cover with 1 gallon vinegar and soak for 6 hours. Drain and discard vinegar. Place cucumbers, sugar and spices in layers in stone jar. Cover 2-3 days until syrup forms. May be stored in a gallon jar or in refrigerator indefinitely. Serve chilled. Excellent appetizer with a sharp cheese and crackers.

Mrs. Meredith Bass
Hazlehurst, Miss.

Dill Beans

4 pounds fresh round string
   beans (blue lake if possible)
Boiling water
6 cloves garlic
12 heads and stems of fresh
   dill
3 teaspoons crushed red
   pepper
2 quarts water
½ cup white vinegar
⅔ cup coarse salt (regular
   salt may be used)

Cook beans in boiling water 5-7 minutes until half cooked. Drain. Place as many beans as possible in six 1-pint jars. Place 1 clove garlic, 2 heads and stems of fresh dill and ½ teaspoon crushed red pepper in each of the pint jars. Bring water, vinegar and coarse salt to a boil. Cool slightly. Remove foam. Cover beans in each jar with this brine. Cover jars loosely, do not screw tight and store in cool place. Beans are ready to eat in 2-3 weeks. 6 pints

Sue Bufkin (Mrs. Homer)
Hazlehurst, Miss.

Delicatessen Dill Pickles

BRINE PROPORTIONS:
   **2 Tablespoons plain table
   salt per 2 cups water (One
   gallon container requires
   2-3 quarts of brine.)**
**Fresh cucumbers (no wax
   coating)**
**Garlic cloves, peeled (6 cloves
   per gallon)**
**Fresh dill or 2 Tablespoons
   dill seed per gallon**
1 slice rye bread

Make a brine of salt and water. Bring to boil. Cool to lukewarm. Place cucumbers into crock or glass container. Place peeled garlic cloves and dill (stem as well as top) in layers as cucumbers are added. Cover cucumbers with lukewarm brine. Place slice of rye bread on top and allow brine to soak bread. Place a plate with a weight on top to submerge pickles. Place crock in warm place for 4-5 days. Don't let crock get cold as the yeast from the bread prefers lukewarm temperature. The liquid will become cloudy and there will be a deposit on pickles. Rinse off and chill pickles before serving.

Note: Garlic and dill can be varied according to individual taste as can the amount of time in solution. Brine must be made according to directions. These pickles are like those served in a delicatessen. They must be stored in refrigerator when completed.

Emy E. Blair (Mrs. H. Duane)

Kosher Dill Pickles

**8 quarts medium size fresh
   pickling cucumbers**
8 fresh dill heads
24-32 cloves garlic
**8 teaspoons crushed red
   pepper**
15 cups water
1 cup white vinegar
1 cup salt
1 teaspoon alum

Clean cucumbers and place as many cucumbers as will fit into eight 1-quart jars. Add to each jar: 1 fresh dill head, 3-4 cloves garlic and 1 teaspoon crushed red pepper. Bring water, white vinegar, salt and alum to a boil and pour into jars of cucumbers; seal. Let cure for 3-4 weeks.
8 quarts

Grace Allred (Mrs. Cecil)
Hazlehurst, Miss.

Bread and Butter Pickles

4 quarts sliced medium-size
  cucumbers
6 medium white onions, thinly
  sliced
⅓ cup coarse-medium salt
  (such as kosher salt)
5 cups granulated sugar
1½ teaspoons tumeric
1½ teaspoons celery seed
2 Tablespoons mustard seed
3 cups cider vinegar
½ teaspoon ground cloves

Do not pare cucumbers; thinly slice and add onions. Add salt; cover with cracked ice; mix thoroughly. Let stand 3 hours; drain thoroughly. Combine remaining ingredients; pour mixture over cucumbers and onions. Heat just to a boil (slowly, take 15-20 minutes if necessary to reach boil). Seal in hot, sterilized jars. Will keep for 1 year. 8 pints

Maryann B. Chapman (Mrs. James P.)

Pickled Okra

Okra
32 cloves garlic
16 teaspoons crushed red
  pepper
16 teaspoons dill weed
3 quarts white vinegar
1 cup coarse salt (regular salt
  may be used)
1 cup water

Wash and dry okra. Remove stem end and pack tightly in jar. To each pint add 2 cloves garlic, ½ teaspoon crushed red pepper, and ½ teaspoon dill weed. Bring wine vinegar, coarse salt and water to boil and cover okra in jars. Seal. Will be ready to eat in 3-4 weeks. Note: Recipe may be adjusted to pickle the amount of okra you might have. 16 pints

Sue Bufkin (Mrs. Homer)
Hazlehurst, Miss.

Peach Pickle

6 pounds peaches
Whole cloves
3 pounds sugar
1 pint vinegar
1 pint water
Stick cinnamon (optional)
Ginger (optional)

Select firm peaches and peel. Stick 2 or 3 cloves in each peach. Make a syrup of sugar, vinegar and water and bring to a boil. Drop peaches in syrup and cook until they are clear and tender. Pack into hot jars, cover with syrup and seal. Stick cinnamon and ginger may be added to syrup mixture if desired. 4 quarts

Virginia Kelly (Mrs. R.L.)
Wrens, Georgia

Green Pepper Relish

4 cups ground onions
1 medium cabbage
10 green tomatoes
12 green peppers
1 small can pimiento
½ cup salt
6 cups sugar
1 Tablespoon celery seed
2 Tablespoons mustard seed
1½ teaspoons tumeric
4 cups vinegar
2 cups water

Grind vegetables or chop in food processor and put in large bowl or pan. Sprinkle with salt and let stand overnight. Mix sugar, celery seed, mustard seed, tumeric, vinegar and water and pour over vegetables. Heat to boiling and simmer 30 minutes. Put in jars and seal. This relish is very good on fresh vegetables, in tuna, egg or potato salad, or on hot dogs and hamburgers. 8 pints

Myrick L. King (Mrs. David L.G., Jr.)

Creamy Pepper Relish
An unusual relish, great for Christmas giving

5 onions, chopped
5 or 6 cups peppers (sweet
    banana, bell and sweet
    red for color)
1 cup sugar
2 Tablespoons flour
2 Tablespoons butter or
    margarine
2 Tablespoons dry mustard
1 Tablespoon pickling salt
1 cup cider vinegar

Chop peppers and onions coarsely and combine with other ingredients in heavy saucepan. Cook until thick. Seal hot in sterilized jars.

Decie Nygaard (Mrs. W.F.)

Peach-Tomato Relish

6 large fresh peaches (4 cups,
   chopped)
6 ripe tomatoes (4 cups,
   chopped)
1 cup ground onions
1 cup diced green pepper
1 small hot red pepper
1 cup cider vinegar
¾ teaspoon salt
2 Tablespoons pickling spices,
   tied in small cloth bag
2 cups light brown sugar,
   packed

Peel and pit peaches; cut into small pieces to equal 4 cups. Peel and cut tomatoes in ½-inch pieces. Combine with all other ingredients in kettle. Bring to a boil and cook on medium heat, uncovered, 1-1½ hours or until thick, stirring frequently. Fill 6 hot, sterilized ½ pint jars and seal. A good accompaniment for meats. Wonderful as an appetizer served with cream cheese and crackers. 3 pints

Maddy S. Kligora (Mrs. John)

Lime Marmalade
A good gift item

1 can beef consomme
3¾ cups sugar
½ cup fresh lime juice
¼ cup lime rind, cut in thin
   strips approximately ½
   inch long
¼ cup lemon rind, cut in thin
   strips approximately
   ½ inch long
3 ounces fruit pectin
Green food coloring (optional)

In a large heavy saucepan, combine all ingredients except pectin. Place over high heat and bring to a boil, stirring constantly. Cook 3-5 minutes. Stir in pectin. Heat to 220° F. on candy thermometer. Boil hard for 1 minute, stirring constantly. Remove from heat, skim off foam with a metal spoon. Stir and skim to cool and to prevent rind from floating to top, approximately 15-20 minutes. Add food coloring if desired. Pour into jelly glasses; cover with ⅛ inch hot paraffin. Serve over cream cheese and crackers or on hot rolls. Especially tasty on Herbed Potato Rolls (see Index) 3 cups

Phyllis K. Kennedy

Strawberry Preserves

An unusual recipe which produces whole strawberries in a light syrup. Wonderful over ice cream or pancakes, or with biscuits and muffins.

2 quarts strawberries, caps removed
6 cups sugar

Place berries in a colander or piece of cheesecloth and hold under boiling water for two minutes. Drain; place in a large saucepan and add 4 cups sugar. Boil slowly for three minutes. Remove from heat and add last 2 cups of sugar. Shake the mixture, do not stir. Cool for 5 minutes. Return to heat and boil for 8 to 10 minutes, shaking the pan continuously (reduce heat if needed to keep from cooking too quickly). Cover the pan and let stand overnight. Every time you pass by the pan, shake it. The next morning, process in hot water bath for 15 minutes. Read instructions on your jar lid box to be sure you prepare them correctly to be sure they will seal. 2½ pints

Mrs. R.B. Barnett
Dunwoody, Georgia

Apple-Peach Conserve

1 can (1 pound, 6 ounces) apple-pie filling
1 package (12 ounces) frozen sliced peaches, thawed
½ cup cranberry-apple juice
Grated rind of 1 lemon

Mix all ingredients in saucepan. Bring to boil and simmer 6 to 8 minutes. Cool and serve as accompaniment for meat or as sauce for pancakes. Yield: 4 cups

Spring Conserve

1 quart strawberries, free of
 blemishes, caps removed
2 cups fresh pineapple, cubed
1 small orange, halved, seeded
 and thinly sliced (cut end
 slices into small slivers)
4 cups sugar

Combine fruit and sugar; let start overnight. The next morning, bring mixture to a boil and cook until it reaches the thickness you desire, testing by dropping small amounts onto a cold saucer. Cooking time will vary from 45 minutes to 2 hours, depending on ripeness of fruit. 1½-2 pints

Emy Blair (Mrs. H. Duane)

Pear Honey

12 cups grated firm cooking
 pears, peeled and cored
12 cups sugar
1 (1 pound 4 ounce) can
 crushed pineapple
1 lemon, thinly sliced

Put pears through coarse blade of food chopper or grate or thinly slice in food processor. Add sugar and cook on low heat, stirring occasionally until clear. Add pineapple and lemon and cook 5-10 minutes longer. Pour into hot sterilized jars and seal. 6-8 pints

Mrs. Meredith Bass
Hazlehurst, Miss.

Pineapple Chutney

1 (1 pound 4 ounce) can sliced
 pineapple, chipped
½ cup vinegar
1 cup brown sugar
½ teaspoon salt
1 or less clove garlic, pressed
¼ cup slivered blanched
 almonds
½ cup golden raisins
½ green pepper, finely chopped
2 Tablespoons crystallized
 ginger, finely chopped
Cornstarch

Cook pineapple, sugar, salt and vinegar slowly about 10 minutes. Stir in remaining ingredients; cook 10 minutes more. Thicken slightly with cornstarch.

Lou Bothwell (Mrs. Eugene)

Breads

Bread Basics

To make a loaf of bread worthy of a jug of wine and thou, it is important to use the right ingredients and the right technique.

Successful bread begins with the proper choice of flour. Most recipes in this book specify all purpose flour and are tested with nationally marketed white enriched flour which is usually a hard wheat blend. Unbleached, whole wheat, rye, and oatmeal flour may be substituted for all or part of the flour in most recipes, although substitution may require a variation in the amount of liquid needed and the length of time required for the dough to rise. Experiment with combinations of whole grain flours for improved nutrition and interesting taste and texture!

Regional brands of flour sold in the South and some states in the West are usually blends of soft wheat.

Generally, hard wheat flour is best for yeast breads; soft wheat flour makes better biscuits and muffins. The real hard wheat flour found in health food stores produces a bread that is more bakery-like in texture and volume, but is never to be used for cakes or pastries or any product where tenderness is desired. Hard and soft wheat flour blends may be used interchangeably, but remember that hard wheat flour absorbs more moisture, requires more mixing and withstands more yeast fermentation than soft wheat flour.

Bread made with milk has a finer texture, more nutritive value, and stays fresh longer than bread made with water.

Kneading doesn't mean mashing and squeezing! To knead properly, turn the dough a quarter turn with every pushing motion. Keep your fingers curved and fold the dough from the far side toward you. Push away from you with the heel of your palm, maintaining a gentle rhythm as you knead. Dough that is sufficiently kneaded looks satiny smooth, has small blisters showing under the surface and is not sticky.

Adequate rising or fermentation time is necessary for good flavor and texture. The second rising may be omitted in some instances where the first rising has been exceptionally lengthy, but is not generally recommended. Punching down the dough for a second or even third rising is recommended for high altitudes where the dough rises to double its bulk in shorter time, making additional risings necessary for superior flavor and texture. When rising time is a problem, the quantity of yeast may be doubled without changing the taste and quality, but good bread is best unhurried.

The secret of good biscuits and muffins often rests with a gentle hand in the mixing process. Remember that muffins should be lightly mixed and lumpy. A few extra strokes can ruin your muffins.

Biscuit dough should be kneaded until just light and soft, but not sticky. Overmixing the dough makes for a tough biscuit. Keep your touch soft and your biscuits will reward you!

Southern recipes with cornmeal as the primary ingredient anticipate the use of white cornmeal which gives an uneven texture, a more interesting crust and, according to any Southerner, a superior flavor. Yellow cornmeal is used when a smoother, cake-like texture is desired.

When a crisp, hard glaze is needed use an egg white slightly beaten with a small amount of water. When a richer, browner glaze is preferred beat the whole egg with a small amount of water and brush on the loaf.

Southern Biscuits

Feather light and delicious, this recipe may
make you famous for your biscuits!

Solid shortening
4 cups self-rising Southern
    soft wheat flour, such as
    White Lily or Martha White
2 heaping Tablespoons
    baking powder
1 cup solid shortening
1½ cups buttermilk

Grease baking sheet with shortening. Prepare a counter space for rolling out dough by generously sprinkling flour on it. Flour a rolling pin. Sift flour and baking powder into medium size mixing bowl. Using a pastry blender, cut in shortening. Add buttermilk and mix thoroughly with wooden spoon. Dough should be light and slightly sticky. If too dry, add more buttermilk. Pick up dough from bowl and place on floured surface. Knead lightly, folding dough inwards and sprinkling flour as needed over dough. Add enough flour so that you can handle dough easily, but maintain light consistency. Using floured rolling pin, roll out dough to ½ inch thickness. Cut with glass or biscuit cutter with diameter of 1½ inches, flouring cutting edge as needed to prevent sticking. Place biscuits on baking sheet. Cook in preheated oven at 450° for about 12 minutes or until lightly browned on top. (Place on baking sheet with sides touching for a soft sided biscuit; ½ inch apart if an all over crust is desired.) Cooked biscuits may be frozen or dough may be refrigerated for 2 days.

Cut biscuits smaller and use with ham for a cocktail party favorite. 48 biscuits

JoAnne T. Neal (Mrs. George P.)

Food Processor Biscuits

2 cups all-purpose Southern
flour
2 teaspoons baking powder
1 teaspoon salt
¼ teaspoon baking soda
3-4 Tablespoons chilled lard or
shortening
1 cup buttermilk

Place metal blade in bowl of food processor and add flour, baking powder, salt and soda. Whirl a few seconds to mix. Add lard or shortening. Process until mixture resembles coarse crumbs, about 10 seconds. Add buttermilk and process until just combined. Turn dough out onto a floured surface. Turn over a few times until surface of dough is no longer sticky. Do not knead; use as little flour as possible. Roll or pat into ½ inch thickness. Cut biscuits with a floured cutter. Bake in a 475° oven for 10 minutes or until browned. 14 biscuits

Barrie C. Aycock (Mrs. Robert R.)

Herbed Potato Rolls
A different, versatile soft roll

5½-6 cups sifted all-purpose
flour
1 package active dry yeast
¾ cup milk
4 Tablespoons butter
¼ cup sugar
1 teaspoon salt
1 can Cream of Potato Soup
1 egg
2 Tablespoons dried parsley
flakes, crushed
1 teaspoon ground sage
½ teaspoon celery seed

In large bowl of electric mixer combine 2 cups flour and yeast. In saucepan, heat milk, butter, sugar and salt to lukewarm; add to dry ingredients. Add soup and egg; beat with mixer at low speed 30 seconds, scraping sides of bowl. Beat at high speed 3 minutes. Stir in seasonings and enough flour to make soft dough. Knead on lightly floured board until smooth, 5-8 minutes. Place in greased bowl; turn once to grease top. Cover and let rise in a warm place until doubled, 50-60 minutes. Punch down. Shape into small balls. Place on greased baking sheet. Let rise until doubled, 25-30 minutes. Bake at 400° for 12 minutes or until lightly browned. May be frozen. 36 large rolls

Phyllis K. Kennedy (Mrs. Crawford)

Mrs. Smith's Refrigerator Rolls

1½ cups buttermilk
½ cup melted shortening
1 teaspoon salt
⅓ cup sugar
2 packages dry yeast
¼ cup warm water
4½ cups all purpose flour
½ teaspoon baking soda
Small amount of melted
  shortening
¼ pound butter, melted

Heat buttermilk until lukewarm (do not overheat or it will separate). Pour over melted shortening, salt and sugar. Cool. Dissolve yeast in warm water, add to buttermilk mixture and mix well. Sift together flour and soda. Add to buttermilk mixture to make a stiff dough (may need to add a little more flour). Knead slightly and place dough in a large greased bowl. Brush top with melted shortening. Cover tightly with waxed paper or foil, then a towel. Refrigerate for at least several hours. (Dough keeps for 2-3 days when refrigerated.) When ready to use, cut off desired amount, roll out to about ½ inch thick and cut with biscuit cutter dipped in flour. Dip in melted butter, fold in half and place in baking pan. Cover with waxed paper or foil and towel* and allow to rise 1 hour or until doubled in bulk. *(At this point the rolls could be refrigerated until 1 hour before desired baking time.) Bake at 425° 10-15 minutes or until golden brown. To freeze, bake only 8-10 minutes, cool and store in plastic bag in freezer. When ready to serve, warm in 250° oven for about 10 minutes. 3 dozen

Connie R. Smith (Mrs. James T., III)

Sour Cream Rolls

So easy to make at the last minute, but avoid the temptation if you're counting calories. They're addictive!

1 cup sour cream
1 stick butter or margarine,
  melted
1 cup self-rising flour

Combine all ingredients in bowl. Stir until well mixed. Bake in tiny, lightly greased muffin tins at 450° for 15 minutes. Leftovers, if any, may be reheated or eaten cold. Great with soup or drinks. 24 tiny rolls

Lee Shelnutt (Mrs. M.T.)

Baps
A French type roll
with a hard crust and a soft inside

4 cups all purpose flour
1 teaspoon salt
¾ cup milk
¾ cup water
¼ cup butter or shortening
1 package dry yeast
1 teaspoon sugar

Sift flour and salt into a large bowl. Dissolve yeast in ¼ cup warm water (100°); set aside. Combine milk and ½ cup water and heat; add butter and stir until melted. Add dissolved yeast to *lukewarm* liquid. Add sugar and stir. Make a well in the center of flour and pour in liquid mixture to form a soft dough. Add more flour if necessary. Turn out onto a floured board and knead 8-10 minutes until smooth and elastic. Put dough in a greased bowl, cover with a damp cloth and let rise 1½ hours, or until doubled in bulk. Set oven at 425°, knead dough lightly and shape into 6 loaves or 18 rolls. Sprinkle with flour and let rise again 5-10 minutes. Bake at 425° for five minutes or until pale golden. For loaves or large rolls, lower heat to 400° and bake 5-10 minutes longer. Note: These may also be shaped to form hamburger buns. May be prepared in advance and warmed in a 300° oven, or frozen. 6 small loaves or 18 dinner rolls

Nathalie Dupree
Rich's Cooking School

To re-heat rolls put them in a wet brown paper bag and then in oven.

Chili Bread
Especially good with quail, dove or any fowl

2 eggs, beaten
1 cup cream style corn
1 cup buttermilk
1½ teaspoons salt
3 teaspoons baking powder
1 cup water ground corn meal
½ cup high quality vegetable
   oil
1 small onion, chopped
2 (4 ounce) cans chopped
   green chili peppers
1 cup grated cheese

Mix eggs, corn, buttermilk, salt, baking powder and corn meal. Add the oil. Pour one half of batter into a greased 9 x 13-inch casserole dish and cover with onion, chili peppers and ½ cup cheese. Carefully pour on rest of batter and top with remaining ½ cup cheese. Bake at 325° for 1 hour. To freeze: mix, freeze and bake later. 6 servings

Carolyn S. Brooks (Mrs. John L.)

Sally Lunn

1 package active dry yeast
½ cup lukewarm milk
⅓ cup sugar
½ cup solid shortening
3 eggs
4 cups all-purpose Southern
   flour (White Lily)
1 teaspoon salt

Sprinkle yeast in warm milk. Set aside. Cream sugar and shortening. Add eggs and mix well. Combine salt with flour and add to mixture, alternating with milk and yeast mixture. Mix well after each addition. Cover and let rise in a warm spot for 1½ hours. Beat well again with electric mixer or by hand. Place batter in a well greased Bundt pan. Cover and let rise again for 1½ hours. Bake in preheated oven for 45 minutes at 350° Best when served hot. 12 servings

Mrs. Guy W. Rutland, Sr.

Beer Bread
An easy bread, suitable for informal dinners

3 cups self-rising flour
3 Tablespoons sugar
1 (12 ounce) can cold beer
½ cup melted butter

Preheat oven to 350°. Mix flour, sugar and beer well. Pour into greased 9 x 5 inch loaf pan or casserole dish. Bake at 350° for 30 minutes. Pour butter over top and cook 10 minutes more or until brown. Best when eaten warm.

Laura G. Ward (Mrs. Peter C.)

African Honey Bread

1 package dry yeast
¼ cup lukewarm water
1 egg
½ cup honey
1 Tablespoon ground coriander
½ teaspoon ground cinnamon
¼ teaspoon ground cloves
1½ teaspoons salt
1 cup lukewarm milk
6 Tablespoons melted butter
4-4½ cups all-purpose flour

Sprinkle yeast into lukewarm water. Stir to dissolve and set aside until mixture foams. Combine egg, honey, spices and salt in a deep bowl and mix well. Add yeast mixture, milk and 4 Tablespoons butter and beat until blended. Stir in flour, ½ cup at a time. When dough becomes too stiff to stir, work in remaining flour with fingers. Turn onto lightly floured surface and knead until smooth and elastic, using a small amount of melted butter on fingers to make dough more manageable. Place dough in a large, lightly buttered bowl, turning to butter all surfaces. Cover and place in a warm spot to rise until doubled in bulk. Butter the bottom and sides of a 3-quart souffle dish or two smaller ones. Punch down dough and knead lightly for 2 minutes. Shape dough into a ball and place in dish, pressing down in corners so that it covers bottom completely. Cover and let rise until double in bulk. Bake at 300° for 50-60 minutes until crust is light golden brown. Turn out on rack to cool. Loaf will peak in the center to resemble an African hut. Eat with butter and honey. 1 loaf, approximately 16 servings

Alpine Cheese Bread

1 loaf French bread
½ pound Swiss cheese
1 medium purple onion,
　chopped
3 eggs, slightly beaten
½ cup milk

Cut top off loaf and scoop out inside. Cut cheese in chunks and put into center of loaf with onion. Beat eggs and milk. Pour liquid over loaf. Bake at 375° for 30 minutes. Slice and serve hot. 12 servings

Martha H. Whitehead (Mrs. Richard)

Moroccan Bread

1 package dry yeast
¼ cup lukewarm water
1 teaspoon sugar
3½ cups unbleached flour
1 cup whole wheat flour
2 teaspoons salt
½ cup warm milk
1 teaspoon sesame seed
1 Tablespoon anise seed
Cornmeal

Soften yeast with ¼ cup sugared water. Let stand 2 minutes. Blend flours and salt. Stir yeast into flours. Add milk and lukewarm water to form a stiff dough. Knead 10-15 minutes adding more flour or water if needed to make workable. Add spices at the end of kneading. Form into 2 balls; let rest 5 minutes. Grease and flatten into 2-inch thick circles. Place on baking sheet sprinkled with corn meal. Cover with damp cloth. Let rise 2 hours. Preheat oven to 400°. Prick sides of bread with fork in 4 places. Bake 12 minutes. Lower oven to 300° and complete baking, 30 minutes. Loaves will be somewhat flat and heavy textured. Serve with any meal with a Middle-Eastern flavor. Toast leftover slices with butter; spread with honey. 2 loaves

Susan M. Morley

Southern Spoon Bread

Hot Spoon Bread, traditionally served with lots of butter, salt and pepper is also delightful with butter and peach preserves for brunch, or dinner with ham. Serve from the casserole dish.

1 cup corn meal
1 teaspoon salt
1 Tablespoon shortening
2 cups boiling water
1 cup milk
2 eggs, separated and beaten

Combine corn meal, salt and shortening; add boiling water, stir and cool. Add milk and beaten egg yolks; mix well. Fold in stiffly beaten egg whites. Pour into greased baking dish* and bake in hot oven at 400° for 30-40 minutes. Serve directly from oven as this dish falls easily.
6-8 servings

*Can be held at this point for a short time before baking.

Agnes S. McLendon

Clark Harrison's Loaf Bread

1 cup water
2 Tablespoons active dry yeast
2 Tablespoons sugar
2 eggs
1 cup shortening
3⅔ cups water
½ cup sugar
4-5 teaspoons salt
5 pounds all-purpose flour

Heat water to 105—115°. *In a small bowl combine:*
1 cup water
2 Tablespoons yeast
2 Tablespoons sugar
Stir and let sit 4-5 minutes.
In a small bowl:
2 eggs
Stir.
In a small skillet:
1 cup shortening
Melt to warm touch.
In a large dish pan:
3⅔ cups water
½ cup sugar
4-5 teaspoons salt
Combine all ingredients; stir with a large spoon. Next stir in half of the 5 pound bag of flour. Now dump in remainder of flour and knead for ten minutes. Place dough in the large greased pan and roll it around until the dough is greased. Cover with a cloth or paper towels and let rise for 1½ to 2 hours. Divide into 5 lumps. Mash each lump into a rectangle, roll rectangle up and mash again and put in a greased baking pan. Cover with a cloth or paper towel and let rise for 1½ to 2 hours. Put in a cold oven and bake 15 minutes at 400°; then reduce heat to 375° and bake 30 minutes or until browned, top and bottom. Turn out on cooling rack, paint top with butter and cover with a wet paper towel.
HINTS: For best results room temperature should be 85°; leave to rise longer in cooler room. Put aluminum foil over loaves on top rack of oven and remove for few minutes to brown. 5 loaves

Clark Harrison

Low Sugar and Low Salt White Bread
Great for those on special diets

2 cups warm water
1 package plus 1 teaspoon
    active dry yeast
1 Tablespoon margarine
3 grains saccharin
5½-6½ cups all-purpose flour
    (hard wheat if possible)
1 Tablespoon sugar
1 teaspoon salt

In mixer bowl put 2 cups warm water; sprinkle yeast over water; add saccharin; stir to mix; add margarine. To this liquid mixture add 2 cups flour, sugar and salt; beat 2 minutes with electric mixer on medium speed, scraping bowl occasionally. Add ¾ cup flour or enough to make a thick batter. Beat at high speed 2 minutes, scraping bowl occasionally. Stir in enough remaining flour with spoon to make a soft dough. Turn out onto lightly floured board and knead until smooth and elastic, 8-10 minutes. (Set timer and knead.) Place in greased airtight bowl; turn dough to grease top. Cover and let rise in warm place free from draft until double, about 1 hour. Punch down dough, divide into 2 balls, cover and let rest 10 minutes. Shape into loaves and place into 2 greased 8½ x 4½ x 2½-inch loaf pans. Cover and let rise in warm place free from draft until double, about 1 hour. Bake in 400° oven 25-30 minutes or until done. Remove from pan and cool on wire racks. 2 loaves

Marceil Joyner (Mrs. John C.)

Sesame Seed Bread

1 loaf bread, thinly sliced
2 sticks butter
3 Tablespoons sesame seeds

Cut each slice bread in half. Melt butter; dip 1 side of bread in butter and place buttered side up on a cookie sheet. Will take 2 or 3 cookie sheets depending on size. Sprinkle with sesame seeds. Place in a 250° oven for 4 hours, or until completely dried out. Store in tin when completely cooled. Serve as an accompaniment to salads. 8-12 servings

Ann Smith (Mrs. George Benton)

Earth Bread

2¼ cups boiling water
2 cups rolled oats
½ cup cracked wheat
¼ cup wheat germ
¾ cup blackstrap molasses
2 Tablespoons melted butter
1½ Tablespoons salt
2 packages dry yeast
1 cup warm milk
1 teaspoon sugar
3 cups stone ground whole
  wheat flour
2-3 cups unbleached flour
1 egg white
1 teaspoon water

Preheat oven to 375°. Pour boiling water over rolled oats, cracked wheat and wheat germ. Add molasses, butter and salt; mix well and let cool until mixture is slightly warm to touch. Meanwhile dissolve yeast in warm milk, add sugar and set aside to let mixture bubble. Combine yeast mixture with whole wheat flour and 1 cup unbleached flour; add oat mixture and mix well. Turn out onto a floured surface. Let rest for a few minutes; then knead, adding some of the remaining flour to achieve a firm, pliable consistency; it will be sticky so do not knead too much at this time. Butter a large bowl and place dough in it; cover and let rise in warm place until double in bulk. Turn out on floured surface and knead 8-10 minutes, adding more flour as necessary. Divide into halves and form 2 loaves; place in buttered 9 x 5 x 3-inch bread tins; dough should fill tins about two-thirds. Let rise again until almost doubled; dough should rise to tops of tins. Brush with egg white mixed with 1 teaspoon water. Bake for 15 minutes, then reduce heat to 350° and continue baking for 40-45 minutes until bread sounds hollow when tapped. Remove loaves from pans and return them to oven. Turn off heat and let bread cool in oven. Remove and place on racks. May be frozen. 2 loaves

Malinda M. Steed (Mrs. Richard)

Rapid-Mix Whole Wheat Bread
Loaves have full, rich, wheat flavor

4½ cups whole wheat flour
2¾ cups all-purpose flour
3 Tablespoons sugar
4 teaspoons salt
2 packages active dry yeast
1½ cups water
¾ cup milk
⅓ cup molasses
⅓ cup margarine

Combine flours. In a large bowl thoroughly mix 2½ cups of the combined flour mixture with sugar, salt and undissolved yeast. Combine water, milk, molasses and margarine in a saucepan. Heat over low heat until the liquids are warm (margarine does not need to melt). Gradually add to dry ingredients and beat 2 minutes with electric mixer at medium speed, scraping sides of bowl occasionally. Add ½ cup of remaining flour mixture, or enough to make a thick batter. Beat 2 minutes at high speed, scraping bowl occasionally. Stir in enough remaining flour mixture to make a soft dough. (If necessary add additional all-purpose flour to obtain desired consistency.) Turn dough onto lightly floured board. Knead until smooth and elastic, about 8-10 minutes. Place in greased bowl; turn dough over to grease top. Cover; let rise in warm place free from draft until doubled, about 1 hour. Punch down; turn onto lightly floured board. Divide in half. Shape into loaves. Place in 2 greased 8½ x 4½ x 2½-inch loaf pans. Cover; let rise in warm place free from draft until doubled, about 1 hour. Bake in preheated 400° oven about 25-30 minutes, or until done. Remove from pans and cool on wire racks. 2 loaves

Marceil Joyner (Mrs. John C.)

Cracked Wheat Bread
A nice nutty flavor!

1 cup milk
1½ Tablespoons shortening
1½ teaspoons salt
1½ Tablespoons molasses
1 package active dry yeast
1¼ cups warm water
1 cup rye flour
1 cup cracked wheat
4-4½ cups all-purpose flour
(hard wheat if possible)

Scald milk; add shortening, salt and molasses. Cool to lukewarm. Sprinkle yeast on warm water in large mixing bowl; stir to dissolve. Stir in rye flour, cracked wheat, 1½ cups all-purpose flour and milk mixture. Beat with electric mixer at medium speed for 2 minutes, scraping bowl occasionally. This beating process activates the yeast. Stir in remaining flour, a little at a time, to make dough that leaves the sides of the bowl. Turn onto lightly floured board and knead until satiny and elastic, about 10 minutes. Place in lightly greased bowl; turn dough over to grease top. Cover and let rise in warm place until double, 1-1½ hours. (Use an airtight bowl if available.) Punch down, cover and let rise again until double, about 45 minutes. Turn dough onto board; divide in half. Shape into balls, cover and let rest 10 minutes. Shape into loaves by beating with fist to flatten out bubbles; then roll as a jelly roll, tucking ends under at seam. Place into 2 greased 9 x 5 x 3-inch loaf pans. Cover and let rise again until double, about 1 hour. Bake at 375° for 45 minutes; cover with foil last 10 minutes to prevent excessive browning. Turn from pans to wire rack to cool.
2 loaves

Marceil Joyner (Mrs. John C.)

Pita
(Lebanese Flat Bread)
Makes enough to eat now and freeze some, too

2 packages yeast
Warm water
2 teaspoons sugar
3 pounds all-purpose flour
2 Tablespoons salt

Dissolve yeast in ¼ cup water with sugar. Combine all dry ingredients in large mixing bowl. Add yeast mixture and enough warm water to make a stiff dough. Knead until dough is stiff enough to roll. Place in bowl, cover with cloth, and let rise 2-4 hours in a warm place. When dough has doubled in size, form into orange size balls and roll in flour. (Orange size balls make loaves approximately 10-12 inches in diameter. Use an egg-size ball for sandwich size loaves.) Lay on flat surface and cover; let stand 30 minutes. Pat and roll with rolling pin until about 10-12 inches in size. Place on lower rack in oven which has been pre-heated to 450°, for 3 minutes; then under broiler for 2 minutes until speckled brown. Remove and cool. Keeps frozen for 4 months. 6 large loaves

Mrs. William Cowles

Williamsburg Orange Muffins

2 cups all-purpose flour
1 teaspoon baking soda
1 stick butter
1 cup sugar
2 eggs, beaten slightly
¾ cup buttermilk
1 cup golden raisins
1 cup nuts (pecans)
Sauce:
1 cup sugar
Juice and rind of 2 oranges
    and 1 lemon

Sift flour and soda. Cream butter and sugar; add eggs. Add sifted flour mixture and buttermilk, alternately in thirds. Add raisins and pecans. Pour into paper lined muffin tins, ½ full. Bake at 375° for 15-20 minutes.

Combine sauce ingredients and pour over muffins while they are warm. This recipe may be prepared completely in most food processors. Yield: 24 muffins or 48 petite size

Sherril Williams (Mrs. Wheat, Jr.)

Onion Cheese Bread
For a change of pace try this for sandwiches

2 packages active dry yeast
½ cup warm water
1½ cups milk, scalded
⅓ cup sugar
¼ cup butter or margarine
1 teaspoon salt
½ pound sharp Cheddar
    cheese, shredded
6-7 cups all-purpose flour
1 egg, beaten
1 envelope onion soup mix

In small bowl, soften yeast in water. In large bowl, combine milk, sugar, butter and salt; stir until butter melts. Cool to lukewarm. Stir in cheese and 2½ cups flour; blend in yeast mixture, egg and onion soup mix. Add enough flour to make a soft dough. Knead on a floured board 10 minutes, or until smooth. Place in greased bowl and grease top of dough; cover and let rise in warm place 1½ hours, or until doubled in bulk. Punch down, cut in half and shape into 2 loaves. Place in 2 greased 9 x 5 x 3-inch pans; cover and let rise 1 hour, or until doubled in bulk. Preheat oven to 375°. Bake about 30 minutes. May be frozen. 2 loaves

Lucia H. Sizemore (Mrs. Thomas A., III)

Tomato-Cheese Batter Bread

1 can condensed tomato soup
½ cup processed cheese
    spread or cheese food
2 Tablespoons butter or
    margarine
¼ cup water
¼ teaspoon baking soda
3-3¼ cups all-purpose flour
2 Tablespoons sugar
1 teaspoon salt
1 Tablespoon dill weed
2 packages active dry yeast
1 egg
12 cup fluted tube or
    Bundt pan

In medium saucepan, heat first 5 ingredients until very warm (120-130°). Lightly spoon flour into measuring cup; level off. In large bowl, combine 2 cups flour, sugar, salt, dill weed and yeast. Add warm liquid and egg to flour mixture. Blend with electric mixer at low speed until moistened; beat 2 minutes at medium speed. By hand, stir in remaining 1-1¼ cups flour to make a stiff batter. Cover and let rise in warm place until light and doubled in size, about 30 minutes. Grease pan with shortening, stir down batter and spoon evenly into pan. Cover; let rise again, approximately 30 minutes. Bake in preheated 350° oven 20-30 minutes until loaf is deep golden brown and sounds hollow when tapped lightly. Remove from pan and cool on wire rack. 25 slices

Popovers
A breeze in the food processor!

⅞ cup all purpose flour
½ teaspoon salt
½ cup milk
2 eggs
½ cup water

Sift into bowl flour and salt. Make well in center and add milk. Stir. Beat eggs until fluffy. Add beaten eggs to milk and flour; beat again. Add water. Beat until bubbles surface. (Batter may be left for 1 hour; beat again before baking.) Heat 1 teaspoon of oil in each cup of muffin tin. Pour batter in and bake 20 minutes at 400°; then 10-15 minutes at 350°.

FOOD PROCESSOR: With metal blade in place, beat eggs until fluffy; set aside. Place flour and salt in bowl and mix with on/off motion several times. Add milk, mix again. Add beaten eggs and mix for 3-4 seconds, or until bubbly.

Butter and spun honey are the perfect accompaniment
12 popovers

Marty D. Halyburton (Mrs. Porter A.)

German Oven Pancake
More like a soufflé than a pancake, it is a great innovation for breakfast!

½ cup sifted all-purpose flour
3 eggs, slightly beaten
½ cup milk
2 Tablespoons melted butter
¼ teaspoon salt

Gradually add flour to beaten eggs, beating with rotary beater. Stir in milk, butter and salt. Pour batter into greased 9-10 inch oven-safe skillet. Bake at 450° for 20 minutes. Serve hot. Cut into wedges. Sprinkle generously with powdered sugar, fresh lemon juice and melted butter, or make a syrup by stirring fresh lemon juice into powdered sugar, adding melted butter. Use approximately ¼ cup of each; adjust to taste. This makes a marvelous breakfast with bacon and fresh fruit. It is easy to make, fun to serve, but plan to get it directly from the oven to the table. 6 servings

Marty D. Halyburton (Mrs. Porter A.)

Bran Muffins

1 cup bran cereal (All Bran)
1 cup buttermilk or sour milk
1 cup all-purpose flour
1 teaspoon salt
½ teaspoon baking powder
¾ teaspoon baking soda
⅓ cup sugar
¼ cup nuts, chopped
1 Tablespoon margarine,
    melted
2 Tablespoons molasses
¼ cup honey
1 egg, slightly beaten

Mix cereal and milk and set aside for 5 minutes. Meanwhile, in food processor or by hand, mix all other ingredients in order as listed and add bran mixture last. Spoon into greased muffin tins, filling cups ⅔ full and bake at 425° for 15-20 minutes. Muffins keep well in an air-tight container. Serves 12

Jeneal Benton (Mrs. Gene R.)

Wheat Germ Muffins
Great! Even the kids like them!

1 cup whole wheat flour*
½ cup all-purpose flour*
1 cup wheat germ
¼ cup brown sugar
1 teaspoon salt
1 teaspoon baking powder
½ teaspoon soda
½ cup milk
½ cup honey
¼ cup cooking oil
1 egg, slightly beaten
*1½ cups white flour may
  be used.

Combine flours, wheat germ, brown sugar, salt, baking powder and soda. Add milk, honey, oil and egg to dry ingredients, and stir just to moisten. Do not over-mix. Fill well greased muffin cups two-thirds full. Bake at 400° for 15 minutes. Serve with butter. 12 muffins

JoAnn P. Whitehead (Mrs. Harry C.)

Date Muffins
A good luncheon companion for chicken or shrimp salad

½ cup butter, creamed
¾ cup brown sugar
½ teaspoon ground cloves
½ teaspoon nutmeg
1 teaspoon cinnamon
¼ cup water
2 eggs
1½ cups all-purpose flour
½ cup broken pecans
1 cup chopped dates

Place all ingredients except pecans and dates in a mixing bowl. Mix well with electric mixer. Fold in pecans and dates. Grease muffin tins and fill ½-¾ full. Bake 25-30 minutes at 350°. May be frozen. 12 muffins

Vonnie Powell (Mrs. J. Montgomery)

Cranberry Nut Muffins

1⅓ cups all-purpose flour
1 teaspoon baking soda
1¼ teaspoons baking powder
½ teaspoon salt
¾ cup sugar
Peel of 1 medium orange
6 Tablespoons butter
1 teaspoon lemon juice
2 eggs
¼ cup orange juice
1¼ cups fresh cranberries
1 cup chopped pecans

Mix together flour, baking soda, baking powder and salt; set aside. Place sugar and orange peel in bowl of food processor and process with metal blade until peel is finely chopped. Add butter and lemon juice and with off/on motion combine until well mixed. Add eggs and orange juice and process until smooth. Add cranberries and nuts; combine with off/on motion. Add flour mixture and combine just until flour disappears. Spoon into well greased tiny muffin tins. Bake in preheated 350° oven until golden brown, approximately 20 minutes. Remove from tins to cool. May be frozen. Serve with Cream Cheese and Marmalade Spread. Muffins may be made just as successfully with electric mixer, using grated orange peel and finely chopped cranberries.
36 tiny muffins

Hobo Bread
Great for Christmas gifts and campers

3 one pound coffee cans
1 cup white raisins
1 cup dark raisins
2 cups boiling water
4 teaspoons baking soda
2 cups sugar
¼ cup oil
½ teaspoon salt
4 cups all purpose flour
½ cup chopped nuts (optional)

Night before baking: Soak raisins in boiling water. Add baking soda and cover container tightly.
Next day: Add sugar, oil, salt, flour and nuts to raisin mixture. Mix well with wooden spoon. Grease and flour coffee cans and fill each ½ full. Bake at 350° for one hour. Take out of oven and let set for five minutes. Remove bread from cans and let cool. Return bread to cans and cover with plastic lids. Store in refrigerator. Will keep up to 6 months. Serve with butter or cream cheese. Yield: 3 loaves, 12 slices per loaf

Mrs. Jack Mielke

Banana Nut Bread
A better banana bread!
Very moist and flavorful

4 ripe bananas
2 large eggs
1 teaspoon lemon juice
Grated rind of ½ lemon
½ cup bran cereal
1½ cups sifted all-purpose
  flour
¾ cup sugar
1 teaspoon salt
1 teaspoon baking soda
¼ cup wheat germ
½ cup chopped walnuts or
  pecans

Beat together in large mixing bowl, bananas, eggs, lemon juice and rind. Add bran and allow to soften for 5 minutes. Beat. Sift together flour, sugar, salt and baking soda. Add to banana mixture and beat. Stir in wheat germ and nuts. Grease and flour one 9 x 5-inch loaf pan or three 5¾ x 3¼-inch miniature loaf pans. Pour batter into pan(s) and bake at 350° for 50-60 minutes. Test with a toothpick. May be frozen.
1 large loaf

Barbara R. Schuyler (Mrs. Lambert, Jr.)

German Butterkuchen
Rich, tasty and worth the effort

1 cup milk
½ cup sugar
1 teaspoon salt
¼ cup butter
1½ packages active dry yeast
1 teaspoon sugar
¼ warm water
2 eggs
3¼ cups unsifted all-purpose
  flour
⅓ cup chopped almonds
Butter Topping:
1 cup sugar
½ cup butter
½ teaspoon cinnamon

Scald milk. Add ½ cup sugar, salt and shortening. Dissolve yeast and 1 teaspoon sugar in warm water; stir into cooled milk mixture. Beat eggs with 1 cup flour. Add the remaining flour alternately with milk and yeast mixture. Mix well after each addition. Add almonds. Dough will be very soft and sticky. Pour into greased 9 x 13-inch pan, spreading evenly. Set in a warm place to rise. Let rise at least one hour. Cut ingredients for topping together to form fine crumb mixture. Sprinkle topping over dough and bake at 375° for 30 minutes. Delicious for breakfast or dessert.

Maddy S. Kligora (Mrs. John)

"Squiggles"

Try these for breakfast in place of pancakes or French toast.
Invite the children to help and plan on a mess!

2 eggs, beaten
1½ cups milk
2 cups all-purpose flour
1 teaspoon baking powder
½ teaspoon salt
2 cups oil
powdered sugar

Combine eggs and milk. Sift together flour, baking powder and salt. Add to egg mixture. Beat until smooth with rotary mixer. In an 8-inch skillet heat oil to 360°. Pour batter in funnel and release from spout or pour from measuring cup in a narrow stream to form spiral shapes or circles. (Cakes may be formed in any shape, including alphabet letters for initials of the children assisting. Shapes should be kept 3-4 inches in circumference for ease in handling.) Fry until golden (3 minutes); turn carefully and brown other side. Drain on paper towel and sprinkle with powdered sugar. Serve hot with syrup. 8 servings

Kimpy Edge (Mrs. J. Dexter, Jr.)

Dutch Pannekoek

Served in Holland with fried bacon or thinly sliced apples
as a filling, this is a brunch or supper dish. Although
basically a crêpe recipe, the pancake is
thicker and larger in size.

1 cup cold water
1 cup cold milk
5 eggs
¼ teaspoon salt
2 cups sifted all-purpose flour
5 Tablespoons butter, melted
Thinly sliced apples or cooked
**   bacon for filling**

In blender or food processor, mix ingredients to form batter. Let stand overnight in refrigerator for best results, but it is not absolutely necessary. Oil and heat an 8 or 10-inch skillet. Pour enough batter to cover bottom well. Add apple or cooked bacon over top; cover with a little more batter. When bubbles appear and pancake lifts easily, turn it and brown slightly on other side. Serve immediately with lots of powdered sugar on top or stack pancakes on plate, cover with a damp tea towel and keep warm in oven for as long as needed.

Joan Roes (Mrs. Hans)

Sour Cream Pecan Coffee Cake

1 cup margarine or butter
2 cups sugar
2 eggs
2 cups flour, sifted
1 teaspoon baking powder
¼ teaspoon salt
½ teaspoon vanilla
1 cup sour cream
TOPPING AND FILLING:
3 Tablespoons brown sugar
½ teaspoon cinnamon
½ cup pecans, chopped

Cream margarine or butter and sugar; add eggs and beat. Sift dry ingredients and add to creamed mixture. Add vanilla, fold in sour cream and mix carefully. Spoon ½ topping mixture into a greased and floured Bundt or tube pan. Cover with ½ of batter. Spoon on rest of topping and cover with batter. Bake at 350° for 55-60 minutes. (Do not overbake.) Toothpick will come out clean. Let sit for 10 minutes. Run sharp knife around edge. Invert on plate. Sprinkle with powdered sugar when cool. Hint: This cake keeps well several days when wrapped in plastic wrap. 12-15 servings

Carolyn Hoose (Mrs. Kenneth A., Jr.)

Puffy French Toast with Orange Sauce

This recipe was served on trains back in the days of first class pullman travel

Batter:
1 cup all-purpose flour
1½ teaspoon sugar
1½ teaspoon baking powder
½ teaspoon salt
¼ teaspoon cinnamon
1 cup milk
1 egg, beaten
8 slices white bread
Oil for frying

Mix dry ingredients. Blend milk and egg; combine with flour mixture and beat until smooth. Dip bread slices into batter. Fry in deep fat 375° until golden brown (about 2 minutes on each side). Drain on paper towels. Serve hot with orange sauce. 8 servings

Orange sauce:
1 Tablespoon cornstarch
½ cup sugar
½ teaspoon salt
1 cup orange juice
2 teaspoons grated orange rind
⅛ teaspoon nutmeg
1 Tablespoon butter
1 orange, sectioned

Mix together cornstarch, sugar and salt in saucepan. Gradually stir in juice; add rind. Cook over medium heat until mixture comes to a boil, stirring constantly. Add nutmeg, butter and orange sections. Beat until well mixed. Yield: 1¼ cups

**Southern Plantation Cookbook
Corinne Carlton Geer**

Danish Pastry Puff

1 cup sifted all-purpose flour
½ cup margarine
2 Tablespoons water
½ cup margarine
1 cup water
1 teaspoon almond extract
1 cup sifted flour
3 eggs
1½ cups powdered sugar
Almond extract
Sliced Almonds
Maraschino Cherries

Cut ½ cup margarine into 1 cup sifted flour. Sprinkle with 2 Tablespoons water and mix with fork. Round into ball and divide in half. Pat each half into a strip 12 x 3 inches and place strips 3 inches apart on an ungreased baking sheet. Mix second ½ cup margarine and 1 cup water in saucepan. Bring to a boil and add almond extract. Remove from heat. Stir in 1 cup flour immediately. (Must be stirred in while liquid is very hot to prevent lumping.) When smooth and thick, add 1 egg at a time, beating until smooth after each. Divide mixture in half and spread over strips of pastry. Bake at 350° for 45-60 minutes until crisp and light brown. Cool. Add to powdered sugar enough almond extract to make spreadable consistency. Frost pastry and sprinkle with almonds and cherries. May be frozen. 2 loaves

Karen DeFazio (Mrs. Richard)

Wales Kringle
A not-too-sweet to serve with coffee

1 cup all-purpose flour
¼ teaspoon salt
½ cup margarine
1 cup water
4 eggs
Glaze:
Confectioners sugar mixed
   with water, almond and rum
   flavorings to taste

Sift flour and salt. Heat water to a boil and add margarine, stir until melted. Add flour and salt at once. Stir until combined. Remove from heat and add eggs, one at a time, stirring after each until smooth. Drop mixture by spoonfuls onto a cookie sheet forming two 12-inch circles or a Kringle (figure 8) shape. Bake at 425° for about 30 minutes or until puffed and brown. Cool slightly and glaze. 4-6 servings

Winnie R. Goodman (Mrs. James E.)

Wine and Cheese Spread
Have your wine, cheese and bread all in one!
This recipe is designed for cooks who like to taste and adjust!

Dehydrated minced onion
Dry wine (red or white)
8 ounce package cream
cheese, softened

Pour wine over dried onion to soften (start with approximately equal amounts of each). When soft, blend with cream cheese in food processor, blender or mixer. Taste and adjust! Spread over warm French or Italian bread or spoon over spaghetti, lasagna or ravioli.

Cream Cheese and Marmalade Spread

1 (8 ounce) package cream
cheese, softened
½ cup marmalade (orange,
grapefruit—your choice)

Blend cream cheese and marmalade in food processor or mixer until well mixed. Adds an extra spark to almost any fruit bread or muffins. Also very good on a warmed slice of pound cake.

Orange Butter

Juice of 2 oranges or
2 Tablespoons undiluted
frozen orange juice
Rind of 2 oranges
1 cup plus 2 Tablespoons
powdered sugar
1 cup butter

Mix all ingredients in blender or food processor. Put in small mold and chill before serving. Excellent on blueberry muffins. Serve for dinner with any bread that is compatible with a fruit spread.

Elise M. Griffin

Desserts and Sweets

Sweetened Condensed Milk
A new old standby for your recipe file

1 cup instant dry milk
⅔ cup sugar
⅓ cup boiling water
3 Tablespoons melted butter

Combine ingredients. Makes same amount as 1 (15-ounce) can condensed milk.

Basic Crêpe Batter

1 cup flour
1 egg plus 1 yolk
1 cup milk
¼ cup water
Cooking oil

Mix flour, egg plus yolk and milk lightly. Let mixture sit at least ½ hour (overnight if possible). Add water. Season crêpe pan with 1 Tablespoon oil; pour excess into batter. Into a hot pan, pour just enough batter to barely cover bottom of pan (tilt pan to cover with batter; pour remainder back into bowl) and cook until edges begin to turn brown. Turn crêpe and cook a few seconds more. Cool on a wire rack. Crêpes may be frozen between sheets of wax paper. Fill with desired filling. 16 crêpes

Nathalie Dupree
Rich's Cooking School

Dessert Crêpe Filling

1 (8-ounce) package cream cheese
1 egg, slightly beaten
¼ cup sugar (or more to taste)
1 teaspoon vanilla
1 pint strawberries, or blueberries, sweetened if desired

In food processor or by hand, blend cream cheese, egg, sugar and vanilla. Spoon about 1½ Tablespoons mixture down the center of each crêpe. Fold and place, seam side down, on a serving plate. Top with fruit.

Lemon Filling For Crêpes

½ cup sugar
¼ cup butter, softened
1 Tablespoon lemon juice
(or more to taste)
grated rind of 1-2 lemons

Cream butter and sugar; add rind and juice to taste. Place a tablespoon of mixture in the center of each crêpe. Roll up and place in a baking dish. Heat at 300° until heated through. Spoon excess sauce from dish over crepes. Crêpes may be frozen after filling. Put frozen crêpes in oven until heated through.

Nathalie Dupree
Rich's Cooking School

Lemon Curd
Versatile and delicious

1 stick butter, softened
1½ cups sugar
4 eggs
Grated rind and juice of 4
lemons

Cream butter and sugar. Add eggs 1 at a time. Add rind and lemon juice. Cook in heavy saucepan over very low heat until thick and shiny. You must stir at all times. If egg whites cook, strain to remove. Store in pint jar in refrigerator up to 2 weeks. Serve in pastry tart shells, over ice cream or on a toasted English muffin. Does not freeze. 1 pint

Mrs. Meredith Bass
Hazlehurst, Miss.

Sabayon à la Creole

1 cup sugar
6 egg yolks
½ teaspoon vanilla
1 cup sweet or dry white wine
1 Tablespoon orange peel
5 Tablespoons Grand Marnier
1 cup heavy cream, whipped

Beat eggs and sugar until ribbon forms. Add vanilla, wine and orange peel. Cook in double boiler over low heat. Whisk until frothy. Cool by placing bowl of double boiler into larger bowl of cold water, continuing to whisk. Add Grand Marnier and whipped cream. Mix rapidly and chill. Serve with lace cookies or over pound cake, fruit, or cooked custards.

Citrus Soufflé

10 egg yolks
1 cup sugar
Zest of 2 lemons
Zest of 2 limes
½ cup lemon juice
½ cup lime juice
¼ teaspoon salt
2 envelopes unflavored gelatin
½ cup rum or Grand Marnier
10 egg whites
1 cup sugar
2 cups heavy cream
1 cup heavy cream
2 Tablespoons sugar
Candied violets (optional)

Beat egg yolks until light and fluffy. Gradually add 1 cup sugar. Beat until mixture forms ribbon. Add zests, juices and salt. Beat thoroughly . Pour into heavy pan and cook over low heat, stirring until thick and coats spoon. Pour into bowl and cool. Sprinkle gelatin over rum or Grand Marnier. Set aside until mixture solidifies. Beat egg whites until foamy. Gradually add 1 cup sugar and beat until like marshmallow. Set aside. Beat 2 cups cream until it mounds (not stiff). Dissolve solidified gelatin over low heat and add yolk mixture. Fold in egg whites and 2 cups whipped cream. Pour into 2-quart soufflé dish with an oiled collar. Chill 3 or more hours. Remove collar. Whip 1 cup cream and 2 Tablespoons sugar. Pour on top of soufflé. Decorate with candied violets. Spoon into iced stemmed sherbet glasses. Do not freeze. 12 servings

Mrs. Carl Welch

HINT

Before peeling oranges, cover with boiling water and let stand 5 minutes. The bitter white membrane can be removed more easily.

Chilled Peach Soufflé
Very light and refreshing

½ cup sugar
1 envelope unflavored gelatin
¼ teaspoon ground nutmeg
⅛ teaspoon salt
½ cup water
4 beaten egg yolks
1 Tablespoon lemon juice
½ teaspoon vanilla
4-5 drops almond extract
4 large peaches
4 stiffly beaten egg whites
½ cup heavy cream

In a 2-quart saucepan, combine sugar, gelatin, nutmeg, and salt. Stir in water. Stir over low heat until gelatin dissolves. Gradually stir hot mixture into beaten egg yolks. Return to saucepan and add lemon juice. Cook and stir until thickened. Remove from heat. Stir in vanilla and almond extracts. Peel, pit, and slice 2 of the peaches (should have 1½ cups). Place sliced peaches in blender and blend until finely chopped. Stir into gelatin mixture. Chill until partially set. Peel, pit and chop remaining peaches; fold into gelatin mixture. Fold in stiffly beaten egg whites. Whip cream; fold into gelatin. Chill until mixture mounds when dropped from a spoon. Turn into a 1½-quart soufflé dish. Chill until firm. Garnish with toasted almonds and peach slices if desired. May be prepared the day before serving. 8 servings

Joan M. Adams (Mrs. John P., Jr.)

MICROWAVE HINT ▬▬▬▬▬▬

Heat brandy for flaming desserts in a glass cup for 10-15 seconds.

MICROWAVE HINT ▬▬▬▬▬▬

To soften "overly dried" dried fruits, sprinkle with ½ to 1 teaspoon water, cover tightly and heat in microwave oven 15 to 45 seconds.

Cold Lemon Soufflé with Wine Sauce
Elegant summertime treat

1 package unflavored gelatin
¼ cup cold water
5 eggs, separated
1½ cups sugar
¾ cup fresh lemon juice
2 teaspoons grated lemon rind
1 cup heavy cream
WINE SAUCE:
½ cup sugar
1 Tablespoon cornstarch
¼ cup water
1 Tablespoon lemon juice
1 teaspoon grated lemon rind
2 Tablespoons butter
½ cup dry white wine

Sprinkle gelatin over water to soften. Mix 5 egg yolks with lemon juice and rind and ¾ cup of sugar. Place in top of double boiler, cook stirring constantly until lemon mixture is slightly thickened—about 8 minutes. Remove from heat and stir in gelatin until dissolved. Chill 30-40 minutes until mixture mounds slightly when dropped from spoon. Beat egg whites until stiff, gradually adding the remaining ¾ cup sugar. Beat cream until stiff. Fold egg whites and cream into yolk mixture until no white streaks remain. Pour into a 2-quart soufflé dish and chill 4 hours or more.
6-8 servings
WINE SAUCE:
    In small saucepan, mix sugar and cornstarch. Stir in water, lemon juice and rind until smooth. Add butter. Bring to boil, lower heat and cook until thickened. Add wine, chill, stirring occasionally.

Frozen Lemon Mousse

2-3 cups graham cracker
    crumbs
1 cup sugar
3 egg yolks
Juice of 2 lemons
1 Tablespoon water
Grated lemon rind
1 large can evaporated milk,
    chilled
3 egg whites, stiffly beaten

Sprinkle two-thirds of crumbs into a buttered 2 quart oblong casserole. Cook sugar, egg yolks, lemon juice and water in top of double boiler until mixture coats spoon. Cool. Add grated lemon rind. Whip chilled milk until stiff. Fold in egg whites and add cooked, cooled mixture. Pour over top of crumbs and sprinkle with remaining crumbs. Freeze. Remove from freezer several minutes before serving to soften.
8 servings

Eleanor R. McCormack (Mrs. Wayne)

Frozen Soufflé with Hot Strawberry Sauce

½ gallon vanilla ice cream,
   softened
12 almond macaroons,
   crumbled
5 Tablespoons Grand Marnier
2 cups heavy cream
½ cup chopped toasted
   almonds
Confectioners sugar
HOT STRAWBERRY SAUCE:
1 quart fresh strawberries,
   cleaned and halved
   or 3 (10-ounce) packages
   frozen sliced strawberries
Sugar
5 Tablespoons Grand Marnier

Soften ice cream slightly. Stir in crumbled macaroons and Grand Marnier. Whip cream until thick and shiny. Fold into ice cream mixture. Spoon into an angel food cake pan. Sprinkle surface lightly with almonds and confectioners sugar. Cover with plastic wrap. Freeze until firm, about 4-5 hours or overnight. Unmold onto cold platter. Return to freezer until serving time. 12 servings
SAUCE:
Just before serving, put berries in a saucepan with sugar (about ½ cup for fresh berries; less for frozen); simmer until soft, but not mushy. Remove from heat; stir in Grand Marnier. Serve frozen soufflé and top with sauce.

Joan M. Adams (Mrs. John P., Jr.)

Mousse à L'Orange

3 egg yolks
⅓ cup sugar
1 Tablespoon unflavored
   gelatin
¼ cup cold water
1 cup fresh orange juice
1 Tablespoon cornstarch
1 Tablespoon grated orange
   peel
3 egg whites
¼ cup heavy cream, whipped
Orange shells
Whipped cream flavored with
   Grand Marnier or Cointreau

Beat egg yolks and sugar until light and fluffy. Sprinkle gelatin over cold water to soften. Then combine gelatin with orange juice, cornstarch and orange peel. Heat this mixture in a saucepan just to the boiling point. Add it gradually to the egg yolks, beating briskly as you do until thickened. Let cool. Fold in beaten egg whites and whipped cream. Pour into orange shells or individual glasses. Top with whipped cream flavored with liqueur. 4-6 servings

Fran Scott (Mrs. Romney E.)

Vanilla Soufflé with Cold Raspberry Sauce
Make the sauce first and serve very cold over the hot soufflé

Soufflé

2 Tablespoons butter
2 Tablespoons flour
1 cup milk, heated
½ cup sugar
¼ teaspoon vanilla
5 egg yolks, beaten
6 egg whites

Preheat oven to 350°
    Melt butter in top of double boiler; stir in flour, cook one minute; add hot milk and sugar. Stir until thick and smooth. Remove from heat, add vanilla. Add beaten yolks and let cool until you can comfortably hold the bowl in palm of hand. Beat whites until stiff but not dry. Add a large spoonful to yolks to lighten the sauce, folding until mixture is slightly foamy. Pour over remaining whites and fold in carefully until thoroughly mixed. Slide into a buttered and sugared 2-quart soufflé dish. Bake 20 minutes or until top of soufflé jiggles only slightly when dish is pushed. 4 servings

Raspberry Sauce

2 Tablespoons cornstarch
½ cup water
¼ cup currant jelly
1 (10-ounce) package frozen raspberries, partially thawed

Over medium heat, blend cornstarch, water and jelly until thick. Stir in raspberries, chill until serving.

Cookbook Committee

Carnival Cream

8 eggs, separated
1 cup sugar
¾ cup rum or brandy
2 envelopes unflavored gelatin
½ cup cold water
½ cup hot water
1 teaspoon vanilla
Lady fingers
1 cup heavy cream, whipped
½ cup chopped almonds
½ cup almond macaroon crumbs

Beat egg whites until stiff; gradually add sugar. Beat egg yolks until thick and yellow; add rum or brandy and fold into whites. Soften gelatin in cold water, dissolve in hot water. Cool and fold into egg mixture. Add vanilla. Line ring mold with lady fingers and pour in mixture. Chill until set. Unmold and fill center with whipped cream mixed with nuts and macaroon crumbs. 10 servings

Susan N. Barton (Mrs. David L.)

Orange Charlotte
A scrumptious orange cloud for dessert!

1⅓ Tablespoons unflavored
    gelatin
⅓ cup cold water
⅓ cup boiling water
1 cup sugar
3 Tablespoons fresh lemon
    juice
1 cup fresh orange juice
1 cup heavy cream
2 teaspoons vanilla flavoring
3 egg whites
Cherries and nuts if desired
    for garnish

Soften gelatin in cold water. Dissolve in boiling water. Add sugar and stir until dissolved over low heat if necessary. Add lemon juice and orange juice to mixture. Chill in refrigerator until mixture begins to congeal slightly. Whip cream, flavor with vanilla and fold into juice mixture. Fold in beaten egg whites. Return to refrigerator until firm. Garnish with cherries and nuts. May be served in individual dishes or crystal bowl. Note: Use a sweet and juicy orange for the best taste. Hint: Frozen concentrate may be used in place of fresh orange juice. 6-8 servings

Mrs. Walter P. McCurdy, Sr.

Peach Crème Brulée
Crème de la Crème

3 cups heavy cream
6 egg yolks
6 Tablespoons sugar
Dash salt
1 teaspoon vanilla
¾ cup light brown sugar
raspberry jam—1 teaspoon
    per peach half
10-12 canned peach halves,
    drained well

Heat cream in top of double boiler. Beat egg yolks, sugar, salt in bowl until light and fluffy. Add warm cream gradually to egg mixture. Pour mix back into double boiler and cook, stirring constantly, until custard coats spoon (do not have water boiling). Cool. Arrange peach halves in shallow baking dish and spoon 1 teaspoon jam in each peach center. Pour the cooled cream mix over peaches and chill overnight. Next day, cover custard with sifted brown sugar about ¼ inch thick. Broil 6-9 inches away from heat until sugar melts and bubbles. Be very careful that sugar does not burn. Refrigerate until ready to serve. 8-10 servings

Almond Custard
Very rich with florentine quality
Well worth the expensive ingredients

3 cups heavy cream
⅔ cup sugar
Dash salt
½ cup almond paste
8 egg yolks
1 teaspoon vanilla
½ cup slivered toasted
   almonds (or sliced)

8 servings

Heat first four ingredients carefully until almond paste melts. Do not boil. Remove from heat and add the beaten egg yolks, vanilla, and almonds. Pour into custard cups and place in hot water bath. Bake at 350° for 20-25 minutes until a knife inserted near rim of cup comes out clean. Serve at room temperature. Hint: Pour a small amount of the hot mixture into the egg yolk mixture stirring all the while. Then pour the yolks into the remaining hot mixture, again stirring all the while so you do not get scrambled eggs.

Classic Flan

½ cup sugar
2 cups heavy cream
¼ cup sugar
3 eggs
1 teaspoon vanilla

The day before serving, melt ½ cup sugar until brown but not too dark. Pour immediately into 1 quart casserole. Scald cream. Beat eggs with ¼ cup sugar and add to cream. Add vanilla. Stir until sugar dissolves. Pour into casserole. Bake inside another dish, pour boiling water in to reach halfway up inside dish. Bake at 325° until knife inserted near center comes out clean, about 1 hour. Chill in form overnight. Turn out upside down to serve. May also be made in individual custard cups lined with the caramelized sugar. Note: Milk may be substituted for cream but flan will not be as creamy.

Beth Koenig (Mrs. William)

Before scalding milk, rinse pan in cold water to avoid coating.

Flan De Queso
A flan with a flair

CARAMEL:
1½ cups sugar
⅓ cup water
CUSTARD:
1 (8-ounce) package cream cheese
4 eggs
1 can sweetened condensed milk plus 1 can water
3 slices white bread
Almond slivers (optional)

Caramel: Heat sugar and water in a heavy saucepan stirring constantly until sugar melts and turns light amber. Pour immediately into an 8-inch square pan tipping until bottom is coated with caramel. Cool while making custard.

Custard: Heat oven to 350°. Put all ingredients except almonds into blender. Cover and process at "stir" until well mixed. Pour into caramel-coated pan. Add almonds. Cover and place in larger pan containing hot water. Bake 1 hour and 15 minutes, or until a silver knife inserted at center comes out clean. Cool about 2 hours then remove custard from mold.
10-12 servings

Susan M. Morley

President's Pudding

½ cup vanilla wafer or graham cracker crumbs
1 envelope Dream Whip
6 ounces cream cheese
1½ cups confectioners sugar
½ cup smooth peanut butter
1 teaspoon vanilla
¾ cup sweet milk
¾ cup crushed salted peanuts

At least 4 hours before serving, prepare 8-10 custard cups placing 2 teaspoons crumbs in each. Whip Dream Whip as directed on package and set aside. Cream together cream cheese, sugar and peanut butter. Add milk and vanilla. Fold in prepared Dream Whip and spoon into custard cups. Top with crushed salted peanuts. Freeze for at least 4 hours. Will keep indefinitely. Note: The size of custard cups determines the number of servings obtained.
8-10 servings

Mrs. Lupo
Mary Mac's Tea Room
Atlanta, Georgia

Devonshire Cream

This is also lovely served in
miniature pastry shells with coffee after dinner

1 (8-ounce) package cream
   cheese, softened
½ cup confectioners sugar,
   sifted
¼ cup heavy cream
1 egg yolk
2 Tablespoons brandy
Fresh fruit of your choice
TO SEAL FRUIT:
2 Tablespoons apricot
   preserves
2 teaspoons kirsch

In bowl of mixer or food
processor beat cream cheese,
sugar, cream and egg yolk until
light. Stir in brandy. Divide into 4
stemmed champagne glasses.
Refrigerate at least 2 hours before
serving. Decorate with any fresh
fruit combination—mandarin
oranges and blueberries are pretty.
Seal fruit with apricot preserves
and kirsch. Heat and paint on.
This will seal and keep colors true.
4 servings

Fran Scott (Mrs. Romney E.)

Strawberry Bread Pudding

1 (10-ounce) package frozen
   strawberries, thawed
2 Tablespoons cornstarch
Few drops red food coloring
2 eggs, slightly beaten
2½ cups milk
½ cup sugar
2 Tablespoons butter, melted
½ teaspoon vanilla extract
¼ teaspoon salt
4 slices bread, cut in ½ inch
   cubes (about 4 cups)

In a small saucepan combine
undrained strawberries and cornstarch. Cook and stir over medium
heat until mixture thickens and
bubbles. Stir in food coloring.
Spread mixture evenly over
bottom of a 6 x 10 x 2-inch baking
dish. In a mixing bowl, combine
eggs, milk, sugar, butter, vanilla
and salt. Add bread cubes; stir to
moisten. Carefully pour custard
mixture over berries. Bake at
350° for 50-55 minutes. Serve
warm. 6-8 servings

Linda D. Bobo (Mrs. W. Earl)

Boston Cream Pie

A very old New England recipe from a nineteenth century "gourmet" cook

CAKE:
1 cup flour
1 cup sugar
2 teaspoons baking powder
Dash salt
½ cup milk
1 Tablespoon butter
2 eggs, separated
FILLING:
2 cups milk
½ cup flour
½ cup sugar
2 eggs, beaten
Dash salt
1 Tablespoon butter
1 teaspoon vanilla
1 cup heavy cream, whipped
FROSTING:
3 squares unsweetened
  chocolate
¾ cup sugar
6 Tablespoons milk
1½ Tablespoons butter
½ teaspoon vanilla

Cake: Sift dry ingredients together. Scald milk and butter; add dry ingredients. Add beaten yolk. Whip egg whites stiff. Fold into mixture. Bake in 2 round cake pans at 375° for approximately 20 minutes.

Filling: Scald milk. Mix flour and sugar and add to beaten eggs in double boiler. Add milk gradually and cook until thick. Remove from heat and add salt, butter and vanilla. Cool and add whipped cream.

Frosting: Melt chocolate, sugar and milk*. Boil 2 minutes. Remove from heat and add butter and vanilla. Beat well.

*A little more milk may be needed to achieve a smooth consistency.

Split both layers of cake. Put filling between layers. Frost top with chocolate. Makes 2-two layer cakes or 1-four layer cake. Refrigerate. 8 servings

Mrs. Alfred J. Westcott
Norfolk, Virginia

Chocolate Pastry Cake

8 ounces sweet chocolate
½ cup sugar
½ cup water
1½ teaspoons instant coffee
2 teaspoons vanilla
2 cups heavy cream
CRUST:
1 (9 or 10-ounce) package pie
crust mix or make your
own pastry: 1 teaspoon
salt, 2 cups flour, ⅔ cup
shortening. Add no liquid.
Blend.

At least 8 hours before serving, in saucepan combine chocolate, sugar, water and coffee. Cook over low heat stirring constantly until smooth. Add vanilla. Cool to room temperature or pastry will melt. Blend ¾ cup chocolate sauce into pastry mixture. Divide pastry mixture into 6 equal parts. Press each part over bottom of an inverted 8-inch round cake pan to ½ inch from edge. Do in relays as to how many pans you have. Bake at 425° for 5 minutes until done. Cool. Then run tip of knife under edges to loosen. Lift off carefully. Whip cream until it just begins to hold soft peaks. Fold in remaining chocolate sauce. Stack baked pastries spreading chocolate cream between layers and over top. Chill at least 8 hours or overnight. 1 cake

Patricia H. Adams (Mrs. P.H.)

Layered Chocolate Cream
A make ahead success

½ cup margarine
1½ cups graham cracker
crumbs
½ cup chopped nuts
8 ounces cream cheese,
softened
1 cup sugar
1½ cups whipped topping
2 small packages instant
chocolate pudding
3 cups milk
Additional whipped topping

Melt margarine in oblong baking dish (11¾ x 7½ x 1¾-inch) in oven; add crumbs and nuts. Press in pan to form crust. Bake at 350° for about 5 minutes. Blend cream cheese and sugar well; fold in whipped topping. Put this on top of crust in mounds and spread. Prepare pudding following package directions except use 3 cups milk. Blend 2 minutes. Layer chocolate on top of cream cheese layer. Top with additional whipped topping and sprinkle with nuts. For a bit of a difference try whipped cream in place of whipped topping. Chill.

Mrs. Richard A. Smith

Boccone Dolce
A favorite all around

4 egg whites
Dash salt
¼ teaspoon cream of tartar
1 cup sugar
1 (6-ounce) package chocolate
    chips
3 Tablespoons water
3 cups heavy cream, whipped
⅓ cup sugar
1 pint fresh strawberries,
    sliced (Save a few whole
    ones for garnish.)

Preheat oven to 250°. Beat egg whites, with salt and cream of tartar until stiff. Gradually add sugar and beat until meringue is stiff and glossy. Line three 8-inch pans with waxed paper, or trace three 8-inch circles on waxed paper and bake on cookie sheet. Spread meringues on circles ¼ inch thick and bake 20-25 minutes until pale gold and still pliable. Remove from oven and peel waxed paper from bottom and allow to dry on racks. Melt chocolate and water in double boiler over boiling water. Whip cream until stiff. Gradually add sugar and beat until very stiff. Place 1 meringue on serving plate, spread with a thin layer of chocolate, ¾-inch layer of cream, and layer of strawberries. Repeat. Top third layer with only cream. Frost sides with remaining cream. Decorate top with whole strawberries. Refrigerate until ready to serve. Hint: Meringue layers may be made ahead and kept in an airtight container.
8 servings

Barbara Johnson (Mrs. Larry)

HINT

When melting chocolate in your double boiler, line the top with wax paper to save chocolate and dishwashing.

HINT

Sift powdered sugar to prevent lumping.

Chocolate Roulade

This elegant and easy dessert recipe may be doubled or frozen

6 ounces semi-sweet chocolate
3-4 Tablespoons water
5 eggs, separated
1 cup sugar
½ cup chopped pecans (optional)
Confectioners sugar
FILLING:
2 cups heavy cream, whipped
¼ cup sugar
Flavoring, if desired (rum, brandy, vanilla extract, etc.)

Oil a 10 x 15-inch jelly roll pan. Line with wax paper extending paper over sides of pan. Oil paper. Place chocolate and water in a saucepan over low heat to melt; set aside to cool. Beat egg yolks until thick and lemon colored. Add sugar. Beat egg whites until stiff. Stir cooled chocolate into egg yolk mixture. Fold in pecans if desired. Fold in a large spoonful of egg whites to soften mixture; then fold in remaining whites as lightly as possible. Spread mixture in prepared pan and bake at 350° for 25-30 minutes. Remove from oven and cool to room temperature. Cover with a lightweight dish towel which is only slightly damp. Refrigerate overnight, if possible. To assemble: Remove cloth and turn roulade out on wax paper which has been dusted with confectioners sugar. Carefully remove all paper from top of cake. trim rough edges. Spread cake with 1½ cups whipped cream to which sugar and any desired flavoring has been added. Roll up like a jelly roll, sprinkle generously with confectioners sugar and decorate with remaining whipped cream. Serve within 2-3 hours or freeze. If frozen, defrost in refrigerator or serve partially frozen. 6 servings

Nathalie Dupree
Rich's Cooking School

Almond Butter Cream Roll
Serve with tart strawberries for a wonderful combination

3 eggs, separated
1 teaspoon cider vinegar
½ cup sugar
½ teaspoon almond extract
½ cup flour, sifted
⅛ teaspoon salt
ALMOND BUTTER CREAM:
⅓ cup butter, softened
3 cups powdered sugar, sifted
Few drops almond extract
About 2 Tablespoons milk or
    cream
1 egg yolk

Oil a jelly roll pan well—also oil brown paper well (cut to fit pan). Beat yolks until they form a ribbon. Beat whites with vinegar until they form soft peaks, gradually adding sugar and extract, beat until stiff. Fold in beaten yolks. Sift flour and salt over top and fold in. Spread batter in pan. Bake at 400° for 12-15 minutes. Turn out on dish towel which has been sprinkled with powdered sugar. Strip off paper and roll up in towel. Let cool. Unroll. Mix all ingredients together for Almond Butter Cream and spread on baked cake. Reroll. Sprinkle with powdered sugar. May be frozen.

Sylvia Dorough (Mrs. Don)

Blitz Torte

½ cup butter, softened
¾ cup confectioners sugar
4 egg yolks, beaten
1 cup flour
1 teaspoon baking powder
½ teaspoon salt
3 Tablespoons milk
4 egg whites
½ cup confectioners sugar
½ cup granulated sugar
1 cup sliced almonds
4 Tablespoons sugar
2 cups milk
½ cup sugar
2 eggs
1 teaspoon vanilla
3 Tablespoons cornstarch
large package Cool Whip
¼ cup almonds, sliced and
    toasted

Mix butter and sugar; beat in yolks. Sift together flour, salt and baking powder and stir into creamed mixture. Stir in milk. Spread batter in 2 greased and floured 8-inch round cake pans.

Make meringue by beating egg whites and adding sugar. Spread on batter in pans and sprinkle with ½ cup sliced almonds and 2 Tablespoons sugar over each layer. Bake at 325° for 40 minutes.

While layers bake, cook milk, sugar, eggs, vanilla and cornstarch in top of double boiler to make custard filling. Cool. Spread custard between cooled layers and frost with Cool Whip leaving a round opening on top. Fill opening with toasted sliced almonds.

Sandy Ford (Mrs. Harold)

Pineapple Torte
Very festive and pretty for a party or spring fling

MERINGUE:
8 egg whites
2 cups sugar
1½ teaspoons vinegar
2 teaspoons vanilla
½ teaspoon cream of tartar
TOPPING:
½ pint heavy cream
1 cup crushed pineapple,
   well drained
½ cup chopped maraschino
   cherries

Prepare several hours in advance of serving.

Meringue: Preheat oven to 450° Allow egg whites to warm to room temperature. Line 2 round cake pans with waxed paper. Beat egg whites until stiff and add sugar, cream of tartar, vinegar, and vanilla. Pour into cake pans, place in pre-heated oven, turn off heat and let stand in oven several hours or overnight. Do not open oven door. (May bake at 300° for 1 hour and 15 minutes.) Carefully remove meringues from pan and allow to cool. 8-10 servings

Topping: Whip cream until stiff. Drain pineapple thoroughly. Drain cherries and chop coarsely. Fold pineapple and cherries into whipped cream and spread a thin layer on top of first meringue. Place second meringue on top. Spread mixture over top and sides. Place in refrigerator for several hours before serving.

Judy L. O'Shea (Mrs. Timothy)

HINT ▬▬▬▬▬▬▬▬▬▬▬▬▬▬

When mailing cookies, pack them in popcorn to keep them from crumbling.

HINT ▬▬▬▬▬▬▬▬▬▬▬▬▬▬

Keep a brand new powder puff in flour canister for dusting greased cake pan.

Chocolate Mousse Torte
A working person's dream; looks difficult but isn't

1 (8-ounce) package semi-
    sweet chocolate squares
6 eggs, at room temperature,
    separated
2 teaspoons vanilla extract
1 (8½ ounce) package
    chocolate wafers
¼ cup orange juice
½ cup heavy cream

In double boiler, over hot (not boiling) water, melt 7 chocolate squares; remove from heat and cool slightly. Stir in egg yolks until well mixed; then stir in vanilla. Beat egg whites until stiff peaks form. Fold beaten egg whites into chocolate mixture; set aside. Dip half of chocolate wafers in orange juice. Arrange wafers, in bottom of 9 x 2-inch springform pan, overlapping slightly, in one layer. Spoon half of chocolate mixture evenly over wafers. Repeat process. Cover pan with plastic wrap or foil; refrigerate at least 5 hours. Dip knife in warm water, loosen cake from side of spring-form pan, and carefully remove side of pan. Coarsely grate remaining chocolate square; press chocolate on side of torte with hand. Whip cream until stiff peaks form, and spoon into pastry tube with medium rosette tip. Decorate top of torte. Refrigerate. To serve: With sharp knife dipped in hot water, cut into thin wedges.
10 servings

Debbie McCurdy

Sherman Strikes Again

4 large peaches (peeled and
    sliced)
½ cup white wine
2 ounces of peach or apricot
    brandy
1 quart peach ice cream

Put peaches in pan, add wine; heat just before servng, add brandy and heat. Ignite and serve flaming over ice cream
4 servings

Pears with Apricot Sauce

6 Bartlett pears
⅓ cup almond paste
1 Tablespoon kirsch
1 cup sugar
3 cups water
2 Tablespoons kirsch
1½ teaspoons vanilla
1 cup dried apricot halves
Kirsch to taste
Toasted slivered almonds

Peel and core pears from bottom making deep cavity. Mix almond paste and 1 Tablespoon kirsch and stuff each cavity three-fourths full. Seal cavity with foil. Dissolve sugar and water in saucepan just large enough to hold pears. Add 2 Tablespoons kirsch and vanilla and simmer 5 minutes. Add pears; barely simmer 4-6 minutes on each side. Remove pears and chill covered. Add apricots to syrup. Cook covered 30 minutes. Drain apricots reserving syrup. Thin purée with enough syrup so that purée will coat pears. Add kirsch to taste. Chill purée. Remove foil from pears; stand them upright. Pour purée over them; thin with more kirsch if necessary. Sprinkle with almonds. 6 servings

Ginger Fruit
A lovely dessert for an Oriental dinner

1 (1-pound) can sliced peaches, drained
1 cup orange juice
2 teaspoons candied ginger, finely chopped
2 bananas
¼ cup sherry or ⅛ cup fruit brandy or cordial (optional)
Mint leaves for garnish (optional)

Combine peaches, juice and candied ginger. Chill several hours to blend flavors. Just before serving peel bananas and run fork tines down sides to flute. Slice on the bias and add to peach mixture. Add sherry, brandy or liqueur if desired. Serve immediately, garnishing with mint leaves.

Judy George (Mrs. Graham W., Jr.)

Chilled Peaches in Chablis
An elegant dessert after a heavy meal

6 small ripe peaches
1 cup sugar
1 cup water
Peel of 1 orange
1 cinnamon stick
1 cup Chablis
Whipped cream

Wash peaches and put in saucepan with sugar, water, orange peel and cinnamon stick, broken in half. Cover saucepan and simmer peaches for 15 minutes. Add Chablis and cook uncovered for 15 minutes or until tender. Hold each peach (using a clean kitchen towel to protect your fingers) and gently rub off skin. Transfer to a deep serving dish, cover and allow to cool. Carefully slice to remove pits. Cook the liquid until reduced to the consistency of light syrup. Pour over peaches and chill in the refrigerator. Serve very cold with whipped cream. Hint: Serve without whipped cream as an accompaniment to chicken. 6 servings

Elise M. Griffin

Strawberries Romanoff
Try this with blueberries too

1 cup heavy cream
4 Tablespoons confectioners
   sugar
1 pint vanilla ice cream,
   slightly softened
Juice of 1 lemon
2 ounces Cointreau
1 ounce white rum
1 quart strawberries

In a 2-quart bowl whip heavy cream with confectioners sugar until stiff. Add vanilla ice cream, lemon juice, Cointreau and rum. Blend the mixture lightly until smooth. Stem strawberries, wash, clean and thoroughly chill. Fill champagne glasses with the fruit. Spoon 3-4 Tablespoons ice cream mixture over the berries.
8 servings

Gale B. Probst (Mrs. William R.)

Brandied Peaches

A wonderful Christmas gift, these peaches are an elegant
finale to your most sophisticated dinner party.

Ripe fresh freestone peaches
1½ cups sugar
1¼ cups water
Brandy
Sweetened whipped cream

Skin peaches and prick all over with a needle. Mix water and sugar in large pan, bring to boil. Halve peaches and simmer in syrup mixture for 5 minutes. Put peaches in sterilized hot quart jars (about 10 peaches fill a quart jar) filling a bit more than half full with syrup. Cool slightly and fill with brandy to cover. Seal immediately. Keep several months turning jars upside down for some of the time. Chill and serve in crystal goblets over whipped cream with a crisp cookie on the side. Hint: If doing a large number of peaches, the peeled and halved fruit will not discolor if placed in a bowl of water. The peaches release some of their juice into the syrup which eventually changes color and sugar content of syrup. If doing many quarts, it may be best to remake syrup halfway through. makes several quart jars

Vivian de Kok (Mrs. Peter)

Fresh Strawberries with Raspberry Sauce

2 (10-ounce) packages frozen
raspberries
2 pints fresh nicely shaped
strawberries
¼ cup confectioners sugar
2-3 Tablespoons kirsh, Grand
Marnier or Cointreau
(optional)

Thaw raspberries, purée and strain out seeds. Rinse strawberries; remove stems. Sprinkle sugar over still wet berries. Refrigerate berries and sauce until ready to serve. Before serving, add liqueur to sauce and pour over strawberries. 6 servings

Sharon Herrli (Mrs. John)

Fruit and Cheese Combinations

Blue—apples, pears (especially Anjou or Bosc pears)
Brick—Tokay grapes
Camembert—apples, pears and plums
Cheddar—Tart apples and melon slices
Edam or Gouda—apples, orange sections, fresh pineapple spears
Muenster or Swiss—apples, seedless grapes, orange sections
Provolone—sweet Bartlett pears

Orange Cheese Dessert Spread

2 cups (8-ounces) shredded Cheddar cheese
1 (3-ounce) package cream cheese, softened
2 Tablespoons butter, softened
3 Tablespoons orange liqueur
½ teaspoon dry mustard
Dash cayenne

Blend in mixer or food processor. Pack into lightly oiled 2 cup mold. Cover and chill until firm. Unmold and let stand at room temperature one hour before serving. Serve with an assortment of sliced fresh fruits and crackers.

HINT ▪▪▪▪▪▪▪▪▪▪▪▪▪▪▪▪▪▪

For its most distinct flavor, cheese should be served at room temperature. Cream, cottage, and Neufchatel cheese should be chilled when served.

Gin's Ice Cream

4 eggs
1½ cups sugar
1 can sweetened condensed
    milk
1½ quarts milk
1½ teaspoons vanilla
4 cups very ripe
    mashed fruit, peaches,
    strawberries, etc.

Beat eggs until very light and fluffy, gradually add sugar. Add condensed milk, fruit, milk and vanilla. Pour into churn and freeze. Makes about 1 gallon

Virginia Kelley (Mrs. R.L.)
Wrens, Georgia

Peach Ice Cream

1 (15-ounce) can sweetened
    condensed milk
1 (15-ounce) can evaporated
    milk
2 cups half and half
2-3 cups crushed ripe peaches
    (more if you like)
1 (13-ounce) container Cool
    Whip
1½ cups sugar
Pinch salt
1 teaspoon vanilla

Mix condensed milk, evaporated milk, and half and half together; add mashed peaches; fold in Cool Whip, add sugar, salt and vanilla. Pour into an ice cream freezer for the freezing process or pour into plastic containers and place in freezer. Remove from freezer and let sit for a few minutes before serving to soften. 10 servings

Mrs. Earle B. May, Jr.

Frozen Peanut Butter Mousse

⅔ cup sweetened condensed
    milk
½ cup crunchy peanut butter
½ cup coffee
1 teaspoon vanilla
1 cup heavy cream

Mix condensed milk with peanut butter. Add coffee and vanilla. Whip heavy cream until thick but not stiff; fold into peanut butter mixture. Freeze in bowl stirring after 30 minutes to keep creamy.

Jane Nardone (Mrs. A. Joseph, Jr.)

Butterscotch Sauce

2 cups light brown sugar,
  packed
½ cup evaporated milk
¼ teaspoon salt
⅓ cup light corn syrup
⅓ cup butter

Combine all ingredients in saucepan. Bring to boil and cook rapidly for 3 minutes. Serve hot or cold.

Agnes Siebert (Mrs. Sam)

Cherry Rum Sauce

1 cup dark cherry preserves
½ cup coarsely chopped nuts
  (almonds, walnuts, pecans)
¼ cup dark rum

Combine all ingredients and stir to blend. Store in jar in refrigerator putting plastic wrap right on sauce. Serve over ice cream, cake or baked custard. Note: Use dark rum only.

Georgia Peanut Butter Sauce
Divine on French vanilla ice cream
(no one ever suspects peanut butter)

1 cup sugar
1 Tablespoon white Karo syrup
¼ teaspoon salt
¾ cup milk
6 Tablespoons peanut butter
½ teaspoon vanilla extract

Mix sugar, Karo, salt and milk. Cook over low heat, stirring constantly until thickened. Add peanut butter and mix well. Remove from heat, let cool, add vanilla.

HINT ■

To cut marshmallows or sticky fruit, rub butter or oil on scissors.

Heavenly Hot Fudge Sauce
The name says it all

4 squares unsweetened
  chocolate
½ cup butter or margarine
Dash salt
3 cups granulated sugar
1 tall can (1⅔ cups)
  evaporated milk, heated
1 teaspoon vanilla

Melt chocolate and butter in top of double boiler. Add salt; then start adding sugar slowly. Add evaporated milk a little at a time. Remove from heat and add vanilla. 1 quart

Merrilee F. Martin (Mrs. J.S.)

Vanilla Sauce

1 cup sugar
4 Tablespoons butter
½ cup cream
¼ cup light Karo syrup
2 teaspoons vanilla

Mix sugar, butter, cream and syrup and boil for 2 minutes, stirring constantly until sauce thickens. Remove from heat and add vanilla.

Agnes Siebert (Mrs. Sam)

Peach Sorbet

1 cup water
2 cups sugar
4 cups peaches
Juice of 2 lemons
Juice of 1 orange

Boil water and sugar 5 minutes. Cool. Purée peaches in processor with steel blade. Add lemon, orange juice and peaches to cool syrup. Pour into shallow metal pan and freeze. As mixture freezes at edges, stir with fork to make smooth two or three times. When almost solid, beat in processor or mixer until smooth. Pour back into pan or individual glasses and freeze 3-4 hours. Serve with lace cookies. Hint: This dessert may be prepared with blueberries, apricots or strawberries.

Jean Schmidt (Mrs. James C.)

Lemon Cream Sherbet

1 cup sugar
2 cups milk
Juice of 2 lemons
Rind of 1 lemon
2 egg whites, beaten
2 Tablespoons sugar
1 cup heavy cream

Add sugar to milk and stir to dissolve. When thoroughly dissolved, stir in lemon rind and juice. Turn into freezer tray and freeze 45-60 minutes. Beat egg whites, adding sugar. Whip cream to a thick custard consistency. Combine with beaten egg whites. Add to frozen mixture and mix lightly. Return to freezer and freeze 2-2½ hours. Do not stir. Garnish with sprig of mint. 6 servings

Margaret S. Westbrook (Mrs. William)

Pineapple Sherbet

2 cups milk, chilled
½ cup pineapple juice
1 Tablespoon grated lemon
   rind
2 teaspoons sugar
1 small can crushed pineapple,
   drained

After milk is chilled, add remaining ingredients. Freeze until hard. Remove and turn into bowl and beat. Return to freezer until ready to serve. 4-6 servings

Margaret S. Westbrook (Mrs. William)

Butterscotch Crumb Squares
Rich, delicious and unusual!

1 cup all-purpose flour
¼ cup rolled oats
¼ cup brown sugar
½ cup butter
½ cup pecans, chopped
1 (12 ounce) jar caramel
   topping
1 quart vanilla ice cream,
   softened

Combine flour, oats and sugar. Cut in butter until mixture resembles coarse crumbs. Stir in pecans. Pat mixture into a 9 x 13-inch pan. Bake at 400° for 15 minutes. Stir, while still warm, to crumble. Cool; then spread half of mixture in a 9-inch square pan. Drizzle half the the topping over this. Spoon ice cream carefully into pan. Drizzle remaining topping over ice cream. Sprinkle with remaining crumbs. Freeze. Cut in squares to serve. 8 servings

Frozen Chocolate Velvet

1½ cups finely crushed
  chocolate wafers
⅓ cup margarine, melted
1 (8-ounce) package cream
  cheese, softened
½ cup sugar, divided
1 teaspoon vanilla
2 eggs, separated
1 (6-ounce) package semi-
  sweet chocolate chips,
  melted
1 cup heavy cream, whipped
¾ cup chopped pecans

To make crust, combine chocolate wafers with margarine. Press into bottom of a 9-inch springform pan and bake at 325° for 10 minutes. Combine cream cheese, ¼ cup sugar and vanilla, mixing until well blended. Stir in well-beaten egg yolks and chocolate. Beat egg whites until peaks form, gradually beat in ¼ cup sugar and fold into chocolate mixture. Fold in whipped cream and nuts. Pour over crumb crust and freeze. Decorate with additional whipped cream or wafer crumbs, if desired. 10 servings.

Lib Tuck (Mrs. Bennett F., Jr.)

Italian Cassata

1 quart chocolate ice cream
1 egg white
1 Tablespoon sugar
1 cup cake crumbs, sponge,
  yellow or white
Small carton chopped fruits for
  fruit cake, soaked in 3
  Tablespoons sherry
½ teaspoon almond extract
½ pint heavy cream, whipped
1 quart vanilla ice cream
1 ounce slivered toasted
  almonds
Stemmed cherries or sliced
  pineapple for decoration

Line a loaf pan smoothly with foil leaving long ends to cover loaf. Soften chocolate ice cream and smooth into pan. Freeze. Beat egg white until stiff, adding sugar. Fold in cake crumbs, fruit, almond extract and ½ of the whipped cream. Freeze. Soften vanilla ice cream, smooth over whipped cream. Freeze. Remove whole loaf from pan, place on cold tray. Remove foil and ice loaf with remaining whipped cream and almonds. Decorate with stemmed cherries or pineapple as desired. Place on serving tray, wrap whole loaf in foil and refreeze. To serve, do not thaw; slice and serve. 10 servings

Judy George (Mrs. Graham)

Lulabell

This recipe is 40 years old and still a favorite!

½ box vanilla wafers (about 50), crushed
6 Tablespoons butter, melted
2 eggs separated
3 Tablespoons bourbon or brandy
1 (8-ounce) bottle cherries, drained and chopped
1 cup pecans, coarsely chopped
2-3 Tablespoons sugar
1 cup heavy cream, whipped

Mix vanilla wafer crumbs with butter, reserving 2 Tablespoons crumbs for top. Press into 8-inch square pan. Beat egg yolks with bourbon or brandy; add cherries and pecans. Beat egg whites with sugar. Fold egg whites and whipped cream into cherry-nut mixture. Pour over crumbs in pan; sprinkle with reserved crumbs on top; cover with plastic wrap. Freeze. To serve, cut into squares. 8-10 servings

Hazel R. Rutland (Mrs. Calvin)

Chocolate Mousse

6 egg whites at room temperature
1 teaspoon cream of tartar
⅔ cup sugar
1 teaspoon vanilla
2 cups heavy cream, stiffly beaten
4 ounces semi-sweet chocolate
½ cup rum (dark or light)
Whipped cream for garnish
Shaved chocolate for garnish

Add cream of tartar to egg whites and beat until stiff. Gradually beat in sugar and vanilla. Continue to beat stiffly as for a meringue. Fold in whipped cream and egg whites together with a wide rubber spatula. Refrigerate. In saucepan, carefully melt, then cool chocolate and rum. Fold COOLED chocolate into meringue. Note: If mixture is too warm, meringue will collapse. Place in bowl or individual serving dishes. Garnish with whipped cream and grated chocolate. Refrigerate. 8 servings

Jean Schmidt (Mrs. James C.)

Food Processor Cheese Cake

CRUST:
1½ cups zwieback crumbs
1 teaspoon cinnamon
½ cup melted butter
½ cup sugar
FILLING:
**3 (8-ounce) packages cream
   cheese**
1 cup sugar
3 eggs
½ cup melted butter, cooled
½ teaspoon orange extract
GARNISH:
**1 pint strawberries or blue-
   berries, cleaned and
   trimmed**
2 Tablespoons apricot jam
1 Tablespoon kirsch

Combine crust ingredients and press into a 9-inch springform pan. Preheat oven to 425°. Process cream cheese and sugar. Add eggs one at a time beating well after each. Pour in butter and orange extract and blend. Pour into prepared crust. Bake 35-40 minutes. Cool and place berries on top. Glaze with heated mixture of 2 Tablespoons apricot jam and 1 Tablespoon kirsch.

New York Deli Cheese Cake
True New York style cheese cake

1 small box graham crackers
¾ cup sugar
4 Tablespoons melted butter
1 teaspoon cinnamon
1½ pounds cream cheese
1 pint sour cream
1 cup sugar
5 eggs, separated
1 Tablespoon flour
1 Tablespoon cornstarch
1 Tablespoon vanilla

Crush crackers. Mix crumbs with ¾ cup sugar, melted butter and cinnamon. Reserve ¾ cup and use the remaining to line a greased springform pan. Mix cream cheese and sour cream; add beaten egg yolks, sugar, flour, cornstarch and vanilla. Beat egg whites until stiff and fold into cheese mixture. Pour into pan. Sprinkle reserved crumb mixture on top. Bake at 325° for 1 hour. Turn off heat, open oven door and let rest for several hours or overnight. May be served with a glazed strawberry or cherry sauce. 10 servings

Pumpkin Cheesecake
A very special cheesecake

CRUST:
1½ cups graham cracker crumbs
⅓ cup ground almonds
½ teaspoon ginger
½ teaspoon cinnamon
⅓ cup butter, melted
FILLING:
4 (8-ounce) packages cream cheese
1¼ cups sugar
3 Tablespoons maple syrup
3 Tablespoons cognac or brandy
1 teaspoon ginger
1 teaspoon cinnamon
½ teaspoon nutmeg
4 eggs (room temperature)
¼ cup heavy cream
1 cup cooked or canned pumpkin
TOPPING:
2 cups sour cream
¼ cup sugar
1 Tablespoon maple syrup
1 Tablespoon cognac or brandy
¼ cup almonds, sautéed in butter

Crust: Preheat oven to 425°. Combine crust ingredients and press into the bottom of a 10-inch springform pan. Bake 10 minutes. Remove pan from oven and reduce temperature to 325°.

Filling: Beat cream cheese until smooth. Gradually add sugar, beating until fluffy and light. Add maple syrup, cognac, ginger, cinnamon and nutmeg. Blend well. Add eggs, one at a time, beating well after each addition. Add cream and pumpkin and mix well. Pour filling into prepared crust. Bake for 45 minutes. Turn off oven. Do not open door during baking time or for 1 hour after oven is turned off. Remove cake.

Topping: Preheat oven to 425°. Blend sour cream, sugar, maple syrup and cognac. Spread over cake and bake for 10 minutes. Allow to cool at room temperature for about 1 hour. Arrange almonds in a ring around the perimeter of cake. Chill at least 3 hours before removing sides of pan. May be frozen. 12 servings

Cookbook Committee

MICROWAVE HINT

Soften lumpy brown sugar by placing in a dish with a slice of apple. Cook for 15 seconds or until soft.

Brown Sugar Pound Cake

1 cup Crisco
½ cup butter
1 box light brown sugar
½ cup white sugar
5 eggs
3 cups cake flour
½ teaspoon salt
½ teaspoon baking powder
1 cup milk
1 teaspoon maple flavoring
1 teaspoon vanilla flavoring
1 cup chopped nuts
ICING:
½ stick margarine
½ cup dark brown sugar
2 Tablespoons milk
1½ cups confectioners sugar

Cream Crisco, butter and sugars together; add eggs one at a time and beat well after each. Sift dry ingredients together and add alternately with milk. Stir in flavorings and nuts. Bake in a greased and floured tube pan at 325° for 1 hour and 15 minutes.
   Icing: Bring first 3 ingredients to a boil in saucepan. Remove from heat and add confectioners sugar.

Jeneal Benton (Mrs. Gene R.)

Mother's Cream Cheese Cake
A fine textured moist cake

3 cups sugar
1½ cups butter, softened
6 eggs
1 (8-ounce) package cream cheese, softened
3 cups flour
1 teaspoon vanilla
1 teaspoon butter flavoring

Cream butter and sugar. Add eggs one at a time. Blend in cream cheese. Add flour and mix well. Add vanilla and butter flavoring. Bake in a tube pan at 325° for 1½ hours. Check for doneness after 1 hour. Do not overbake.

Ann Benton

Fresh Apple Cake
Crunchy and Different

2 cups sugar
3 cups flour
1 teaspoon soda
1 teaspoon salt
1 teaspoon cinnamon
1½ cups Wesson oil
3 eggs
1 teaspoon vanilla
3 cups chopped red apples
   (do not peel)
1 cup chopped nuts

Sift together dry ingredients; add oil, eggs and vanilla. Stir in the apples and nuts. Grease, but do not flour a tube pan. Bake at 350° for 1 hour. Cool 10 minutes in pan and turn out on plate. Serve with sweetened whipped cream.

Melva Jansen (Mrs. Klaus)

Carrot Cake

1 package good quality spice
   cake mix
1 package (4 serving size)
   vanilla instant pudding mix
¼ cup water
½ cup cooking oil
1 cup sour cream
4 eggs
1 cup chopped walnuts or
   pecans
3 cups grated carrots (can be
   grated in blender)

Preheat oven to 350°. Combine all ingredients except nuts and carrots. Mix on low speed briefly, just to blend. Beat at medium speed 1 minute. Stop and scrape down sides of bowl, then beat for 1 minute more. Fold in carrots and nuts. Pour batter into well greased and floured Bundt or tube pan. Bake at 350° for 40-60 minutes, or until the cake springs back when touched lightly with finger, towards the center. Let cool on rack in pan for 15 minutes. Turn out onto serving plate. Glaze if desired.

Susan L. Kreitzman
The Nutrition Cookbook
Harcourt, Brace, Jovanovitch

Pineapple Cake

CAKE:
2 cups sugar
3 eggs
**1 20-ounce can crushed pine-
apple (sweet, in syrup) with
juice**
2 cups all-purpose flour
1 cup chopped nuts (pecans)
Dash salt
1 teaspoon vanilla
**2 teaspoons baking soda
(add last)**
FROSTING:
1½ cups confectioners sugar
**1 (8 ounce) package cream
cheese, softened**
½ cup butter, softened
1 teaspoon vanilla

Cake: Beat or mix ingredients by hand. Spread into greased 9 x 13-inch pan. Bake at 350° for 40-45 minutes.

Frosting: Mix with electric beater. Frost cake while warm. Refrigerate before cutting.

Dannie Martin (Mrs. Fielder)

Tia Maria Pecan Cake
Aunt Mary's Favorite Pecan Cake

**9 large eggs separated (7 yolks
2 yolks, 9 whites)**
1½ cups sugar
⅓ cup orange juice
**2½ cups pecan meal (finely
ground pecans)**
⅓ cup flour
CREAM FILLING:
¾ cup sweet butter
2 squares bitter chocolate
2 egg yolks
1½ cups confectioners sugar
**⅓ cup Tia Maria (any coffee
liqueur)**
Pecans (optional)

Beat egg whites until stiff and add ½ cup sugar. Beat 7 yolks with 1 cup sugar until thick. Add orange juice to yolks and beat until thick again. Fold yolk mixture slowly into whites; then fold in pecan meal. Sift flour over mixture and fold in. Pour into three well greased and slightly floured 9-inch cake pans. Bake 375° for 15-18 minutes till edges loosen.

Cream Filling: Melt chocolate slowly, put in small bowl. Add butter, yolks, sugar. Beat and add the liqueur slowly until light and fluffy. When layers are cold, frost cake. Cover with pecan pieces or whole pecans.

Susan Barton (Mrs. David L.)

Napoleon Cake
Napoleon may even have enjoyed Waterloo if he'd had this

1 frozen loaf pound cake (store bought)
1 (6-ounce) package chocolate chips
⅛ cup boiling water
⅛ cup brandy
4 egg yolks
1 teaspoon vanilla
½ cup butter, softened

Slice pound cake horizontally into 5 or 6 slices. Frost layers with following mixture: In blender or food processor place chocolate chips, water and brandy. Blend 20 seconds on high. Add egg yolks, vanilla and butter. Blend. Frost cake. Store in refrigerator. May be frozen.

Pat Barton (Mrs. William L.)

Kim's Poppy Seed Cake
The sherry makes the difference

1 package good quality yellow cake mix
1 package (4 serving size) vanilla instant pudding mix
2 ounces poppy seeds
4 eggs
1 cup cooking oil
1 cup cream sherry
2 teaspoons vanilla extract

Combine all ingredients in bowl of electric mixer. Mix on low speed briefly to blend ingredients. Beat at medium speed for 1 minute. Stop and scrape down sides of bowl; then beat for 1 minute more. Pour batter in well greased and floured bundt or tube pan. Bake at 350° for 40 minutes to an hour, until cake springs back when pressed with finger near the center. Let cool in pan on rack for 15 minutes. Turn on serving plate. Glaze if desired.

Susan L. Krietzman
The Nutrition Cookbook
Harcourt Brace Jovanivitch, Inc.

Pumpkin Spice Cake

1 package spice cake mix
1 cup canned pumpkin
½ cup salad oil
1 small package vanilla instant pudding
3 eggs
1 teaspoon cinnamon
½ cup water

Mix ingredients. Pour into greased and floured Bundt pan. Bake 45 minutes at 350°. Let sit in pan 15 minutes before removing.

Cookbook Committee

Chocolate Town Cupcakes
So chocolatey, you need not even frost them!

½ cup butter
1 cup granulated sugar
1 teaspoon vanilla
4 eggs
1¼ cups all-purpose flour
¾ teaspoon baking soda
1½ cups (1-pound can)
    Hershey's chocolate
    flavored syrup

Cream the butter, sugar and vanilla until light and fluffy. Add the eggs, one at a time, beating well after each addition. Combine the flour and baking soda. Add alternately with the chocolate syrup to the creamed mixture. Pour the batter into paper-lined muffin cups filling each ½ full. Bake at 375° for 20 to 25 minutes. Frost with your favorite icing. 30 servings

Peggy M. Youngblood (Mrs. Robert M.)

Shawneetown Chocolate Cake

1 pound box dark brown sugar
3 eggs
2 squares unsweetened
    chocolate
½ cup butter
2 cups flour
1 teaspoon soda
½ cup buttermilk
1 cup boiling water

Mix sugar and eggs. Melt chocolate and butter in double boiler. Combine sugar-egg mixture with chocolate-butter mixture. Sift flour and soda and add to mixture. Add buttermilk and boiling water. Mix until well blended (batter will be thin). Pour into 2 greased and floured 8-inch square pans. Bake at 350° for 20-25 minutes or until firm. Frost with a white butter icing. Chill 1 cake and put the other in the freezer for next week.

Edna Snider (Mrs. George E.)

Hummell Futter
"Heavenly Food"
Sinfully rich, simple and divine

2 eggs, beaten
1 cup sugar
1 teaspoon baking powder
1 Tablespoon flour
1 (8-ounce) package whole
    pitted dates, chopped
2 cups pecans, coarsely
    chopped
Sliced bananas
Sliced oranges
1 cup heavy cream, whipped

Gradually add sugar to well beaten eggs. Blend in flour and baking powder. Stir in dates and nuts. Spread in a greased 9-inch pan and bake at 350° for 30 minutes. When cool, crumble on a small tray or in individual dishes. To serve, cover with sliced bananas and oranges. Top with whipped cream. 8-10 servings

Judy H. Lewis (Mrs. William)

Gingerbread with Maple Cream
An old-fashioned favorite with a new-fashioned topping

GINGERBREAD:
½ cup sugar
½ cup butter
1 egg, beaten
1 cup molasses
1 cup hot water
2½ cups sifted flour
1½ teaspoons soda
1 teaspoon cinnamon
1 teaspoon ginger
½ teaspoon powdered cloves
½ teaspoon salt
1½ cups raisins
MAPLE CREAM TOPPING:
1 cup sour cream
¼ cup pure maple syrup

Cream butter and sugar; add beaten egg and molasses. Sift all dry ingredients together and add to creamed mixture. Add hot water and beat until smooth. Fold in raisins. Pour in well buttered 9 x 13-inch baking pan and bake in preheated 350° oven until tests done. Cut and serve while warm (good cold, too) and top with maple-sour cream mixture.

Barbara R. Johnson (Mrs. Larry)

Lemon Pecan Cake
A delicious light fruit cake!

1 pound margarine
2 cups sugar
6 eggs, separated
2 ounces pure lemon extract
4 cups all-purpose flour
1 box white raisins
½ pound candied cherries
½ pound candied pineapple
1 teaspoon baking powder
1 quart chopped pecans
   (or more)
Dash salt

Cream margarine and sugar. Add beaten egg yolks, then extract. Add baking powder to flour. Then add fruit and pecans to flour and mix well. Beat egg whites until stiff. Add butter and sugar mixture to flour mixture and mix well. Add beaten egg whites and fold in thoroughly by hand. Bake at 250° for 2 hours or until done. Bake in generously greased large tube pan or 2 smaller pans. Other fruits may be added, or for a moister cake add 1 cup of orange marmalade or applesauce.

Maureen T. Vandiver (Mrs. Roy W.)

Million Dollar Bourbon Cake
A favorite of a French chef we know, from his wife's collection

2 teaspoons nutmeg (Freshly
   grated is best)
1 cup bourbon
4 cups pecans, coarsely
   chopped
2 cups raisins
3 cups flour, sifted
2 teaspoons baking powder
1 cup butter, softened
2 cups plus 4 teaspoons sugar
6-7 eggs (depending on size),
   separated
Dash salt

Soak nutmeg in bourbon at least 15 minutes. Put pecans and raisins in a bowl with 1 cup sifted flour. Combine remaining 2 cups flour with baking powder and sift twice more. Cream butter and sugar; add egg yolks 1 at a time and beat until smooth. Add flour and bourbon alternately; blend well. Fold in raisin-nut-flour mixture. Beat egg whites and salt until stiff. Gently fold in egg whites. Put batter in a 9-inch tube pan which has been greased and lined with wax paper. Bake at 325° for 1 hour and 15 minutes. Let stand 30 minutes before removing.

Rainey Vivier (Mrs. Pierre)

Fruit Cake
A rich moist cake; almost like a confection

½ pound figs
1 pound candied cherries (half red, half green)
1 pound candied pineapple
1 pound freshly grated or frozen coconut
1 pound white raisins
3 pounds pecans (3 quarts)
1 package dates
1 pound butter
2 pounds sugar (4 cups)
1 dozen eggs
2 pounds (8 cups) plain flour
1 Tablespoon baking powder
1 teaspoon salt
2 Tablespoons nutmeg
2 Tablespoons cinnamon
2 Tablespoons vanilla

Butter mixing pan well (choose a large utensil that cake can be baked in, such as a deep roasting pan). Finely chop fruit and nuts by hand or in food processor. Cream butter and sugar until fluffy. Add 1 egg at a time, beating well after each addition. Add spices to flour. Add half of flour-spice mixture to creamed mixture and blend well. Use remaining flour-spice mixture over fruit and nuts, mixing to coat well. Add fruit and nuts to batter and mix. Bake for 1½ hours at 325° in same pan as mixed in. Remove from oven at 15 minute intervals and stir well with long handled spoon, counting stirring time as part of cooking time. When batter has been cooked and stirred for 1½ hours, pack in shallow pans lined with foil and seal. Do not overcook. Mixture will not be firm. Cake keeps indefinitely, always stays moist. 6 loaves

Virginia Kelly (Mrs. R. L.)
Wrens, Georgia

White Fruit Cake
Make in fall; serve in winter

2 quarts chopped pecans
1 pound candied cherries
1 pound candied pineapple
1 pound coconut
1 box white raisins
2 cans condensed milk

Cut and mix fruit and nuts with 1 can condensed milk; stir. Pack firmly in oiled and floured tube pan. Pour other can of condensed milk over mixture in pan. Bake at 350° for 1 hour. Make this cake in early fall, wrap in cheese cloth and store in cool dark place. Pour ¼ cup bourbon or rum over cake once a month. By December the cake is really delicious.

Mrs. Ivy Lee Snipes

Food Processor Pastry

2 cups all-purpose flour
1 teaspoon salt
⅔ cup unsalted butter
1 egg yolk in ¼ cup water
1 teaspoon sugar

Put all ingredients in bowl of processor. Process on and off to mix, then turn on until a ball forms, about 40 seconds. Refrigerate 2-3 hours or freeze 30-45 minutes before working dough.
1 (10-inch) shell

Coconut Cream Pie

1 (10-inch) baked pie shell
⅔ cup sugar
¼ cup cornstarch
½ teaspoon salt
3 cups milk
4 egg yolks beaten
2 Tablespoons butter
4 teaspoons vanilla
1 (10-ounce) flaked coconut
½ cup heavy cream, whipped

In saucepan, stir together sugar, cornstarch and salt. Blend milk and egg yolks and gradually stir into sugar mixture. Cook over medium heat, stirring constantly until mixture thickens and comes to boil. Boil and stir one minute. Remove from heat and blend in butter and vanilla. Add ¾ can of coconut. Pour into pie shell. Refrigerate. Before serving, top with whipped cream (you may sweeten this to taste) and sprinkle with the rest of the coconut.

Rosamond Buckler (Mrs. Robert)

Cottage Coconut Pie

3 eggs
1 cup sugar
½ cup butter, melted
½ cup cottage cheese
1 small can coconut
1 teaspoon vanilla
1 unbaked pie shell

In mixer or food processor, beat eggs; add sugar, butter, cottage cheese, coconut and vanilla. Mix well and pour into unbaked pie shell. Bake 1 hour at 300° until golden brown.
8 servings

Jane H. Nardone (Mrs. A. Joseph, Jr.)

Peach Custard Pie

1 unbaked (9-inch) pie shell
6-8 large peaches
3 eggs
1 cup sugar
pinch salt

Peel peaches and cut into large slices; place in pie shell. Beat eggs, sugar and salt together and pour over peaches. Bake at 400° for 15 minutes. Reduce heat to 325° and continue baking for another 45 minutes. Serve warm or cool. 6 servings

Jeanine Andrews (Mrs. Edward B.)

Pumpkin Praline Chiffon Pie
This could become a new tradition at your Thanksgiving table

1 (10-inch) pie shell, unbaked
6 Tablespoons butter
⅓ cup light brown sugar
½ cup chopped walnuts
1½ cups canned eggnog
¾ cup sugar
2 envelopes unflavored gelatin
1 teaspoon cinnamon
½ teaspoon ginger
¼ teaspoon nutmeg
3 eggs, separated
1 (16 ounce) can pumpkin
¼ teaspoon cream of tartar
1 cup heavy cream, whipped

Several hours before serving, while your pie shell partially bakes, cream butter and brown sugar. Stir in walnuts and spread on bottom of partially baked pie shell. Bake 5 minutes longer until shell is golden brown. Combine ½ cup sugar, gelatin, cinnamon, ginger and nutmeg in medium saucepan. Beat in egg yolks and eggnog. Heat, stirring constantly, over low heat until gelatin is dissolved. Stir in pumpkin. Pour in large bowl. Chill stirring often until mixture mounds on spoon. Beat egg whites with cream of tartar until they hold peaks. Fold into pumpkin mixture; also fold in whipped cream. Spoon into crust. Chill several hours until firm. Garnish with walnuts and cream if desired. 6-8 servings

Holiday Pie
Even those who don't care for mince pie
will love this creamy combination

1 cup Non-Such mincemeat
1 large tart unpeeled apple,
    diced fine
3 Tablespoons sherry, brandy
    or rum
1 cup sugar
3 eggs, beaten
2 cups canned pumpkin
1 teaspoon cinnamon
¼ teaspoon ginger
1 Tablespoon melted butter
½ teaspoon salt
1 teaspoon allspice
1 cup milk
1 (9 or 10-inch) pie shell,
    unbaked

Mix in a bowl mincemeat,
apple and sherry, brandy or rum.
Combine in a separate bowl sugar,
eggs, pumpkin, cinnamon, ginger,
butter, salt, allspice and milk.
Place mincemeat mixture in
bottom of pie shell. Pour pumpkin
mixture over mincemeat mixture.
Bake at 350° for 45 minutes until
firm. Serve plain or with dollop
of whipped cream flavored with
brandy, sherry or rum. 8 servings

Mrs. Charles A. Neubauer

Apple Cream Pie
An old standby with a new twist

⅔ cup sugar
2 Tablespoons flour
⅛ teaspoon salt
1 cup sour cream
1 egg, slightly beaten
1 teaspoon vanilla
3-4 cups chopped tart apples
1 (9-inch) pie shell, unbaked
TOPPING:
½ cup sugar
¾ cup flour
⅓ cup butter
1 teaspoon cinnamon (optional)

Combine sugar, flour and salt.
Add sour cream, egg and vanilla
and beat until smooth. Fold in
apples and pour into unbaked pie
shell.
Topping: Combine flour and
sugar and cut in the butter.
Sprinkle over pie and bake at
425° for 25-30 minutes.
6-8 servings

Mrs. Charles A. Neubauer

Pecan Pie

1 cup sugar
½ cup melted butter (no
    substitutions)
1 cup light corn syrup
4 eggs, beaten
1 teaspoon vanilla extract
¼ teaspoon salt
1 (9-inch) unbaked pie shell
1-1½ cups pecan halves

Combine sugar, butter and corn syrup. Stirring constantly, cook over low heat until sugar is dissolved, about 20 minutes. This is a slow process. Cool. Add eggs, salt and vanilla. Mix well. Pour filling into pie shell and arrange pecan halves in a pin wheel design; start at outer edge and work to the center. Bake at 325° for 50-55 minutes. 8 servings

Dunja S. Awbrey (Mrs. James J.)

Amelia Island Mud Pie

CRUST:
21 Oreo cookies, crushed
6 Tablespoons butter, melted
FILLING:
1 quart chocolate ice cream,
    softened
2 Tablespoons instant Sanka
    coffee
2 Tablespoons ground coffee
2 Tablespoons brandy
2 Tablespoons coffee liqueur
1 cup heavy cream, whipped
1 (12-ounce) jar fudge sauce
    (or your favorite homemade)
Toasted almonds and cherries
    to garnish

Mix cookie crumbs with butter. Press into 9 or 10-inch pie pan. Freeze.
Filling: Whip ice cream with coffee, brandy and liqueur. Whip cream, add 4 Tablespoons whipped cream to ice cream mixture and continue to whip. Spread in frozen pie shell. Freeze until very hard. Dip knife in hot water, spread fudge sauce on top of frozen pie working quickly. Cover with whipped cream. Garnish with toasted almonds and cherries. Freeze. 8 servings

Sharon Hooten (Mrs. James)

"The" Strawberry Pie

1 (9-inch) pastry shell, baked
2 cups strawberries
3 Tablespoons cornstarch
¾ cup sugar
2 Tablespoons lemon juice
2 cups whole or halved
   strawberries

In saucepan crush 2 cups strawberries, cornstarch and sugar. Cook, stirring constantly, until mixture boils. Boil 2 minutes. Cool slightly and fold in lemon juice and halved strawberries. Pour into crust. Chill. Serve topped with whipped cream. 6 servings

Hazel Mattingley

Toffee Ice Cream Pie

18 vanilla or brown edge
   wafers
½ gallon vanilla ice cream,
   slightly softened
1 cup chopped toffee bar
   (Heath Bar)
1½ cups sugar
1 cup evaporated milk
¼ cup butter or margarine
¼ cup light corn syrup
Dash salt

Line bottom and sides of 9-inch buttered pie plate with wafers. Spoon half of ice cream into shell. Sprinkle ½ cup of chopped toffee candy over ice cream. Spoon remainder of ice cream over toffee layer. Store in freezer until serving time.

Sauce: Prepare toffee sauce by combining sugar, milk, butter, corn syrup and salt in a saucepan. Bring to a boil over low heat; boil 1 minute. Remove from heat and stir in remaining toffee candy; cool, stirring occasionally. Serve pie topped with cool or warm sauce. 8 servings

Joan M. Adams (Mrs. John P., Jr.)

French Apple Cobbler
A delicious change from the standard apple pie

FILLING:
5 cups peeled, sliced tart
  apples
¾ cup sugar
2 Tablespoons flour
½ teaspoon cinnamon
¼ teaspoon salt
1 teaspoon vanilla extract
¼ cup water
1 Tablespoon margarine,
  softened
BATTER:
½ cup sifted plain flour
½ cup sugar
½ teaspoon baking powder
¼ teaspoon salt
2 Tablespoons soft margarine
1 egg, slightly beaten

Filling: In medium bowl, combine apples, sugar, flour, cinnamon, salt, vanilla and water. Turn into a 9-inch square pan. Dot apples with margarine.

Batter: Combine all batter ingredients. Beat with wooden spoon until smooth. Drop batter in 9 portions on apples, spacing evenly. Batter will spread during baking. Bake 35-40 minutes at 375° or until apples are fork tender, and crust is golden brown. Serve warm with cream.
6-8 servings

Mrs. William Schley Howard

Chocolate Chess Pie
Everyone's favorite

½ cup butter
1½ ounces unsweetened
  chocolate
1 cup light brown sugar, firmly
  packed
½ cup granulated sugar
1 Tablespoon flour
2 eggs, well beaten
2 Tablespoons milk
1 teaspoon vanilla
1 (8-inch) unbaked pie shell

In saucepan melt butter and chocolate over moderate heat. Remove pan from heat and add brown sugar and granulated sugar mixed with flour. Beat in eggs, milk and vanilla. Prick bottom of pie shell with fork and bake at 400° for 10 minutes or until it is lightly colored. Cool. Pour mixture into shell and bake at 325° for 35-40 minutes or until filling is set. Hint: Pie may be prepared the day before using. Serve topped with whipped cream or ice cream sprinkled with chocolate shavings for a lovely dessert. 6-8 servings

Nancy Kirby (Mrs. Jeff D., III)

Almond Macaroons
Hard to find, but easy to make

1 (8-ounce) can almond paste
¾ cup sugar
2 egg whites, unbeaten
¼ cup all-purpose flour, sifted
Dash salt

Beat paste to soften. Beat in sugar and unbeaten egg whites gradually. Mix thoroughly. Add flour and salt and mix well. Drop by teaspoonfuls onto lightly greased cookie sheet. Bake at 300° for 25-30 minutes. Remove onto racks immediately or these will stick. These freeze well.
3 dozen

Butter Pecan Turtles
Chew these turtles slowly to make them last!

CRUST:
2 cups all-purpose flour
1 cup firmly packed brown
** sugar**
½ cup softened butter
1 cup pecan pieces
CARAMEL LAYER:
⅔ cup butter
½ cup brown sugar
TOPPING:
1 (6-ounce) package chocolate
** chips**

Mix crust ingredients with electric mixer until particles are fine. Line pan with foil before putting crust into it to make removal easier. Pat into 9 x 13 x 2-inch pan. Sprinkle pecans over crust. Combine caramel layer ingredients in saucepan and cook, stirring until entire surface boils. Boil ½-1 minute until ingredients combine, stirring constantly. Pour over crust. Bake at 350° for 18-20 minutes. Remove from oven and sprinkle with chocolate chips, spreading slightly by swirling. Cool completely. Cut into bars.

Mrs. James P. McMahan

Ardy's Blonde Brownies

⅔ cup butter
2 cups brown sugar
2 teaspoons vanilla
3 eggs
1 teaspoon baking powder
1 teaspoon salt
2 cups flour
1 cup chopped nuts
1 (6-ounce) package chocolate
   chips

Melt butter in saucepan and remove from heat. Add remaining ingredients one at a time. Pour into a 9 x 13-inch pan. Bake at 350° for 35-40 minutes.

Barbara R. Johnson (Mrs. Larry)

Christmas Spritz
Make these the first week in December;
by Christmas they will be buttery delicious

1½ cups unsalted butter
1 cup sugar
1 egg
1 Tablespoon milk
1 teaspoon vanilla
½ teaspoon almond extract
4 cups all purpose flour, sifted
1 teaspoon baking powder
½ teaspoon grated lemon peel

Cream butter and sugar; add egg, milk, vanilla and almond extract, beat well. Sift together flour and baking powder and add to creamed mixture; add lemon peel. Force dough through a cookie press onto ungreased cookie sheet in the shape of an "S". Bake at 400° for 8-10 minutes until light golden brown. About 9 dozen

Melva Jansen (Mrs. Klaus)

London Tea Cakes

¾ cup butter
¼ cup sugar
3 egg yolks
¼ cup water
1½ cups flour
½ teaspoon soda
½ teaspoon salt
½ teaspoon vanilla
1 (12-ounce) jar raspberry jam
2 egg whites
½ cup sugar
Sliced almonds or ground
   pecans

Cream butter and sugar; add egg yolks and water. Combine flour, soda and salt; add to mixture. Add vanilla. Spread thin on jelly roll pan. Bake 10 minutes at 350°. Spread raspberry jam over. Make meringue with egg whites and sugar and spread over jam. Sprinkle with nuts; return to oven to brown. Cool and cut in squares.

Oatmeal Lace Cookies

These are a nice accompaniment for a sorbet

½ cup flour
¼ teaspoon baking powder
½ cup sugar
¼ teaspoon nutmeg (optional)
½ cup quick cooking oats
2 Tablespoons heavy cream
⅓ cup melted butter
1 Tablespoon vanilla
2 Tablespoons white corn
  syrup

Sift together flour, baking powder and sugar. Add oats, cream, butter, vanilla and corn syrup. Mix until well blended. Drop by ¼ teaspoons onto ungreased cookie sheet allowing 3-4 inches between as these cookies spread. Bake at 375° for 4-6 minutes until lightly browned. Remove from oven and let stand 30 seconds before removing from pan. If cookies become too hard to remove, return to oven for a few seconds to soften. 4 dozen

Jean Schmidt (Mrs. James C.)

Chocolate Macaroons

2½ Tablespoons margarine
4 squares unsweetened
  chocolate
2 cups sugar
4 eggs
2 teaspoons vanilla
2¾ cups all-purpose flour
3½ teaspoons baking powder
1 cup confectioners sugar

In a saucepan over low heat, melt: margarine, sugar and chocolate and mix to a smooth paste. Transfer to a large bowl and add eggs one at a time stirring well after each addition. Add vanilla. Sift flour and baking powder and add to mixture. Put confectioners sugar in a pie plate. Drop cookie mixture by teaspoonfuls into sugar and roll to form 1-inch balls (If mixture is too soft to form balls, add a little more flour.) Place balls 1 inch apart on a greased cookie sheet and bake for 8 minutes at 350°. Do not overcook. Cookies will still be soft. Allow to cool completely and remove from sheet with a spatula. 4 dozen

Peggy P. Weitnauer (Mrs. John H., Jr.)

Cowboy Cookies

1 cup shortening
1 cup brown sugar
1 cup white sugar
2 eggs
2½ cups flour
1 teaspoon soda
½ teaspoon baking powder
½ teaspoon salt
2 teaspoons vanilla
1 (12 ounce) package
    chocolate chips
2 cups oats
1 cup chopped nuts

Cream shortening and sugar. Add eggs. Sift dry ingredients and add to shortening mixture. Mix well and add other ingredients. Stir until evenly mixed. Drop by teaspoonfuls onto greased cookie sheet. Bake at 350° for 12 minutes. May be frozen. 7 dozen

Elizabeth Crotwell (Mrs. Wm. V.)
Birmingham, Alabama

Smackeroos

½ cup shortening
1 cup brown sugar
1 egg
1 cup flour
¼ teaspoon salt
1 teaspoon vanilla
24 maraschino cherries

Blend shortening and sugar until smooth. Add egg and blend. Add flour, salt and vanilla; blend well. Fill small muffin tins two-thirds full. Put cherry in center of each. Bake at 375° for 12-15 minutes. Variation: Substitute date or nut if desired. May be frozen. 24 small muffins

Karen DeFazio (Mrs. Richard A.)

Drop Sugar Cookies

1 cup butter
1½ cups confectioners sugar,
    sifted
1 egg
1 teaspoon vanilla
¼ teaspoon salt
2½ cups flour
1 teaspoon baking soda
1 teaspoon cream of tartar
1 cup pecans, chopped
    (optional)

Cream butter and confectioners sugar well. Add egg and vanilla. Sift dry ingredients and add to creamed mixture. (Add nuts if desired.) Chill dough overnight. Drop by teaspoonfuls onto greased cookie sheet and bake at 350° for 8-10 minutes. Remove from oven and sprinkle sugar on still warm cookies. 6-7 dozen

Kaye Waters (Mrs. Allan)

Old Fashioned Raisin Squares

1 cup water
1 cup seedless raisins
½ cup salad oil
1 egg beaten
1 cup sugar
1¾ cups all-purpose flour
¼ teaspoon salt
1 teaspoon ground allspice
1 teaspoon ground nutmeg
½ teaspoon ground cloves
½ cup chopped walnuts or
    pecans
Powdered sugar (optional)

Combine water and raisins; bring to a boil. Add salad oil; cool to lukewarm. Add remaining ingredients except powdered sugar, blending well. Spoon batter into a greased 9 x 13 x 2-inch pan. Bake at 375° for 25 minutes. Sprinkle with powdered sugar, if desired. Cut into 2 inch squares. 2 dozen

Lucia H. Sizemore (Mrs. Thomas H., III)

Pecan Tassies

CHEESE PASTRY:
1 (3-ounce) package cream
    cheese, softened
½ cup butter, softened
1 cup sifted all-purpose flour
PECAN FILLING:
1 egg
¾ cup brown sugar
1 teaspoon vanilla
2 teaspoons butter
Dash salt
⅓ cup coarsely broken pecans
24 pecan halves

Cheese Pastry: Blend cream cheese and butter; stir in flour. Chill slightly about 1 hour. Shape in 2 dozen 1 inch balls. Place in tiny ungreased 1¾ inch muffin cups. Press dough against bottoms and sides of cups.

Pecan Filling: Beat together egg, sugar, butter, vanilla and salt, just until smooth. Sprinkle broken pecans in pastry lined cups; add egg mixture over pecans and top with pecan halves. Bake at 325° for 25 minutes or until filling is set and crust is golden. Remove from oven; run sharp knife around edges to loosen any filling which has stuck to tin. Cool and remove from tins. Hint: These may be frozen. 6-8 servings

Jean Schmidt (Mrs. James C.)

Cheese Cake Tarts
Beautiful sweet for a coffee

1 box vanilla wafers, crushed
2 pounds cream cheese,
    softened
⅓ teaspoon salt
1 cup granulated sugar
4 eggs, well beaten
1 teaspoon lemon juice or
    vanilla extract
1 can fruit pie filling

Use miniature muffin tins and paper liners. Place 1 teaspoon vanilla wafer crumbs in the bottom of each tin. Beat cream cheese, salt, sugar, eggs and flavoring together. Fill cups ¾ full. Bake at 350° for 12-15 minutes. Allow to cool. Decorate tops with pie filling of your choice using small amount of fruit on each one. Hint: Tarts may be frozen before adding toppings. 75 tarts

Nancy Kirby (Mrs. Jefferson D., III)
Ann McCrory (Mrs. Charles O.)

Toffee Bars
These are wonderful served with fresh fruit

2 cups plain flour
1 cup brown sugar (packed)
½ cup butter
⅔ cup butter
½ cup brown sugar
1-2 cups whole pecans
2 cups chocolate chips

At least 8 hours before serving, mix together flour, brown sugar and butter with fingers. Press this crust mixture into an ungreased 9 x 13-inch pan. Combine butter and brown sugar in saucepan and bring to rolling boil; pour this hot mixture over crust. Sprinkle pecans over all this and bake at 350° for 20 minutes or until brown and bubbling. Remove from oven and sprinkle with chocolate chips. Let melt about 10 minutes; then spread with spatula. Do not put back in oven. After mixture cools, if chocolate is still sticky, put in refrigerator for about 15 minutes and chocolate will set up. 20 bars

Margaret D. Stent (Mrs. F. Terry)

Hawaiian Bars
Excellent for a coffee or a buffet

¼ **pound butter or margarine**
2 **cups white sugar**
4 **large eggs**
1½ **cups all-purpose flour**
½ **teaspoon salt**
½ **teaspoon baking soda**
1 **(20-ounce) can crushed**
   pineapple, well drained
1 **cup chopped nuts**

Melt butter in pan; cool slightly. Add sugar. Beat eggs until thick and creamy. Add butter and sugar. Beat well. Sift dry ingredients; add to above mixture. Add pineapple and nuts. Bake on greased 15 x 11-inch cookie sheet with sides at 350° for 30-45 minutes until done. Makes 36 large bars about ½ inch thick. Store in airtight container. 36 bars

Alice I. Noble (Mrs. David A.)

Buckeyes
These taste exactly like chocolate covered peanut butter cups

1½ **cups creamy peanut butter**
½ **cup softened butter**
1 **pound confectioners sugar**
1 **teaspoon vanilla**
1 **(12-ounce) package semi-**
   sweet chocolate chips
¼-½ **block parrafin**

In food processor or by hand, combine peanut butter, butter and sugar. Mix thoroughly. Transfer mixture to a large bowl and continue mixing until mixture can be shaped to form balls. Add ¼ cup water if needed. Melt chocolate and parrafin over low heat. Shape peanut butter mixture into 1 inch balls. Pierce each ball with a toothpick and dip into chocolate mixture to partially cover. Set aside on wax paper until hardened.

Barbara Ender (Mrs. Steven)
Watkinsville, Georgia

Congo Squares

1 **cup butter**
1 **box brown sugar**
3 **eggs**
2¾ **cups flour**
1 **cup nuts**
1 **(6 ounce) package chocolate**
   chips

Melt butter and add brown sugar. Add eggs one at a time beating well. Add flour. Mix well and add nuts and chocolate chips. Bake in a greased and floured 9 x 13-inch pan at 350° for 30-45 minutes. Cool and cut into squares.

Mrs. Edna Peacock

Cheese Cake Cookies
Cheese cake lovers love cheese cake cookies!

⅓ cup butter
⅓ cup brown sugar, packed
1 cup flour
½ cup walnuts
¼ cup sugar
1 (8-ounce) package cream
  cheese, softened
1 egg
2 Tablespoons milk
1 Tablespoon lemon juice
½ teaspoon vanilla

Heat oven to 350°. Cream butter with brown sugar. Add flour and walnuts; mix to make crumbs. Reserve 1 cup for topping. Press remainder into bottom of an 8-inch square pan. Bake at 350° for 12-15 minutes until lightly browned. Blend sugar with cream cheese until smooth. Add eggs, milk, lemon juice and vanilla. Beat well. Spread over baked crust. Sprinkle with remaining crumb mixture. Bake at 350° for 25 minutes. Cool. Cut into 2-inch squares. Store in the refrigerator.
16 squares

Maddy Kligora (Mrs. H. John)

Ranger Cookies

1 cup margarine
1 cup brown sugar
1 cup white sugar
2 eggs
1 teaspoon vanilla
2 cups sifted flour
1 teaspoon soda
½ teaspoon baking powder
½ teaspoon salt
2 cups oatmeal
2 cups corn flakes
1 cup coconut

Cream margarine and sugars. Beat in eggs and vanilla. Mix flour, soda, baking powder and salt. Stir into creamed mixture. Combine oatmeal, corn flakes and coconut; mix well and add to first mixture. Roll in small balls; press down on ungreased cookie sheet with a fork. Bake at 350° for 10-12 minutes. May be frozen.
75-85 cookies

Jane O. Duckworth (Mrs. E. J.)

Lemon Squares

1 cup butter
2 cups flour
½ cup powdered sugar
¼ teaspoon salt
4 eggs
2 cups sugar
4 Tablespoons flour
5 Tablespoons lemon juice

Blend first four ingredients and press into a 9 x 13-inch pan. Bake 15 minutes at 350°. Do not let top brown. Cool 5 minutes. Beat together remaining ingredients and pour over pastry. Bake at 350° for 25 minutes. Remove from oven and while warm, sprinkle with powdered sugar. When cool cut into squares.

Joy Butler

Amaretto Kisses
Almond lovers delight

1 (6-ounce) package chocolate
    chips
½ cup sugar
3 Tablespoons light corn syrup
½ cup chocolate amaretto
    liqueur (or regular amaretto)
2½ cups finely crushed vanilla
    wafers
1 cup finely chopped pecans

Melt chocolate in bowl of double boiler over hot, not boiling, water, stirring until chocolate is melted. Remove from heat; stir in sugar and corn syrup. Add liqueur and blend well. Combine nuts and vanilla wafer crumbs in bowl and stir in chocolate mixture. Mix well. Form into 1 inch balls; roll in granulated sugar. Store in airtight container several days before serving.

Birds Nest Cookies

½ cup butter, creamed
¼ cup brown sugar
1 egg yolk
1 cup flour
1 egg white
1 cup pecan meal or ground
    pecans
Jam—strawberry, blackberry,
    blueberry—your choice

Beat butter, brown sugar and egg yolk together. Add flour. Form balls and push flat. Beat egg white lightly. Roll cookie in egg white; then roll in ground nuts. Bake for 8 minutes at 350°. Make a dent with a thimble in center of each cookie and fill with dot of jam or jelly. Return to oven and bake 10 more minutes. Store in an air-tight container. 2 dozen

Susan Barton (Mrs. David L.)

Granny Squares
Especially pretty at Christmas

32 single graham crackers,
    crushed
2 Tablespoons sugar
⅔ cup butter, softened
1 (15-ounce) can condensed
    milk
1 cup coconut
1 teaspoon vanilla
1 cup mixed candied fruit
½ cup walnuts or pecans

Mix crumbs, sugar and butter as for a pie crust. Pack in an 8-inch square pan reserving ⅓ of crumbs for topping. Bake at 350° for 10 minutes. Mix remaining ingredients and pour on top of crumbs. Sprinkle reserved crumbs on top. Bake at 350° for 20 minutes. This can be made in a food processor.

Mrs. Charles A. Neubauer

Easy Chocolates
Those who don't like coconut don't even know it's in these!

1 box confectioners sugar
½ cup melted butter
1 can condensed milk
2 cups flaked coconut
2 cups chopped pecans
12 ounces chocolate chips
½ block paraffin

Combine sugar, butter, milk, coconut and pecans and chill 1 hour. Melt chocolate pieces and paraffin in double boiler over hot, not boiling, water. Roll candy mixture in 1-inch balls; insert toothpick in each. Return to refrigerator for 30 minutes. Dip in chocolate mixture. Remove toothpick. Spoon small amount of chocolate mixture over toothpick hole. Chill and store in refrigerator. Variation: Add an 8-ounce jar of chopped, drained maraschino cherries.

Linda P. Hightower (Mrs. Charles R.)

Divinity Fudge
Constant beating is the secret that makes this Divinity divine

2 cups sugar
½ cup light corn syrup
½ cup cold water
2 egg whites
1 teaspoon vanilla
1 cup chopped pecans (more
 if you like)

Mix sugar, syrup and water in saucepan over low heat. Stir only until sugar dissolves, then cook to soft ball stage. Beat egg whites stiff, continue beating and pour half the syrup slowly over the beaten egg whites. While continuing to beat this mixture, cook the rest of the syrup to the hard ball stage. Add this gradually to the syrup and egg white mixture. Add vanilla and continue beating until the candy is thick enough to drop from a spoon. Add the chopped pecans and place by spoonful on a buttered cookie sheet. 3 dozen servings

Virginia Carson (Mrs. Francis)

Caramelized Almonds
For a special touch
sprinkle over ice cream, pumpkin pie or chocolate mousse

1 cup slivered blanched
  almonds
½ cup sugar

In a heavy skillet over medium heat, stir sugar and almonds constantly until a light caramel color. Spread on a greased cookie sheet. Break apart when cool. Store in an airtight container.

Georgia Pralines

1 cup brown sugar
2 cups granulated sugar
1 cup water
1 Tablespoon butter
¼ teaspoon salt
1 teaspoon vanilla
3 cups pecan halves

Line baking sheets with waxed paper. In saucepan combine sugars and water. Stir over medium heat until sugars are melted. Bring to boil; boil to soft ball stage (236°F.). Remove from heat; stir in butter, salt and vanilla. Beat until syrup starts to become creamy. Stir in pecans. Drop by teaspoon onto baking sheets. If candy becomes too hard to drop from spoon, place pan over hot water; stir a few drops hot water into mixture to soften. 24 pralines

JoAnn P. Whitehead (Mrs. Harry C.)

Swedish Nuts
This is a lovely Christmas present

1 pound pecans or combination
  pecans and almonds,
  shelled
3 egg whites
Dash salt
1 cup sugar
½ cup butter

Toast pecans at 325° until light brown. Beat egg whites with salt until frothy. Add sugar and beat until stiff. Fold in nuts. Melt butter in a 10 x 15 x 1-inch jelly roll pan. Spread nut mixture over butter and bake at 325° for 30 minutes. Stir carefully every 10 minutes until light brown. Cool on paper towels and break into pieces.

International Fare

Chinese Party
MENU

Egg Drop Soup
Boiled Rice
Chicken Wings in Red Sauce
Barbecued Spareribs
Steamed Fish
Cabbage in Cream Sauce with Peanuts
Pears in Ginger Sauce
Almond Cakes
Chinese Tea

Most of this dinner can be prepared in advance. The following schedule will help you have everything ready at the same time and still not be in the kitchen a long time just before serving.

Early in the day or the day before the dinner:
1. Make chicken soup
2. Bake almond cakes.
3. Barbecue spareribs, refrigerate.
4. Make Sweet and Sour Sauce, refrigerate.
5. Buy fish, select serving dish to steam and serve in.
6. Buy pears and fresh ginger root (powdered ginger no substitute).
7. Cook chicken wings and refrigerate.
8. Cut scallions for garnish and refrigerate.
9. Select all serving dishes and utensils.

1 hour before dinner:
1. Wash rice and cook.
2. Clean and cut cabbage into 1 inch pieces.
3. Fry peanuts, set aside with cabbage. Open soup can.
4. Peel and slice pears and pour hot syrup over them.
5. Make cornstarch thickener.
6. Warm chicken wings.
7. Warm ribs and sauce slowly.

15 minutes before serving:
1. Steam fish.

Just before serving:
1. Reheat soup. When boiling add reconstituted cornstarch, egg and transfer to serving tureen. Garnish with chopped scallions.
2. Transfer wings to serving dish.
3. Transfer ribs to platter, mask with sauce; serve extra sauce.
4. Cook cabbage, transfer to serving dish, garnish with peanuts.
5. Rice may be served in casserole it was cooked in or transferred to appropriate serving dish.
6. Put water on for tea, warm tea pot.

Bon Appetit!

Chicken Egg-Drop Soup

4 cups chicken broth
½ cup finely diced water
chestnuts
2½ Tablespoons cornstarch
2½ Tablespoons cold water
½ cup green part of scallions,
cut in ¼ inch pieces
1 egg, slightly beaten

Add water chestnuts to the broth in pan and simmer 1 minute. Mix cornstarch and water together until smooth and stir into soup. Continue stirring until soup thickens. Add scallions. Turn off heat. Slowly pour in beaten egg, stirring gently with chopsticks or fork. Serve at once. This part may be done after soup has been transferred to tureen if service is to occur at dining room table.

It is important to not waste meat, bones, skin and vegetable peelings...a plastic bag in the freezer to "catch" each scrap is practical and this corresponds to the "stock pot" of former years. When a sizeable amount is collected, a very good broth may be made as follows:

Thaw contents of freezer bag and with about 1 quart add 2 quarts water and a slice of ginger root and 2 teaspoons salt. Bring to boil. Cover pan and turn heat to simmer for 15 minutes. Turn off heat and cool in broth...discard "solids", strain broth and refrigerate for future use. Will keep in refrigerator a few days.

Boiled Rice

1 cup long grain rice, rinsed
1¾ cups cold water

Place rice in a 2 quart saucepan that has a tight lid. Add water. Turn heat to high and bring to hard boil; watch carefully as this probably will take 3-4 minutes. Cover; turn heat to low and simmer for 20 minutes. Remove from heat. Without uncovering pan, let rice relax for another 20 minutes. Stir briskly with chop sticks or fork to loosen rice before serving. 3 cups cooked rice

FOR LARGER QUANTITIES OF RICE: Follow table below. Note that as quantity of rice is increased, proportionately less water is used. Cooking time: Once the rice is brought to a rolling boil, the simmering and the relaxing time is the same, regardless of the amount cooked. Rice triples in volume when cooked.

Rice	Cold Water	Pan Size
2 cups	3¼ cups	2 quart
3 cups	4 cups	4 quart
4 cups	5 cups	4 quart

Four cups raw rice is about the maximum amount to cook well. If more is needed, use additional pan with desired amount.

Chicken Wings in Red Sauce

3 or 4 wings per serving, separated at joints, washed and dried
2 Tablespoons dry cocktail sherry
3 Tablespoons soy sauce (imported)
1 Tablespoon honey
4 slices fresh ginger root
3 scallions or 2 small onions, cut into 1 inch pieces
4 star anise seeds

Heat 2½ quart saucepan with small amount of cooking oil until very hot. Add chicken wings and coat well with hot oil. Add other ingredients, cover, bring to a boil, reduce heat and simmer for about 1 hour. Stir often. This dish is better made ahead and reheated. Also freezes well.

Barbecued Spareribs

1 slab (about 2 pounds) fresh, young spareribs. Have butcher cut slab in half lengthwise so ribs are about 2 inches long
MARINADE:
4 Tablespoons imported soy sauce
4 Tablespoons hoisin sauce
2 Tablespoons dry sherry
½ teaspoon 5 spice powder
5 Tablespoons honey
1 clove garlic, minced or pressed

Preparation time: 10 minutes
Marinating time: 2-3 hours (or overnight in refrigerator)
Cooking time: 1 hour 20 minutes (more or less)

Marinade: Mix all ingredients, brush on spareribs on all sides. Place ribs in a large pan and pour over remaining marinade. Set aside 2 or 3 hours at room temperature (or overnight) in the refrigerator.

To cook: Set oven at 375°. Pour water to cover bottom of roasting pan. Place ribs on roasting rack and set over water. Do not let ribs touch water. Place pan on mid rack in oven. After 30 minutes or so, baste with remaining marinade. After 1 hour or so total cooking time, remove from oven and pour off water. Raise temperature to 450°F. Return ribs for 8-10 minutes or until nicely crisp and brown.

To serve: Cut into individual ribs to be eaten with fingers. Pile on serving plate. Serve with Hot Mustard Sauce or Sweet and Sour Sauce.

Note: Once cooked, ribs may be frozen and reheated.

Steamed Fish

1½ pounds fresh fish, whole,
   fillets or chunks
½ teaspoon shredded fresh
   ginger root
1 scallion, cut in 2 inch pieces
½ teaspoon fermented black
   beans
1 Tablespoon soy sauce
1 Tablespoon dry sherry
1 Tablespoon peanut or corn
   oil

If using a whole fish, clean, wash and dry inside and outside. Put whole fish into a heatproof dish that fits into your steamer. Mix remaining ingredients and pour all over fish and rub some inside. Heat water until boiling and steam for 30 minutes or until done. Do not peek into steamer during steaming process; large, thick pieces may require 5 additional minutes while thin pieces may require less; decide first. Note: Regular salt may be substituted for fermented black beans although some flavor will be lost.

Cabbage in Cream Sauce with Fresh Peanuts

½ cup fresh, raw peanuts
Oil
1 head cabbage, cut in half
   and then sliced into 1 inch
   square pieces, rinsed and
   drained
Salt and pepper to taste
½ cup chicken broth or water
1 Tablespoon dry cocktail
   sherry
½ can cream of chicken soup

Fry peanuts in a little oil. Drain on paper. In a wok, large skillet or stew pot, measure 2 Table-spoons oil and heat very hot. When oil "ripples" add cabbage all at once and stir to coat with oil. Add salt and pepper. Stir well and add broth or water to make vegetable steam. Cover with lid for 5 seconds. Uncover and stir again. Recover for another 5 seconds. Add sherry and recover for 5 seconds. At this point, cabbage should be crisp-tender. If not, recover for another 5 seconds or so. When crisp-tender, make well in center and add chicken soup mixing well with liquid in pan. Transfer to serving dish and garnish with peanuts.

Chinese Almond Cakes

¾ cup sugar
1 teaspoon baking powder
½ teaspoon salt
¾ cup softened margarine
1 egg
2 Tablespoons water
2 teaspoons almond extract
2½ cups unbleached flour
42 whole almonds

In a large bowl blend sugar, baking powder, salt, margarine, egg, water and almond extract well. Gently measure flour and gradually add to above mixture. Shape dough into 1 inch balls; place on greased cookie sheet about 2 inches apart. Flatten balls slightly with glass dipped in granulated sugar. Press a whole almond firmly into center of each cookie. Bake at 350° for 8-12 minutes until firm but not brown. Do not overbake. These freeze well.

Pears in Ginger Sauce

1 cup sugar
2 cups boiling water
5-6 pieces fresh ginger root
4 firm pears

Make syrup using sugar, boiling water and ginger root. Dissolve sugar and let steep for ½ hour. Peel and core pears and slice into glass serving bowl. Discard ginger and pour syrup over pears. Let stand at room temperature until ready to serve. A beautiful garnish is a peeled and sliced Chinese gooseberry (Kiwi Fruit) which may be added just after the syrup.

Sweet and Sour Sauce

½ scallion, cut in 1-inch pieces
2 green peppers, cut in 1-inch
pieces
4 slices canned pineapple, cut
into 8 pieces each
12 maraschino cherries
1 carrot, parboiled and cut into
1 inch cubes (optional)
6 Tablespoons catsup
5 Tablespoons vinegar
5 Tablesoons sugar
2 Tablespoons cornstarch
1 cup water

Heat small amount of oil in wok and quickly stir-fry fruit and vegetables; remove from wok and set aside. In a small bowl, mix catsup, vinegar, sugar, cornstarch and water. Heat 4 Tablespoons oil in wok and when hot pour catsup mixture all at once into wok. Stir until sauce thickens. Add fried fruit and vegetables and stir quickly. Transfer to serving bowl or pour over meat that has specially been prepared for Sweet and Sour recipes. Note: If you have leftover jam, preserves or jelly in the refrigerator, try using it in place of sugar in this recipe; also substitute honey or add a few slivers of fresh ginger root and stir-fry along with the other vegetables and fruit.

Hot Chinese Mustard

2 Tablespoons water
¼ teaspoon vinegar
¼ teaspoon peanut oil
Dry Coleman's mustard

In a very small bowl add water, vinegar and peanut oil. Into this mixture, fold in dry Coleman's mustard until a thin paste forms. The mustard swells, so add a teaspoon at a time; you can always add a drop or two of water if you have too much mustard powder; this keeps sealed in a small jar in refrigerator or add small amounts to your regular mustard to "jazz it up".

Deen Terry
The Chinese Cooking School
Atlanta, Georgia

Danish Christmas Dinner
MENU

Pork Roast
Gravy
Brown Potatoes
Red Cabbage
Sweet and Sour Pickles
Danish Rice Pudding

Glaedelig Jul!

Merry Christmas from Denmark!

This is a traditional dinner that has been served on Christmas Eve in my Danish family for generations. It is a Christmas tradition that I now share yearly with my Atlanta friends.

Pork Roast

1 (10-15 pound) pork ham with skin left on

Slice the pork skin with sharp knife in thin slices through the fat. Salt all sides of pork. Cook at 325° for 40 minutes per pound. During cooking pour cold water over roast several times. When finished cooking, before removing from oven, turn temperature up to 400° to brown the rind; this will also make it crisp. Save all the juice and drippings for the gravy.

Gravy

4 Tablespoons margarine
4 Tablespoons flour
Drippings and juice from roast

Melt butter in saucepan, stir in flour and mix to a paste. Gradually add drippings and juice from roast stirring until smooth. Will require 4 cups of juice at least; if more liquid is needed use cold water. Add salt and pepper if needed, also Kitchen Bouquet for color.

Brown Potatoes

2 sticks margarine
1 cup sugar
4 cans small white potatoes,
    drained (1 can per two
    people)

Melt butter in large frying pan, add sugar, stir and heat until melted and light brown. Add potatoes; simmer for 15-20 minutes turning potatoes as necessary to brown them on all sides with a slight sugar coating.

Red Cabbage

2 medium heads red cabbage
2 large apples, shredded
1 cup vinegar
2 Tablespoons butter
1 cup sugar
2 cups cranberry juice
2 teaspoons salt

Cut cabbage very fine; mix with shredded apples. Cook cabbage and apples in vinegar and butter for 1½ hours. Add sugar, cranberry juice and salt, adding more sugar or salt if needed. Cook another 30 minutes or until cabbage is done.

This freezes well. Serve as a vegetable with pork roast, Danish meatballs, pork chops, etc. Also excellent cold on an open face sandwich.

Danish Rice Pudding
(Christmas Dessert)

1 cup rice
4 cups milk
½ pint heavy cream, whipped
Vanilla
Chopped or sliced almonds
Blueberry sauce or syrup

Cook rice in milk over very low heat until all milk has been absorbed, 20-30 minutes. Cool. This can be prepared ahead of time and stored in the refrigerator. Before serving add the whipped cream, vanilla and almonds. It should be a smooth pudding; if too thick, add a little more milk. Serve with blueberry sauce or syrup. At Christmas we serve it with 1 whole almond in one dessert. The person who finds the almond then receives a prize.

Winnie R. Goodman (Mrs. James E.)

Cold French Buffet

MENU

Tomates Farcis
Potage Crème d'Asperges
Filet de Boeuf
Legumes pour le Grand Aioli
Peches à la Franz Josef

An elegant buffet, suitable for a luncheon or dinner. Everything may be prepared beforehand, and no rewarming is necessary.

Tomatoes Farcis (stuffed tomatoes)
Potage Creme d'Asperges (cream of asparagus soup)
Filet de Boeuf (fillet of beef)
Legumes, Sauce Aioli (vegetables, garlic mayonnaise)
Peches a la Franz Josef (peaches stuffed with buttercream)

Tomates Farcis
(Stuffed Tomatoes)
Serve these little hors d'oeuvres with cocktails.
In France, something that can be eaten in a single bite is
called an amuse-gueule, something to "amuse your mouth".

1 basket cherry tomatoes
Herbed cheese, such as
   Boursin
3 Tablespoons finely chopped
   parsley

Cut a slice from the smooth end of each tomato. With your fingertip, scoop out the seeds. Dip the cut edge into the parsley to make a green rim. Beat the cheese until smooth. Place in a pastry bag fitted with a medium star tip and pipe a rosette of cheese into each tomato. Chill until serving time.

Potage Crème D'Aspèrges
(Cream of Asparagus Soup)

2 Tablespoons butter
3 Tablespoons flour
1 cup milk
1 small onion, sliced
2 cups chicken stock
1 generous pound fresh
  asparagus
1 cup heavy cream

Add flour to hot melted butter. Cook over low heat 3 minutes. Whisk in the milk and stock. Add the onion. Let this simmer while cooking the asparagus. Wash asparagus. Snap off butt ends. Cut into 2-inch pieces. Place tips loosely in a cheesecloth bag. Place all asparagus in 4 cups salted water that has just come to a rolling boil. Remove tips as soon as they are tender, about 8 minutes. Boil the other pieces about 5 more minutes. Reserve the tips to use as a garnish. Place asparagus stem pieces in the simmering sauce. The asparagus cooking water should now be reduced to about 1¾ cup. Stir this liquid into the sauce. If necessary, continue boiling water until it is reduced enough. Simmer the soup, partially covered, 45 minutes or until asparagus pieces are very soft. Sieve soup through a food mill or a strainer, pressing through all of the tender pulp. This is necessary to eliminate the unpleasant texture of the tougher peels. If you want to purée the soup in a food processor, the asparagus should be peeled below the tips with a vegetable peeler before cooking. Chill soup. Stir in the cream and season to taste before serving. Garnish each serving with a few asparagus tips. 6-7 servings

Filet De Boeuf
(Filet of Beef)

1 beef fillet
3 Tablespoons butter

Trim the beef of all sinews, tough membranes and excess fat. The "chain", the long, thin piece of meat along the side, should be removed. (It may be ground for steak tartare or cut in bits and quickly sautéed.) If desired, lard the fillet using a larding needle and thin strips of pork fat. Tuck the tail end of the fillet under so that the piece of meat is approximately the same thickness along the entire length. This prevents the tail, or thin end, from overcooking. Tie the fillet in several places with kitchen string to insure juiciness and a compact shape. Heat butter in a skillet or shallow roasting pan. Quickly brown the fillet over a fairly high burner heat, turning the fillet to brown on all sides. Place pan in a 475° oven. Cook 20 minutes, turning it occasionally. Cook to an internal temperature of 135° for medium rare. Seven minutes per pound will give you an estimate of time required, but the thermometer is much more accurate. Remove from pan and let rest at least 15 minutes before serving. Season slices with salt and freshly ground pepper. This may be served warm or cool, with or without the aioli sauce.

Légumes Pour Le Grand Aioli
(Vegetables, garlic mayonnaise)

1 bunch broccoli
1 head cauliflower
1 bunch carrots

Cut broccoli and cauliflower into flowerets. Peel carrots. If using miniature carrots, leave them whole. Otherwise, cut into julienne strips ½ inch wide and 3-4 inches long. Bring 3 large pots of water to a boil. For every 4 quarts water, add 2 teaspoons salt. Gently boil each vegetable until just tender enough to be pierced with the point of a knife, about 5 minutes for broccoli and 10 minutes for carrots and cauliflower. Drain vegetables and quickly refresh by pouring cold water over them until they are cool to the touch. This locks in the color and stops the cooking. Drain on a towel. Arrange the vegetables on lettuce leaves and serve with the aioli. 6 servings

Aioli Mayonnaise

This sauce is served with practically anything in the South of France: grilled fish or chicken, fish soup, vegetables. It's easily made in a food processor or blender.

1 slice bread, crust removed
2 Tablespoons white wine vinegar
3 large garlic cloves, skinned and crushed well
2 egg yolks
½ cup olive oil
½ cup vegetable oil
½ teaspoon salt

Soak the bread in the vinegar. Chop the crushed garlic in processor bowl. Blend in the bread. Add the egg yolks, 3 Tablespoons of the oil and the salt. Blend 4 seconds. Pour in the remaining oil in a slow steady stream. Taste for seasoning.

Pêches à la Franz Josef
(Peaches stuffed with buttercream)

4 peaches
3 egg yolks
Rounded ½ cup sifted
    confectioners sugar
Quick dash of salt
9 Tablespoons soft unsalted
    butter
3 Tablespoons very finely
    chopped almonds (or
    praline powder)
Scant Tablespoon rum,
    Cognac or B & B
GARNISH:
Mint leaves

Drop peaches in pot of boiling water for 15 seconds. Immediately refresh with cold water. Peel and rub all over with lemon or fruit fresh to prevent discoloration. Beat together the yolks, salt, and sugar until light and thick. Beat in half of the butter. Then beat in the remaining butter Tablespoon by Tablespoon. Beat in the nuts, and liqueur to taste. Cut peaches in half. Top with buttercream. Chill if made ahead of time. Take peaches from refrigerator 20 minutes before serving to resoften the buttercream. Top peaches with a mint leaf. 4 servings

Diane Wilkinson
School of Cooking
Atlanta, Georgia

French Nouvelle Cuisine
A DINNER MENU FOR 4

Rack of Lamb Provençale
Sweated Vegetables
Onion Soup in the French Manner, Gratineéd
Orange and Onion Salad
Crêpes Normande

A typical Nouvelle Cuisine menu, with fine, fresh ingredients, fast cooking time, without the use of flour, and little preparation time.

Rack of Lamb Provençale
(2-3 pound racks are needed to serve 4)

1 (2½-3 pound) rack of lamb
2 cloves garlic, peeled and cut in slivers
1 teaspoon rosemary
1 teaspoon thyme
2-3 Tablespoons olive oil
Salt and pepper
½ cup white wine
½ cup chicken stock
SWEATED VEGETABLES:
Onions
Celery
Carrots
Salt, pepper, butter

Scrape bones. Make incisions in lamb with point of knife and insert slivers of garlic. Heat oil in roasting pan, put in lamb, baste and sprinkle with herbs and salt and pepper. Roast, basting often in 375° oven for 1¼ hours or until meat registers 140°F (or rare)

To serve: Tranfer the lamb to platter, decorate chop bones with paper chop frills and keep warm. Lamb may be carved into individual portions in the kitchen before serving. Discard any fat from roasting pan and deglaze pan juices with wine and stock. Bring to boil, simmer 1-2 minutes, strain, taste for seasoning and serve sauce separately.

Sweated Vegetables: Slice vegetables, place in pan with seasoning and butter with wax paper over them. On low heat, cook until tender.

Onion Soup in the French Manner, Gratinéed

4 Tablespoons butter
2 pounds onion (preferably
    Bermuda onion), peeled and
    thinly sliced (about 7 cups)
1 teaspoon salt
1 Tablespoon flour
2 quarts brown beef stock,
    freshly made or canned; if
    you use concentrated
    canned type, dilute it with
    equal amount of water
Freshly ground black pepper
6-8 one inch slices of French
    bread
About 4 ounces Swiss and
    imported Parmesan cheese,
    freshly grated, mixed.
    Should equal 1 cup.

Melt butter over moderate heat in a heavy 5-6 quart casserole. When foaming, add onions and salt. Stirring occasionally, fry them 20-30 minutes, letting onions become a deep rich brown. This will give the soup color and flavor. Don't hurry this, or onions will char and have a particularly unpleasant flavor. Now stir in flour, off heat; return to heat, stirring constantly for a minute or two, then pour in the stock. Bring stock to a boil, stirring until it boils, and reduce heat to a simmer; partially cover casserole, and simmer for 20-30 minutes. Taste for seasoning. You may add considerably more salt than indicated to give the soup more body and flavor. Nothing's worse than undersalted soup, especially onion—this soup is dictated by its stock so if your stock is poor, so will be your soup. Make the croûtes. Preheat oven to 325°. Arrange slices of bread side by side on a baking sheet, then slide it into the upper third of the oven and toast them for about 15 minutes. If you brush them with a good oil or butter, they will add more flavor to the soup.

Variation: Soupe a l'Oignon Soufflé

For 1 quart, make a soufflé mixture with 1 teaspoon butter, 1 teaspoon flour, ¼ cup milk, 1 Tablespoon grated Swiss cheese, salt and white pepper to taste, 2 egg yolks and 2 beaten egg whites. Float this mixture on top of soup in which you have already placed slices of toasted bread. Put in 375° oven for 10 minutes or until soufflé rises and is golden brown.

When you are ready to serve the soup, preheat the oven to 375°. Arrange the croûtes side-by-side on top of the soup, and sprinkle them evenly with cheese. (You may ladle the soup into individual bowls before adding a croûte to each, and sprinkle it with cheese.) Bake soup in middle of oven for 10-15 minutes, or until cheese has melted and formed a light brown crust. If it is not brown enough for your taste, slide casserole or individual bowls under broiler for a few seconds or so to brown tops further. Serve at once.

Orange and Onion Salad

Boston lettuce, red leaf
    lettuce or Romaine
Naval oranges, peeled and
    sectioned
Red onions, thinly sliced
VINAIGRETTE DRESSING:
¼ cup white wine vinegar with
    tarragon
¾ cup salad oil
Pinch sugar
1 teaspoon salt
Freshly ground pepper

Whisk dressing ingredients to combine, and taste. If too oily, add more salt. Combine lettuce, oranges and onions; toss with dressing. If desired add toasted slivered almonds.

Crêpes Normandes

8 cooked crêpes
3 tart apples, pared, cored
    and thinly sliced
2 Tablespoons melted butter
½ cup heavy cream
½ cup sugar

Lay 4 crêpes in bottom of 4 heatproof plates. Brush crêpes with melted butter, lay another crêpe on each one and brush again with butter. Put apple slices on top and pour over the cream. Sprinkle generously with sugar and broil for 6-8 minutes or until sugar has caramelized and apples are tender.

Nathalie Dupree
Rich's Cooking School
Atlanta, Georgia

French Nouvelle Cuisine
A LUNCHEON MENU FOR 4

Stuffed Tomato Salad with Flounder Goujonnettes
Wholemeal Soda Bread
Profiteroles with Ginger Ice Cream and Raspberry Puree

Some of the elements of Nouvelle Cuisine represented here are the shorter cooking time for the fish and vegetables, the fresh ingredients, the ginger in the ice cream and the overall lightness of the meal. The soda bread, although English, complements the salad nicely.

Wheatmeal Soda Bread

**2 pounds whole wheat flour
(Hodgson Mill)
2 teaspoons* baking soda
4 teaspoons* cream of tartar
2 teaspoons* sugar
3 Tablespoons* butter
2 teacups* (approximately) milk
All purpose flour**

***when measuring, use
tableware instead of
regulation measuring spoons**

Mix dry ingredients in a large bowl. Rub in butter with fingers. Add milk to make a soft dough that is firm but sticky. Turn dough onto board that has been sprinkled with enough all-purpose flour to make dough easy to handle. Knead 8-10 times. Shape into a large round. Flour the handle of a wooden spoon and make a deep cross in the dough. Place on a greased baking sheet and bake 25-35 minutes or until done. Serve this moist bread warm with lots of butter.

Stuffed Tomato Salad with Flounder Goujonnettes

4 medium size, firm tomatoes,
   peeled
12 large shrimp, cooked and
   peeled
2 flounder fillets, cut in
   diagonal strips
16-20 lettuce leaves
2 teaspoons fresh mixed herbs
   (parsley, mint, tarragon),
   chopped
HERB MAYONNAISE:
1 egg yolk
Salt and pepper
1 Tablespoon vinegar
½ Tablespoon mustard
⅓ cup vegetable oil
⅓ cup olive oil
1 Tablespoon lemon juice
2 Tablespoons grapefruit juice
1 Tablespoon catsup
2 teaspoons fresh mixed herbs
   (parsley, mint, tarragon),
   chopped

½ pound small snap beans,
   split in half lengthwise
VINAIGRETTE:
½ Tablespoon Dijon mustard
1 Tablespoon vinegar
3 Tablespoons oil
Salt and pepper

Tomato Shells: Cut off the top of each tomato, scalloping the edges, to make a cup. With a teaspoon carefully remove the seeds. Sprinkle with salt, turn upside down and leave to drain.

Flounder: Poach the flounder fillets in boiling salted water for 2-3 minutes or until tender but still quite firm to avoid their being broken up when mixed with the mayonnaise. Drain thoroughly and dry on a towel. Cool and mix carefully with herb mayonnaise.

Herb Mayonnaise: Using blender, food processor or mixer, mix yolk, salt and pepper and mustard. Add oil slowly, drop by drop, to incorporate it well. Then mix in other ingredients and taste for herbs and seasonings.

Green Bean Salad: Cook the green beans in a large pan of boiling salted water for about 5-7 minutes or until barely tender. Drain, refresh under cold running water and drain thoroughly. Mix the green beans with enough vinaigrette to moisten.

To assemble: Place the strips of flounder inside the tomatoes, standing up. Decorate with the shrimp by placing them, facing each other, inside the tomato also. On each plate arrange a bed of lettuce leaves. Place the stuffed tomato in the center. Arrange the green bean salad in a wreath around the tomato. Sprinkle the fresh herbs on the flounder.

Ginger Ice Cream

4 cups milk
10 egg yolks
1½ cups sugar
5 Tablespoons chopped
    candied ginger (can be
    done in food processor)
1-1½ cups heavy cream,
    whipped until it holds a
    soft shape

Bring the milk to a full rolling boil. In another saucepan, beat the egg yolks with the sugar until thick and light. Whisk in all the hot milk slowly—don't whisk too hard or you will get too much foam—and return to heat. Heat gently, stirring constantly with a wooden spoon, until the custard thickens slightly; if you draw your finger across the back of the spoon, it will leave a clear trail. The foam should subside by the time the custard is done. Do not overcook or boil the custard or it will curdle. Remove the custard at once from the heat, strain it into a bowl, and stir in the chopped candied ginger. Let cool and pour into a churn. After about 5 minutes of churning or when the ice cream is partly set, add the lightly whipped cream to the mixture and continue freezing the mixture until set. Remove dasher, taste, and either stir in ginger from bottom of freezer or throw away if ice cream is flavored enough. Serve immediately or replace lid covered with aluminum foil, wrap churn in towels or a blanket, and let ice cream cure. Serve in cream puffs with raspberry or strawberry purée (use blender or food processor to purée fresh berries, sweeten lightly, if necessary).

Sarah Rhodes
Martha Summerour
Rich's Cooking School
Atlanta, Georgia

Hungarian Cookery—A Collection of Recipes

Classic French cookery is believed to have its roots in the famous marriage between the young Italian Catherine De'Medici and a French youth who was to become King Henry II. This sixteenth century nuptial happening has had far reaching culinary reverberations, and historically inclined gourmets tend to agree that Italy, not France is the true cradle of gastronomy. But about 100 years earlier, another country had received the enriching civilized Italian touch, a touch that would begin the development of one of the most exciting and savory cuisines in the world. In 1475, King Matthias of Hungary married an Italian noblewoman, Beatrice, daughter of the King of Naples. Beatrice brought with her, as a sort of culinary dowry, an array of chefs, fine china, cookware, cookery books and exotic ingredients. The wedding feast of Beatrice and Matthias was a study in ultra-sophisticated gastronomic excess. From that day on King Matthias became obsessed with fine food and drink. During the time of his reign Hungary became one of the world's richest and most powerful nations. All the arts were of the utmost importance in the royal court, but the art of cookery provided the greatest pleasures.

During the next century, after the death of the great king, Hungary entered a dark period…the country suffered a long Turkish occupation. This occupational influence brought changes and new dimensions to Hungarian food. The famous Hungarian strudel is a direct descendant of Turkish filo; the Turks eventually introduced two gifts of the new world—paprika and tomatoes—to Hungarian cooks; and Turkish pita bread became Hungarian Langos. The strong Turkish cultural impact on the Hungary of Matthias, which in turn was built on a strong foundation of Magyar cookery techniques, has produced a cuisine of great subtlety and delicacy; a combination of peasant and aristocratic tastes that is unmatched anywhere in the world.

The soul of modern Hungarian cookery is paprika, not the tasteless red dust often used for coloring the top of egg salad, but lovely full flavored Hungarian rose paprika. I buy it several pounds at once from a shop in New York called, appropriately enough, Paprikas Weiss, but it is available in the "gourmet" section of local super markets in little red cans.

The following is a collection of my favorites to share with you in good taste…

Blueberry Soup*

2 (10 ounce) packages frozen blueberries
2 cups water
1 lemon, sliced
1 cinnamon stick
⅓ cup granulated sugar
1 cup half and half
Fresh blueberries (optional)

Combine first 5 ingredients in a saucepan. Bring to a boil. Reduce heat and simmer for 10 minutes. Remove lemon and cinnamon stick, and purée soup in the blender. This soup should be very smooth and velvety. Cool, then chill thoroughly in the refrigerator. Just before serving, stir in half and half. If fresh blueberries are in season, garnish each bowlful with a few. 6 servings

Cold Hungarian Tomato Soup

4 pounds vine ripened tomatoes
2 onions, chopped
½ cup fresh parsley
Slivered zest of ½ lemon
1 Tablespoon sweet Hungarian
   paprika
1 Tablespoon sugar
Salt and freshly ground
   pepper to taste
Juice of 1 lemon
Sour cream

Peel, seed and juice the tomatoes. Chop them coarsely into a large, non metallic pot. Add the onions, parsley, lemon zest, paprika, sugar, salt and pepper. Bring to a simmer and simmer for 5-7 minutes. Stir in the lemon juice. Put the soup into the blender in batches and flick the blender on and off. This soup should be lumpy; not a puree. Pour into a glass bowl and chill. Serve with a dollop of sour cream on top of each bowlful. 6-8 servings

Stiriai Metelt
(Noodle Pudding)

½ pound wide egg noodles
4 eggs
⅔ cup sugar
1 cup sour cream
Grated rind of 1 lemon
¾ cup yellow raisins
4 Tablespoons butter

Preheat oven to 375°. Cook noodles according to package directions. Meanwhile, beat eggs with sugar. Beat in sour cream. Stir in lemon rind and raisins. Drain noodles. Rinse under hot running water. Place in large bowl and toss with butter. Stir in egg, sour cream mixture. The noodles should be well coated with the mixture. Pour the noodles into an oblong buttered 1½ quart baking dish. Spread them evenly in the dish. Bake for 30-40 minutes, until the top is lightly browned and crispy and the pudding is set. (A knife inserted near the center will emerge clean.) Serve warm.
6 servings

Bogracs Gulyas
(Kettle Goulash)

4 Tablespoons bacon fat
5 large onions, chopped coarsely
2 large green peppers,
   chopped coarsely
3 cloves garlic, minced
1½ Tablespoons Hungarian
   Paprika
3 pounds well trimmed stewing
   beef, cut into 1 inch cubes
Salt and freshly ground pepper
   to taste
1 (6 ounce) can tomato paste
Sour cream at room
   temperature

Preheat oven to 325°. Heat fat in a deep heavy pot. Cook the onions, peppers, and garlic until the onions are limp and transparent. Add paprika. Stir over very low heat until vegetables are well coated and paprika has lost its raw taste. Add beef and remaining ingredients except sour cream. Stir well to combine. Simmer in preheated oven for 1½-2 hours or until the meat is tender. Adjust oven temperature during cooking time so contents of pot remain at a simmer. Serve in shallow soup bowls with a tablespoon of sour cream atop each serving.
6 servings

Erdelyi Zsivanypecsenye
(Bandit's Meat)

2 pounds well trimmed flank
   steak
Paprika
Salt and freshly ground pepper
½ pound bacon, each slice
   cut in half
1 Tablespoon bacon fat

Slice the flank steak, against the grain, about ¼ inch thick. Spread wax paper over your work surface. Place the beef slices on the paper. Cover with another sheet of wax paper. With a kitchen mallet or the flat side of a wide knife, gently pound the pieces until they are about ⅛ inch thick. Remove top sheet of paper. Sprinkle upper side of each slice with paprika, salt and pepper. Roll each slice into a sausage like shape. Wrap with a bacon slice and secure with a toothpick. Melt bacon fat in a wide, heavy skillet. When sizzling, add the beef rolls and brown quickly on all sides. When browned, pour into a colander over a bowl to drain away all fat. Return rolls to skillet. Cover and cook over very low heat for 10 minutes, shaking pan frequently. Serve at once.
6 servings

Pork Paprikash*

1 Tablespoon butter
1 Tablespoon corn oil
1 pound mushrooms, trimmed and sliced
1 Tablespoon butter
2 Tablespoons corn oil
2 pounds well trimmed pork tenderloin, sliced ¼ inch thick
Salt and pepper
1 large onion, chopped
1 small clove garlic, minced
1 teaspoon sweet paprika
½ cup dry, white wine
½ cup chicken stock
1 teaspoon Dijon mustard
¼ cup sour cream at room temperature
¼ cup half and half at room temperature
½ cup fresh, chopped parsley

Heat butter and oil. Sauté the mushrooms in a heavy skillet until just limp. Scrape into a bowl and set aside. Heat remaining butter and oil in the skillet. Sprinkle the pork slices with salt and pepper and add to the skillet. Cook over high heat, turning the slices in the hot oil until browned, about 2 minutes. Add the pork slices to the mushrooms. Add the onions and garlic to the fat remaining in the skillet. Sauté them until the onions are limp and transparent. Add the paprika and stir over low heat until the onions are well coated. Transfer the onions to the bowl with the pork. Add the wine and stock to the skillet and cook over high heat for 3 minutes. Use a wooden spatula or spoon to scrape up any brown bits adhering to the pan. Stir in the mustard. Return the onions, mushrooms and pork to the skillet. Simmer for 5 minutes. Combine the half and half and sour cream. Blend some of the liquid in the pan into the cream. Then stir the mixture back into the pork and mushrooms. Simmer over very low heat for 3-5 minutes, or until tender. Do not boil. Sprinkle with parsley and serve at once.
6 servings

Green Beans in Sour Cream

2 pounds fresh green beans,
  trimmed
4 Tablespoons butter
1 large onion, cut in half and
  thinly sliced info half
  moons
1 green pepper, cut in half
  and thinly sliced
1 can plum tomatoes, well
  drained and chopped
½ cup chopped parsley
½ teaspoon dried basil
Salt and freshly ground pepper
  to taste
1 Tablespoon flour
1 cup sour cream at room
  temperature

Steam the beans over boiling water until crisp tender, 7-10 minutes. Rinse under cold water and drain well. Melt butter in a heavy skillet. In it, saute the onion and green pepper until tender. Add tomatoes and cook until they begin to render their juices. Add beans, parsley, basil, salt and pepper. Cook until it is all piping hot. Whisk flour into sour cream. Stir some hot liquid from the skillet into the sour cream, then stir cream mixture into the vegetables in the skillet. Simmer for 5 minutes. Taste and adjust seasonings. Serve at once.
6 servings

Squash with Sour Cream and Dill*

2 pounds yellow squash,
  peeled, seeded and cut
  lengthwise into long thin
  strips (to seed squash,
  after peeling, cut in half
  lengthwise and remove
  seeds with a teaspoon)
Salt
2 Tablespoons corn oil
2 Tablespoons enriched flour
1 cup sour cream at room
  temperature
1½ teaspoons white wine
  vinegar
1 Tablespoon dried dill or 2
  Tablespoons fresh snipped
  dill
Salt and pepper

Sprinkle squash with a generous amount of salt in a glass or enameled bowl. Let stand for 20-30 minutes. Rinse, drain and pat dry. Heat oil, toss squash in oil for about 5 minutes. Squash should still be crisp. With a wire whisk, stir flour into sour cream. Pour over squash and stir. Simmer gently about 5 minutes. Stir in vinegar, dill, salt and pepper. Serve hot. 6 servings

Susan L. Krietzman
*Courtesy **The Nutrition Cookbook**
Harcourt Brace Jovanovitch

all other recipes
Susan L. Krietzman
In Good Taste School of Cookery
Atlanta, Georgia

Ron Cohn's Palacsinta
(Hungarian Crêpe Dessert)
The carbonated water makes an unusually light crêpe

CREPES:
3 eggs
1¼ cups flour
1 cup milk
1 teaspoon sugar
Pinch of salt
1 cup carbonated water or
   1 cup combination
   carbonated water and
   cherry liqueur
Clarified butter for cooking
APRICOT JELLY:
12 ounces dried apricots
½ cup sugar
Brandy or cherry liqueur to
   taste
TOPPING:
½ pound sugar
3 egg whites
1 cup walnuts, finely ground

Crepes: Mix flour, milk, sugar and salt to make a smooth pancake like dough. Let rest for 1 or 2 hours. Stir in carbonated water at last minute, just before cooking. Heat 8-inch crêpe pan. When hot, add ¼ teaspoon butter. Pour ladle full of dough into pan, twist to cover entire pan. When top of the batter bubbles turn over and cook 4 or 5 seconds longer. Add more butter for each Palacsinta. Keep warm covered with wax paper. Fill with apricot jelly.

Apricot Jelly: Put dried apricots in saucepan with water to cover, cook over low heat until apricots disintegrate into a jelly. Add liqueur and sugar to taste. Place some jelly across one end of pancake and roll.

Topping: Top with powdered sugar which has been standing with a vanilla bean, or mix topping ingredients until fluffy. Put 2 Tablespoons of this mixture on top of filled Palacsinta and place in broiler until lightly browned.
12-14 crepes

Ron Cohn
Hal's Restaurant
Atlanta, Georgia

A Family Italian Dinner for Eight
MENU

Spinach Soup
Baked Fish and Potatoes
Zucchini Frittata
Green Salad
Zuccotto

Italian cooking seeks to procure the best fresh ingredients and preserve their identity. The traditional Italian recipes are mainly derived from homespun creations, rather than from chef and restaurant recipes.

Spinach Soup

2 pounds spinach—before cooking or 2 packages frozen spinach, thawed and drained
4 Tablespoons olive oil
2 cloves garlic, crushed
4 Tablespoons flour
8 cups chicken stock (or canned chicken broth)

Cook and purée spinach. Heat oil in heavy pan, add crushed garlic and when brown remove. (Watch carefully. The garlic will burn very easily.) Blend in the flour, add puréed spinach and stock; bring to a boil and cook gently for half an hour. Serve with croûtons of toast and grated Parmesan cheese.

Baked Fish and Potatoes

2 pounds boiling potatoes
¾ cup olive oil (or half salad
    oil and half olive oil)
1 heaping Tablespoon finely
    chopped garlic
⅓ cup chopped parsley
Salt and pepper to taste
8 fish fillets, with skin on
    (Blue fish is superb, but
    any firm-fleshed fish will
    work.) If frozen, thaw before
    using, and dry as much
    as possible

Preheat oven to 450°. Peel potatoes and slice thinly. Wash in cold water and pat dry. (If they are not dry, they have a tendency to "steam-cook".) Mix oil, garlic, parsley, salt and pepper together. Put potatoes into 16 x 10-inch baking dish, pour half of the oil mixture over and mix well. Place the dish in the upper third of the oven. Bake until the potatoes are half-cooked, about 15 minutes. Place fish fillets, skin side down, over the potatoes. Pour remaining oil mixture over the fish, add a sprinkle of salt, and continue baking. After 10 minutes, baste and cook for another 5 minutes. Serve hot, using all of the cooking juices.

Zucchini Frittata
(Italian Egg Pancake with Zucchini)

2½ Tablespoons olive oil
1 clove garlic, peeled and
    crushed, but left whole
4 zucchini, sliced ¼ inch thick
Flour
3 Tablespoons minced parsley
½-¾ teaspoon salt
⅛ teaspoon pepper
3 Tablespoons butter
10 eggs, lightly beaten
1 teaspoon salt
⅛ teaspoon pepper

Heat oil in large skillet, add garlic and saute 1-2 minutes. Remove. Lightly coat zucchini with flour and stir fry over medium heat until golden, about 8 minutes. Remove oil from skillet and add parsley and salt and pepper. Remove from heat. In 10-12 inch skillet melt butter over high heat. Add eggs and remaining salt and pepper as soon as butter foams. Reduce heat to low and add zucchini mixture. Fry over direct heat, slowly, loosening edges and allowing uncooked portion to run underneath. Also prick with fork to allow uncooked portion to seep to bottom. When all but top is softly set, run under broiler 10-15 seconds. Cut into wedges or cool to room temperature before serving (as is frequently done in Italy). Grated cheese may be added before broiling.

Zuccotto
(Dome-shaped Florentine Dessert)

1 (12-16 ounce) sponge cake
3 Tablespoons brandy or
   cognac
2 Tablespoons sweet liqueur
3 Tablespoons cointreau
5 ounces semi-sweet chocolate
3 cups cold heavy cream,
   whipped
¾ cup confectioners sugar
¾ cup fruit (Any combination
   of candied and fresh; must
   use some candied. Frozen
   strawberries, crushed and
   drained, may be used for
   some of the fresh fruit.)
4 ounces shelled nuts,
   preferably ½ of which are
   unskinned almonds

Line a 3-quart round bottomed bowl such as Tupperware with damp cheese cloth or spray with Pam. Cut cake into ⅜ inch thick slices. Cut each of these slices on the diagonal, to form 2 triangular sections. Mix all cordials and moisten each cake section and place cake against insides of bowl with narrowest end of sections at bottom. Continue until inside of bowl is completely lined with cake, filling any gaps. Press edges together to completely seal bowl. There will be some cake left; it is to be used later. Whip cream in chilled bowl, adding powdered sugar. Grate chocolate and add to whipped cream; divide into three parts. Assemble by placing a layer of ½ of the fruit, and then ⅓ of the cream; all of the nuts, and the ⅓ of the cream; ½ of the fruit and ⅓ of the cream. This should completely fill the bowl. Trim edges of cake around rim of bowl. Cover and seal top of bowl completely with moistened cake sections. Be sure this is even since this will become the bottom of the finished dessert. Cover with plastic wrap; refrigerate overnight and/or up to two days. May be frozen. To serve: Loosen edges, cover with flat plate, turn over and serve. Do this before serving dinner, if using frozen. Slice as you would any cake.

Rosellen Amisano

Japanese Tempura Dinner

Make dinner a Far Eastern adventure with a crisp Japanese delicacy—tempura. Cover a low table with a bamboo mat and bring in plenty of soft floor pillows. (Plan on no more than six to eight people.) Cooking at the table while guests watch is the heart of the fun: you batter-dip the shrimp and vegetables, then deep-fry in an electric skillet. Serve drained and piping hot in individual baskets. Guests use chopsticks to dunk the tidbits in a trio of condiments.

Shrimp Tempura

Ice cubes keep the batter well chilled without diluting

**Raw shrimp, peeled and
  deveined
Assorted fresh vegetables:
  asparagus spears, spinach,
  green beans, mushrooms,
  sweet potatoes, parsley
Cooking oil
1 cup sifted all-purpose flour
1 cup ice water
1 slightly beaten egg
2 Tablespoons cooking oil
½ teaspoon salt
½ teaspoon sugar
TEMPURA CONDIMENTS:
Grated fresh gingeroot
Equal parts of grated turnip
  and grated horseradish,
  mixed
½ cup prepared mustard
  mixed with 3 Tablespoons
  soy sauce**

Wash and dry shrimp and vegetables thoroughly; slice or cut into strips or bite size pieces, if necessary. Fill electric skillet half full with cooking oil; heat to 360° on deep fat thermometer. To prepare the batter: Combine flour, ice water, egg, the 2 Tablespoons cooking oil, the salt and sugar. Beat just until ingredients are moistened, a few lumps should remain. Stir in 1 or 2 ice cubes. Use immediately. Dip shrimp and vegetables, a few at a time, in cold batter. Fry in hot oil until browned; drain on paper toweling. Serve in individual paper lined baskets.

Cookbook Committee

Jr. League of DeKalb Publications
P.O. Box 183 • Decatur, GA 30031 • 404-377-2973

Please send me _____ copies of **PUTTIN' ON THE PEACHTREE**
@ $16.95/copy (Georgia residents add $1.18 sales tax per book).

Please send me _____ copies of **PEACHTREE BOUQUET**
@ $14.95/copy (Georgia residents add $1.05 sales tax per book).

Please add $3.00 shipping and handling per book.
Gift wrap available for an additional $2.00 per book.

Enclosed is my check for $_____ payable to "JLD Publications"

Ship to: Name:_____

Address:_____

City:_____ State:_____ Zip Code:_____

All proceeds from cookbook sales will be returned to the community through volunteer projects of the Jr. League of DeKalb County. Many thanks!

Jr. League of DeKalb Publications
P.O. Box 183 • Decatur, GA 30031 • 404-377-2973

Please send me _____ copies of **PUTTIN' ON THE PEACHTREE**
@ $16.95/copy (Georgia residents add $1.18 sales tax per book).

Please send me _____ copies of **PEACHTREE BOUQUET**
@ $14.95/copy (Georgia residents add $1.05 sales tax per book).

Please add $3.00 shipping and handling per book.
Gift wrap available for an additional $2.00 per book.

Enclosed is my check for $_____ payable to "JLD Publications"

Ship to: Name:_____

Address:_____

City:_____ State:_____ Zip Code:_____

All proceeds from cookbook sales will be returned to the community through volunteer projects of the Jr. League of DeKalb County. Many thanks!

Re-Order Additional Copies

I would like to see **PUTTIN' ON THE PEACHTREE** and **PEACHTREE BOUQUET** in the following stores:

Store:_____

Address:_____

Store:_____

Address:_____

Store _____

Address:_____

Store _____

Address:_____

I would like to see **PUTTIN' ON THE PEACHTREE** and **PEACHTREE BOUQUET** in the following stores:

Store:_____

Address:_____

Store:_____

Address:_____

Store _____

Address:_____

Store _____

Address:_____